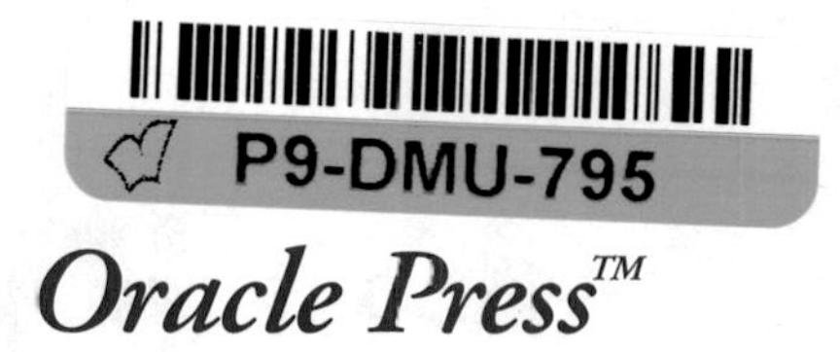

Oracle E-Business Suite Development and Extensibility Handbook

About the Authors

Anil Passi is an Oracle ACE with over a decade of consultancy experience in Oracle E-Business Suite. He is also a speaker on Oracle E-Business Suite development techniques and regularly gives seminars about best practices in E-Business Suite development.

Anil is the co-founder of FocusThread UK Ltd., a fast growing E-Business Suite and SOA (Service Oriented Architecture) consultancy company that is an industry leader in Oracle E-Business Suite online training (http://focusthread.com/training). In addition, he runs a popular E-Business Suite knowledge portal, http://apps2fusion.com, where experts publish their papers on Oracle E-Business Suite.

Vladimir Ajvaz is an SOA architect at Imperial College in London, where he applies a wide variety of technologies, including Oracle Fusion middleware and E-Business Suite, in pursuit of creating information and technology architecture of composite applications that enables greater flexibility in implementing and delivering efficient business processes.

Prior to joining Imperial, Vladimir worked at Oracle Corporation for almost a decade in a senior consulting role, where he directly engaged with the customers as well as Oracle product development teams across the globe. During this time, he regularly coached and gave seminars and presentations about application technologies and their practical implementations.

The authors can be contacted at apps.extensions@googlemail.com with questions, suggestions, and comments related to this book.

About the Technical Editor

Sailen Kotecha is a business solutions architect and senior Oracle Applications specialist with more than 18 years of experience in the field. Working with E-Business Suite since 1990, he has seen the product evolve into its current form and has an excellent understanding of the underlying architecture and tools. He has worked in many industry sectors both public and private and is well respected by his peers for his strategic foresight and vision. Sailen lives with his wife in Melbourne, Australia.

Oracle Press™

Oracle E-Business Suite Development and Extensibility Handbook

Anil Passi
Vladimir Ajvaz

New York Chicago San Francisco
Lisbon London Madrid Mexico City Milan
New Delhi San Juan Seoul Singapore Sydney Toronto

The McGraw-Hill Companies

Cataloging-in-Publication Data is on file with the Library of Congress

Oracle E-Business Suite Development and Extensibility Handbook

1 2 3 4 5 6 7 8 9 0 DOC DOC 0 1 9

ISBN 978-0-07-162942-3
MHID 0-07-162942-4

Sponsoring Editor
Lisa McClain

Editorial Supervisor
Jody McKenzie

Project Editor/Manager
Vipra Fauzdar, Glyph International

Acquisitions Coordinator
Meghan Riley

Technical Editor
Sailen Kotecha

Copy Editor
Sally Engelfried

Proofreader
Andy Saff

Indexer
Write Away Indexing Services

Production Supervisor
George Anderson

Composition
Glyph International

Illustration
Glyph International

Art Director, Cover
Jeff Weeks

Cover Designer
Pattie Lee

To my mother, brother, uncle, and the loving memory of my father.

—Vladimir Ajvaz

To my parents, wife Anjali, son Nikhil and the rest of my family members.

—Anil Passi

Contents at a Glance

Contents

Acknowledgments

We would like to thank everyone who helped us to make this book a reality. It was really a great pleasure to work with Lisa, Meghan, Jody, Vipra, and the rest of the production team from McGraw-Hill and Glyph International. A big thanks to Sally, our copy editor, who turned our manuscript into a book that is actually legible. We are deeply indebted to Sailen Kotecha for his effort in reviewing the material; his feedback on the drafts was highly valuable and appreciated. Thanks also to Atul, Neha, and the rest of the FocusThread team for providing us with uninterrupted access to E-Business Suite and SOA platform environments. We would also like to thank our family members, partners, and friends who tolerated and supported us as our deadlines were getting closer.

Introduction

The idea for writing a book about Oracle E-Business Suite development, customization, and extensibility techniques stemmed from everyday practical experiences as well as the seminars, presentations, and courses taught by the authors on this subject. Although the Internet seems awash with information related to Oracle Applications, most of it is still largely unstructured when it comes to the practical aspects of custom development and Oracle tool use for the purposes of customization in Oracle E-Business Suite.

Writing a book on this subject was a challenging task, mainly due to the myriad of tools and products used within Oracle E-Business Suite, including JDeveloper, Oracle Forms, Oracle Reports, Oracle Database, SQL Plus, Oracle Application Server, Oracle Workflow, BI Publisher, XML Gateway, BPEL Process Manager, and others. Oracle Applications also use a wide variety of programming languages and standards such as SQL, PL/SQL, Java, C, XML, Web Service Description Language (WSDL), shell scripts, Service Oriented Architecture (SOA), and many others.

The motivation to write this book came from our fruitless struggles to suggest to our colleagues a single resource on how to use the tools in the context of E-Business Suite extensions. This book is an attempt to fill that gap, and its main aim is to provide a head start to anyone who is beginning to learn Oracle E-Business Suite R11i /R12 development and extensibility techniques, as well as more seasoned E-Business Suite developers who haven't had a chance to work with the tools and the development methodologies covered in this book.

This book is a guide that describes the fundamentals in a compact form and provides step-by-step examples of the key technologies in Oracle E-Business Suite that will benefit not only beginners, but also a seasoned professional. It focuses on covering the essentials for the purposes of satisfying these immediate needs.

We strongly recommend that you always consult related manuals and user and development guides that accompany E-Business Suite products and are available at the Oracle Technology Network website and Metalink. This book is not a substitute for the user and development guides that come with the E-Business Suite product, and some of the topics in this book deserve a book in their own right.

Who Should Read This Book

This book is for developers and professionals who are either already working or intend to work on extending, customizing, and personalizing E-Business Suite releases 11i and R12. When writing the book, we had three types of readers in mind: university graduates who recently joined a consulting organization without prior exposure to E-Business Suite, Oracle professionals with extensive Oracle tools knowledge but without previous exposure to E-Business Suite, and experienced Oracle E-Business Suite professionals who didn't have exposure to some of the techniques covered in this book.

We assume that you are familiar with at least the basics of the programming languages and tools such as SQL, PL/SQL, Java, XML, and others used within the suite. This book is not going to teach you how to program in those languages or tools. Instead, we provide guidance on how to use them in the context of E-Business Suite custom development and extensions.

About the Examples

The step-by-step examples in this book are quite simple and largely self-explanatory. Their purpose is to get you started quickly with a particular tool, methodology, programming language, or development framework in E-Business Suite. Please bear in mind that in order to keep things simple and short, in many instances we didn't follow the usual coding standards such as code commenting, variable anchoring to database data types in PL/SQL, and the like; therefore, do not assume that the examples are production-grade code.

We have tested the examples against the R12.0.4 version of E-Business Suite VISION installation on Linux, but all of the examples should also work against the VISION installation of release 11i (11.5.7+) with the latest Applications Technology patches applied. This implies that in order to follow the examples in this book, you'll need an access to the demonstration (VISION) installation of E-Business Suite, although most of the examples can be tried on any development instance of E-Business Suite.

Additionally, we assume that examples are deployed against a custom application that, in this book, we called "Custom Development" with the short name *XXCUST.* How to create the custom application is covered in the System Administrator's Guide for each release of Oracle Applications. For example, for release R12.1 this is documented in Oracle Applications System Administrator's Guide—Configuration Release 12.1, which can be downloaded from Oracle Technology Network (OTN) or Metalink (Oracle Support online resource).

The Structure of the Book

At the beginning of each chapter we provide a summary of how a particular technology or development framework works and then we move on to the examples; at the end of the chapter we provide good practices as applicable. The first four chapters (Chapter 1, "Introduction to Oracle E-Business Suite"; Chapter 2, "E-Business Suite Architecture"; Chapter 3, "Application Object Library [AOL]"; and Chapter 4, "Multiple Organizations Feature") are exceptions to this rule, as they are intended to introduce some of the key concepts in E-Business Suite to those readers who are new to it.

The chapters are largely independent from one another, although we recommend that readers without prior exposure to E-Business Suite not skip the first four chapters.

CHAPTER 1

Introduction to Oracle E-Business Suite

In this introductory chapter, we'll give a high level functional overview of Oracle E-Business Suite from an application developer's point of view. This chapter is primarily aimed at the readers who are familiar with Oracle tools but new to E-Business Suite; those who have already gained experience in working with E-Business Suite can safely skip this chapter.

We also look at what options are available to implementation teams and developers to change the standard product features, and later in the chapter we briefly discuss the concept of E-Business Suite environments.

At the end of this chapter we look at how information is shared and reused within different modules in Oracle Applications in order to highlight the importance of data sharing between different modules within E-Business Suite.

What Is Oracle E-Business Suite?

Oracle E-Business Suite is a software package that allows organizations to manage key business processes; it is known on the market by various names such as Oracle Enterprise Resource Planning (ERP), Oracle Apps, Oracle Applications, Oracle Financials, e-Biz and EBS (E-Business Suite). In this book we refer to it as either E-Business Suite, or Oracle Applications.

In the past, it was a common practice for businesses and organizations to develop in-house software to automate their business processes. Most of the software that was developed in-house largely matched the precise needs of the business. However, the fundamental business flows and processes such as accounting, procurement, human resource/employee management, and order management are based on common principles across all organizations. For example, most organizations require a system to make purchases from suppliers and a system to make payments to the suppliers, events known as transactions that need to be accounted for in the financial reporting. Enterprise Resource Planning (ERP) software prepackages different types of these functionalities into out-of-the-box software package, so that customers who purchase such software packages do not have to develop the same software applications time and again.

Product Families

Oracle E-Business Suite is a product offering that covers almost all of the business flows widely used in most organizations. Businesses can implement as many modules as necessary due to the modular but still integrated nature of the E-Business Suite architecture. This allows unified information to be available across the enterprise; it also reduces information technology (IT) expenses and helps run business more efficiently.

On the contrary, managing heterogeneous software solutions developed in-house that use different systems and technologies can be extremely costly and complex. Any time you update one system, you must go back and review all the integration points and potentially update the interfaces between the systems. Oracle E-Business Suite is engineered to work as an integrated system on a common IT infrastructure. You can directly pass information from one application to another without incurring incremental integration costs.

The product offering in E-Business Suite is organized into product families. Some of the key product families are as follows:

- Financials
- Procurement
- Customer Relationship Management (CRM)
- Project Management
- Supply Chain Planning and Management
- Discrete Manufacturing
- Process Manufacturing
- Order Management
- Human Resources Management System (HRMS)
- Applications Technology

In E-Business Suite, each product family usually consists of individual applications. For example, some of the applications that make up the Oracle Financials product family are General Ledger, Payables, Receivables, Cash Management, iReceivables, iExpenses, and others. It is beyond the scope of this book to cover the functionality of products such as General Ledger, Oracle Purchasing, and the like. There is a wealth of information about the functionality of E-Business Suite products publicly available, and we suggest the following resources for further reading:

- **Oracle Technology Network (Documentation section)** www.oracle.com/technology/documentation/applications.html
- **Oracle E-Business Suite** www.oracle.com/applications/e-business-suite.html
- **Oracle Metalink (requires registration)** metalink.oracle.com

NOTE
Throughout this book, we'll sometimes refer to E-Business Suite applications as modules. The terms application *and* module *will be used interchangeably.*

Professional User Interface

When the Oracle ERP product was initially launched, the screens were built in character mode. The end users interacted with the system through dumb terminals, which provided a character-based interface that connected to the back end server. Both Oracle Forms (then known as SQL*Forms) and Oracle Database were run at the back end tier. Initially, the R10.7 version of Oracle Applications ran in character mode, as did all the previous releases. However, when Oracle released its GUI version called SmartClient, the SmartClient screens were built with Oracle Forms 4.5 and ran at the desktop client tier, accessing the database over the network. Although SmartClient provided a better user experience, it was difficult to maintain, as software updates needed to be distributed on every individual client desktop. Last in that release, Oracle announced R10.7 NCA (Network Computing Architecture), which was an attempt to integrate the latest web technologies into Oracle's business applications using three-tier architecture, including database and application servers; end users interacted with the system using the browser from their client desktops. The latest releases of E-Business Suite, R11i and R12, are also based on multi-tier architecture, and the details will be covered in the next chapter.

Nowadays, in the latest releases of E-Business Suite R11i and R12, we refer to the professional user interface as an interface that is built with the Oracle Forms developer tool. Such Forms-based screens run within a Java applet at the client desktops, and in their appearance and behavior they are similar to desktop applications. Office personnel who often performs data entry tasks usually prefer using this type of user interface as it allows speedy data entry.

Web User Interface

As mentioned in the previous section, most of the screens in Oracle E-Business Suite were initially developed using Oracle Forms. However, over the last few years, Oracle has started to deliver new screens using pure web-based technology. These web-based screens do not run within a Java applet, unlike Forms-based screens. Instead, the HTML-based screens are run with a browser such as Firefox or Internet Explorer. Oracle initially started developing HTML-based pages in E-Business Suite primarily to provide a light footprint application or Self-Service–based applications. Here are some examples of the Self-Service applications:

- **HR Self-Service** End users maintain their own personal records, such as name, address, and so on.
- **iProcurement** Users create requisitions to buy goods such as stationery by themselves directly rather then having a central purchasing team creating that order for them.
- **iRecruitment** Users apply for a different job internally within their organization.
- **iExpenses** Employees submit their expenses for approval via a web interface.

The reasons that justify the broad adoption of an HTML-based interface is ever increasing; here we list just a few of them:

- Commitment to the open industry standards usually leads to the increased product interoperability.
- A pure HTML-based web application is lightweight and it runs without the need for a Java applet in the browser.
- An adoption of the new components and emerging technologies such as AJAX, Rich Internet Applications (RIA), and others ensures a better end user experience.

As a result of the preceding factors, even the new back office screens are now being developed as HTML-based pages using Oracle Application Framework (OA Framework). The sophisticated user interface features that were previously offered only through Oracle Forms are increasingly becoming available to HTML-based screens that run exclusively within desktop browsers, without the need for Java applets.

Nowadays, Oracle E-Business Suite developers find themselves working with both Oracle Forms and OA Framework, as the current releases (Release 11i and Release 12) contain a mixture of screens using both the technologies. Later in the book, we cover both Oracle Forms in Chapter 6 and E-Business Suite Oracle Applications Framework development techniques in Chapter 9.

Configurations, Personalizations, Extensions, and Customizations

Oracle E-Business Suite was designed and developed to take into consideration various standard business flows that are common to most organizations. However, each business can have its own unique requirements. For example, a company may want to allow all of its employees to make purchases up to $10 without having such purchases approved. Another company may have a business rule that each employee's approval limit depends on his or her position within the organization. Oracle E-Business Suite is a package that has to meet not only the needs of both these types of companies, but also the needs of numerous other companies that may have a completely different set of requirements and business needs. That's why Oracle E-Business Suite has been developed in a configurable manner, so that each customer can buy this package and configure it to meet his or her specific business requirements. However, if business requirements cannot be met purely by using setup and configuration options, implementations have to resort to other options such as system personalizations, extensions, and customizations, which may or may not require custom code to be written by an E-Business Suite technical developer.

Configurations

E-Business Suite is an off the shelf software package that is both configurable and extensible. Changes are mostly made to ERP products by means of setup and configurations. Performing a setup usually means making changes to the product, without writing computer programs. System or product configuration is normally performed by functional analysts.

Personalizations

In E-Business Suite, the underlying technologies that render the user interface at presentation layer allow system implementers and end users to declaratively personalize the content of application forms and web pages. If business needs cannot be met by system configuration and setup, this is the first option to look at as it provides the safest way to change the system.

The major technologies that enable user personalizations in E-Business Suite are Oracle Forms and Oracle Application Framework (OAF), often referred to as Forms Personalizations and OA Framework Personalizations. We cover both Forms and OAF personalizations later in this book in chapters that cover the corresponding tools (Oracle Forms in Chapter 6 and OAF Personalizations in Chapter 9).

Customizations and Extensions

If, due to the generic nature of the product or any other reason, certain business requirements cannot be met through the product configuration and personalization, the technical development team is required either to extend the existing product functionality or introduce completely new custom modules that seamlessly integrate with the standard product and functionality. Depending on the underlying technology, both customization and extension terms are often used interchangeably, and usually they mean one thing: extending the product functionality by means of writing custom code that is either tightly or loosely coupled with E-Business Suite applications code and, in some cases, even completely decoupled from product code.

E-Business Suite developers are advised to err on the side of caution when dealing with customizations and extensions. It is important to stress that Oracle Support Services (OSS) do not support custom code logic in customizations developed to extend the standard product functionality. The general rule of thumb is that if something is not documented, then it is not supported by OSS. Most of the tools used by developers to build product customizations have corresponding support guidelines published on Metalink. Here are some examples:

Note 578466.1 Oracle Workflow Customization Policy Clarification

Note 395441.1 Oracle Application Framework Support Guidelines for Customers Release 12

More generic policy regarding the customizations is explained in Metalink Note 209603.1: Oracle Support Services Policy Regarding Customizations. Ultimately, if unsure about any aspect of customization policy, system implementers and developers should contact Oracle Support Services for clarification.

That said, if tools such as Oracle Forms, JDeveloper for Oracle Applications, Oracle Workflow Builder, and others that we use to build customizations do not behave as documented, we are entitled to address an issue with Oracle Support and raise a support call. The best course of action is to create a very simple test case that is not dependent on our custom code but is of generic nature. As we said earlier, all the documented features of Oracle tools and Oracle Applications are fully supported and will be dealt with by Oracle Support.

Concept of E-Business Suite Environments

In organizations that implement or already have implemented E-Business Suite, you will find multiple copies of Oracle E-Business Suite installations in use. The installations can be either on the same machine or on different physical machines. Each such installation is called an instance or an environment of Oracle E-Business Suite and consists of E-Business Suite software, an Oracle database including the data files, and Oracle server software.

An instance has a unique purpose; for example, if the customer is already running their business operations on E-Business Suite, they will always have a production instance. An E-Business Suite developer should never directly make any code changes to the production environment. The code changes must be first done to a development environment, and from there on promoted to test, and finally to production systems. The promotion of code changes must be scripted where possible to avoid human error.

An E-Business Suite developer engaged in the task of extending or customizing a module within an E-Business Suite at a customer site will typically find that customer is either in the implementation or production phase. The environments that support the implementation process are different from those required to support a post "go-live" running production instance of E-Business Suite. For instance, during the implementation phase, it is usually required to perform a master system configuration; develop and perform system testing of interfaces, conversions, and customizations; test the performance of the final system and infrastructure design; perform a UAT (User Acceptance Test); and train the end users and go live with the production system. Obviously, the production system requires fewer environments. Customers that are already running "live" production systems need support and development environments for the future system enhancements. They also need to test patches that fix production issues and a separate UAT environment for the final sign-off prior to applying changes to the production environment.

When it comes down to detail, every implementation is different in terms of used number and types of environments that support either the implementation process or live production system. Here is a brief description of some of the environments that exist during an Oracle E-Business Suite implementation process:

- **Master environment** This environment is used for the main configuration setup of the system. Although it does not contain any transactional data, it is important that the master environment is managed by a very strict change control as this environment contains production (master) setup.

- **Development environment** This is where developers design and build extensions and customizations. The developers are usually granted very powerful access rights for both E-Business Suite and the operating system that hosts the system. For instance, the developers may be granted System Administrator or Application Developer responsibilities.

- **Testing environment (also known as UAT)** Developers usually do not have an APPS database schema password to this environment. This is where users sign off on customizations and configuration changes.

- **Deployment environment** Once the users have finished their User Acceptance Testing on a UAT instance, patches/scripts can then be promoted to a Deployment instance for final checks. Effectively, applying patches on a Deployment instance is a dry run before applying code changes to a Production instance.

- **Patching environment** Oracle delivers their code changes, bug fixes, and product updates through *patches*. The patches can be downloaded from the Oracle Support website and applied by E-Business Suite database administrators (Apps DBAs). Apps DBAs can use the patching environment to perform sanity checks for patches delivered by Oracle.

- **Support environment** If a user reports an issue on the production system, it is a good idea to reproduce the problem on a copy of the production system. Such copied instances are referred to as *clones*. The support environment is exclusive to the support staff, where developers do not make changes directly. This environment is usually the most frequently cloned environment in cases where E-Business Suite implementation is running a live production instance. Frequent cloning helps the E-Business Suite support staff to reproduce production issues.
- **CRP environment** The conference room pilot environment is where someone, usually an implementation team, gets buy-in to their product offering from the wider user and business community during an implementation. This environment is usually used for sign-off during new implementations.
- **Migration environment** For new implementations of Oracle Applications, developers are tasked with migration of data from the old legacy systems into Oracle E-Business Suite. This is where repeated data migration can take place before the migration code gets frozen and ready for user testing.
- **Production environment** This is where the business runs its day-to-day operations.

Generally, E-Business Suite technical developers shouldn't be too concerned about the variety of environments, as their focus is predominantly concentrated on the development environment. In very simple terms, the life cycle of extensions and customizations could be summarized as follows: the developer performs the development and unit testing in the development environment, and the code gets promoted to the testing environment. Following successful testing, the changes are applied to the production environment.

There can be more than one development environment for any implementation as well as a live site, especially when some of the bigger modules are being implemented with different timelines. Nevertheless, the changes in each development environment should ideally be tested on a common test (UAT) environment.

The changes in the development environment must be scripted in all cases where possible. As a rule of thumb, everything except for functional configuration can be scripted. To promote functional setup and configuration, the implementers of E-Business Suite can use the iSetup module, which is used to promote functional changes between various E-Business Suite environments.

NOTE
The process of automating of the code delivery helps avoid human errors; changes can quickly be promoted to other test instances, and this approach also ensures a tight control over the changes that affect production instances.

Concept of Common Entities and Common Data

Sometimes people refer to the common data as *shared entities*, but you can also think of them as business objects or entities that are common to a number of different business functions. For example, entities such as customers and suppliers can be referenced by multiple Oracle Applications modules.

You may have heard that Oracle Applications are built around a single data model, which, in essence, means that within a single database you can find a single definition of your customers, suppliers, employees, inventory items, products, and all the other important aspects of a business or an organization. In contrast to this idea of a single data model, organizations tend to build or implement new applications to meet their business needs as they grow, ending up with "point-to-point" solutions between the systems because new applications need to share the existing data with other applications in the organization. As the systems alongside the business continue to grow, the number of interfaces between disparate applications will also grow. For example, Human Resources–related data about employees could be stored in one database, while financial data is stored in another system.

Figure 1-1 represents such systems, where the applications are added one after another as the business needs grow, and as a result, end-to-end interfacing between them starts to look incomprehensible. It is perfectly possible to make such applications collaborate to connect different business processes; however, when major changes occur in one application, it will start having a domino effect on other components of the system and make it more expensive to maintain. Oracle E-Business Suite is trying to address this issue by integrating around a single common data model. The idea of this model is to allow us to create and maintain a single common business definition of employees, students, customers, suppliers, products, and other aspects of a business or an organization, so everyone in that organization has an instant access to the common data shared by different applications. All the applications collaborate with each other, share the same information, and can be run in one global installation of a single database. Oracle E-Business Suite is designed and shipped as a preintegrated set of applications, but organizations and businesses are free to implement a single application, multiple applications, or all of the applications that comprise Oracle E-Business Suite. This modular approach is a key integration enabler that allows us to integrate with already existing applications.

It is important for developers to keep this in mind, as almost all of the custom development efforts in Oracle Applications will reference the common or shared entities. In addition, they are not documented in a single user or implementation guide as a part of the Oracle Applications documentation library. If you search the Oracle Applications documentation library online or Metalink (Oracle's support services website), you'll see that common entities are referenced in different

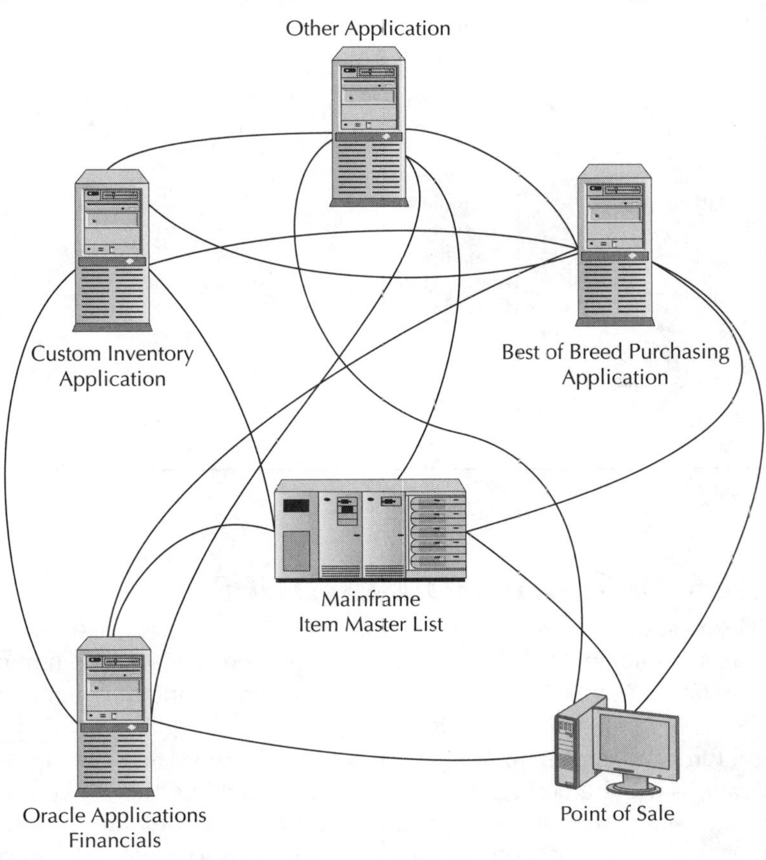

FIGURE 1-1. *Fragmented point-to-point interface model*

implementation and user guides for the multiple products that your organization has implemented. If you think of the common data as business objects shared and referenced by multiple modules, as indicated in Figure 1-2, you can then say that the common data represents reusable entities defined as a one-time exercise in one product and then shared and reused by other applications. For example, suppliers defined in Oracle Payables are shared between Payables, Assets, and Purchasing applications. Similarly, items defined in Oracle Inventory are shared by Purchasing, Order Management, and Receivables. Further examples of the shared entities are Organizations, Locations, Employees, Units of Measure, and Items.

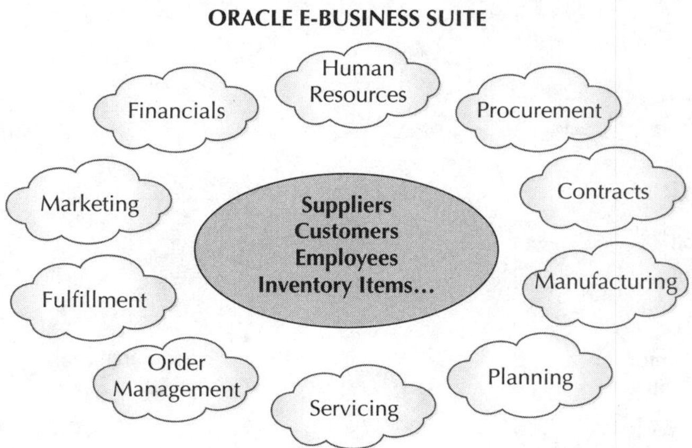

FIGURE 1-2. *Shared data model*

Examples of Common Entities

Figure 1-3 gives a simplified view of an example of data sharing between the different products in Oracle Applications. In the figure there are three common entities that are shared across the modules: Items, Customers, and Suppliers.

- **Items** Order Management and Purchasing and many other Oracle applications use the definitions of items configured in Oracle Inventory. Items are usually the things that an organization or a company makes, purchases, or sells. Different applications use items for different purposes. In Oracle Inventory, items are used for stocking process, planning, and cost; in Payables, items are used in supplier invoices; in Receivables, they are used as units to bill the customers.

- **Customers** In Figure 1-3, the customer purchase orders are created in Order Management (OM). Sales orders define what products are shipped to the customers. After shipping the products to your customers, you invoice the customers through Receivables, and Oracle Inventory adjusts the quantity of the products currently held. The customers created in Order Management are shared with Receivables and vice versa.

- **Suppliers** In the example, the suppliers are defined through the Oracle Purchasing module. The suppliers are business or trading partners that deliver goods or services of some kind. The supplier invoices are entered into the Oracle Payables and matched to the purchase orders in the Oracle Purchasing module. You can create suppliers in different modules such as Payables or Purchasing.

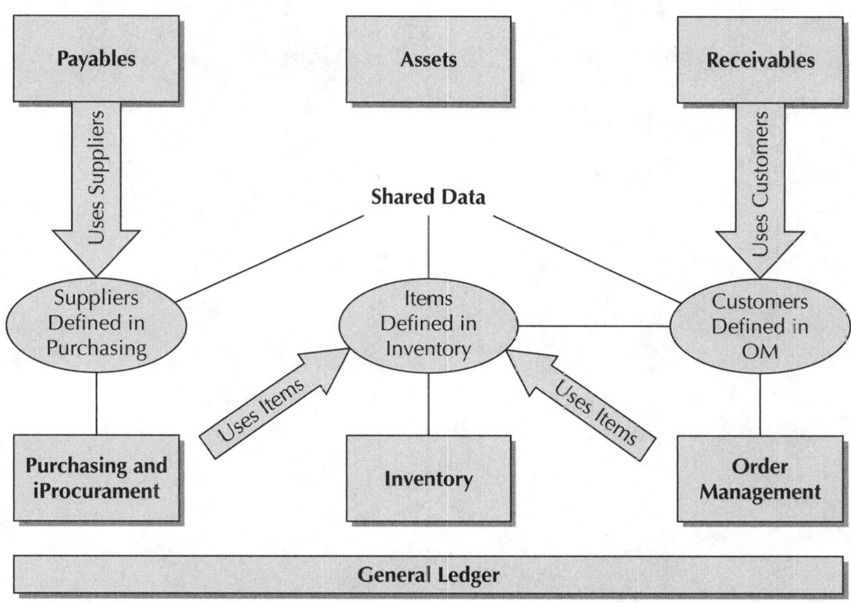

FIGURE 1-3. *Example of data sharing*

Summary

In this chapter, we introduced customizations, personalizations, E-Business Suite instances, and the concept of data sharing. However, this is by no means a complete list of topics that developers should keep in mind when venturing into building custom code and extensions. We also highlighted the difference between system configuration, personalization, and customization. It is important to understand that the custom logic in the code that we develop to extend product functionality is not supported by Oracle but by ourselves. However, the tools and various technology frameworks used with E-Business Suite are supported by Oracle Support, and any issues with them are usually dealt with promptly by Oracle Support staff.

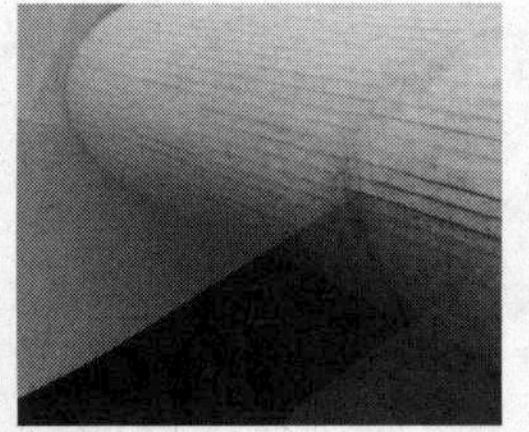

CHAPTER 2

E-Business Suite Architecture

n this chapter, we'll discuss key components that make up the basic building blocks of the E-Business Suite architecture from the technical perspective. For the purposes of this book, we will only take into consideration the latest major releases of E-Business Suite, R11i and R12.

Between these two releases there has been some significant changes in the system architecture, and where it is relevant we will highlight these throughout this chapter and the rest of the book.

Architecture Overview

ERP (Enterprise Resource Planning) and CRM (Customer Relationship Management) systems need to be capable of collecting, processing, presenting, analyzing, and storing the data. To collect data from the end users, Oracle Applications includes in its technology stack support for two distinctly different user interfaces: Forms and the HTML-based interface also known as the Self-Service interface. In addition, mobile users can interact with the system through PDA devices.

These different user interfaces cater to different types of users: the Forms-based or Professional interface is better suited for users who interact with the system daily, such as an accounts clerk who is required to enter the data quickly. On the other hand, the HTML-based Self-Service interface is better suited for casual users, such as an employee who infrequently enters expense claims and subsequently checks the progress of the expense claim in the system through the Self Service HTML-based screens. Mobile users such as warehouse workers are the class of users who often perform their duties away from network connected desktops. For them, the mobile interface makes it possible to interact with the system using mobile devices.

In addition to user interaction, another important aspect of the system is the capability of scheduled background processing for long running and reporting tasks. This is achieved through the Concurrent Processing component, which, in the landscape of various Oracle products and technologies, is particular to Oracle Applications.

NOTE

The Concurrent Manager is a logical part of the E-Business Suite architecture; however, it is not really part of the technical architecture. In reality, there is no technology stack component called "Concurrent Manager." We'll cover Concurrent Manager in more detail later in this chapter.

Lastly, all of the collected and processed data is kept in Oracle Database server. The database server is responsible for storing and retrieving of the business and other organizational data.

Figure 2-1 shows that Oracle Applications are built with the help of traditional Oracle Developer tools such as Oracle Forms and Oracle Reports; however, the trend for HTML-based user interfaces has forced architectural changes in Oracle Applications to introduce more components from the Oracle JDeveloper tool to facilitate rapid development of the standard HTML-based screens. This is particularly evident in R12, where most of the application's user interfaces are converted into HTML-based screens.

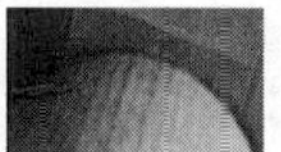

NOTE

In R12, not all screens built with Oracle Forms have HTML-based counterparts. Forms-based screens are still being used across many applications in E-Business Suite R12.

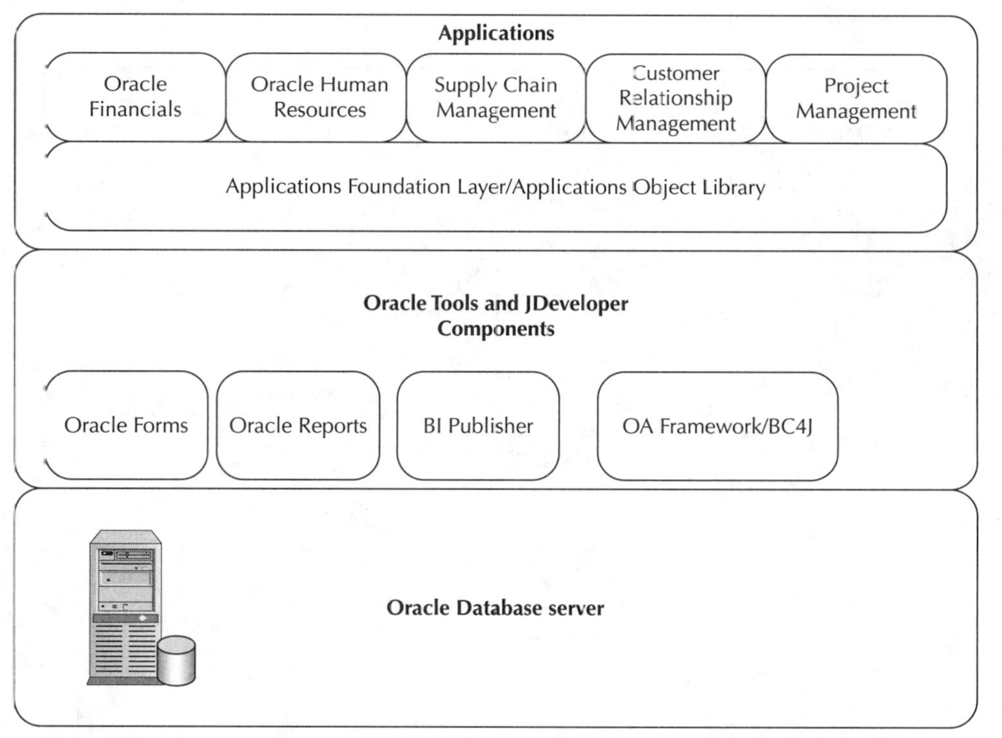

FIGURE 2-1. *System overview*

Oracle Applications R11i and R12 are based on a three-tier architecture, as depicted in Figure 2-2.

Multi-tier architecture is a type of client-server architecture that logically separates the presentation, application logic, and data management and storage layers. Three-tier architecture is the most common type of multi-tier architecture in which user interface, business rules (logic), and application data are maintained independently of each other.

- **Client tier** This layer includes the user interface, such as networked desktop computers, laptops, and portable devices (such as PDAs, iPhones, and similar items). User interface interacts with the end users by presenting the data to them and allowing them to enter the data into the system.
- **Application tier** Also known as the middle or mid-tier, this layer is responsible for business logic processing as well as managing the applications. The application tier enables communication between the client tier and the database tier.
- **Database tier** This layer is responsible for storing and retrieving the data in Oracle Database.

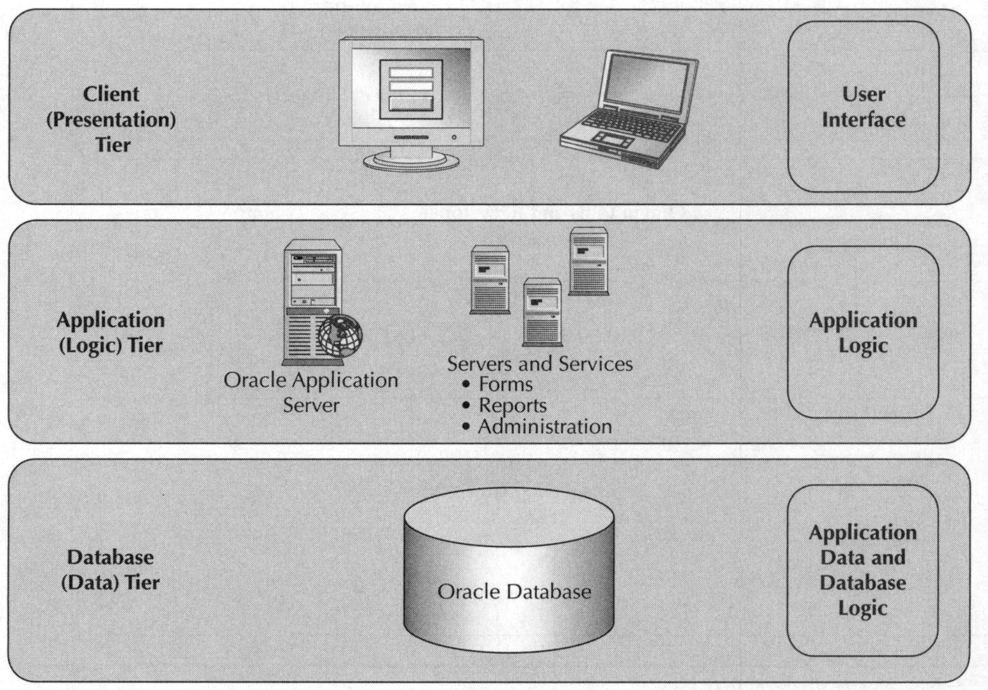

FIGURE 2-2. *Three-tier architecture in Oracle Applications*

The main differences between Oracle Applications R11i and R12 are in the application tier. The differences are related to both the file system structure as well as the technology stack components.

E-Business Suite System Architecture

We'll now look a little deeper into the individual components that make the Oracle Applications infrastructure, with emphasis on the differences between Oracle Applications R11i and R12. We believe that covering the differences in parallel will be beneficial to developers who haven't had exposure to one or the other of these two releases. The development techniques and tools between releases remain largely similar; however, what has changed are the tools versions and the location of technology stack components.

Figure 2-3 shows a more detailed diagram of the system architecture for both releases of Oracle Applications.

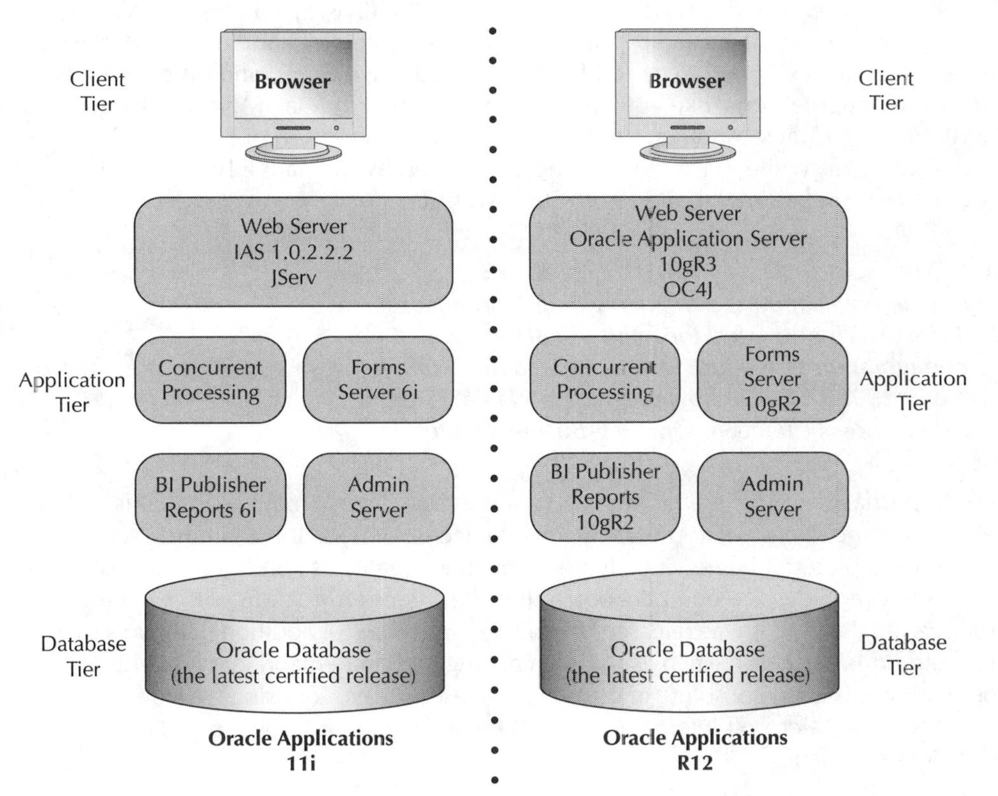

FIGURE 2-3. *System components in Oracle Applications*

Client or Desktop Tier

The client or desktop tier offers two types of user interfaces in Oracle Applications: Forms-based and HTML-based. Both of these user interfaces are run via a supported web browser (currently Firefox or Internet Explorer). Forms-based screens run within the Oracle Forms Client applet. An end user uses a browser to log in to Oracle Applications through the Personal Home Page, which acts as an entry point for all applications in Oracle E-Business Suite.

Oracle Forms Client Applet

If you are familiar with Java applets that run in Java-enabled browsers, Oracle Forms Client applet is no different. It provides interactive features to web applications that cannot be easily provided by HTML. In its appearance, Oracle Forms client applications are similar to Windows desktop applications. As with other applets, Oracle Forms Client applet is deployed as packaged JAR (Java Archive) files. JAR files include all the libraries required for Oracle Applications forms. After the initial download, JAR files are cached in the browser's disk cache. The client Java libraries consist of the Forms and Extended Windowing Toolkit (EWT) Java classes. EWT is Oracle's Java library. It is used by Oracle Forms to create and handle user interface widgets such as text input boxes, tables, buttons, tabs, windows, and others. Oracle Forms Client applet runs, like any other Java applet, within a Java Virtual Machine (JVM). In R11i, Oracle Applications usually uses its own version of JVM called Oracle JInitiator, while in R12 this has been replaced by the native JVM (Sun J2SE Plug-in) that can be downloaded from Sun's website.

NOTE
Oracle now supports Sun Native Plug-in in release 11i. For Windows desktops, the installation and configuration procedure is documented in Metalink Note: 290807.1 - Deploying Sun JRE (Native Plug-in) for Windows Clients in Oracle E-Business Suite 11i.

Oracle JInitiator Oracle JInitiator is a Java Runtime Environment (JRE) that is delivered to the client desktop computers. It replaces the default JVM in browsers such as Internet Explorer. It has essentially the same functionality as Sun Microsystems' plug-in but includes the bug backports, important for certification with Oracle products. At the time it was released, it provided a number of additional features over the standard JVM plug-in, such as JAR file caching and on-demand loading. This approach has become obsolete in post-R11i releases in favor of using the standard Java plug-in. In Microsoft Internet Explorer, Oracle JInitiator is implemented as an ActiveX component.

Sun J2SE Plug-in (Native Plug-in) Similar to R11i installations, the desktop or client tier in R12 offers both Professional Forms User Interface (Oracle Forms) and HTML-based screens. HTML-based screens still require a certified web browser such as Firefox or Internet Explorer, while Professional Forms uses Sun J2SE Native Plug-in. In R12, Oracle JInitiator is not a required component to run Forms-based screens (R11i was also recently certified to use the native plug-in). One of the reasons Oracle departed from the previous strategy of having its own certified version of JVM in JInitiator was to reduce the number of desktop management issues usually related to conflicting JVMs on user's desktops. Oracle's JInitiator has its own JVM which, on occasion, conflicted with JVMs from other vendors. Dropping JInitiator in favor of a native plug-in could reduce a number of such incidents.

Oracle Applications Forms are still run as Java applets on the desktop client computers, and it may take additional time to download necessary JAR files when the Forms interface is run for the first time. After the initial load, the JAR files are kept in the cache and will be updated only if there is a newer version or the copies in the cache expire.

Application Tier

The application tier, also known as the middle tier, is where most of the application's functionality is performed, including business logic control or validation of the data entered though the client tier, among many other functions. The application tier also acts as an intermediary between the client tier and the database tier. As shown previously in Figure 2-3, the following are the principal components of the Oracle Applications application tier:

- Web server
- Forms server
- Concurrent Processing server
- Reports server (R11i)
- BI Publisher
- Admin server (R11i)

It is important to note that the terminology *server* is used to denote a "logical" server rather than a "physical" server machine. Logical servers can have as many physical server machines as necessary to satisfy various requirements such as performance, scalability, security, and so on. For smaller implementations, testing, or development, often all of the nodes are installed on a single (physical) machine.

Web and Forms components are referred to as services rather than servers in R12, and this is due to the changes in the architecture of these individual components in Oracle Applications Server 10g.

Web Server

When talking about the Web server in the Oracle Applications technology stack, you might think of other releases of Oracle Applications Server middle-tier technology that are comprised of the actual web server and some kind of servlet engine that runs Java-based applications. There are many other components that are part of Oracle Applications Server, but the most relevant to Oracle Applications developers are Web Listener and Servlet Engine. The Web Listener component is also called Oracle HTTP Server, powered by Apache. Its purpose, as with any other web listener, is to process HTTP requests by either fulfilling them itself or forwarding them to other components of the Applications Server or layers of Oracle Applications technology stack. The following list shows Applications Server versions in R11i and R12:

- **R11i**
    - OracleAS 1.0.2.2.2 (Applications Server)
        - Oracle HTTP Server powered by Apache (Web Listener based on Apache 1.3.19)
        - Apache JServ Servlet Engine (Apache JServ 1.1.2 Servlet Engine)
- **R12**
    - OracleAS 10gR3 (Applications Server)
        - Oracle HTTP Server powered by Apache (Web Listener based on Apache 1.3.34)
        - OC4J (Oracle Components for Java 10.1.3—a J2EE-compliant engine based on Orion server from Ironflare Corporation)

Oracle HTTP Server is an entry point for both HTML-based Self-Service and Oracle Forms-based applications. For HTML-based applications, the executing of the application logic and Java code occurs within a servlet engine: Apache JServ in R11i and Oracle Components for Java (OC4J) in R12.

Self-Service Applications and OA Framework Self-Service applications and OA Framework (Oracle Applications Framework or OA Framework)–based applications are two terms that are often used interchangeably. Oracle Applications Framework is the Oracle Applications development and deployment Java-based platform for HTML-based business applications.

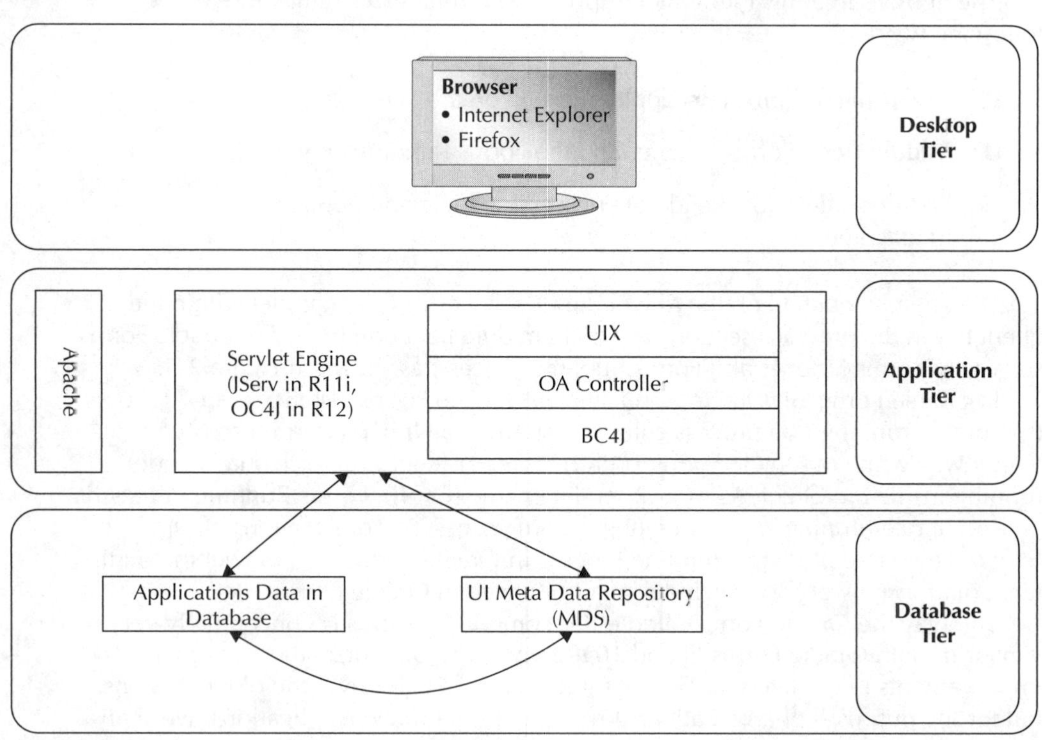

FIGURE 2-4. *OA Framework architecture*

OA Framework is based on JSP technology, which executes in a servlet engine. When the browser issues an OA.jsp request for one of the Self-Service pages, page processing takes place within a servlet engine which, in turn, can access the application data as well as user interface metadata from the database. Figure 2-4 shows the main components in the OA Framework infrastructure.

Forms Server

The Forms server component runs Oracle Applications screens developed with the Oracle Forms tool. Two different versions of this component are used in E-Business Suite R11i and R12:

- **R11i** Oracle Developer 6i installed in ORACLE_HOME 8.0.6
- **R12** Oracle AS 10gR2 installed in ORACLE_HOME 10.1.2

The Forms server fits into Oracle Applications three-tier architecture in the following way:

- **Client tier** Forms Java applet running on the client desktop
- **Middle tier** Forms Listener and the Forms Runtime Engine
- **Database tier** Backend data processing logic and applications data management

We already touched on the role of the Oracle Forms Client applet within the client tier in the previous section. The main middle tier components of Oracle Forms server are Forms Listener and Forms Runtime Process, as shown in Figure 2-5.

In Oracle Forms 6i (Oracle Applications 11i), the Forms Listener is an executable running as a process called f60srvm on a Unix platform (ifsrv60 on Windows), while in Oracle Forms 10gR2, Forms Listener is a servlet (Java code) running inside the OracleAS 10gR2 servlet engine (OC4J). Forms Runtime Process is an executable running as an operating system process in both versions of Oracle Forms. The name of Forms Runtime Process in Oracle Forms 6i is f60webmx on the Unix platform (ifweb60 on Windows) and f90web in Oracle Forms 10gR2.

The way the Oracle Forms middle-tier component works is conceptually very similar in both Oracle Forms 6i and 10gR2 versions. Of course, there are many improvements in the latest version of Oracle Forms 10gR2 over the older versions, but for the purposes of applications development in Oracle Applications, we shall

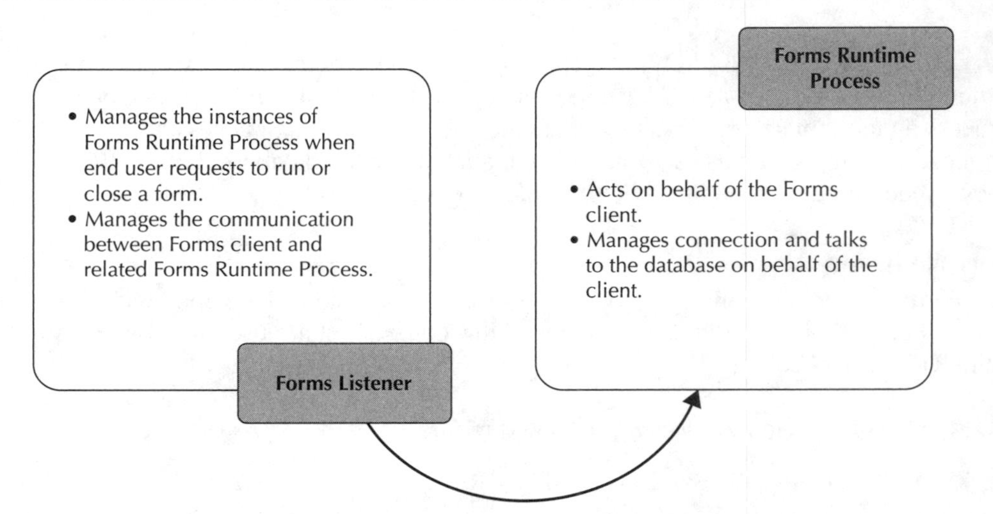

FIGURE 2-5. *Forms server components*

take for granted that they are very similar in architecture. If we generalize the roles of the Forms Listener and the Runtime Process, then we can say that the Forms Listener accepts connections from the client, which then "spawns" and manages the Forms Runtime processes responsible for communication with Oracle Applications database as depicted in Figure 2-6.

Concurrent Processing Server

Aside from allowing users to interact with the system through the user interface, in Oracle Applications you can schedule a background (noninteractive) processing of long-running transactions, batch jobs, and reports. In Oracle Applications, this is referred to as *concurrent processing*, implying that multiple jobs can be run as concurrent programs simultaneously on one or more nodes. The key advantage of having this type of node is that it allows for computationally intensive operations to be run on either a separate physical server or at a different time when, for example, the key business users are not logged in. A concurrent program can be scheduled to be run either periodically or as a one-off task. In the jargon of Oracle Applications,

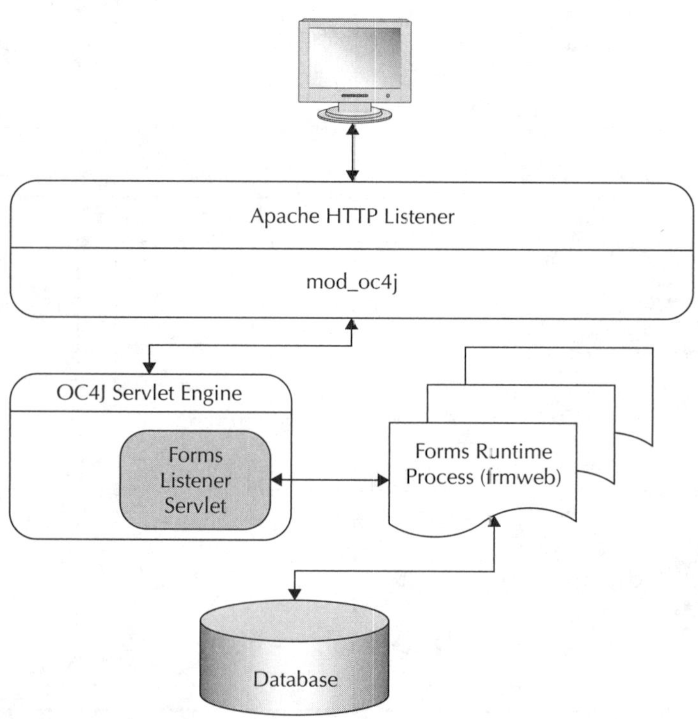

FIGURE 2-6. *Overview of Oracle Forms 10gR2 component used in R12*

you submit a concurrent request through Oracle Applications forms for the concurrent program that needs to be run.

As shown in Figure 2-7, concurrent requests are managed by Concurrent Managers. The following list of events summarizes what happens when a user submits the concurrent request:

1. User navigates to the Submit Request form in Oracle Applications and submits the request to run a report (for example, Gather Table Statistics).
2. The details of the concurrent requests are recorded in the FND_CONCURRENT_REQUESTS table.
3. The Concurrent Managers are scheduled to poll the request table for the new requests.

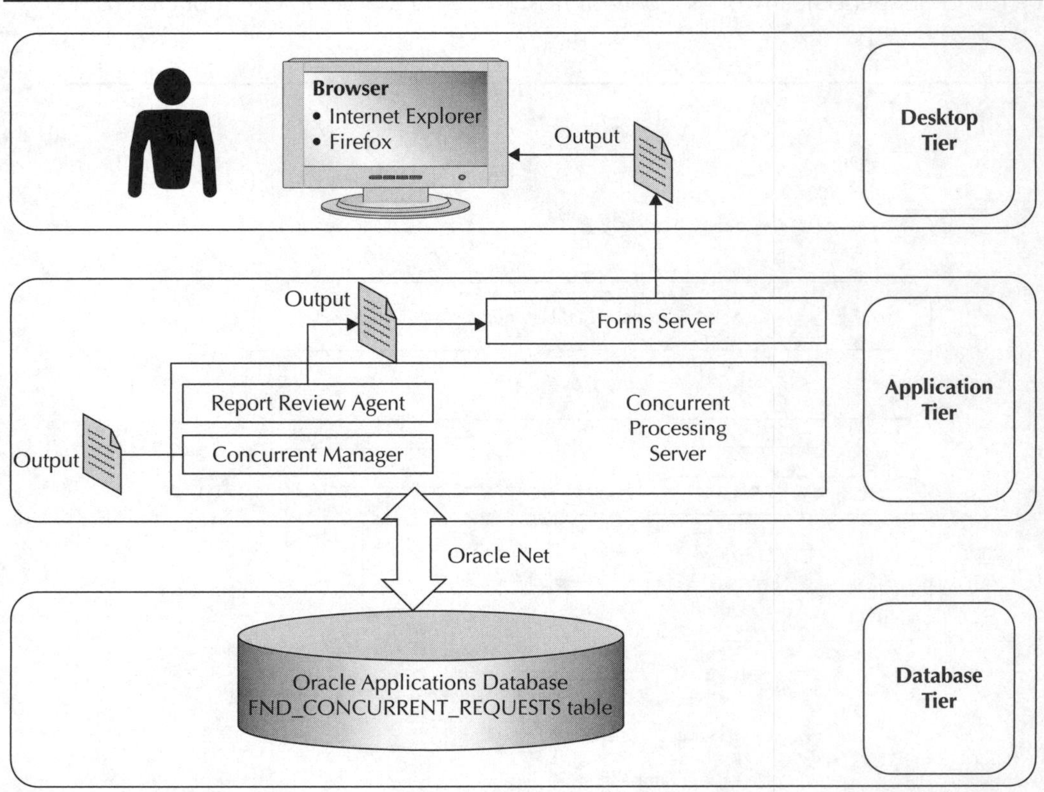

FIGURE 2-7. *Overview of concurrent processing*

4. Depending on the type of the submitted concurrent request, the Concurrent Manager spawns an appropriate process to fulfill the request. The type of the request could be a host program such as the Unix shell script, Oracle Reports, a SQL or PL/SQL program, a C executable, Java, and others.

5. Upon the program completion, the Concurrent Manager updates the status in the FND_CONCURRENT_REQUESTS table. For the requests that complete normally, the status column is updated to Normal. Failed requests are recorded with the status set to Error. Other statuses are Warning, Canceled, and Terminated.

6. The Concurrent Processing server generates the log and/or output file for the concurrent request. When the user needs to see the output file, such as a generated report, a program called Report Review Agent passes the output file to the Forms server, which in turn passes the report page by page for viewing back to user.

The key process in Concurrent Processing is Internal Manager. Internal Manager is an executable that controls startup and stopping of all the other managers; system administrators can activate and deactivate it from command line. The fault tolerance for the Internal Manager is provided by Internal Monitor Process, which monitors the Internal Manager and attempts to restart it if it detects its failure. The Internal Manager can run and control other managers on any node. Concurrent processing also offers specialized managers such as Conflict Resolution Manager. Concurrent programs can be defined as incompatible with other programs, so they should not run together if there is a danger of jeopardizing data integrity, for example. The Concurrent Resolution Manager prevents running incompatible programs by queuing conflicting requests in its own queue. Most of the work, though, is performed by Standard Managers that accept any type of concurrent requests such as PL/SQL, SQL, reports, and other programs all the time.

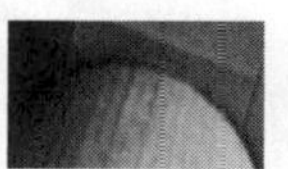

NOTE
Although concurrent processing is one of the key components in the E-Business Suite architecture, we should think of it as an AOL (Applications Object Library) component.

Reports Server in R11i

The Reports server is a middle-tier component in the R11i technology stack. As of R12, this component is not present in the middle-tier architecture as a standalone component in Oracle Applications. The purpose of the Reports server is to satisfy the reporting needs for an organization. The Reports server fits into the three-tier architecture in the following way:

- The client tier contains the web browser, where the request is initiated.
- The server software is installed on the application (middle) tier.
- The data required by the reports runtime engine is stored in Oracle Database.

Figure 2-8 describes the Reports server (Oracle Reports 6i) components and processing overview:

1. The user clicks the report link in the browser. The HTTP request from the browser is passed on to the Apache Web server (Listener).
2. The Apache Web server passes the request to the Reports Web CGI. Reports Web CGI is a standard CGI web component that enables dynamic communication to the Reports server.
3. The Reports Web CGI processes the request and identifies an executable command and arguments and runs the command that is executed by the Reports server.
4. The Reports server checks if it already has the report output file in its cache. If it finds it, it will return the report output file from the cache.

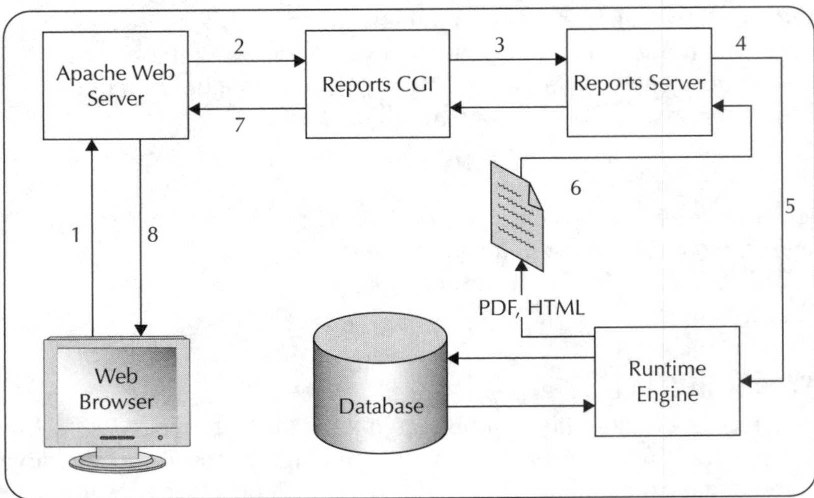

FIGURE 2-8. *Reports server architecture*

5. If the output file is not in the cache, the Reports server sends the command line to one of its available runtime engines for execution.
6. The runtime engine executes the report.
7. The Reports Web CGI receives the report output from the Reports server. The output is passed back on to the web server.
8. The web server passes back the report output to the end user's browser.

In R11i, the Reports server is located on the same node as the Concurrent Processing server.

Oracle Reports in R12

As mentioned in the previous section, the Reports server is not part of the system architecture in Oracle Applications R12. Oracle Reports are still part of the technology stack hosted in OracleAS 10.1.2 Oracle Home; however, the traditional Oracle Reports are run through the Concurrent Processing node by directly calling the executable rwrun.

Admin Server

The main purpose of the Admin or Administration server is to maintain the applications database objects, apply patches, and perform upgrades of Oracle Applications. It doesn't have to be a separate physical server machine as it does not require a lot of processing. Most of the processing occurs on the database server side where updating and maintenance of Oracle Applications database objects takes place. In Oracle Applications R12, the idea of having a separate Admin node is obsolete; the administration and maintenance tasks can be performed from any application tier node.

Oracle Home Directories and File System in Oracle Applications

ORACLE_HOME refers to the installation directory where an Oracle software component is installed. The environment variable ORACLE_HOME is usually defined to point to the top directory where some Oracle software component such as the application or database server is installed. These top-level installation directories are called "Oracle Home." E-Business Suite R11i and R12 use many different versions of Oracle products, resulting in the diverse structure of the underlying file system. Figure 2-9 shows the different versions of ORACLE_HOMEs used in R11i and R12.

At the time of writing, Release 12 is installed and configured to utilize the features of the very latest Oracle middle-tier products: OracleAS 10.1.3 and Oracle

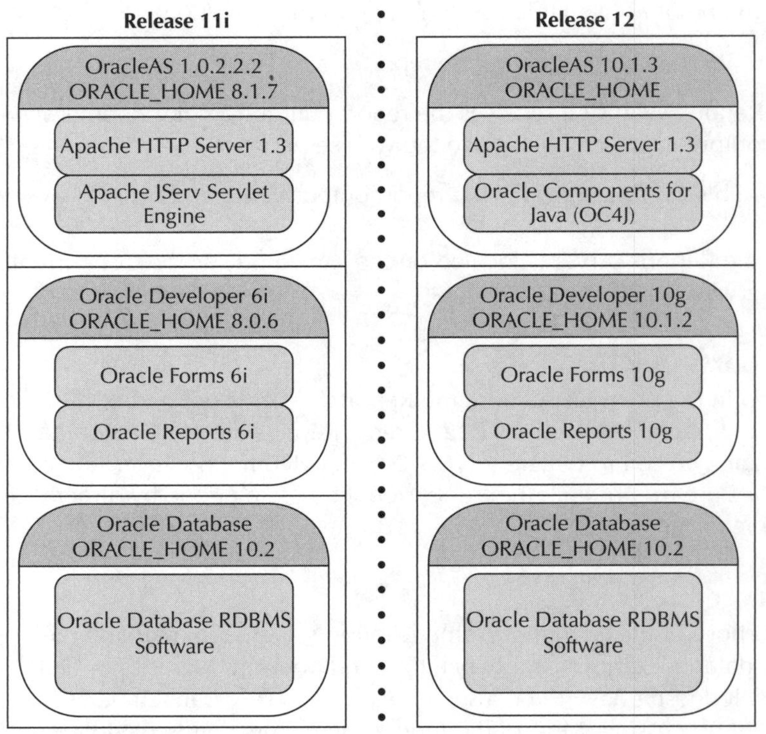

FIGURE 2-9. *ORACLE_HOMEs in R11i and R12*

Developer 10g. Oracle Applications database also tends to be certified against one of the latest releases of Oracle Database software.

File System in Oracle Applications

Various Oracle products are used by Oracle Applications, and its own utilities are stored in various directory structures. As we mentioned in the previous section, environment variables such as ORACLE_HOME can be set up in your Unix or Windows environment to point to the important top-level directory structures of your Oracle Applications installation. The following are the most important top-level directories in Oracle Applications:

- **<APPL_TOP>** Contains Oracle Applications product directories such as General Ledger (GL), Purchasing (PO), and many others.
- **<COMMON_TOP>** Contains common directories and files such as log files and Java libraries shared across different products.

- **<ORACLE_HOME>** Contains the technology stack components such as Oracle Database RDBMS and Oracle Developer Tools (Forms, Reports) software.
- **<DATA_TOP>** Contains database data files for Oracle Applications.
- **<INST_TOP>** This is new to R12. It contains various configuration files to provide the ability to share Applications and technology stack code between multiple instances.

Because of the substantial changes in file system structure between Release 11i and Release 12, we are going to look at them separately.

File System in R11i

The file system in R11i can be divided into three main parts: APPL_TOP, COMMON_TOP, and the technology stack, as illustrated in Figure 2-10. The technology stack is comprised of Oracle Developer 6i components in 8.0.6 ORACLE_HOME, Oracle Applications Server 1.0.2.2.2 in 8.1.7 ORACLE_HOME, and Oracle Database in its own ORACLE_HOME. The database can be any version that is certified to run against the version of E-Business Suite in question.

Database Node in R11i

The Database node is installed in its own directory, which is named after the version of the database installed. Figure 2-10 shows the Oracle Database as 10gR2.

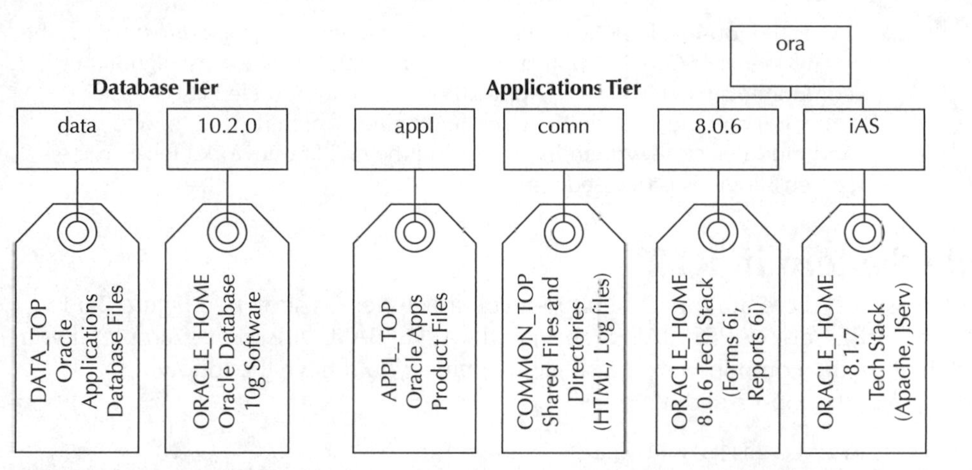

FIGURE 2-10. *File system in R11i*

Oracle Applications database data files (.dbf) are installed in the separate data directory. Installing the Oracle software components in their own ORACLE_HOME separate from other components is sometimes referred to as *split configuration* in Oracle Applications. It allows for flexible update of individual components of Oracle software.

Applications Node in R11i

The Applications node is installed in the appl, comn, and ora directories.

- The APPL_TOP directory (appl) contains the main Oracle Applications environment file (<ctx_name>.env on Unix or <ctx_name> on Windows; <ctx_name> is usually <SID>_<hostname>), all product-related directories and subdirectories, and Oracle Apps technology files and directory structures.
- The COMMON_TOP directory (comn) contains the files and directory structures that are shared among the products. For example, the admin directory under COMMON_TOP is the default location where Concurrent Managers write the output and log files from concurrent program requests. Another example is the html directory, which contains various HTML-based pages and screens. Java classes are also installed under COMMON_TOP in the java directory.
- The technology stack (ora directory)
    - 8.0.6 is the top-level ORACLE_HOME 8.0.6 technology stack directory for Oracle Developer 6i (Forms 6i and Reports 6i).
    - iAS is the top-level ORACLE_HOME 8.1.7 technology stack directory for the components of Oracle Application Server 1.0.2.2.2. The most significant components used in Oracle Applications R11i are Oracle HTTP Server (Apache) and the Apache JServ servlet engine, which runs components and modules code written in Java. All of the OA Framework (Self-Service) screens' logic is processed within JServ.

File System in R12

In Release 12, there are three main top-level directories, as shown in Figure 2-11: <APPS_BASE>/db, <APPS_BASE>/apps, and <APPS_BASE>/inst. For example, if you install all of the components on a single machine, you'd have the following structure of the top-level directories:

```
 [avisr12@r12 R1204]$ pwd/oracle/apps/R1204
[avisr12@r12 R1204]$ ls
apps  db  inst
```

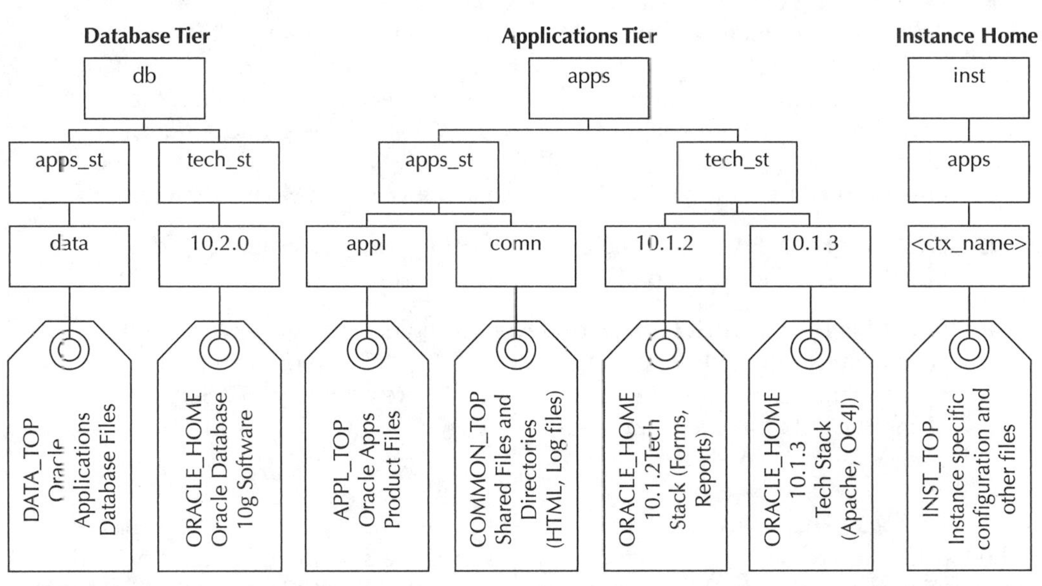

FIGURE 2-11. *File system in R12*

From the preceding listing, we can see that the <APPS_BASE> directory is the top directory where Oracle Application software is installed, and in this case it is /oracle/apps/R1204.

Database Node in R12

The Database node is installed in the db directory and is split into two directories, apps_st and tech_st, which contain Oracle Applications database data files (.dbf) and Oracle Database software. This split configuration of the database ORACLE_HOME from the other components allows for better flexibility when separate components of the system need to be upgraded independently.

Applications Node in R12

The Applications node is installed in the apps directory. This node is split into applications (apps_st) and technology (tech_st) stacks. There are four main top-level directories in this node:

- **APPL_TOP** Contains the main Oracle Applications environment file (<ctx_name>.env on Unix or <ctx_name> on Windows; <ctx_name> is <SID>_<hostname>, which in our case is APPSR124_r12.env), all product-related directories and subdirectories, and Oracle Apps technology files and directory structures.

- **COMMON_TOP** Contains the files and directory structures that are shared among the products. For example, the admin directory under COMMON_TOP is the default location where Concurrent Managers write the output and log files from concurrent program requests. Another example is the html directory, which contains various HTML-based pages and screens. Java classes are also installed under COMMON_TOP in the java directory. The environment variable $JAVA_BASE points to this top-level Java directory.
- **ORACLE_HOME 10.1.2** The top-level technology stack directory for Oracle Developer 10g (Forms and Reports).
- **ORACLE_HOME 10.1.3** The top-level technology stack directory for the components of Oracle Application Server 10.1.3. The most significant components used in Oracle Applications R12 are Oracle HTTP Server (Apache) and Oracle Components for Java (OC4J), which runs most of the code written in Java.

In R12, Oracle has introduced a new concept of Instance Home, and INST_TOP is the top-level directory. This directory contains instance-specific configuration and log files. Separating the instance-specific structures from other ORACLE_HOMEs allows an easy deployment of the shared file system for components that are not instance specific. Therefore, multiple nodes and instances of Oracle Apps can share applications and technology stack components, which is illustrated in Figure 2-12.

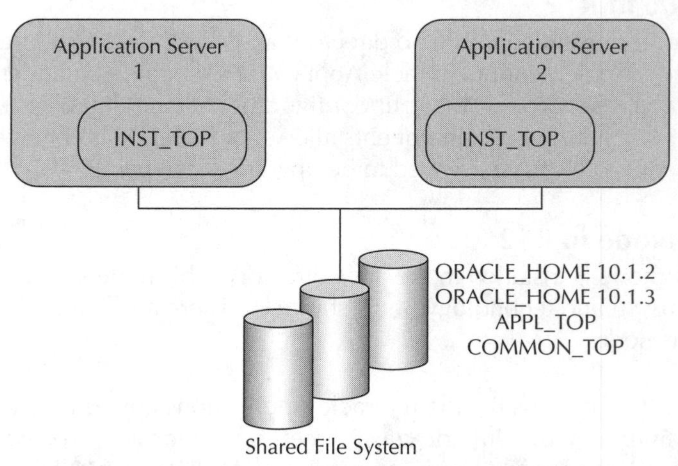

FIGURE 2-12. *Application tier components in R12*

Environment Files in Oracle Applications

Environment files are the type of configuration files usually used to set up a working environment to point to the various top-level directory structures such as COMMON_TOP and other environment variables such as NLS_LANG relevant to Oracle Applications configuration. During the installation, several environment files are created, usually in the root of different ORACLE_HOMEs. For applications developers, the most important environment file is the consolidated environment file APPS<CTX_NAME>.env in the APPL_TOP directory, where <CTX_NAME> is the configuration context name, usually in the format <DATABASE_SID>_<HOSTNAME>. For example, our installation on Linux has APPSR124_r12.env environment file with the following content:

```
[avisr12@r12 appl]$ view APPSR124_r12.env
# ####################################################################
. /oracle/apps/R1204/inst/apps/R124_r12/ora/10.1.2/R124_r12.env
. /oracle/apps/R1204/apps/apps_st/appl/R124_r12.env
```

The last two lines set up both the applications and technology stack environments. If you look at the R124_r12.env in the APPL_TOP directory, you'll notice that there are many variables set through this environment file such as FND_TOP, AD_TOP, NLS_LANG, APPLOUT, APPLLOG, and many others. On Windows, the equivalent consolidated environment file in %APPL_TOP% is called envshell.cmd; executing it opens another command line window with sourced environment. On Unix/Linux platforms, the environment file is sourced by executing . *APPS<CTX_NAME>.env* (note the dot is followed by a space and the name of the consolidated environment file, followed by return), which in the example looks like:

```
[avisr12@r12 appl]$ . APPSR124_r12.env
```

Database Tier

Oracle Applications store and manage applications data in Oracle Database. Both releases are certified against one of the latest releases of the Oracle Database product (as of this writing, Oracle Apps uses the 10gR2 database). The function of the database tier is very similar in both releases, and we will discuss it in more detail in the sections to follow.

Database Objects

The Oracle Applications database stores applications data and database-side code. For example:

- Data database objects
    - Database tables
    - Sequences
    - Indexes
- Database code
    - PL/SQL code
    - Triggers
    - Views
    - Synonyms
    - Java code in database

Oracle Applications Database Schemas

In the Oracle Applications database design, there are two main types of Oracle Database schemas:

- **Product schemas** Contains only data-related objects such as product database tables and sequences. An example is the GL (General Ledger) product. All of the data-related tables are owned by the GL schema in the database.
- **APPS schema** Contains database code–related objects for all the products, such as PL/SQL code, views, triggers, and others.

APPS Database Schema

To achieve a higher reuse of data sharing, Oracle Applications utilize an APPS database schema. Imagine for a second if all the database code and data objects were owned and stored in the product-specific schemas such as GL (General Ledger), AP (Payables), PO (Purchasing), and others. In this scenario, it would be really difficult to manage the access rights for all the objects that, for example, a database stored procedure needs to access in other product schemas. The approach used in Oracle Applications is to have database synonyms in the APPS schema for each database table and sequence in individual product schemas, and in addition

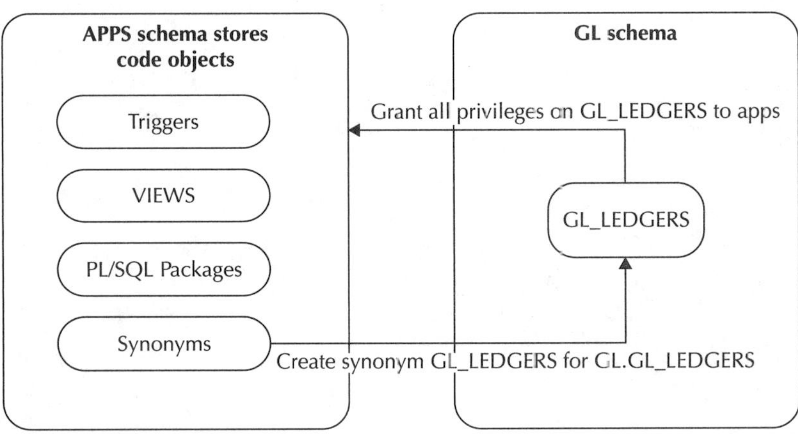

FIGURE 2-13. *APPS schema in Oracle Applications*

to that, each product schema grants full privileges to APPS schema, as depicted in Figure 2-13. This way, a database user with access to the APPS schema has full access to all of the products data in all schemas.

Other Schemas in Oracle Applications

There are two additional schemas in an Oracle Applications database:

- **APPLSYS** This schema contains objects from the Oracle Applications foundation and technology layer. Examples of the products in this category are AD (administration utilities) and FND (Applications foundation).
- **APPLSYSPUB** This schema is a special one and is used only for the purposes of the initial user login process to validate a user's credentials.

Summary

In this chapter we covered the very basics of E-Business Suite architecture. We discussed the three-tier architecture and their corresponding individual components without going into too much detail, as almost all of the components are covered from the developer's perspective in their own chapters later in this book. The changes in technology stack between releases R11i and R12 are substantial, and we highlighted the main differences between the two releases. In R12, the technology stack is in line with the latest releases of Fusion Middleware, making the integration with other systems and emerging technologies such as SOA much more versatile.

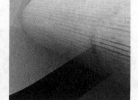

CHAPTER 3

Application Object Library (AOL)

n this chapter, we are going to outline the most important functions of Application Object Library (AOL), a particularly important subject to developers, as it provides a foundation for most of the extensions in Oracle E-Business Suite.

AOL is a part of the Applications Technology layer and, as the name suggests, AOL provides common functionality for all E-Business Suite products through a library of reusable database objects, programs, and code. Apart from providing an efficient development framework to developers, AOL has many other functions such as providing E-Business Suite with security infrastructure, tools to manage concurrent processing, tools to manage users and audit their activity, and many other features.

AOL is one of the key parts of E-Business Suite that must be given due attention by both application developers and system administrators. It is documented in various places within the Oracle Applications documentation library such as Oracle Applications Flexfields Guide, Oracle Applications Developer's Guide, and Oracle Applications System Administrator's Guide. Here, we look at some of the main AOL functions from an application developer's perspective.

Overview of Security Architecture

A user's login details get authenticated against a table that holds the login and password details. In some cases, the authentication of a user happens entirely in Oracle Applications; in other cases, a user can be authenticated in partnership with an external system like Active Directory/LDAP. Regardless of how the authentication happens, once the users are authenticated they are presented with a list of responsibilities that in turn are assigned a menu and request group. The following illustration represents hierarchy of the function security in Oracle Applications:

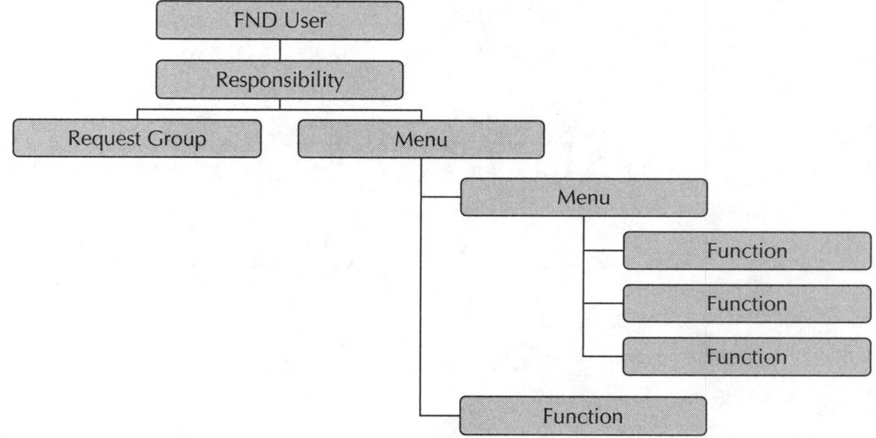

A *responsibility* is a collection of business functionalities, such as UI screens and reports, that is granted to Oracle Applications users for the purpose of access control to the screens and data that are related to the user's role within the organization. In other words, what a user can do in Oracle Applications is determined by assigned responsibilities. The responsibility is assigned a menu, which represents a hierarchy of functions and other menus, and a request group, which allows access to programs and reports relevant to the organizational role.

A *menu* is a reusable grouping of application functionality and consists of functions and other menus. As shown in the illustration, menus can have multiple functions attached to them. You can think of functions as units of an application's functionality such as UI screens. For example, every HTML and Forms-based screen is associated with a corresponding function, which can get attached to menus so that users can access it through an assigned responsibility.

A *request group* is a grouping of reports and concurrent programs that is assigned to a responsibility. For example, custom reports have to be attached to a request group before the end users can access them through the responsibility.

The following are frequently asked questions related to the function security:

- **Why does a screen's functionality change when it is attached to different functions?** This happens because the screens are developed in such a manner that their functionalities can differ depending upon the parameters that are passed into that screen. Menus never pass parameters to the screens, but a function can. When a given screen is attached to two different functions, each function can pass different parameters to the screen. Consequently, even though the same screen is reachable via two different menus, the functionality exposed by the screen can vary, depending upon the parameters passed by the function to the screen. The typical example is when a screen is developed to cater to both Data Entry and Read Only modes. For example, if the page flow requires this screen in Read Only mode, you can create a function for this screen and pass parameter to it so that the underlying code can pick it up at runtime and render the screen in Read Only mode.

  To recap, a responsibility is attached to a menu, and a menu can have several menu items. Each menu item can be attached to a function, and the function is attached to a screen. At the time of defining a function, you specify a screen name and optional parameters with their default values.

- **Is a menu item always attached to a function?** No. Sometimes a menu item is attached to another menu. By doing so, you effectively create submenus within the menu, which creates a menu nesting. However, a function must be attached to a menu in order for it to be accessed by the end user.

- **Does a function always pass parameters and parameter values to a screen?** No. If the screen has not been developed to be dependent on any parameter, then of course there is no need to pass any parameters. However, you will still have to define a function if you want a screen to become accessible.

Applications in E-Business Suite

Oracle E-Business Suite is a combination of various applications such as Payables, General Ledger, Payroll, Human Resources, and many others. We can refer to them as modules, but formally these are known as *applications*. The main purpose of an application is to divide an E-Business Suite instance logically into different business functions.

An application is defined by its long (full) name, short name, and base path, which points to the top directory for that application on the file system structure. Customizations should be registered with a custom application, which should be created to host the extensions and custom modules. The grouping of custom objects under the custom application helps protect them from upgrades and patches.

An Example: Attaching a Concurrent Program to an Application

Concurrent programs provide a mechanism in E-Business Suite by which executables such as Reports, PL/SQL, and SQL Scripts can be run. Each concurrent program has an executable. Each concurrent program and its executable are attached to an application. The location of the executable file on the server may vary depending upon the application with which it is associated.

For example, the report's executables are RDF files, SQL*Plus executables are SQL files, and Unix Shell Scripts are PROG files (in Oracle Apps). All these executables must be registered with an application.

Each application is mapped to a specific directory path on the server. For example, application XXPO (which, for example, holds PO Customizations) may map to directory /home/oracle/apps/appl/xxpo.

To develop or customize a report in a Purchasing module, assuming the executable name is XXPOPRINT.rdf, you need to register the executable with the XXPO application. Hence, this RDF must be transferred to directory /home/oracle/apps/appl/xxpo/reports/<US>.

When the end user runs this report from the application, Oracle Apps will identify the executable XXPOPRINT as being attached to the XX Purchase Order application. This application will have a short name of XXPO and will be mapped to directory /home/oracle/apps/appl/xxpo/reports/US for reports, which is where the file XXPOPRINT.rdf resides on the server. Hence, the name of the application will help the Oracle Apps environment locate the executable file on the server.

Each application has a base path, which is also the name of a corresponding operating system environment variable. These environment variables are also called top directories, and there is one for each module. For example, the Purchase Order application has a corresponding environment variable named $PO_TOP.

System administrators can define a custom application from the System Administrator responsibility using the following navigation path:

```
(N)Application|Register
```

Profile Options in Oracle Applications

Profile options provide a great deal of flexibility to Oracle Applications developers. They are a key component of Oracle Applications and must be understood properly.

You can think of a profile option as a global variable in Oracle Applications; however, the value of this global variable changes depending upon factors like the following:

- The user who has logged in
- The responsibility used by the user
- The application being used by the user via the responsibility
- The server to which that user is connected

The order of precedence is very important. The applications check the user value first, then responsibility, application, and site levels, in that order.

The profile options keep the application flexible and also avoid hard-coding in the programs because business rules in various countries and different organizations can be different. Oracle delivers profile options that avoid hard-coding of logic within programs and lets the implementation team on site decide the values of those global variables.

Oracle has delivered hundreds of preseeded profile options that have varying purposes. Here are some of the different actions they can take:

- **Turn the debugging on to generate debug messages** Say one of one thousand users reports a problem, and you wish to enable debugging for that specific user. In this case, you can turn on the debugging profile option for that specific user.
- **Control program flow** For example, a profile option can control which user can give discounts to his or her customers at the time of data entry. The profile option Discount Allowed could be created and set to a value of either Yes or No for each order entry user.
- **Control access** Let's assume an organization has departments D1 and D2. Managers of both departments have the HRMS Employee View responsibility. But you do not want the manager of D2 to be able to see the list of employees in organization D1. You can set a profile option for the username of each of these users. The value assigned to such a profile option will be Name of the Organization, for which they can see the employees. Of course, the SQL in the screen that displays a list of employees will filter the data based on the "logged in user's profile option value." (In reality, this functionality is implemented in Oracle HRMS using the Security Profiles profile option.)

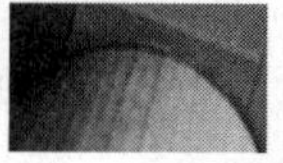

TIP
Developers performing customizations must not modify the seeded definitions of profile options.

Example Use Case for Profile Options

In this example, we'll assume that you are an Oracle Applications developer building a screen in the Order Entry module. Here is the high-level list of requirements for the screen that is to be developed:

- The screen should be flexible enough to ensure that different users of the screen can give different levels of discounts. For example, a clerk Order Entry user can give no more than a 5 percent discount. But a Sales Manager can enter an order with 15 percent discount.
- There should not be any hard-coding regarding the maximum permissible discount.

- There will be a discount field in the screen.
- When the discount value is entered in the discount field, an error will be raised if the user violates the maximum permissible discount.

Follow these steps to build the screen:

1. Define a profile option named ONT Maximum Discount Allowed. This profile option will be created using the short name ONT_MAX_DISCOUNT. The short name is the internal name used by AOL.
2. Insert the following code in the when-validate-item of the discount field (assuming the screen is built in Oracle Forms):

```
IF :oe_line_block.discount_value >
   fnd_profile.value('ONT_MAX_DISCOUNT')
THEN
message( 'You can't give discount more than '
|| fnd_profile.value('ONT_MAX_DISCOUNT') || '%' ) ;
raise form_trigger_failure ; -- raise error after showing message
END IF ;
```

NOTE
In practice, the message dictionary should be used to display the message text instead of the hard-coded message text value.

Here is how the client implementing Oracle Order Entry could configure his or her system:

1. Navigate to System Administration and click the System Profile menu.
2. For the Clerk user JOHN, set the value of profile ONT Maximum Discount Allowed to 5. For Sales Manager User SMITH, set the value of profile ONT Maximum Discount Allowed to 15.

If the implementing company has hundreds of Order Entry Clerks and dozens of Order Entry Sales Managers, the profiles can be set at a higher level.

In this example, each Order Entry Clerk can be assigned the responsibility XX Order Entry Clerk Responsibility. Each Sales Manager can be assigned the responsibility named "XX Order Entry Sales Manager Responsibility." Thereafter, you can assign the profile option value to both of these responsibilities.

XX Order Entry Clerk Responsibility can have a profile value of 5 percent assigned against it, and XX Order Entry Sales Manager Responsibility can have a profile option value of 15 percent assigned.

In the when-validate-item of the discount field, the following code could be written:

```
IF :oe_line_block.discount_value > fnd_profile.value('ONT_MAX_DISCOUNT')
THEN
message( 'You can't give discount more than '
|| fnd_profile.value('ONT_MAX_DISCOUNT') || '%' ) ;
raise form_trigger_failure ;-- raise error after showing message
END IF ;
```

Note that the coding style does not change even though the profile option is now being assigned for responsibility. The reason is that the API fnd_profile.value will follow logic similar to this:

- Does the profile option value exist for the user?
  - ***Yes*** *Use the profile option value defined for the user.*
  - ***No*** *Does the profile option value exist for the responsibility?*
    - ***Yes*** *Use the profile option value defined for the current responsibility that user has logged into.*
    - ***No*** *Use the profile option value defined for the site level.*

Creating Custom Profile Options

Custom profile options are useful when you are building extensions to Oracle Applications Forms/Interfaces. In order to keep your code flexible and configurable, you can define custom profile options and then reference them in your source code. To create custom profile options, navigate to the responsibility Application Developer and click the Profile menu. You can decide the levels at which to set your custom profile option. It is also possible to specify whether an end user will be able to view or edit the value of this profile option.

For example, a user must not be allowed to change the maximum discount he or she can offer to a customer. However, you may want a user to change his or her default printer through a profile option.

Tables Used by Profile Options

Profile options definitions are stored in the tables FND_PROFILE_OPTIONS and FND_PROFILE_OPTIONS_TL. Column PROFILE_OPTION_NAME contains the short name of the profile option, whereas USER_PROFILE_OPTION_NAME contains the descriptive name of the profile option.

The values assigned to the profile options at different levels are stored in table FND_PROFILE_OPTION_VALUES.

TIP
You should always use the public API to access the profile options in programs or screens. You must never update FND_% or any other tables in Oracle Applications directly.

Main PL/SQL APIs for Profile Options

In order to interact with profile options programmatically, you must use the APIs. For performance reasons, the profile option values are cached. The moment a profile option value is read for the first time for a user session, its value gets cached (for that session). The caching can happen both at server-side and client-side. Some of the key APIs and their purpose are listed in Table 3-1.

API Name	Purpose
fnd_profile.put	Passes as parameters the name of the profile option and the value to which it must be set. Updates the value of profile option in the cache, in the context of logged in user. Values in the database table FND_PROFILE_OPTION_VALUES are not updated. A PUT on the server affects only the server-side profile cache, and a PUT on the client affects only the client-side cache. By using PUT, you destroy the synchrony between server-side and client-side profile caches. Hence widespread use of FND_PROFILE.PUT is not recommended.
fnd_profile .value	Returns the value of the profile option for the current logged in context. Passes the name of the profile option as a parameter. If the profile option value does not exist in the cache, then table FND_PROFILE_OPTION_VALUES is queried and the cache gets populated.
fnd_profile .save_user	Sets the value of the profile option into table FND_PROFILE_OPTION_VALUES for the current logged in user. Also populates the cache.
fnd_profile.save	Sets the value of the profile option into table FND_PROFILE_OPTION_VALUES at any level. Also populates the cache. The following are some common examples for using this API : FND_PROFILE.SAVE('PROFNAME_HERE', 'P_VAL', 'SITE'); FND_PROFILE.SAVE('PROFNAME_HERE', 'P_VAL', 'APPL', 321532); FND_PROFILE.SAVE('PROFNAME_HERE', 'P_VAL', 'RESP', 321532, 345234); FND_PROFILE.SAVE('PROFNAME_HERE', 'P_VAL', 'USER', 123321);

TABLE 3-1. *Profile Options APIs*

Descriptive Flexfields (DFFs)

Organizations that implement E-Business Suite often want to capture additional information specific to their enterprise through the screens. This is achieved through the configuration of descriptive flexfields (DFF), which provide a mechanism for capturing additional data in application tables through user-defined fields without the need to customize the underlying database schema.

In other words, descriptive flexfields add extra information to a transaction. Each screen usually consists of a group of fields, and these fields capture the data entered by the user. Of course, most fields have a business purpose; for example, in the Purchase Order entry screen, the supplier field captures the name of the supplier from whom you purchase the goods. Oracle develops the screens in a generic manner, so that they can be used by any company in the world. However, different companies have different or additional needs to capture extra details about a transaction. For example, in purchasing, one company might require a Shipping Special Instructions field, whereas other company might require a Telephone Number of Purchaser field. To meet the requirements of different companies, Oracle Applications comes with a preseeded set of flexible fields. Descriptive flexfields allow you to customize your applications to capture data that would not otherwise be tracked by your application. These fields can be used to capture values for additional fields as per business requirements. Given that these are generic fields, they are named ATTRIBUTE1, ATTRIBUTE2...ATTRIBUTE*n*.

To activate these fields, you have to configure the descriptive flexfields, but before you can do that, you must ensure that you have access to the Application Developer responsibility. Follow these steps to identify the flexfield:

1. Identify the table into which you wish to capture additional information. Ensure that this table has columns named ATTRIBUTE1...*n* in the database.
2. Navigate to the responsibility Application Developer.

Within Application Developer responsibility, follow the instructions as illustrated in Figure 3-1:

The steps that follow configure a DFF on the Purchase Order Screen. To try it out,

1. Click the menu option Flexfield | Descriptive | Register.
2. Query the table that will capture the additional information.
3. Note the title of the descriptive flexfield, as this will be used to perform the query in the Segments screen. (It is in the Segments screen that you will define the new fields that you want to enable for the end users, so that data can be entered into ATTRIBUTE1..15 database columns.)

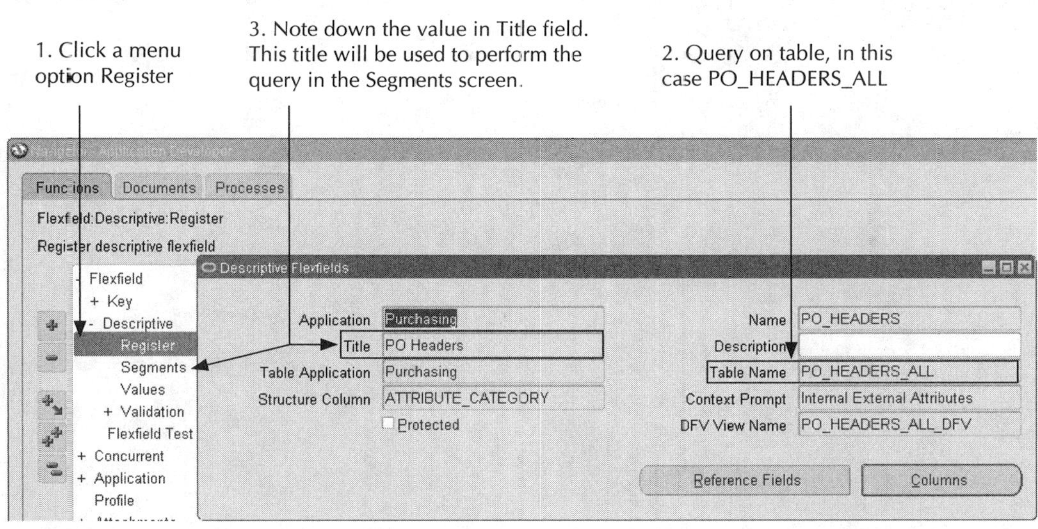

FIGURE 3-1. *Descriptive flexfield registration and the relation between the table and the DFF title*

Once the descriptive flexfield title has been identified, you need to define the segments, as shown in Figure 3-2.

In order to define the flexfield segments, in the Application Developer responsibility, follow the navigation path (N)Flexfield | Descriptive | Segments.

1. Query on the descriptive flexfield title that you noted from the Register DFF screen.
2. Unfreeze the flexfield by unchecking the check box. (It is not possible to amend the flexfield segment if it is in a frozen state.)
3. Select Global Data Elements and click the Segments button (the button is not visible in Figure 3-2).
4. Give a user-friendly name to this field and map this field to an ATTRIBUTE column. Also attach a value set (explained in next section). A value set is used to ensure that only validated values are entered into descriptive flexfields by the user.
5. Make the flexfield segment required or nonrequired as per business requirements.

Freeze the flexfield again after making the changes.

After following the previous steps, you should see the flexfield segment appear in the Purchase Order Entry screen as shown in Figure 3-3.

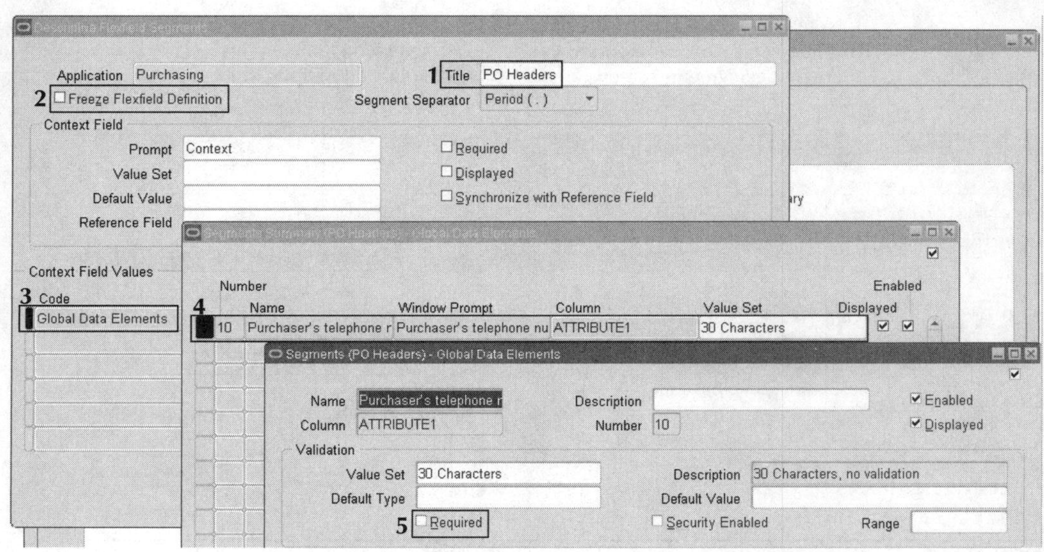

FIGURE 3-2. *Descriptive flexfield segments*

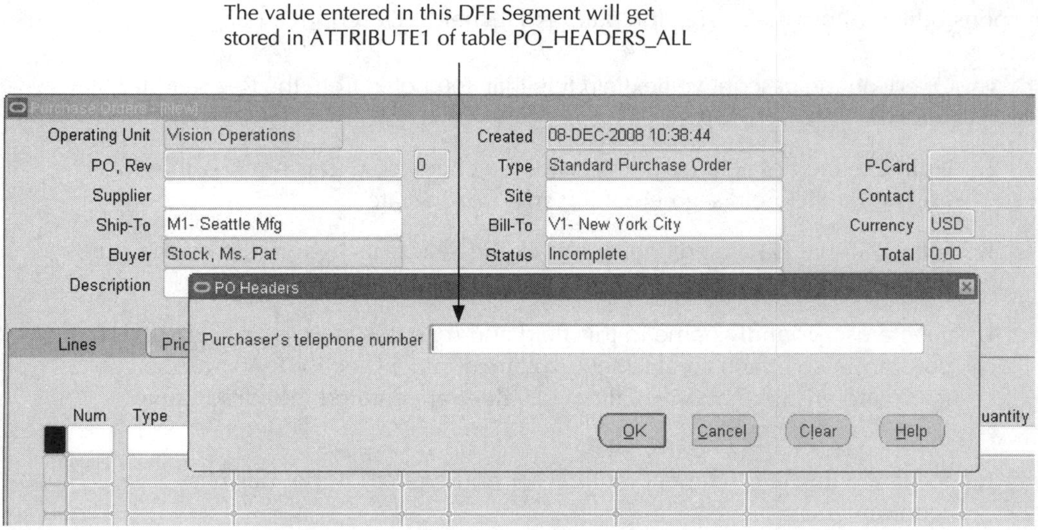

The value entered in this DFF Segment will get stored in ATTRIBUTE1 of table PO_HEADERS_ALL

Operating Unit Vision Operations | Created 08-DEC-2008 10:38:44
PO, Rev 0 | Type Standard Purchase Order | P-Card
Supplier | Site | Contact
Ship-To M1- Seattle Mfg | Bill-To V1- New York City | Currency USD
Buyer Stock, Ms. Pat | Status Incomplete | Total 0.00
Description

PO Headers
Purchaser's telephone number
OK Cancel Clear Help

Lines Pric
Num Type uantity

FIGURE 3-3. *Descriptive flexfield segment as seen by the end user*

Descriptive Flexfield FAQs

We have compiled a list of frequently asked questions about descriptive flexfields in this section to serve as a useful reference when working with DFFs.

What Are Global Data Elements?

One flexfield can have multiple structures. A structure is a grouping of fields or segments. All DFFs have a default structure named Global Data Elements. If you add segments within global segments, then those segments will always be visible in the screen regardless of context (Reference). However, if you have other structures defined in a DFF, then at any given point in time, only the segments or fields within one of the structures will be displayed on screen.

What Is the Significance of the Reference Field in the DFF Segment Screen?

In certain cases you might want descriptive flexfield segments to appear on a screen based on the value of another field in that screen. For example, you may want to display Telephone Number Segment when the user is entering a purchase order that requires approval, but not for a purchase order that does not require approval. We know that the field APPROVAL_REQUIRED_FLAG holds this value and therefore we would make this the REFERENCE field. This field must be enabled as a reference field in the descriptive flexfield register screen (accessed by clicking the Reference button). Please note that it is not mandatory for a descriptive flexfield to have a reference field.

How Does the Reference Field Control Which Segments Are Displayed?

Let's assume that on the Purchase Order screen there is a field named Approval Required, and the internal name of the field is APPROVAL_REQUIRED_FLAG. Let's further assume that our requirement is as listed:

Condition	Fields to Be Displayed on the Purchasing Screen
APPROVAL_REQUIRED_FLAG='Y'	Purchaser's Telephone Number Reason for Purchase
APPROVAL_REQUIRED_FLAG='N'	Verbally Agreed with Manager[Yes/No]
APPROVAL_REQUIRED_FLAG is Y or N or Blank	Special Delivery Instructions Alternate Delivery Address

To meet this requirement, your DFF will be defined as follows:

Section	Field	Value
Context Field	Reference Field	APPROVAL_REQUIRED_FLAG
Context Field Value	Code	Global Data Elements Special Delivery Instructions Alternate Delivery Address Y Purchaser Telephone Number Reason for Purchase N Verbally Agreed with Manager

What Is Purpose of the Protected Check Box in a Descriptive Flexfield Register Screen?

The protected check box in the DFF Register screen can be checked for some flexfield definitions. This type of flexfield is called a protected descriptive flexfield. For example, Oracle might deliver a preseeded flexfield for localization as per country legislations. Such flexfields might be protected so that a developer or administrator cannot accidentally unfreeze the flexfield to make changes. You must complete the descriptive flexfield segments setup before enabling the Protected check box. The protected (Oracle-seeded) DFF definitions should not be altered without specific instruction from either Oracle Support or official product documentation.

Multiple Context Field Value Codes with Displayed Check Box Enabled

Reference fields help the flexfield engine automatically decide the context segments that must be displayed to the user. However, in some cases, you may want the end user to decide the context. In this case, the Displayed check box can be enabled as shown in Figure 3-4.

The following are the steps for defining the flexfield:

1. **Analyze the group of segments that must be displayed conditionally.** Analyze the possible additional fields and group them into contexts. For example, let's assume for internal purchase orders you wish to capture the Internal Project reference code. However, if the purchase order is external, you wish to capture the number of warranty years. (These examples are merely for explanatory purposes, as Oracle Apps does provide means of tracking similar details via standard functionality.)

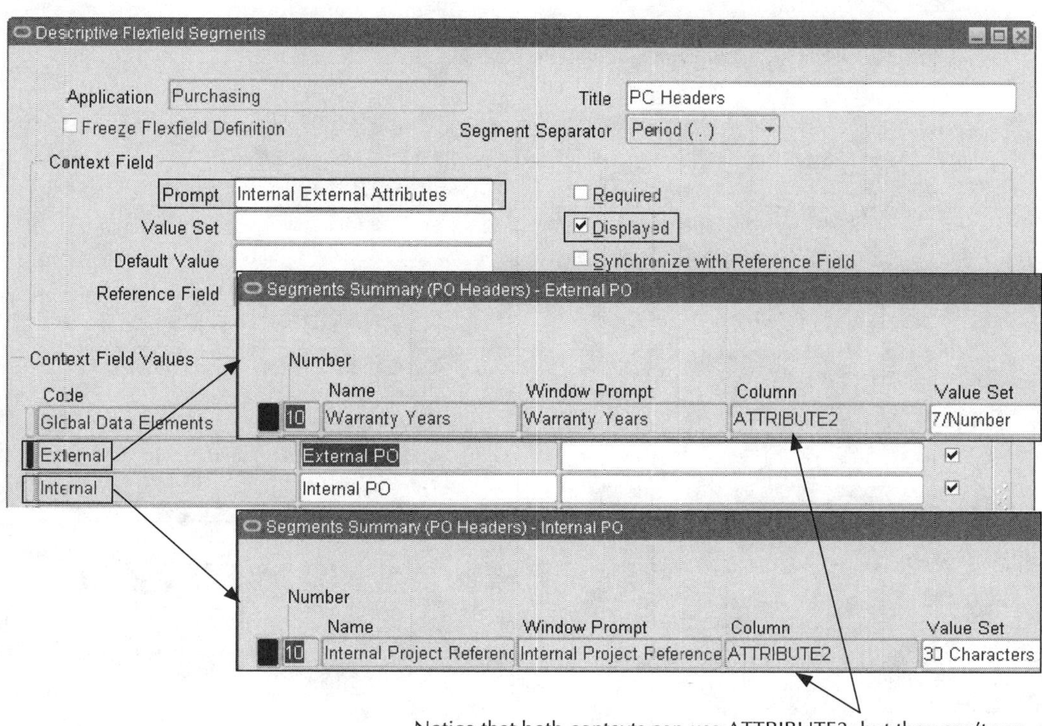

FIGURE 3-4. *Defining multiple contexts for a descriptive flexfield*

2. **Create the contexts for each possible group of fields to capture additional information.** In this case, you will create two different contexts as shown in Figure 3-4, one for internal and the other for external purchase orders. The beauty of creating multiple contexts is that the same Attribute column can be reused. However, if an Attribute column has already been used in Global Data Elements, then the same attribute cannot be used for any other context.

Once you complete the setup of different contexts, you can navigate to the Purchase Order Entry screen. Figure 3-5 depicts the steps the end user takes to capture additional information.

The user will see Purchaser's telephone number regardless of the context selected, as this segment is a part of Global Data Elements. However, the user will either see the Warranty Years field or the Internal Project Reference field, depending upon the context he or she selects as shown in Figure 3-5.

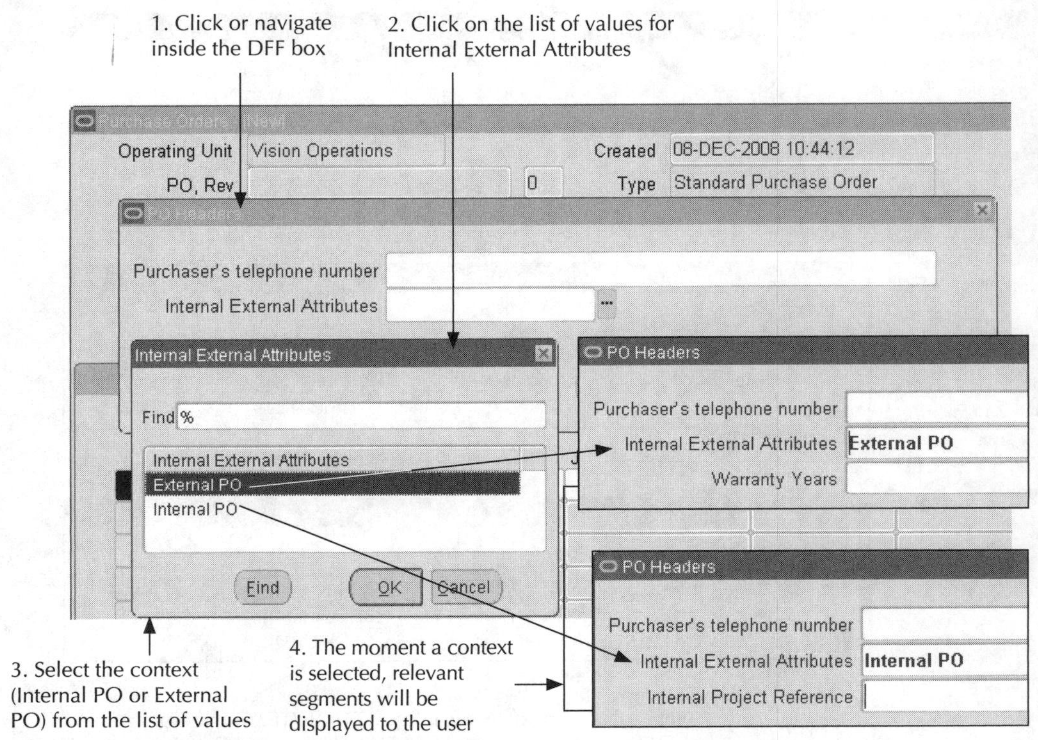

FIGURE 3-5. *Users can pick the descriptive flexfield context for entering relevant data.*

Key Flexfields (KFFs)

Key flexfields in E-Business Suite allow businesses and other organizations to create user-definable, unique composite keys such as accounting codes, item codes, and many others. The key difference between descriptive and key flexfields is that DFFs usually collect user-defined additional information related to entities, while KFFs provide user-defined, unique keys or identifiers for entities.

To illustrate the difference between KFFs and DFFs, let's take a look at an example. Assume for a minute that there is no such thing as key flexfields and all you have on a screen or inside a table is a descriptive flex.

Assume that the basic requirement is to be able to capture values in the following additional fields for a purchase order and invoices transaction:

- Company name: GM
- Cost Centre: IT

- Project: OFP (Oracle Fusion Project)
- Expense Type: OCC (Oracle Consultant Cost)

If you had only DFFs available as a configuration option, when the business raises a purchase order to IT Consulting Company, the PO_DISTRIBUTIONS_ALL table would store values for following columns in a record:

- ATTRIBUTE1 : GM
- ATTRIBUTE2 : IT
- ATTRIBUTE3 : OFP
- ATTRIBUTE4 : OCC

When an invoice is received from the consulting company, the payables clerk would capture the Invoice Line accounting as follows in AP_INVOICE_DISTRIBUTIONS_ALL:

- ATTRIBUTE1 : GM
- ATTRIBUTE2 : IT
- ATTRIBUTE3 : OFP
- ATTRIBUTE4 : OCC

In other words, if DFFs were used for capturing the accounting details as in the example, then the four text values for fields (ATTRIBUTE1…4) would be physically duplicated in each module for the related transactions.

Imagine further when this transaction flows to the Oracle General Ledger. Given the nature of DFF, the Oracle Database would again have to store the four columns physically into table GL_JE_LINES. If so, the table GL_JE_LINES would have the following values in its DFF (Descriptive Flex) columns:

- ATTRIBUTE1 : GM
- ATTRIBUTE2 : IT
- ATTRIBUTE3 : OFP
- ATTRIBUTE4 : OCC

As you can see, such a design using a descriptive flexfield is flawed, as it causes duplication of data at various places. It is also possible that the same combination of GM-IT-OFP-OCC would be required against thousands of other purchase order records, and the text GM-IT-OFP-OCC would be duplicated across many tables and many records in each such table.

Clearly, the descriptive flexfield does not fit into this scenario. Let's now consider a new approach using a key flexfield. In this example, you have a table named GL_CODE_COMBINATIONS with the following columns:

- CODE_COMBINATION_ID
- SEGMENT1
- SEGMENT2
- SEGMENT3
- SEGMENT4

You capture a *single* record in the table GL_CODE_COMBINATIONS as shown:

Column Name	**Column Value**
CODE_COMBINATION_ID	50493 ** a unique number value
SEGMENT1	GM
SEGMENT2	IT
SEGMENT3	OFP
SEGMENT4	OCC

The preceding combination of four fields can now be uniquely identified by a value of 50493 in a column named CODE_COMBINATION_ID.

Now, in the PO_DISTRIBUTIONS_ALL table, you will have a column with the value CODE_COMBINATION_ID = 50493 that refers to the unique key combination of the record in the KFF table.

In the Account Payables module, even though a clerk enters the values for four columns (one for each segment), the database stores only the reference value 50493 in the column CODE_COMBINATION_ID of the Payables Distributions table. Ditto for the entry in the GL_JE_LINES table in the Oracle General Ledger module: only the ID that references those four columns will be stored. Therefore, all the tables (Purchase Order Distributions, Payables Distributions, and General Ledger Journal Lines) will reference just the CODE_COMBINATION_ID. This concept of having a unique ID that maps to a combination of other values is called key flexfields.

Key Flexfield FAQ

As we did with the descriptive flexfields, we have compiled a list of frequently asked questions about key flexfields in the sections that follow. The list is not exhaustive by all means, but it gives you the answers to some common questions about KFFs.

Does Every Key Flexfield Always Have a Dedicated Table?

Yes. Every key flexfield has a table dedicated to store the unique combination for a group of fields. For the GL accounting key flexfield, there is a table named GL_CODE_COMBINATIONS. Another example is grades in Oracle Human Resources. An HR grade can be defined as a combination of, say, Clerk + Senior or Clerk + Junior. These combinations will be stored in the PER_GRADES table.

Do All the Tables That Are Used for Storing Key Flexfields Have Columns Named SEGMENT1, SEGMENT2...SEGMENT*X*?

Yes. It is a standard practice used by Oracle to give generic names like SEGMENT1, SEGMENT2...SEGMENT*X* to these columns. These segment columns are generic columns so that each E-Business Suite customer can reference them by whatever name he or she likes and by giving the desired prompt name to the key flexfield segment.

Does Oracle Deliver Key Flexfields out of the Box?

Oracle delivers many KFFs out of the box, but you will have to configure their segments as per business needs. You can also create new KFFs in Oracle Apps; however, this is a very rare requirement and is not covered in this book.

What Are the Steps for Configuring a Key Flexfield?

Navigate to the Application Developer responsibility and click the menu Flexfield | Key | Register. In this screen, you can get the title of the flexfield against a table name. Next, navigate to the KeyFlexfield segments screen (Flexfield | Key | Segments) and query using the flexfield title. In the KFF Segments screen, the desired segments can be configured in a manner similar to that for descriptive flexfields.

Unlike the descriptive flexfields setup, the configuration of key flexfields is usually a one-off exercise, normally performed by functional analysts during the initial implementation.

What Are Cross Validation Rules (CVRs)?

Cross validation rules (CVRs) are used to prevent the creation of invalid segment combinations. For example, a Location key flexfield can have two structures, say one for each country, the U.K. and the U.S. For the U.S. flexfield structure, you can define a cross validation rule that excludes COUNTY=NY and CITY=ABERDEEN. At the time of defining cross validation rules, you also specify the accompanying error message that the end user will receive if he or she uses the wrong combination of values in segments.

Whenever any component of the Oracle Applications attempts to create a new segment combination, the flexfield engine checks all the cross validation rules against that KFF structure to ensure that the combination is valid. If the combination fails to pass a rule, the error message associated with that rule is displayed to the end user. CVRs are applied to all users in Oracle Apps, but they are not applied to existing combinations.

Lookups in Oracle Apps

Lookups are an approach of creating a configurable "list of values" in E-Business Suite. The main purpose of a lookup is to keep programs flexible and easier to configure. One of the simplest examples of a lookup type is gender. A "gender lookup" will have definitions as shown next:

Code	Meaning
M	Male
F	Female
U	Unknown

Let us assume that there is a table for employees named PER_ALL_PEOPLE_F and it has the following columns:

- FIRST_NAME
- LAST_NAME
- DATE_OF_BIRTH
- GENDER

The screen that displays an employee's gender will display a value of Male, Female, or Unknown. However, the database column PER_ALL_PEOPLE_F.GENDER will store a value of M, F, or U. Hence, the screen displays the meaning, whereas the database columns reference the lookup via a lookup code. If in the future your organization wants the users to see "Undisclosed" instead of "Unknown," you will have to make a change to just one record in the lookups table via the lookup screen. By doing so, you will avoid having to update thousands of records in PER_ALL_PEOPLE_F. Your new lookup will look like the following:

Code	Meaning
M	Male
F	Female
U	Undisclosed

Here lies the power of the lookups; you do not need to modify thousands of records in a transactional table. A simple change via the lookup screen will suffice. Using the lookup screen, you can either create new custom lookups or modify existing lookups.

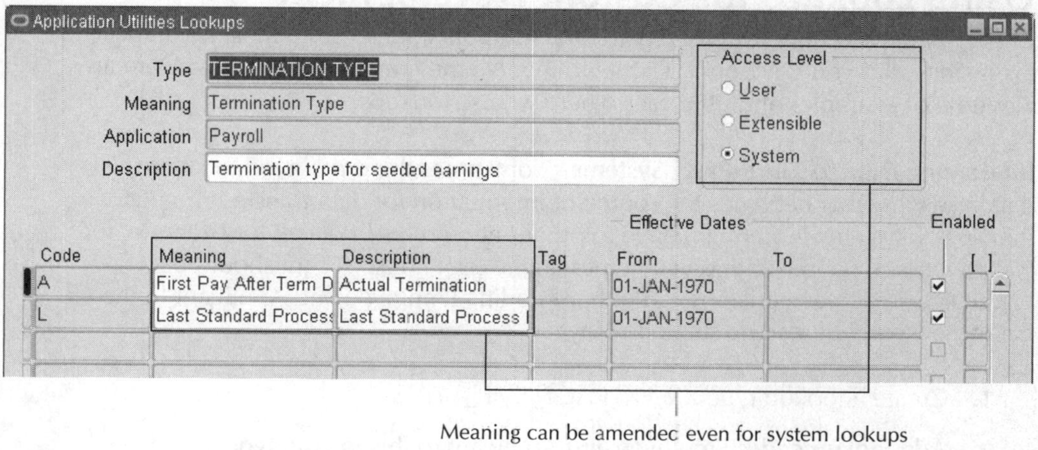

FIGURE 3-6. *Example of a system-defined lookup*

Security of Lookups

Some preseeded lookups given by Oracle cannot be modified. For example, Oracle has a lookup type called a termination type as shown in Figure 3-6. Oracle has some rules defined within the Payroll Engine program that read the value of a termination type code for employees before calculating their final salaries. Obviously, such lookup codes, if changed, can affect the logic within the Payroll Engine. For this reason, Oracle flags some lookups as system lookups, and the Lookup Entry screen will not let you modify those lookup codes.

The following table shows the differences between system, extensible, and user lookup types:

Access Level	Change Text of Meaning	Add New Lookup Codes	Modify Enabled Flag
User	Yes	Yes	Yes
Extensible	Yes	Yes	No
System	Yes	No	No

Validating Flexfield Segments Against Lookups

A lookup type cannot be directly attached to a flexfield segment to do validations; however, it is indirectly possible to do so. To do this, create a value set of Table type that validates against FND_LOOKUP_VALUES using the desired lookup. In this manner, you can validate flexfield segments against lookup values.

Using Lookups for Custom Development

Lookups are used quite extensively in Oracle Applications, and almost all of the extensions that you develop are likely to involve the creation of lookups. Here are a couple of examples and use cases where we use lookups.

Interfacing Data to Third-Party Systems Sometimes there is a need to create a database view that becomes the source of information for data transfer to other third-party systems. You might have to put filtration rules in place; for example, for HRMS Extract, people with person types Employee and Applicant should be extracted. To achieve this, instead of hard-coding Employee and Applicant in the database view, you can do the following:

1. Create a lookup type XX_EXTRACT_EMP_TYPES.
2. Add lookup codes Employee and Applicant to this lookup type.
3. In the database view, join the HR Person Types from HR Tables with FND_LOOKUP_VALUES for this lookup type.

Development of Custom Screens In custom screen development, there is often a need to provide a list of values (LOV) on a field, as per business requirements. If the LOV data is not available in standard Oracle tables, then it is recommended you maintain a lookup that drives such a lookup value.

Value Sets

A value set is a set of different values. These values either be a static set of values or dynamically generated from data in the application tables. Value sets are attached to flexfield segments to ensure that invalid items or values are not being entered into the flexfield segments. Another usage of the value set is to validate the value of parameters being passed to concurrent programs. In reality, the concurrent program parameters are displayed using a descriptive flexfield mechanism. Hence, value sets can be attached only to descriptive flexfield segments, key flexfield segments, or concurrent program parameters.

To create value sets, navigate to the Application Developer responsibility and follow the navigation path (N)Application | Validation | Set.

The different types of value sets are shown in the following table:

Validation Type	Possible Validations Performed	Further Description
None	Length of data entered, data type (number or characters), validates date to be a valid format entered by the user.	For example, an Oracle seeded value set named "20 characters" restricts the entered value in a segment to a maximum of 20 characters.
Independent	Validates against a static list of values.	Value Set attached to the segment "Item Categories" as per Figure 3-7 is an Independent Value Set.
Dependent	Each value in this value set belongs to a parent value from an independent value set. When attaching a dependent value set to a segment, it must be ensured that its corresponding independent value set is attached to a prior segment.	The value set attached to the segment "Item Class Category" as per the example in Figure 3-7 is a Dependent value set. The values that can be entered in the segment of this value set will depend on the value entered in the segment attached to its parent value set.
Table	The data input is checked against values in a database table or a view. Effectively, the value selected in the segment is checked by executing a SQL Query.	For example, to validate that a valid Purchase Order Number is being entered in a Flexfield segment, the Table value set will be based upon the table PO_HEADERS_ALL.

In addition to the validation types listed above, there are additional validation types such as Translatable and Pair, which are rarely used by the developers.

Figure 3-7 depicts the relationship between an independent value set and a dependent value set. This example illustrates:

- Segment 1 of the flexfield is attached to the independent value set Item Categories.
- Segment2 of the flexfield is attached to the dependent value set Item Class Category.

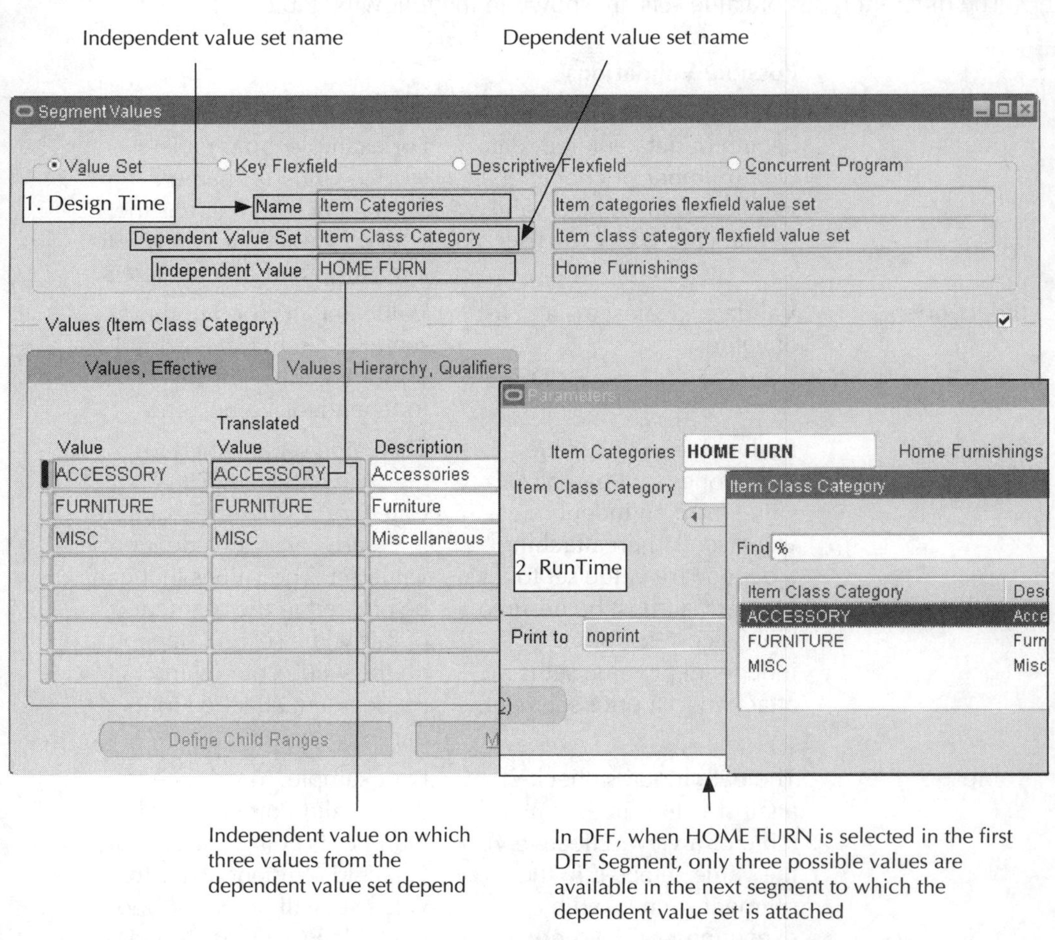

FIGURE 3-7. *Design time and runtime view of dependent value set*

When a value of HOME FURN is selected in the list of values for Segment1, the user's data entry for SEGMENT2 will then be restricted to child values for HOME FURN: ACCESSORY, FURNITURE, or MISC.

Value Set of a Validation Type Table

You can use a value set of table type when you wish to display a list of values to the user from the result of a SQL Statement. A SQL Statement is composed of column lists, a FROM clause, and a WHERE clause. In the example shown in Table 3-2,

Component	Purpose	Examples
Table application	To identify the application name to which the table belongs. This field is optional and can be left blank.	Purchasing
Table name	To specify the table that is equivalent to the FROM clause in a SQL Statement. This can be a single table name or a view name of a comma-separated list of tables. As a rule, you can extract the text from a SQL Query to extract everything between the FROM and WHERE clauses.	po_headers ph
Value	To name the column in database table. The value entered by the user in the flexfield segment will be validated against the value column name entered in the value field. You may use a SQL expression in place of a column name, but you cannot use any special bind variables.	SEGMENT1. Segment1 displays the purchase order number from PO_HEADERS.
Meaning	To name the column in your validation table that contains descriptions for the values in the Value column. This field is optional, and you can leave this blank.	COMMENTS. Flexfield list of values will display the value of this column if specified.
ID	To store the value in this column in the database. If you leave the ID field blank, then the value from the value column will be stored in database (in your ATTRIBUTE*nn* column or SEGMENT*nn* column) of the underlying flexfield table.	PO_HEADER_ID. Internal ID of the purchase order number will be stored in the ATTRIBUTE*nn* or SEGMENT*nn* column.
Where/Order By	To filter the list of values that is displayed to the user in the flexfield segment by applying a WHERE criteria. As a rule, you can extract the text from a SQL Query to extract the entire text beginning from WHERE clauses, including the keyword WHERE.	WHERE PH.SEGMENT1 LIKE 900%. In this example, only those purchase orders will be displayed in the list of values that have their purchase order numbers beginning with 900%.

TABLE 3-2. *Value Set Validation Based on a Database Table*

the value entered in the flexfield segment will be cross-checked against the table PO_HEADERS. In this example, when entering data in the flexfield segment, the user will see the PO number and purchase order comments in the list of values. However, it is the po_header_id value that will get stored in the database.

Dependent and Reference Values

The WHERE clause in the table-based value sets can be dependent upon a value in another segment. Within the WHERE clause of a table value set, you can reference the value in another segment in the same flexfield set by using following notation:

```
WHERE <COLUMN_NAME>=:$FLEX$.<VALUE_SET_NAME>
```

Let's have a look at an example where a concurrent program has the following parameters:

Parameter Num	Parameter Name	Value Set Name
1	P001	VS001
2	P002	VS002
3	P003	VS003

Making a Table Value Set Dependent on Another Value Set

In this case, if the value set VS002 is of the type table, its WHERE clause can contain:

```
WHERE user_id = :$FLEX$.VS001
```

The value selected in parameter 2 will hence become dependent on the value selected in parameter 1.

Defaulting a Value in a Flexfield Segment Based on Another Segment

In a flexfield definition, it is possible to default a value into a flexfield segment by executing a SQL Statement. The SQL used for defaulting a value into the segment must return no more than one value. To default a value in parameter 3 via a SQL Statement that depends upon parameter 1, specify the default property of the segment as follows:

```
Default Type = SQL Statement
Default Value = select user_id from fnd_user where user_name =
   :$FLEX$.P001
```

Message Dictionary

FND Messages is a name given to the repository of messages and instructions in Oracle Applications. All the programs written with Oracle Forms, concurrent programs, and others display informative messages to the Oracle Application users to help them use the application as per business rules, while respecting the data integrity. The key components of this message dictionary are the message name, message application, and message text. The message name contains the internal name of the message (with a maximum of 30 characters), whereas the message text contains the user-friendly text (with a maximum of 2000 characters). All the programs written in Forms, Reports, Java, or PL/SQL contain references to the message name and their application short name.

The Purpose of Message Dictionary

The following list summarizes the main reasons why developers use messages in E-Business Suite:

- To make messages dynamic for end users so that hard-coding of message texts is avoided
- To facilitate multilanguage capability
- To allow a functional team to amend messages/instructions for end users

All the programs reference the message via the message name; this avoids the need to hard-code message text.

How a Message Is Created

Developers usually use the Forms-based interface in Oracle Applications to create a message. In Application Developer Responsibility, we navigate to (N)Application | Messages.

Using that screen, the new messages can be created by entering records. The contents entered in field message text become visible to the end user. The content of the message can optionally have *tokens*, which act as placeholders for dynamically substituted values at runtime. For example, let's assume there is a FND Message with a structure as follows:

Field	Value
Message Application	General Ledger
Message Name	XX_GL_ENTRY_WRONG
Message Text	This journal line must be entered in &XX_PERIOD_NAME

The end user will never see the text XX_GL_ENTRY_WRONG or the text "This journal line must be entered in &XX_PERIOD_NAME." Examples of the text that is visible to the end user are as follows:

- This journal line must be entered in MAR-08

  or

- This journal line must be entered in APR-08

In this case, XX_PERIOD_NAME is the name of the token. The program that invokes the message XX_GL_ENTRY_WRONG will set the value of the token at runtime to MAR-08, APR-08, or any other value.

Displaying a Message from Different Tools

When developing custom extensions in Oracle Applications, you can expect to use a variety of development tools and programming techniques such as Oracle Forms, Reports, PL/SQL program units, OA Framework, and others. In the next few sections, we'll highlight the specific techniques used to display messages from different tools.

Oracle Forms

In Oracle Forms, you can use APIs from FND_MESSAGE to display the message on the screen. Here is a simple example:

```
fnd_message.set_name('SQLGL', ' XX_GL_ENTRY_WRONG ');
fnd_message.set_token(' XX_PERIOD_NAME ', 'MAR-08');
fnd_message.show;
```

PL/SQL Concurrent Program

The same API from FND_MESSAGE can be used in PL/SQL to display the message in output or the log file of the concurrent program:

```
fnd_message.clear;
fnd_message.set_name ('SQLGL', ' XX_GL_ENTRY_WRONG');
fnd_message.set_token(' XX_PERIOD_NAME ', 'MAR-08');
--Now get the final string
l_message_var := fnd_message.get;
--Display the message text in output of concurrent program
 fnd_file.put_line(fnd_file.OUTPUT, l_message_var);
```

Java Concurrent Program

From a Java concurrent program, you can use a code snippet as shown:

```
public void runProgram(CpContext pCpContext) {
CpContext mCtx = pCpContext;
```

```
Message msg = new Message("SQLGL", "XX_GL_ENTRY_WRONG");
msg.setToken(" XX_PERIOD_NAME ", "MAR-08", true);
returnMsg = msg.getMessageText(mCtx.getResourceStore());
```

OA Framework Controller

The controller of the OA Framework page will display the same message if you use the following code:

```
String sReturnMsg = oapagecontext.getMessage("SQLGL", " XX_GL_ENTRY_
WRONG ", new MessageToken[] {new MessageToken("XX_PERIOD_NAME ", "MAR-
08") });
```

Table Used by Messages Dictionary

The messages are stored in a table called FND_NEW_MESSAGES. The unique key for this table is comprised of columns APPLICATION_ID, MESSAGE_NAME, and LANGUAGE_CODE. For this reason, the same message name can map to a different message text, depending upon the application to which it is registered.

Given that messages are stored in a table, it is not very performance efficient to query the database tables each time the messages are displayed. Consequently, these messages are cached in varying ways by each technology in question. When you define a new message or if you modify the existing message text, it is always a good practice to generate message files. If yoy do so, the messages from the tables are extracted into a flat file on the server. The contents of this file can then be cached by Oracle Applications. Oracle Applications DBAs can generate the message file, by running the adadmin utility and selecting the Maintain Applications Files | Generate Message Files option.

Auditing in Oracle Apps: User Audits and Data Change Audits

The data stored in Oracle Applications can be extremely sensitive. For that reason, it is necessary to have a framework that facilitates the data change tracking as well as end user activity performed on the system. In this section, we'll briefly cover the subject of auditing in Oracle Apps from a developer's perspective.

In E-Business Suite, there are two types of auditing:

- Audit of end users' activity
- Audit of data changed by end users

In the next sections, we'll cover a couple of typical auditing scenarios that a developer needs to be aware of in Oracle Applications.

Audit of End Users' Activity

End user activity in Oracle Applications can be monitored at four possible levels. The levels of auditing are defined as per the values in the seeded lookup type SIGNONAUDIT. This lookup contains four possible values at which auditing can be performed. One of these four values can be assigned to a profile option named Sign-On:Audit Level as shown in the following table:

Profile Option Value	Result of Setting Profile
NONE	Auditing is disabled. This is the default behavior.
USER	Users' login time and logout time are recorded in table FND_LOGINS.
RESPONSIBILITY	Auditing at user level plus users' access to responsibilities is tracked via table FND_LOGIN_RESPONSIBILITIES.
FORM	User level auditing, responsibility auditing, list of forms accessed by the user, and the duration of each form's access are recorded in table FND_LOGIN_RESP_FORMS.

Auditing is enabled as soon as the profile option Sign-On:Audit Level is set to a value other than NONE. In addition to preceding auditing tables, two further tables can be used for tracking user activity:

Table Name	Purpose
FND_UNSUCCESSFUL_ LOGINS	A column name ATTEMPT_TIME gives the timestamp when an unsuccessful login attempt was made by a user.
FND_USER	A column named LAST_LOGON_DATE contains the timestamp of the last successful user login.

Audit Monitoring

There are two ways a System Administrator can report or query the user activity.

Audit Monitoring Option 1: Run Seeded Reports Oracle delivers some reports that can be run as concurrent programs. The names of these concurrent programs begin with Signon Audit%:

```
SQL> select user_concurrent_program_name
from fnd_concurrent_programs_vl
where user_concurrent_program_name like 'Signon Audit%'

List of Signon Audit reports are
Signon Audit Concurrent Requests
Signon Audit Forms
```

```
Signon Audit Responsibilities
Signon Audit Unsuccessful Logins
Signon Audit Users
```

Audit Monitoring Option 2: Monitor the User Screen Oracle delivers a screen that lets you query on a username. This screen lists the username, responsibility name, form name, timestamp, and the Oracle internal process ID for the user's Forms session. To access this screen, navigate to the System Administrator responsibility: (N)Security | User | Monitor.

Audit of Data Changes

Data auditing allows you to know who changed the data and when; the framework also monitors old and the new values. In Oracle Applications, it is possible to audit changes to data in any table without writing a single line of code. The entire code is generated by the Oracle Applications auditing engine.

To enable auditing for data changes in a given table, follow these steps:

1. Enable the audit profile.
2. Identify the application name to which table being audited belongs.
3. Enable audits for the desired application.
4. Create an audit group within an application containing the list of tables to be audited.
5. Specify the column names to be audited.
6. Run the audit concurrent program.

We are now going to outline a step-by-step example of enabling an audit on a table named FND_LOOKUP_VALUES.

Step 1: Enable the Audit Trail profile option. Set the profile option AuditTrail: Activate to Yes at the site level.

Step 2: Select the applications and schemas. Log in to the System Administrator responsibility and navigate to (N)Security | AuditTrail | Install. Query on the desired schema for which auditing should be enabled. This can be found by running the SQL as shown:

```
SELECT at.owner, fav.APPLICATION_NAME
  FROM all_tables at, fnd_application_vl fav, fnd_tables ft
WHERE ft.table_name = 'FND_LOOKUP_VALUES' AND
       ft.application_id = fav.application_id and
       at.table_name = ft.table_name
```

In this example, the query will return the schema named APPLSYS for the table FND_LOOKUP_VALUES.

Step 3: Create a new audit group containing the list of tables. In the System Administrator responsibility, select Security -| AuditTrail -| Groups. Create a new audit group for the application name (the Application Object Library in this case). Give a user-friendly audit group name and set Group State to Enable Requested. Add the tables to be audited, in this case FND_LOOKUP_VALUES.

Step 4: Define table columns to be audited. This step is optional in case you wish to audit only the unique keys on the table. To define additional columns for auditing, log in to the System Administrator responsibility and navigate to (N)Security | AuditTrail | Tables. Query the table name and add the columns that need to be audited.

Step 5: Run the concurrent program AuditTrail Update Tables. Run the AuditTrail Update Tables program to activate the auditing. This program will create a shadow table for each audited table and also create a trigger on each audited column in the audited table. Names of the supporting audit objects created by this process can be found by running the following SQL, assuming the table being audited is FND_LOOKUP_VALUES:

```
SELECT object_name, object_type
  FROM all_objects
WHERE object_name LIKE 'FND_LOOKUP_VALUES_A%'
OBJECT_NAME             OBJECT_TYPE
---------------------   ----------------------
FND_LOOKUP_VALUES_A     TABLE
FND_LOOKUP_VALUES_A     SYNONYM
FND_LOOKUP_VALUES_AC    TRIGGER
FND_LOOKUP_VALUES_AC1   VIEW
FND_LOOKUP_VALUES_AD    TRIGGER
FND_LOOKUP_VALUES_ADP   PROCEDURE
FND_LOOKUP_VALUES_AH    TRIGGER
FND_LOOKUP_VALUES_AI    TRIGGER
FND_LOOKUP_VALUES_AIP   PROCEDURE
FND_LOOKUP_VALUES_AT    TRIGGER
FND_LOOKUP_VALUES_AU    TRIGGER
FND_LOOKUP_VALUES_AUP   PROCEDURE
FND_LOOKUP_VALUES_AV1   VIEW
```

Row Who Columns

Each Oracle Applications table contains a set of columns called Row Who Columns. These columns provide default auditing at a very basic level, and they are always updated when a new record gets created in a table or when an existing record gets updated. Hence, it is important that when writing a custom code to perform DML (Data Manipulation Language) on a custom table, you must assign values to the following columns:

Column Name	Description
CREATION_DATE	Date with timestamp when the record was created.
CREATED_BY	USER_ID of the user that created this record. To find the username, query fnd_user table for this user_id.
LAST_UPDATE_DATE	Date timestamp when the record was last updated. When a record is inserted, the value in this column is same as that of CREATION_DATE.
LAST_UPDATED_BY	Which system user modified this record. When a record is inserted, the value in this column is same as that of LAST_UPDATE_DATE.
LAST_UPDATE_LOGIN	References the login_id from fnd_logins.

Common Debugging Framework in Oracle Applications

Prior to Oracle E-Business Suite 11i, each module used in Oracle EBS had its own debugging methodology. Moreover, within the same module, each toolset applied its own methodology too. For this reason, there were several debugging-related profile options and debug tables for each module. Some toolsets produced a debug file, whereas others dumped data into debug tables or sent debug messages to pipe.

Given the lack of consistency, Oracle Apps customers had to develop their own custom modules to manage debugging in custom code. Oracle Support staff also had to learn different debugging methodologies depending upon which technology or module they were debugging.

For example, Oracle Purchasing used a debug table named PO_WF_DEBUG, Oracle Time Labor used a table named HXC_DEBUG_TEXT, and Fixed Assets used a table named FA_PLSQL_DEBUG. In addition to different debug tables, there were different profile options for debugging, like FA: Debug Filename, HR: FastFormula debug level, PA: Debug Mode , GL: Debug Mode, GL: Debug Log Directory, HZ: API Debug File Name, POR: Debugging, and PJM: Debug File Directory, to name a few. Overall, there was lack of consistency when it came to debugging different programs.

However, with the Common Debugging Framework initiative, Oracle introduced a common set of profile options and tables that can be used to debug any application across all technologies.

In this debugging framework, a centralized table named FND_LOG_MESSAGES captures debug messages. For a program written in any technology—Oracle Forms,

Oracle Reports, PL/SQL, Java Concurrent Program, or OA Framework—all the debug messages can be stored in a central table named FND_LOG_MESSAGES.

In order to enable debugging, three possible profile options can be set as follows:

Profile Option Name	Description
FND: Debug Log Enabled	This profile option must be set to Yes to enable debugging. To enable debugging for an entire site, set this profile at Site Level. To capture debug messages for just one user, set this profile to Yes for a specific user.
FND: Debug Log Level	Can be set to one of the following values: Statement [Level 1] Procedure [Level 2] Event [Level 3] Exception [Level 4] Error [Level 5] Unexpected [Level 6]
FND: Debug Log Module	Set this to % to debug all the modules. Set this to po% when debugging a purchasing module. To debug multiple modules, specify a comma-separated value; for example, po%,hr%,fnd%.

The Statement level extracts debug messages at all levels, and the Unexpected level produces the least number of debug messages.

We suggest that DBAs run the concurrent program Purge Debug Log and System Alerts to purge the old debug messages in FND_LOG_MESSAGES.

API to Capture Debug Messages in Custom Code

FND logging can be used to implement debugging in your custom code. For example, when writing custom code for the purchasing module, fnd_log.string can be called as shown in the following example:

```
fnd_log.STRING(log_level => fnd_log.level_statement
              ,module    => 'xxpo.packagename.procedurename'
              ,message   => 'debug message here');
```

In the following listing, we show a sample custom PL/SQL program that uses FND logging:

```
CREATE OR REPLACE PACKAGE BODY xxpo_approval_pkg IS
  g_debug_procedure_context VARCHAR2(30);
  g_debug_header_context CONSTANT VARCHAR2(80)
                  := 'xxpo_approval.plsql.xxpo_approval_pkg.';
```

```
  PROCEDURE debug_stmt(p_msg IN VARCHAR2) IS
  BEGIN
    fnd_log.STRING(log_level => fnd_log.level_statement
                  ,MODULE    => g_debug_header_context ||
                                      g_debug_procedure_context
                  ,message   => p_msg);
  END debug_stmt;
  PROCEDURE debug_begin_procedure IS
  BEGIN
    fnd_log.STRING(log_level => fnd_log.level_procedure
                  ,MODULE    => g_debug_header_context ||
                                g_debug_procedure_context
                  ,message   => 'Begin ' || g_debug_procedure_context);
  END debug_begin_procedure;
  PROCEDURE set_debug_context(p_procedure_name IN VARCHAR2) IS
  BEGIN
    g_debug_procedure_context := p_procedure_name;
    debug_begin_procedure;
  END set_debug_context;
  PROCEDURE debug_end_procedure IS
  BEGIN
    fnd_log.STRING(log_level => fnd_log.level_procedure
                  ,MODULE    => g_debug_header_context ||
                                      g_debug_procedure_context
                  ,message   => 'End ' || g_debug_procedure_context);
  END debug_end_procedure;
END xxpo_approval_pkg;
```

Autonomous Transaction in Debugging

When using the debugging techniques as described in this chapter, it is important to be aware that FND_LOG.STRING eventually calls procedure FND_LOG.STRING_UNCHECKED_INTERNAL2. This procedure uses pragma AUTONOMOUS_TRANSACTION with the commit. Consequently, your debug messages will always be committed, even if the calling process performs a rollback.

Debugging an API from SQL*Plus

You can enable FND logging for just one single PL/SQL API. Here is how we can do it from SQL*Plus:

1. From SQL*Plus, issue the following:

```
fnd_global.apps_initialize(fnd_user_id, fnd_resp_id, fnd_appl_id);
fnd_profile.put('AFLOG_ENABLED', 'Y');
fnd_profile.put('AFLOG_MODULE', '%');
fnd_profile.put('AFLOG_LEVEL','1'); -- Level 1 is Statement Level
fnd_log_repository.init;
```

2. Call the desired API.
3. Call step 1 again, but this time set AFLOG_ENABLED to N.

Summary

Application Object Library (AOL) is one of the key foundation modules in E-Business Suite. It provides a common framework for developing applications that look and behave consistently. In addition to that, AOL provides an essential infrastructure for administration of concurrent processing, security, user auditing, printing, document attachments, and many other components of Oracle Applications. In this chapter, we have discussed only the essential features from the developer's perspective.

Achieving most of the common tasks, such as capturing of additional user data from the screens through the configuration of descriptive flexfields rather than customizations, will enhance productivity and supportability of an implementation. On the other hand, developers who use lookup codes and messages defined in the message dictionary future-proof their applications by not using the hard-coded values. These are just very simple examples of how AOL can be used in custom development; when faced with any development task in Oracle Applications, the first thing to ask yourself is how the components of AOL can be used to meet the requirements.

CHAPTER 4

Multiple Organizations Feature

-Business Suite is an enterprisewide product that is quite often implemented globally. One of its key features is to hold data for multiple companies, legal entities, divisions, and other organizational structures in a single installation of E-Business Suite while providing data separation at the organization level to maintain security between logical boundaries of individual organizations.

Multi-Org (short for *multiple organizations*) is both a concept as well as an E-Business Suite product feature that we are going to look at in this chapter in some detail. There have been some significant changes in the functionality of the Multi-Org feature between R11i and R12, and we are going to discuss them separately. We'll also discuss the impact on of upgrading to R12 on Multi-Org custom objects that have been created prior to R12.

Overview of Multi-Org

In any large organization, there is always a need to secure data at various levels. One of the important levels in E-Business Suite at which data can be secured is the Operating Unit level. For example, if a multinational organization has operations in the U.K., France, and the U.S., then a payables clerk in the U.K. operating unit will usually not be allowed to create or query the invoices that belong to French and U.S. operations. On similar lines, a payables clerk in a U.S. operating unit will usually not be allowed to create or view invoices of U.K. and French operations. Multi-Org is a concept that facilitates implementing security of data at the Operating Unit level.

NOTE

In this example, we assume that U.S. operations corresponds to one single operating unit. In reality, there can be several operating units applicable within a single country, as per the business requirements.

In the previous chapter, you learned that the only way business users can access the screens or concurrent program reports is via responsibilities. In this example, for payables clerks there would be three responsibilities, such as UK Payables Clerk, France Payables Clerk, and US Payables Clerk. Each of these responsibilities would be attached to the same menu structure, hence giving access to the same set of screens to the clerks in all three countries.

When users from any of these responsibilities log into E-Business Suite, they should be able to see only those invoices that belong to their organization. However, there is only one table that stores the invoice header records, which is a table named AP_INVOICES_ALL. Therefore, the screens and reports need to be written to take account of the operating unit. To make the data separation happen, you need two elements. First, all records in the transaction tables need to be labeled with the operating unit associated with those transactions. Second, you need to establish which operating unit each user who tries to access the data has access to. In the example, the AP_INVOICES_ALL table has an operating unit column identifying the owner, and the responsibility is labeled with the operating unit to which that it has access.

The preceding example corresponds to the design principles behind the Multi-Org model in R11i. The Multi-Org model in R12 has been enhanced further. We will discuss the Multi-Org model for both R11i and R12 versions in this chapter.

It must be noted that not every single table in Oracle E-Business Suite has its data maintained at the operating unit level. Oracle has recognized that certain types of data should be shared across operating units. For example, a trading party named FocusThread might sell its services and products from its offices in both the U.S. and the U.K. A company named Acme that has offices in both those countries might buy services from both FocusThread U.K. and FocusThread U.S. operations. In this case, the trading party FocusThread will be visible to both Acme U.S. and Acme U.K. However, a data entry clerk of Acme U.K. will only be able to see the customer accounts of FocusThread U.K., and the data entry clerk of Acme U.S. will only be able to see the customer accounts of FocusThread U.S. In such a case, the HZ_PARTIES table, which registers FocusThread as a trading party, will not have an Operating Unit column and therefore will not be secured. However, the HZ_CUST_ACCOUNTS_ALL table will have entries for both FocusThread U.K. and FocusThread U.S., and this table will have an org_id column that will facilitate implementation of Multi-Org on that table. In fact, any table in E-Business Suite that has its name ending with _ALL supports Multi-Org. Another example of a table supporting Multi-Org is the AP_TAX_CODES_ALL table because the tax codes used by operating units will most likely be different.

NOTE
HZ_% tables belong to the Trading Community Architecture (TCA) module. You can learn more about TCA from the Reference Guide available at the documentation library for both Release 11i and R12.

Multi-Org in R11i

At the technical level, three things must happen for Multi-Org to work. First, a flag that points to an operating unit must be set as soon as a user logs into a responsibility. Second, all the SQLs executed within a user session must be able to read the value of that flag and filter data appropriately. Third, the transactions that support Multi-Org must have underlying tables labeled with the operating unit values.

In case of R11i, this flag is set using a profile option named MO: Operating Unit, which is usually set at the responsibility level. Oracle executes a PL/SQL procedure named fnd_global.apps_initialize each time a user either logs in or switches his or her responsibility in E-Business Suite. This PL/SQL stored procedure reads the value of the profile option MO: Operating Unit, along with the user login–related contexts, and populates certain database session variables. One of the variables that is populated is called CLIENT_INFO. The value of this variable is a string that contains the organization ID and is related to the value of the profile option MO: Operating Unit. The same CLIENT_INFO variable value also contains other information such as Security Group ID. Therefore, a substring operation must be performed to extract the value of Organization ID from the CLIENT_INFO variable. To separate the data, a database view is created in the APPS schema based on the transactional Multi-Org table containing a WHERE CLAUSE that extracts the value of the organization ID from the CLIENT_INFO variable and joins that to a column named org_id in the Multi-Org table.

As seen in Figure 4-1, one of the tables in E-Business Suite is AP_INVOICES_ALL. This table exists in the AP schema, which contains all the Accounts Payables tables. However, all the screens and concurrent programs in E-Business Suite are designed to connect to the APPS schema. This approach allows the application to maintain data security in a generic manner.

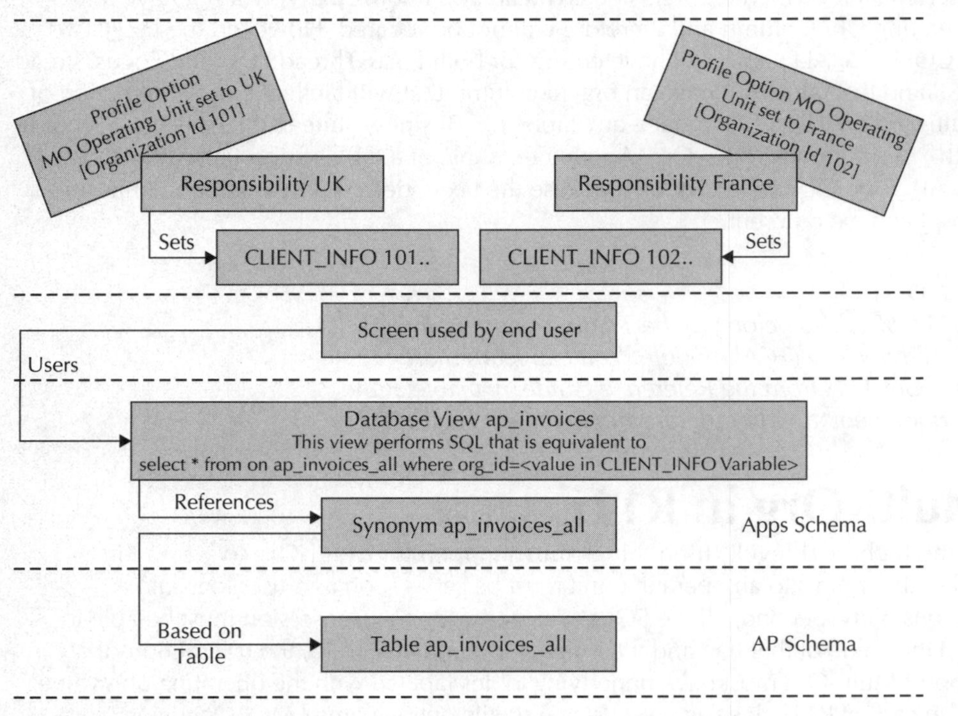

FIGURE 4-1. *Multi-Org design in R11i*

The Oracle product team delivers a synonym named AP_INVOICES_ALL in the APPS schema. The name of this synonym is exactly the same as the table name that exists in the AP schema, and it points to the table AP.AP_INVOICES_ALL. Finally, a Multi-Org view named AP_INVOICES is seeded by the Oracle product team.

Let's take a look at how such a Multi-Org table is created, along with corresponding synonym and the view.

First, while connected to the AP schema, the Multi-Org table that includes the ORG_ID column gets created:

```
create table AP_INVOICES_ALL
(
INVOICE_ID NUMBER(15) not null
,.....
,ORG_ID NUMBER(15) default to_number(decode(substrb(userenv('CLIENT_
INFO'),1,1)
..    ,' ',null,substrb(userenv('CLIENT_INFO'),1,10)))
) ;
```

Still connected to the AP schema, you grant all privileges on the AP_INVOICES_ALL table to the APPS schema:

```
grant all on AP_INVOICES_ALL to APPS with grant option;
```

Next, you connect to the APPS schema, where you create a synonym of the same name as the table:

```
create or replace synonym ap_invoices_all for ap.ap_invoices_all;
```

Last, still connected to APPS schema, you create a view called AP_INVOICES:

```
CREATE OR REPLACE VIEW AP_INVOICES AS
SELECT * FROM ap_invoices_all
WHERE
      nvl(org_id,nvl(to_number(decode(substrb(userenv('CLIENT_INFO')
      ,1,1),' ',NULL,substrb(userenv('CLIENT_INFO'),1,10))),-99))
      =
      nvl(to_number(decode(substrb(userenv('CLIENT_INFO'),1,1),
      ' ',NULL,substrb(userenv('CLIENT_INFO'),1,10))),-99);
```

To create a custom Multi-Org object, you must follow the steps similar to those outlined here. However, the custom table (XX%_ALL) will always be created in a custom schema. From this schema, all the privileges are granted to APPS for the custom XX%_ALL table, following which a synonym of same name (XX%_ALL) is created in the APPS schema. Finally, a view (XX% without the _ALL suffix) is created in the APPS schema.

Setting the Multi-Org Context in SQL*Plus

Some developers prefer to unit test their code from SQL*Plus or an equivalent tool. When performing such unit tests, it becomes essential to set the context of your SQL session so as to simulate a responsibility login. This can be done by calling exactly the same API that gets invoked during a responsibility login. In a Multi-Org environment, if you run select count(*) from ap_invoices without setting the Multi-Org context, you will get no records returned. However, if you set the context using a code similar to the following, a nonzero count will be returned, assuming there are some invoices in the respective operating unit.

```
DECLARE
  l_user_id      INTEGER;
  l_resp_id      INTEGER;
  l_resp_appl_id INTEGER;
BEGIN
  SELECT user_id INTO l_user_id FROM fnd_user WHERE user_name =
     'OPERATIONS';
  SELECT responsibility_id INTO l_resp_id FROM fnd_responsibility_vl
        WHERE responsibility_key LIKE 'PAYABLES_OPERATIONS';
  SELECT application_id INTO l_resp_appl_id FROM fnd_responsibility_vl
        WHERE responsibility_key LIKE 'PAYABLES_OPERATIONS';
  fnd_global.apps_initialize(user_id      => l_user_id
                            ,resp_id      => l_resp_id
                            ,resp_appl_id => l_resp_appl_id);
END;
/
```

Internally, PL/SQL API fnd_global.apps_initialize reads the value of the profile option MO: Operating Unit and sets the CLIENT_INFO variable using API dbms_application_info. After executing fnd_global.apps_initialize, CLIENT_INFO will be populated as shown next:

```
SELECT userenv('CLIENT_INFO') FROM dual;
204 -1  0
```

Alternatively, you can directly call dbms_application_info API as shown next to set the ORG_ID context:

```
dbms_application_info.set_client_info ( 204 ) ;
--Note : 204 is the organization_id that corresponds to MO:
    Operating Unit in
--this example. Master table for Organizations is
    HR_ALL_ORGANIZATION_UNITS
```

Note that dbms_application_info will not set the responsibility context in your SQL session; it simply sets the CLIENT_INFO variable. Therefore, making a call to fnd_global.apps_initialize is the preferred option. By executing fnd_global.apps_ initialize appropriately, not only is your session set for Multi-Org, but also other global variables are populated that allow you to unit test concurrent request submissions from a SQL session using API fnd_request.submit_request.

NOTE
In some cases, merely calling fnd_global.apps_initialize does not fully simulate the responsibility login session, as with HRMS responsibilities that use the Date-Track functionality, which inserts a record in table fnd_sessions.

Multi-Org in Release 12

In the Multi-Org model of E-Business Suite 11i, there is a one-to-one relation between a responsibility and an operating unit. This approach has worked well over the years; however, there are some limitations because organizations sometimes want the ability to allow responsibilities to be able to access data from multiple operating units.

For example, a large global organization might have a common shared service center for European operations where all European invoices are centrally processed. Additionally, there might be another shared service center for American operations. Let us presume all invoices received in Europe are scanned and placed in an electronic queue. The payables clerk working for the European shared service center can enter invoices for any operating unit within Europe. Each scanned image of the invoice will then be read by the shared service center operator and entered into the E-Business Suite using the Payables invoice screen. Different scanned images of invoices might correspond to different operating units such as France, the U.K., and Austria. If the payables clerk working in a shared service center is using E-Business Suite 11i, he or she will have to switch the responsibility each time an invoice from a different operating unit is keyed in, which is not ideal for efficient processing of transactions.

Additionally in R11i Multi-Org model, a large organization will have to maintain several responsibilities. If a change has to be made to one responsibility, for example a menu exclusion, then such changes may have to be replicated across all related responsibilities for different operating units. R12 overcomes these limitations by allowing you to attach multiple operating units to a responsibility.

In R12, the new Multi-Org model is implemented using HRMS Organization Hierarchy and Security Profiles. In Oracle HRMS, it is possible to create an organization hierarchy that contains a tree-based nested structure of the organizations and departments in a company.

After that, a security profile can be created in Oracle HRMS to which the organization hierarchy can be attached. This security profile is then attached to a responsibility, which in turn has access to all organizations in the hierarchy. The diagram in Figure 4-2 illustrates this concept.

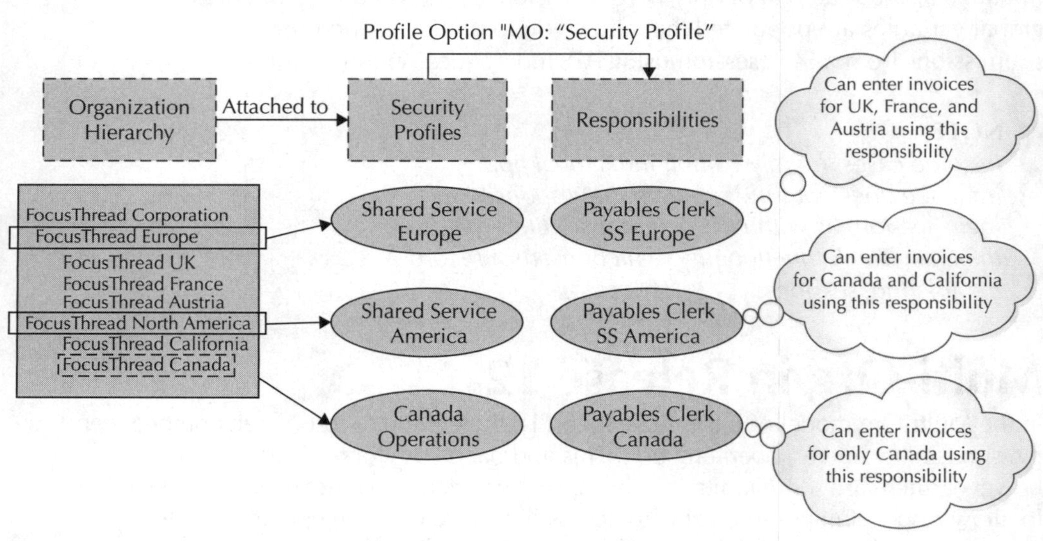

FIGURE 4-2. *Multi-Org model in R12*

Once the security profile has been defined, it can be attached to any responsibility using the profile option MO: Security Profile. This design approach overcomes the restriction of a one-to-one relationship between a responsibility and operating unit. If your implementation team does not set the profile MO: Security Profile in R12, then Multi-Org in R12 can be made to work exactly the same as in R11i by setting profile option Initialization SQL Statement - Custom to mo_global.init('S',null);.

This new design is also known as MOAC (Multi-Org Access Control). In MOAC, more than one operating unit is accessible from a single responsibility. All the screens that operate on Multi-Org tables have an Operating Unit field. This is applicable to screens developed using both OA Framework and Oracle Forms. The value of the Operating Unit field is defaulted using MO: Default Operating Unit.

Technical Details of the MOAC Design

In R12, as soon as a user logs into a responsibility, mo_global.init API is executed. This API first checks if MOAC is enabled by querying the FND_MO_PRODUCT_INIT table. If MOAC is enabled, a list of organizations to which this responsibility has access is prepared. This information is prepared by reading the Organization Hierarchy attached to profile option MO: Security Profile. A record is then inserted in table mo_glob_org_access_tmp for each operating unit that can be accessed from that responsibility.

Table mo_glob_org_access_tmp is a global temporary table, which means that its records are visible only to the single SQL session that inserted the record. Each time a user logs into a responsibility, the list of organizations that can be accessed by that session is recorded in this global temporary table.

Multi-Org views created in R11i no longer exist in R12. Each Multi-Org view from R11i has been replaced by a synonym for its R11i counterpart. A row-level security (also known as Virtual Private Database) is applied to these Multi-Org synonyms. The purpose of this row-level security is to restrict the access to only those records that have an org_id that matches the organization_id in table mo_glob_org_access_tmp. In order to achieve this, Row Level Security (RLS) generates the WHERE clause dynamically each time the table that has RLS is accessed. This dynamically generated WHERE clause is also known as the predicate. Generation of the predicate is made possible by attaching a PL/SQL function MO_GLOBAL.ORG_SECURITY to the synonym. This PL/SQL function is executed whenever a reference is made to a synonym that is secured for Multi-Org.

A comparison between R11i and R12 of the steps required to create Multi-Org objects is listed in Table 4-1. For illustration purposes, this example assumes that you want to create a custom table XXPO_EXTRA_INFO_ALL in a custom schema XXPO.

R11i	R12	Comment
Create table XXPO_EXTRA_INFO_ALL in XXPO schema with column org_id. Also, grant all privileges to APPS for XXPO_EXTRA_INFO_ALL as discussed earlier.	Create table XXPO_EXTRA_INFO_ALL in XXPO schema with column org_id. Also, grant all privileges to APPS for XXPO_EXTRA_INFO_ALL as discussed earlier.	No difference
Create synonym XXPO_EXTRA_INFO_ALL in the APPS schema	Create synonym XXPO_EXTRA_INFO_ALL in the APPS schema for the custom table.	No difference
Create or replace view XXPO_EXTRA_INFO in the APPS schema, as "select * from XXPO_EXTRA_INFO_ALL where org_id=<client_info>"		View is no longer created in R12. Instead, a synonym is created without _ALL.
	Create another synonym XXPO_EXTRA_INFO in APPS, referring to table XXPO_EXTRA_INFO_ALL in custom schema	Synonym is created without _ALL in its name.
	Execute PL/SQL API fnd_access_control_util.add_policy	Apply Row Level Security to XXPO_EXTRA_INFO

TABLE 4-1. *Comparison Between 11i and R12 for Creation of Multi-Org Tables*

The following code explains the precise steps involved when creating custom Multi-Org tables in R12. In this example, we are creating table XXPO_EXTRA_SHIPPING_INFO_ALL in the XXPO schema. In addition, we demonstrate how the entries in global temporary table affect the Row Level Security:

```
--Connect to XXPO Schema and create table and give grants
CREATE TABLE XXPO_EXTRA_SHIPPING_INFO_ALL (
 EXTRA_INFORMATION_ID          INTEGER NOT NULL,
 LAST_UPDATE_DATE              DATE NOT NULL,
 LAST_UPDATED_BY               NUMBER NOT NULL,
 LAST_UPDATE_LOGIN             NUMBER,
 CREATION_DATE                 DATE,
 CREATED_BY                    NUMBER,
 ORG_ID                        NUMBER     );
GRANT ALL ON XXPO_EXTRA_SHIPPING_INFO_ALL TO APPS ;

--Connect to APPS Schema and execute the following:
CREATE OR REPLACE SYNONYM XXPO_EXTRA_SHIPPING_INFO_ALL for
   XXPO.XXPO_EXTRA_SHIPPING_INFO_ALL ;
CREATE OR REPLACE SYNONYM XXPO_EXTRA_SHIPPING_INFO for
   XXPO.XXPO_EXTRA_SHIPPING_INFO_ALL ;

BEGIN
fnd_access_control_util.add_policy(p_object_schema    => 'APPS'
      ,p_object_name     => 'XXPO_EXTRA_SHIPPING_INFO'
      ,p_policy_name     => 'ORG_SEC' ,p_function_schema => 'APPS'
      ,p_policy_function => 'MO_GLOBAL.ORG_SECURITY'
      ,p_statement_types => 'SELECT, INSERT, UPDATE, DELETE'
      ,p_update_check    => TRUE ,p_enable          => TRUE
      ,p_static_policy   => FALSE);
END;

DECLARE
l_user_id      INTEGER;
l_resp_id      INTEGER;
l_resp_appl_id INTEGER;
l_app_short_name fnd_application_vl.APPLICATION_SHORT_NAME%TYPE;
BEGIN
SELECT user_id INTO l_user_id FROM fnd_user WHERE user_name =
'EBUSINESS';
SELECT responsibility_id INTO l_resp_id FROM fnd_responsibility_vl WHERE
responsibility_key LIKE 'RECEIVABLES_VISION_OPERATIONS';
SELECT application_id INTO l_resp_appl_id FROM fnd_responsibility_vl
WHERE responsibility_key LIKE 'RECEIVABLES_VISION_OPERATIONS';
SELECT application_short_name INTO l_app_short_name FROM fnd_application_
vl fav ,fnd_responsibility_vl frv WHERE frv.responsibility_key =
'RECEIVABLES_VISION_OPERATIONS' AND fav.application_id =
frv.application_id; fnd_global.apps_initialize(
```

```
user_id => l_user_id ,resp_id => l_resp_id ,resp_appl_id => l_resp_appl_
id ); mo_global.init( p_appl_short_name => l_app_short_name ) ;
END;
```

If you are using the VISION R12 instance, after executing the previous statements, the results can be tested in APPS schema, as shown in Table 4-2.

As shown in Table 4-2, only the records for org_id = 204 are returned. This happens because the responsibility Receivables, Vision Operations (U.S.), has access to the operating unit Vision Operations that corresponds to operating unit 204. The security profile attached to this responsibility does not allow access to the operating unit Widgets Product Line, which has org_id 206. Therefore, a select on xxpo_extra_shipping_info does not return records for org_id 206 in the example, as shown in Table 4-2.

The Technical Impact of MOAC on Release12 Upgrade

When an E-Business Suite instance is upgraded from R11i to R12, it becomes the responsibility of the implementation team to ensure that existing custom Multi-Org views are replaced by synonyms that are secured using Row Level Security. An additional impact of upgrading to R12 is that for every custom form that references Multi-Org data, an Operating Unit field must be created. This is applicable to both professional Oracle Forms and OA Framework–based screens. The value in this field will be defaulted using the profile option MO: Default Operating Unit. This field will also be attached to the list of values.

Additionally, all the concurrent programs in R12 can either be run for a single operating unit or multiple operating units. By default, all the concurrent programs upgraded from R11i will be a single operating unit. For single operating unit–based concurrent programs, an Operating Unit field will be presented in the Submit Request window at the time of submission of a concurrent program. This field will be mandatory, and the user will be forced to select the operating unit from the list of values. Therefore, the Multi-Org synonyms in the concurrent program will return data for one single operating unit.

Step	Result
Insert record in XXPO_EXTRA_SHIPPING_INFO_ALL with ORG_ID=204	
Insert into XXPO_EXTRA_SHIPPING_INFO_ALL with ORG_ID=206	
SELECT org_id FROM xxpo_extra_shipping_info	204 returned
SELECT organization_id FROM mo_glob_org_access_tmp	204 returned

TABLE 4-2. *Testing MOAC on a Custom Object*

To enable the concurrent program to be run for multi-org users as per the Multi-Org Security Profile, follow these steps:

1. Navigate to the System Administration responsibility and navigate to Concurrent | Program to open the Concurrent Program definition screen in OA Framework.
2. Search for the concurrent program definition that you want to run for all the operating units that are applicable to the responsibility.
3. Click the Update icon for that program, and select the Request tab. Change the value of the Operating Unit Mode field to Multiple. (By default, this is set to Single.)

After making this change, the Operating Unit field in the Submit Request window of the concurrent program will be disabled. References to Multi-Org synonyms within your concurrent program will have access to all the operating units for that responsibility.

When submitting concurrent programs with a single operating unit programmatically from PL/SQL, you can set the context to the relevant operating unit, as shown next:

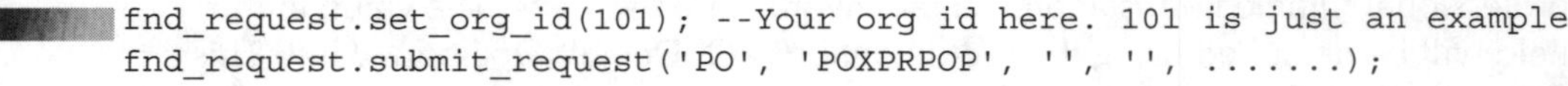

```
fnd_request.set_org_id(101); --Your org id here. 101 is just an example
fnd_request.submit_request('PO', 'POXPRPOP', '', '', .......);
```

NOTE
*To set your SQL*Plus session to a single org_id, call API MO_GLOBAL.SET_POLICY_CONTEXT ('S', p_org_id), where p_org_id is the desired org_id.*

Following is a list of additional impact areas of MOAC on the custom code that is upgraded from R11i to R12:

1. All the custom code that uses FND_PROFILE.VALUE ('ORG_ID') must be revisited.
2. The custom code that uses CLIENT_INFO variable should also be revisited.
3. If a custom code SQL query joins multiple tables that are secured by the MOAC policy, such a query will invoke Row Level Security for each secured table in the FROM clause. This will cause the PL/SQL package MO_GLOBAL.ORG_SECURITY to be invoked for each secured table in the FROM clause. Such queries can impact performance. Therefore, it is recommended that you use an RLS-based synonym just for the driving table in the query. The remainder tables should be _ALL. The joins in the SQL statement will filter the corresponding operating unit records from _ALL tables.

4. Table creation definitions may contain a default clause for the ORG_ID column. In case MOAC is enabled, you will have to specify the org_id explicitly in the insert statements. Therefore, the default clause on the ORG_ID column must be removed from all custom tables.

Summary

Multi-Org is one of the key concepts in E-Business Suite and needs to be understood well by both functional analysts and developers alike. In this chapter, we discussed the main features of Multi-Org with emphasis on technical insights in both R11i and R12.

In R11i, users have to log into different responsibilities to access the data in different operating units, while in R12, the enhanced Multi-Org Access Control (MOAC) feature allows users to access and report on data for multiple operating units at the same time within a single application's responsibility. We discussed the technical details of both approaches and provided practical guidance on how to create Multi-Org-enabled custom objects. In addition, we outlined the process of upgrading Multi-Org custom objects created in R11i to R12 and highlighted the upgrade impact areas that developers need to be aware of.

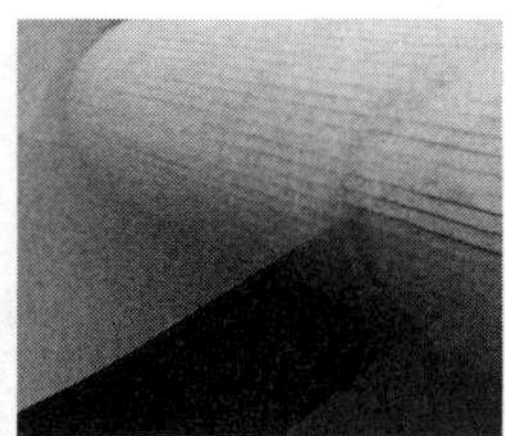

CHAPTER 5

Development of Concurrent Programs

esigning, developing, and customizing *concurrent programs* is one of the key skills Oracle Applications developers must have. When we earlier discussed E-Business Suite architecture, you learned that concurrent processing plays a pivotal role in the management of key business processes within the E-Business Suite by allowing the background job submission alongside the core online transaction processing. In this chapter, we'll concentrate on the practical aspects of concurrent program development in Oracle Applications. In practical terms, the process of concurrent program development is unchanged between E-Business Suite in R12, R11i, and even earlier releases.

What Is a Concurrent Program?

The word *program* in the "concurrent program" is used in its broader sense in the context of concurrent processing in Oracle Applications. Most of us assume that a computer program is something that can be run as an operating system executable or series of executable instructions that return some kind of a result or perform some operations. In Oracle Applications, the concurrent program has a subtly different meaning. Rather than being just an executable file or a piece of code, the concurrent program is a collection of definitions that describe an executable file or module that is actually executed, the parameters and types of parameters that are passed to a such executable, and the definition of the programs that are incompatible to run simultaneously with the concurrent program being defined because they could interfere with its execution. Say, for example, you are asked to create and periodically run a SQL script to purge temporary data from some custom application module that you have developed in house. You could define that script to be run as a concurrent program in Oracle Applications and use the full power of concurrent processing to schedule and manage concurrent requests for your newly defined program.

The concurrent programs definitions are stored in the following database tables in the APPLSYS schema:

- **FND_CONCURRENT_PROGRAMS** Contains information about the name and description of the concurrent program, execution method, standalone flag, print style, and other attributes that define the program.
- **FND_EXECUTABLES** Contains attributes about concurrent program executables, including the concurrent program executable name alongside the name of the actual executable file on the operating system such as shell script, Oracle Report, Java class, and others. The execution method is associated with the concurrent program executable to help the Concurrent Manager identify how and with what tool to run the physical executable file.

The following illustration depicts the relationship between the application, concurrent program, and executable code:

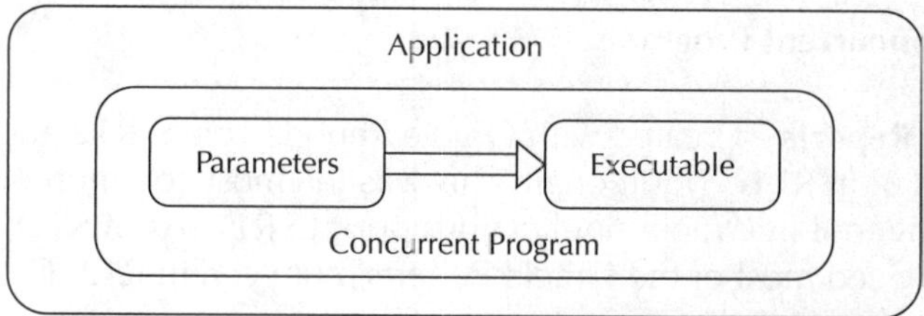

The link between the concurrent program and the actual physical executable file is through the concurrent program executable record; the concurrent program executable stores information that tells Concurrent Managers where to find the physical executable file on the file system and what tool is suitable to execute it.

There are three ways of creating a concurrent program definition in Oracle Applications:

- Through the Forms-based interface screens Concurrent Programs (FNDCPMCP) and Concurrent Program Executable (FNDCPMPE)
- Through the AOL loader utility FNDLOAD and afcpprog.lct control file
- Using PL/SQL API (FND_PROGRAM)

The concurrent programs must be associated with an existing application. For example, if you develop a concurrent program for a custom application XXCUST (the short name for the custom application module in this example), you would than normally create the definition of the concurrent program against the application "Custom Development" (user-friendly name for our custom application).

What are the candidates for concurrent programs? This usually depends on requirement details, but as a rule of thumb, any application with noninteractive functionality that can be deferred to be executed in the background, such as a long running query or data import from the third-party application, could be implemented as a concurrent program.

Types of Concurrent Programs

There are about 12 different types of concurrent programs in Oracle Applications at the time of the writing of this book. The type of the concurrent program is determined by the Execution Method attribute and is inherited from concurrent program executable definition. You can divide concurrent programs into the following groups based on the tools or programming language they are created with:

Oracle Tool Concurrent Programs

- **Oracle Reports** Created with Oracle Reports 10g in R12 and Oracle Reports 6i in R11i. Traditionally this was the most common operational reporting tool in Oracle Applications prior to R12. As of R12, BI Publisher has replaced most of the Oracle Reports, but even in R12, Oracle Reports are still used.
- **PL/SQL** Based on the database procedure stored within the PL/SQL package. This is a common type of concurrent program.
- **SQL*Loader** A database command-line utility used to load data from external flat files into the Oracle Applications database. Used very often for data conversions and importing data from third-party applications and other types of data import.
- **SQL*Plus** Executes SQL scripts as well as anonymous PL/SQL blocks. Useful for noncomplicated SQL reports, data purge routines, and updates that need to be executed repeatedly.

Java-based Concurrent Programs

- **Java stored procedure** Executes Java stored database procedures. Not used very frequently.
- **Java concurrent program** Executes a Java program that resides outside of the Oracle database. Due to the popularity of Java and availability of various Java libraries, this type is becoming very popular.

C or Pro*C-based Concurrent Programs

- **Immediate** Written in C or Pro*C. With this type of concurrent program, the subprograms are written in C or Pro*C and linked with a Concurrent Manager executable that runs the concurrent program within the same OS process. This type is rarely used these days for custom development.
- **Spawned** Also written in C or Pro*C. The difference between immediate and spawned is that the spawned type of concurrent program is compiled as a standalone executable on the target platform and as a result runs in a separate process from the Concurrent Manager process. This type is rarely used these days for custom development.

Script or Command-based Concurrent Programs

- **Host** Executes operating system commands on the host machine. Typically this type is used to execute shell scripts to perform operations native to the operating system such as coping, moving, and transferring of files.
- **Perl concurrent program** Executes Perl scripts.

Although there are many different types of concurrent programs, in practice, the most frequently used are Oracle Reports, SQL and PL/SQL, SQL*Loader, Java, shell scripts, and host (OS) commands. We'll take a detailed look at the most common types of concurrent programs.

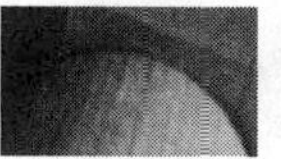

NOTE
Oracle Reports development techniques are discussed in Chapter 7 in more detail.

How to Define a Concurrent Program

Before you can define a concurrent program in the Oracle Applications database, you need to write the code or scripts in SQL, PL/SQL, Java, or any other permitted development tool that will fulfill the functional requirements. Once you are happy with how the code logic executes as a standalone program, you can register it with Application Object Library (AOL) and link it with a named concurrent program in Oracle Applications. A more detailed overview of this process is in the following steps:

1. Write the program logic in any of the allowed tools.
2. Create and register with AOL the Concurrent Program Executable. Specify the execution method and associated operating system file name of the executable file or a script. Different types of concurrent programs require different attributes; for example, a PL/SQL concurrent program executable needs to provide the PL/SQL package and procedure name.
3. Create and register with AOL the concurrent program, link it to the Concurrent Program Executable, specify program parameters, and define any incompatibilities with the other concurrent programs.
4. Make the concurrent program available to the end users. To achieve that, add the concurrent program to an appropriate Request Group for the user's responsibility. The Request Group is just a list of concurrent programs that can be assigned to responsibilities to provide access control over which programs a user can run.

In the next section, we take a closer look at this process by providing a step-by-step approach to creating the concurrent programs in Oracle Applications.

Creating a Hello World Concurrent Program

It has become almost a ritual in computer learning books to get started with the writing of a simple Hello World program. This book is no exception, and it is probably the best way to explain the basic steps of creating concurrent programs. And so, without further ado, let's start building our Hello World concurrent program that will take two parameters, NAME and MY_DATE, to produce the text output *Hello <NAME>. Date entered is <MY_DATE>*, where <NAME> and <MY_DATE> are the values specified in the respective parameters passed from the concurrent request submission form.

Design and Write Your Program

The requirements for the Hello World program are very simple. The program's purpose is to demonstrate how concurrent programs are created, where the executable files go, and how to pass parameters to a simple program. We chose to implement this program as a SQL*Plus concurrent program, and to do that we have created the HELLOWORLD.sql script:

```
SET VERIFY OFF
SET LINESIZE 70
SET HEADING OFF

WHENEVER SQLERROR EXIT FAILURE ROLLBACK;
WHENEVER OSERROR EXIT FAILURE ROLLBACK;
/* ---------------------------------------------------------------*/

SELECT 'Hello ' || UPPER('&1') || '. Date selected is ' ||
         fnd_date.canonical_to_date('&2')
FROM dual;

EXIT;
```

The SQL script takes two parameters, &1 and &2. We also use the FND_DATE.CANONICAL_TO_DATE function, which takes a character string in the canonical date format and converts it to a PL/SQL date. In Oracle Applications, canonical date format is a standard format used to express a date as a string: *YYYY/MM/DD H24:MI:SS*.

NOTE
*Parameters are passed to the SQL script in the same order they are defined later in the Concurrent Programs (FNDCPMCP) form. It is the relative order that matters and not the actual sequence numbers. The parameter numbers &1, &2, and so on should be in ascending order to match the ascending parameters sequence order in the Concurrent Programs form. For example, you can sequence parameters in the Concurrent Programs form as 10 for Parameter A, 15 for Parameter B, and 20 for Parameter C; the corresponding SQL*Plus script parameters would be &1, &2, and &3.*

If you execute the HELLOWORLD.sql script from SQL*Plus now, it should produce the required output:

```
$ sqlplus -s apps/welcome @HELLOWORLD Joe "2008/12/28 00:00:00"
Hello JOE. Date selected is 28-DEC-08
```

Place the SQL Script in the Appropriate Directory

When you are happy that the script fulfills the requirements, even if they are very simple as in this example, you should place HELLOWORLD.sql in the $PROD_TOP/sql directory, where <PROD_TOP> is a product top-level directory. For the purposes of demonstration, we have created an application called Custom Development. The top-level directory of our Custom Development application is XXCUST_TOP:

```
[avisr12@r12 sql]$ pwd
/oracle/apps/R1204/apps/apps_st/appl/xxcust/12.0.0/sql
[avisr12@r12 sql]$ ls
HELLOWORLD.sql
```

Create the Concurrent Program Executable

The next step is to create the concurrent program executable that will link an entry in the database with the physical path and the name of the SQL script. Assuming that you are signed on as the OPERATIONS Oracle Applications user, navigate from the Application Developer responsibility (N) Application Developer | Concurrent | Executable.

In the Concurrent Program Executable form, enter the details as shown in Figure 5-1.

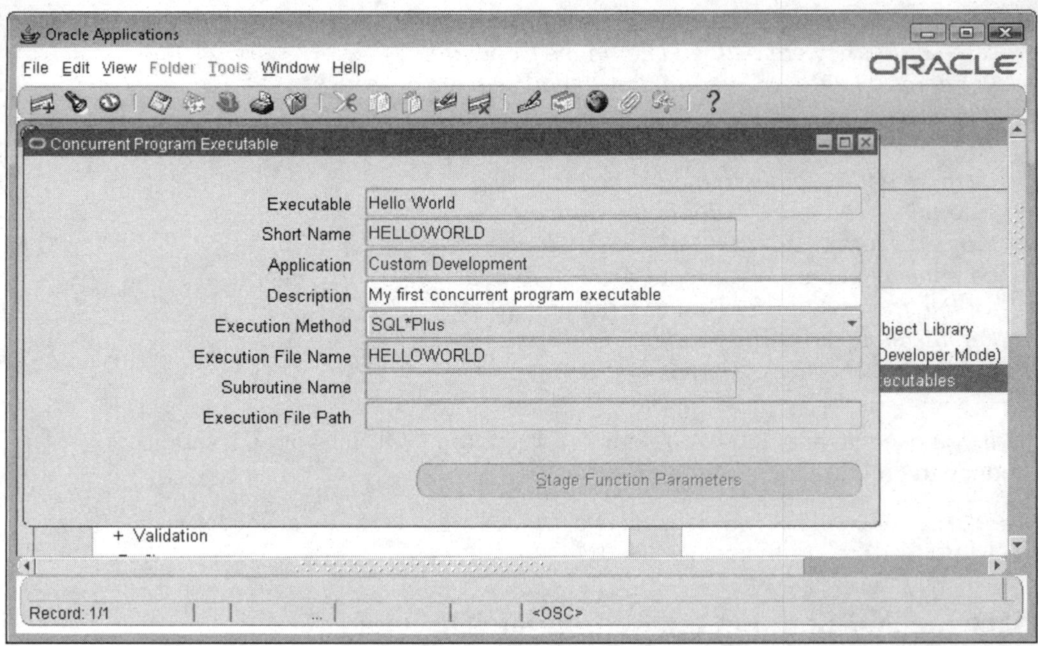

FIGURE 5-1. *The definition of the Hello World concurrent program executable*

The Executable field is just a free text logical name for the concurrent program executable. The Short Name is an executable identifier that is used later in the Concurrent Program form. An executable must be associated with an application, and this is defined in the Application field. This field associates the executable with the product top-level directory, which is XXCUST_TOP for the Custom Development application. Description is just a free text field where you document the purpose of the executable. The Execution Method field identifies the tool that is needed to run the executable that we are defining in this form. In this case, the executable is SQL*Plus and the runtime process will search the $XXCUST_TOP/sql directory to find the SQL script to execute. The Execution File Name field specifies the name of the HELLOWORLD physical executable file. You'll notice that the standard file extension for SQL scripts, .sql, is assumed and you should not attempt to specify the execution file name with the file extension .sql for SQL*Plus concurrent program executables.

The fields that are not used in this example are Subroutine Name and Execution File Path. The first is applicable only to immediate and spawned concurrent programs written in C or Pro*C, while the execution file path is used for Java concurrent programs.

Create the Concurrent Program

Now that you have defined the concurrent program executable, you can proceed with the definition of the concurrent program itself: (N) Application Developer | Concurrent | Program.

In the Concurrent Programs (FNDCPMCP) form, enter the details as shown in Figure 5-2.

The Program field is a free text logical name for the concurrent program that you are defining. Short Name is an internal name of the concurrent program. The Application field is also mandatory, as every concurrent program must be associated with an application, and in this case it is assigned to the Custom Development application. The Description field documents the purpose of the concurrent

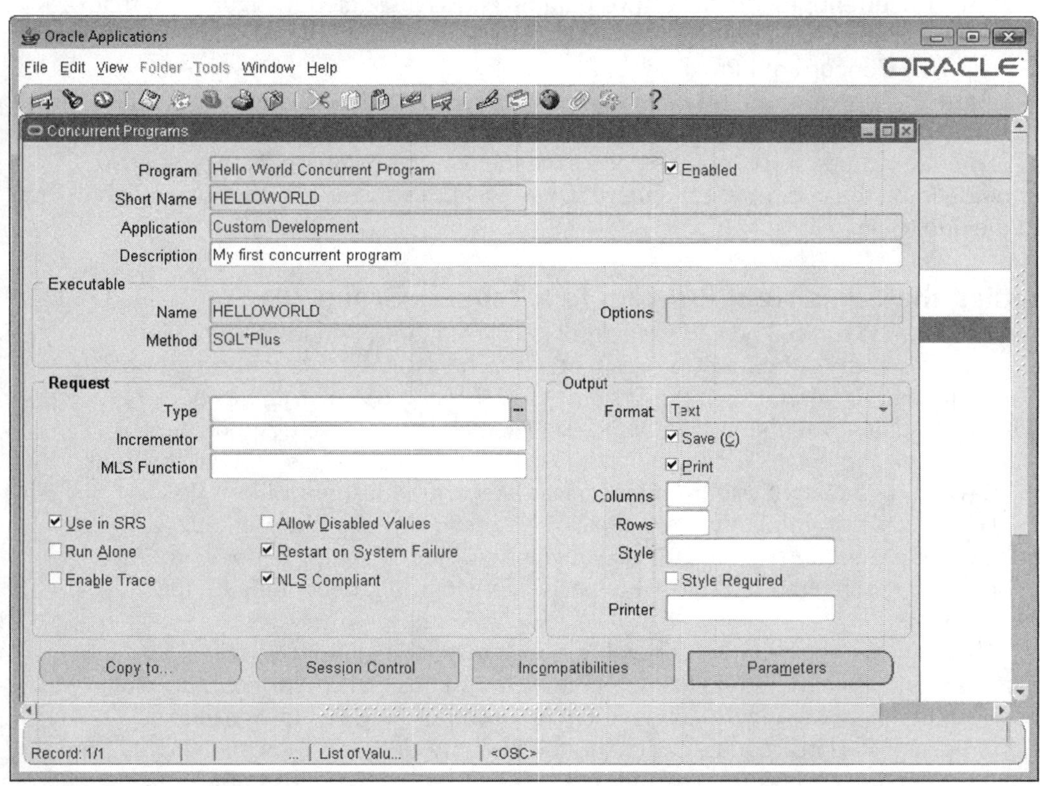

FIGURE 5-2. *The definition of the Hello World concurrent program*

program; the Name field in the Executable region within the form window specifies which executable to run. You define your Hello World concurrent program to run your earlier defined Hello World executable, which in turn is defined to run the HELLOWORLD.sql script that resides in $XXCUST_TOP/sql.

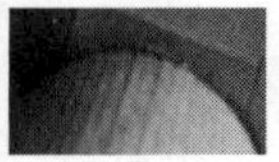

NOTE
You need to make sure that the Use in SRS check box is checked if you want to allow the end users to submit this or any other request to run this program from a Standard Request Submission (SRS) window. SRS is a concurrent processing functionality that provides a common interface for running concurrent programs from the GUI.

The concurrent program takes two parameters, as illustrated in Figure 5-3, that you define in the Concurrent Program Parameters window: (N) Application Developer | Concurrent | Program (B) Parameters.

Table 5-1 provides the list of values used to define the NAME and MY_DATE parameters.

Enter the values from Table 5-1 and save them to the database. Now you are done defining the concurrent program; however, at this stage, it is still not available to the end users.

Assign the Concurrent Program to a Request Group

Before it can be run by the end users through the Standard Request Submission (SRS) window, the concurrent program needs to be assigned to a request group. This can be achieved through the System Administrator (SYSADMIN) responsibility, which is usually available to the OPERATIONS user in the Oracle Applications VISION environment. You can navigate to the Request Group screen by following the navigation path (N)System Administrator | Security | Responsibility | Request.

For the sake of simplicity, in Figure 5-4 we opted to assign the Hello World concurrent program to the already existing System Administrator Reports group, although in real life this will probably be a different group, depending on the requirements.

This step will enable any user with the System Administrator responsibility attached to it, such as an OPERATIONS user, to run this Hello World concurrent program. If you are wondering what the relationship is between the System Administrator Reports request group and the System Administrator responsibility, the link between the two is provided through the Request Group fields in the Responsibilities screen in for the System Administrator responsibility, as shown in Figure 5-5. The navigation path to the Responsibilities screen is (N) System Administrator | Security | Responsibility | Define.

Seq	Parameter	Description	Value Set	Default Value	Prompt
10	NAME	First Parameter (Char)	100 Characters	(leave empty)	Name
20	MY_DATE	Second parameter (Date)	FND_STANDARD_DATE	Current Date	My Date

TABLE 5-1. *Defining Parameters in the Concurrent Programs Form*

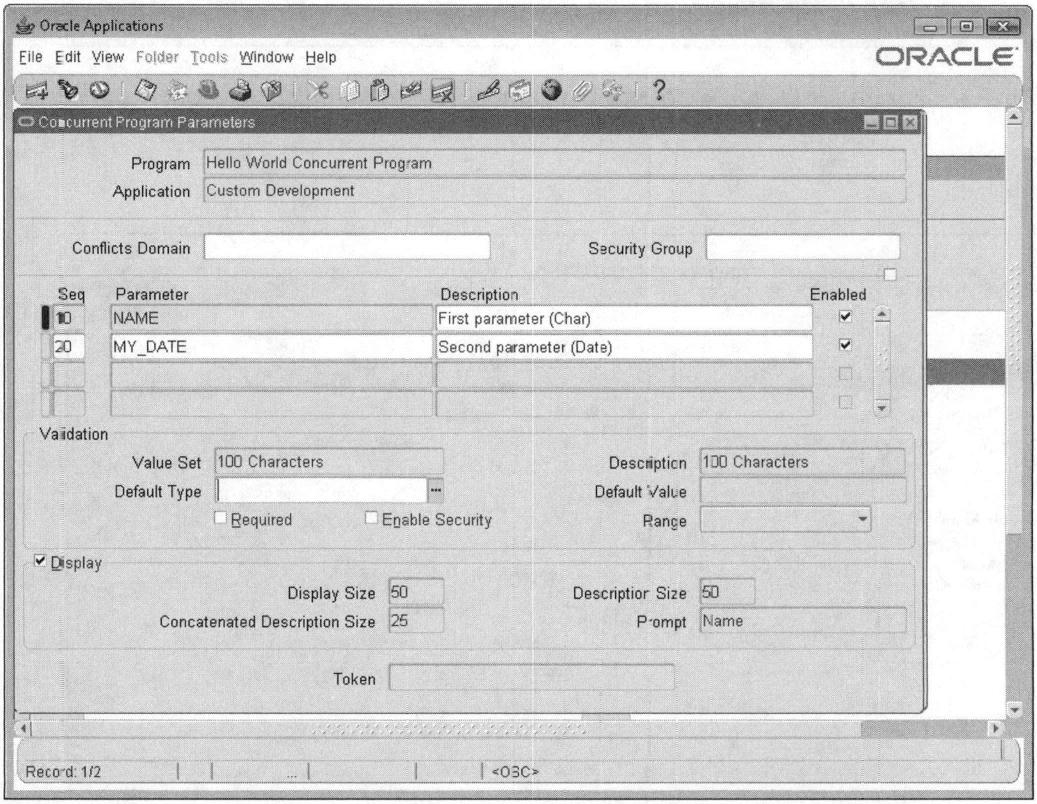

FIGURE 5-3. *The Concurrent Program Parameters window*

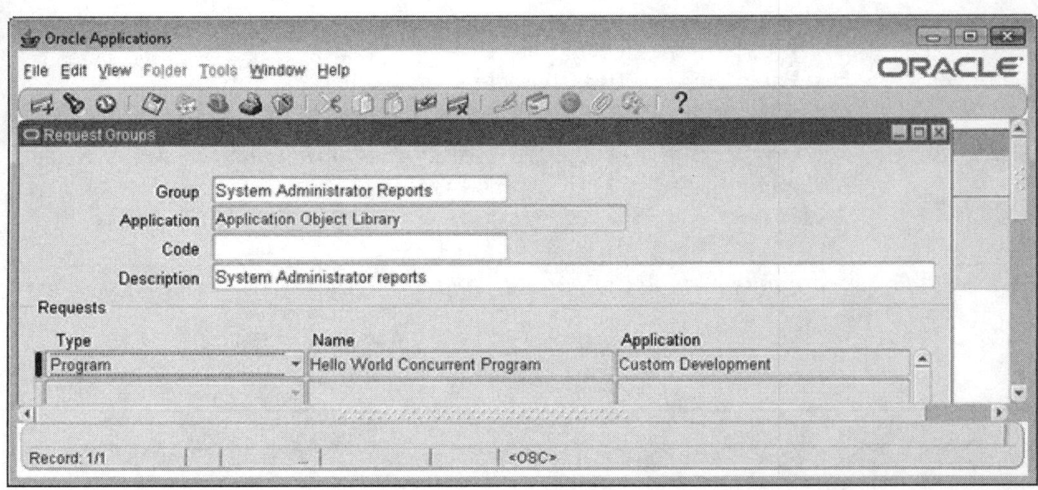

FIGURE 5-4. *Assign the Hello World program to the System Admin Reports request group.*

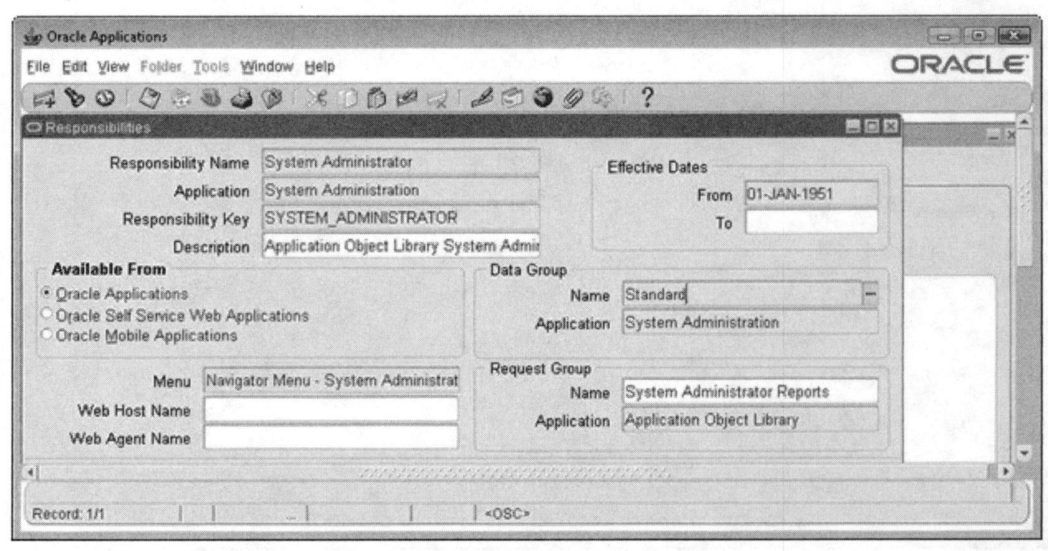

FIGURE 5-5. *Request Group System Administrator Reports assigned to the System Administrator responsibility*

At this point, you can run the Hello World concurrent program by submitting it through the Standard Request Submission (SRS) window, which is the most common way of scheduling and submitting of concurrent requests in Oracle Applications. You can navigate to the SRS screen by navigating to the System Administrator responsibility, then going to the View item on the menu and selecting Requests from the list: (N) System Administrator | (M) View | Requests | (B) Submit a New Request.

If you choose to run a single request, you'll be able to query your Hello World Concurrent Program, and the Parameters window will pop up to prompt you to enter the Name and My Date parameters that you defined earlier. If you enter the two values and submit the request, the program will be submitted to the Concurrent Manager to be executed.

You can check the current execution status by clicking the Find button in the Find Requests window: (N) System Administrator | (M) View | Requests | (B) Find Requests.

You can see in Figure 5-6 that the concurrent request has completed successfully. The output and the log details from the concurrent requests can be

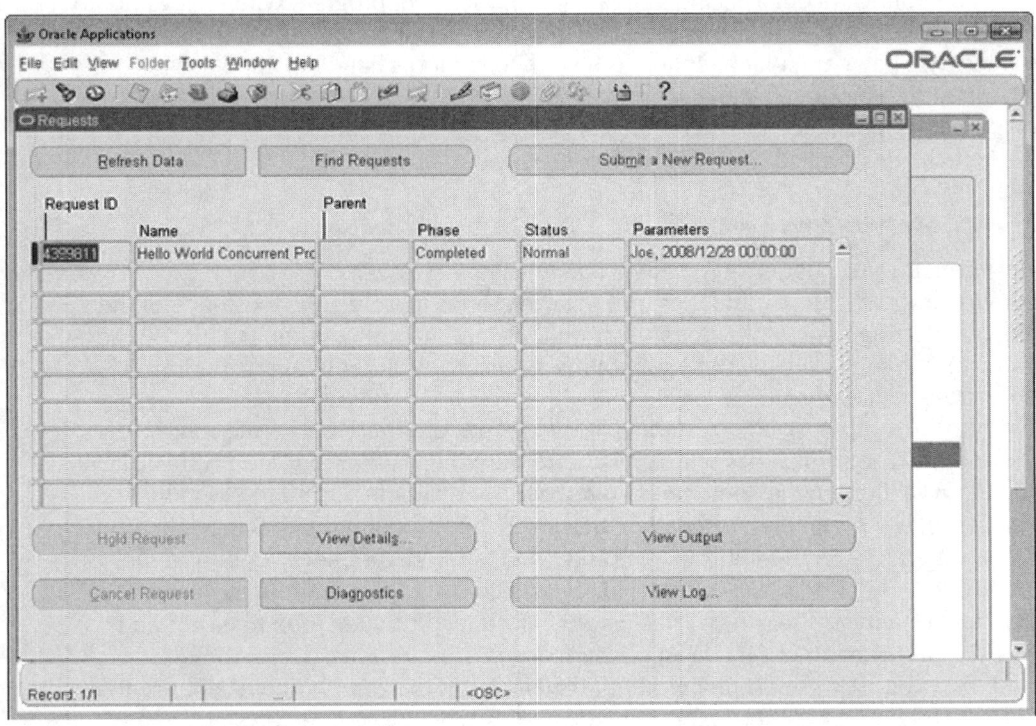

FIGURE 5-6. *Hello World successfully executed*

accessed by clicking the corresponding buttons in the form. This action opens another browser window; however, as expected from our simple program, the output is a simple line of text with the parameters substituted on the fly by the run-time process: *Hello JOE. Date selected is 28-DEC-08.*

Clicking the Log File button opens a browser window with the detail information about the concurrent request execution, parameters passed, request ID, name of executable, and other information that you may find useful, especially when looking for the clues when the execution of the concurrent program completes with an error.

Examples of Concurrent Programs

We shall now take a look at the most frequently used types of the concurrent programs. Aside from Oracle Reports, in practice, it is quite common to create your concurrent programs with other Oracle tools such as SQL*Plus scripts, SQL*Loader, and PL/SQL. However, you should use other techniques if they meet your requirements more closely; for example, you can create a host concurrent program' for an operating system–specific task or a Java concurrent program when a Java library that can fulfill the requirements is readily available. In the following examples, we suggest you pay particular attention to how different tools handle parameters passed by concurrent programs and how concurrent programs' executables are defined for different types of execution methods.

Let's have a look at each of these techniques in more detail.

Host Program

Host concurrent programs typically execute some OS-specific tasks such as copying, moving, or reading files; polling directories to detect the existence of the file; transferring data via FTP or similar utilities; and handling other situations where you can utilize readily available operating system tools and utilities to perform operations.

In this example, you'll create a host concurrent program to execute a simple shell script. The shell script will copy an arbitrary output file from the $APPLCSF/$APPLOUT directory to some target directory (for example, /tmp directory) that will be passed as a parameter to the concurrent program through the SRS form. If you are using an R12 VISION instance, you'll find that there are plenty of output files in the $APPLCSF/$APPLOUT directory that you can use to move about to demonstrate the functionality of the script. This example is created on the Linux platform and R12 (12.0.4) version of Oracle Applications.

Host programs are usually written as shell scripts of your choice. We'll use the Korn shell command interpreter in the examples. You can follow the steps in the next sections to create a host concurrent program to execute your shell script, which will copy a file from the $APPLCSF/$APPLOUT directory to a target directory of your choice.

Create the Shell Script and Place It in the PROD_TOP/bin Directory

Here is the shell script called COPY_A.prog:

```
#/bin/ksh
######################################################################
PROGRAM_NAME=`basename $0`
echo $PROGRAM_NAME "has started"
echo " "
echo " "
echo "Parameters passed to the shell script by the system:"
echo "**************************************************"
echo "Name of the concurrent program is $0"
echo "Database user/passwd is $1"
echo "UserID is $2"
echo "Apps user name that submitted the request is $3"
echo "Concurrent RequestID is $4"
echo " "
echo "Following are user parameters submitted via SRS form: "
echo "**************************************************"
echo "File to copy:     $5"
echo "Target directory: $6"
#####################################################
# Check if the user parameters are non empty        #
#####################################################
if [ "$5" != "" ] &&  [ "$6" != "" ]
then
  echo "Executing cp $APPLCSF/$APPLOUT/$5 S6"
    ##################################
    # Check that file actually exists#
    ##################################
    if [ ! -f $APPLCSF/$APPLOUT/$5 ]
    then
      echo  $APPLCSF/$APPLOUT/$5 " does not exist. Nothing to copy"
      echo "Exiting with status 1"
      exit 1
     fi
#################################################
# If file exists, copy it to target directory #
#################################################
cp $APPLCSF/$APPLOUT/$5 $6
else
  echo "Please enter a non empty file and directory"
  echo "Exiting with status 1"
  exit 1
fi
```

You need to make sure that you save the shell script as COPY_A.prog (with the extension .prog) in the bin directory of the product top-level directory. In this case, that directory is the Custom Development $XXCUST_TOP/bin directory (/oracle/apps/R1204/apps/apps_st/appl/xxcust/12.0.0/bin). Once the file is created, change the executable permissions on the script:

```
[avisr12@r12 bin]$ chmod 775 COPY_A.prog
[avisr12@r12 bin]$ ls -l COPY_A.prog
-rwxrwxr-x  1 avisr12 dba 1468 Dec 29  2008 COPY_A.prog
```

Create a Symbolic (Soft) Link to $FND_TOP/bin/fndcpesr

With host concurrent programs, you may find dealing with parameters passed to the shell script to be a little cumbersome. Ideally, each parameter should be available as a separate variable in the shell script. The way to achieve that is to create a symbolic or soft link to $FND_TOP/bin/fndcpesr by executing the following command from the directory where you placed your shell script ($XXCUST_TOP/bin):

```
[avisr12@r12 bin]$ ln -s $FND_TOP/bin/fndcpesr COPY_A
```

You can execute the ls command to verify that the link has been created:

```
[avisr12@r12 bin]$ ls -l
lrwxrwxrwx  1 avisr12 dba   60 Dec 29 06:42 COPY_A ->
oracle/apps/R1204/apps/apps_st/appl/fnd/12.0.0/bin/fndcpesr
-rwxrwxr-x  1 avisr12 dba 1468 Dec 29  2008 COPY_A.prog
```

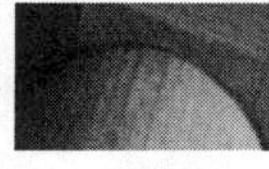

NOTE
The soft link is created to COPY_A (without the .prog extension). In other words, the soft link name should have the same name as the shell script but without the .prog extension.

NOTE
There is an alternative way of processing the parameters in the host concurrent programs. We'll take a look at the different way of dealing with parameters in the next section.

Register the Concurrent Program with AOL and Associate It with a Request Group

Just as in the Hello World concurrent program in the previous section, you first need to register the concurrent program executable and assign a COPY_A host (shell) program to it. The navigation path is (N) Application Developer | Concurrent | Executable.

Executable	Short Name	Application	Description	Execution Method	Execution File Name
Host Demo Copy A	XXCUST_ COPY_A	Custom Development	Demo host program using fndcpesr	Host	COPY_A

TABLE 5-2. *Concurrent Program Executable Definition*

Table 5-2 lists the values associated with the fields in the Concurrent Program Executable screen in our example.

Once you've created the concurrent program executable, you can proceed and create the concurrent program itself and associate two parameters with it. The navigation path is (N) Application Developer | Concurrent | Program.

The values we entered in the example to define our host concurrent program are listed in Table 5-3.

We also define parameters by clicking the Parameters button in the Concurrent Programs form: (N) Application Developer | Concurrent | Program (B) Parameters.

The values for parameters that we used in our example are listed in Table 5-4.

Finally, assign your newly defined host concurrent program to the System Administrator Reports request group using the Request Groups form available from the System Administrator responsibility: (N) System Administrator | Security | Responsibility | Request.

The Demo Host Program concurrent program is now available to be run if the user signed on is assigned the System Administrator or other responsibility that you have specifically allowed access to your concurrent program through the request group management feature of AOL.

Program	Short Name	Application	Description	Name
Demo Host Program	XXCUST_COPY_A	Custom Development	Demo host program using fndcpesr	XXCUST_ COPY_A

TABLE 5-3. *Concurrent Program Definition*

Seq	Parameter	Description	Value Set	Default Value	Prompt
10	FILE_TO_COPY	File to copy	100 Characters	(leave empty)	File to copy
20	TARGET_DIR	Target directory	100 Characters	/tmp	Target directory

TABLE 5-4. *Values Entered in the Parameters Screen*

Execute the Concurrent Program (Script) from SRS Form

Last, navigate to the Submit Request window, which allows you to run your concurrent program: (N) System Administrator | (M) View | Requests | (B) Submit a New Request.

Enter **Demo Host Program** in the Name field, and the Parameters window automatically pops up. There are two parameters that we defined for this program; for the File to copy parameter, you enter any of the output files that can be found in the $APPLCSF/$APPLOUT directory. On the middle-tier box, we selected o4399977.out; if you are following this example on your Oracle Applications instance, you can enter any other file from this directory. The default target directory in the example is /tmp (on the Linux platform, usually anyone can write to the /tmp directory).

After you click the Submit button, the concurrent program is run by the Concurrent Manager and completes successfully with the normal status. The script has written the informational and other messages into the log file, which can be accessed by clicking the View Log button in the Requests screen.

Let's now examine the log file and check what parameters have been passed to the $0, $1, $2, $3, $4, $5, and $6 shell script variables:

```
+---------------------------------------------------------------------------+
Custom Development: Version : UNKNOWN

Copyright (c) 1979, 1999, Oracle Corporation. All rights reserved.

XXCUST_COPY_A module: Demo Host Program
+---------------------------------------------------------------------------+

Current system time is 29-DEC-2008 16:22:15

+---------------------------------------------------------------------------+

COPY_A.prog has started
```

```
Parameters passed to the shell script by the system:
****************************************************
Name of the concurrent program is /oracle/apps/R1204/apps/apps_st/appl/
xxcust/12.0.0/bin/COPY_A.prog
Database user/passwd is APPS/apps
UserID is 1318
Apps user name that submitted the request is OPERATIONS
Concurrent RequestID is 4400001

Following are user parameters submitted via SRS form:
****************************************************
File to copy:     o4399977.out
Target directory: /tmp
Executing cp /oracle/apps/…/logs/appl/conc/out/o4399977.out /tmp
+---------------------------------------------------------------------------+
Executing request completion options...

+------------- 1) PRINT   --------------


Printing output file.
               Request ID : 4400001
         Number of copies : 0
                  Printer : noprint

+---------------------------------------+


Finished executing request completion options.

+---------------------------------------------------------------------------+
Concurrent request completed successfully
Current system time is 29-DEC-2008 16:22:16

+---------------------------------------------------------------------------+
```

From the output produced by the COPY_A.prog shell script, you can see that the first five parameters, $0, $1, $2, $3, and $4, are passed by the system—that is, the Concurrent Manager itself:

- **$0** The name of the concurrent program.
- **$1** Database user ID (usually APPS) and password
- **$2** Oracle Applications user ID (the USER_ID value in the FND_USER table)
- **$3** Oracle Applications user who submitted the request (OPERATIONS in this case)
- **$4** Concurrent request ID

As of parameter $5, $6, and so on, the shell script variables receive the values from the end user parameters when the concurrent request was submitted through the SRS form.

TIP
If you've got more than five end user parameters, use the Unix/Linux shift command to place the value into the $9 variable and so on. Of course, this is dependent on the scripting language used, but it usually works in the Unix type of shell scripts.

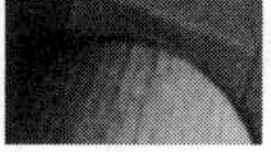

NOTE
In Oracle Applications, R12 (12.0.4), the log file is created in the usual $APPLCSF/log directory and file name is l<reqestId>.req, where reqestId is the concurrent program unique identifier. However, the output file o<requestId>.out does not get created. The variable $4 could be used within the shell script to create an output file in the $APPLCSF/out directory and we could redirect the desired output from the shell script to this file.

If you hadn't created the symbolic link to the $FND_TOP/bin/fndcpesr executable in the previous example, the Concurrent Manager in Oracle Applications would have passed all of the parameters to the $1 variable in the shell script. In this case, you need to use some kind of editing utility such as sed on Unix-like systems to extract the values and parameters from the variable $1. To demonstrate this alternative way of creating a host concurrent program, you can create a shell script called COPY_B and save it into the $XXCUST_TOP/bin directory, similar to what we did earlier with COPY_A.prog. This time, we save the shell script without the .prog extension and give it appropriate execution permissions (for example, on Linux, you would give it the permission chmod 775 COPY_B). Here is the code listing for the COPY_B shell script:

```
#/bin/ksh
###################################################################
PROGRAM_NAME=`basename $0`
echo $PROGRAM_NAME "has started"
echo " "
echo " "
echo "Parameters passed to the shell script by the system:"
echo "****************************************************"
echo "Parameter \$1: $1"
echo " "
```

```
echo "Parameters extracted by sed utility:"
echo "****************************************************"
PARAM1="`echo $1 | sed 's/ /@/g;s/"//g'| cut -f1 -d@`"
echo "Executable: $PARAM1"
PARAM2="`echo $1 | sed 's/ /@/g;s/"//g'| cut -f2 -d@`"
echo $PARAM2
PARAM3="`echo $1 | sed 's/ /@/g;s/"//g'| cut -f3 -d@`"
echo $PARAM3
PARAM4="`echo $1 | sed 's/ /@/g;s/"//g'| cut -f4 -d@`"
echo $PARAM4
PARAM5="`echo $1 | sed 's/ /@/g;s/"//g'| cut -f5 -d@`"
echo $PARAM5
PARAM6="`echo $1 | sed 's/ /@/g;s/"//g'| cut -f6 -d@`"
echo $PARAM6
PARAM7="`echo $1 | sed 's/ /@/g;s/"//g'| cut -f7 -d@`"
echo $PARAM7
PARAM8="`echo $1 | sed 's/ /@/g;s/"//g'| cut -f8 -d@`"
echo $PARAM8
PARAM9="`echo $1 | sed 's/ /@/g;s/"//g'| cut -f9 -d@`"
echo $PARAM9
PARAM10="`echo $1 | sed 's/ /@/g;s/"//g'| cut -f10 -d@`"
echo $PARAM10
#####################################################
# Check if the user parameters are non empty        #
#####################################################
if [ "$PARAM9" != "" ] &&  [ "$PARAM10" != "" ]
then
  echo "Executing cp $APPLCSF/$APPLOUT/$PARAM9 $PARAM10"
    ###################################
    # Check that file actually exists#
    ###################################
    if [ ! -f $APPLCSF/$APPLOUT/$PARAM9 ]
    then
      echo  $APPLCSF/$APPLOUT/$PARAM9 " does not exist. Nothing to
copy"
      echo "Exiting with status 1"
      exit 1
     fi
##############################################
# If file exists, copy it to target directory #
##############################################
cp $APPLCSF/$APPLOUT/$PARAM9 $PARAM10
else
  echo "Please enter a non empty file and directory"
  echo "Exiting with status 1"
  exit 1
fi
```

Now, if you change the value of the File Execution Name field to the COPY_B value for the concurrent program executable Host Demo Copy A that we defined in the earlier exercise, the change will take effect immediately. That is, if we run the concurrent program Demo Host Program, the following output can be found in the log file:

```
+---------------------------------------------------------------------------+
Custom Development: Version : UNKNOWN
Copyright (c) 1979, 1999, Oracle Corporation. All rights reserved.
XXCUST_COPY_A module: Demo Host Program
+---------------------------------------------------------------------------+
Current system time is 02-JAN-2009 22:04:44
+---------------------------------------------------------------------------+
COPY_B has started

Parameters passed to the shell script by the system:
****************************************************
Parameter $1: COPY_B FCP_REQID=4400616 FCP_LOGIN="APPS/apps"
FCP_USERID=1318 FCP_USERNAME="OPERATIONS" FCP_PRINTER="noprint"
FCP_SAVE_OUT=Y FCP_NUM_COPIES=0  "o4400585.out" "/tmp"

Parameters extracted by sed utility:
****************************************************
Executable: COPY_B
FCP_REQID=4400616
FCP_LOGIN=APPS/apps
FCP_USERID=1318
FCP_USERNAME=OPERATIONS
FCP_PRINTER=noprint
FCP_SAVE_OUT=Y
FCP_NUM_COPIES=0
o4400585.out
/tmp
Executing cp /oracle/apps/…/logs/appl/conc/out/o4400585.out /tmp
+---------------------------------------------------------------------------+
Executing request completion options...
+------------- 1) PRINT   -------------+
Printing output file.
               Request ID : 4400616
         Number of copies : 0
                  Printer : noprint
+--------------------------------------+
Finished executing request completion options.
+---------------------------------------------------------------------------+
Concurrent request completed successfully
Current system time is 02-JAN-2009 22:04:44
+---------------------------------------------------------------------------+
```

From the output, you can see that the shell variable $1 contains all the values passed to it by the concurrent program, including those that are passed by the end user:

```
Parameter $1: COPY_B FCP_REQID=4400616 FCP_LOGIN="APPS/WELCOME"
FCP_USERID=1318 FCP_USERNAME="OPERATIONS" FCP_PRINTER="noprint"
FCP_SAVE_OUT=Y FCP_NUM_COPIES=0  "o4400585.out" "/tmp"
```

In the example, we used the sed utility available on the Linux host machine to extract the values of the parameters:

```
PARAM<n>="`echo $1 | sed 's/ /@/g;s/"//g'| cut -f<n> -d@`"
```

where <n> is the number of the parameter that we want to extract. For example, end user parameters File to copy and Target directory, which we used in the exercise, are extracted by following commands in the script COPY_B:

```
PARAM9="`echo $1 | sed 's/ /@/g;s/"//g'| cut -f9 -d@`"
PARAM10="`echo $1 | sed 's/ /@/g;s/"//g'| cut -f10 -d@`"
```

SQL*Loader Concurrent Programs

The SQL*Loader type of the concurrent programs are frequently used when importing data into Oracle Applications from other systems (although they can be used in any scenario where we can efficiently use the Oracle SQL*Loader utility). This is a very well documented database utility and can cope with a huge amount of data quite efficiently. The methodology of creating of this type of concurrent program is very simple. As an illustration, follow this simple guide on how to create a SQL*Loader program.

Create the SQL*Loader Control File

1. First, you must successfully create a control file for the SQL*Loader utility. The listing that follows is an example of a simple control file:

```
LOAD DATA
 INFILE *
 INTO TABLE XXCUST_SQLLOAD_DATA
 FIELDS TERMINATED BY "," OPTIONALLY ENCLOSED BY '"'
 TRAILING NULLCOLS
 (
    DATA_FIELD1
  , DATA_FIELD2
  , REQUEST_ID     "FND_GLOBAL.conc_request_id"
  , creation_date  SYSDATE
  , created_by     "fnd_global.USER_ID"
```

```
 )
BEGINDATA
"City","London"
"City","New York"
"City","Tokyo"
"City","Bombay"
"City","Paris"
```

The control file for this example is called DATALOAD.ctl and it is placed in the $XXCUST_TOP/bin directory. It is the PROD_TOP/bin directory that will be scanned by the Concurrent Manager to find the control file, as defined in the concurrent program executable. The definition of the data file assumes that the data is loaded inline into the XXCUST_SQLLOAD_DATA table, although more often than not, data gets loaded separately and the name of the data file is specified within the control file. We also created the XXCUST_SQLLOAD_DATA table in the APPS schema:

```
SQL> create  table XXCUST_SQLLOAD_DATA
 (
  DATA_FIELD1      VARCHAR2(100),
  DATA_FIELD2      VARCHAR2(100),
  REQUEST_ID       NUMBER       ,
  CREATION_DATE    DATE         ,
  CREATED_BY       NUMBER
 )  ;
Table created.
```

NOTE
Never create database tables on the production system in the APPS schema. Coding standards assume that all tables in Oracle Applications are created in the product schemas. In this case, that would be the XXCUST custom schema, but for illustration purposes, we created tables in the APPS schema.

At this stage, you can test your control file by manually invoking the SQL*Loader utility from the command line:

```
sqlldr USERID=apps/<passwd> CONTROL=DATALOAD.ctl LOG=dataload.log
```

If you are happy with the outcome, you can proceed with the registering of our SQL*Loader control file in AOL.

Create a Concurrent Program Executable as SQL*Loader Type

The concurrent program executable is defined with the value SQL*Loader for the Execution Method field in the Concurrent Program Executable form. Also, you need to specify the name of the control file to be passed to the SQL*Loader utility by defining the Execution File Name field. In this case, populate the Execution File Name field with the name of the control file DATALOAD without the .ctl extension.

Create a Concurrent Program with an Optional Data File Parameter

When creating a concurrent program based on a SQL*Loader concurrent program executable, you have an option either to provide the name of the data file in the control file itself or pass the full name and directory of the data file as an argument in the concurrent program. If the data file is specified as a parameter, the Concurrent Manager passes this value as data=<data_file>, where <data_file> is the full path to the data file. Our example does not specify the data file at all; instead, the data is passed inline within the control file beginning with the SQL*Loader key word BEGINDATA.

PL/SQL Program

The PL/SQL stored procedure is another popular type of the concurrent program in Oracle Applications extensions. The popularity of this type of the concurrent program for the concurrent processing is probably related to the fact that PL/SQL is still seen by most developers to be the most efficient way of manipulating data in Oracle databases; another important factor for using PL/SQL is that the Oracle Applications database comes with a huge library of PL/SQL programs and APIs that are freely available to developers for reuse in their own custom modules and extensions.

The methodology of creating a PL/SQL concurrent program is similar to creating a SQL*Plus host or any other concurrent program. First, you have to write the code in PL/SQL and save it into the Oracle Applications database in the APPS schema. Once you are happy with the functionality of your PL/SQL code, you can register it with AOL through the Concurrent Program Executable screen by specifying PL/SQL Stored Procedure in the Execution Method field and the fully qualified name (<PACKAGE_NAME.STORED_PROCEDURE>) of the PL/SQL stored procedure defined in the Execution File Name field. Once again, you need to pay special attention to how you pass and deal with parameters in the PL/SQL procedure type of the concurrent programs.

We will illustrate how to do this with an example in which we'll create a PL/SQL procedure to delete all rows from the table XXCUST_SQLLOAD_DATA, which we have created and populated with the data in the previous section. We'll also pass a couple of parameters just to demonstrate how to deal with them within a PL/SQL program. Here is the PL/SQL script:

```
  CREATE OR REPLACE
PACKAGE xxcust_conc_demo_pkg
IS
PROCEDURE delete_demo_data
  (


    errbuf OUT VARCHAR2 ,
    retcode OUT NUMBER ,
    p_date_from IN VARCHAR2 ,
    p_date_to   IN VARCHAR2 );
END xxcust_conc_demo_pkg;
/
CREATE OR REPLACE
PACKAGE BODY xxcust_conc_demo_pkg
AS
PROCEDURE delete_demo_data
  (
    errbuf OUT VARCHAR2 ,
    retcode OUT NUMBER ,
    p_date_from          IN VARCHAR2 ,
    p_date_to            IN VARCHAR2 )
                         IS
  l_del_rows_count NUMBER := 0;
BEGIN
  fnd_file.put_line (fnd_file.log , 'Deleting data from the table.');
  fnd_file.put_line (fnd_file.log, chr(10));
  DELETE
    FROM XXCUST_SQLLOAD_DATA t
    WHERE t.creation_date
    BETWEEN FND_CONC_DATE.STRING_TO_DATE(p_date_from)
    AND FND_CONC_DATE.STRING_TO_DATE(p_date_to);


  l_del_rows_count := sql%rowcount;
  COMMIT;


fnd_file.put_line (fnd_file.log, 'Deleted ' ||
  l_del_rows_count || ' records.');
  fnd_file.put_line (fnd_file.log, chr(10));
  fnd_file.put_line (fnd_file.log , 'Procedure completed.');
  errbuf  := '';
  retcode := 0;
EXCEPTION
```

```
WHEN OTHERS THEN
  ROLLBACK;
  errbuf  := SQLERRM;
  retcode := 2;
  fnd_file.put_line (fnd_file.log, '****ERROR OCCURRED****');
  fnd_file.put_line (fnd_file.log, SQLERRM);
  RAISE;
END delete_demo_data;
END xxcust_conc_demo_pkg;
/
```

In this example, the procedure DELETE_DEMO_DATA is contained within the PL/SQL package XXCUST_CONC_DEMO_PKG. DELETE_DEMO_DATA is executed by the Concurrent Manager, which expects two mandatory OUT parameters, errbuf and retcode, as defined in the example. Much like with the SQL*Plus concurrent programs, you can also pass a number of end user parameters to the PL/SQL procedure by defining them through Concurrent Programs | Parameters form in Oracle Applications. Our choice was to create two parameters of the FND_STANDARD_DATE type similar to how we created the FND_STANDARD_DATE type of parameter in the Hello World host program. The sequence order defines how the end user parameters are passed to the PL/SQL procedure; in the example, we handle two FND_STANDARD_DATE parameters as the VARCHAR2 variable:

```
PROCEDURE delete_demo_data
  (
   errbuf OUT VARCHAR2 ,
   retcode OUT NUMBER ,
   p_date_from            IN VARCHAR2 ,
   p_date_to              IN VARCHAR2 )
```

We've only used one PL/SQL API, fnd_file.put_line, to illustrate how easy is to redirect the output from the concurrent program to the log and output files. There are many other PL/SQL APIs available to concurrent programs; take a look at the following packages in your Oracle Applications database APPS schema to examine the internals of concurrent processing APIs:

- FND_CONCURRENT
- FND_FILE
- FND_PROGRAM
- FND_REQUEST
- FND_REQUEST_INFO
- FND_SET
- FND_SUBMIT

All of these APIs are documented in greater detail in *Oracle Applications Developer's Guide.*

Java Concurrent Program

Java is another popular development tool, and in Oracle Applications, you can create Java concurrent programs in both R11i and R12. Availability of various Java libraries in Oracle Applications makes it easy to reuse the existing products' functionality when building the extensions; an example is the BI Publisher products', which comes with numerous Java libraries that can be used in your custom extensions and concurrent programs.

Let us consider the scenario where we need to write a Java concurrent program that will use Java classes from a java.util.zip package to create a ZIP file out of two files provided as input files. In other words, when submitting the Java concurrent request, we'll provide three parameters: File A, File B, and Zipped File Name. Two files, A and B, will be compressed and zipped by the Java utility, and a ZIP file will be created on the file system. Follow the steps outlined to create this example Java program, and we'll discuss the most important components of the Java concurrent program, as well as how to pass parameters to it.

Create Java Code and Place It into the Appropriate Directory

Before we proceed to building the Java code, you need to decide which tool to use. In our opinion, the natural choice is the version of Oracle JDeveloper for Oracle Applications, and as of the writing of this book, JDeveloper for OA can be obtained via Metalink by downloading patch 5856648. This version of JDeveloper (10.1.3.1) is used to build Oracle Applications Framework customizations and extensions; it is also shipped with Oracle Applications libraries but does not provide all that we require for Java concurrent programs.

Before you start building the code in JDeveloper, you need to create some additional Java libraries that are specific for concurrent processing. To do this, go to your Oracle Applications middle-tier machine to the $JAVA_TOP directory. From here, assuming that your installation is on a Unix-style box, you can issue the following command to create the Java library related to concurrent processing:

```
[avisr12@r12 tmp]$  zip -r conclib ./oracle/apps/fnd/cp/*
```

This command will create the file conclib.zip in the $JAVA_TOP directory. Now you can transfer conclib.zip onto the desktop machine where you run JDeveloper and create the concurrent processing library in your JDeveloper project. If necessary, repeat the same steps to create a library for the classes in the $JAVA_TOP/oracle/apps/fnd/util directory in your Oracle Applications installation. Similar steps need to be performed on the Windows platform, and utilities such as WinZip can easily be used for this task. Now the Java code should successfully compile:

```
package oracle.apps.xxcust.cp;
import oracle.apps.fnd.util.*;
import oracle.apps.fnd.cp.request.*;
import java.io.FileInputStream;
import java.io.FileOutputStream;
import java.io.IOException;
import java.util.zip.ZipEntry;
import java.util.zip.ZipOutputStream;

public class ZipDocs implements JavaConcurrentProgram
{
   String fileA;
   String fileB;
   String outFile;

   public void runProgram(CpContext pCpContext)
   {
        // Get parameter list from CpContext.
        ParameterList params = pCpContext.getParameterList();
        // ReqCompletion object is used later to set the
        // completion status for the concurrent request.
        ReqCompletion compl = pCpContext.getReqCompletion();
        // Get handles for OUT and LOG files. This will be used
        // to write the output to the concurrent program log and
        // output files.
        OutFile concOutFile = pCpContext.getOutFile();
        LogFile concLogFile = pCpContext.getLogFile();

        while (params.hasMoreElements())
        {
                NameValueType aNVT = params.nextParameter();
                if ( aNVT.getName().equals("FILEA") )
                        fileA = aNVT.getValue();
                if ( aNVT.getName().equals("FILEB") )
                        fileB = aNVT.getValue();
                if ( aNVT.getName().equals("OUTFILE") )
                        outFile = aNVT.getValue();
                               }
            // Files to be added to the ZIP file.
            String[] files = new String[]{fileA, fileB};
            // Buffer to read the files.
            byte[] buf = new byte[1024];

            try {
                String zippedFile = outFile;
```

```
                ZipOutputStream out =
                    new ZipOutputStream
                       (new FileOutputStream(zippedFile));

                for (int i=0; i<files.length; i++) {
                    concLogFile.writeln("Adding file "
                    + files[i].toString()
                    + " to zip file ",LogFile.STATEMENT);

                    FileInputStream in=new FileInputStream(files[i]);
                    out.putNextEntry(new ZipEntry(files[i]));
                    int len;

                    while ((len = in.read(buf)) > 0) {
                        out.write(buf, 0, len);
                    }
                    out.closeEntry();
                    in.close();
                }
                out.close();
                concLogFile.writeln("ZIP file creation completed"
                                                   ,LogFile.STATEMENT);
                compl.setCompletion(ReqCompletion.NORMAL,
                            "Request completed with status Normal");
            } catch (IOException e) {
             compl.setCompletion(ReqCompletion.ERROR, e.toString());
            }
    }
}
```

If the rebuilding of this project was successful, the compiled Java ZipDocs.class from JDeveloper output directory can be transferred to the $JAVA_TOP/oracle/apps/xxcust/cp directory. We created this directory to keep all the Java code that is used for concurrent processing in customizations.

Create Concurrent Program Executable

When defining the concurrent program executable, specify the values listed in Table 5-5.

The value specified in the Execution File Path field tells the Concurrent Manager where to look for the compiled Java class, and Execution File Name is the name of our main Java class.

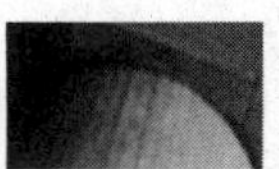

NOTE
Use the Java package naming style "." instead of "/" in the Execution File Path field.

Executable	Short Name	Application	Execution Method	Execution File Name	Execution File Path
Java Demo Executable	XXCUST_ ZIP_FILES	Custom Development	Java Concurrent Program	ZipDocs	oracle.apps .xxcust.cp

TABLE 5-5. *The Executable Definition for the Java Concurrent Program*

Create Concurrent Program and Its Parameters

As always, you also need to create the concurrent program that is based on the executable you created earlier. In the Concurrent Program Parameters form, create three parameters: File A, File B, and Zipped File Name. The values are listed in Table 5-6.

It is important that the names of the tokens defined in the Concurrent Program Parameters form match the values in your Java code so they can be correctly passed upon concurrent request submission:

```
while (params.hasMoreElements())
     {
              NameValueType aNVT = params.nextParameter();
              if ( aNVT.getName().equals("FILEA") )
                   fileA = aNVT.getValue();
              if ( aNVT.getName().equals("FILEB") )
                   fileB = aNVT.getValue();
              if ( aNVT.getName().equals("OUTFILE") )
                   outFile = aNVT
    }
```

Seq	Parameter	Description	Value Set	Token	Prompt
10	File A	First file	100 Characters	FILEA	File A
20	File B	Second file	100 Characters	FILEB	File B
30	Zipped File Name	Zipped file	100 Characters	OUTFILE	Zipped File Name

TABLE 5-6. *Values Defined in the Concurrent Program Parameters Form*

After assigning your Java concurrent program to an appropriate request group, you are ready to run your request in Oracle Applications. Say, for example, when prompted to enter the values for File A, File B, and Zipped File Name values, you can pass the names of the files that already exist in the /tmp directory, such as /tmp/filea.txt, fileb.txt. The ZIP file could also be created in the /the tmp directory by specifying some arbitrary name for the Zipped File Name parameter (for example, /tmp/zippedfile.zip).

Java Concurrent Program Code Logic

All Java concurrent programs implement the JavaConcurrenProgram interface in the oracle.apps.fnd.cp.request package. The signature of the interface is as follows:

```
public interface JavaConcurrentProgram
{
      void runProgram(oracle.apps.fnd.cp.request.CpContext cp) { }
}
```

This implies that you have to implement the runProgram() method in your Java code, and concurrent processing will pass the CpContext object through this method. It is the CpContext object that allows you to get the handles for concurrent processing output and log files so you can write to them from Java code. Through the introspection feature in JDeveloper, you can see that CpContext allows you to access many other items specific to the Oracle Applications context, such as FND Global values, JDBC connections, profile values, and many others. We recommend you use the getJDBCConnection() method to get the connection to the Oracle Applications database and use the commit() and rollback() methods to commit or roll back the transactions. Don't forget to release the connection by invoking releaseJDBCConnection() on the CpContext object.

Best Practices

In this section, we are going suggest how to define the best methodology for designing an efficient process of concurrent program development; this is by no means meant to be an exhaustive list of rules.

It almost goes without saying that the key action is to select the most appropriate tool in which to write the concurrent program executable; for example, if the purpose of the concurrent program is to frequently produce a professional-looking report, then, instead of being tempted to convert a nicely formatted SQL script into a concurrent program, you should consider using the BI Publisher tool to create such a report. There are no hard and fast rules about how to select the most appropriate tool, but most of the time the selection decision is driven by the tool's capabilities to meet the requirements. Every project should have a checklist in which there is an item that refers to development tools selection criteria used for the development of custom concurrent programs.

When defining the parameters that are passed to concurrent programs from SRS, you should fully utilize Value Sets feature from AOL to define lists of values that meet your requirements. This not only improves the user experience but allows also for all sorts of validations to be performed when passing the parameters.

Errors and failures must be gracefully handled in your code, and the methodology largely depends on the underlying tool. Generally, the Concurrent Manager expects to be notified by your code about the status of execution, and different tools use different techniques and APIs to do this. For example, in Java code you call the setCompletion API:

```
try
{
....
 setCompletion(ReqCompletion.NORMAL,
                                "Request completed with status Normal");
} catch (IOException e) {
              compl.setCompletion(ReqCompletion.ERROR, e.toString());
             }
```

Apart from signaling concurrent request status to the Concurrent Manager, it is a good practice to record necessary information in the log file that will help you understand and debug the problem. You do this by sending the error stack or any other relevant information to the log file. The level of logging is different for every concurrent program and can be dictated by the complexity, importance, performance, and many other factors. The information in the log file should be separated from the output file, and you should use the appropriate APIs to redirect to each of them. In case of the host concurrent program (a shell script on Linux), there are no APIs that can do this; therefore, you have to create log and output files programmatically and redirect appropriate output from the shell script to them.

When dealing with the host concurrent programs, the Concurrent Manager passes an unencrypted APPS password. This is usually not a good idea for nondevelopment systems such as UAT and production. To remedy this security issue, you can set ENCRYPT or SECURED values in the Execution Options field of the Concurrent Program screen. This is covered in the *System Administrator Guide*, Chapter 6, "Defining Concurrent Programs and Requests," in the section "Protecting Your Oracle User Password."

When it comes to deployment, Oracle Applications offers FNDLOAD utility, which allows you to extract your seed data from the development environment and deploy it to the target environments such as CRP (Customer Room Pilot), UAT (User Acceptance Testing), and production. Let's apply this technique to our Java concurrent program and execute the following command from the command line:

```
$FND_TOP/bin/FNDLOAD apps/apps 0 Y DOWNLOAD
$FND_TOP/patch/115/import/afcpprog.lct xxcust_java_zip.ldt PROGRAM
CONCURRENT_PROGRAM_NAME=XXCUST_JAVA_ZIP APPLICATION_SHORT_NAME=CUSTOM
```

The command will produce a log file in the same directory where it is run, as well as the LDT file xxcust_java_zip.ldt with all of the data in the Oracle Applications database that defines the structure of your concurrent program, including the executable definition, value sets, and the concurrent program definition. To upload the definition of your concurrent program into a different environment, run the same utility but in UPLOAD mode this time:

```
$FND_TOP/bin/FNDLOAD apps/apps 0 Y UPLOAD
$FND_TOP/patch/115/import/afcpprog.lct xxcust_java_zip.ldt
```

The key parameter to the FNDLOAD utility is the concurrent program configuration file afcpprog.lct. This configuration file instructs FNDLOAD to download and upload the concurrent program definitions. The other two parameters are the short program name (XXCUST_JAVA_ZIP in the example) and the short application name (CUSTOM in our example).

Summary

Concurrent processing in Oracle Applications has a long history and is widely used for job scheduling. In this chapter, we covered some practical development techniques of creating concurrent programs in E-Business Suite. You saw that the concurrent program executables can be written with a wide variety of tools, including Oracle Reports, PL/SQL, Java, C, Pro*C, and even shell scripts. Developers are only limited by their imagination as far as the types of programs can be created for concurrent processing.

In a nutshell, the methodology of creating concurrent programs consists of writing the program logic first, registering the executable with AOL, and linking the executable with the concurrent program itself. AOL provides a number of APIs that help the execution management and interaction between the programs and Concurrent Managers that execute them, and developers are encouraged to use them whenever possible. In general, the use of public AOL APIs will make the code more robust and manageable.

CHAPTER 6

Forms in Oracle Applications

racle Forms is a tool that enables rapid development of enterprise applications. In E-Business Suite, it is used to build screens that allow data to be entered and retrieved from the database as required. The screens based on Oracle Forms in E-Business Suite are also known as Professional User Interface.

In this chapter, we aim to explain the most basic principles of Oracle Forms custom development for E-Business Suite applications. The latest release of E-Business Suite, R12, has been upgraded to the most up-to-date version of Oracle Forms 10g, while the previous release, R11i, uses Oracle Forms 6i. The concepts and techniques we are going to cover in this chapter are largely applicable to the both releases of Oracle Applications.

Oracle Forms Tool: An Overview

In Oracle Forms, data that is stored in database tables is entered or displayed through fields that are also known as *items*. These fields belong to a collection of data referred to as a *record*. One or more records are grouped together into a *block*. The fields must be attached to a canvas in order for them to be visible on a screen, and the canvas is contained within a window, which is displayed to an end user. You can think of the canvas as a whiteboard onto which different items and fields can be placed, and the window can display one or more stacked canvases. Fields from differing blocks can be displayed on the same window. A combination of all these components put together is called a *form*, as illustrated next:

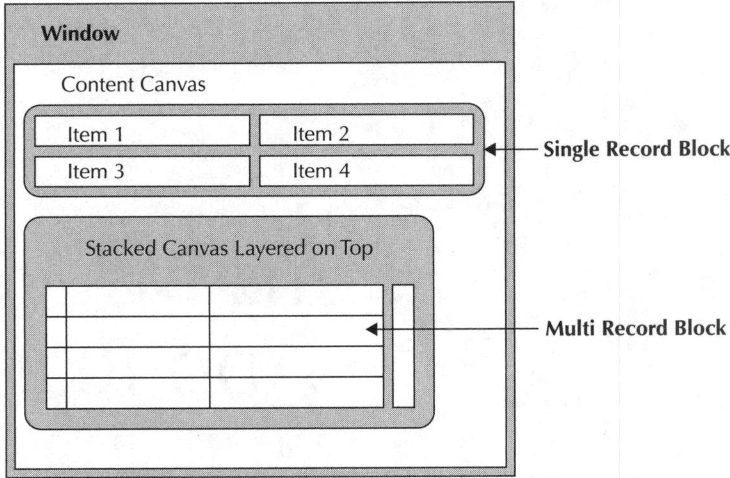

The canvas is a surface in the background on which you place user interface items such as text items, check boxes, radio groups, and so on. There are three canvas views: content view, stacked view, and toolbar canvas view. Content canvas view is the base view that occupies the entire content frame of the window in which it is displayed. Each window has one content canvas. A stacked canvas is displayed on top of another canvas, usually containing items in a group separate from the items in the underlying content canvas view. A toolbar canvas view contains the tool icon buttons that the window displays at the top or to the side of a window.

Simple screens that allow data entry into the tables without the need for data validation can be quickly developed using wizards in Oracle Forms. In such simple forms, data validation is usually delegated to the database server, which provides data integrity imposed by database constraints and triggers if they exist on the table. But programming standards in E-Business Suite generally prohibit the use of database triggers for the purposes of data validation; therefore, in E-Business Suite, Oracle Forms initiates and performs required data validation on database update, inserts, and delete operations.

In this chapter, we are going to use the E-Business Suite R12 VISION instance to demonstrate the concepts and typical development tasks. The Oracle Forms 10g version will be used for the examples in this chapter. Where applicable, we will explain the steps for R11i if they differ.

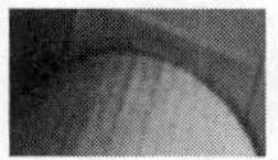

NOTE
R12 uses version Oracle Forms 10g, whereas R11i uses Oracle Forms 6i.

The Oracle Forms Builder tool can be downloaded from Oracle Technology Network (OTN) at www.oracle.com/technology/index.html. Before we discuss Oracle Forms in the context of Oracle Applications, we will give a quick overview of some of the key components.

Forms

At design time, the Oracle Forms tool creates a file with the extension.fmb. When the form is compiled by the tool, an executable with the extension .fmx is created. It must be noted that FMB files are not used by the runtime engine. If your E-Business Suite instance is hosted on a Linux or Unix environment, then your FMB file must be generated on the server itself. The FMX file compiled and transferred from the Windows operating system to a Linux or Unix operating system will not work.

PL/SQL libraries can be attached to a form; think of PL/SQL library as reusable code that can be shared among multiple forms. The code within the libraries can reference and programmatically modify the property of components within the forms to which they are attached. Code in the library can also make calls to the database stored procedures. On the file system, these libraries have a .pll extension; once generated, an executable with the .plx extension gets created.

Blocks

At the heart of a form are blocks that can optionally be based on database objects. Examples of such database objects are tables, views, synonyms, or stored procedures. A block can be created either manually or by using the wizard in the Oracle Forms tool. When a query is executed on a block, it effectively gets translated into a SQL statement that retrieves the data displayed to the user. When changes are made to fields that are based on database columns, the DML (Data Manipulation Language) statements are executed in order to apply the changes made by the user.

Items

Users interact with items that are physical components on the screen, such as data entry fields, check boxes, radio buttons, and others. Each item has a property named Item Type that determines the type of item.

Triggers

Triggers provide a mechanism for the programmable code to interact with various actions that take place within the form. An example of a trigger is the PRE-FORM trigger, which is executed by the forms engine just before the form is started. PRE-FORM is a trigger at the Form Level. Similar to that there are various triggers that can either be created at Form Level, Block Level, or Item Level. One of the common Block Level triggers is WHEN-VALIDATE-RECORD, which is executed when navigation moves out from a record, provided some changes were made to any of its fields. Similarly, an Item Level trigger WHEN-VALIDATE-ITEM is executed as soon as the navigation moves away from a field, provided its value was changed. The triggers are very well documented within the help files that comes bundled with the Oracle Forms Developer tool.

Some triggers can be created at different levels; for example, the WHEN-NEW-ITEM-INSTANCE trigger can be created at Item Level, at Block Level, and also at Form Level. When this trigger is at Item Level, it will fire when the cursor moves to that specific item. When the WHEN-NEW-ITEM-INSTANCE trigger exists at Block Level, then this trigger executes as and when the cursor enters into any of the editable items within that block. Similarly, when this trigger exists at Form Level, it executes when the cursor enters into any of the editable items within the entire form. With the help of system-level global variables, it is possible to find out the name of the item, block, or form that initiated the trigger, even though the trigger may be trapped at Block Level or Form Level. Triggers have a Execution Hierarchy property that can be either Override, Before, or After. You will notice that in the forms delivered by Oracle Applications, this trigger will always have Execution Hierarchy set to Before at Item Level and set to After or Override at Block and Form Levels. This information will be useful in the sections that follow when we discuss the use of CUSTOM.pll and Forms Personalizations.

Property Palette

Each of the components discussed so far has a number of properties. To modify the properties at design time, right-click the object and select Property Palette. Most of the properties can also be set at runtime programmatically.

Forms Delivered by Oracle E-Business Suite

E-Business Suite comes bundled with over three thousands forms. Some of these forms are foundation forms and the rest of them belong to the modules such as Oracle Procurement, Oracle Receivables, Oracle Cash Management, and so on. In addition to the forms delivered by the product teams, there are approximately two thousand PL/SQL libraries shipped by Oracle. All the forms and libraries exist as physical files on the forms server. As discussed in Chapter 2 about E-Business Suite Architecture, the forms server resides on the middle tier, where the main reference data is cached for performance reasons to reduce the number of network calls to the database server.

To access the forms, users first have to log in to a responsibility. The responsibility contains menu items, and the menu items are attached to form functions. The form function is attached to the actual physical form. Each form that is accessed by the user via a menu must be registered against an application. The Forms Registration screen can be accessed from the responsibility Application Developer by navigating to the Application | Form screen. The information in Table 6-1 is required in order to register a form with E-Business Suite.

Name of the Field	Purpose
Form	The short name of the form.
Application	The application against which the form is registered. Based on this information, the FMX file is located on the forms server at runtime using the base path from the Application definition.
User Form Name	A user-friendly description of the form.
Description	A business description of the form.

TABLE 6-1. *Information Required for Registering a Form in Oracle E-Business Suite*

Location of the Form Files on Server

As seen previously, the forms are registered against an application. The definition of an application defines a directory location or a base path for that application. For example, in the Application Registration screen accessed through the Application Developer responsibility, the Purchasing application has a short name PO and its base path is PO_TOP. The base path of an application corresponds to an environment variable on the forms server. Therefore, on the forms server, an environment variable PO_TOP points to the top directory location of the Purchasing application. In R12, the path to the PO_TOP directory on our middle-tier server looks like this:

```
[avisr12@r12 US]$ echo $PO_TOP
/oracle/apps/R1204/apps/apps_st/appl/po/12.0.0
```

Each top directory such as PO_TOP contains subdirectories; one of the directories under <PRODUCT_TOP> is the forms directory:

```
[avisr12@r12 US]$ ls -x $PO_TOP
admin  bin  forms  help  html  lib  log
mds  mesg  out  patch  reports  sql  xml
```

Within the Forms directory, there is a further subdirectory for each installed language. The installations of E-Business Suite normally have the <PRODUCT_TOP>/forms/US directory; for example, for Oracle Purchasing, this would be $PO_TOP/forms/US. In the case of multiple language installations, there will be further subdirectories under the $PO_TOP/forms directory, one for each installed language. It is important to know that all the runtime form files (FMX files) are located in their respective language subdirectories. Therefore, all Purchasing forms executables in the English language will be located in $PO_TOP/forms/US.

As we mentioned earlier, PL/SQL libraries (PLL files) can be attached to the forms. These PLL files and their corresponding runtime PLX files are located in the directory $AU_TOP/resource. At runtime, whenever the code from the attached library is invoked, in order to locate the library files, the Oracle Forms engine first searches the current directory and thereafter searches within all the directories as per the $FORMS_PATH environment variable; and finally, it searches the directory locations within $ORACLE_PATH. In E-Business Suite, at the middle-tier machine where the forms server resides, the environment variable $FORMS_PATH will always contain a reference to the directory $AU_TOP/resource, where all the libraries can be found.

NOTE

In R11i, the name of this environment variable is $FORMS60_PATH.

Object Type	Location
Forms source code	$AU_TOP/forms/US
Libraries (both PLL and PLX)	$AU_TOP/resource
Forms runtime executables	$<APPLICATION>_TOP/forms/<Language> For example $PER_TOP/forms/US for HRMS Forms

TABLE 6-2. *Location of Files for Forms in E-Business Suite on Midtier*

In addition to the runtime forms and libraries, Oracle E-Business Suite also ships the forms design-time files. The English language versions of these FMB files are located in $AU_TOP/forms/US.

Table 6-2 lists a summary of the location of standard E-Business Suite forms objects. For multilanguage installation, replace US with the corresponding language.

The patches delivered by Oracle can add or modify the contents in these directory locations. Therefore, any of the objects delivered by Oracle must not be modified; otherwise you can lose the changes made to the standard forms. Additionally you must never remove any validations performed by standard Oracle Forms, as that may lead to data corruption in E-Business Suite.

Custom Forms in E-Business Suite

Oracle has well-defined guidelines that must be followed when creating custom forms in E-Business Suite. By following these guidelines, your custom forms will look and feel exactly the same as standard forms, and your custom development will remain upgrade safe. Effectively, when creating custom forms, the guidelines and procedures followed by you are the same as those followed by Oracle's product development team. All the forms in Oracle E-Business Suite are based on TEMPLATE.fmb. As with other forms in E-Business Suite, the TEMPLATE.fmb file can be found in the $AU_TOP/forms/US directory.

The TEMPLATE form includes an example window with sample blocks, as well as many referenced objects such as windows, canvases, blocks, Lists of Values (LOVs), and other objects. It inherits the object groups from the APPSTAND form, which is a platform-specific form. By starting out with the TEMPLATE form when developing custom forms in E-Business Suite, developers ensure that they will get the same look and properties of the standard product forms. Examples of such properties specific to Oracle Applications are the toolbar, the menu, the calendar, applications property classes, required Form Level triggers, required procedures, LOVs, parameters, and many others.

Preparing the Desktop for Custom Forms Development

Forms Developer 10g and 6i versions can be downloaded from the URL www.oracle.com/technology/software/products/forms/index.html.

If you are using Windows Vista, in order to install Forms Developer 10g, you must follow the instructions as per Metalink Note 559067.1.

Once Oracle Forms Developer has been installed, you need to configure Oracle TNS for the Oracle Home where Forms Developer is installed so it can connect to the target database.

Open TEMPLATE.fmb

In order to begin development, you must base your custom form development on the TEMPLATE form (TEMPLATE.fmb). This ensures that your custom form will inherit the shared core form components and libraries. The TEMPLATE form has attached several libraries such as FNDSQF, APPCORE, APPDAYPF, and others that contain many of the Application Object Library utilities.

Let us assume that you want to store all your FMB and PLL files in the folder C:\code\forms on your Windows desktop. Transfer TEMPLATE.fmb from $AU_TOP/forms/US from the middle-tier machine to the C:\code\forms directory on your desktop. Now in Oracle Forms try to open TEMPLATE.fmb. You will get a message "FRM-18108: Failed to load the following objects". If you click on OK, you will get another error listing the missing libraries (FRM-10102 errors). At this stage, you must not save TEMPLATE.fmb once it is opened.

The reason we see those errors is because the TEMPLATE form itself depends on other forms and libraries. Before you begin to transfer all the dependent objects from the server, you must set the FORMS_PATH environment variable on your computer. In order to do so, right-click My Computer, click on Properties, and in the Advanced setting, click on the button labeled Environment Variable. For R12, name of the environment variable will be FORMS_PATH and its value set to C:\code\forms. For Release 11i, you can change the value of FORMS60_PATH in the registry to include your directory, which is C:\code\forms in our example. After changing the environment variable, you must restart the forms builder for this change to take effect.

In order to open TEMPLATE.fmb successfully, we have two options. The first option is to transfer everything from the $AU_TOP/forms/US and $AU_TOP/resource directories from the middle-tier machine to the C:\code\forms directory on the desktop. However, in R12 instance, this will equate to transferring files over 3GB to your desktop. Therefore, the second option is to be selective for the files being transferred from the server. From $AU_TOP/forms/US, transfer the APP*.fmb and FND*.fmb forms to folder C:\code\forms. Similarly, from $AU_TOP/resource, transfer the APP*.pll, FND*.pll, VERT*.pll, PS*.pll, HR*.pll, GMS*.pll, FV*.pll, IGI*.pll, GLOBE.pll, JA.pll, JE.pll, JL.pll, VERT.pll, GHR.pll, PQH_GEN.pll, PSAC.pll, CUSTOM.pll, and OPM.pll libraries. If you still receive message for some other missing libraries, then transfer those as well. Sometimes the error message for a missing library can be misleading. For example, you might get the error, "Cannot find APPDAYPK.pll," despite the file being present in the C:\code\forms directory. In such cases, try to open APPDAYPK.pll itself to see the dependent libraries that remain to be transferred to your desktop.

Once all the required objects have been transferred to C:\code\forms, you will be able to open TEMPLATE.fmb without any errors and at that point you can start developing the custom form.

Steps for Developing Custom Forms in E-Business Suite

Follow these steps to create custom forms in E-Business Suite:

1. **Create TEMPLATE form** Make a copy of TEMPLATE.fmb and rename it to your custom form name. Your form name will begin with XX. For developing HRMS-related screens, use HRTEMPLT.fmb.
2. **Develop form** Develop your form as per programming guidelines and standards in Oracle Applications Forms Development Guide. Detailed guidelines are available at http://download.oracle.com/docs/cd/B34956_01/current/acrobat/120devg.pdf.
3. **Generate runtime file** Transfer the FMB file to midtier and compile it to generate an FMX compiled file.
4. **Register** Register the form with Custom Application.
5. **Create form function** Create a form function attached to the form.
6. **Attach to menu** Attach the form function to the menu.
7. **Assign to responsibility** Assign the menu to the responsibility.

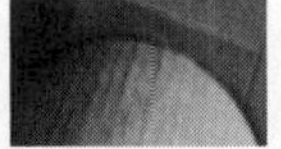

NOTE

The custom forms based on TEMPLATE.fmb will not run successfully from the Forms Developer tool on your desktop due to the dependencies on Oracle Applications–specific AOL objects and user exits that are not available in Forms Developer. For this reason, the custom form must be generated and tested from the middle-tier machine where the Oracle Applications forms server resides after registering the custom form with AOL and assigning it to a menu and a responsibility.

Extending Forms Using CUSTOM.pll

As mentioned in the previous section, all professional forms in Oracle Applications are based on the TEMPLATE.fmb form file. The TEMPLATE.fmb references the APPSTAND.fmb form file, which has APPCORE.pll attached to it. In addition, APPCORE.pll is attached to CUSTOM.pll. Therefore all the forms that are developed in Oracle Applications indirectly attach CUSTOM.pll. In other words, every form in Oracle Applications is capable of making calls to CUSTOM.pll by sending events to it. These events can be captured within CUSTOM.pll to write additional processing logic for standard E-Business Suite forms without making changes to the form itself.

At this stage, you may be wondering how CUSTOM.pll, even though it can be called by each form, actually gets called from each and every form. The answer to that lies in Form Level triggers in TEMPLATE.fmb as depicted in Figure 6-1.

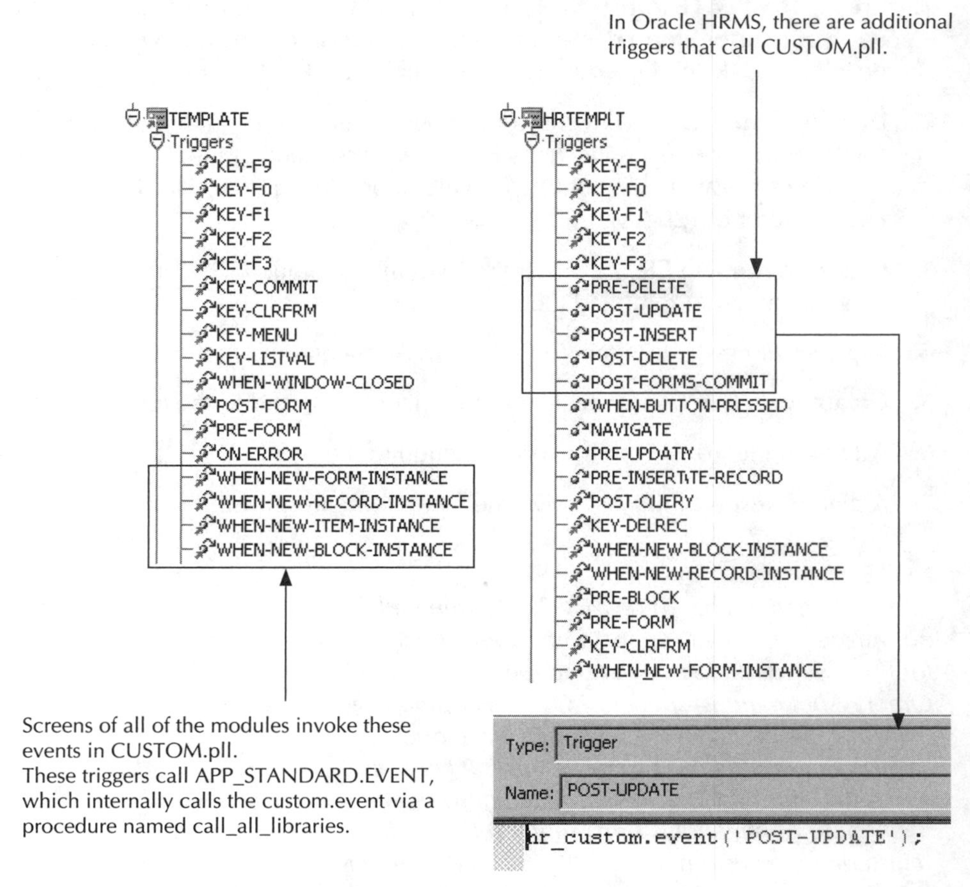

FIGURE 6-1. *Form Level triggers in TEMPLATE.fmb*

For the triggers at Form Level, the Execution Hierarchy property is set to either Override or After. When defined by the developer at a lower level such as at Block or Item Level, these triggers will have the Execution Hierarchy property set to Before. Hence the triggers at the lower level will be executed first, following which the triggers at Form Level will be executed. The triggers at the Block or Item Level usually contain the business logic, whereas the triggers at the Form Level call APP_STANDARD.EVENT, which internally calls the procedure custom.event through a procedure called call_all_libraries.

Therefore, each form in Oracle Application calls code in CUSTOM.pll via the triggers defined at Form Level. For example, if by accident an Oracle product development team member set the Block Level WHEN-VALIDATE-RECORD trigger's execution hierarchy to Override, then CUSTOM.pll would not be called, unless the developer made a call to APP_STANDARD.EVENT in the trigger at a lower level.

As shown in Figure 6-1, not all the triggers make calls to CUSTOM.pll. For performance reasons, Oracle does not pass all the triggers to CUSTOM.pll. Additionally, as per Figure 6-1, forms developed for Oracle HRMS use HRTEMPLT.fmb. The HRMS form template makes calls to CUSTOM.pll for some additional set of triggers such as PRE-DELETE, POST-UPDATE, and so on. Note that changes made to CUSTOM.pll have no impact on OA Framework–based pages.

Given that CUSTOM.pll receives various trigger events from each standard form, it is possible to write additional custom logic to enhance the functionality of the standard seeded screens. The name of the event is passed as a parameter to the CUSTOM.EVENT procedure within CUSTOM.pll. In addition to that, names of the form, block, and item with which a user was interacting at the time when the event was triggered can be captured from the system-level global variables, such as system.current_form, system.current_block, and system.current item. Other form system variables can also be accessed inside CUSTOM.pll. In order to fetch the value of these variables or to access values of form items, a routine name_in must be used. To set the values of form items, a routine copy must be used.

When extending the functionality of the form using CUSTOM.pll, it is important to identify the correct trigger for CUSTOM.pll in order to write your extension logic. This can be done by navigating from the menu to Help | Diagnostics | Custom Code | Show Custom Events, as shown in Figure 6-2. If the Diagnostics menu is not visible, ensure that the Hide Diagnostics Menu Entry profile option is set to No. When the Show Custom Events option is enabled, a message box will be displayed as and when any triggering event gets sent to CUSTOM.pll. This message box provides the name of the triggering event, as shown in Figure 6-3.

First, navigate to the screen that you wish to extend using CUSTOM.pll. Let us say your requirement is to display a message when a user navigates to a specific block. In this case, you can enable Show Custom Events just prior to navigating to that block so that you can see in a message window the list of events that are being sent to CUSTOM.pll, as shown in Figure 6-3.

The message format is <FormName>.<BlockName>.<FieldName>:<TriggerName>.

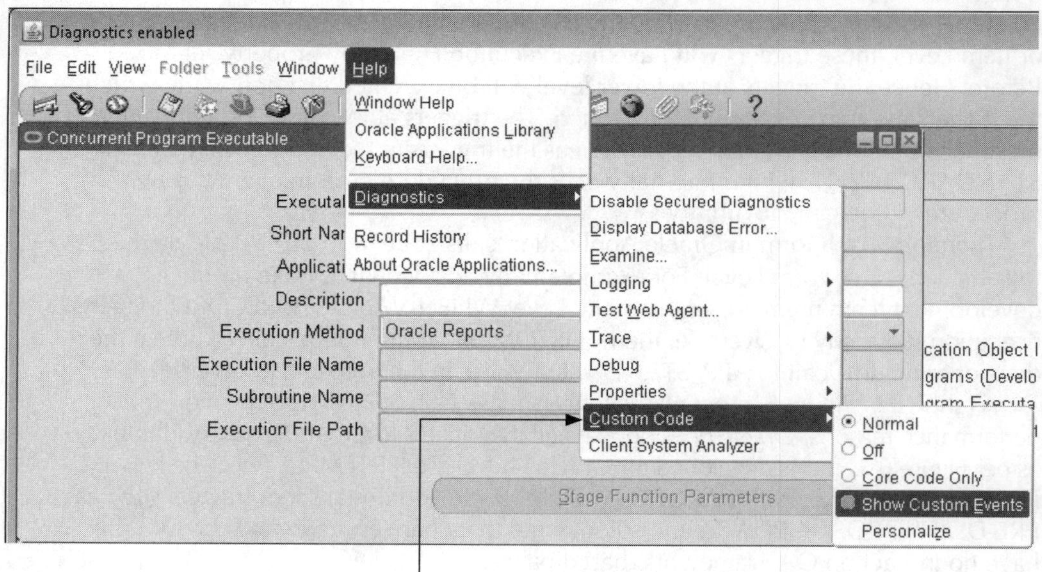

Once you enable Show Custom Events, Oracle will display the name of each and every event that can be trapped using CUSTOM.pll. Using this technique, you can identify the custom event that you need to trap to achieve the desired result.

FIGURE 6-2. *Display a list of triggers for which CUSTOM.pll is called for a screen.*

Example of an Extension Using CUSTOM.pll

In this example, we will use CUSTOM.pll to change the Executable field into uppercase within the Concurrent Program Executable screen. For this exercise, it is assumed that you have already been able to open TEMPLATE.fmb in Oracle Forms, therefore you have all the basic forms objects on your desktop. The purpose of this example is to explain all the steps for using CUSTOM.pll. In reality, you will be using Forms Personalization to achieve simple tasks such as this.

From the menu, navigate to Concurrent | Executable to open the Concurrent Program Executable screen, where you can define executables for concurrent programs. As shown in Figure 6-4, in the Executable field, it is possible to enter an executable name in either uppercase or lowercase. Using CUSTOM.pll, we will enforce that any new executable name defined is always in uppercase.

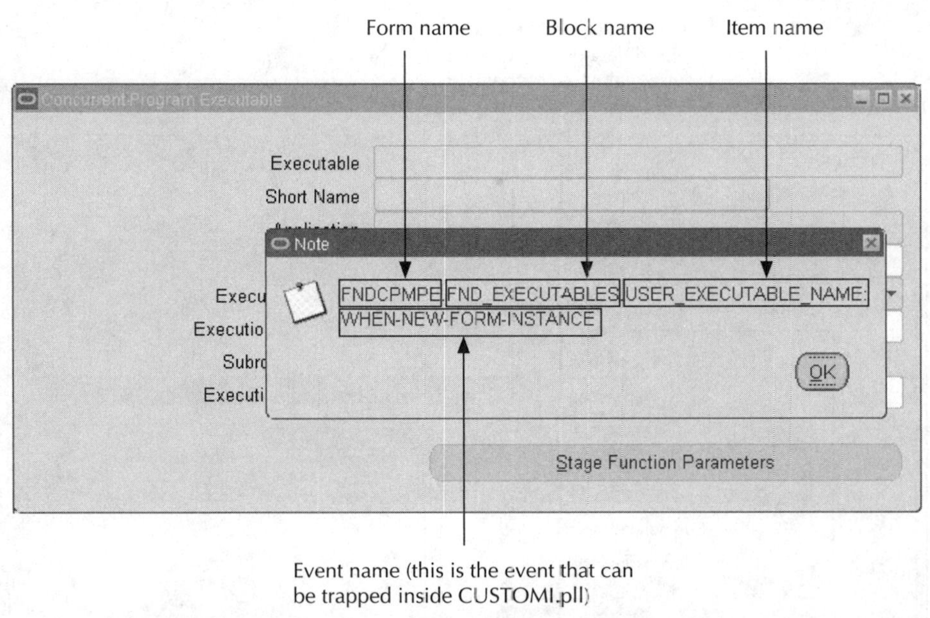

FIGURE 6-3. *Enabling Show Custom Events displays a list of events passed to CUSTOM.pll.*

Follow these steps to make the Executable field uppercase using CUSTOM.pll:

1. **Enable show custom events** Log in to the Application Developer responsibility and enable Show Custom Events.
2. **Gather information** A message box will appear when this form is opened, indicating that the form name is FNDCPMPE, the block name is FND_EXECUTABLES, the field name is USER_EXECUTABLE_NAME, and the event name is WHEN-NEW-FORM-INSTANCE. Note down the names of these components as these will be required in programming CUSTOM.pll. To double-check the name of field, navigate to the Executable field and use the Help/Diagnostics/Examine menu to see the name.
3. **Write code in CUSTOM.pll** Open Oracle Forms Builder, highlight PL/SQL Libraries, and navigate from the menu to File | Open. Open the CUSTOM.pll file and expand the nodes. Within the node Attached Libraries, you will see FNDSQF and APPCORE2. If you do not find APPCORE2.pll

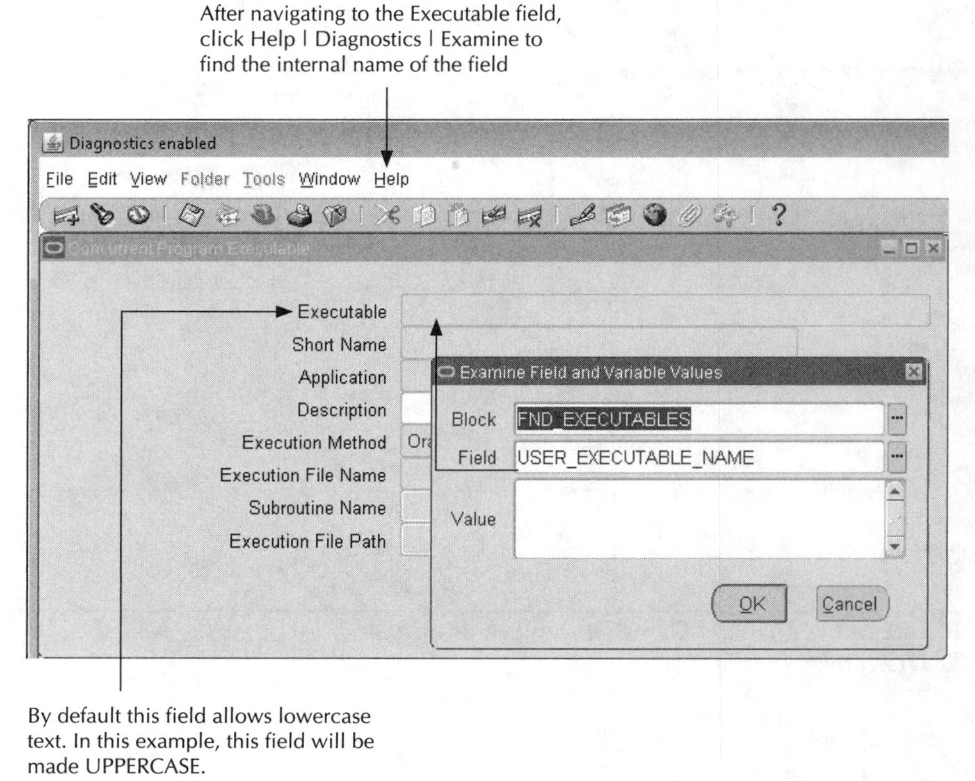

After navigating to the Executable field, click Help | Diagnostics | Examine to find the internal name of the field

Diagnostics enabled

File Edit View Folder Tools Window Help

Concurrent Program Executable

Executable

Short Name

Application

Description

Execution Method

Execution File Name

Subroutine Name

Execution File Path

Examine Field and Variable Values

Block FND_EXECUTABLES

Field USER_EXECUTABLE_NAME

Value

OK Cancel

By default this field allows lowercase text. In this example, this field will be made UPPERCASE.

FIGURE 6-4. *Make the Executable field UPPERCASE using CUSTOM.pll.*

attached, click the plus (+) icon on the left-hand pane and browse to select APPCORE2.pll. Then click the Attach button and when prompted, click the Yes button to remove the path. After attaching APPCORE2.pll, open the package body named Custom in CUSTOM.pll. Write your logic in a procedure called event, using the following sample syntax:

```
procedure event(event_name varchar2) is
form_name       varchar2(30) := name_in('system.current_form');
block_name      varchar2(30) := name_in('system.cursor_block');
begin
if form_name='FNDCPMPE' then
  if event_name='WHEN-NEW-FORM-INSTANCE' then
```

```
        app_item_property2.set_property('FND_EXECUTABLES.USER_
            EXECUTABLE_NAME'
                                            ,CASE_RESTRICTION, UPPERCASE);
      end if ;
    end if ;
    end event;
```

After making the programming changes to CUSTOM.pll, scroll down to the bottom of the package body Custom and make these changes to the version history of CUSTOM.pll:

```
This code should appear as a sublisting under
#3fdrcsid('$Header: CUSTOM.pld 120.1 2009/03/03 18:43:00 appldev
ship $');
```

4. **Transfer CUSTOM.pll to $AU_TOP/resource** Log in to the forms server and change the directory to $AU_TOP/resource. Ensure you have a backup of CUSTOM.pll either in the source control system or on the file system. Next, transfer CUSTOM.pll from your desktop to $AU_TOP/resource.

5. **Generate CUSTOM.pll** Use the command frmcmp_batch, replacing the appspassword with the relevant value on your system. After running this command, CUSTOM.plx will be created in $AU_TOP/resource:

```
cd $AU_TOP/resource
##For R12 use frmcmp_batch
frmcmp_batch module=CUSTOM.pll userid=apps/appspassword out-
put_file=./CUSTOM.plx compile_all=special module_type=LIBRARY
batch=yes
##For 11i Use f60gen command as shown below
f60gen module=CUSTOM.pll userid=apps/appspassword output_file=./
CUSTOM.plx module_type=LIBRARY
```

6. **Test your changes** Log out and log back in to the Concurrent Program Executable screen. You will notice that it is no longer possible to enter the concurrent program executable name using lowercase letters.

As you saw in step 3, APPCORE2.pll is attached to CUSTOM.pll. A very common mistake is to attach APPCORE.pll to CUSTOM.pll. Doing so can cause circular references because CUSTOM.pll itself is attached to APPCORE.pll. Therefore, Oracle ships APPCORE2.pll, which duplicates most of the APPCORE routines in APP_ITEM_PROPERTY2, APP_DATE2, APP_SPECIAL2, APP_MENU2, and APP_FIELD2. It is also possible to attach further libraries to CUSTOM.pll, as you will see in the section "Best Practice for CUSTOM.pll."

Events That Can Be Captured Using CUSTOM.pll

As a general guideline, all the forms in Oracle Applications send the following triggering events to CUSTOM.pll:

```
SPECIAL1-45                      WHEN-NEW-FORM-INSTANCE
WHEN-NEW-BLOCK-INSTANCE          WHEN-NEW-RECORD-INSTANCE
WHEN-NEW-ITEM-INSTANCE           WHEN-VALIDATE-RECORD [Most forms]
```

In addition to the preceding events, CUSTOM.pll sends the following events to HRMS forms:

```
PRE-DELETE              PRE-INSERT              PRE-UPDATE
POST-DELETE             POST-INSERT             POST-UPDATE
POST-FORMS-COMMIT       WHEN-CREATE-RECORD      KEY-DELREC
```

In certain cases, it becomes necessary to disable the effect of CUSTOM.pll temporarily. This can be done by selecting Help | Diagnostics | Custom Code | Off from Oracle Applications. When you select this option, you will be prompted to confirm the disabling of CUSTOM.pll. This change will be effective only for your current session into which you have logged in, and will not impact any other users of E-Business Suite.

Common Usages of CUSTOM.pll

CUSTOM.pll provides a mechanism to enhance the standard functionality of Oracle Applications forms by enabling you to write extra processing logic. The programming style in CUSTOM.pll is the same as that for Oracle Forms. Some of the common usages of CUSTOM.pll are as follows:

- Enabling and disabling the Hide and Show fields
- Changing the list of values in a LOV field at runtime
- Defaulting values into fields
- Validating additional record level
- Enabling the Special menu
- Zooming and navigating to other screens

You can do much more as well, all without modifying the form files.

Despite the wide use of CUSTOM.pll in Oracle Applications implementations, changes to properties such as INSERT_ALLOWED, UPDATE_ALLOWED, or REQUIRED must be extensively tested, as these can potentially break the standard application processing logic.

Limitations of CUSTOM.pll

CUSTOM.pll requires a programmer for each task regardless of how trivial the task is. Also, there exists only one CUSTOM.pll for the entire instance, therefore multi-developer mode is limited.

Let us assume that three developers have made changes to CUSTOM.pll and promoted their changes for testing to a UAT environment. We assume that the changes are performed by each developer sequentially, that is, Developer 2 carries forward the version of CUSTOM.pll that has changes done by Developer 1, and Developer 3 carries forward the version of CUSTOM.pll that was worked upon by Developer 2. Finally, Developer 3 moves the CUSTOM.pll to the test environment for UAT. Now, if Developer 2 changes fail in UAT, the changes introduced by Developer 3 code must not proceed to production.

You will later learn that Forms Personalization can overcome these limitations. However, some project implementations made changes to CUSTOM.pll for several years before Forms Personalization was introduced. They may not decide to re-engineer their existing extensions using Forms Personalization. Additionally, there are certain changes that cannot be achieved by using Forms Personalization. Therefore, it is important to implement the best practice approach when using CUSTOM.pll.

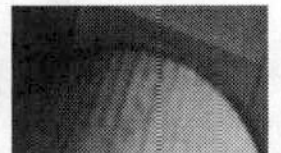

NOTE

CUSTOM.pll could potentially be dangerous if used without due care. For example, because it is called by every form, if the developer forgets to reference a form_name or trigger name, the code may be executed by every form in E-Business Suite. This will result in severe performance degradation!
Also, as there is only one CUSTOM.pll per installation, if it is used heavily at the site, it could extend many forms. Each extension is a set of IF statements. Every form in E-Business Suite will have to evaluate many IF statements to establish if they need to run the code, so this will cause additional performance problems as the number of customizations increase.

Best Practice for CUSTOM.pll

Customers that are already on E-Business Suite version 11.5.10CU2+ will keep their usage of CUSTOM.pll to a minimum because Forms Personalization is available in their technology stack. However, some customers have implementations going

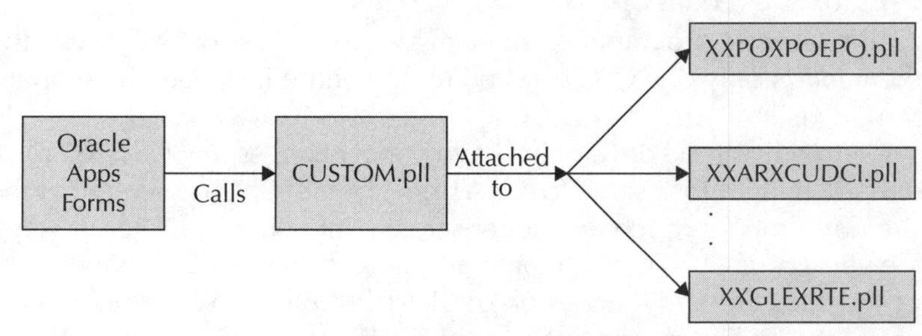

FIGURE 6-5. *CUSTOM.pll best practice approach*

back over decade when Forms Personalization did not exist. Therefore, minor enhancements and bug fixes continue to be made to CUSTOM.pll. In order to overcome the limitations of CUSTOM.pll, it is recommended that a new PLL file be created for each form that is extended using CUSTOM.pll. As shown in Figure 6-5, a new PLL file has been created for extensions to forms POXPOEPO, GLEXRTE, and ARXCUDCI. Using this approach, changes done by the first and third developer can be moved to production following their successful UAT.

Using this approach, each form will have its own equivalent of CUSTOM.pll. Each developer's deployment script or patch will contain only the developer's business logic for CUSTOM.pll. Once a CUSTOM.pll is attached to an individual PLL, each such individual PLL must reside on the form server in $AU_TOP/resource.

With this methodology, CUSTOM.pll is simply used as a stub that makes calls to respective PLLs having custom code for each form. For example, the developer implementing this approach will follow these steps:

1. Create XXPOXPOEPO.pll (if it does not already exist).
2. Attach APPCORE2.pll to XXPOXPOEPO.pll.
3. Add a "do nothing" procedure as follows within package XXPOXPOEPO.pll:

```
procedure check_warn_duplicate_supplier is
begin
NULL ; --Does nothing. Each developer checks similar code to
source control
end check_warn_duplicate_supplier ;
```

4. Check in XXPOXPOEPO.pll to source control and attach it to CUSTOM.pll.

5. In CUSTOM.pll, write the code as follows:

```
IF form_name = 'POXPOEPO' AND block_name = 'XXXWHATEVER'
THEN
XXPOXPOEPO.check_warn_duplicate_supplier ;
END IF;
```

6. Check CUSTOM.pll into source control.

7. Make changes to XXPOXPOEPO.pll with the business logic for changes:

```
procedure check_warn_duplicate_supplier is
begin
---Actual code execution business logic here
end check_warn_duplicate_supplier ;
```

Steps 1 to 6 are responsible for creating a stub. The changes made until step 6 do not impact the business functionality. Therefore, in this example, the changes made by Developer 2 until step 6 can be promoted to production alongside all the changes made by Developer 1 and Developer 3. Effectively, the changes made in step 7 must be promoted to production only after the successful UAT. Figure 6-6 depicts the chain of this sequence.

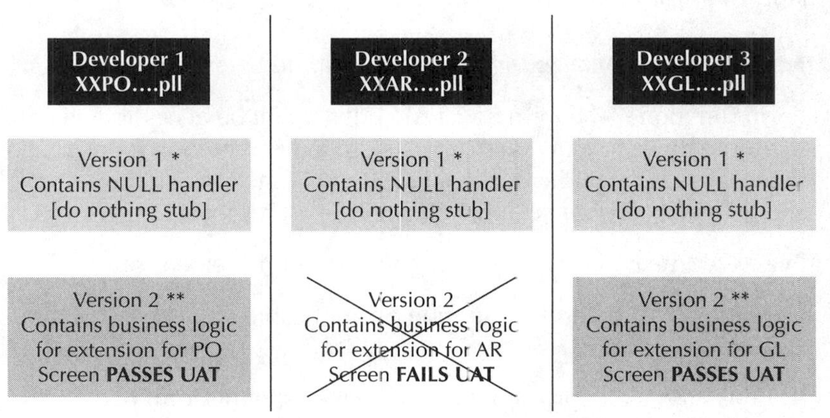

FIGURE 6-6. *CUSTOM.pll best practice methodology*

When implementing this methodology, it is no longer required to attach APPCORE2.pll to CUSTOM.pll. Instead, APPCORE2.pll should be attached to the individual PLL files if required.

Extending Forms Using Forms Personalization

As you have seen, CUSTOM.pll is a programmatic methodology for extending Oracle Forms. In CUSTOM.pll, you have to program to achieve even the most trivial extension, such as changes to a prompt. To overcome this and other limitations of CUSTOM.pll, the concept of FP (Forms Personalization) was introduced starting from E-Business Suite version 11.5.10.2. Using FP, you can navigate to any Oracle Forms–based screen in E-Business Suite and then click Help | Diagnostics | Custom Code | Personalize. This will take you to the Forms Personalization screen, where you can capture the details for your extension. When personalizations are saved, those details are stored in database tables, and the personalizations and their associated actions can then be parsed and executed by the FND libraries at runtime.

As with CUSTOM.pll, the changes made via Forms Personalizations are never overwritten by Oracle patches. Therefore, such extensions are upgrade safe, unless the upgrade process replaces the fundamental design of the form altogether.

A developer should ask the following questions when extending the functionality of any form:

- **Form to be personalized** Which form should be extended?
- **Form function** The form being extended might be accessible via different menus, with each menu item attached to a different form function. Should the extension be applicable to all such form functions for this form? Also, should this extension be applicable to a set of responsibilities or set of users?
- **Events** Which events should be captured for this extension?
- **Conditions** Should this extension be applicable only when certain conditions are true?
- **Actions** What actions should the extensions to this form perform?

Table 6-3 shows the corresponding answers and how they map to Forms Personalization features.

As shown in Table 6-3, both CUSTOM.pll and Forms Personalization are called from the same set of events and triggers. If extensions are present in both places for any given form, the extensions in Forms Personalization are executed first, and after that the code in CUSTOM.pll is executed. Figure 6-7 shows the screen from which

Question	Forms Personalization Feature
Form to be personalized	Navigate to the form I question and click Help I Personalize. This will open the Form Personalization screen; this screen is always opened in the context of the form being extended.
Form function	In the Forms Personalization screen, you can select either the Form or Function context. When Function is selected, the personalizations are restricted to the form function from which the Personalization Screen was invoked.
Events	The events that can be trapped in Forms Personalization are the same as those in CUSTOM.pll. For Block and Item Level events, it is possible to specify the block name and the item name. You will create one personalization for each event that you wish to trap in a form.
Conditions	It is possible to specify the conditions that have constructs similar to IF..THEN..ELSE in PL/SQL. These conditions can reference the value of the fields in the form being personalized. The extensions will take effect only when the conditions specified are true in the context of data being entered.
Action	Actions can be either to display error messages, to change the navigation, to change the item properties, and so on.

TABLE 6-3. *Components of Forms Personalization*

Forms Personalizations can be created. To restrict personalizations to one or more responsibilities or one or more users, entries can be made in the Context Level region of the Forms Personalization screen.

If the conditions within the personalizations are evaluated to true, then all the actions attached to that personalization are executed. As shown in Figure 6-8, there are four possible types of such actions: Property, Message, Builtin, and Menu.

The action type Property is commonly used to achieve the following:

- Initialize global variables and assign values to global variables.
- Assign a value to items or global variables or parameters.
- Change the list of values (LOV) properties; for example, change its record group.
- Hide, show, enable, or disable fields, tabs, canvas views, and so on.
- Change Navigation properties and default WHERE clauses of blocks.
- Make items mandatory.

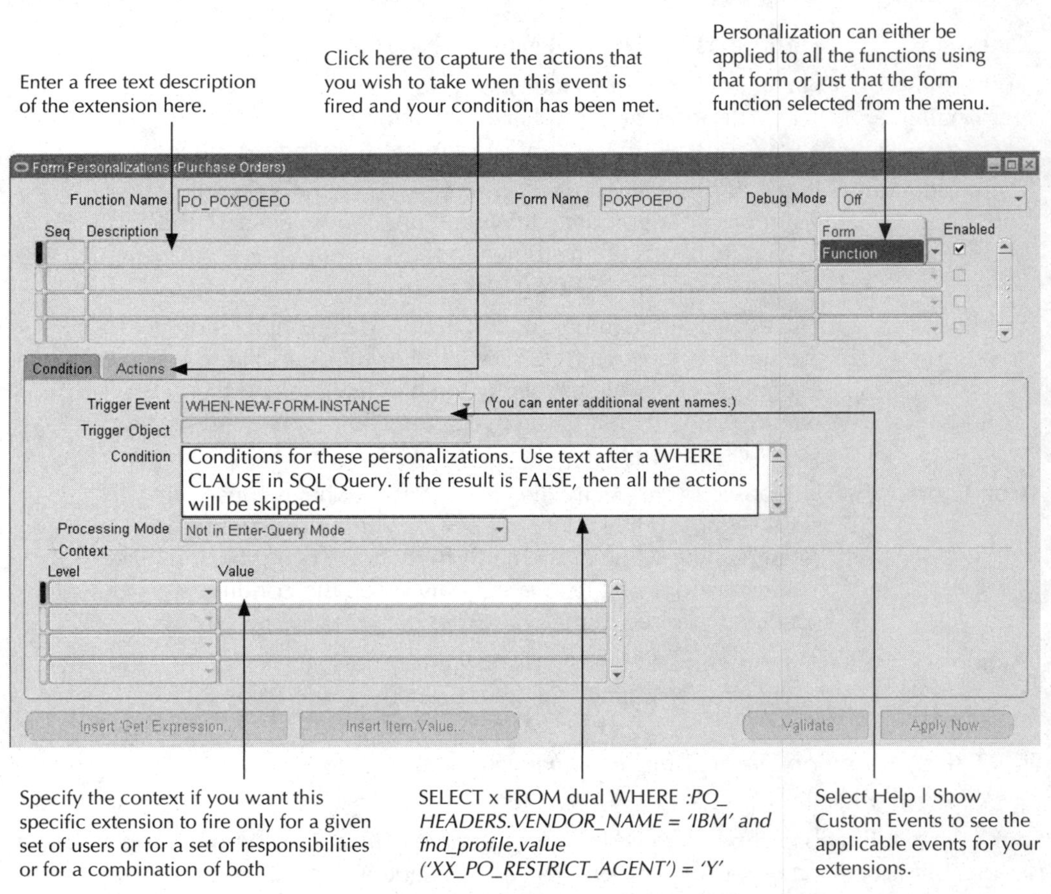
Enter a free text description of the extension here.
Click here to capture the actions that you wish to take when this event is fired and your condition has been met.
Personalization can either be applied to all the functions using that form or just that the form function selected from the menu.
Form Personalizations (Purchase Orders)
Function Name PO_POXPOEPO
Form Name POXPOEPO
Debug Mode Off
Seq Description
Form
Function
Enabled
Condition Actions
Trigger Event WHEN-NEW-FORM-INSTANCE
(You can enter additional event names.)
Trigger Object
Condition
Conditions for these personalizations. Use text after a WHERE CLAUSE in SQL Query. If the result is FALSE, then all the actions will be skipped.
Processing Mode Not in Enter-Query Mode
Context
Level
Value
Insert 'Get' Expression...
Insert Item Value...
Validate
Apply Now
Specify the context if you want this specific extension to fire only for a given set of users or for a set of responsibilities or for a combination of both
SELECT x FROM dual WHERE :PO_HEADERS.VENDOR_NAME = 'IBM' and fnd_profile.value ('XX_PO_RESTRICT_AGENT') = 'Y'
Select Help | Show Custom Events to see the applicable events for your extensions.

FIGURE 6-7. *Forms Personalization components*

The action type Builtin is commonly used to achieve the following:

1. Call other form functions (passing parameters).
2. Execute DO_KEY triggers, for example, EXECUTE_QUERY.
3. Execute a PL/SQL stored procedure by passing the form field values as parameters.
4. Create record groups that can be attached to the existing LOVs.
5. Raise FORM_TRIGGER_FAILURES to abort processing in case of errors.

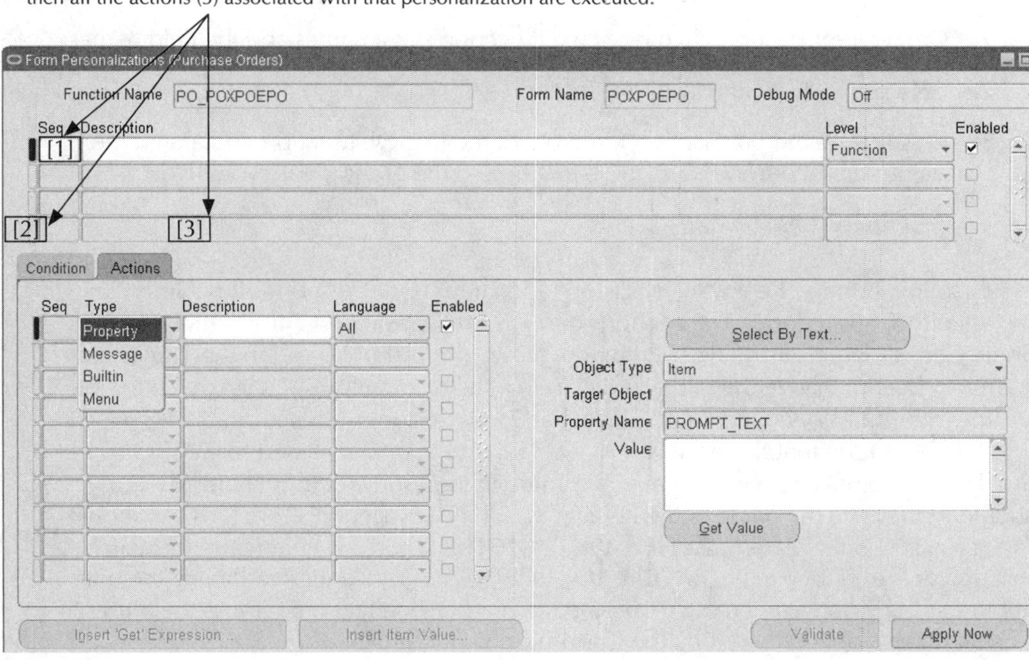

FIGURE 6-8. *Actions in Forms Personalization*

The action type Menu is used to create new tools menus with the arbitrary labels.

The action type Message is used to display messages to the end users via a message box or as a hint in the console window.

Examples of Forms Personalizations

Let us now take a look at simple examples to demonstrate the steps of how to perform Forms Personalizations. These are made up examples and can be very easily tried on the R12 VISION instance using the OPERATIONS username or any other user with similar privileges.

Default a Value from a PL/SQL Function

In this example, we will execute a stored PL/SQL function by passing to it certain parameters. The value returned from the PL/SQL function will be assigned to a field on Oracle Form. In this example, in the Receivables responsibility we use a Transactions screen that is used to create invoices, credit memos, and other transactions. In this case, let us assume that our business requirement is to default the Customer Transaction Type from the Transaction source. Our high-level steps to implement this requirement will be:

1. Gather information to figure out the triggering event names and the field names.
2. Create a PL/SQL function.
3. Personalize the Transaction form to call the PL/SQL function and assign the value returned from the PL/SQL function to the Transaction type field.
4. Test the results.

First, log in to the Receivables, Vision Operations (USA) responsibility and navigate to Transactions | Transactions to open the Transaction Entry screen. Enable Show Custom Events from the Help menu. Now click List of Values in the Transaction source field and change the value in the Source field to any transaction source for the Vision Operations operating unit. Given that Show Custom Events is enabled, you will be able to see that the WHEN-VALIDATE-ITEM trigger is passed to CUSTOM.pll and Forms Personalization whenever the value in the source field is changed. You should note down the name of the item for which this triggering event fires. As shown in Figure 6-9, in this case it's WHEN-VALIDATE-ITEM, and the item name for which this trigger is executed is BS_BATCH_SOURCE_NAME_MIR. After you make the note about the triggering event that will be used in our personalization, disable the Show Custom Events option by setting the Custom Code property to Normal.

Next, navigate to the Transaction Source field, and click Help | Diagnostics | Examine. This will display the name of the items and fields you need to use in your personalization. As shown in Figure 6-10, the name of the block for both the fields is TGW_HEADER and the name of the Source field is BS_BATCH_SOURCE_NAME_MIR, whereas the name of the Transaction Type field is CTT_TYPE_NAME_MIR.

Next, create a sample PL/SQL function in the database using the code that follows. Please note that this is a made-up example; in a real-life scenario, you should never do any hard coding in your programs.

```
CREATE OR REPLACE FUNCTION xx_get_trx_type_from_source
(p_trx_source IN VARCHAR2)
  RETURN VARCHAR2 AS
BEGIN
  IF p_trx_source LIKE 'Loan%' THEN
    RETURN 'Auto Vehicle Sls Inv';
  ELSE
    RETURN 'Invoice';
  END IF;
END xx_get_trx_type_from_source;
```

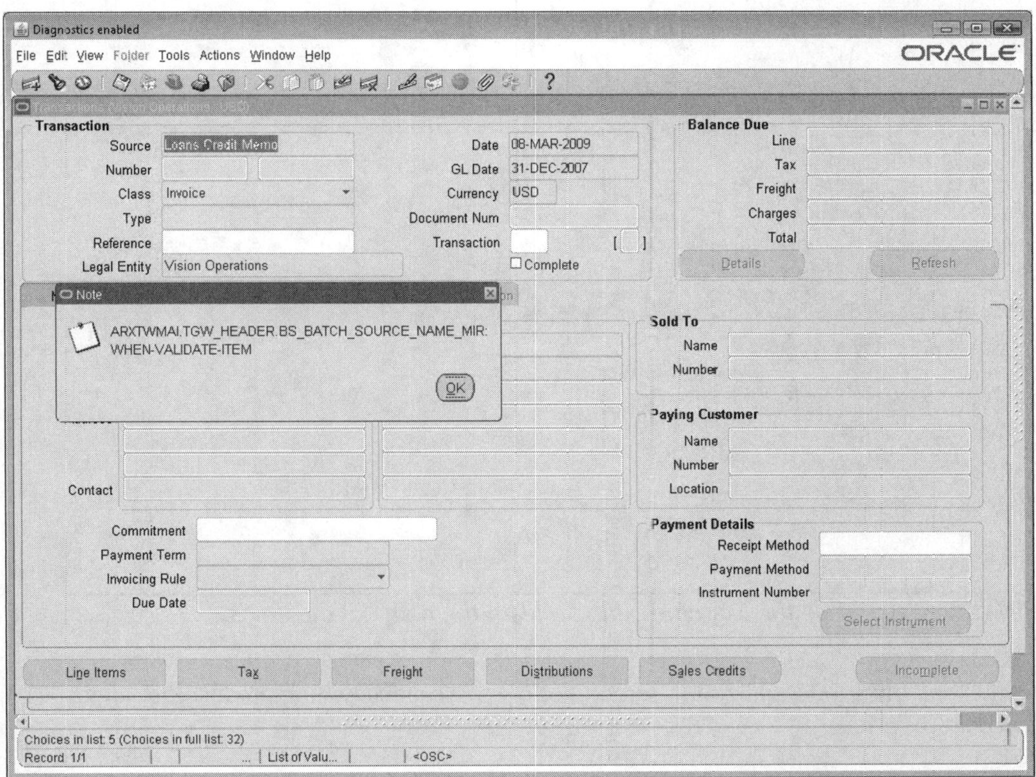

FIGURE 6-9. *The WHEN-VALIDATE-ITEM is executed when a transaction source is changed.*

As per the example, if the user selects a transaction source that begins with Loan, the Transaction Type field will be defaulted to the value Auto Vehicle Sls Inv. In all other cases, the Transaction Type field will be defaulted to the value Invoice. Therefore, the PL/SQL function xx_get_trx_type_from_source takes the transaction source as an input parameter and returns the corresponding transaction type. In a real-life scenario, the default transaction type will most likely be mapped to the transaction source via a descriptive flexfield or by means of some other mapping.

To create your personalization, while the cursor is in the transaction entry screen, navigate to Help | Diagnostics | Custom Code | Personalize. This will open the Forms Personalization screen.

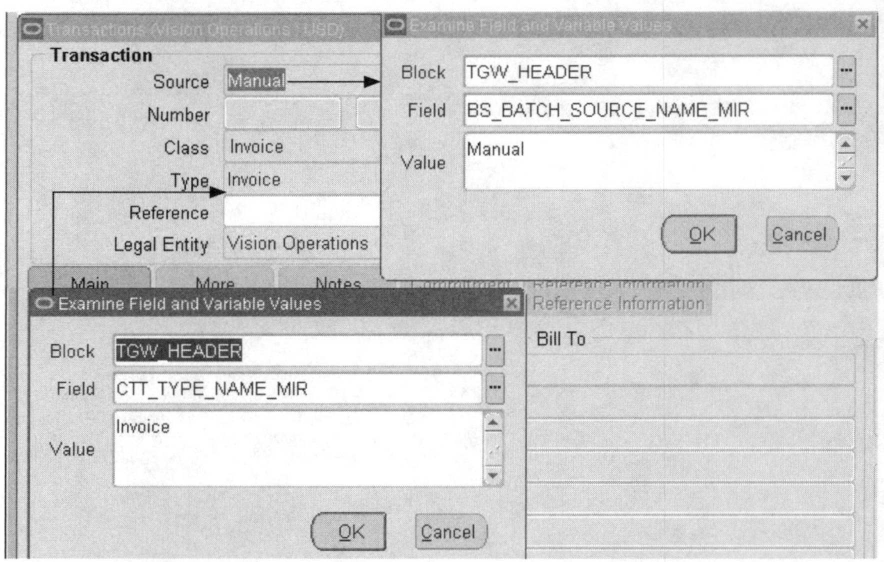

FIGURE 6-10. *Use the Examine utility to learn the name of the fields.*

In the Forms Personalization screen, follow these steps (which are also depicted in Figure 6-11):

1. Enter **1** in the Seq field and type **Default Transaction Type** in the Description field. Leave the level defaulted to Function.
2. On the Condition tab, in the Trigger Event field, enter **WHEN-VALIDATE-ITEM**.
3. In the Condition field, enter the following text:

```
:system.current_field='BS_BATCH_SOURCE_NAME_MIR'
```

4. Click the Actions tab and create an action with Sequence=1, Type=Property, Object Type=Item, Target Object=TGW_HEADER.CTT_TYPE_NAME_MIR, Property Name= VALUE, and the Value field as shown next (including the =):

```
=select xx_get_trx_type_from_source(${item.TGW_HEADER.BS_BATCH_
SOURCE_NAME_MIR.value}) from dual
```

Click Validate and then click Apply Now. Next, close both the Forms Personalization screen and the Transaction Entry screen. To test your changes, open the Transaction Entry screen again, and click the LOV Torch icon when the cursor is in the Source field. Select Source=Loans and Operating Unit=Vision Operations from the list of values. Immediately after the selection of Loans, the value in Transaction Type field will change to Auto Vehicle Sls Inv.

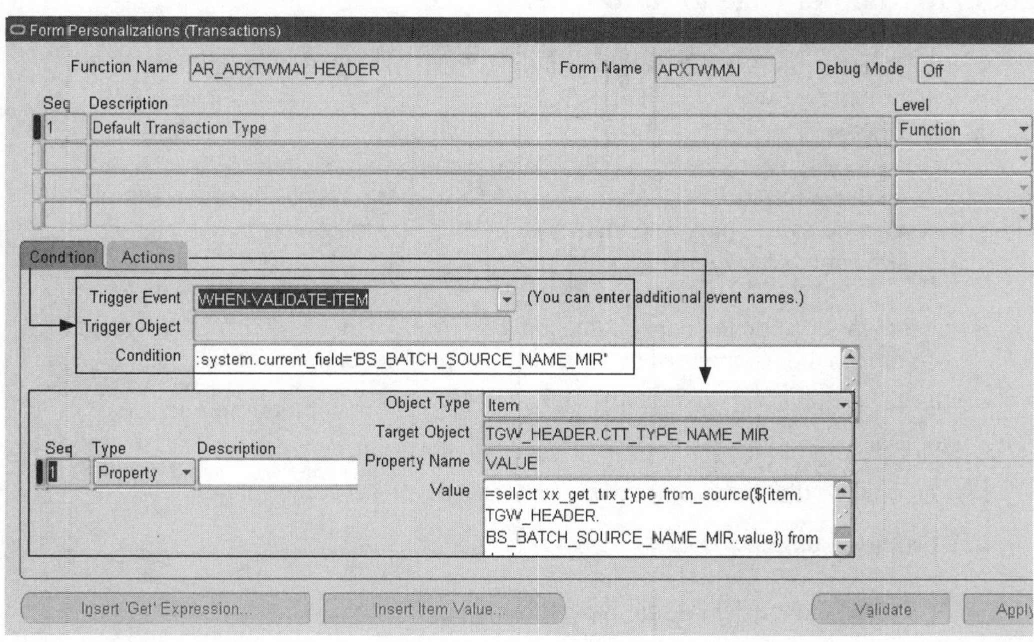

FIGURE 6-11. *Create a personalization to execute a PL/SQL function.*

Behind the scenes, the following sequence of events happens:

1. The WHEN-VALIDATE-ITEM trigger is passed to the Forms Personalization framework and then to CUSTOM.pll.
2. A personalization is found for the form function, with a Default Transaction Type description of this Forms Personalization.
3. The condition :system.current_field='BS_BATCH_SOURCE_NAME_MIR evaluates to TRUE when the value in the Source field is changed because the trigger WHEN-VALIDATE-ITEM was executed as a result of the change to the Source field.
4. All the actions are executed sequentially (although in this case it happens to be a single action).
5. The PL/SQL function xx_get_trx_type_from_source is executed, with the value in the Source field (TGW_HEADER.BS_BATCH_SOURCE_NAME_MIR) passed as an input parameter. The result of the PL/SQL function gets assigned to the Transaction Type field (TGW_HEADER.CTT_TYPE_NAME_MIR).

Zoom to Another Page to Auto-Query

Forms Personalization can also be used to zoom to another page. In this example, you will add a new menu in the toolbar to the Transaction entry screen in Receivables. The new item will be added using Forms Personalization. The label of this item will be Bill To Customer Details. The customer screen will open when you click this newly created toolbar menu item. The Bill-To customer selected in the Transaction entry screen will be automatically queried in the Customer screen. The end result of these personalizations will be as shown in Figure 6-12. The following are the high-level steps to implement this requirement:

1. Gather information to figure out the function name of the Customer Maintenance screen and the parameter it expects for auto-querying of the customer.
2. Personalize the Transaction entry form to create a new menu item in the toolbar.
3. Personalize the Transaction entry form to call the Customer page.
4. Test the results.

Log in to the Receivables, Vision Operations (USA) responsibility and navigate to Transactions | Transactions. This opens the Transaction entry screen. Use the Examine utility from Help | Diagnostics to find the field that stores Bill-To Customer ID. In the Examine window, click the List of Values icon on the Field item and search for the item %BILL%CUSTOMER%. Using this technique, you can see that a field named BILL_TO_CUSTOMER_ID exists in this form within the block TGW_HEADER. The name of this field will be used when passing a parameter to the Customer screen.

Next, you need to find the name of the AOL Function to which the Customer screen is attached. In the System Administrator responsibility, query the responsibility definition for Receivables, Vision Operations (USA), and notice that User Menu AR_NAVIGATE_GUI is attached to this responsibility. Further, a submenu named AR_CUSTOMERS_GUI is attached. Upon querying the definition of the submenu, notice that an AR Customer Search function is attached to this responsibility with its prompt labeled Customers. Query this AOL Function in the Function Definition screen. Notice that this function invokes an OA Framework page as shown next:

```
OA.jsp?page=/oracle/apps/ar/cusstd/srch/webui/
ArPrtySrchPG&OAPB=AR_BRAND_FUNC&OAHP=AR_CUS_STD_ROOT&OASF=AR_CUS_SRCH
```

In the Profile Options screen, make sure that the FND: Diagnostics profile option is set to Yes for your username. Now navigate back to the Receivables, Vision Operations (USA) responsibility and go to the Customers | Customers screen. Then click the About this page link at the bottom-left corner of the browser window. This shows the page definition: notice that the controller attached to this page is ArPrtySrchCO. This controller file is a Java class file that exists on midtier in the

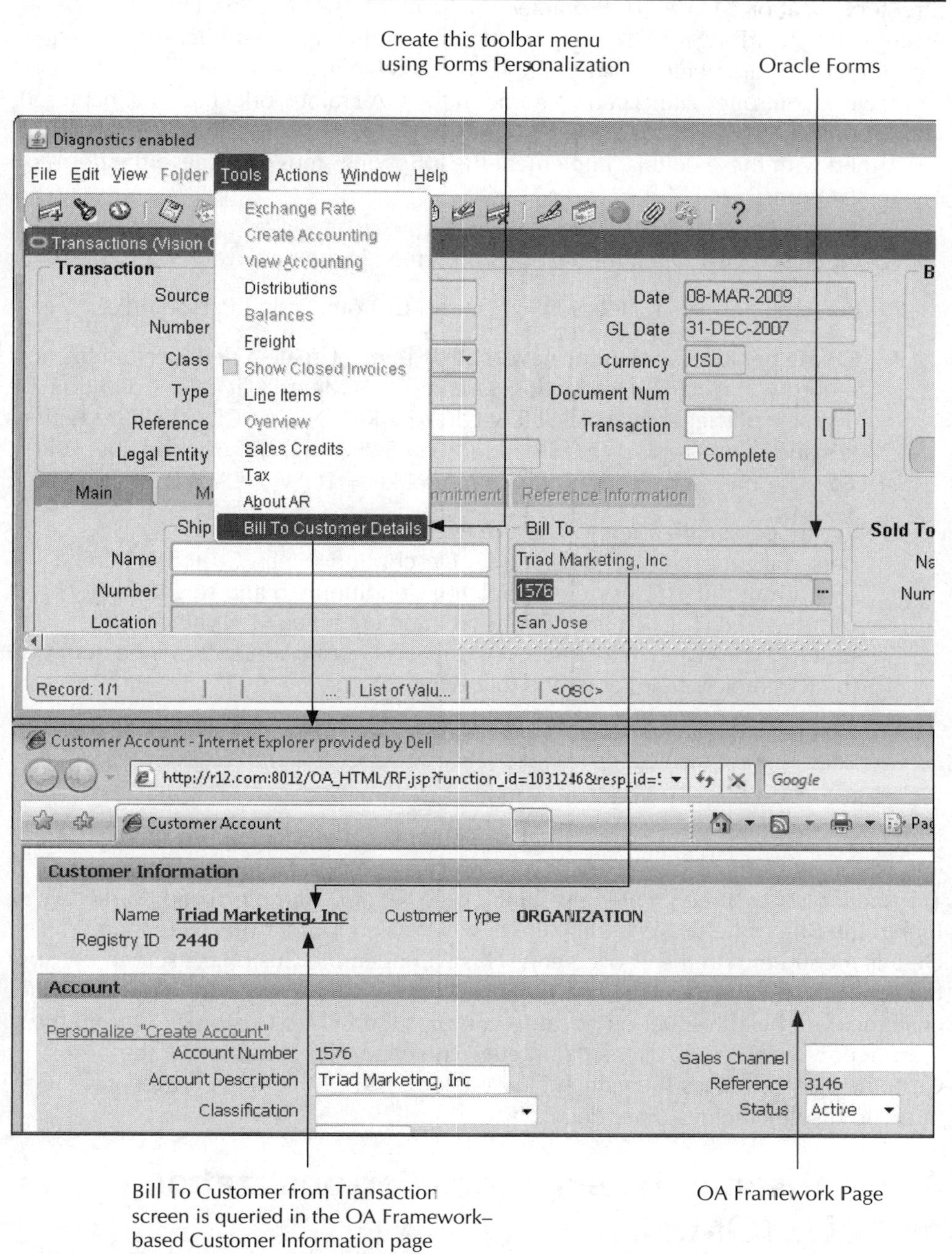

FIGURE 6-12. *Create a Tools menu and open the OA Framework Customer page to Auto-query.*

directory location $JAVA_TOP/oracle/apps/ar/cusstd/srch/webui. Upon examination of ArPrtySrchCO, you should discover that this controller can auto-query a customer if a parameter CUSTOMER_ID is passed to it. The details of how the OA Framework controller works can be found in the OA Framework chapter (Chapter 9) in this book.

Armed with these details, implement the following steps to achieve the desired personalizations:

1. **Open screen** Open the Transaction screen in the Receivables responsibility.
2. **Personalize** Click Help | Diagnostics | Custom Code | Personalize.
3. **Create personalization for new toolbar item** Create a new personalization record with Seq=2, Description=Create Tools Menu. Click the Condition tab and select Trigger Event= WHEN-NEW-FORM-INSTANCE. Click the Actions tab and enter Seq=1, Type=Menu, Menu Entry=MENU1, Menu Label=Bill To Customer Details and Enabled in Block(s)= TGW_HEADER.
4. **Create personalization to capture event MENU1** Create a new personalization record with Seq=3, Description=Open Customer Screen for current Bill To Customer. Click the Condition tab and select Trigger Event=MENU1. Click the Actions tab, and enter Seq=1, Type=Builtin, Builtin Type=Launch a Function, Function Name=AR Customer Search. In the Parameters field, enter the following value:

```
=select 'OAPB=AR_BRAND_FUNC&OAHP=AR_CUS_STD_ROOT&OASF=AR_CUS_
SRCH'||'&CUSTOMER_ID='||${item.TGW_HEADER.BILL_TO_CUSTOMER_
ID.value} from dual
```

Now click Validate to ensure there are no errors. Save the records and close the Forms Personalization screen and the Transaction entry screen. Now reopen the Transaction entry screen. Enter any valid customer (for example, Triad Marketing, Inc) in the Bill-To field. Next, click the newly created toolbar Bill To Customer Details menu item in the Tools menu. This will open the Customers screen because the action type Launch a Function will open the AR Customer Search function. The customer will be auto-queried because you pass the Bill-To Customer ID from the Transaction entry screen as the parameter. The controller class against the Customers screen reads the value of parameter CUSTOMER_ID and executes the query to display the customer details.

Comparison Between Forms Personalization and CUSTOM.pll

Even though Forms Personalization and CUSTOM.pll are driven by the same set of triggering events, there are certain limitations in Forms Personalization due to the difference in the architecture of the two technologies. Table 6-4 compares Forms Personalization and CUSTOM.pll.

Task	CUSTOM.pll	Forms Personalization
Change LOV query	Yes	Yes
Change field properties such as Mandatory, Display, and so on	Yes	Yes
Zoom to another screen	Yes	Yes
Disable a menu entry when certain conditions are met	Yes	No
Display messages, warnings, hints, and so on	Yes	Yes
Display messages with questions and conditionally execute code based on users' response to the question	Yes	No
Execute PL/SQL stored procedures	Yes	Yes
Change navigation and navigational properties	Yes	Yes
Change block properties such as Query Where Clause and so on	Yes	Yes
Change applicable across multiple screens, such as changing the window title for all screens within one organization or responsibility	Yes	Yes**
Use a PL/SQL stored procedure that has OUT parameters in Condition.	Yes	No

**In Forms Personalization, you will need to personalize each and every impacted form separately. However, in CUSTOM.pll this can be achieved with a few lines of code so changes can be effective across all the relevant screens.

TABLE 6-4. *Comparison between Forms Personalization and CUSTOM.pll*

Best Practices When Implementing Forms Personalizations

As always, it is good to follow the best practices in Forms Personalization. We have compiled a list of best practices from our experiences gained by working on projects that involved a number of forms personalizations:

- **Global variable naming convention** All the global variables defined must begin with XX. This will ensure there is no conflict with global variables defined by Oracle.
- **FNDLOAD** Use FNDLOAD to transfer Forms Personalizations from one environment to another. If the functional team makes changes to the test environment and the development team makes changes to the development environment for the same form, the changes performed on the test environment will be lost when the FNDLOAD extract from the Development environment is promoted.
- **Master environment** Maintain a master environment where developers, functional staff, and support staff perform their personalizations. An FNDLOAD extract can be made from this master environment.
- **Tools menu** To create new tool menus, always use MENU1-MENU15, as Oracle guarantees never to use these during development. The same is not true for SPECIAL menus, however, as Oracle development may release a patch utilizing the same SPECIALx as you may have personalized.
- **Sequence** Keep in mind that the Forms Personalization code fires prior to the CUSTOM.pll code (in case you have the same form extended from both FP and CUSTOM.pll).
- **Clear global variables** Make sure you clear the custom global variables after you are finished with them. This will ensure that the screen works under normal scenarios as well. Global variables can be used when integrating two different screens using Forms Personalizations.
- **Changes to production** Never make changes to Forms Personalizations directly in test or production. Always make changes in the development environment and transfer using FNDLOAD.
- **Bug reporting** Forms Personalizations can be disabled by turning the custom code off. Before reporting any form-related bug to Oracle, try reproducing the issue by turning Custom Code off.

Further Readings on Forms Personalizations

Metalink has various articles that explain step by step different features of Forms Personalizations. Such articles are listed in the following table:

Metalink Note	Description
429604.1	How to Use Parameters in Forms Personalizations
578984.1	How to Launch URL in Forms Personalizations
726324.1	Forms Personalization and Customizing LOV
279034.1	Information About the Oracle Applications Forms Personalization Feature in 11i (contains PowerPoint presentations and video demonstrations)

Summary

In this chapter, we discussed Oracle Forms tools, customization, and extension techniques with emphasis on Forms Personalizations and using the CUSTOM.pll library. When building a custom form from scratch, you must use the TEMPLATE form, which comes with the installation of Oracle Applications. The development process consists of building, generating, and testing the custom form. The build is performed on a developer's desktop machine, which must have access to any referenced forms and attached libraries. The FMB form file is then transferred onto a middle-tier machine where the forms server resides in order to be generated. The form is compiled from the command line on a middle-tier box. After compilation, the form is registered with AOL and added to a menu and responsibility in order to be tested from Oracle Applications by the developer. Finally, after successful testing, the custom form is deployed by copying the generated FMX file to the target environment, provided that the target environment is running on the same platform as the development environment.

In addition to customizing the existing forms and building the custom ones from scratch, the preferred technique is to always use the Forms Personalization feature, which has been available since R11i. This technique is considerably easier to support and maintain. If certain requirements cannot be currently met by using Forms Personalization, wherever possible we prefer to use CUSTOM.pll as described in this chapter, as this technique is preferred to customizing the existing Oracle-delivered forms file directly.

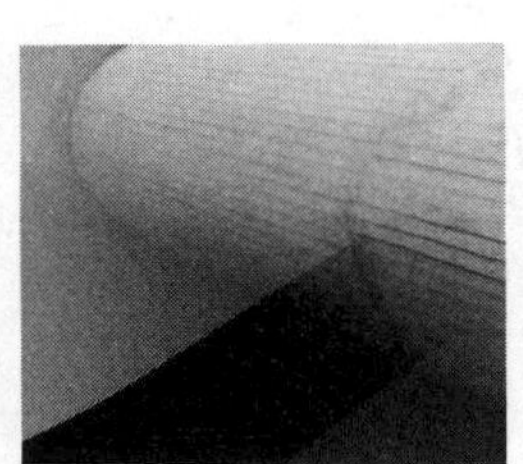

CHAPTER 7

Reports Development and Customization in Oracle Apps

racle Reports is a reporting tool that queries data from the Oracle database and presents it in the desired format. It has been part of the E-Business Suite technology stack ever since the conception of Oracle Applications. Like many other technology components discussed in this book, Oracle Reports consists of the design-time development tool (Oracle Reports Developer), which is run from the developer's desktop, and the runtime component (Reports Server/Services), which runs as a component of Oracle Application Server.

Currently, E-Business Suite 11i uses Reports Developer 6i, whereas Reports Developer 10g is used in R12. In the context of Oracle Applications, the development methodologies for both versions of the Oracle Reports tool are the same. In this chapter, we are going to use the latest version of Oracle Reports 10g against an E-Business Suite R12 VISION installation.

Main Components of Oracle Reports

The two main components of Oracle Reports are the Data and Layout models. The Data model is the place where the SQL statements are written to fetch the data from the database tables. In the Layout model, you perform the design of an appearance of the report output.

Data Model

The Data model consists of SQL Statements that query data to be displayed in the report. The query contains columns that can be bundled together into groups. Therefore, a query can have one or more groups, and a group can have one or more columns. This hierarchy, in effect, determines the layout of the report. For example, if a report is to display all purchase orders by vendor, then Vendor becomes the parent group and Purchase Order becomes the child group. Therefore, for each vendor, one or more purchase orders will be displayed.

The columns within the group act as the data source for the fields in the layout. Effectively, the column names in groups are mapped to the fields in the layout, so it is important to give user-friendly names to the columns. This can be achieved by specifying an alias for the columns in a SQL Query.

Joining Queries with Links

You could potentially develop a complex report by writing one single SQL Query in the Data model, and thereafter break that query into multiple groups, as per the hierarchy desired in the layout. However, in practice, to have one massive and complex SQL Query can be cumbersome to maintain and might not be performance efficient. Oracle Reports allows you to join different queries using links. These links enforce an outer join between the two queries. The fact that links in the Data model are always outer joins ensures that all the records from parent query can be displayed even though the child queries may or may not return any records.

Formula Columns, Summary Columns, and Placeholder Columns

Columns selected in the SQL Query of the Data model are not the only columns available for report development. In addition to those, a developer can create three further types of columns: formula, summary, and placeholder columns.

Formula columns are nothing but PL/SQL functions. Whenever a reference is made to a Formula column, the PL/SQL code attached to that Formula column is executed. The difference between PL/SQL stored procedures and the PL/SQL within the Formula column is that the code in the Formula column can reference other Data model column values programmatically, because this code runs within the context of the report. For performance reasons, usage of Formula columns must be kept minimal, and where possible the logic within the Formula column should be computed within the SQL Query of the Data model itself.

The formula columns can also be used to generate the SQL Statement text dynamically within the Data model. One example of this usage is to build WHERE clauses for the SQL Statement dynamically in the Data model. In this case, the SQL Query in the Data model will reference a Formula column in its WHERE clause, and the Formula column will return a text value to facilitate building the WHERE clause.

The summary columns perform aggregate functions such as SUM, COUNT, MAX, MIN, AVG, and the like.

A placeholder column serves the purpose of a global variable within the report. The value of the placeholder column can be modified within the Formula column. As per general programming guidelines, the usage of the global variables must be kept to a minimum, and the same rules apply for the usage of placeholder columns.

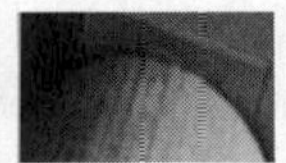

NOTE

Another way of creating global variables in Oracle Reports is to create a local program unit of type Package Specification and then create a variable within it. This variable can then be accessed by using syntax package_name.variable_name.

Layout Model

The Layout model dictates what the end user gets to see in the output of the report. Essentially, the Layout consists of a layer of frames and items within those frames. To visualize the frames, one could imagine a pyramid, with one slab stacked over the other. Each such slab equates to a frame.

By default, a frame is created in the layout for each group in the Data model. Within the group frame, a repeating frame is created. Think of the repeating frame as a FOR LOOP that iterates over the result of the SQL Statement to print data for each record. The repeating frames contain the fields that are meant to be printed multiple times depending upon the number of records fetched from the corresponding group in the Data model.

Newcomers to Oracle Reports development are advised to keep a copy of each version of the report as the layout is modified. This makes it easy to roll back to a prior working version of the report. There is also an option to re-create the default layout by right-clicking anywhere on the Layout and selecting the Report Wizard item. Reverting back to the default layout for an existing report will make it lose all the existing formatting for that report. Reports delivered out of the box by Oracle will already have refined layouts. Therefore, it is not recommended to rebuild the default layout for Oracle Apps reports.

Given that a complex report will consist of several layers, it helps if the developer temporarily fills the layers with varying colors, so that each frame can be located with ease. These color fillings can be removed once the development of the report has been completed.

One important property in the Layout Editor is the Confine mode, which is ON by default. Confine mode prevents you from accidentally moving an object to the wrong layer. For example, it makes no logical sense to move the Line Number field from Lines Repeating Frame to Header Repeating Frame. With Confine mode, such actions can be prevented.

Another important functionality of the Layout model is vertical and horizontal elasticity. When the vertical elasticity of a layout component is set to Variable, then its height can either shrink or expand depending upon the volume of data being printed. Other possible values for this property are Contract, Expand, and Fixed. The Vertical Elasticity property is useful when printing reports on preprinted stationery—for example, pay slip printing.

There is a very tight coupling between the Data model and the Layout model of a report. A repeating frame always corresponds to a group within the Data model. Similarly, a layout field corresponds to a column within the Data model. Nevertheless, the reverse is not always true, which means that a group or a column does not always have to correspond to a component in the Layout model.

Triggers in a Report

There are five kinds of triggers in a report:

- **Before Parameter Form** The first trigger to fire.
- **After Parameter Form** Fires after the Before Parameter Form trigger.
- **Before Report** Fires after the After Parameter Form. Additionally, this trigger fires before the data is fetched.

- **After Report** Fires after the report output has been sent to its destination; for example, a printer.
- **Between Pages** Fires just before each page is formatted, except the very first page.

Oracle Apps reports are run from the Submit Request window where the parameters are presented to the users. Therefore, in Oracle Reports, the After Parameter Form trigger will fire immediately after the Before Parameter Form.

Reports Delivered by Oracle Apps

Oracle delivers hundreds of reports out of the box. The reports files have .rdf extensions. Each report is registered as a concurrent program executable. You saw in Chapter 5, "Development of Concurrent Programs," that the executables are always attached to an application. The following sequence of events occurs when a user submits a report from the Submit Request screen:

1. Concurrent Manager finds the executable attached to the concurrent program.
2. Concurrent Manager discovers that the executable belongs to the application Oracle Human Resources.
3. Concurrent Manager finds the execution file name for this report.
4. The <Execution File Name>.rdf is located in $PER_TOP/reports/US (we'll assume that this report is for the Human Resource module and developed in English language here; for other languages, the RDF file is located in the corresponding language subdirectory).
5. The report is run by the Reports executable.
6. The output of the report is made visible through the output of the concurrent request.

NOTE
When defining concurrent programs, it is possible to define parameters for the program. In Oracle Reports, every parameter must be registered in the Concurrent Program screen. The value of the Token field in the Concurrent Program Parameters window must match the name of the parameter defined in the Oracle Report.

Dynamic ORDER BY Clauses

Many of the reports in E-Business Suite use dynamic WHERE and ORDER BY clauses. This information is useful when customizing the standard reports. For example, the dynamic ORDER BY clause is achieved by following these steps:

1. Create a Formula column of Character type in the Data model. Do this by selecting Insert | Data Item | Formula Column and then click anywhere in the Data model.

2. The properties of the Formula column are usually amended to 2000 characters long. The Value If Null property is also amended to contain the default WHERE clause column names. For example:

   ```
   pov.vendor_name, pvs.vendor_site_code
   ```

3. Assuming the name of the Formula column is orderby_clause, the query in the Data model will contain:

   ```
   SELECT
         pov.vendor_name Vendor,
         pov.segment1 Vendor_Number,
         pov.vendor_type_lookup_code Vendor_Type
   FROM
         po_vendor_sites pvs, po_vendors pov
   WHERE
         pov.vendor_id = pvs.vendor_id
   ORDER BY &orderby_clause
   ```

4. Right-click the Formula column and select PL/SQL Editor.

5. The logic for building the ORDER BY clause can be written here:

   ```
   FUNCTION orderby_clauseFormula RETURN VARCHAR2 IS
   BEGIN
     IF :P_orderby = 'VENDOR TYPE' THEN
         return('pov.vendor_type_lookup_code');
     ELSE
       RETURN('pov.vendor_name');
     END IF;
   END;
   ```

Another way of implementing logic similar to this is by referencing a parameter name in the SQL query. The SQL query can contain a notation similar to:

```
SELECT … FROM … WHERE … &LP_VENDOR_ID
```

where LP_VENDOR_ID is the name of a parameter. In the BeforeReport trigger, the code shown next will be used:

```
FUNCTION beforereport RETURN BOOLEAN IS
BEGIN
  IF (:P_VENDOR_ID IS NOT NULL) THEN
    :LP_VENDOR_ID := 'and pov.vendor_id = ' || TO_CHAR(:P_VENDOR_ID);
  END IF;
  RETURN(TRUE);
END;
```

Parameters used for building dynamic WHERE clauses as shown previously are known as lexical parameters. In our examples, we have used BEFORE REPORT TRIGGER to manipulate lexical parameters. It must be noted that lexical parameters can be amended from AFTER PARAMETER FORM TRIGGER as well.

Multi-Org Initialization

An API named SRW.USER_EXIT('FND SRWINIT') is called from the Before Report trigger. This User Exit is responsible for setting the Multi-Org security and initializing the global variables in the context of the currently logged-in user. This ensures that the user is able to report on only those records that are permissible to view as per the data security setup in Oracle Apps. Similar to this API, from the After Report trigger, SRW.USER_EXIT('FND SRWEXIT') should be called.

Reports Customization and Custom Reports Development

Understanding the basic concepts of Oracle Reports makes it easier to understand the steps for customization of existing Oracle reports. The report must be customized in such way that customized changes to the report are not lost when Oracle patches are applied.

When customizing the report, follow these steps:

1. Identify the concurrent program to be customized and query it from the concurrent program definition screen. This program will have the Oracle Reports method. The navigation path for this screen from the Application Developer responsibility is Concurrent | Program.

2. Note down the name of the concurrent program executable. The executable name in the concurrent program definition window is the short name of the executable.

3. Query the executable from the concurrent program executable screen. Query the executable definition by using the short name captured from the concurrent program screen.
4. Note down the name of the Execution File Name for this concurrent program executable.
5. Copy the <Execution File Name>.rdf file to your custom top directory and rename it as per your naming conventions.

You have now created a copy of the reports RDF file. However, the standard concurrent program and its executable will still point to the executable delivered by Oracle. Therefore, you must create a new executable and a new concurrent program. The new concurrent program will be made to reference the new executable. Follow the steps listed next:

1. Create a new executable in the Concurrent Program Executable screen. This executable must be registered against a custom application. As a result, the RDF file will be picked up from the directory that corresponds to the custom application.
2. Query the standard concurrent program in the Concurrent Program Definition screen. Click the Copy To button and ensure that the Include Parameters and Include Incompatible Programs check boxes are checked. Give a user-friendly name to your new program. Also give an appropriate short name and your custom application name.
3. Attach the executable created in step 1 to the concurrent program created in step 2.
4. Include your new concurrent program to the desired request group.

By following the previous steps, you are creating a copy of the existing concurrent program with a new name; you are also making this concurrent program point to the new executable, which is registered against the custom application. The new RDF executable file resides in the custom directory, which on your VISION instance points to $XXCUST_TOP/reports/US. If the name of the standard report being customized is GLGVFNAV, then its corresponding custom report will be named with an XX prefix (XX<CUST>GLGVFNAV). Of course, you must adhere to the naming conventions imposed in your organization.

By implementing the previous steps, you'll have the new concurrent program that submits a report. However, the report being run is going to produce the same output as that of the standard report because it is not yet customized.

To customize the report, copy the renamed report from the server to your desktop, modify the report to meet your business requirements, and then redeploy the modified report to your server.

Sometimes the standard Oracle reports may have dependency on attached libraries. Therefore, you will see an error when opening those reports. The libraries are present in the $AU_TOP/plsql directory. These PLL files can be copied to a directory on your desktop. Next, an environment variable REPORTS_PATH is created at your desktop that points to the directory path that contains PLL files copied from $AU_TOP/plsql at middle tier.

The steps for developing a custom report are similar to that for customization of the standard reports, except that you will have to create a new concurrent program instead of copying it from an existing one. Additionally, ensure that the user parameter P_CONC_REQUEST_ID exists in the Data model of the report.

Reports Customization Example

In this example, we will customize the standard Oracle Purchase Order Print Report in E-Business Suite. The standard Oracle Purchase Order Print Report displays the buyer name in the output of the report. As per the business requirement in this example, you need to add a new field to the report so as to display the name of the final approver for the purchase order. The report layout before customization is as shown in Figure 7-1.

You need to display the final approver in the layout by customizing the standard report. In this example, we have printed the report for Purchase Order Number 508. The final approver for this purchase order is Brown, Ms. Casey, as shown in Figure 7-2.

First, you need to identify the report that is being customized. To do so, log in as a user with the Application Developer responsibility and navigate to the Concurrent | Program screen. Query on the concurrent program Printed Purchase Order Report (Portrait). Notice the name of the executable is POXPRPOP. Close that screen and open the Concurrent Program Executable screen, and query the concurrent program executable with the short name POXPRPOP. Notice that the concurrent program Execution File Name is POXPRPOP, its execution method is Oracle Reports, and it is registered with the application Purchasing. Therefore, you know that a file POXPRPOP.rdf will certainly exist in the $PO_TOP/reports/US directory on the machine where the concurrent server is running.

Navigate to the Purchasing, Vision Operations (USA) purchasing responsibility that has access to this concurrent program. If you are not using the VISION environment, you should use another purchasing responsibility that has access to the Printed Purchase Order Report (Portrait) concurrent program. Alternatively, this report can be added to the desired request group. Once you are in the responsibility with access to this program, navigate to View | Requests | Submit a New Request | Single Request | OK. Enter **Printed Purchase Order Report (Portrait)** in the Name field and tab out. You will be presented with the Parameter Entry screen, where you can select parameters as shown in Table 7-1.

Parameter Name	Value
Print Selection	All
Purchase Order Numbers From	508 (or any relevant value)
Purchase Order Numbers To	508 (r any relevant value)

TABLE 7-1. *Parameters Passed to the Report in This Example*

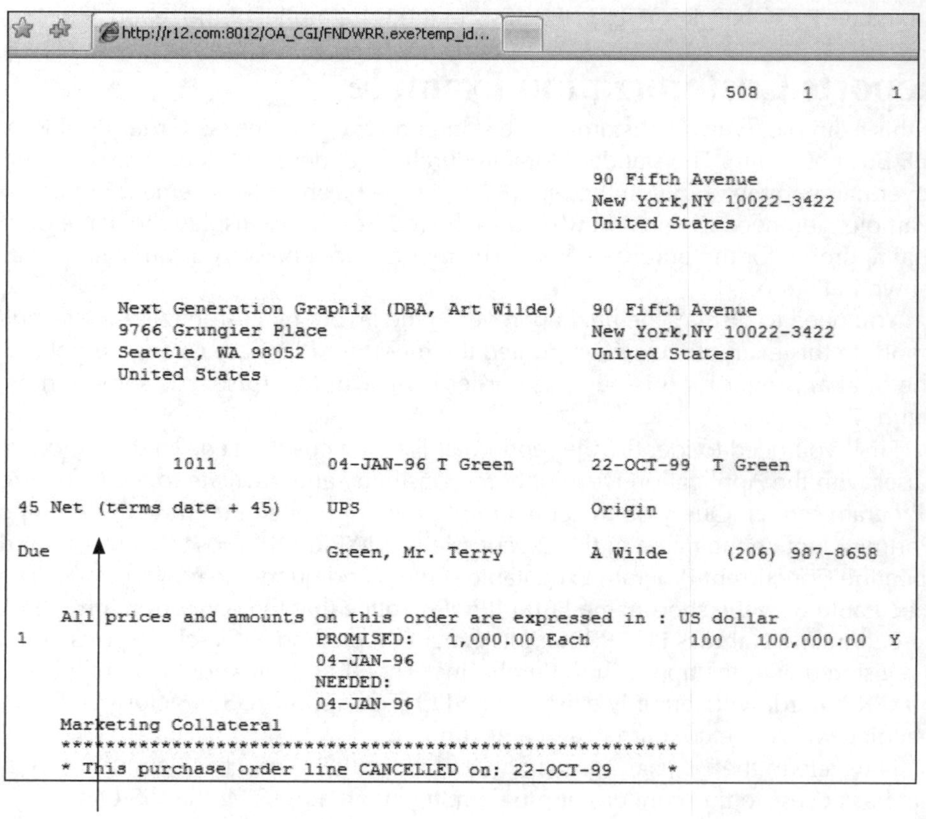


```
                                                         508    1    1

                                           90 Fifth Avenue
                                           New York,NY 10022-3422
                                           United States

     Next Generation Graphix (DBA, Art Wilde)  90 Fifth Avenue
     9766 Grungier Place                   New York,NY 10022-3422
     Seattle, WA 98052                     United States
     United States

          1011        04-JAN-96 T Green    22-OCT-99  T Green

45 Net (terms date + 45)   UPS             Origin

Due                   Green, Mr. Terry     A Wilde    (206) 987-8658

    All prices and amounts on this order are expressed in : US dollar
1                    PROMISED:   1,000.00 Each      100   100,000.00  Y
                     04-JAN-96
                     NEEDED:
                     04-JAN-96
    Marketing Collateral
    ******************************************************
    * This purchase order line CANCELLED on: 22-OCT-99   *
```


FIGURE 7-1. *Output of the standard Purchase Order Print Report in E-Business Suite*

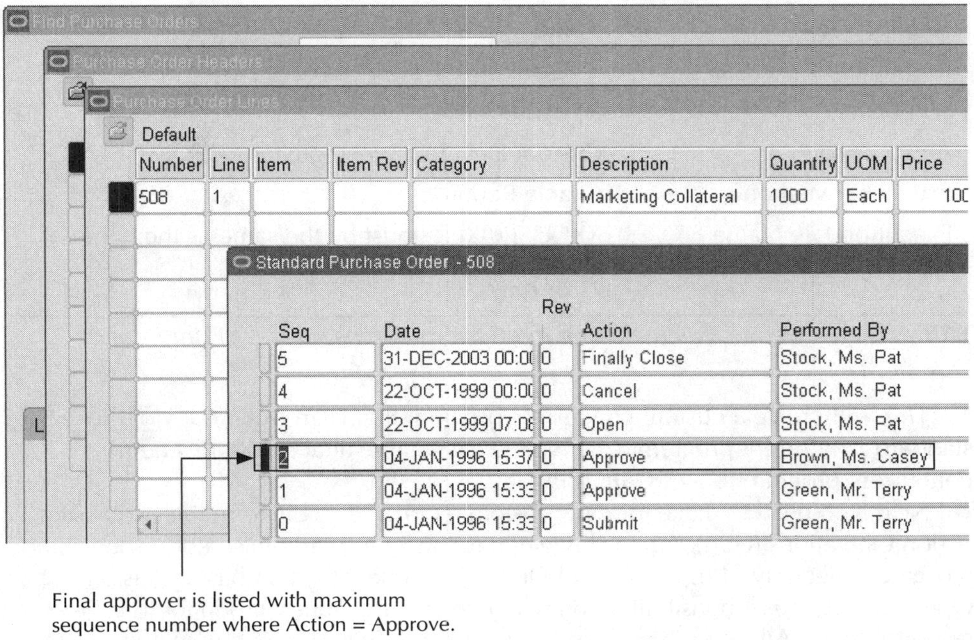

Final approver is listed with maximum sequence number where Action = Approve.

FIGURE 7-2. *This example purchase order has approver Brown, Ms. Casey.*

Click OK in the Parameter window and then click the Submit button. Find the request that you have submitted, and you will be able to see the output as shown in Figure 7-1. As per the standard guidelines, each custom report must be copied with a new name to the custom top directory. Use a similar command to the following on a Unix-like platform:

```
cp $PO_TOP/reports/US/POXPRPOP.rdf $XXCUST_TOP/reports/US/XXCUSPOXPR.rdf
```

Before you begin the customization, you can register the executable XXCUSPOXPR .rdf as a concurrent program. Navigate to the Application Developer responsibility, navigate to the Concurrent | Executable screen, and create an executable as shown in Table 7-2.

Save the executable data and close the screen. Now open the Concurrent Program definition screen by navigating to Concurrent | Program. Query on the Printed Purchase Order Report (Portrait) concurrent program, click Copy To, and enter the details shown in Table 7-3.

Field Name	Value
Executable	XXCUSPOXPR
Short Name	XXCUSPOXPR
Application	Custom Development (equates to $XXCUST_TOP)
Execution Method	Oracle Reports
Execution File Name	XXCUSPOXPR (must be the same as the name of the RDF file on the server)

TABLE 7-2. *Define Executable for the Custom Purchase Order Print Report*

This will create a custom concurrent program that is an exact copy of the standard concurrent program. Change the executable attached to this new concurrent program to XXCUSPOXPR.

Next, you need to make this new custom report accessible from the Purchasing, Vision Operations (USA) responsibility. Go to the System Administrator responsibility, navigate to Security | Responsibility | Define, and query the Purchasing, Vision Operations (USA) responsibility. You will note that the request group for this responsibility is All Reports, and the application is Purchasing. Again, within the System Administrator responsibility, navigate to Security | Responsibility | Request and query on the request group All Reports with the Purchasing application. Add the concurrent program XXCUS Printed Purchase Order Report (Portrait) to this request group. Now go to the Purchasing, Vision Operations (USA) responsibility and navigate to View | Requests | Submit New Request. You should be able to run the custom report with exactly the same parameters that you used for the standard Purchase Order Print Report. Note that the output of the custom concurrent program remains the same because the custom executable is a copy of the standard report.

Field Name	Value
Program	XXCUS Printed Purchase Order Report (Portrait)
Short Name	XXCUSPOXPR
Application	Custom Development
Include Incompatible Programs	Yes (set check box to checked value)
Include Parameters	Yes (set check box to checked value)

TABLE 7-3. *Copy the Standard Concurrent Program to Create Its Customized Version*

To customize this report, transfer XXCUSPOXPR.rdf from the server to your desktop and open it in the Reports Developer. To create the custom report, follow these steps:

1. Identify the repeating frame into which the new field will be placed.
2. Identify the group attached to that repeating frame.
3. Create a new Formula column within that group.
4. Develop the Formula column.
5. Create a field in the layout that references the new Formula column.
6. Transfer the report and test it on the server.

In Oracle Reports, we wish to display the new field just below the field f_poh_payment_terms. Both the payment terms and the final approver fields will be at the purchase order header level. To identify the name of the repeating frame, right-click the F_poh_payment_terms fields in Layout Editor and select the Select Parent Frame option. From the menu, select Tools | Property Inspector; the parent frame for this field is M_header_info, which belongs to repeating frame R_headers. Repeating frame R_headers is attached to group G_headers.

To create a new Formula column that returns the final approver, double-click Data Model within the Object Navigator and click the View menu to ensure that the tool palette is enabled. Click the f(x) Formula column icon in the tool palette and then click inside G_header, where the existing columns are listed. This will create a Formula column named CF_1 within the group G_headers. Double-click this new Formula column and rename it XXCF_Get_Latest_Approver. Make sure that the data type of this Formula column is Character and its width is 240. Click PL/SQL Formula, paste the code as shown next, and click Compile.

```
FUNCTION XXCF_Get_Latest_Approver RETURN Char IS
  CURSOR c_get_latest_approver IS
    SELECT ppx.full_name
      FROM per_people_x ppx, po_headers_all pha, po_action_history pohis
     WHERE pohis.object_id = :poh_po_header_id
       AND pohis.object_type_code = 'PO'
       AND pohis.action_code = 'APPROVE'
       AND pha.po_header_id = pohis.object_id
       AND ppx.PERSON_ID = pohis.employee_id
     order by pohis.sequence_num desc;
  l_full_name per_all_people_f.full_name%TYPE;
BEGIN
  OPEN c_get_latest_approver;
  FETCH c_get_latest_approver
```

```
    INTO l_full_name;
  CLOSE c_get_latest_approver;
  RETURN l_full_name;
END;
```

Navigate back to Layout Editor. Select Insert | Field and create a new field under F_poh_payment_terms. Double-click the new field, rename it XXF_Get_Latest_Approver, and attach it to the custom Formula column XXCF_Get_Latest_Approver. Alter the position of the field as appropriate, provided it remains within the R_headers repeating frame. Attach a Final Approver prompt to this field by clicking Insert | Text Label. After making this change, the layout will appear as shown in Figure 7-3.

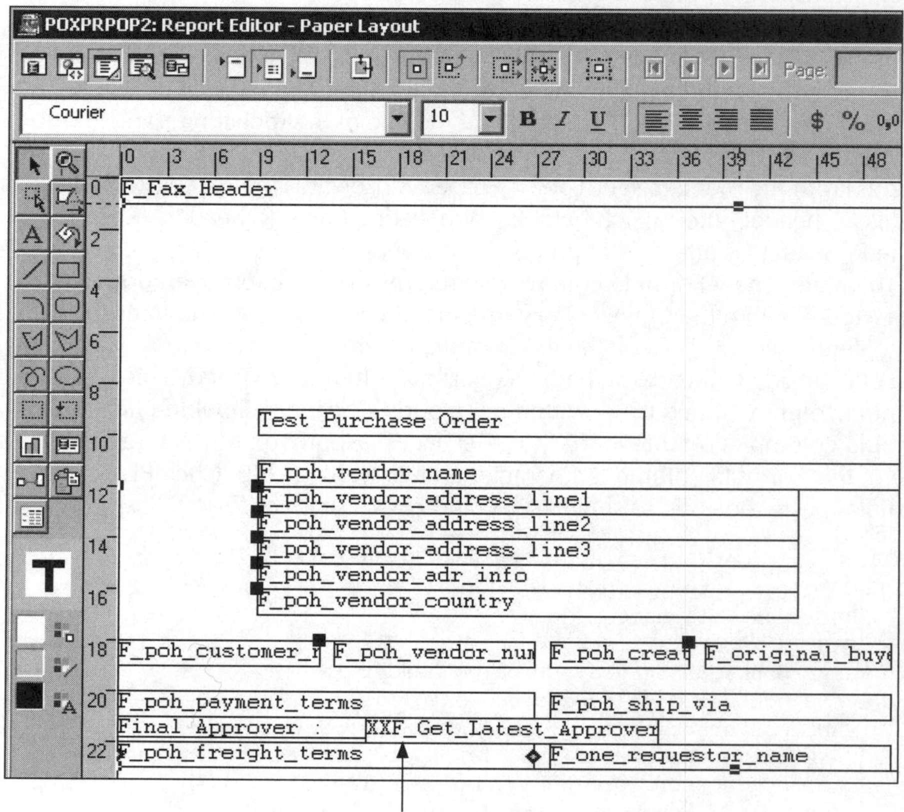

FIGURE 7-3. *Layout Editor of the report where the new field is added*

After transferring the report to the server, run the custom report again, and you will notice that the output is displayed as shown in Figure 7-4.

As demonstrated in this example, you must never modify the RDF file that resides under the standard application top directory. To customize the report, you take a copy of the standard report, modify it to meet the business requirements, and then register it with the custom application by creating a new concurrent program executable and concurrent program.

Best Practices for Developing Reports in E-Business Suite

Reports should be designed to improve the productivity of end users. There are many coding standards that, if followed, ensure ease of maintenance, performance efficiency, good structure and style, efficient debugging, exception handling, and the like. Here, we list only a few of the best practices that Oracle Reports developers usually practice.

Exception Handling

When writing PL/SQL within Oracle Reports—for example, in formula columns—you must handle exceptions so that the log file of the concurrent program report pinpoints the exact location and the cause of the problem:

```
BEGIN
[Your select statement here]
EXCEPTION  /*Handle other exceptions too as required*/
WHEN Others THEN
SRW.Message ('100','ERROR 01: Error in formula column ..-' || SQLERRM);
END;
```

One of the most common causes of such exceptions is that the text value returned from PL/SQL contains more characters than the maximum permissible as per the column property.

Additionally, if any unhandled error is encountered in the Report Level Trigger—for example, in the Before Report trigger—then the concurrent program must be aborted:

```
EXCEPTION
WHEN OTHERS THEN
    RAISE SRW.PROGRAM_ABORT;
```

Variable and Column Names for Customizations

When Oracle patches are applied, your customized reports remain untouched. However, the version of the report delivered by Oracle might change with Oracle patches. When patches deliver a bug fix to the standard report, the customized

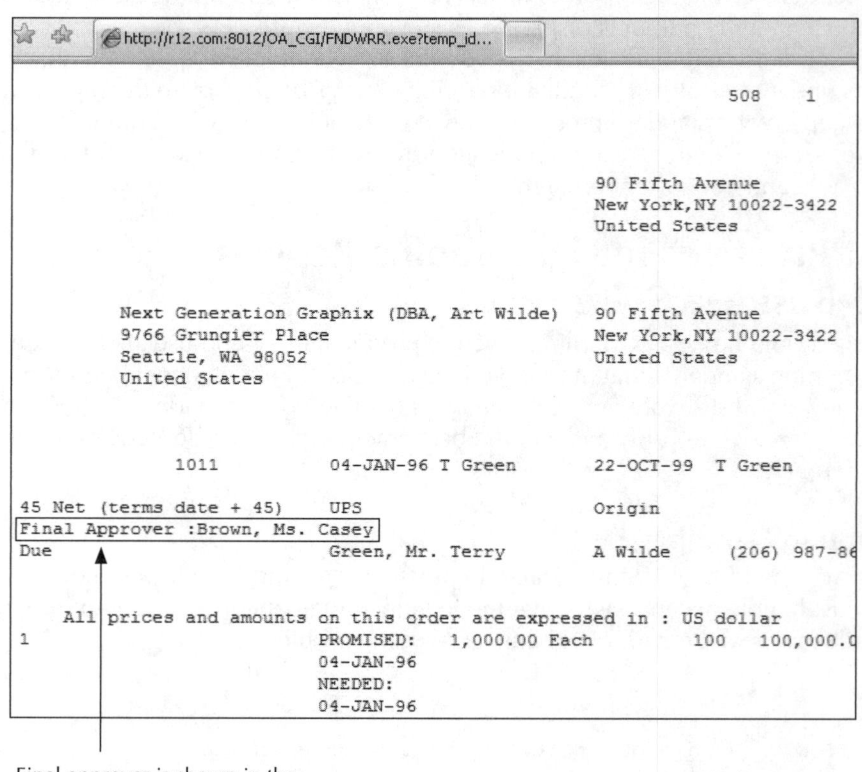

FIGURE 7-4. *Report output after customization displays the final approver*

version of that report can go out of sync with the standard report. In many cases, the developer has to reapply customizations on top of the latest version of the standard report. The developer reapplying the customization may not be the same person as the developer that originally built the customizations.

For that reason it is important that each customization is documented and those customizations are developed so that they are easily identifiable in a report. You must name all your columns, frames, and variables starting with XX_. When modifying SQL queries in the Data model, alias names for all the tables and columns must begin with xx_. This will ensure quick detection of customized code within the report.

It is also useful to print the name of the standard report that was customized in the log file of the concurrent request; you can do this by writing code in Before Report Trigger, as shown next:

```
srw.message ('10','Customization of Purchase Order Detail Report POX-
POSTD version 01.10 dated 09-Feb-2009.');
```

Additionally, full customization history must be maintained in a Comments property at report level. To do this, simply right-click the report name in Reports Developer, select Property Inspector, and click Comments to capture customization comments.

Debugging and Performance Tuning

Many standard Oracle Reports have the parameter P_DEBUG. Thereafter, in the report code, many debug messages are printed within the report provided the debug Parameter is set to Yes. You can apply the same technique for printing debug messages in your custom reports. It is important to display a message in the log file stating that debugging is enabled. For this you can print a warning through Before Report Trigger, if P_DEBUG=Y:

```
IF NVL (:p_debug,'N') = 'Y' THEN
srw.message ('100','WARNING: Debug Flag is ON.');
END IF;
```

Thereafter, use this parameter in your code where it is necessary to print messages. The debug messages will be surrounded by the IF CONDITION as shown earlier. Messages printed using srw.message will appear in the log file of the concurrent program.

Sometimes it is necessary to run the SQL trace to track, fine-tune, or troubleshoot performance issues with SQL queries being executed. SQL trace can be enabled by querying the concurrent program definition and checking the Enable Trace check box. Once the check box is selected and saved for the concurrent program in question, the trace file for that concurrent program will be created in the USER_DUMP_DEST directory on the database server. The path of this directory can be found by running the following from SQL Plus:

```
select value from v$parameter where name like 'user_dump_dest'
```

Note that the concurrent program tracing using the Enable Trace option will not show the values of bind variables in the generated trace file. To see the bind variable values, you should trace the concurrent program session by following Metalink Note 179848.1. Also, Metalink Note 296559.1 is very useful as it explains common tracing techniques in Oracle Applications.

The generated trace files can be opened in the text editor to examine the SQL statements and their bind variable values. Oracle also provides the TKPROF utility, which formats the raw trace files to produce a report that is much easier to read and understand. For example:

```
tkprof <tracefileName>.trc output=traceResult.prf
```

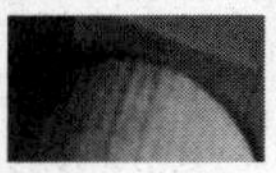

NOTE
SQL statement tuning is covered in more detail in Chapter 15, "Performance Coding Guidelines."

TKPROF can help identify the problematic SQL statements that require further tuning. Queries for which the results do not change for the duration of the report should have their results cached. You can use Before Report Trigger to cache those values instead of performing unnecessary joins in the main SQL or calling APIs for iteration of each record. Caching can be achieved by using session variables in PL/SQL Package Specification of Program Units. Alternatively, the placeholder columns can be used for maintaining the cache.

You should avoid creating extremely large and complex SQL Statements because it will take a significant amount of time to parse them. At the same time, usage of formula columns within repeating frames must be avoided in the report frames that produce a large number of rows. Using lexical parameters can also prevent the creation of multiple UNION clauses and/or OR conditions, thereby reducing the parsing overhead.

Summary

Oracle Reports have been the reporting tool of choice in E-Business Suite for many years. Recently, however, it has been progressively replaced by the BI Publisher tool. Although you can still find Oracle Reports in R12, it is clear that Oracle's preference is to use BI Publisher rather than Oracle Reports to develop new reports. For that reason, when creating new custom reports, Oracle Applications developers should consider using the BI Publisher tool rather than Oracle Reports in both Oracle Applications R11i and R12.

We suggest that Oracle Applications developers use Oracle Reports only to modify and maintain the existing reports that have already been designed with the Oracle Reports Developer tool. In this chapter, we provided an example of how to modify and customize the standard report delivered by Oracle product team.

CHAPTER 8

BI Publisher in Oracle Applications

BI Publisher was introduced in E-Business Suite 11i (release 11.5.10). When it was the first released, it was called XML Publisher, so references to either BI Publisher or XML Publisher refer to the same software. BI Publisher offers greater flexibility and functionality over the Oracle Reports tool, which was the traditional reporting tool in Oracle Applications for many years. In R12, BI Publisher is the reporting tool of choice.

Many developers who are familiar with the Oracle Reports tool but not BI Publisher will find it easy to make comparisons between Oracle Reports and BI Publisher features, and for that reason we'll start this chapter by comparing the two tools.

Comparison Between BI Publisher and Oracle Reports

In Oracle Reports, a single executable RDF file contains the data source, layout, business logic, and the language-specific prompts. However, BI Publisher separates these components into different layers. Following are some of the key limitations of Oracle Reports that are overcome by BI Publisher:

- **Multiple layouts** If you wish to publish the data from a report in more than one format—for example, in both an Excel and HTML layout—then multiple RDF files have to be prepared. If any bug fixes are required, fixes will have to be applied to both RDF files.
- **Multiple language** Global implementations for a large organization usually require the same report to be developed in multiple languages. In case of Oracle Reports, developers will have to create different copies of the same RDF files and place them in the <application top>/reports/<language> directory. In case of any bug fixes to data or any changes to layout, all the copies of reports have to be amended.
- **Trivial tasks** Even trivial tasks like changing the prompt or minor changes to the layout require a developer in Oracle Reports. Using BI Publisher, these tasks can be implemented by trained support staff or business analysts.
- **Distribution** The distribution capabilities in the Oracle Reports tool within E-Business Suite are very restrictive. To distribute the output of Oracle Reports, many companies implementing E-Business Suite have to purchase third-party products or even build their own in-house reports distribution framework. With BI Publisher, a mechanism named *bursting* can automate distribution of the reports using industry standard delivery protocols.

- **Securing the output** When distributing the output of Oracle Reports in E-Business Suite, it is not possible to secure the output using a password. BI Publisher facilitates password protection of the documents.

Due to the previously listed limitations, the cost of customization and maintenance is very high for Oracle Reports in multilanguage implementations. In the case of BI Publisher, the data layer, presentation layer, and the translation layer are separate. Additionally, BI Publisher is based on open standards and thus overcomes many of the limitations of Oracle Reports. In addressing some of the limitations of Oracle Reports and adopting open standards, Oracle has allowed implementations to potentially reduce the overall cost of build, customization, and ongoing maintenance of reports.

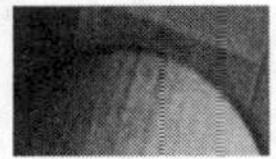

NOTE
Oracle Reports is still used in E-Business Suite because many of the reports delivered by Oracle E-Business Suite in the past were developed using Oracle Reports.

BI Publisher: Introduction and Example

BI Publisher software is a J2EE application that can be deployed to any J2EE container. Data input to BI Publisher reports is XML and the layout of BI Publisher reports are internally converted into XSL-FO, which is a W3C standard. The outputs generated by the application are as per industry standards such as PDF, RTF, and HTML. The delivery protocols are industry standards as well—for example, Internet Printing Protocol (IPP), WebDAV, FTP, and so on.

BI Publisher separates data, layout, and translation into three distinct layers. A mandatory ingredient for running a report in BI Publisher is XML data. Given that this data must always be in XML format, it is not relevant how the XML data is generated.

Therefore, in E-Business Suite, a BI Publisher report can be developed based on any data source that can generate XML—for example, a database SQL query returning XML, Oracle Reports resulting in XML, PL/SQL that generates XML, a Java program that can write XML, and so on.

The presentation layer that is responsible for generating the layout uses a template file. This BI Publisher template file can be created using any of the desktop tools such as MS Word, Excel, or Acrobat Reader. When creating BI Publisher templates using MS Word, all the commonly used MS Word features such as tables, forms, header, footers, and so on can be used. Additionally, it is possible to write conditional formatting logic within the BI Publisher template itself. In addition to this, special fonts can be embedded into the template to support barcodes in the final output.

BI Publisher Example Using an XML File

In this section, you will see step-by-step instructions that illustrate how the BI Publisher template can be built to display the contents of XML data. For this exercise, you will be required to install BI Publisher plug-in software for Microsoft Word, and you must have Microsoft Word 2000. The BI Publisher desktop can be downloaded from Metalink using patch 5887917, or version 10.1.3.x or version 5.6.x can be downloaded from the Oracle website at www.oracle.com/technology/software/products/publishing/index.html. Templates developed using both versions can be used in E-Business Suite.

Once the software has been downloaded and installed, you will find an Oracle BI Publisher menu entry in Microsoft Word at the very end of the menu list that simplifies the creation of rich text format (RTF) templates. Within the Oracle BI Publisher menu, you will find options to create data fields, tables, charts, and so on using the wizards. These wizards are very useful for quick development of the report. Data fields are fields that you can create in MS Word that can be linked to XML elements in the data source. It is also possible to create and manipulate variable values within these fields. However, to fully understand the fundamentals of BI Publisher, it is important for developers to build some sample reports without using any wizards. Taking this manual approach for developing your first report helps you understand some of the "behind the scenes" syntaxes that can get masked when using wizards. This knowledge is very useful when it comes to customizations of complex layouts for existing reports. Therefore, for building this sample exercise, none of the Oracle BI Publisher wizards will be used.

You will follow these steps to complete the exercise:

1. **Prepare XML data** Create an XML file with a customer and its invoice listing using Notepad or an equivalent tool.
2. **Load the XML file** Load the XML data file. The file can be uploaded using the Oracle BI Publisher menu path Data | Load XML Data.
3. **Develop the template** Use the BI Publisher syntax to loop through the records and reference data from the XML file. You will also display running totals.
4. **Save the file** Save the file with an .rtf extension.
5. **View the output** Use the preview feature of BI Publisher plug-in to view the final output that BI Publisher report will produce.

In this example, the structure of the XML file used will be a list of customers, with the list of invoices nested within the customer group. The name of the repeating customer group is G_CUSTOMER_LIST, and the name of the nested repeating invoice group is G_INVOICE_LIST. Effectively, this is a master/detail relation between the customers and their invoices. Save the XML file as shown in the following code into a flat file named CustomerList.xml anywhere on your desktop.

```
<CUSTOMER_REPORT>
          <REPORT>
              <COMPANY>FocusThread Limited</COMPANY>
              <REPORT_TITLE>Customer - Invoice Listing</REPORT_TITLE>
              <COMPANY_SITE>http://focusthread.com</COMPANY_SITE>
          </REPORT>
          <G_CUSTOMER_LIST>
              <CUSTOMER_NAME>Acme</CUSTOMER_NAME>
              <G_INVOICE_LIST>
              <INV_DESCR>Anti Virus Software</INV_DESCR>
              <INV_AMT>80</INV_AMT>
              </G_INVOICE_LIST>
          </G_CUSTOMER_LIST>
          <G_CUSTOMER_LIST>
              <CUSTOMER_NAME>Brompac</CUSTOMER_NAME>
              <G_INVOICE_LIST>
                <INV_DESCR>Servers</INV_DESCR>
                <INV_AMT>3000</INV_AMT>
              </G_INVOICE_LIST>
              <G_INVOICE_LIST>
                <INV_DESCR>Keyboard</INV_DESCR>
                <INV_AMT>20</INV_AMT>
              </G_INVOICE_LIST>
          </G_CUSTOMER_LIST>
</CUSTOMER_REPORT>
```

Once the XML file has been saved, create a new RTF file using Microsoft Word. Then click the Oracle BI Publisher menu in MS Word, select Data | Load Sample Data, and browse to select the file CustomerList.xml. You will get a message: "Data Loaded Successfully." Click OK to proceed.

To display the output as shown in Figure 8-1, we will require two "for loops." The first loop is for iterating over all the customer entries and the second loop is to iterate through the list of invoices for each customer. The tabular region listing the invoices will be within the Customer Loop. The inner loop will begin inside the table to display each invoice record.

Table 8-1 indicates how this template is built step by step. Figure 8-2 shows how the template will appear after the steps of Table 8-1 have been implemented in the RTF, which will be stored as XXCUSINV.rtf on your desktop.

Once you build XXCUSINV.rtf, it will look exactly the same as Figure 8-2. Click the Oracle BI Publisher menu within MS Word and select Validate Template. Ensure that there are no errors reported when the template is validated. To see the

Step	Implementation Step
Loop through customers	Create a loop using the syntax <?for-each: G_CUSTOMER_LIST?>.
Display customer name	Value is displayed using the syntax <?CUSTOMER_NAME?>.
Initialize variable RtotalVar	This variable tracks the running total of INV_AMT for each customer. The syntax is <?xdoxslt:set_variable($_XDOCTX,'RtotalVar',0)?>.
Create table in MS Word	Create a table with two rows. Enter column headings in first row.
Loop through invoices	In the first column of the second row in the MS Word table, create a new loop for iterating over invoices within the customer loop. Use the syntax <?for-each: G_INVOICE_LIST?>.
Display invoice description	Value is displayed using the syntax <?INV_DESCR?>. This value is displayed within the invoice loop, in the first column.
Display invoice amount	Value is displayed using the syntax <?INV_AMT?> in the second column.
Increment running total	Get the current value of the RtotalVar variable and add to it the INV_AMT of current record. The syntax is <?xdoxslt:set_variable($_XDOCTX, 'RtotalVar',xdoxslt: get_variable($_XDOCTX,'RtotalVar')+INV_AMT)?>.
Declare variable to hold page total	Add this syntax to the field INV_AMT, which you need to print the page totals: <?add-page-total:xxPageTotalField;'INV_AMT'?>.
Display running total	Use the syntax <?xdoxslt:get_variable($_XDOCTX,'RtotalVar')?> to display the running total. This retrieves the value of variable RtotalVar.
Finish loop for invoices	After displaying the running total for the invoice, close the nested invoice loop using the syntax <?end for-each?>.
Finish loop for customers	Close the outer loop for customers using the syntax <?end for-each?>. This is done outside the table.
Show page total	Show the page total using the syntax <?show-page-total: xxPageTotalField?>.
Create inline template	Instead of placing form fields in the header/footer, create a nested template anywhere in the RTF using the syntax <?template:xxCompanyHeader?>place contents here<?end template?>. Then reference that template by calling <?call: xxCompanyHeader?> from the header or the footer of MS Word.

TABLE 8-1. *Steps for Building the Template for Layout as per Figure 8-1*

Company: FocusThread Limited
Report Name: Customer – Invoice Listing
Company URL: http://focusthread.com

Customer Name: Acme

Invoice Item	Invoice Amount	Customer Running Total
Anti Virus Software	80	80

Customer Name: Brompac

Invoice Item	Invoice Amount	Customer Running Total
Servers	3000	3000
Keyboard	20	3020

FIGURE 8-1. *Output of sample BI Publisher report using data in CustomerList.xml*

output of this template, click Oracle BI Publisher and select Preview | PDF, as shown in Figure 8-3. This will display the output in PDF format, which will resemble the report output shown in Figure 8-1. We will use the very same RTF template when developing the BI Publisher report in E-Business Suite in the subsequent sections of this chapter.

<?call:CompanyHeader?>

<?for-each: G_CUSTOMER_LIST?>
Customer Name: <?CUSTOMER_NAME?> <?xdoxslt:set_variable($_XDOCTX,'RtotalVar',0)?>

Invoice Item	Invoice Amount	Customer Running Total
<?for-each: G_INVOICE_LIST?> <?INV_DESCR?>	<?INV_AMT?> <?xdoxslt:set_variable($_XDOCTX, 'RtotalVar',xdoxslt:get_variable($_XDOCTX, 'RtotalVar')+INV_AMT)?> <?add-page-total:xxPageTotalField; 'INV_AMT'?>	<?xdoxslt:get_variable($_XDOCTX, 'RtotalVar')?> <?end for-each?>

<?end for-each?> Page Total: <?show-page-total:xxPageTotalField?>

<?template:CompanyHeader?>
Company: <?COMPANY?>
ReportName: <?REPORT_TITLE?>
Company URL: <?COMPANY_SITE?>
<?end template?>

FIGURE 8-2. *Template used in the example to display customers and their invoices*

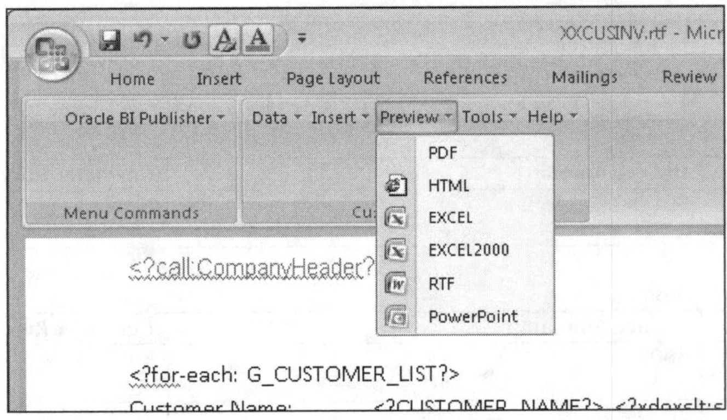

FIGURE 8-3. *View the output of the RTF layout in PDF format.*

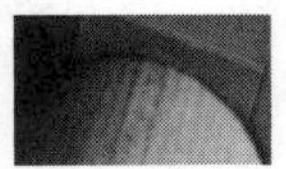

NOTE
The RTF template is created using MS Word tool. Therefore keywords "RTF Template" and "MS Word Template" are used interchangeably.

After you develop the RTF template as just shown, you will notice that even though the RTF layout produces the desired output, it is not very user-friendly, as it contains the syntax for referencing XML elements and embedding the XML tags into the RTF template can make the RTF template look cluttered. For this reason, Oracle also provides an option to create fields within the RTF template. These fields can then be attached to the code snippet using the Advanced property, as shown in Figure 8-4.

For example, the Oracle BI Publisher desktop wizard can automatically create a table layout in the RTF template that has directives for "begin for loop" and "end for loop." To try this, take a copy of XXCUSINV.rtf and rename it XXCUSINV01.rtf. Move the cursor to just above the sentence "<?template:xxCompanyHeader?>". Using the Oracle BI Publisher menu, click Insert | Table From and drag G_INVOICE_LIST from data source to Template and select Drop All Nodes. Click OK. You will notice that a table has been created in the RTF template by the wizard. This table has two rows, and the second row contains a field titled F.

As shown in Figure 8-4, right-click the F field and select BI Publisher properties. In the Advanced tab, you will find the code "<?for-each:G_INVOICE_LIST?>". This is exactly the same code that you write when you build the RTF template manually.

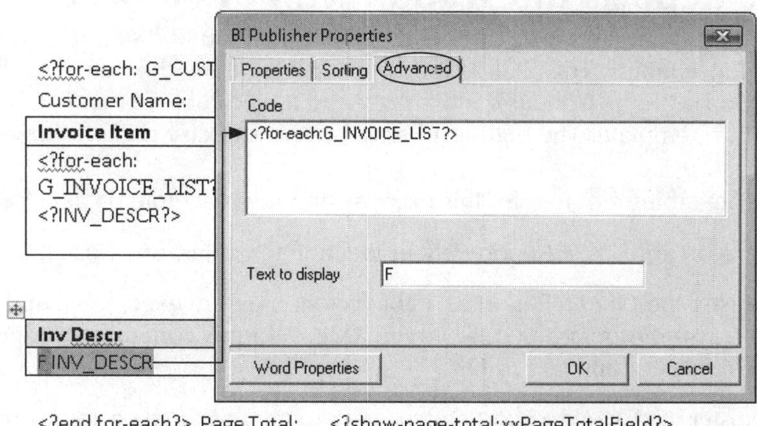

FIGURE 8-4. *Field property where code snippets can be embedded*

In other words, you can write code in BI Publisher either by typing the code snippet directly into MS Word Template or by writing the code in the Advanced Code property of the fields. The end result is the same whether you write the logic inside the field property or directly into the MS Word template.

In the Oracle BI Publisher desktop software, you can click Oracle BI Publisher | Tools | Options | Build and enable the Hidden check box. This hides any fields created using the wizard in the RTF template. Developers may enable the Hidden property for building some components in the layout. Therefore, the best way to browse all the fields in a template is to select Oracle BI Publisher | Tools | Field Browser. This will show all the fields within the template alongside the supporting code snippets.

After you understand these concepts, we recommend that you read the Oracle BI Publisher developer guide that comes along with the BI Publisher desktop software. In the subsequent sections of this chapter, we will carry forward the template XXCUSINV.rtf that we built and use it for integrating with Oracle E-Business Suite.

Integration of BI Publisher with E-Business Suite

As you have learned, it is possible to run a report using the BI Publisher tool that displays the data from an XML file. In E-Business Suite, you can use various approaches to generate the XML file. You will see different techniques in which XML data can be generated and then integrated with XXCUSINV.rtf in E-Business Suite.

Oracle Reports Integration with BI Publisher

In this exercise, you will create a set of tables and then build a simple Oracle Report that reads those tables. This will be followed by integrating the output of that Oracle Report with the Concurrent Manager and the BI Publisher engine using the XXCUSINV.rtf template. The high-level steps for this exercise are as follows:

1. Create tables required for this exercise and insert sample data.
2. Develop an Oracle Report data model to fetch data from those tables.
3. Register the Oracle Report as a concurrent program executable and concurrent program of output type XML. Add this concurrent program to the request group.
4. Register the Oracle Report concurrent program as the data source (called data definition) with the BI Publisher.
5. Register the template XXCUSINV.rtf in BI Publisher Template Manager, attaching it to the data source. (This data source happens to be the Oracle Report concurrent program.)
6. Run the concurrent program to test the output.

For this exercise, a Release 12 VISION instance will be used for deployment. Therefore, Reports Designer version 10g will be used. However, this exercise is equally applicable on a Release 11.5.10 instance. The custom application used for this exercise is called Custom Development, with its corresponding top directory being $XXCUST_TOP.

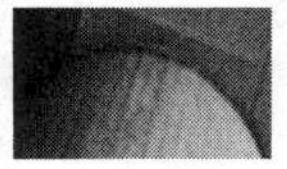

NOTE
The tables for this exercise are being created in the apps schema; however, in real-life projects, these must be created in custom schemas with appropriate synonyms in the apps schema.

Create the tables and sample data in those tables using the following scripts:

```
create table xx_customers
(  customer_id integer ,customer_name varchar2(100) ) ;
create table xx_cust_invoices
(  customer_id integer ,inv_descr varchar2(100) ,inv_amt number ) ;
INSERT INTO xx_customers ( customer_id, customer_name) VALUES
(1000,'Acme') ;
INSERT INTO xx_customers ( customer_id, customer_name) VALUES
(1001,'Brompac') ;
```

```
INSERT INTO xx_cust_invoices ( customer_id, inv_descr, inv_amt ) VALUES
(1000,'Anti Virus Software','80' ) ;
INSERT INTO xx_cust_invoices ( customer_id, inv_descr, inv_amt ) VALUES
(1001,'Servers','3000' ) ;
INSERT INTO xx_cust_invoices ( customer_id, inv_descr, inv_amt ) VALUES
(1001,'Keyboard','20' ) ;
commit;
```

Next, open the Reports Builder tool and connect it to database. Click File | New Report and select the option to build a new report manually. This will open the Data Model editor. Click the SQL Query icon in the left-hand tool palette, and then click anywhere on the Data Model window. Enter a query that selects some static values from dual, as shown here:

```
select 'FocusThread Limited' as COMPANY ,'Customer Invoice Listing' as
REPORT_TITLE ,'http://focusthread.com'  as COMPANY_SITE from dual
```

Change its group name to G_COMPANY, then click SQL Query in the tool palette again, and enter the following SQL statement in the Query window:

```
select * from xx_customers
```

Click OK. This will create a group named G_CUSTOMER_ID. Change this group name from G_CUSTOMER_ID to G_CUSTOMER_LIST by using the group property palette. Click the SQL Query icon again and then click the Data Model window to create the third query. In the SQL Query window, enter the following:

```
select * from xx_cust_invoices
```

Change the name of the group that is created to G_INVOICE_LIST. Now click the Data Link icon in the tool palette of the Data model, and then drag the link from CUSTOMER_ID in Query2 to CUSTOMER_ID (labeled CUSTOMER_ID1) in Query3. The end result will be a Data model as shown in Figure 8-5. Save the report as XXCUSINV.rdf on your desktop.

In this case, you have not created a layout for this report. The sole purpose of this report is to produce XML output that can be fed to the BI Publisher template XXCUSINV.rtf. Therefore, XXCUSINV.rdf serves the purpose of a data source, and a layout is not required to be developed for this report. Also, the reason you renamed the groups was to ensure that their names matched the XML nodes in the static XML you used building XXCUSINV.rtf.

Next, log in to E-Business Suite and navigate to the Application Developer responsibility. Click Concurrent | Executable. Create a new executable with its name, short name, and execution file name being XXCUSINV. Application will be the name of your custom application, which in this case is Custom Development; the Execution Method for this concurrent program executable will be Oracle Reports.

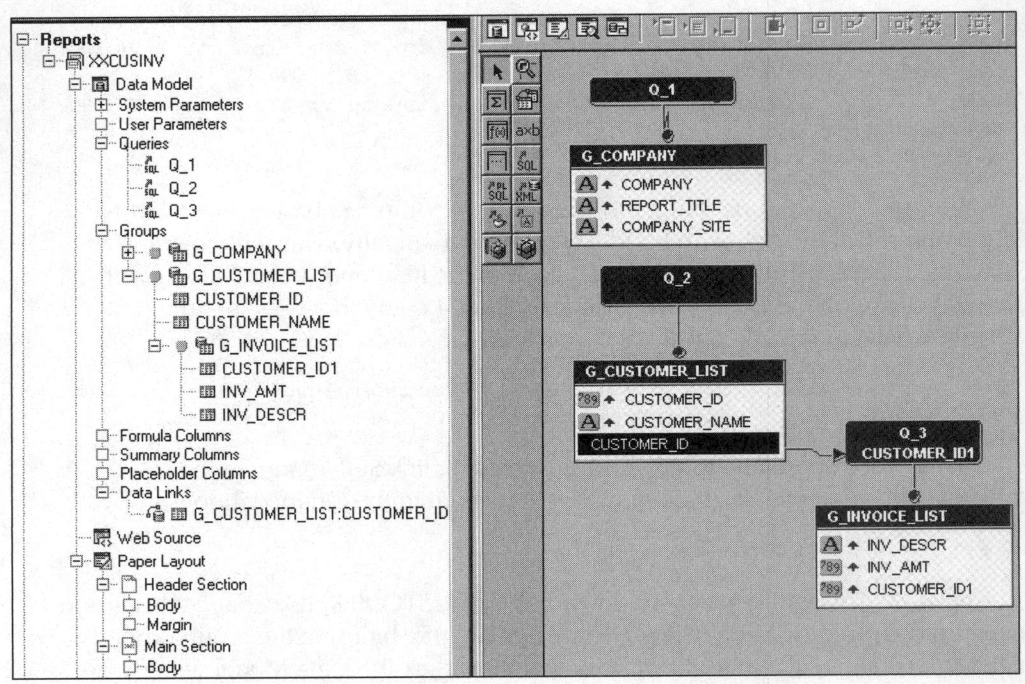

FIGURE 8-5. *Data model of the query in Reports Builder*

After creating the executable, create a concurrent program named XX Customer Invoice Listing, with a short name and executable name of XXCUSINV. Attach the Custom Development application to this program. Assign any of the standard styles such as landscape or A4 because the concurrent program style is irrelevant given that layout style is generated by the BI Publisher template. Change the output format to XML, and save the concurrent program definition. Add this concurrent program to the System Administrator Reports request group by navigating to the System Administrator responsibility: Security | Responsibility | Request. If you do not have access to System Administrator, then you may attach the concurrent program to another request group, assuming you have access to the corresponding responsibility.

Transfer the file XXCUSINV.rdf in binary mode from your desktop to the Custom Top directory, which as per the convention in this book is $XXCUST_TOP/reports/US.

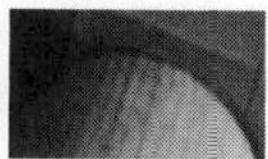

NOTE
In Oracle Report XXCUSINV.rdf, we have merely created a Data model with three SQL Statements and linked two of those queries together for a master detail relationship. We did not create a layout in the Oracle Report because the Oracle Report engine will produce XML data output without a layout within the report definition. This is an important point to note, as this explains why the format triggers within Oracle Reports are not executed when reports are converted from normal Oracle Report to XML output format.

Next, you need to register the Oracle Reports concurrent program as a data definition so the report output will become available to the BI Publisher engine at runtime. To register a data definition, navigate to the XML Publisher Administrator responsibility, select the Data Definitions menu, and click the Create Data Definition button. Create a new data definition with any meaningful name—for example, XX Customer Invoice Listing Data Def. Ensure that the data definition code matches the concurrent program short name, as this allows the Concurrent Manager to provide the list of templates that are available for a concurrent program at the time of submission. Click Apply.

After creating the data definition, you can register the template XXCUSINV.rtf. When you create a template, you assign it to a data definition and upload your template layout file. At initial creation, you upload one template file for a specific language and territory combination. This file then becomes the default template file for that data definition. Click the Templates tab and then click the Create Template button. Enter any user-friendly name for the template—for example, XX Customer Invoice Listing Template. Assign a meaningful value to the template code, for example, XXCUSINVTEMPLATE, and enter your custom application name in the Application field. In this example, the application name is Custom Development. Select the RTF value from the drop-down list for the field labeled Type. In the Data Definition field, enter the definition that we created, i.e. "XX Customer Invoice Listing Data Def". In the Template File field, click Browse to select XXCUSINV.rtf from your desktop. Enter English in the Language field and click Apply.

Navigate to System Administrator or the relevant responsibility, click Concurrent Requests, and then click Submit a New Request. Run the program XX Customer Invoice Listing. You will be able to see the generated PDF output is an exact replica of the output that you saw when running the report against static XML data. As evident from this process, the developers can unit test the layout of their reports using the preview section of the Oracle BI Publisher Desktop software.

NOTE
When registering templates, it is also possible to flag them as subtemplates, so that they can be referenced by any other template. A company logo and company address details are most common use cases for registering subtemplates.

Using a Data Template with BI Publisher

As seen in the previous example, the only reason Oracle Reports was used with BI Publisher was to generate XML output. In this section, instead of using Oracle Reports, we will use something known as a data template for creating the XML. A data template is nothing but an XML file that contains a list of SQL Statements that must be executed to produce the desired output. The data template itself is an XML file, which can very easily be created using Notepad.

In this case, there is no need to register a new concurrent program executable. When using data templates, you should use a seeded concurrent program executable named XDODTEXE, which is a Java concurrent program. In this example, you will build exactly the same report you built using a static XML File and Oracle Report. Therefore, you will use the same RTF template: XXCUSINV.rtf.

The steps for implementing this example are as follows:

1. **Prepare data template** Create a data template file and save it as XXCUSINV_DT.xml. This file can be created in Notepad. The details of building a data template are discussed in the latter part of this example, when we will create a file named XXCUSINV_DT.xml.

2. **Define data definition** Log in to the XML Publisher Administrator responsibility and create a new data definition with any user-friendly name. Enter a name to the code of this data definition. In this example, the data definition code will be XXCUSINV_DATA_DEF. As soon as the data definition is created, you will see an option to upload the data template. Click the Add File button beside the prompt data template. Click Browse and select XXCUSINV_DT.xml from your desktop. Click Apply.

3. **Create template** Again, using the XML Publisher Administrator responsibility, create a template of type RTF. Give it a user-friendly name and attach to it the data definition created in previous step. Browse to select the file XXCUSINV.rtf in the Template File section with appropriate language, which in this case is English.

4. **Create concurrent program** Create a concurrent program with any user-friendly name—for example, XX Customer Invoice Listing Data Def. The short name of this concurrent program must be exactly the same as the "code" in Data Definition, which in this example is XXCUSINV_DATA_DEF. The executable attached to this concurrent program will be XDODTEXE. The output format of this concurrent program must be set to XML. Add a parameter for the customer ID with token P_CUSTOMER_ID. Add this concurrent program to a request group.

After having implemented these steps, you will be able to run the concurrent program that will execute the corresponding data template attached to the data definition. Figure 8-6 explains the sequence of events that take place when a user submits a concurrent program that references a data template. The output of this report will be exactly same as the output as you saw in the previous example with static XML and Oracle Reports.

When you submit the concurrent program from the Submit Request window, the user can click the Options buttons and ensure that appropriate layout template is being defaulted. In this example, you will have only one template attached to this concurrent program; therefore, the XXCUSINV.rtf layout will be defaulted.

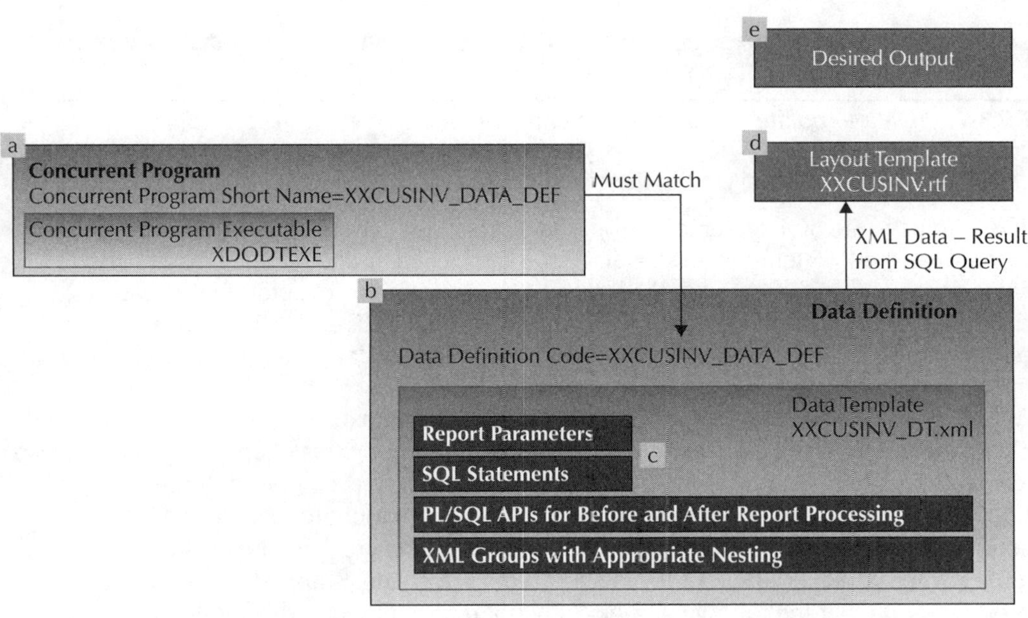

FIGURE 8-6. *Data template, data definition, layout template, and concurrent program*

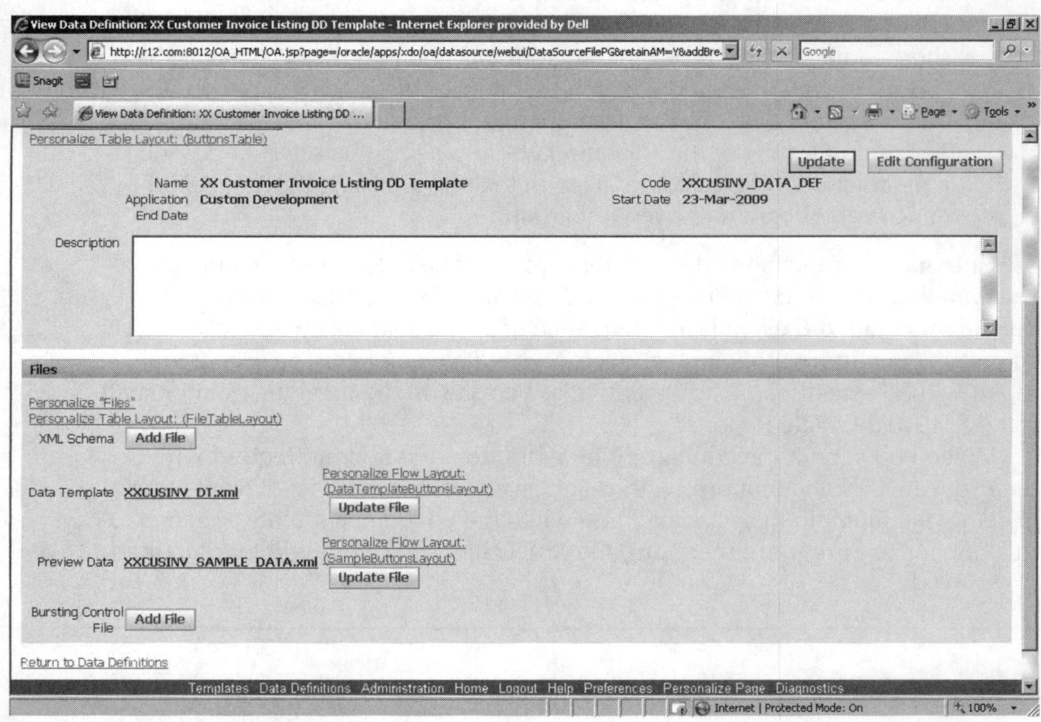

FIGURE 8-7. *Data template attached to the data definition*

The output of the SQL Statements from the data template (XXCUSINV_DT.xml) will be fed into the RTF template XXCUSINV.rtf. The RTF template remains exactly the same as the one you created in the very first example of this chapter. Figure 8-6 displays the link between the various components that deliver the BI Publisher report using a data template. Additionally, Figure 8-7 displays the screenshot of how a data template is attached to a data definition.

The data template used in this example is as shown next. We will discuss each component within this data template. At the time of writing this chapter, the data template Designer Tool was not publicly available, so we used one of the seeded Oracle data templates as a reference. Run this SQL statement to extract one of the seeded data templates from the database. The data templates are always stored in a table named XDO_LOBS. R12 has over 150 data templates shipped as a part of the product. Note that the following query may not return any records in Release 11i.

```
SELECT file_data FROM xdo_lobs WHERE lob_type = 'DATA_TEMPLATE'
and file_name like 'ARLCRPT.xml'
```

Open and save the contents of file_data to your desktop as ARLCRPT.xml. Rename ARLCRPT.xml to XXCUSINV_DT.xml and modify it to ensure that the contents of the new data template are as shown next in XML:

```
<?xml version = '1.0' encoding = 'UTF-8'?>
<!-- $Header: XXCUSINV_DT.xml 120.3 2006/04/20 21:20:14 kmaheswa noship
$ -->
<dataTemplate name="XXCUSINV_DT" defaultPackage="XX_CUS_INV_PKG" ver-
sion="1.0">
<parameters>
   <parameter name="P_CUSTOMER_ID" dataType="character"/>
</parameters>
<dataQuery>
   <sqlStatement name="Q_PARAMS">
      <![CDATA[select 'FocusThread Limited  as COMPANY
             ,'Customer Invoice Listing' as REPORT_TITLE
            ,'http://focusthread.com'  as COMPANY_SITE from dual]]>
   </sqlStatement>
   <sqlStatement name="Q_HEADERS">
      <![CDATA[select CUSTOMER_ID, CUSTOMER_NAME from
                  xx_customers xxcus WHERE &P_QUERY_WHERE]]>
   </sqlStatement>
   <sqlStatement name="Q_LINES">
      <![CDATA[SELECT INV_DESCR, INV_AMT FROM xx_cust_invoices xxinv
              where xxinv.customer_id=:CUSTOMER_ID]]>
   </sqlStatement>
</dataQuery>
<dataTrigger name="beforeReport" source="XX_CUS_INV_PKG.before_report"/>
<dataStructure>
   <group name ="G_COMPANY"  source="Q_PARAMS">
      <element name="COMPANY" value="COMPANY"/>
      <element name="REPORT_TITLE" value="REPORT_TITLE"/>
      <element name="COMPANY_SITE" value="COMPANY_SITE"/>
   </group>
   <group name ="G_CUSTOMER_LIST"  source="Q_HEADERS">
      <element name="CUSTOMER_ID" value="CUSTOMER_ID"/>
      <element name="CUSTOMER_NAME" value="CUSTOMER_NAME"/>
          <group name ="G_INVOICE_LIST"  source="Q_LINES">
              <element name="INV_DESCR" value="INV_DESCR"/>
              <element name="INV_AMT" value="INV_AMT"/>
          </group>
   </group>
</dataStructure>
</dataTemplate>
```

To understand this data template, we need to study each component one by one. The very first element, dataTemplate, indicates the name of the template. This element can be attached to a default PL/SQL package, which in this case is XX_CUS_INV_PKG.

Within the parameters section, it is possible to enlist all the parameters used by the BI Publisher report. In this example, we have created a parameter token named P_CUSTOMER_ID for the customer ID. When P_CUSTOMER_ID is passed a NULL value via a concurrent program, then the requirement is that the BI Publisher report displays all the customers and their invoices from table xx_customers and xx_cust_invoices.

A PL/SQL package variable of exactly the same name, p_customer_id, should be created within the default package. This PL/SQL package variable will be automatically assigned a value by the concurrent program executable XDODTEXE as soon as the concurrent program runs. Therefore, whatever value is passed to the customer ID parameter in the concurrent program gets assigned to variable XX_CUS_INV_PKG .P_CUSTOMER_ID.

The dataQuery element contains all the SQL Statements that can be used by this data template. Every SQL Statement is listed within the sqlStatement node. Each SQL Statement is tagged by a name. In this example, the names of the SQL queries are Q_PARAMS, Q_HEADERS, and Q_LINES. Note that the SQL Statements listed in the data template are not executed in the sequence that they are listed. In fact, SQL Statements get executed only if they are attached to a group.

The dataTrigger element contains the triggers that can be executed just before and after the report processing. This example uses the before report trigger that invokes the PL/SQL API named XX_CUS_INV_PKG.before_report. Within this API, you read the value of parameter P_CUSTOMER_ID and build the appropriate WHERE clause. The WHERE clause is then assigned to another PL/SQL package variable named P_QUERY_WHERE. The name of this variable must match the lexical parameter used in the SQL Statement of the data template. Therefore, the SQL Statement for Q_HEADERS contains a lexical parameter &P_QUERY_WHERE in its WHERE clause, which derives its value from the variable XX_CUS_INV_PKG.P_CUSTOMER_ID.

Both beforeReport and afterReport triggers execute PL/SQL functions that return True or False. The beforeReport trigger should be placed in a data template before the <dataStructure> section and the afterReport trigger after the <dataStructure> section. A beforeReport trigger executes before the dataQuery section is executed. The beforeReport and afterReport triggers can also be passed parameters using the following notation:

```
<dataTrigger name="beforeReport"
source="xx_pkg.my_before_report_function(:ParameterName)"/>
```

The dataStructure element contains the list of groups within the data template. Each group references a query defined within the dataQuery section of the data template. The groups can be nested within one another so that the child group can reference the value of a parent cursor using a bind variable. In this example, G_INVOICE_LIST is nested within G_CUSTOMER_LIST. The query attached to G_INVOICE_LIST [Q_LINES] references CUSTOMER_ID of G_CUSTOMER_LIST [Q_HEADERS] using the bind variable notation: CUSTOMER_ID. The nesting of groups effectively creates a Master Detail relationship between the queries. The element section within each group creates the XML alias for columns in SQL Statements. It is also possible to create summary columns within the groups—for example, Sum, Average, Count, Maximum, and Minimum.

It is also possible to link queries using the <link> element in data templates. However, the bind variable approach is considered to be more performance efficient.

The supporting PL/SQL package specification and body can be created as shown next:

```
CREATE OR REPLACE PACKAGE XX_CUS_INV_PKG AS
   P_QUERY_WHERE                VARCHAR2(240);
   p_customer_id                 NUMBER(15);
   FUNCTION before_report RETURN BOOLEAN;
END XX_CUS_INV_PKG;
/

CREATE OR REPLACE PACKAGE BODY XX_CUS_INV_PKG AS
 FUNCTION before_report RETURN BOOLEAN IS
 BEGIN
   IF p_customer_id IS NOT NULL THEN
      p_query_where := '  xxcus.customer_id = :p_customer_id';
   ELSE
      p_query_where := '  1=1';
   END IF;
   RETURN TRUE;
 EXCEPTION
   WHEN OTHERS THEN
      RAISE;
 END before_report;
END XX_CUS_INV_PKG;
/
```

From the preceding example, it is clearly evident that the data template is very tightly integrated with Oracle's PL/SQL engine. The parameters are linked to PL/SQL session variables, whereas the data triggers are linked to PL/SQL functions. Once the data template has been prepared and attached to a data definition, run the concurrent program that is related to a layout template, which in turn is attached to the data template via the data definition. After running the concurrent process, to view the XML generated by the data template, select the desired request ID, click the Diagnostics button, and then click the View XML button. This will show to you the XML generated by the SQL Statements in the data template. This information is very useful for debugging any issues that you may face when developing BI Publisher reports with a data template.

Using BI Publisher with OA Framework

In previous examples, you have seen different ways of generating the XML data while using the same RTF layout template. In this example, you will generate a BI Publisher report using OA Framework. You must read the Chapter 9, "OA Framework: Concepts, Development and Extensions," before trying the steps in this example. In OA Framework, you do not need to use a data template or an Oracle Report to generate a BI Publisher report. Instead, the XML data is sourced from something known as view objects.

In this example, you will develop a very simple page with a button on it. When you click the Show BI Report button, the BI Publisher report will be displayed to the user on the screen. Behind the scenes, the following events will happen when the button is clicked:

1. **Trap button click event** The OA Framework page is attached to a controller class, and its method processFormRequest is executed when the button is clicked.

2. **Retrieve data** Inside the processFormRequest, you execute a query on a view object. A view object query retrieves the data from customer and invoice tables used in this example.

3. **Generate XML** In OA Framework, the view objects have a method named writeXML that can dump the entire data returned by their SQL Query into XML. Therefore, you invoke writeXML on the view object and its output is written to a byte output stream.

4. **Generate PDF output** The BI Publisher API named TemplateHelper .processTemplate is executed, to which the template name and result of writeXML() are passed as input parameters. The complete list of parameters passed to the BI Publisher API for this example is shown in Table 8-2.

5. **Display PDF output** The BI Publisher API returns a stream for PDF output, which is then redirected to the browser.

Figure 8-8 shows the end result of the exercise in this example.

BI Publisher API Parameter	Value Passed
AppsContext	In OA Framework, the application module has a method that returns a handle to the current database session; using this, you can return the AppsContext object.
Template	The short code of the template, which in this example will be XX_CUST_INV_TEMPLATE.
Template Application Short Name	The application short name, which in this example is CUSTOM, but in your case will be the relevant custom application short name on your instance.
Data Input Stream	The XML generated using ViewObject.writeXML() is converted into byte array input stream, which is passed as parameter to the TemplateHelper API.
Language and Territory	The language and the locale, which you can get from the current OA Framework session using oadbtransaction.getCountry and oadbtransaction .getUserLocale.
Data Output Stream	A new ByteArrayOutput stream, which you create; the template helper API writes the BI Publisher output contents (PDF in this case) into the ByteArrayOutput. The byte array received from TemplateHelper is written into the ServletResponse of the user's browser session. This makes it possible for the user to see the BI Publisher output.

TABLE 8-2. *Parameters Passed to the BI Publisher API*

The steps for building this example can be broken down into two parts. In the first part, we will show the steps for building the OA Framework page. Ensure that your development environment has been set up on JDeveloper. Transfer the xdo directory and its contents from $JAVA_TOP/oracle/apps on the server to myclasses. After the transfer is complete, you will have a directory named <JDEV_USER_HOME>/myclasses/oracle/apps/xdo on your desktop. The transfer of files with extension ".class" must be done in binary mode. XDO is the short name of the XML Publisher application. $JAVA_TOP/oracle/apps/xdo contains the BI Publisher API TemplateHelper.processTemplate. This API is used for generating the output for the BI Publisher report.

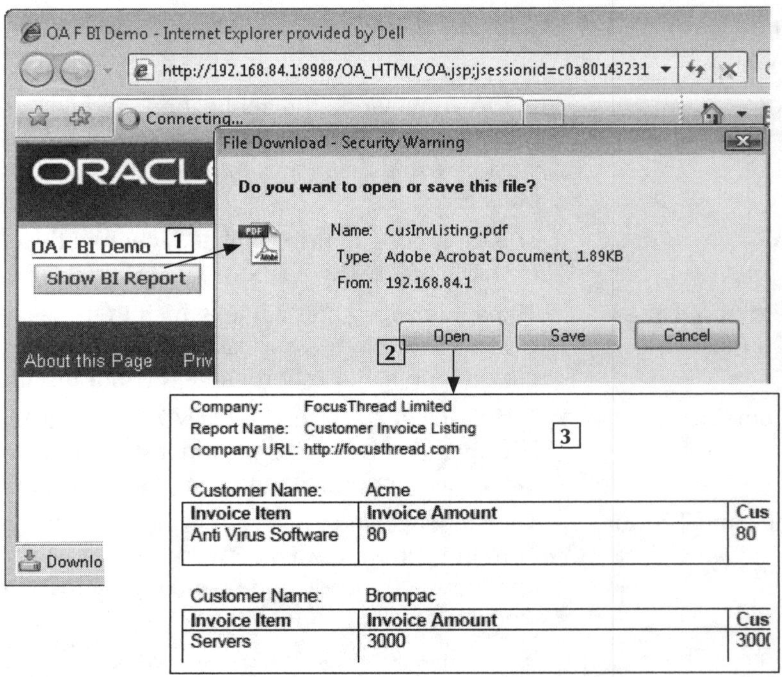

FIGURE 8-8. *OA Framework with a BI Publisher example*

Create a new OA Workspace and a new OA Project in JDeveloper. Select an appropriate value in the DBC (Database Connectivity) file. Enter appropriate values for username, password, application short name, and responsibility key and ensure that the user has access to the responsibility being entered. Right-click Application Sources and select New | ADF Business Components | Application Module. Create a new application module named OAFBIDemoAM in the package xxcust.oracle.apps.bi.server.OAFBIDemoAMImpl. Next, create three view objects in the same package, as shown in Table 8-3.

After the view objects have been created, you will notice that the attribute names of the view objects are named as CustomerName, InvDescr, InvAmt, and so on. The writeXML() method will create XML elements of exactly the same names as that of view object attributes. Therefore, you must rename these attribute names so they match their references in the RTF template that you developed earlier in this chapter. For example, the RTF template makes reference to "Customer Name" as CUSTOMER_NAME. Therefore, the CustomerName attribute in the view object xxCustomersVO must be renamed CUSTOMER_NAME. After renaming the

View Object Name	SQL
xxReportHeaderVO	Select 1 as DummyHeader, 'FocusThread Limited' as COMPANY, 'Customer Invoice Listing' as REPORT_TITLE, 'http://focusthread.com' as COMPANY_SITE from dual
xxCustomersVO	Select 1 as dummy_header, customer_id, customer_name from xx_customers
xxCustInvoicesVO	Select * from xx_cust_invoices

TABLE 8-3. *View Objects for This Example Exercise*

attributes, you will have attribute names in the view objects as xxReportHeaderVO (COMPANY, REPORT_TITLE, COMPANY_SITE), xxCustomersVO (CUSTOMER_ID, CUSTOMER_NAME), and xxCustInvoicesVO (INV_DESCR, INV_AMT). It is not necessary to rename the attributes that contain internal IDs as those are not being referenced in the RTF template.

After creating the view objects, you need to create view links. View links create relationships between the view objects. To generate the XML required for the report, the writeXML() method will execute the queries on all the child view objects until the point in time when it keeps finding further child view objects via view links. It is also possible to restrict the nesting level of view objects because writeXML() takes a parameter for the maximum number of levels for which child view objects are automatically queried. Right-click the xxcust.oracle.apps.bi.server package to create two view links as shown in Table 8-4.

Next we need to attach the view objects to the application module. Double-click the OAFBIDemoAM application module, and in the Data model section, drag all three view objects beneath the application module. The application module identifies these view object instances as xxReportHeaderVO1, xxCustInvoicesVO1,

View Link Name	Source Attribute	Destination Attribute	Source-Destination Cardinality
xxCusHeaderVL	xxReportHeaderVO. Dummyheader	xxCustomersVO. DummyHeader	1 To *
xxCusInvVL	xxCustomersVO. CUSTOMER_ID	xxCustInvoicesVO. CUSTOMER_ID	1 To *

TABLE 8-4. *View Links for This Example Exercise*

and xxCustomersVO1. These instance names can be changed, but leave them as is for this example. Once the relationship between the application module and view objects is in place, you can test the application module to see the XML that it will generate. Right-click the application module OAFBIDemoAM and select Test, then click Connect. Double-click the xxReportHeaderVO1 view object to query its data. Then select View | Data As XML as shown in Figure 8-9.

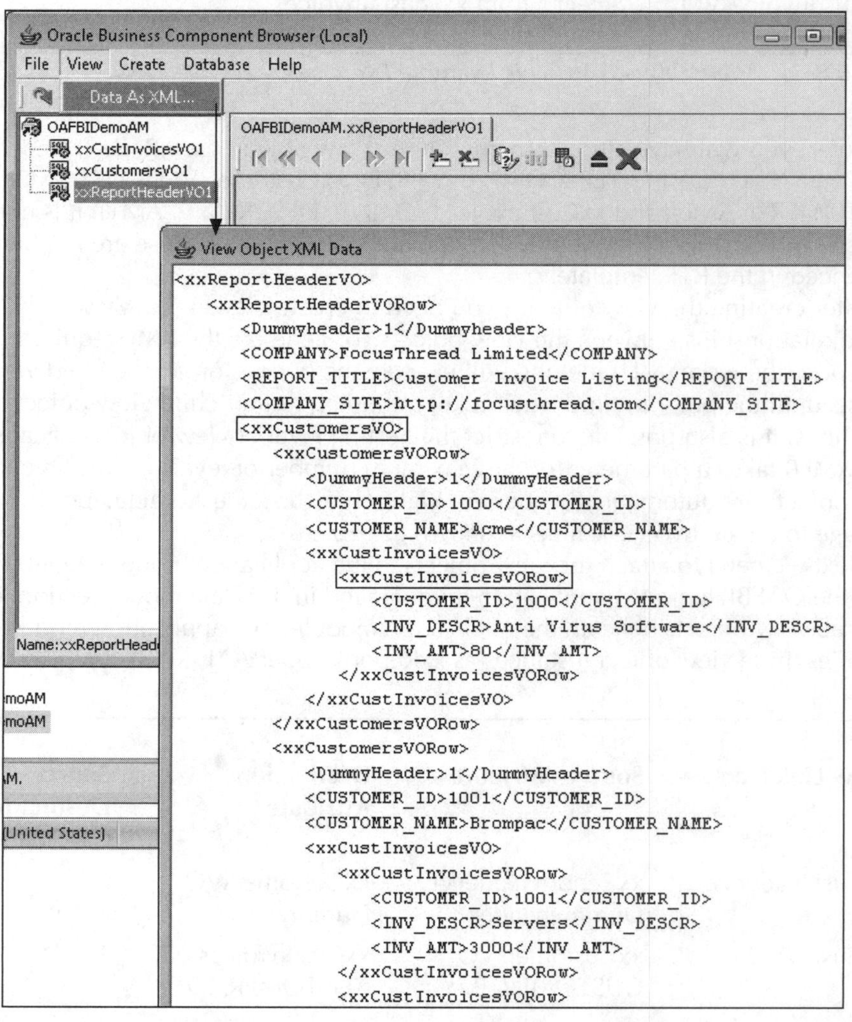

FIGURE 8-9. *Preview the XML that writeXML() method will generate.*

This will give you a preview of XML data generated via the writeXML() method. When you inspect this data, you will notice there is no repeating element named G_CUSTOMER_LIST or G_INVOICE_LIST. However, you made references to these elements in the RTF template when looping through the records in XML. Therefore, in the RTF template, when looping through the records, you have to replace G_CUSTOMER_LIST with xxCustomersVORow and replace G_INVOICE_LIST with xxCustInvoicesVORow. Save the new template as XXCUSINV_OAF.rtf.

Back in JDeveloper, create an xxCusInvDemoPG page within the package xxcust.oracle.apps.bi.oafdemo.webui. To do this, right-click the project and select the options New | OA Components | Page. In this example, you will create page xxCusInvDemoPG in the package /xxcust/oracle/apps/custom/oafdemo/webui. The element after /xxcust/oracle/apps must be a valid application short name. In this case, the application short name happens to be Custom. A default region named region1 was automatically created when the new OA Page was created. Now attach the application module OAFBIDemoAM to region1 and give this region a window and page title.

Right-click region1 to create a new controller named xxOAFBIDemoCO in the package xxcust.oracle.apps.custom.oafdemo.webui. Right-click region1 and select New:Item to create a new item. This will create an item named item1. Rename item1 to submitReport. Change the item style of submitReport to submitButton and change the prompt of this button to Show BI Report.

Next, you must register the data definition and template using the XML Publisher Administrator responsibility. Create a data definition named XX Customer Invoice OAF Data Definition and give an appropriate short name to that data template. Click the Create Template button to create a template with Name="XX Customer Invoice OAF Template", Application="Custom Development", and template code="XX_CUST_INV_TEMPLATE", and assign "XX Customer Invoice OAF Data Definition" to this template. Upload the modified XXCUSINV_OAF.rtf file against the template. Now you can write the program in the Controller class and run the page to produce the results as shown in Figure 8-8. The source code of the controller class is shown next:

```
package xxcust.oracle.apps.custom.oafdemo.webui;
import java.io.ByteArrayInputStream;
import java.io.ByteArrayOutputStream;
import javax.servlet.ServletOutputStream;
import javax.servlet.http.HttpServletResponse;
import oracle.apps.fnd.common.VersionInfo;
import oracle.apps.fnd.framework.OAApplicationModule;
import oracle.apps.fnd.framework.OAException;
import oracle.apps.fnd.framework.server.OADBTransactionImpl;
import oracle.apps.fnd.framework.webui.OAControllerImpl;
import oracle.apps.fnd.framework.webui.OAPageContext;
import oracle.apps.fnd.framework.webui.beans.OAWebBean;
import oracle.apps.xdo.oa.schema.server.TemplateHelper;
```

```
import oracle.cabo.ui.data.DataObject;
import oracle.xml.parser.v2.XMLNode;
import xxcust.oracle.apps.bi.server.OAFBIDemoAMImpl;
import xxcust.oracle.apps.bi.server.*;
import oracle.jbo.XMLInterface;
public class xxOAFBIDemoCO extends OAControllerImpl {
    public static final String RCS_ID = "$Header$";
    public static final boolean RCS_ID_RECORDED =
        VersionInfo.recordClassVersion(RCS_ID, "%packagename%");
public void processRequest(OAPageContext pageContext, OAWebBean
webBean)
    { super.processRequest(pageContext, webBean); }
public void processFormRequest(OAPageContext pageContext,
OAWebBean webBean) { super.processFormRequest(pageContext, webBean);
OAApplicationModule oaapplicationmodule =


pageContext.getApplicationModule(webBean);
DataObject dataobject =
pageContext.getNamedDataObject("_SessionParameters");
HttpServletResponse httpservletresponse =
(HttpServletResponse)dataobject.selectValue(null, "HttpServletRe-
sponse");
try {
ServletOutputStream servletoutputstream =
httpservletresponse.getOutputStream();String sFileDetails = (newString-
Builder())
.append("attachment;filename=CusInvListing.pdf").toString();
httpservletresponse.setHeader("Content-Disposition", sFileDetails);
httpservletresponse.setContentType("application/pdf");
byte abyte0[] = xxGetXMLByteArray(pageContext, webBean);
ByteArrayInputStream bytearrayinputstream =
new ByteArrayInputStream(abyte0);
pageContext.getApplicationModule(webBean).getOADBTransaction();
ByteArrayOutputStream bytearrayoutputstream = new ByteArrayOutput-
Stream();
TemplateHelper.processTemplate(((OADBTransactionImpl)pageContext
.getApplicationModule(webBean).getOADBTransaction()).getAppsContext(),
"CUSTOM", "XX_CUST_INV_TEMPLATE", ((OADBTransactionImpl)pageContext.
getApplicationModule(webBean)
.getOADBTransaction()).getUserLocale().getLanguage(),
((OADBTransactionImpl)
pageContext.getApplicationModule(webBean).getOADBTransaction())
.getUserLocale().getCountry(),bytearrayinputstream, TemplateHelper
.OUTPUT_TYPE_PDF, null, bytearrayoutputstream);

byte abyte1[] = bytearrayoutputstream.toByteArray();
```

```
httpservletresponse.setContentLength(abyte1.length);
servletoutputstream.write(abyte1, 0, abyte1.length);
servletoutputstream.flush();
servletoutputstream.close();
} catch (Exception exception) {
httpservletresponse.setContentType("text/html");
throw new OAException(exception.getMessage(), (byte)0); }
pageContext.setDocumentRendered(false);
} //End of processFormRequest

public byte[] xxGetXMLByteArray(
OAPageContext oapagecontext, OAWebBean oawebbean)
throws OAException
{
ByteArrayOutputStream bytearrayoutputstream = new
ByteArrayOutputStream();
try {
  OAFBIDemoAMImpl oaapplicationmodule =
        (OAFBIDemoAMImpl)oapagecontext.getApplicationModule(oawebbean);
  xxReportHeaderVOImpl xxvo = oaapplicationmodule.getxxReportHeaderVO1();
//You can set your where clauses on VO to filter Data
//by using vo.setWhereClause()
  xxvo.executeQuery();
  ((XMLNode)xxvo.writeXML
          (2, XMLInterface.XML_OPT_ALL_ROWS))
.print(bytearrayoutputstream);
    } catch (Exception exception)
   { throw new OAException(exception.getMessage(), (byte)0); }
  return bytearrayoutputstream.toByteArray();
}
}
```

Ideally, the operations on view objects are performed from the application module. However, for the convenience of demonstration, we have written the entire logic within the controller class. After you follow these steps, you will be able to run the OA Framework page and click the button to generate the BI Publisher report.

Converting Oracle Reports Output to BI Publisher

Prior to the introduction of BI Publisher, reports with complex layouts were always delivered in E-Business Suite using Oracle Reports. Besides the complex layout, these reports also have complex calculations within various formula columns. One example of such a report is the Invoice Print Selected Invoices report in Oracle Receivables. To convert any Oracle E-Business Suite Report to BI Publisher, implement the following steps. Using this methodology, the Oracle Report is retained because it becomes the source of the XML data. The following steps are the generic guidelines that can be applied across the board for integrating any existing Oracle Reports in E-Business Suite with BI Publisher.

1. **Identify and run concurrent program** Identify the concurrent program that is associated with the report that you wish to develop using BI Publisher. Run the report to view the output.

2. **Copy concurrent program** Query for the concurrent program that runs the report being converted using the Concurrent Program Definition screen. Click Copy To and create a new concurrent program with its name beginning with XX. Ensure that the Include Parameters check box is checked at the time of copying the concurrent program. Change the output format of the new concurrent program to XML. Add this concurrent program to a request group.

3. **Run to produce XML** Run the new concurrent program and save its XML output to a file on your desktop machine. Try to run the report for specific transactions so that the size of the XML file is kept to a minimum. The sole purpose of this step is to get sample XML data, so that you get the structure of the source XML data. Using this XML data, you can design your BI Publisher template layout. Save the XML output to your desktop machine; for example, save it as XXABCD.xml.

4. **Design template** Design your layout template as per the XML data. To do this, create a new RTF file and save it as XXABCREP.rtf for this example. Load XXABCD.xml in this RTF template using Oracle BI Publisher | Data | Load Sample XML Data.

5. **Register data definition** Create a data definition to register your concurrent request as a data definition. This makes the XML output of Oracle Report available to BI Publisher at runtime. In the XML Publisher Administrator responsibility, navigate to the Data Definitions page. Enter all the required fields, ensuring that the data definition code matches the concurrent program short name.

6. **Create template** Create a template using the XML Publisher Administrator responsibility. Assign it a data definition and upload your template layout file, which is XXABCREP.rtf in this case. Assigning the data definition makes the template available to the data source at runtime. During initial creation, you upload one template file for a specific language and territory combination. This file automatically becomes the default template file.

7. **Change default template** It is possible to associate one data definition with multiple layout templates. In such cases, you can assign the default template to the concurrent program, by querying the concurrent program using the System Administration responsibility. In the Update Concurrent Program screen, click the Onsite Setting tab and enter the default template in the Template field.

8. **Run concurrent program** Run the new concurrent program to produce the output using BI Publisher.

By following the preceding steps, you can convert any Oracle Report to a BI Publisher report. In such cases, the Oracle Report is still retained to generate XML data. The predefined layout of the Oracle Report is ignored when it is used with BI Publisher. Therefore, it becomes the developer's responsibility to design a new layout template. Oracle also provides a utility to convert your reports to a data template and RTF. This conversion utility is discussed next.

Utility to Convert Oracle Reports to a Data Template

Converting Oracle Reports to a data template is a three-step process. The first step is to create an XML file that will contain the Oracle Reports Definition. Only reports developed using toolset version 9i or above can be converted into XML. Second, after the Oracle Report has been converted to XML, a Java-based utility, DataTemplateGenerator, can be run to create a data template, supporting the PL/SQL package specification and package body. Third and finally, the RTF layout can be created using a Java utility named RTFTemplateGenerator.

When working on Reports 6i (eBusiness Version 11i), you must first convert that report to Reports 9i or Reports 10g by opening and then saving that report with the 9i/10g Reports tool. Release 12 reports are based on Oracle Reports 10g version and hence can be converted directly into XML. This conversion can either be carried out on your desktop or on the server side itself.

In this example, you will convert the Payables report named Supplier Audit Report, which has the executable APXVDDUP.rdf. The following steps were carried out on a Release 12 instance on the server side. As shown in Figure 8-10, first you execute the utility rwconverter, passing it APXVDDUP.rdf. This utility converts APXVDDUP.rdf to APXVDDUP.xml.

```
cd $AP_TOP/reports/US
rwconverter batch=yes source=./APXVDDUP.rdf dest=./APXVDDUP.xml
dtype=xmlfile  overwrite=yes
```

Next you execute the Java utility DataTemplateGenerator as shown next. This will create the data template XML file along with the supporting PL/SQL objects.

```
cd $AP_TOP/reports/US
java oracle.apps.xdo.rdfparser.DataTemplateGenerator ./APXVDDUP.xml
```

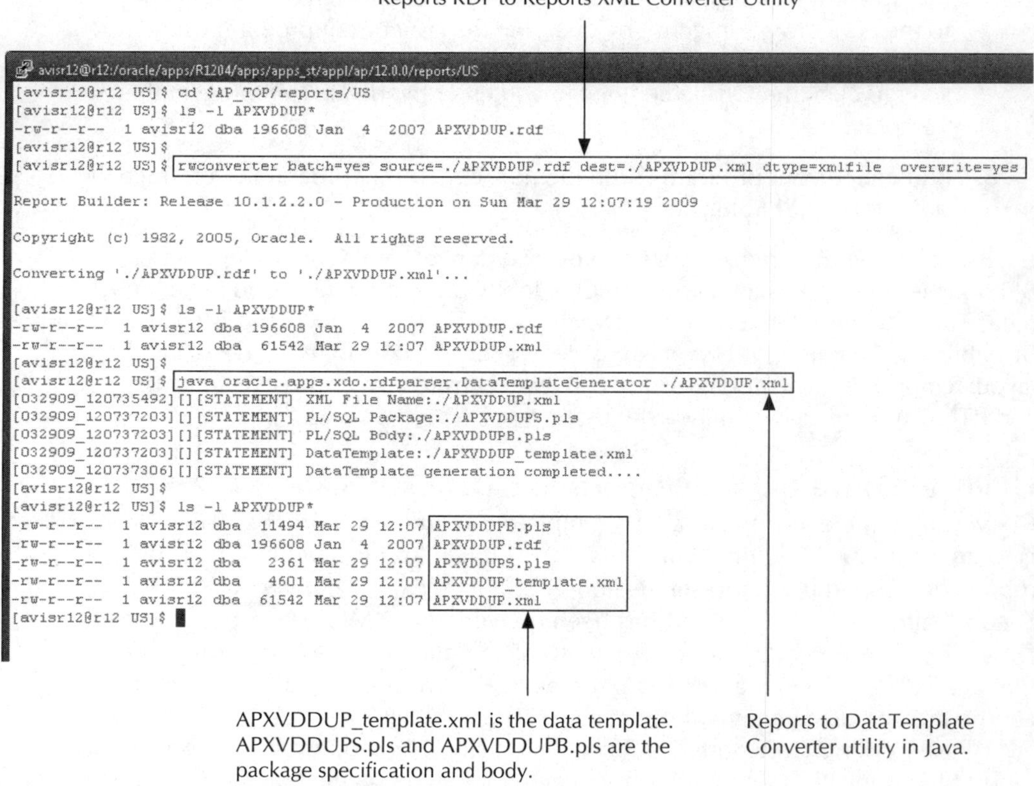

FIGURE 8-10. *Steps at a glance for converting Oracle Reports to a data template*

Finally, the RTF layout file can be generated by calling API RTFTemplateGenerator:

```
[avisr12@r12 US]$ java oracle.apps.xdo.rdfparser.RTFTemplateGenerator
./APXVDDUP.xml
[032909_123704095][][STATEMENT] File ./APXVDDUP.rtf, ./APXVDDUP.log has
been generated successfuly...
```

By running the utility DataTemplateGenerator, a layout template named APXVDDUP.rtf is generated. After running these commands, you will have seven files, as shown in Table 8-5.

When working on implementation projects, you will rename APXVDDUP.rdf to XX<%>APXVDDUP.rdf so that all the objects created have a custom naming convention.

File Name	Purpose
APXVDDUP.rdf	Original Oracle Reports file in Release 12, Oracle Reports version 10g
APXVDDUP.xml	XML definition of the RDF file when converted using rwconverter
APXVDDUP_template.xml	Data template file that should be uploaded against a new data definition
APXVDDUPS.pls	PL/SQL package specification creation script. This will be run in Apps Schema to create a PL/SQL package used by the data template
APXVDDUPB.pls	PL/SQL package body creation script. This will also be run in Apps Schema to create a PL/SQL package body used by the data template
APXVDDUP.rtf	The layout template that can be modified further and uploaded against the template in the XML Publisher Administrator responsibility
APXVDDUP.log	Contains the log of converting layout in RDF to RTF. Typically this log file will list the objects that could not be converted; for example, it will list format trigger functions F_NLS_END_OF_REPORTFormatTrigg and F_NLS_NO_DATA_EXISTSFormatTrig

TABLE 8-5. *Files Created After the Conversion Utility Is Run*

There is no support for PL/SQL in the RTF template, so PL/SQL logic must be implemented as XSL code. Figure 8-11 illustrates the resulting layout template file created by Reports Conversion Utility.

To facilitate converting the PL/SQL of format triggers in RDF, the resulting RTF template contains form fields that hold the format trigger names that are called. These form fields are highlighted in Figure 8-11. You can refer to the log file to examine the PL/SQL code for these format triggers. You can then use XSL to convert these PL/SQL format trigger codes to XSL. The Oracle BI Publisher development guide for Release 12 contains various sample code and syntaxes for writing XSL syntax within the BI Publisher template.

To summarize, when it comes to converting existing Oracle Reports to BI Publisher, you can either convert the layout using the conversion utility or draw the layout template by yourself. You make this decision depending upon how much your layout requirements of BI Publisher output differ from layout within Oracle Reports.

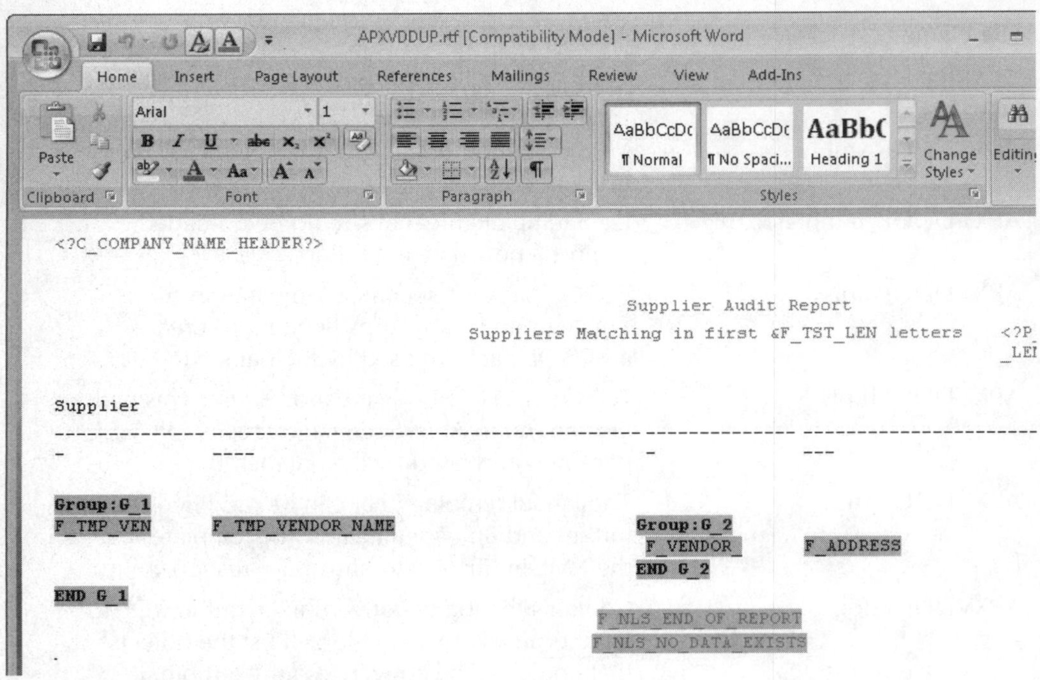

FIGURE 8-11. *APXVDDUP.rtf created by running the RTFTemplateGenerator utility*

Bursting in E-Business Suite

In the bursting process, the XML output of the data definition is fed as a stream to BI Publisher. The bursting engine within BI Publisher can then process the XML data stream by applying some rules that can be applied to generate output based on a certain template and deliver those outputs using different delivery mechanisms. Prior to the introduction of bursting, several implementation projects used either home-grown solutions or third-party solutions. However, bursting makes it very easy to distribute the contents of a report using various delivery mechanisms.

In E-Business Suite Release 12, the bursting process works out of the box. In Release 11i of E-Business Suite, you must ensure that patches 5472959 and 5968876 have been applied by your DBAs.

To implement bursting for any report, follow these three steps:

1. **Temp directory** Navigate to the XML Publisher Administrator responsibility and click Administration. In the Configuration tab, expand Properties | General and ensure that a directory has been assigned in the Temporary Directory field.
2. **Bursting control file** Prepare the bursting control file in XML and upload it against the data definition as shown in Figure 8-7. The BI Publisher developer guide in this URL contains various steps for preparing the bursting file: http://download-west.oracle.com/docs/cd/B40089_02/current/acrobat/120xdoig.pdf.
3. **Burst the output** Call the bursting concurrent program XML Publisher Report Bursting Program from the After Report Trigger and pass it the request_id of the current program that has generated the XML output. The bursting program is a Java concurrent program that reads and parses the XML output produced by a specific request_id and applies the rules defined in the bursting control file to format and distribute the contents.

Figure 8-12 shows an example of a bursting control XML file when viewed from a browser.

Figure 8-12 shows a bursting control file example that e-mails the output of the invoice report to customers. This bursting control file will break the output for each invoice. Depending upon the transaction type of the invoice, the output will be e-mailed to the customer using a specific layout. The location of the layout template can be picked from the database using the following notation, where XXAR is the custom application against which the template with the short code XXAR_INV_FIXED_LAYOUT is registered. The language in this case is English, or "en," and the location is US.

```
location="xdo://XXAR.XXAR_INV_FIXED_LAYOUT.en.US/?getSource=true"
```

In this example, we are using two different layouts, depending upon the invoice transaction type. This example uses the e-mail server installed on the local host to distribute the contents; however, any SMTP server can be used for e-mailing the output. An alternate mechanism to access the layout template is to reference it from the file system as shown next:

```
<xapi:template type="rtf" location="/templates/XXAR_INV_FIXED_LAYOUT
.rtf" />
```

In addition to e-mails, bursting can also distribute the output using fax, printer, WebDAV, FTP, Secure FTP, AS2, HTTP, or custom delivery channels. For distributing the contents to a printer, you must have a Common Unix Printing

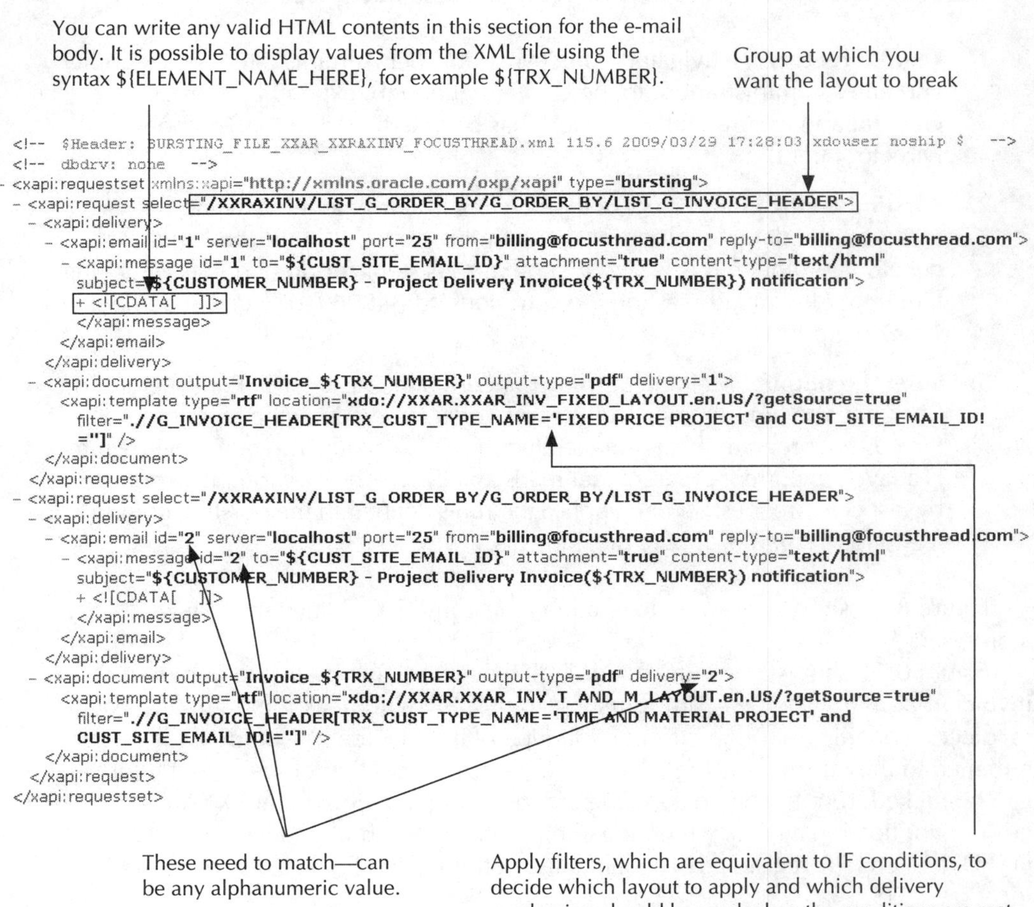

FIGURE 8-12. *Sample bursting control file to distribute output of the Receivables Invoice Report*

System (CUPS server) running on a server. The printer to be used be must be registered on the CUPS server, and the notation for referencing the printer is ipp://printServerAddressHere:portNumberHere/printers/printername. For example, if the CUPS is installed on the local host itself listening for requests at port number 631, then it can be referenced using the following notation:

```
<xapi:print id="xxPrinterName" printer="ipp://localhost:631/printers/
xxPrinterName" copies="1"/>
```

Finally, the bursting process should be called after the XML data has been generated. Therefore, the general practice is to invoke the bursting concurrent process from after the report trigger, using the code snippet shown here:

```
CREATE OR REPLACE PROCEDURE xxcust_SubmitBursting(p_request_id IN INTE-
GER) AS
    n_request_id NUMBER;
    l_layout_result boolean;
  BEGIN
  l_layout_result := fnd_request.add_layout(template_appl_name => 'XDO',
                          template_code => 'BURST_STATUS_REPORT',
                          template_language => 'en',
                          template_territory => 'US',
                          output_format => 'PDF');
  n_request_id := fnd_request.submit_request(application => 'XDO',
                      program => 'XDOBURSTREP',
                      description => NULL,
                      start_time => NULL,
                      sub_request => FALSE,
                      argument1 => p_request_id,
                      argument2 => 'Y' ) ;
  END xxcust_SubmitBursting;
/
```

Good Practices for Developing BI Publisher Reports in E-Business Suite

There are several good practices you should follow when developing reports using BI Publisher:

1. Avoid information clutter.
2. Focus on the business purpose.
3. Write separate reports for each business purpose.
4. Set the margins as follows:
    - Left: 0.5 inches
    - Right: 0.5 inches
    - Top: 0.75 inches
    - Bottom: 0.75 inches

    You may need to increase the size of the header and footer depending on the data to be included.

5. Use the standard font size of Arial 9pt. Do not use a smaller font as this will cause readability problems when the report is translated to a glyph-based language such as Chinese, Japanese, or Korean (CJK).
6. Try to eliminate column wrapping from all reports except archives, since wrapped reports are extremely difficult to read.
7. Do not use underlining or italics in your reports. For example, do not use *Customer Name or* Customer Name.
8. Do not use a colon to separate strings and values. For example, do not use "Total for VAT Box:".

Summary

In this chapter, we discussed the advantages of using the BI Publisher tool over Oracle Reports. You learned how to install the BI Publisher desktop tool and which BI Publisher reports can be developed and unit tested. In the initial part of the chapter, you learned the basic syntax that allows you to develop the BI Publisher reports manually. It is important that you develop your very first simple report using the manual approach so that you get insight into the inner workings of the BI Publisher framework. After you understand the basics, you can then progress with developing reports with the help of wizards within the BI Publisher desktop tool.

Next, you learned about the integration between BI Publisher and Oracle E-Business Suite. We discussed the simple working example of leveraging XML output from an Oracle Report concurrent program and generating the desired output using BI Publisher. By demonstrating the usage of data templates in BI Publisher, we emphasized that RDF reports are not mandatory for developing BI Publisher reports in Oracle E-Business Suite. Any XML data source can feed the data into the BI Publisher engine to generate the output. We also walked you through a step-by-step working example to demonstrate how easy it is to integrate an OA Framework page with a BI Publisher report.

In the bursting section, we explained how to distribute and deliver the output of a BI Publisher report in E-Business Suite. Finally, you saw the steps for converting an existing E-Business Suite Oracle Report into a BI Publisher report.

We recommend you use BI Publisher over Oracle Reports, unless you are customizing a standard report in Oracle E-Business Suite for minimal layout changes to the seeded layout.

Using the techniques in this chapter, you will be able to develop reports in E-Business Suite using different technologies to suit your business requirements.

CHAPTER 9

OA Framework: Concepts, Development, and Extensions

racle Applications Framework, also referred to as OA Framework or OAF, is Oracle's J2EE rapid development framework for HTML-based screens in Oracle E-Business Suite. The framework consists of two components, a runtime that exists on the midtier and a design time component accessible from JDeveloper called OAF extensions.

You may have heard of other Java-based frameworks such as Spring, Struts, and so on. Similar to those, Oracle Applications uses OA Framework as its development tool. OA Framework facilitates rapid development of the web-based applications that are integrated with 11i and Release 12 installations. OA Framework was designed by Oracle's Applications Technology Group (ATG), which is the primary reason it fits very nicely into the security model of E-Business. OAF is just another framework, but it has been developed internally by Oracle, hence its tight integration to E-Business Suite.

In this chapter, we'll take a look at how OA Framework evolved over the years, provide the overview of its architecture, draw the comparison between Oracle Forms and OAF development techniques, and more importantly, we'll closely examine the detailed examples of how to create extensions and customizations with OA Framework.

OAF: A Historical Perspective

OA Framework is the current technology used for developing web-based screens in Oracle E-Business Suite. However, the technology used for developing the very first version of HTML-based screens in Oracle Apps did not use Java or XML; it used the PL/SQL toolkit. To appreciate the need for the type of technology offered by OA Framework, in the following sections we'll take a look at how the web-based screens have evolved in Oracle Apps.

NOTE

Some Oracle E-Business Suite CRM products like iStore and iSupport still use old technology such as AK Developer in version 11i and R12. In this chapter, we will cover only the basic concept of AK Developer, as the core emphasis of this chapter is OA Framework.

PL/SQL-Based Web Pages

Initially, HTML-based screens were developed in PL/SQL. The PL/SQL stored procedures used the PL/SQL toolkit to return the HTML output to the browser. The sequence of events for displaying one such page is as follows:

1. The user clicks a menu that is attached to an AOL function (not a PL/SQL function), which is attached to a PL/SQL stored procedure.
2. Security check is done to ensure that the PL/SQL stored procedure is registered to be used for generating a web screen in Oracle Apps; the table FND_ENABLED_PLSQL performs this check as it contains the list of web-enabled stored procedures.
3. Following the successful security check, the PL/SQL stored procedure is executed.
4. The PL/SQL stored procedure builds HTML content for the page and also queries the data from tables if required. Data queried from the tables is then formatted by HTML to achieve the desired format in the web browser.
5. The entire HTML content is then displayed to the end user within the browser.

The HTP PL/SQL package can be used to generate HTML tags in PL/SQL. Some examples of HTML PL/SQL APIs are htp.htmlOpen, htp.htmlClose, htp.headOpen, htp.headClose, htp.bodyOpen, htp.bodyClose, htp.comment, htp.base, htp.title, htp.script, htp.formOpen, htp.formClose, htp.formCheckbox, and htp.formText. These and other APIs return formatted HTML markup, making it easier for a developer to deal with data-centric applications.

Limitations of the PL/SQL-Based Approach

The initial web pages of Oracle Apps were built in PL/SQL. Product updates released by Oracle are quite common in Oracle Applications. Consequently, the PL/SQL packages that represent the web page are updated by the patches; this reason alone causes a great many limitations to the capability of extending those web pages. Customers had two options to customize the page:

- Copy the existing seeded PL/SQL package and create a new custom PL/SQL package.
- Make the changes directly to the standard PL/SQL code as delivered by Oracle.

In the first case, the customized PL/SQL is attached to a new function and a new menu. However, this could lead to Data corruption if the underlying Data model was changed and the end user keeps using the customized version of the old screen. In the latter case, the customizations will be lost as soon as a patch that modifies the PL/SQL code is applied.

It is clear from these examples that customizations were either dangerous (which could lead to data corruption) or unprotected (customizations could be lost). Even trivial changes such as the changes to a prompt could be lost by applying the new patches as delivered by Oracle Support.

Some additional drawbacks of this approach were as follows:

- To perform a minor change such as changing the text of the prompt on the screen, the implementers and customers need the help of a PL/SQL developer.
- The entire user interface, navigation, and business validations code resided within the PL/SQL APIs.

To overcome these limitations, Oracle developed a metadata repository known as AK Developer that was configurable, so that a programmer was not required for trivial tasks such as prompt changes, hiding a field on the screen, or making a field read-only.

AK Developer

AK Developer is a repository where the structure and definition of the web pages can be stored. A web page typically consists of regions, and each region consists of region items. The region can be based on a database table or a database view, which dictates the source of the data displayed in that region. Similarly, the region consists of *region items* that can be connected to the columns in the database table or view. Each region item has further properties such as mandatory, updatable, displayed, and the like. In AK Developer, these region item properties are configurable, as AK Developer is shipped with the screens for maintaining the regions and region items.

The main benefit of AK Developer over the pure PL/SQL web approach is that the programmer's involvement is not required for tasks as trivial as changing the prompts or hiding of the fields. The following are some common examples of customizations made via AK Developer:

- Changing the prompt of the field
- Making a field mandatory
- Hiding or rendering fields

- Enabling descriptive flexfields by rendering ATTRIBUTE columns
- Attaching an LOV to a field

The structure of the page is stored in the AK_REGIONS and AK_REGION_ITEMS tables. The metadata in these tables can be configured through the screens in the AK Developer responsibility. Yet we need a mechanism that can read the metadata from AK tables and render the pages in a web browser. Different modules in Oracle Applications use different toolsets to read the AK Developer metadata. For example, PL/SQL, JSP files, and Java can read the metadata in AK tables and then display them in a web browser. Response to user actions such as button clicks is handled by code written in PL/SQL, JSP, JavaScript, or Java.

As seen in the following table, different modules in Oracle Apps can use AK Developer in completely different way.

Module	How It Integrates with AK Developer
HRMS	Pages are driven by PL/SQL cartridges but reference AK metadata to render the structure of page.
iProcurement	Pages are driven by Java and XML; the XML regions map to AK regions.
iStore	JSP pages internally use AK regions as metadata.

Advantages of AK Developer over PL/SQL Web Cartridges

The introduction of AK Developer was the first step in the direction of defining the HTML-based screens in a metadata repository. This approach enabled customers to perform a number of personalizations without writing a single line of code. The following are the main advantages of AK Developer over PL/SQL web cartridges:

- Trivial changes do not have to be made by a programmer.
- The presentation layer is separated from the data layer.

Limitations of AK Developer

Even though using the AK Developer repository provided a number of advantages over pure the PL/SQL toolkit-based approach, the main disadvantage was the loss of customer-applied customizations when Oracle patches with the new versions of AK regions were applied. In addition, for shared regions, the changes made to the region items were globally reflected in all the screens and responsibilities that reused those regions or region items.

OA Framework with AK Developer Repository

The initial version of OA Framework proper used Model View Controller (MVC) architecture, with the view layer still using AK Developer as metadata repository. The view layer in the MVC design pattern is responsible for displaying the page and its structure in the browser. This version of OA Framework overcomes the disadvantage of undoing the AK Developer changes after applying patches. Personalizations are allowed and are stored in the following tables: AK_CUSTOMIZATIONS, AK_CUSTOM_REGIONS, and AK_CUSTOM_REGION_ITEMS. The changes made to the prompt, rendering, and other properties were retained during the upgrades because Oracle patches would never modify the data in AK_CUSTOM% tables. Effectively, with this approach, a layer of the client's customizations is added on the top of AK Developer's existing repository. To display the page, OA Framework first needs to read the core AK Developer tables to construct the seeded structure of the page. Once the page structure has been constructed, the AK_CUSTOM% tables are read to apply the client's customizations on top of it, following which the page is displayed to the end user.

Limitations of OA Framework with AK Developer

AK Developer is a standalone module that is not integrated with JDeveloper. The page development and design process is divided in two parts: one part of the application development is performed in JDeveloper and the rest of it is built in AK Developer. For this reason, this process is not a particularly convenient development methodology. In addition to that, the AK Developer supported a very limited set of properties for the page components.

Current Technology: OA Framework with MDS

Metadata Service (MDS) is a repository that is used for rendering of an OA Framework page. On a database level, it is implemented as a group of database tables that stores the structure and properties of the page components. The tables that belong to the MDS repository begin with a JDR% prefix. The metadata itself is defined as XML files at design time using JDeveloper, which then gets transferred into the database tables inside the MDS repository: JDR_PATHS, JDR_COMPONENTS, JDR_ATTRIBUTES_TRANS, and JDR_ATTRIBUTES.

A lot of modules such as Self Service HRMS and iProcurement defined their pages in AK Developer. When the technology stack of these modules was changed from AK Developer to MDS, Oracle made a provision to migrate those AK Definitions to MDS. Effectively, the content from AK% tables was moved to JDR`% tables during so-called JRAD (Java Rapid Application Development) migration. Modules that were migrated from AK to MDS will have profile option FND: Migrated To JRAD set to Yes at their respective application level.

The life cycle for deployment of MDS pages for standard OA Framework screens is as follows:

1. An Oracle Applications developer builds the pages using JDeveloper, which results in XML files being created due to the declarative nature of the development methodology.
2. These XML files are bundled into a patch that customers can download and apply.
3. The patching process copies these XML files to $<PRODUCT>_TOP/mds on the server; for example, $ICX_TOP/mds or $PER_TOP/mds.
4. The Java-based XMLImporter utility is run to load the files from $<PRODUCT>_TOP/mds into JDR% tables.

For example, as a developer you will notice that the definitions of OA Framework pages are in the directory location $PER_TOP/mds for HR Self Service applications. However, during runtime, the page definitions are not read from $PER_TOP/mds by OA Framework. Instead, the page definitions are read from the database tables (MDS repository).

Migrated to MDS Applications

For those applications that have been migrated from AK Developer to MDS, their corresponding $<PRODUCT>_TOP/mds will contain a file named regionMap.xml. This file contains the mapping from the region codes in AK Developer to MDS pages. During the migration process, even the region mapping file gets loaded by Oracle patches into the JDR% tables through the XMLImporter utility.

The following sequence of events happens when the AOL function is accessed through an application's menu:

1. If the menu points to a function referencing AK region, the AOL engine checks whether the application to which that AK region belongs has been migrated to JRAD. This check is done by reading the value of the JRAD profile option FND: Migrated To JRAD.
2. The data in the regionMap is read from the MDS cache or JDR% tables.
3. The OA Framework page that maps to the AK region in the function gets displayed.

Overall, there are some advantages and disadvantages of using OA Framework with MDS. One of the obvious advantages is that MDS is completely integrated within JDeveloper for design and development purposes. In addition to that, the personalization features in MDS provide a lot more options than personalizations in AK Developer.

On the other hand, the declarative design of UI screens usually means the page design process is not WYSIWYG (What You See Is What You Get).

Comparison Between Oracle Forms and OA Framework

As we already mentioned, OA Framework is used to build HTML-based screens in Oracle E-Business Suite. Conceptually OA Framework is very different from Oracle Forms; however, some comparisons are possible. Table 9-1 compares the features between two technologies.

Entity Type/ Operation	Oracle Forms	OA Framework
Screen	Screens are called forms, developed with Oracle Forms Developer tool, saved as FMB files, and deployed as FMX files.	Screens are called pages, developed declaratively via JDeveloper, saved as XML files, and deployed by loading into the Oracle Apps Database into a group of tables known as MDS.
Blocks	A form is divided into blocks; blocks contain the fields, buttons, and other components. All the components within block are known as items.	A page is divided into regions. Regions contain fields, buttons, tables, and other components. Technically, page components are JavaBeans during the runtime. In fact, the region itself is a JavaBean.
Triggers	Pockets of code fire as the user navigates from one field to another or when user takes certain actions such as a button click.	Pages can be attached to a Java class known as controllers. There are three methods in the controller class: ■ processRequest()fires just before the page is displayed to the user. ■ processFormData()fires when page is submitted to the server. This method transfers the data from page fields into the server cache. ■ processFormRequest() fires after processFormData. In processFormRequest, logic can be written to trap the event such as a button click.

TABLE 9-1. *Oracle Forms Versus OA Framework–Based Screens*

Entity Type/ Operation	Oracle Forms	OA Framework
Look and feel	Visual attributes in Oracle Forms control the look and feel, such as colors, fonts, and so on.	A custom CSS can be applied to different page components. This topic will be covered in detail in Chapter 10 about custom look and feel.
Reusable objects	Object groups are reusable components. For example, a group of blocks can belong to an object group. This object group can be referenced by many different forms, hence inheriting the blocks within the object group. Any changes made to blocks within an object group can automatically be reflected in each form.	Shared regions in OA Framework can be referenced across multiple pages. A classic example is the list of values (LOV) region. For example, a LOV region will display Employee Name and Employee Number. Instead of developing one such LOV region in each page, this LOV region can be referenced and used across multiple pages.
Commit	The COMMIT_FORM or DO_KEY('COMMIT_FORM') commands can be invoked from any trigger that allows restricted procedures.	Commit always takes place in the Application Module's (AM) Java code. When a commit takes place, the data from OA Framework Cache is transferred to the database.
Override default insert, update, delete, or lock operation	You write logic in ON-INSERT, ON-UPDATE, ON-DELETE, or ON-LOCK triggers to override default insert, update, delete, and locking behavior.	You write logic in the entity object's Java class by writing code in onInsert(), onUpdate(), onDelete or onLock().

TABLE 9-1. *Oracle Forms Versus OA Framework–Based Screens (continued)*

Entity Type/ Operation	Oracle Forms	OA Framework
Personalizations to change the behavior of screens	Personalizations can be done to Oracle Forms in E-Business Suite. These personalizations are stored in tables named beginning with FND_FORM_CUSTOM_% and are safe from upgrades.	Personalizations performed on OA Framework pages are stored in the MDS layer, that is, JDR% tables. These personalizations are safe from upgrades. The personalization feature in OAF is much more powerful than its counterpart in Oracle Forms. For example, new items and regions can be added to a standard Oracle page using personalizations.

TABLE 9-1. *Oracle Forms Versus OA Framework–Based Screens (continued)*

OA Framework Architecture

OA Framework is based on the MVC (Model-View-Controller) design pattern. However, for ease of understanding, we will split OA Framework components into various layers. Each layer plays a unique role in the OA Framework architecture. Figure 9-1 shows each of the layers represented in the elliptical shape. We will be discussing the roles of each layer in OA Framework in the subsequent sections of this chapter.

MDS: Pages in OA Framework

At design time, page definitions are stored in XML files. However, for an OA Framework page to be accessed from a menu within a responsibility in Oracle Applications, the page definition must get loaded into the Oracle Database. As mentioned earlier, the JDR% tables are collectively known as MDS. Oracle's patches deploy the XML page files to the $<PRODUCT>_TOP/mds directory (e.g., $PER_TOP/mds). However, the files in that directory are only for reference purposes because those files are not used at runtime. You can see in Figure 9-1 that MDS sits outside the OA Framework layers.

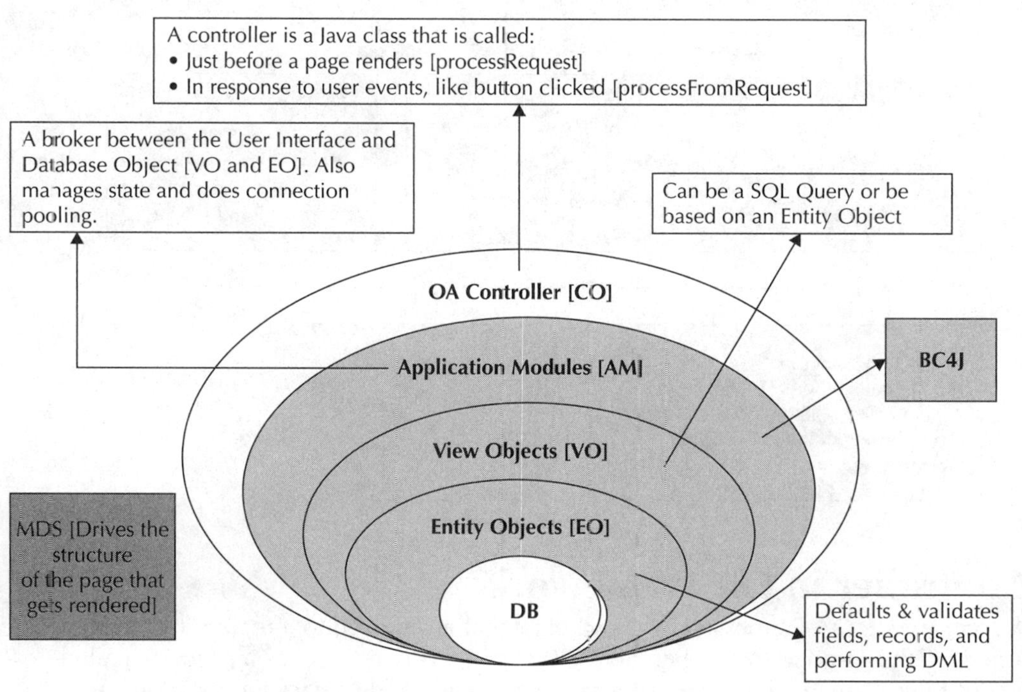

FIGURE 9-1. *Layers in OA Framework: each layer is aware of just one layer below it.*

A page consists of regions, and the region can consist of various region items. Regions and region items can be of differing types. They can also be nested within other regions. At runtime, both regions and region items are instantiated as JavaBeans within the application server.

The page definition is stored in the database tables. To avoid performance-related issues, the OA Framework engine caches the page structure into the memory cache on middle-tier server machines. When any given page or region is accessed for the very first time, its definition gets loaded in the MDS cache. Subsequently, each successive access to that page or region happens from the memory, hence reducing the performance overhead of querying the page definitions from the database tables.

The steps executed by the OA Framework engine for displaying the OAF page are shown here:

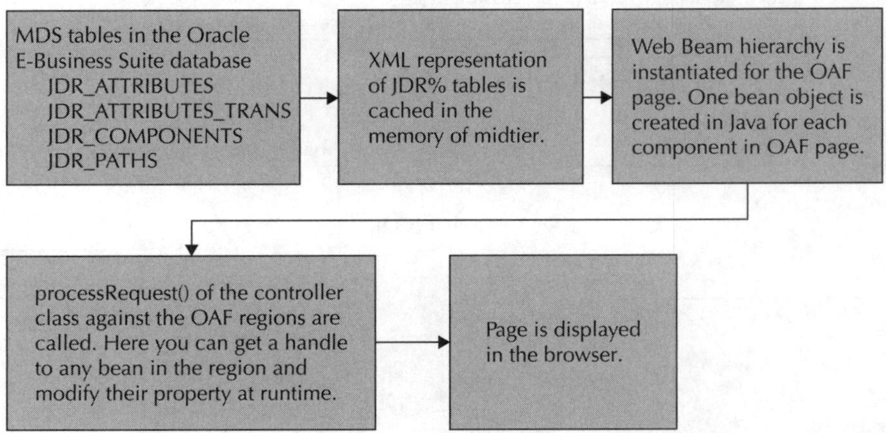

Controller in OA Framework

A controller in OA Framework is a Java class that is attached to a region. Its main function is to respond to and handle user actions. Every region has a property called a controller class to which the name of the Java class and its package location can be attached. However, it is not mandatory to attach a controller class to a region.

Java controllers in OA Framework are based on the OAController interface, which defines three methods that can be implemented in the controllers that implement the OA Framework controller:

- processRequest()
- processFormData()
- processFormRequest()

The listed methods are invoked by OA Framework during the page processing at different stages.

Method processRequest() (PR)

The processRequest() (PR) method is called by OA Framework just before a region gets displayed. This method is quite often used for executing queries on view objects by calling the methods of an Application Module that is attached to the page so that data can be displayed to the user.

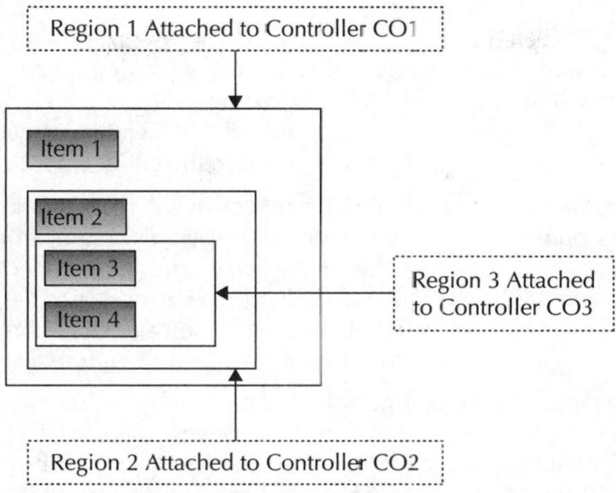

FIGURE 9-2. *Controllers attached to regions*

As illustrated in Figure 9-2, one page can have multiple regions, and each region may have a controller class attached to it. If a page has nested regions, then a controller class against each and every region will be invoked, with the controller against the outermost region being the first to be called.

processFormData() (PFD)

When a user submits the page, the processFormData() method in the controller class is invoked. The responsibility of this method is to transfer the values from the fields on the screen into the cache. This cache is not the same as the MDS cache. You can think of it as being a sort of a data cache for the user session.

Let us consider the design of a basic page in OA Framework, which allows a user to take the following actions on the screen:

1. The user queries data from a table. This data is then displayed to the user on screen.
2. The user modifies the data that is visible on the screen.
3. The user clicks a Submit button.
4. The user's changes are applied to the database table.

Table 9-2 lists the typical steps that an OA Framework developer needs to undertake in order to produce the screen that meets the requirements.

Step	How It Happens	Behind the Scenes
User queries data	Query is executed on a view object	View object is usually based on an entity object, which is based on a database table. The query is executed on that table. Data returned from SQL Query is stored in the entity object cache.
User modifies the data in the screen	User makes the changes on the screen	Nothing happens in OA Framework, as the data changes only happen in the user's browser. The fields on the screen may be mapped to view object attributes, but the view object or the entity object is not affected until the page gets submitted to the server (by clicking on a Submit button, for example).
User clicks Submit button	User makes the changes to the data on the screen and clicks a button that submits the page to the application server	**Cache Population** Fields in the screen are mapped to view object attributes. processFormData() of the controller attached to that page is called at this stage. PFD transfers the values from the screen fields to the view object cache. However, the view object in this case is based on the entity object; the user's changes are transferred into the entity object cache. Effectively, PFD is responsible for fetching the values from fields and transferring them into the OA Framework cache. This cache is encapsulated within Application Module. The data flow is screen fields to view object attributes to entity object attributes to database table column. **Validations** At the time when the cache is populated, the setAttribute method is called for each column as well as each row on the view object. Within the setAttribute method, the view object automatically calls the corresponding set(Attribute Name) method in the underlying entity objects (if applicable). This executes the column-level validation in the entity object. Once all the attribute values have been set, OA Framework calls the validateRow() method for each view object row the user modified. This executes any row-level view object validation. Finally, within the validateRow() method, the view object calls validateEntity() for validating data in underlying entity objects. **Commit or Rollback** Once the cache has been populated and validated by PFD, the processFormRequest() method gets called. Inside this method, the developer can issue a commit or rollback through the Application Module. When a commit takes place, the data changes are transferred from the cache to the database table.

TABLE 9-2. *Typical OA Framework Page Design*

processFormRequest() (PFR)

If the processFormData() (PFD) method does not raise any unhandled exceptions, then processFormRequest() of the controller class is called. If at the time of processing PFD any unhandled exceptions are thrown during the validation, then PFR does not fire. Usually developers issue a commit via processFormRequest(). The code in PFR that initiates a commit is called only after the validations have been successfully completed in view object (VO) and entity object (EO). Multiple controller classes can be attached at different levels within a page. In that case, processFormRequest() against each of the controllers is called for each nested region within that page.

Page Context

During the page processing, OA Framework creates an instance of the OAPageContext class and passes it as a parameter to processRequest(), processFormData(), and processFormRequest() methods. In addition to OAPageContext, OA Framework also passes OAWebBean to the mentioned controller methods, as shown in the following table:

Parameter	Purpose
OAPageContext	This parameter provides application context and also the current user's session-related details such as profile options, current responsibility, and the like. However, two of the most common usages of this parameter are ■ To get parameter values passed to the page ■ To navigate to another page
OAWebBean	Use this parameter to get a handle to any of the beans within an OA Framework page.

The OAPageContext class is frequently used when developing with OA Framework. One of the most common tasks developers use this object for is reading the request parameters by invoking the getParameter() method. For example, OAPageContext helps you navigate from one page to another or allows you to get a handle to the Root Application Module.

Business Components for Java

As you saw in the section "OA Framework Architecture," Business Components for Java (BC4J) is nothing but a collective name for Application Module (AM), view object (VO), and entity objects (EO) put together.

Let us assume the following scenario. User1 and User2 are querying some purchasing data using an OA Framework page. The page displays a Purchase Order header and purchase order line records. Let us further assume that the purchase order queried by User1 returns two line records, whereas for User2 just

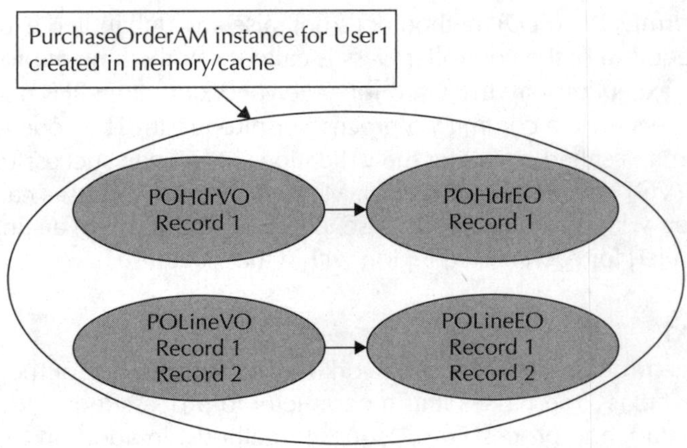

FIGURE 9-3. *How BC4J objects are instantiated for User1 in our example*

one purchase order line record is retrieved. In this case, behind the scenes, for each user OA Framework will create an Application Module instance. The end result is that the PurchaseOrderAM instance will be created twice in memory, once for each user. Each instance of PurchaseOrderAM will encapsulate instances of the POHdrVO view object and POHdrEO entity object for each user.

As shown in Figures 9-3 and 9-4, separate physical instances of BC4J are instantiated in the memory of the midtier server. When the Application Module instance is released, then all its underlying components such as view and entity objects are removed from the memory.

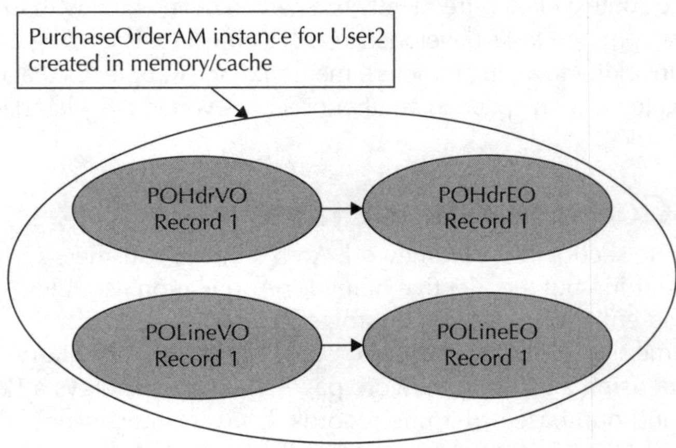

FIGURE 9-4. *How BC4J objects are instantiated for User2 in this example*

Application Module (AM)

An Application Module (AM) encapsulates server side objects, which are view objects, entity objects, view links, and entity associations. Effectively, an Application Module is a container for these objects.

Every OA Framework page accessed through Oracle Applications must have an Application Module attached to its top-level region. This top-level region is of the pageLayout region type and serves as a container for other regions and page components. When the user clicks a link that points to an OA Framework page, the Application Module attached to the pageLayout region becomes the Root Application Module. The Root AM holds a BC4J transaction object that facilitates JDBC operations.

Application modules can also be attached at lower-level regions within the page. In such cases, AMs become nested AMs. The nested AMs reference the Root AM's transaction object. Some transactions span multiple pages, which usually means that the transaction is committed to the database at the very last page. In such cases, the Root AM is retained when the user navigates from one page to another. Let us assume that a user navigates from page1 to page2 to page3, with the database commit taking place on page3. In this scenario, when page1 is submitted, the data from page1 is pushed to the cache but not committed to the database. Similarly, when the user navigates from page2 to page3, again processFormData() transfers the data from page2 into the cache of the Root AM instance for that user. Given that three pages comprise a single transaction, the developer codes the navigation from page1 to page2 to page3 in such a way so as to retain the Root AM when navigating through all three pages (page1 to page2 to page3). Therefore, when a commit is issued via the PFR from the page controller in page3, the changes from all three pages are applied to the database.

A page can be submitted in different ways. The submission of the page initiates the PFD of the controller class, which in turn populates the VO and EO cache. A Submit button click is just one of the ways a page can be submitted. Other events that can submit a page are changing the value in a drop-down list, selecting a subtab, checking or unchecking of a check box that fires a submit action, and so on.

View Object

The purpose of a view object is to query the data from database. A view object can either be a SQL Statement or it can be based on entity objects. As a rule of thumb, if a region is read only, then its view object can be based directly on a SQL Statement. However, if the region allows a user to make changes to the data interactively, then its view object should be based on entity objects. A classic example of a read-only region is a list of values (LOV) region; you will find that view objects used by LOVs are not based on entity objects. In theory, data can be validated in both view objects and entity objects; however, it is recommended that data validations are performed in entity objects.

Any view object that is hand coded, that is, not automatically generated from an entity object, is known as Expert mode view object. We will discuss the significance of Expert mode view objects when we discuss the extensions in more detail in the following sections.

Entity Object

Entity objects in BC4J are responsible for doing inserts, updates, and deletes to database tables. Entity objects also serve as a central point for business logic and validations related to a table. Each instance of an entity object represents a single row in the database table.

Theoretically, inserts, updates, and deletes can be done from anywhere in the BC4J layer— in fact, even from the controller. This is possible because any of these layers can request a JDBC connection via the Application Module. However, this practice is not recommended. OA Framework makes a provision of letting developers override default insert/update/delete behavior of entity objects by allowing them to make calls to PL/SQL APIs. You do this by extending your entity object class from OAPlsqlEntityImpl. This approach is useful in scenarios where you already have developed complex PL/SQL APIs. For example, when a FND_USER record is created, the records get inserted into FND_USER and WF_LOCAL_ROLES. Oracle provides an API named FND_USER_PKG.CREATE_USER. An Oracle developer can develop an OA Framework screen that creates records in FND_USER by leveraging the existing the FND_USER_PKG API. On similar lines, if you have already developed some complex PL/SQL APIs, they can be reused in OA Framework by using PL/SQL-based entity objects.

In Oracle Apps, _ALL tables are used to partition organization-specific data. You must create entity objects on the _ALL tables instead of basing them on organization-restricted views (these are views in R11i but synonyms based on Row Level Security in R12).

When creating an entity object, you must include all table columns in the EO. Also ensure that setters and getters for each such column are generated. Some of the key methods in entity objects are shown in the following table:

EO Method Name	Method Information
create()	Is invoked as soon as a blank record is created in the cache. Use this to generate a primary key and also to use default attribute values.
set<AttributeName>	Is invoked during cache population. Use this to perform column-level validation.
validateEntity()	Is invoked immediately after all the attributes of EO have been set in the cache. Use this for cross-attribute validations.

When creating entity objects based on custom tables, ensure that your table has Row Who Columns (LAST_UPDATE_DATE, LAST_UPDATED_BY, CREATED_BY, CREATION_DATE, and LAST_UPDATE_LOGIN). The JDeveloper Entity Object Creation Wizard will create corresponding EO attributes for each of these columns. In the create() and doDML() methods of EO, these attributes will be automatically set by OAF in the context of current logged in user.

Optimistic Locking OA Framework uses optimistic locking, which means unlike Oracle Forms, the record is not locked as soon as it gets modified by the user in the screen. In Oracle E-Business Suite, many tables have a column named OBJECT_VERSION_NUMBER (OVN). OA Framework uses this column to check if a user is modifying stale data. When creating an entity object in JDeveloper, it is possible to flag the OVN column that will be used for locking by checking the Change Indicator check box, as shown in Figure 9-5.

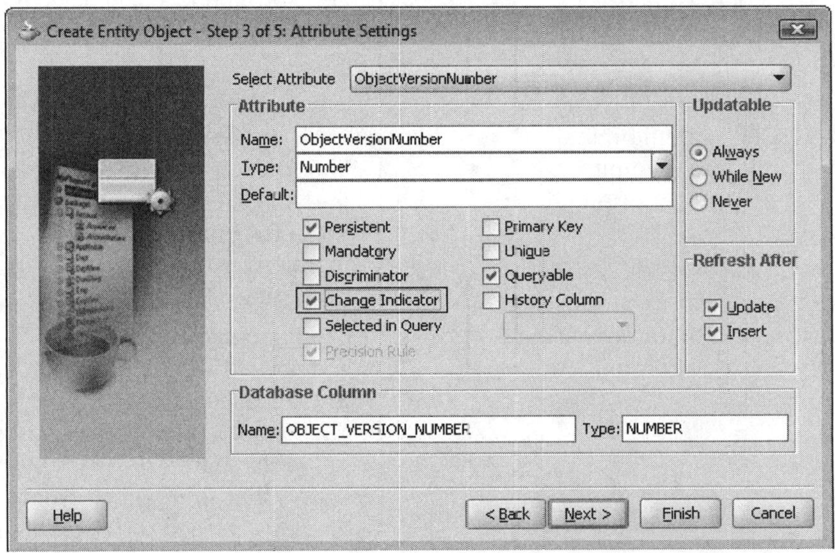

FIGURE 9-5. *Change Indicator in entity object to flag the OVN attribute for locking*

To understand how the locking mechanism works, let's take a look at an example where two users simultaneously query the same record:

User	Action	OVN Value	Behind the Scenes
User1	Queries party record with name "FocusThread" from TCA	1	Entity object cache for that user contains Name="FocusThread" and OVN=1
User2	Queries party record with name "FocusThread" from TCA	1	Entity object cache for that user will contain Name="FocusThread" and OVN=1
User1	Modifies name from "FocusThread" to "Focus-Thread" and navigates to review page to commit	1	Entity object cache for that user will contain Name="Focus-Thread" and OVN=1
User2	Modifies name from "FocusThread" to "Focus Thread" and navigates to review page to commit	1	Entity object cache for that user will contain Name="Focus Thread" and OVN=1
User1	Clicks a button that initiates commit	2	OA Framework engine first checks if current value of record in database still have OVN=1. This being the case, OVN is incremented by 1, to result in OVN=2 in database
User2	Clicks a button that initiates commit	1	OA Framework engine first checks if current value of record in database still has OVN=1. Given that OVN is not equal to 1 in the database, OA Framework knows that some other user has already changed the data. Hence, an error is returned.

Not all tables in E-Business Suite have an OVN column. In those cases, OA Framework internally uses Row Who columns, that is, timestamp in LAST_UPDATE_DATE and user ID in LAST_UPDATED_BY. For this reason, OA Framework enforces that tables used for entity object creation must contain Row Who columns.

Where to Write Code

OA Framework provides a great flexibility and, most of the time, logic of performing a business validation can be written either in CO, AM, VO, or EO. However, as per the best practices guidelines, the following table lists the right places where code must be written:

Programmers action	**CO**	**AM**	**VO**	**EO**
Manipulating page beans programmatically (for example, hiding, rendering, and so on)	X			
Handling events such as a button click	X			
Changing the page navigation to another page	X			
Accessing values of the page fields and parameters password to a page	X			
Executing a query on a view object	X*	X	X	
Validating field and item values				X
Taking miscellaneous server side actions—for example, operating on multiple view objects		X		
Returning server side values to the client (browser)		X		
Calling PL/SQL APIs		X	XX**	X**
Programmatically defaulting to field values			X***	X

*For this to happen, get a handle to AM from the controller, and then get handle to VO via AM. Once you do this, the query can be executed against it.

**If the EO is of type PL/SQL, then override doInsert(), doUpdate(), and doDelete().

***Defaulting can happen at various levels; however, if defaulting happens at the EO level, then all the view objects based on that EO inherit the default value.

JDeveloper: Development Methodology

JDeveloper is used for developing OA Framework–based pages in E-Business Suite. For this reason, the very first step is to download the JDeveloper. Once the right version of JDeveloper has been downloaded, the next step is to perform some minor configurations to your desktop and JDeveloper. After your configurations are complete, you can begin development. JDeveloper provides various wizards to quickly create pages in OA Framework. In the following sections, you will not only learn the configurations steps, but also take a look at the files that JDeveloper creates behind the scenes.

JDeveloper and Desktop Configuration

In this section, we will go through the steps required to get your desktop ready for development of OA Framework applications. It is assumed that you have access to an E-Business Suite VISION environment.

Download JDeveloper for OA Framework

You must download the right version of JDeveloper depending upon the version of your E-Business Suite. This information is available from Metalink Note 416708.1 and is listed in the table shown next:

E-Business Version and Patching Level	Download JDeveloper from Patch
Base 11.5.10 (patch 3438354)	Patch 4045639
11.5.10 CU1 (patch 4017300)	Patch 4141787
11.5.10 CU2 (patch 4125550)	Patch 4573517
11.5.10 RUP3 (patch 4334965)	Patch 4725670
11.5.10 RUP4 (patch 4676589)	Patch 5455514
11.5.10 RUP5 (patch 5473858)	Patch 6012619
11.5.10.RUP6 (patch 5903765)	Patch 6739235
Base R12	Patch 5856648
R12.0.1 (patch 5907545)	Patch 5856648
R12.0.2 (patch 5484000 or 5917344)	Patch 6491398
R12.0.3 (patch 6141000 or 6077669)	Patch 6509325
R12.0.4 (patch 6435000 or 6272680)	Patch 6908968
R12.0.5 (No new ATG code released)	Patch 6908968 (same as R12.0.4)
R12.0.6 (patch 6728000 or 7237006)	Patch 7523554
R12.1	Patch 7315332

The JDeveloper that you will download from Metalink comes bundled with BC4J, MDS, and FND libraries that match the version of libraries that are deployed on the server. The easiest way to double-check the version of your E-Business Suite instance is to run a query on the ad_bugs table. For example, to confirm if you are on R12.0.4, run the following SQL query. If the query returns a record, then you are on R12.0.4 or higher.

```
SELECT creation_date
FROM ad_bugs
WHERE bug_number IN ( '6435000','6272680');
```

After downloading the zip file from Metalink, extract it to any directory on your desktop. Let us assume you have downloaded the zip file from Metalink to c:\oaf\r124. For R12 RUP3, the file name is p6908968_R12_GENERIC.zip. The next step is to unzip this file in c:\oaf\r124. This will create three directories: jdevbin, jdevdoc, and jdevhome.

Please note that for Oracle Applications 11i, the JDeveloper version is 9i, whereas in R12 the JDeveloper version is 10g.

How to Configure the Environment for OA Framework Development

To configure JDeveloper for OAF development, you must create an environment variable JDEV_USER_HOME on your desktop. On a Windows desktop, this can be performed by navigating to System Properties | Advanced tab, and then clicking Environment Variables. Create a new user variable named JDEV_USER_HOME, and a variable value that points to <install directory >\jdevhome\jdev—e.g., c:\oaf\r124\jdevhome\jdev. Please note that it is not mandatory to use <install directory>\jdevhome\jdev\. You can use any directory on your desktop as your JDEV_USER_HOME. In fact, having a JDEV_USER_HOME independent of your JDeveloper installation directory will isolate your development area from future upgrade of JDeveloper, such as when your E-Business Suite instance gets upgraded to R12.1.

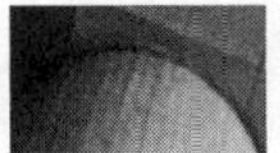

NOTE
The instructions in this chapter to prepare your desktop for OAF Development are applicable to Windows machines only. These steps will not work on a Mac or Unix installations.

If you are a consultant who works with multiple customers, you may set JDEV_USER_HOME to c:\oaf\dev\<ClientName>. Of course, when you do development for a specific customer, you will then switch the value of JDEV_USER_HOME to an appropriate value and then start JDeveloper. In this book, we will assume that the JDEV_USER_HOME is set to c:\oaf\r124\jdevhome\jdev.

Copy the file c:\oaf\r124\jdevbin\Tutorial.zip to c:\oaf\r124\jdevhome and unzip Tutorial.zip. If you get the message, "This folder already contains this file," click Yes to All. To start JDeveloper, double-click c:\oaf\r124\jdevbin\jdev\bin\jdevW.exe. If you get the message, "Would you like to migrate from a previous version of JDeveloper?" simply click No, assuming this is the first time you are running JDeveloper.

Tutorial Workspace

In JDeveloper, you create a workspace that encapsulates your development efforts. Within the workspace, you create a project. For example, when doing development on HRMS, you may decide to create an Oracle Applications Workspace called xxhrms, and within that, you can create projects like xxiRecruitment, xxLearningMgmt, xxSelfServiceHR, and so on. It is important to note that a workspace created for OA Framework must be a workspace configured for OA Framework. The steps are very well documented in the tutorials that come with JDeveloper.

In this book, we will not try to show you how to create a very simple Hello World page; the OA Framework tutorial that comes bundled with JDeveloper goes into a great deal of detail on how basic pages get created from scratch. To access this help, open the index.htm in C:\oaf\r124\jdevdoc or your equivalent jdevdoc directory. On this page, click link Oracle Application Framework Toolbox Tutorials and expand the Content section in the left hand side pane. In that navigation tree, you will find Chapter 2, "Hello, World!"

By now, you should be able to open the sample tutorials delivered by Oracle in JDeveloper. Simply select File | Open and open C:\oaf\r124\jdevhome\jdev\ myprojects\ toolbox.jws. Once you open the workspace, all the projects within that workspace are opened as well. In R12, you will receive a message, "Do you want to migrate these files?" Click Yes. The reason you receive this message is because these tutorial files were developed with Oracle in JDeveloper 9i, which you are now trying to open using JDeveloper 10g.

Configuring the OA Framework Project

One of the first mandatory steps before you can run any page in JDeveloper is to get hold of a so-called DBC (Database Connectivity) file. DBC is specific to each instance of Oracle E-Business Suite. When running pages from JDeveloper, you have to be authenticated against Oracle E-Business Suite instance. It is this E-Business Suite instance for which you will require the DBC file. The DBC file, among other things, lists the machine on which the E-Business Suite database is running, the name of the database, and the port number at which database listener is listening to the requests.

Log in to your midtier using a tool such as putty, ssh, or other similar tool. You will have to log in as a Unix user who owns a midtier installation of Oracle Apps. Once logged in, you can go to the $FND_SECURE directory as shown:

```
cd $FND_SECURE
ls ltr *.dbc
```

Locate the relevant DBC file, which most likely will be listed at the end. Double-check that this DBC file is indeed the correct file by opening this file in text editor. Copy this file in ASCII mode to c:\oaf\r124\jdevhome\jdev\dbc_files\secure onto your desktop. A sample DBC file will look as shown in the following listing:

```
#DB Settings
#Tue May 13 23:36:30 BST 2008
GUEST_USER_PWD=GUEST/ORACLE
APPL_SERVER_ID=
5EB4D8C6752C9CBAE0408F516C030FC126162113943872805134358175301238
APPS_JDBC_DRIVER_TYPE=THIN
JDBC\:processEscapes=true
GWYUID=APPLSYSPUB/PUB
TWO_TASK=R124
FNDNAM=APPS
DB_PORT=1533
DB_HOST=r12.com
```

It is obvious from the sample DBC file that it contains all the information required to establish a database connection to Oracle Apps Database except the password details.

NOTE
DBAs sometimes run a process named Autoconfig that can change the APPL_SERVER_ID. For example, Autoconfig can be run after patches delivered by the Application Technology Group have been applied. Autoconfig is also run after a new application is registered with E-Business Suite. Therefore, it is important to ensure that you are using the latest DBC file from the server, so that APPL_SERVER_ID is always correct.

Connecting JDeveloper to Oracle Apps Database for Design and Runtime Use

The first step in connecting JDeveloper to Oracle Apps Database is to ensure that you have a valid username and password for the Oracle E-Business Suite instance that corresponds to your DBC file. The following table lists the information that you must note down before creating a relationship between JDeveloper and an E-Business Suite instance.

Information	Where to find	Its usage
FND username	Your application login	Used in the JDeveloper runtime project property
FND user password	Your password for Oracle Application	Used in the JDeveloper runtime project property
DBC file	$FND_SECURE	Used in the JDeveloper runtime project property
Responsibility short name	This is the responsibility assigned to your username. You must not use a responsibility that is not assigned to your username.	Used in the JDeveloper runtime project property
Responsibility application short name	Application short name attached to this responsibility, such as AK, AP, PA, ICX, and so on	Used in the JDeveloper runtime project property
Apps password	Ask your DBA	For design time connection from JDeveloper to your Oracle Apps Database. This is used when creating entity objects.
Database machine name	From the DBC file, get the value of DB_HOST	For connecting JDeveloper to the database
Database port number	From the DBC file, get the value of DB_PORT	For connecting JDeveloper to the database
Database name	From the DBC file, get the value of TWO_TASK	For connecting JDeveloper to the database

Creating a Database Connection A database connection is required to connect JDeveloper with the Oracle E-Business Suite database. In JDeveloper, select File | New | Connections (under the General category) | Database Connection. Click the Next button, give your connection a user-friendly name, and click Next. In the

UserName field, enter **apps**, set the password to an appropriate value, and then click Next. Enter the host name, JDBC port, and SID as shown in the previous table. Click Next to test the connection. Ensure that the Status of Test Connection is Success.

NOTE
The database connection is not required for running the pages in JDeveloper. The purpose of creating the database connection is to facilitate creating entity and view objects.

Configuring the Project Property To access an OA Framework page in E-Business Suite, a user must be authenticated using his or her FND username and password. Once the login is authenticated, the user navigates to a responsibility from where he or she can access a menu. The menu in turn is attached to an AOL function that points to an OA Framework page.

When running the same page from JDeveloper, the user is not presented with a list of responsibilities nor prompted to enter FND username and password in JDeveloper. Running a page in OA Framework can be as simple as right-clicking a page and selecting Run. The selection of FND username, password, and responsibility occurs behind the scenes, as these details are held against project properties.

Specify the Runtime Connection project properties under Oracle Applications in the left-hand pane, as shown in Figure 9-6. The DBC file in this case will be picked from c:\oaf\r124\jdevhome\jdev\dbc_files\secure. You can use your own username that you use to log in to Oracle E-Business Suite. This user must have access to the responsibility specified in the project runtime property. These are free text fields, so care must be taken to enter the correct and valid values.

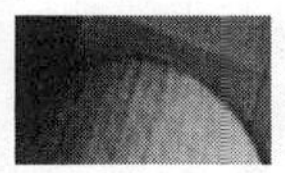

TIP
If you are using single sign-on, ensure the profile option Applications SSO Login Types is set to BOTH at the user level for this user.

Running Hello World from Tutorial

Once you open c:\oaf\r124\jdevhome\jdev\myprojects\toolbox.jws and configure the project property for Tutorial.jpr, you can right-click the project to rebuild the files. Next, right-click the page you wish to run and select Run as shown in Figure 9-7.

Location of Files on the File System

Java uses the CLASSPATH argument, which tells JVM (Java Virtual Machine) the location of classes and packages as defined by the user. When a Java application is

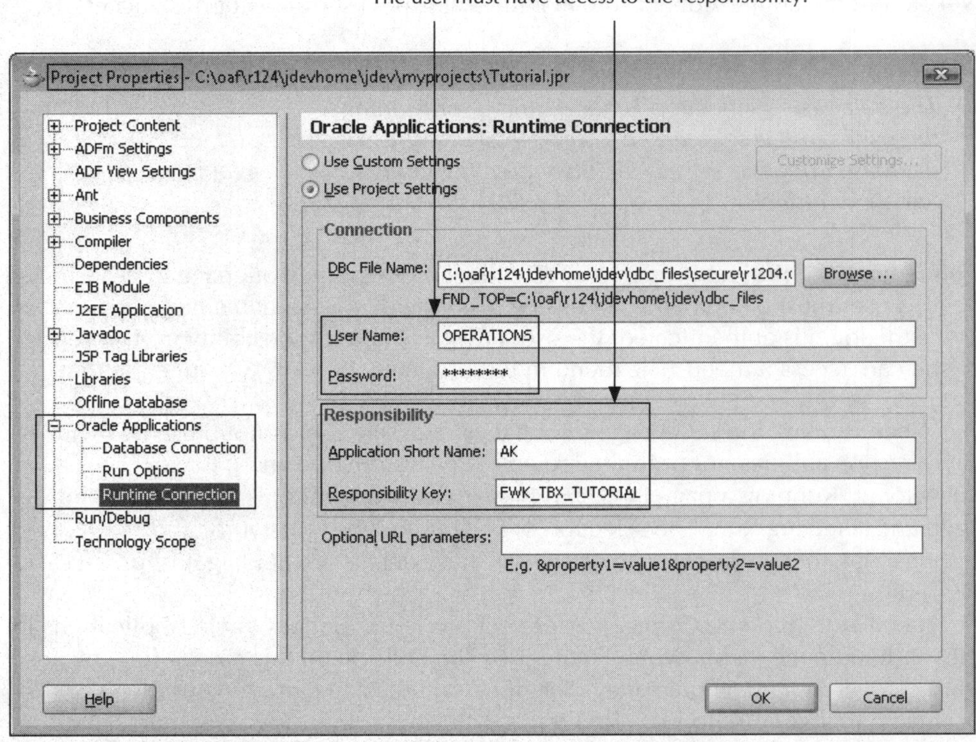

FIGURE 9-6. *Configure your JDeveloper project before running the page.*

running, it searches the required Java files in all the locations within the CLASSPATH argument. It is quite common that in both Unix-like and Windows operations systems, the CLASSPATH is defined as an environment variable.

In Oracle E-Business Suite, the CLASSPATH variable contains numerous directories and JAR files. One of the directory locations within the CLASSPATH variable is JAVA_TOP, and this is where Java code for Oracle Apps is deployed. When users run an OA Framework page, the required class files are searched and loaded into JVM from JAVA_TOP at runtime.

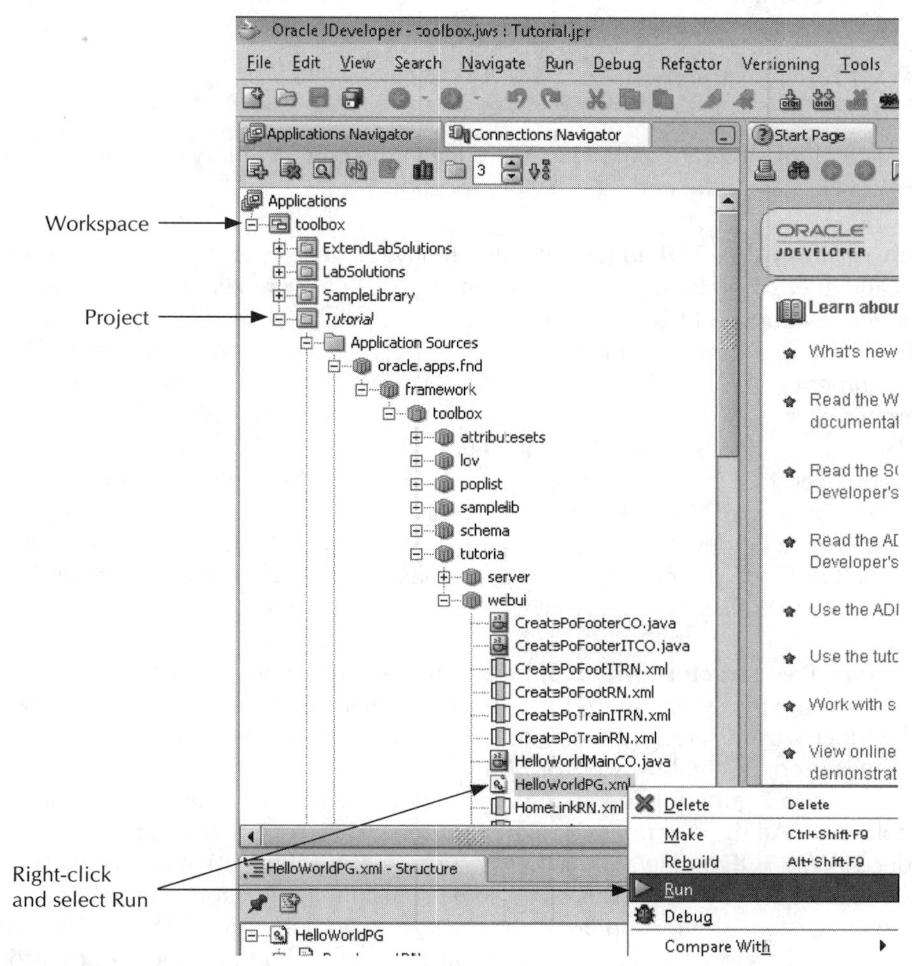

FIGURE 9-7. *To run a page, right-click that page's XML file and select Run.*

Similar to other Java applications, the classes in Oracle Applications are grouped within packages. In this context, a package identifies the location of a file on the file system. For example, a file Utility.class exists within different packages as shown next, with each Utility.class having a different functionality.

```
oracle.apps.fnd.security.Utility.class
oracle.apps.pay.utils.Utility.class
oracle.apps.igs.recruitment.server.Utility.class
```

These class files physically exist in the location on the file system as shown next:

```
$JAVA_TOP/oracle/apps/fnd/security/Utility.class
$JAVA_TOP/oracle/apps/pay/utils/Utility.class
$JAVA_TOP/oracle/apps/igs/recruitment/server/Utility.class
```

The calling program will make reference to the correct Utility.class by executing the Java class from the correct directory location.

Equivalent of JAVA_TOP in JDeveloper In Java, a developer writes logic into JAVA files and after compilation a corresponding CLASS file is created. Oracle Apps product development teams do not deliver JAVA (source code) files of their OA Framework applications to their customers. $JAVA_TOP is a purely runtime environment where the CLASS, XML, and JAR files are deployed. At runtime, JVM searches classes in specific packages within the $CLASSPATH environment variable, which leads to search being performed in $JAVA_TOP at runtime.

However, in JDeveloper, there is no $JAVA_TOP. The equivalent directory for $JAVA_TOP is <JDEV_USER_HOME>/myclasses.

When you do development, all your JAVA and XML files get created in <JDEV_USER_HOME>/myprojects. When you compile/build your OA Framework project, CLASS and XML files get created in <JDEV_USER_HOME>/myclasses.

Directory Tree Structure within $JAVA_TOP As you know, the directory tree created on the file system maps to the packages that are created for Java objects. JDeveloper wizards create the directory tree behind the scenes to match the packages used for creating MDS or BC4J objects.

As seen in Figure 9-8, there are different package naming conventions that must be followed. All the components within brackets (< >) are optional. Immediately under $JAVA_TOP/oracle/apps is the short name of an application that is registered in Oracle E-Business Suite. This can also be a custom application short name; however, custom application development should go under the $JAVA_TOP/xxcust/oracle/apps directory tree provided that XXCUST is the short name for your custom application in our example.

For custom OA Framework objects, some DBAs prefer creating a new directory location that is totally independent of $JAVA_TOP. Such a directory location can then be added to the CLASSPATH so that the Oracle Framework engine can find your custom objects at runtime. Regardless of whether you use a custom directory or $JAVA_TOP/xxcust, your custom code will have packages with the naming convention of xxcust.oracle.app, and when deployed, it will be stored under the <CLASSPATH> $JAVA_TOP/xxcust/oracle directory.

Entity objects are always created in packages whose name ends with .schema.server. The view objects should be created in a package that ends with .server but not within .schema.server. All the page definitions and controllers should be created

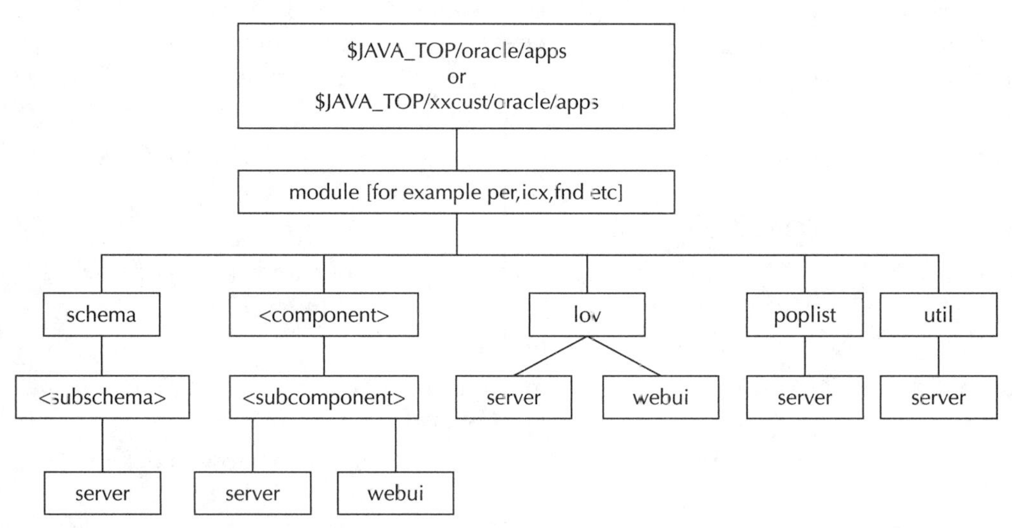

FIGURE 9-8 *Directory tree for some common objects like entity objects, view objects, and so on*

within packages that end with .webui. For custom LOVs (lists of values), the package name for a view object should be xxcust.oracle.apps.<applshortname>.lov.server and the package for a LOV region should be xxcust.oracle.apps.<applshortname>.lov.webui.

In this book, we use XXCUST as a short name of our custom application; however, for your implementation this could be replaced by a short name of your company. For example, if you are developing an extension for a company called FocusThread, then the package naming convention could be xxft.oracle.apps.<applicatioshortname>.

The <applicatioshortname> in the package name must be a valid application short name when creating OA Framework pages. When creating BC4J objects, you can use any text for <applicatioshortname>; however, it is a good practice to ensure the use of a valid application short name.

Files Created by JDeveloper in OA Framework When creating OA Framework pages or BC4J objects, JDeveloper creates a mixture of files behind the scenes. The following table looks at these files. Please note that a file will reside in a myclasses subdirectory after the file has been compiled or after the project or workspace has been rebuilt.

Object	File	Location in Desktop	Location After Deployment
Entity object	*EO.xml	myprojects myclasses	$JAVA_TOP
Entity object	*EOImpl.java	myprojects	Not mandatory to deploy to $JAVA_TOP
Entity object	*EOImpl.class	myclasses	$JAVA_TOP
Entity object	*EODefImpl.java	myprojects	Not mandatory to deploy to $JAVA_TOP
Entity object	*EODefImpl.class	myclasses	$JAVA_TOP
View object	*VO.xml	myprojects myclasses	$JAVA_TOP
View object	*VOImpl.java	myprojects	Not mandatory to deploy to $JAVA_TOP
View object	*VOImpl.class	myclasses	$JAVA_TOP
View object	*VORowImpl.java	myprojects	Not mandatory to deploy to $JAVA_TOP
View object	*VORowImpl.class	myclasses	$JAVA_TOP
Application Module	*AM.xml	myprojects myclasses	$JAVA_TOP
Application Module	*AMImpl.java	myprojects	Not mandatory to deploy to $JAVA_TOP
Application Module	*AMImpl.class	myclasses	$JAVA_TOP
Pages and regions	*PG.xml *RN.xml	myprojects	MDS database via xmlImporter
Substitution file	.jpx	myprojects	MDS database via jpxImporter
BC4J list	server.xml	myprojects myclasses	Not mandatory to deploy to $JAVA_TOP but good practice to deploy it
Project file	.jpr	myprojects	Not mandatory to deploy to $JAVA_TOP
Workspace	.jws	myprojects	Not mandatory to deploy to $JAVA_TOP

It is not mandatory to deploy JAVA files of your custom development to $JAVA_TOP/xxcust/ as they are source code for your customization; however, it is a good to store them in $JAVA_TOP/xxcust/ or an appropriate custom code directory location for documentation purposes unless your organization uses specialized tools for release management of the custom code.

Concepts of OA Framework Personalizations

As you already have learned in the previous sections, OA Framework pages and regions are physically stored in Oracle Apps Database in JDR% tables (MDS repository). Almost every implementation of E-Business Suite has a need to make a certain degree of changes to some of these pages. OA Framework has an elegant mechanism to implement these changes in such a manner that the changes are not wiped out when patches delivered by Oracle are applied. This is made possible by means of personalizations and extensions.

Personalizations do not involve any programming, whereas extensions do require programming. Hence we will cover extensions as a separate section of this chapter, "OA Framework Extensions." As you will see in this section, extensions are a combination of programming and personalizations.

Personalizations done to OA Framework pages are also stored in the database MDS repository. However, the personalizations are stored in the layer above the layer in which core page definitions reside. When a user accesses a page, OA Framework first reads the seeded definition of pages and regions as delivered by Oracle's product teams and then applies each layer of personalizations on top, so as to override the original definition of the seeded page. When Oracle delivers patches that upgrade OA Framework pages, the layers that store the personalizations are never modified. For this reason, your personalizations are able to survive patching and upgrades.

It must be noted that the personalization layer above the core layer does have a dependency on the core page definition. To make an analogy from database modeling, this is similar to a foreign key reference. For example, if you change the prompt of an item CustomerItemNumber, then the personalization layer will make a reference to the internal name of the item of core page, that is, the personalization layer will make a reference to text CustomerItemNumber. If in the future Oracle removes this field altogether from the seeded page, then OA Framework will indeed throw an error when displaying the page. Consequently, personalizations are conceptually safe so long as the basic fabric of underlying page definition remains unchanged. As a rule of thumb, Oracle very rarely removes the existing regions or items from their core pages. Indeed, Oracle usually keeps adding new items to the page, and this does not break the existing personalizations.

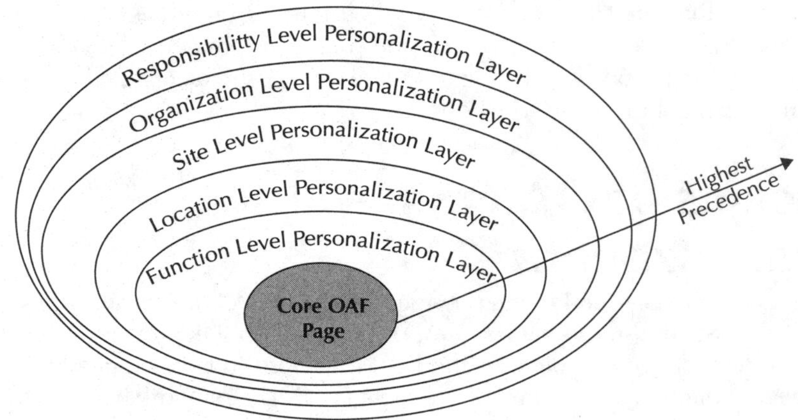

FIGURE 9-9 *The responsibility layer personalization gets the highest precedence.*

There are two types of personalizations in OA Framework. One is user-level personalization, which, as the name suggests, an end user can perform. Another is admin personalization, done by administrators (implementers). In this book, whenever we make reference to OA Framework personalization, it relates to the admin type of personalization. For user personalizations, we will explicitly state "user personalizations."

Admin Personalizations

Admin personalizations are done by administrators (or implementers); however, it is very important not to confuse this with System Administrators. Admin personalizations can be done by developers, functional staff, or support staff alike, provided they have certain profile options assigned to them.

Admin personalizations can be done at various layers, as illustrated in Figure 9-9.

The higher-level layer does not override all the changes done at the layer beneath. The delta changes done at each layer are carried forward to the next layer. Let us take an example of a page that has EmpNumber and EmpName fields:

Layer	Prompt of EmpNumber	Prompt of EmpName
Core Page layer	Employee Number	Employee Name
Function layer personalization	No personalization at this layer	Emp Name
Site layer personalization	Emp Number	Full Name
Responsibility layer personalization	No personalization at this layer	Person Full Name

As shown in preceding table, when a user accesses the page from the responsibility that contains a personalized prompt, they will see the prompts "Emp Number" and "Person Full Name," respectively. When the same page is accessed from other responsibilities that were not personalized, the end user will see prompts Emp Number" and "Full Name".

Two profile options should be set for a user to be able to perform personalizations:

- Profile option Personalize Self-Service Defn
- Profile option FND: personalization region Link Enabled

The profile option Personalize Self-Service Defn must be set to Yes for personalizations to be performed. If this profile option is set to Yes at site level, then any user in the system can perform personalizations, provided this profile is not set to No at his or her user level. Therefore, on production systems you will never set this profile option to Yes at site level.

The profile option FND: personalization region Link Enabled is used to enable the personalization link at region level. This profile has three possible values: Minimal, No, and Yes. If it is set to No, the user will still be able to see the personalize page link on top of the page, provided the profile Personalize Self-Service Defn is set to Yes. If FND: personalization region Link Enabled is set to Yes, then users will see the Personalize link for each region in every OA Framework page, provided the profile Personalize Self-Service Defn is set to Yes.

It is recommended that you use the Functional Administrator responsibility to change the value of the two profile options that were just discussed. When these profile options are changed using Functional Administrator responsibility, the change takes an immediate effect.

If a lot of personalizations have been done, then pages can look different from the vanilla E-Business Suite installation as shipped by Oracle. You can disable all the personalizations in the system by setting a profile option Disable Self-Service Personal to Yes at the site level. When this profile is set to Yes, then personalizations done at all the levels are ignored, and the product functionality and its appearance are the same as delivered originally by Oracle. There are a few points to keep in mind when setting profile Disable Self-Service Personal to Yes:

- Disable Self-Service Personal can be set at the application level as well.
- When set to Yes, personalizations delivered by Oracle as localizations will be disabled as well. These are the personalizations at location level.
- When set to Yes, at site level even OA Framework extensions will be disabled.

- Before raising a service request with Oracle, ensure that an issue with the OAF page can be reproduced if Disable Self-Service Personal is set to Yes.
- Personalizations can be re-enabled by setting this profile option to No or a blank value.

When you click the Personalize link, you will be presented with the entire hierarchy of the page being personalized, as shown in Figure 9-10.

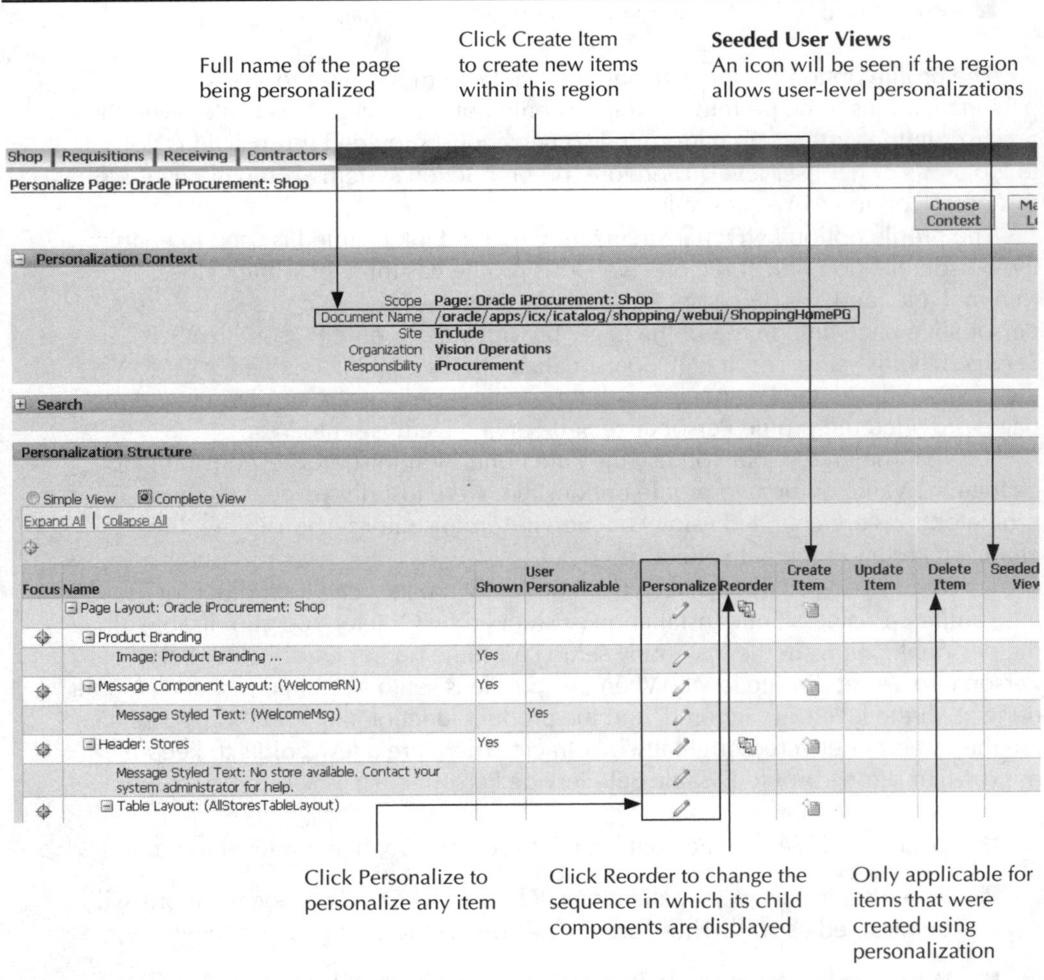

FIGURE 9-10 *Options available to the user when the page is personalized*

There are three possible routes for applying personalizations to a page:

- Navigate to the page being personalized and click the Personalize Page link.
- Navigate to the Functional Administrator responsibility, click the Personalization tab, and search any document using its document name.
- Import the personalization from the file system.

The most common types of personalizations are as follows:

- Changing the labels, prompts, or tip texts
- Hiding or showing components
- Changing the order in which items or regions appear on the page
- Adding new items to the page, like buttons, links, drop-down lists, LOVs, flexfields, and so on
- Embedding other regions into the page

Exporting and Importing Personalizations

During implementations a lot of personalizations are performed in the development environment and then tested on the test environment. In order to remove the duplication of effort, Oracle allows for these personalizations to be exported to XML files on the file system. Once exported, these exported files can be moved to the test and production environments, where they can be imported into the MDS repository. The directory location where the personalization files are extracted, or are imported from, is dictated by the value of the profile option FND: personalization Document Root Path. Once that profile option has been set up, you can download or import personalizations by navigating to the Functional Administrator responsibility.

To export personalizations, follow these steps:

1. Log in to the Functional Administrator responsibility.
2. Navigate to the Personalization tab.
3. Click Import/Export.
4. Search the personalizations that you want export.
5. Export the personalizations.
6. Go to the midtier machine and navigate to the directory as specified in the profile option.
7. Archive the files using a utility such as zip or tar; for example, on a Unix-like system, issue tar –cvf xxpersonalizations.tar ./*.

To import the exported personalizations to another environment, perform the following steps:

1. Copy xxpersonalizations.tar to the directory as specified in the profile option.
2. Navigate to that directory.
3. Unzip or extract the personalization file, for example, extract tar –xvf xxpersonalizations.tar.
4. Log in to the Functional Administrator responsibility.
5. Navigate to the Personalization tab.
6. Click Import/Export.
7. Select and import the personalizations that were exported from the source environment.

Items That Can Be Created Using Personalizations Different types of items can be added to an OA Framework page through personalizations, as listed in Table 9-3. It is important to note that with later versions of rollup patches in E-Business Suite, new items might get added to this list.

User-Level Personalizations

User-level personalizations allow an end user to create different views on top of the standard results region within the search pages. User-level personalizations are available only on those search pages where Oracle's product development team has enabled that feature. In OA Framework, table and advanced table styled regions have a User Personalization property. If this property is set to True, then users can create *user views*. These user views allow users to predefine query filters on the displayed data, as well as order columns, sort data, make changes to column prompts, and hide or show columns.

If a user creates a view with a user personalization, then such views are not visible to other users. However, if an administrator creates the views, those are called seeded views, which can be made available to all users.

Using this functionality, end users can create as many personalized queries as they need. Each such view is given a label. All the available views can be retrieved by using a drop-down list on top of the inquiry region.

For end users to create user views, they can click a Save Search button in the inquiry region. This button is visible if and only if the inquiry region was developed with the User Personalization property set to True. For end users to create these views, they do not need to have the Personalize Self-Service Defn profile option set to Yes.

Item That Can Be Added via Personalization	Purpose
Attachment link	Displays links for attachments in a single row.
Attachment table	Displays the link of attachments in a tabular format.
Button	Creates a link to another page or URL. (The button added via personalization does not submit the page.)
Export button	Exports data from the page into CSV or Excel. Specify the view object instance from which the data is exported.
Flex	Adds a descriptive flexfield to the page.
Flexible layout	Embeds an external region of style StackLayout into the page.
Form value	Adds a hidden field.
Formatted text	Adds a new HTML text.
Image	Enables a user to access an image from the database.
Link	Creates a hyperlink to another page.
Message check box	Allows creation of a check box.
Message choice	Allows creation of a drop-down list. The view object that returns the list for the drop-down must already exist.
Message file upload	Enables uploading of a file from a client machine to the middle tier.
Message download	Allows downloading of a file from the middle tier to the client's machine.
Message inline attachment	Displays a list of inline attachment links. The default number of maximum links displayed is 5, but this can be overwritten.
Message LOV input	Creates an item with a list of values. The region for the LOV must exist in MDS.
Message radio group	Creates a set of radio buttons on an OA Framework page.
Message styled text	Creates a display-only item on the page.
Message text input	Creates a user-enterable field in an OA Framework page.
Raw text	Creates custom HTML contents on a page.
Separator	Creates a separator line.
Stack layout	Adds a reference to the stack layout region.
Static styled text	Adds instruction text.
Tip	Adds a link that a user can click to see instruction text for a tip.
URL include	Embeds contents of an external HTML page from a URL into the standard OA Framework page.

TABLE 9-3. *Personalizable Items*

For an administrator to create seeded views, the Personalize Self-Service Defn profile option must be set to Yes. When personalizing the region that is enabled for user personalizations, the administrator can click an icon under the Seeded User Views section in the personalization page.

OA Framework Extensions

The difference between extensions and personalizations is that extensions can involve some level of programming. Extensions can be done to the BC4J objects and also to the controller classes. The extensions to the controller code are not officially supported by Oracle, and this is documented in Metalink Note: 275846.1: Oracle Application Framework Support Guidelines for Customers; however, from our experience we can say that changes to the controller code are performed almost routinely on client sites. Once the extensions have been performed, the information related to the definition of extensions—that is, what has been extended is stored in the MDS repository. Usually, the BC4J extension is a replacement—of the original BC4J object by an extended BC4J object. The new object extends the original object itself, and this replacement process is referred to as substitution.

The substitution of a BC4J component always involves the creation of a new BC4J object. In the Java terminology, the new BC4J object classes extend the Java classes of the existing BC4J object. Whenever OAF makes reference to a BC4J object, OA Framework looks up in the MDS repository to see if the substitution exists. If a substitution is found, then the extended BC4J object is returned to the calling program. If the substitution is not found, then the original BC4J object is executed.

Once deployed, the substitution information about BC4J objects is loaded inside the MDS repository (JDR% tables in the database). Therefore, if you wish to delete a BC4J substitution, you will have to delete the corresponding substitution directive from the MDS repository. This can be done by using jdr_util.deleteDocument PL/SQL API. In effect, the substitution information of all BC4J objects is stored inside the MDS repository. To put it simply, think of BC4J objects substitution (view objects, entity objects, and Application Modules) as site-level personalization to the respective BC4J objects. The understanding of this concept is very significant. It means that if, for example, a view object has been substituted, such a substitution will be effective for all the screens where this view object is being referenced.

When you specify the substitution in JDeveloper, it produces the <projectName>.jpx file. This JPX file is created in the myprojects directory. It is this XML file that must be loaded into the database using the jpxImporter utility. The JPX file contains the name of the original BC4J object and also the name of the extended BC4J object.

A sample JPX file from JDeveloper 9i is shown next:

```
<?xml version="1.0" encoding='windows-1252'?>
<!DOCTYPE JboProject SYSTEM "jbo_03_01.dtd">
<JboProject
   Name="xxiProcRcvExt"
   SeparateXMLFiles="true"
   PackageName="" >
   <DesignTime>
      <Attr Name="_version" Value="9.0.3.13.75" />
      <Attr Name="_jprName" Value="xxiProcRcvExt.jpr" />
      <Attr Name="_ejbPackage" Value="false" />
      <Attr Name="_NamedConnection" Value="goauat" />
   </DesignTime>
<Substitutes>
  <Substitute OldName ="oracle.apps.icx.por.req.server
.PoReqDistributionsVO" NewName ="xxcust.oracle.apps.icx.por.req
.server.xxcustPoReqDistributionsVO" />
  <Substitute OldName ="oracle.apps.icx.por.rcv.server
.ReceiveMyItemsVO" NewName ="xxcust.oracle.apps.icx.por.rcv.server
.xxcustReceiveMyItemsVO" />
  <Substitute OldName ="oracle.apps.icx.por.req.server.PoRequisition-
LinesVO" NewName ="xxcust.oracle.apps.icx.por.req.server.xxcustPoRequi-
sitionLinesVO" />
  <Substitute OldName ="oracle.apps.icx.por.rcv.server.ReceiveReqItems-
VO" NewName ="xxcust.oracle.apps.icx.por.rcv.server.xxcustReceiveReq-
ItemsVO" />
</Substitutes>
</JboProject>
```

A sample script, which we tested on a Linux box, to load the JPX file into Oracle Apps database is shown in the following listing. This script takes the apps password as parameter:

```
APPS_PWD=$1
export APPS_PWD
MACHINE_NAME=0
PORT_NUMBER=0
export MACHINE_NAME
export PORT_NUMBER
getPortMachine()
{
   MACHINE_NAME=`sqlplus -s apps/$APPS_PWD <<EOF
                  set pages 0
                  set lines 1023
                  select fnd_profile.value('CSF_EMAP_DS_HOST')
                     from dual ;
                  exit
```

```
                EOF`
   PORT_NUMBER=`sqlplus -s apps/$APPS_PWD <<EOF
                        set pages 0
                        set feed off
                        select fnd_profile.value('CSF_MAP_DB_PORT')
                            from dual ;
                        exit
               EOF`
}
getPortMachine
"Echo now loading BC4J Substitution into Database"
adjava \
oracle.jrad.tools.xml.importer.JPXImporter ./xxcustiProcGl01.jpx \
-username apps \
-password $APPS_PWD \
-dbconnection "(description=(address_list=(address=(community=tcp
.world)(protocol=tcp)(host=$MACHINE_NAME)(port=$PORT_NUMBER)))
(connect_data=(sid=$TWO_TASK)))"
```

The definition of an extended controller class could also be held in the MDS repository, and a controller class can be extended at all those levels at that are allowed for personalizations. This is particularly useful in scenarios where you want your controller object extension to be applicable for only a limited number of responsibilities, instead of making the extension available across all responsibilities.

Identifying the Type of Required Extension

To identify the right place for performing an extension, you first need to figure out which functionality of Oracle you wish to extend. Once you know that, the next task is to figure out which part of OA Framework delivers that functionality.

Therefore, the most important aspect of the OA Framework extension is to be able to figure out how the standard functionality works. Given that at the time of writing this book Oracle does not provide the Java source code for applications written with OA Framework, at times it can become difficult to identify the location of the code that contains the functionality that you wish to extend. Of course, there is always an option to use widely available Java decompiler tools such as JAD to reverse engineer the Java files, provided that it is legal to do so where you live and use such tools.

If using the Java decompiler is not an option, you can consider debugging OA Framework in a manner that allows you to see the list of classes and methods that are being executed. This can be done by setting the profile option FND Diagnostics, which enables a Diagnostics link on the top-right corner of the screen. When you click the Diagnostics link, it presents four options: Show Log, Set Trace Level, Show Log on Screen, and Show Pool Monitor. Select the option Show Log on Screen and, for example, to see all the debug messages related to iProcurement, enter **icx%** in the Module field. If you wish to see the highest level of debugging, then it is best to select the radio button Statement. This technique will help you see all the OAF method calls and can help you identify the objects that should be extended to meet your requirements.

View Object Extension

It is quite often the case that there is a need to display additional information on screens that display data fetched from view objects. To show additional information, two things must be done. First, you need to create an additional field on the page, which can be done using personalization. If the underlying view object already contains the column value that you wish to display, then an extension is not required because the field created via personalization can be mapped to the existing view object attribute.

A view object extension will be required in those cases where the value that must be displayed to the user on the screen does not already exist in the underlying view object. In such cases, you will create a new view object. This new view object extends the existing view object, which is why it inherits all the features and columns of the existing view object. This is referred to as view object extension.

Another common reason for view object extension is to override the WHERE clause programmatically. The standard product code quite often programmatically sets the WHERE clauses either in VOImpl(view object Implementation) or AMImpl(Application Module Implementation), or even sometimes from the controller itself.

You must follow these steps to create a view object extension:

1. Identify the view object to be extended.
2. Open that view object in JDeveloper.
3. Create a new view object in the xx<cust>.oracle.apps package. This new view object extends from the parent view object.
4. Create a substitution in JDeveloper; the substitution contains the directive to replace the existing view object with the new view object at runtime.
5. To test the substitution directly from JDeveloper, change the project property by navigating to project properties and select Run/Debug | Edit to modify the run configuration. Here you can append the line -Djbo.project=<name of jdev project here>, where <name of jdev project here> is the name of the JDeveloper project.
6. To test the substitution form application, deploy the new view object files to the $JAVA_TOP/xxcust directory on the relevant midtier box and load the JPX file into the database.

Here are a couple of things you need to be aware when performing the view object substitutions in Oracle Applications:

- **Row class** You must always create a VORowobject class for an extended view object. This is done by navigating to the project property, selecting the Java node in the left-hand pane, then checking the check box labeled Generate Java File within View Row Class.
- **Expert mode** Extensions done to view objects created in expert mode are not 100 percent safe. This is because a physical copy of the SQL Statement exists in the extended view object. During the extension, you will most likely add or modify that SQL Statement. If Oracle were to modify the SQL within the view object, then changes delivered by Oracle product teams will be effective only to the base view object that has been substituted.
- **Binding style** There are three possible binding styles for OA Framework view objects: Oracle Named, Oracle Positional, and JDBC Positional. The binding style of your extended view object must be the same as that of the view object being extended. To select the appropriate binding style, navigate to the View Object property and select SQL Statement in the left-hand pane. Here you will find the Binding Style property just below the Expert Mode check box.

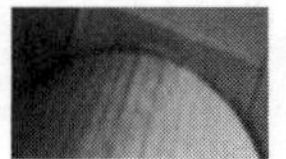

TIP
In case of JDeveloper 9i for E-Business Suite 11i, view objects do not have a Binding Style property. The equivalent property in JDeveloper 9i is Use ?Style *Parameters.*

Entity Object Extensions

In most cases, you will extend entity objects to add extra validation to some fields or even records. Another common reason for extending entity objects is to assign default values to the attributes. Sometimes default values in an entity object may be overridden by default values executed by Oracle's code at View Object (VO) level or Controller (CO) level. Thus you need to anticipate the correct level for placing your defaults when designing extensions. Having said that, even though entity objects are the most obvious place to perform the defaulting, it is not always the best place to do so.

The steps for extending the entity object are similar to those for extending view objects. However, unlike the view objects, entity objects do not have an expert mode.

Application Module Extension

You will find that the Application Module is the least common extension that is done in OA Framework. Application Modules are usually the place from where Oracle seeded code initiates PL/SQL JDBC calls. Sometimes, there is a need to supplement that PL/SQL call by some additional PL/SQL calls. In such cases, you can extend the Application Module. Steps for extending the AM are similar to those of extending a view object and entity object.

Let us assume that an Application Module has following methods:

```
public String createFndUser(parameters) {....}
public boolean validateLoginPassword(parameters) {....}
public boolean validateFndUser(parameters) {....}
```

Let us say that you wish to raise a business event each time an invalid login happens. In that case, you will program your extended Application Module as shown in the following listing:

```
public boolean validateLoginPassword(parameters)
{
//We will call the parent method to validate the Login and Password.
//If authentication fails, then let us perform additional processing
if !(super.validateLoginPassword(parameters))
  {
  //raise your business event here or do additional processing}
  }
```

Controller Extension

Extending an existing controller code as delivered by Oracle product teams is a bit of controversial subject. We would like to draw attention to Metalink Note: 395441.1 - Oracle Application Framework Support Guidelines for Customers, which clearly states that Oracle does not recommend that customers extend controller objects associated with regions in seeded E-Business Suite product pages. Although it is technically possible to extend controller code, there are multiple reasons why it is not feasible for Oracle to support the controller code extensions. The most obvious reason is that controller code is subject to change at any time, and Oracle cannot guarantee that extended controller code will and should work after the updates.

In practice, however, the controller code gets extended quite regularly by customers. A typical scenario is when web beans are created programmatically on the fly in the controller code instead of declaratively, and therefore it is not possible to use the personalization framework to change the web bean properties. There are other numerous occasions that require controller code to be extended to meet customer needs; however, you must make sure that before undertaking such customizations, your customers are aware of the consequences with regard to the support options for such extensions as documented in Metalink Note 395441.1. In this section, we'll discuss a number of the most commonly used techniques to extend seeded controllers.

To extend an existing controller, first create a new class file that extends the original controller's Java class. Next, using personalization, personalize the region to which the original controller is attached.

Once in the personalization screen for the region, replace the existing controller with your newly created extended controller. The controller can be extended at any of the levels at which personalization can be done. Unlike substitutions to BC4J, controller extension does not necessarily need to happen at site level. Therefore, for any given region, one responsibility can be personalized to use controller class, say CO1, and another responsibility can be configured to use controller class CO2.

If in your extended CO class you override processRequest(), then OA Framework will invoke the overridden method in your custom class. OA Framework will not execute the method in the original controller class unless you call super.processRequest() in your extended class. To ensure that your extensions are safer, it is a good idea to ensure that the super Java keyword is used to invoke the overridden method from the parent controller class.

TIP
If you make a call to super.processFormRequest() from an extended controller, and if the parent processFormRequest() performs OAPageContext .forwardImmediately(), then the code in your extended controller may not get executed.

Executing SQL Statements from an Extended Controller

It is not recommended you use JDBC connections from controllers. However, sometimes in your extended controllers, you may need to execute SQL Statements. You have three options to achieve this.

Option 1 Create a new view object with the required custom SQL Statement and attach that view object to the Application Module of that page. Then call the SQL by executing a query on the custom view object. The disadvantage of this approach is that you will have to extend the Application Module as well, in order to attach the custom view object. If you recall from the introductory sections in this chapter, it is not possible to use a view object unless it is associated to one of the AM instances. Also, if the Application Module is a root AM, then such AM may not be extensible.

Option 2 Get the database connection within the controller and call SQL Statements or PL/SQL APIs by doing one of the following:

```
OADBTransactionImpl oadbtransactionimpl =
(OADBTransactionImpl)oapagecontext.getRootApplicationModule()
.getOADBTransaction();
CallableStatement callablestatement =
oadbtransactionimpl.createCallableStatement("begin :1 :=
xx_get_Fnd_user_desc(:2); end; ", 1);
```

or:

```
OADBTransaction oadbtransaction = (OADBTransaction)oapagecontext
.getApplicationModule(oawebbean).getTransaction();
java.sql.Connection connection = oadbtransaction.getJdbcConnection();
```

There is nothing to stop you from doing this; however, referencing JDBC connections inside the controller is not recommended. Avoid this option.

Option 3 (Recommended) Create the view object on the fly from a SQL Statement. This view object will be automatically attached to the Application Module of the page. Let's say that, in the extended controller, for a given value of FND_USER .USER_NAME, you need to find FND_USER.DESCRIPTION.

Follow these steps:

1. Create a new Java class that extends from the original controller class.
2. In the extended controller, import oracle.apps.fnd.framework .OAApplicationModule and oracle.jbo.ViewObject.
3. Build the SQL Statement that you wish to execute in a string variable. Ensure that you use bind variables as shown in the example shown next.
4. Execute the query on the view object.
5. Get the desired results from the rows of this view object:

```
package oracle.apps.fnd.framework.toolbox.tutorial.webui;
import oracle.apps.fnd.common.VersionInfo;
import oracle.apps.fnd.framework.OAException;
import oracle.apps.fnd.framework.webui.OAControllerImpl;
import oracle.apps.fnd.framework.webui.OAPageContext;
import oracle.apps.fnd.framework.webui.beans.OAWebBean;
//-----------------------------------------------------
import oracle.apps.fnd.framework.OAApplicationModule;
import oracle.jbo.ViewObject;
/*
```

```
 * Controller for oracle.apps.fnd.framework.toolbox.
 * tutorial.webui.HelloWorldP page
*/
public class HelloWorldMainCO extends OAControllerImpl
{
  // Used for source control
  public static final String RCS_ID="$Header: HelloWorldMainCO
.java 115.6
2004/01/19 10:14:57 atgopxxOnTheFlyVOQuery noship $";

  public static final boolean RCS_ID_RECORDED = VersionInfo
.recordClassVersion(RCS_ID, "oracle.apps.fnd.framework.toolbox
.tutorial.webui")
  /**
   * Layout and page setup logic for region
   * @param pageContext the current OA page contex
   * @param webBean the web bean corresponding to the region
  */
public void processRequest(OAPageContext pageContext, OAWebBean
webBean
  {     super.processRequest(pageContext, webBean);
 //First get the Application Module
 OAApplicationModule oam = pageContext
.getApplicationModule(webBean);
 //Let's say you need to get the description of FND_USER Named
OPERATIONS
String sWhereClauseValue = "OPERATIONS" ;
 //Build the select statement for this on the fly view object
String xxOnTheFlyVOQuery = "select description xxdesc from
fnd_user ";
//Specify the Where Clause for the same
xxOnTheFlyVOQuery = xxOnTheFlyVOQuery + "where user_name = :1 ";
//First see if this VO is already attached to view object
ViewObject xxOnTheFlyViewObject = oam.findViewObject("xxFNDUserD
escVO");
if(xxOnTheFlyViewObject == null)
xxOnTheFlyViewObject = oam
.createViewObjectFromQueryStmt("xxFNDUserDescVO", xxOnTheFlyVO-
Query);
            //By now we are sure that the view object exists
            xxOnTheFlyViewObject.setWhereClauseParams(null);
            //Set the where clause
            xxOnTheFlyViewObject.setWhereClauseParam(0,
sWhereClauseValue);
            xxOnTheFlyViewObject.executeQuery();
            oracle.jbo.Row row = xxOnTheFlyViewObject.first();
            //get the value of description column from view
object record returned
if(row != null)
{
```

```
String mFndUserDescription = row.getAttribute(0).toString();
System.out.println("Result from Dynamic VO is =>" +
mFndUserDescription );
}
//Remove the view object, as this is no longer required
xxOnTheFlyViewObject.remove();
  }
```

OAF Extensions: Fully Worked Example

In this example, you will be extending an Oracle iProcurement noncatalog requisition page. In the iProcurement responsibility under the Shop tab, you will find a subtab named Non-Catalog Request. On that page, there is a list of values (LOV) icon next to the supplier name. In the LOV region, you will find supplier-related details; however, the standard functionality of an Oracle-delivered LOV region does not display the supplier site's e-mail address. Once you search and select a supplier, the selected supplier is copied to the Non-Catalog Request page. Let us assume that our business requirements for this extension are as follows:

- To display the supplier site e-mail in the LOV region.
- To create a field named Supplier Site Email in the Non-Catalog Request page. The value for this field should be copied from the supplier selected in the LOV.
- To return Supplier Site Email, selected from LOV, to the Supplier Site Email field in the Non-Catalog Request page. Once it returns the value of the e-mail address, the value itself should be stored in ATTRIBUTE15 of the requisition line record.

In this example, you will learn how to:

- Set up JDeveloper for OA extensions.
- Identify which objects to extend.
- Create a new view object that extends the standard view object so as to add a new column attribute.
- Substitute the original view object with your extended view object.
- Make BC4J substitution work in JDeveloper.
- Add a new field to the LOV region.
- Add a new field to the iProcurement page.
- Copy the value from the field in the LOV region into a field on the main page.
- Deploy the changes.

We are using an R12 VISION instance in this example. However, these steps will pretty much work for Release 11i as well. If there are differences, we will highlight the difference between R12 and 11i steps as applicable using this notation: *11i*. In this example, we also used an installation of JDeveloper on the Windows desktop, and our middle tier is a Linux box.

Finding the Objects to Be Extended

Ensure that the FND: Diagnostics profile option and the personalization profile options are set to Yes:

- An About this page link appears at the bottom of every OA Framework page when the profile option FND: Diagnostics is set to Yes.
- When you click the About this page link, the entire MDS structure of the page is displayed in the browser together with all the BC4J components used by that page.

Following this approach, you will be able to find out that the name of the OA Framework page that contains the supplier field with the LOV is NonCatalogRequestPG. (Sometimes the name of the page is also visible from the URL.) Additionally, you will find that name of the LOV region in this case is ReqSupplierLovRN.

To find the name of the view object used by LOV, navigate to the iProcurement responsibility and click the Non-Catalog Request tab. Then click the LOV icon next to the Supplier Name field, and in the LOV screen, click About this page. Here you will find that name of the view object used is ReqSupplierVO. In some cases, the About this page link does not work in LOV pages. If you experience this problem, then open ReqSupplierLovRN.xml in JDeveloper or in any text editor available to you. Here you will also find that the view object used by LOV is ReqSupplierVO. You will be adding the Supplier Site Email address to this view object by means of an extension.

JDeveloper Set Up for iProcurement Extension

Before you run iProcurement pages from JDeveloper, make sure that you are able to access the page from an appropriate responsibility. Following that, it is important to be able to run the page being extended from JDeveloper itself.

To set up a database connection to the E-Business Suite from JDeveloper, select File | New| General-Connections | Database Connection. Alternatively, you can click the Connections Navigator pane and right-click the Database node to select New Database Connection. Make sure that you can connect to the database.

To run the page from JDeveloper, you will first have to copy the files from the midtier machine to your desktop where JDeveloper is installed. There are two types of files that you must transfer: the MDS definitions of pages and the runtime classes under the $JAVA_TOP directory.

Pages are nothing but XML files that reside in $ICX_TOP/mds in the example. To run iProcurement pages from JDeveloper, you must copy those pages from the $ICX_TOP/mds to C:\oaf\r124\jdevhome\jdev\myprojects\oracle\apps\icx folder to the desktop. You may have to create a directory tree structure manually on your desktop in c:\oaf\r124\jdevhome\jdev\myprojects\oracle\apps\icx. Also, it is not required to create an mds directory under the myprojects directory.

In order to copy the runtime files to the desktop, you need to copy all the files under the $JAVA_TOP/oracle/apps/icx directory to c:\oaf\r124\jdevhome\jdev\myclasses\oracle\apps\icx. If you are using FTP to transfer the files, make sure that CLASS files are transferred in binary mode, whereas XML files are transferred in ASCII mode.

Once you have transferred the files, start JDeveloper. Next, create an Oracle Applications Workspace and an Oracle Applications Project in JDeveloper. In the example, we have used xxicx01 as a workspace name. The name of the project can be the same as the workspace name, for example, xxicx01. The project properties must be set up in such a way that you are able to log in to the iProcurement responsibility from JDeveloper. To find out the short name of the iProcurement responsibility and its associated application short name, run the SQL as shown next:

```
SELECT fa.application_short_name, responsibility_key
FROM fnd_responsibility_vl fr ,fnd_application_vl fa
WHERE responsibility_name = 'iProcurement'
AND fa.application_id = fr.application_id
```

To set up project properties, double-click the project name in the left-hand pane named Application Navigator. Within project properties, expand the Oracle Applications tree and enter the following properties:

Property Name	**Value**
DBC File Name	Full path to the .dbc file name, for example, c:\oaf\r124\jdevhome\jdev\dbc_files\secure\r12.dbc.
UserName	FND username that has access to iProcurement. For example, in a VISION instance, username OPERATIONS can be used.
Password	FND username password
Responsibility Application Short Name	Application short name of the application to which the iProcurement responsibility belongs—in this case, ICX.
Responsibility Key	Responsibility key of the responsibility to which the selected user must have access—in this case, SELF_SERVICE_PURCHASING_5.

Again within project properties, select Oracle Applications and this time select Run Options. Ensure that in Selected Options the value OADiagnostics is included. Also remove OADeveloperMode from the Selected Options. OADeveloperMode is usually used when building a new application. If OADeveloperMode is enabled for the project when doing extensions, it will cause various warnings to be displayed in the standard Oracle OAF screens. Therefore, it is recommended to remove OADeveloperMode when doing extensions.

NOTE
To explain the analogy between the JDeveloper and E-Business Suite runtime in this context, OADiagnostics in JDeveloper corresponds to a profile option named FND: Diagnostics, and OADeveloperMode corresponds to the profile option FND: Developer Mode.

One of the last steps in preparation is to copy the XML files for BC4J objects that you wish to extend from myclasses (originally sourced from $JAVA_TOP on the midtier box) into the myprojects directory in the JDeveloper installation on the desktop. Here you simply copy the XML files that define the BC4J objects that you will later extend. In the example, you need to extend the ReqSupplierVO view object that belongs to the package oracle.apps.icx.lov.server. Thus you first ensure that a directory tree c:\oaf\r124\jdevhome\jdev\myprojects\oracle\apps\icx\lov\server already exists. Next, copy all the XML files from c:\oaf\r124\jdevhome\jdev\myclasses\oracle\apps\icx\lov\server to c:\oaf\r124\jdevhome\jdev\myprojects\oracle\apps\icx\lov\server. When you do this, the XML file server.xml will also get copied to myprojects directory.

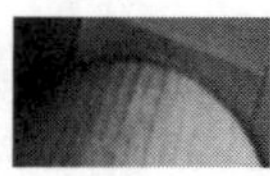

NOTE
The server.xml file is important when performing extensions of BC4J objects in Release 11i because to open the BC4J objects being extended, you need to import the server.xml from the package that contains the BC4J objects of your interest. The BC4J object being extended must be opened in JDeveloper. This can be done by selecting File | Import in JDeveloper 9i. Next select Import from Existing Sources and then click the Add button to browse the server.xml. You may find that in some cases server.xml is missing from the package within $JAVA_TOP. In such cases, you can copy any other server.xml and edit it in Notepad and then place it within an appropriate directory in myprojects. In rare cases, you may have to edit server.xml so that it contains just those BC4J objects that you wish to extend. Then you won't have to open other BC4J objects that are not being extended.

Running the Page From JDeveloper

In R12, you will be using the JDeveloper 10g version for OA Framework development. In JDeveloper 10g, when you expand the project node within the workspace, you will find an Application Sources node. As soon as you copy the MDS definitions of the pages to the myprojects directory on your desktop, you will be able to right-click that page to run it. In this example, expand the nodes as shown in Figure 9-11 and right-click to run the page.

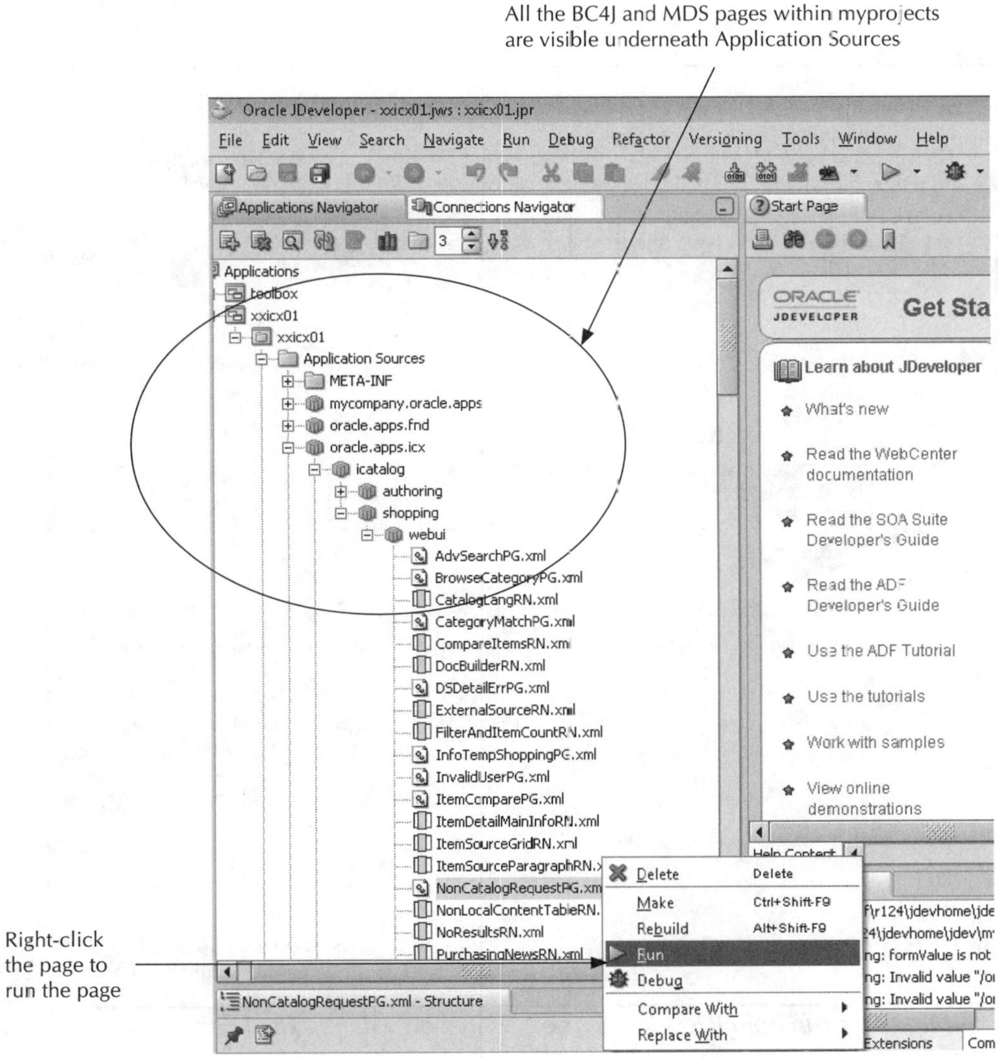

All the BC4J and MDS pages within myprojects are visible underneath Application Sources

Right-click the page to run the page

FIGURE 9-11. *Running the iProcurement NonCatalogRequestPG from JDeveloper in R12*

In Release11i, you will have to explicitly open the page within the project by browsing to the directory in myprojects\oracle\apps\icx\iccatalog\shopping\webui and selecting NonCatalogRequestPG.xml.

Once you run the page, you will be able to see the page as shown in Figure 9-12. You will see two regions: the main Non-Catalog Request page in the background, and the pop-up LOV region page.

When a user clicks the torch icon next to the Supplier Name field, it pops up a window that happens to be the LOV region for the supplier name and site. You need to add a new field in the Results section to display Supplier Site Email next to

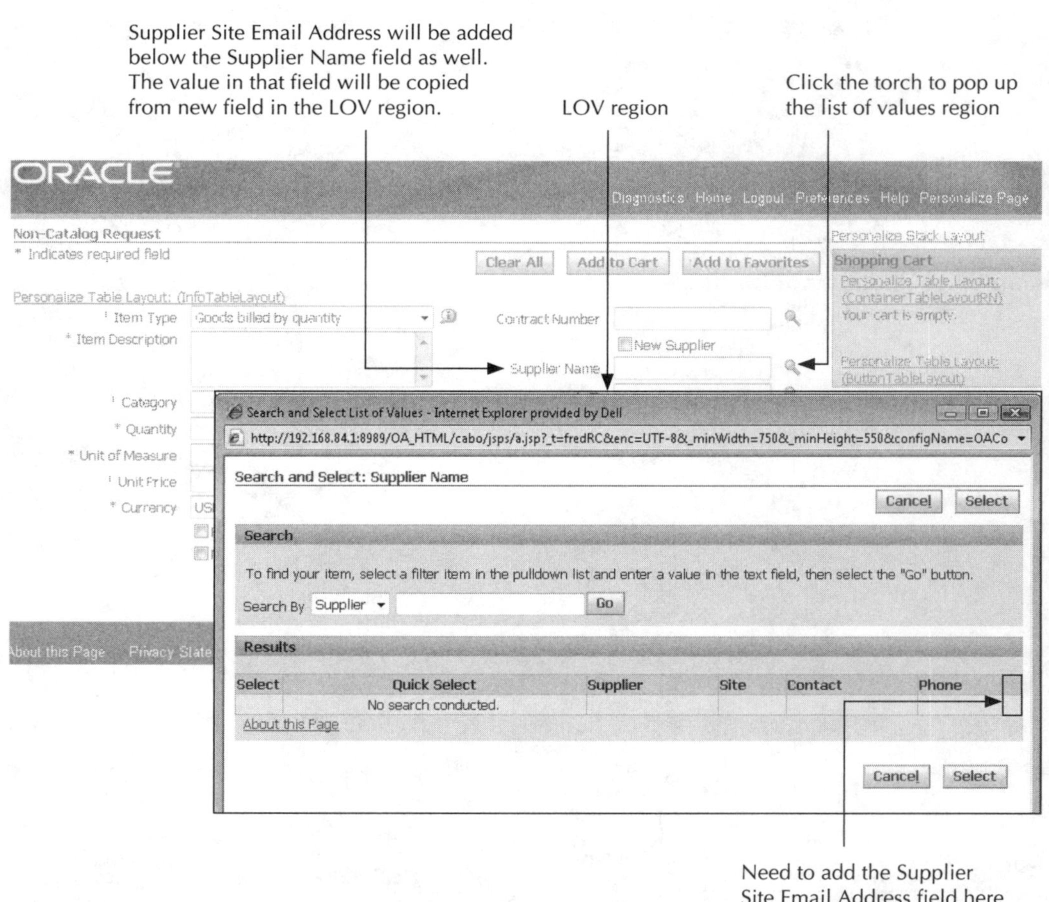

FIGURE 9-12. *Page run from JDeveloper. The LOV region will be extended to add e-mail.*

the Phone field. Once the user selects a record from the results section, the Supplier Site Email of the selected record must be copied back to a field on the main page, under the Supplier Name field. The site e-mail address thereafter should be stored in ATTRIBUTE15 in the requisition line table. Effectively, in this extension the aim is to create two fields, one in the LOV region and the other in the Non-Catalog Request page. Both of the new fields will display Supplier Site Email.

JDeveloper 10g allows you to browse through all the BC4J and MDS pages in the myprojects directory. Therefore, in the Application Sources underneath the JDeveloper project, you will see the entire directory tree for files that you transferred from $ICX_TOP/mds. We also copied all the XML files from myclasses\oracle\apps\icx\lov\server to myprojects\oracle\apps\icx\lov\server. Hence you will also be able to see the BC4J objects of the oracle.apps.icx.lov.server package in the Application Sources node. This package contains the view object ReqSupplierVO that you wish to extend.

Creating a Custom New View Object

An original BC4J object must be opened in the JDeveloper project before it can be extended. As you have already seen, the XML files pertaining to the BC4J object being extended must be copied to the myprojects folders first. You will not be able to create an extension for the BC4J object, unless that object has been opened within the JDeveloper project. JDeveloper 10g (R12) automatically makes these BC4J objects available under Application Sources. However, in order to open the BC4J objects in JDeveloper 9i (for Release 11i), certain steps must be followed.

11i: The steps for JDeveloper 9i are listed next:

1. Within the project, select File | Import.
2. From the window that pops up, select Import From Existing Sources.
3. Click the Add button, and then browse to select server.xml from the folder that contains the BC4J object being extended.

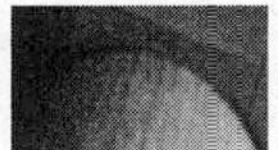

NOTE

Sometimes you might get an error when opening a BC4J view object in JDeveloper 9i. To work around that issue, edit server.xml in the myprojects folder using Notepad. Editing should be done in such a manner as to remove all BC4J object entries from server.xml other than the objects that you wish to extend. By doing so, when you import server.xml, only the BC4J objects that you wish to extend will be opened in JDeveloper.

Additionally, in some rare cases, you may find server.xml missing from $JAVA_TOP for a given package. In such cases, you can create a server.xml file manually. There are plenty of server.xml files around that can serve as examples, and you can copy and edit those to meet your needs, depending upon the objects that you wish to extend.

Once the desired BC4J object has been opened, you can proceed with the creation of an extended view object as shown in Figure 9-13.

The name you'll give your extended view object is xxReqSupplierVO, and it will be created within the package xxcust.oracle.apps.icx.lov.server. The existing view object already makes a join to the table PO_VENDOR_SITES_ALL. Therefore, in the extended view object's SQL, you will add PoVendorSitesAll.e-mail_address as XX_VEN_SITE_EMAIL. This will be added to the select list, just prior to the FROM clause within the view object's SQL Statement.

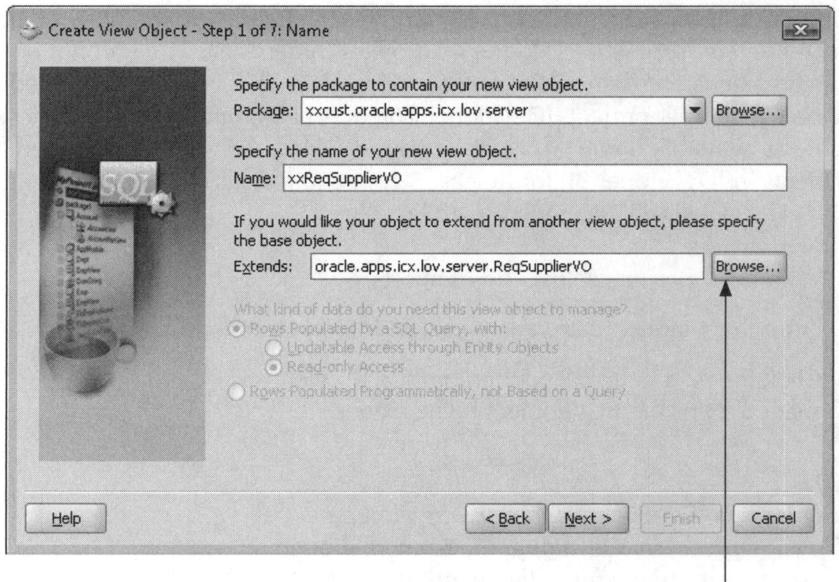

FIGURE 9-13. *Create a new view object that extends ReqSupplierVO.*

To create a new view object, follow these steps:

1. Right-click Project and select New. A pop-up window will open; expand the Business Tier node and select ADF Business Components.
2. On the right-hand side pane, select View Object to create a new view object. Click Next, and you will be presented with the Create View Object window.
3. Enter the values in the fields presented so that the package name is xxcust.oracle.apps.icx.lov.server, the view object name is xxReqSupplierVO, and the value in the Extends fields is oracle.apps.icx.lov.server.ReqSupplierVO. You can also click Browse beside the Extends field and select the view object ReqSupplierVO under the package oracle.apps.icx.lov.server. In the next window, you will find the SQL Statement inherited from the parent view object.
4. Modify the SQL Statement and add the text **,PoVendorSitesAll.e-mail_address as XX_VEN_SITE_EMAIL** just prior to the FROM clause of the SQL Statement. Introduction of this new column in a select statement results in creation of a new View Object Attribute.
5. Click the Test button and ensure that the query syntax is valid. Click the Next button to continue. Addition of a new column in the SQL SELECT list creates a new view object attribute.
6. Ensure that the binding style for the new view object is the same as for the parent view object. In this example, the binding style of the new view object should be Oracle Positional.
7. Ensure that the new view object attribute has the following properties:

   Name=xxVenSiteEmail
   Type=String
   Mapped to Column or SQL=Yes (*11i*: This property does not exist in 11i.)
   Selected in Query=Yes
   Queryable=Yes
   Updatable=Always
   Alias=XX_VEN_SITE_EMAIL
   Expression=XX_VEN_SITE_EMAIL

These view object attribute values are illustrated in Figure 9-14.

Click Next until you reach the Java step. Ensure that the Generate Java File check box is checked for the View Row Class. Click Next and then Finish to complete the creation of the view object.

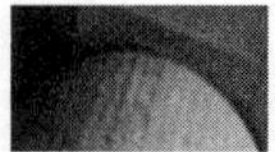

NOTE

When following the steps mentioned earlier, if you get an error message, "Each row in the Query Result Columns must be mapped to a unique query attribute in the Mapped Entity columns," follow the workaround shown here. In all other cases, ignore this note. Create a new view object and enter the values in the field, so that Package=xxcust.oracle.apps.icx.lov.server, Name=xxReqSupplierVO, and Extends= oracle.apps.icx.lov.server.ReqSupplierVO. You can click the button labeled Browse for Extends and select the view object ReqSupplierVO under the package oracle.apps.icx.lov.server. In the next window, when presented with the SQL Statement step, click Next without modifying the SQL Statement. Keep clicking Next until you reach step 5 of 7, Attributes. Here you will be presented with the list of existing attributes. Click the New button to create a new attribute with the name xxVenSiteEmail with the usual values for the attribute property. The remainder of the steps remain the same. Remember that with this workaround you have not yet modified the SQL Statement to include the Vendor Site Email address. Hence a transient VO Attribute was created, which is not yet mapped to the results of the SQL Statement. Now, double-click to open this new view object again, and click Next to modify the SQL Statement as desired. Modify the SQL Statement to include Vendor Site Email, click Next, and ensure that the View Object attribute is named xxVenSiteEmail, as shown in Figure 9-14.

***11i* Steps for a Creating a View Object in 11i** When creating the new view object in Release 11i, right-click the project and select New Business Components Package. Enter the package name as xxcust.oracle.apps.icx.lov.server and click Finish. Now right-click the new BC4J package that you have created and select New View Object. The remainder of the steps are the same as those for R12.

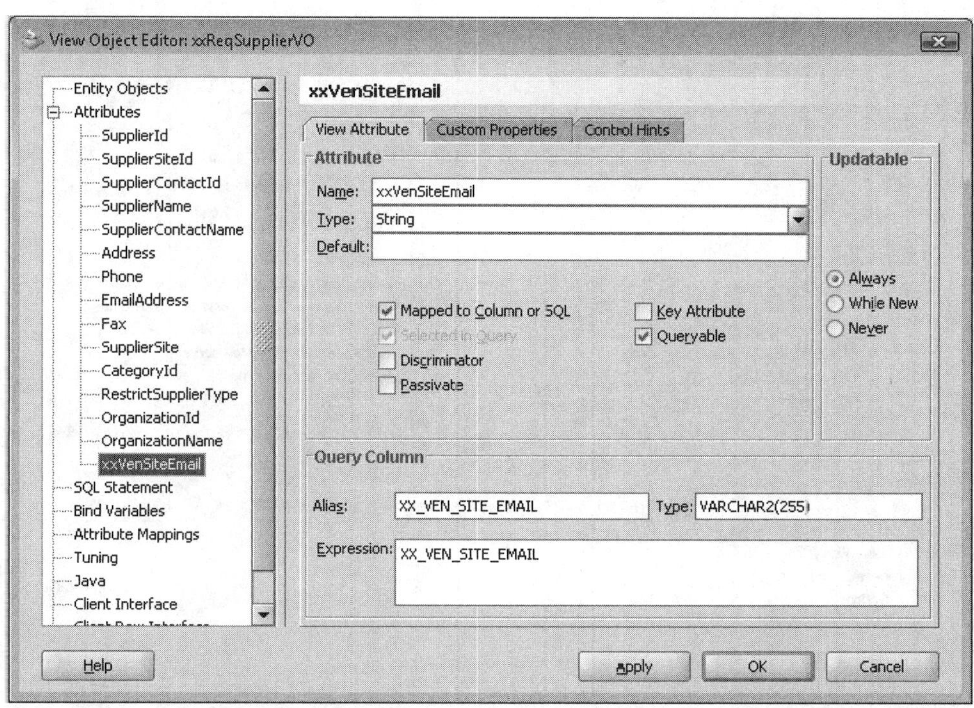

FIGURE 9-14. *New attribute added to the extended view object*

Substituting the View Object

Once the new view object has been created, you need to tell OA Framework to start using the new view object (xxReqSupplierVO) instead of the original view object (ReqSupplierVO). The pages will not be able to reference the Supplier Site Email field unless OAF is told to use the extended view object. In order to create the substitution, you can navigate to the Project Properties, and then click the Substitutions node within Business Components. Here you will be able to specify that xxReqSupplierVO replaces all occurrences of ReqSupplierVO, as shown in Figure 9-15.

NOTE

**11i*: To perform this substitution in Release 11i, in JDeveloper, right-click the project name and select Edit Business Components Project. The Business Components Project Editor window will pop up where you can enter the substitutions.*

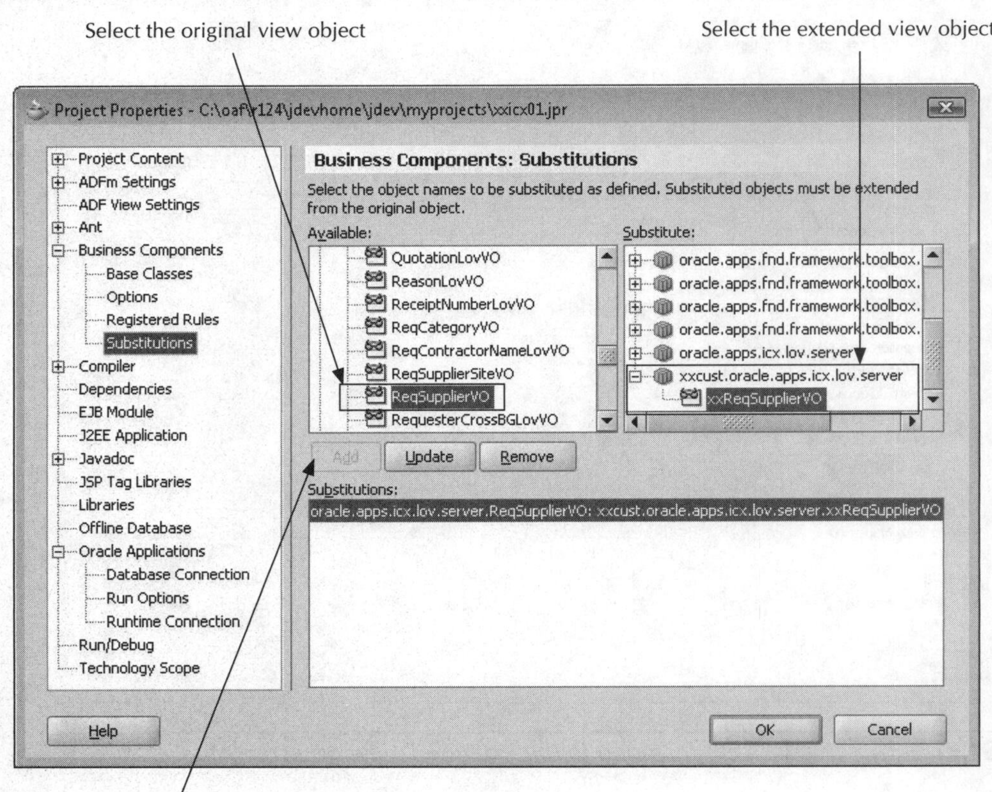

FIGURE 9-15. *View object substitution*

For BC4J extensions to be tested from JDeveloper, again within project properties, select Run/Debug. Now click Edit to modify the default Java Configuration. A new window will pop up. In the field Java Options, scroll to the very end and append the following entry: **-Djbo.project=xxicx01**. In this case, xxicx01 is the name of the JDeveloper Project.

NOTE
**11i*:- For 11i, that is, JDeveloper version 9i, you click project settings and select Runner at the very bottom of left-hand pane. Here you will be presented with Java Options, into which you can enter the -Djbo directive at the very end of the field.*

You enter the -Djbo directive because even though the project's JPX file contains the BC4J substitution details, the JDeveloper runtime does not read the project's JPX file. To make sure that the JDeveloper runtime reads the JPX file, you must configure the runtime system property -Djbo.project=*Name,* where *Name* is the JPX file name without the .jpx extension.

If you do not wish to enter the -Djbo.project directive, you can instead load the project's JPX file into the database using the jpximporter utility. In fact, you will have to load the substitution into the database at the time of deployment.

However, please note that importing the JPX file is optional when testing changes merely from JDeveloper. To run jpximport from the desktop machine where JDeveloper is installed, you can issue the following commands from the command prompt on your desktop:

```
cd C:\oaf\r124\jdevbin\oaext\bin
jpximport.bat C:\oaf\r124\jdevhome\jdev\myprojects\xxicx01.
jpx -username apps -password myappspassword -dbconnection
"(description=(address_list=(address=(community=tcp
.world)(protocol=tcp)(host=r12.com)(port=1533)))
(connect_data=(sid=R124)))"
```

Make sure that the port number, SID, ProjectName.jpx, machine name, and so on correspond to your E-Business Suite environment. The results of this command will appear as shown next:

```
Imported document : /oracle/apps/icx/lov/server/customizations/site/0/
ReqSupplierVO
Import completed successfully
```

NOTE

11i: *In Release 11i (JDeveloper 9i), the location of jpximport.bat is in <JDEV_INSTALL_DIRECTORY> \jdevbin\jdev\bin.*

Once the substitution has been imported, you can double-check the entry in MDS by running the following commands in a SQL Plus session that is connected to the Apps schema:

```
set serveroutput on ;
BEGIN
jdr_utils.listdocuments('/oracle/apps/icx/lov/server/',TRUE);
END;
/
```

This command returns:

```
Printing contents of /oracle/apps/icx/lov/server/ recursively
/oracle/apps/icx/lov/server/customizations/site/0/ReqSupplierVO
```

As you will notice, a site-level personalization has been created for this view object. Effectively, now you have a new document in the MDS repository called /oracle/apps/icx/lov/server/customizations/site/0/ReqSupplierVO. You can see the contents of this document by using jdr_utils.printDocument as shown next:

```
exec jdr_utils.printdocument
('/oracle/apps/icx/lov/server/customizations/site/0/ReqSupplierVO');
```

This will result in the XML listed next, which indicates that this personalization directive is responsible for the replacement of the standard view object by your custom view object:

```
<?xml version='1.0' encoding='UTF-8'?>
<customization xmlns="http://xmlns.oracle.com/jrad"
xmlns:ui="http://xmlns.oracle.com/uix/ui" xmlns:oa="http://xmlns
.oracle.com/oa" xmlns:user="http://xmlns.oracle.com/user"
version="10.1.3_1086" xml:lang="en-US"
customizes="/oracle/apps/icx/lov/server/ReqSupplierVO">
<replacewith="/xxcust/oracle/apps/icx/lov/server/xxReqSupplierVO"/>
</customization>
```

Now that the view object is substituted, the attribute xxVenSiteEmail will be available to use. With the substitution in place, you should not need to make any reference to xxReqSupplierVO because all the references to ReqSupplierVO will automatically be converted into a reference for xxReqSupplierVO.

Given that the definition of this substitution is stored in the MDS repository, it will be possible to export this personalization and then import it into a different E-Business Suite instance, using the Functional Administrator responsibility as indicated in the earlier sections. This means that you don't have to run the jpximport utility again on your UAT and Production E-Business Suite instances.

Creating Personalizations to Add New Fields to the Page

To complete the example, you need to create three personalizations:

1. To show Supplier Site Email in the Supplier LOV region.
2. To create a display field Supplier Site Email in the Non-Catalog page.
3. To create an LOV Mapping, so that value from Supplier Site Email field in the LOV region (in step 1) is copied to the field in the Non-Catalog page (created in step 2).

Let us walk through these steps in detail. To create a new field in LOV region, first navigate to the LOV region, and then click the Personalize Page link. In case you do not find a personalization link on the LOV page, you can personalize the LOV region from the Functional Administrator responsibility: first, click the Personalization tab. Then, in the Document Path field, enter /oracle/apps/icx/lov/webui/ReqSupplierLovRN and click Go, as shown in Figure 9-16. Next, click the Personalize Page link for region ReqSupplierLovRN. This will present you with the Choose Personalization Context screen; click Apply and ensure that the Site Include check box is enabled. Now, you click the Create Item icon next to Table: (SupplierLovTableRN), as shown in Figure 9-17. This table is a region that displays the search result of LOV in tabular format. You need to add a new field for Supplier

It is possible to personalize any OA Framework page in E-Business Suite using the Functional Administrator responsibility.

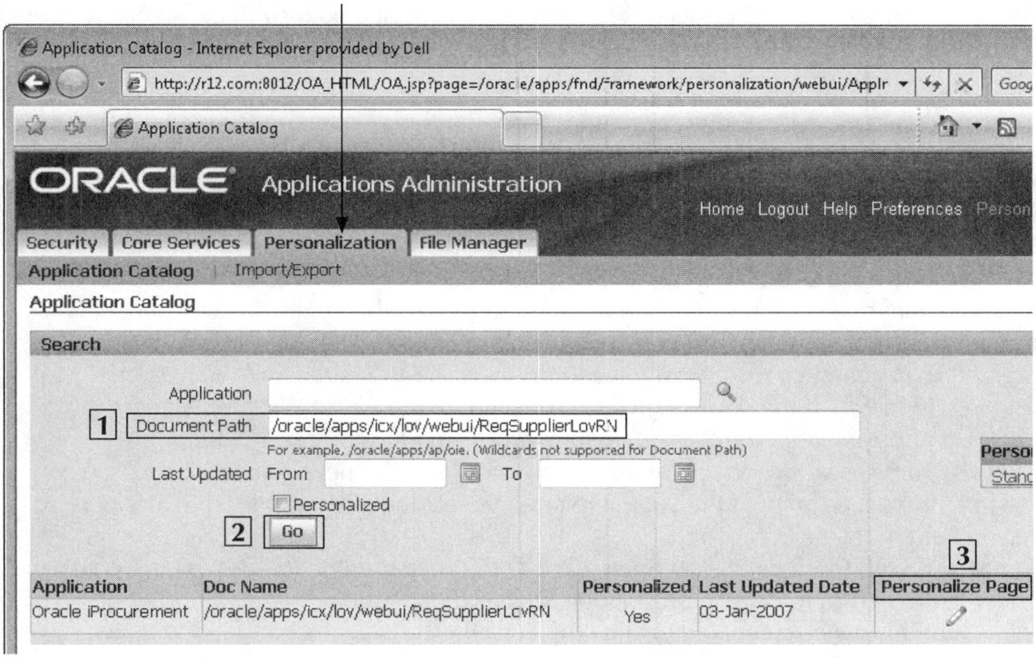

FIGURE 9-16. *Personalize the LOV page using the Functional Administrator responsibility.*

Site Email, so you need to create a new item within this tabular region through personalization. Enter following values in the Create Item screen:

Field	Value	Comments
Level	Site	
Item Style	Message Styled Text	So that item style is display only
ID	xxVendorSiteEmailFieldLOV	A unique name for field created via personalization
Prompt	Vendor Site Email	
View Attribute	xxVenSiteEmail	Name of the view object attribute that is the source of data for this item being created
View Instance	ReqSupplierVO	You have not entered xxReqSupplierVO because ReqSupplierVO will automatically be translated into xxReqSupplierVO by substitution.

The Create New Item screen will appear similar to the image in Figure 9-18.

By following these steps, you will be able to see the Supplier Site Email address field in the LOV region. When you perform a search for a supplier in the LOV region, you should now see the appropriate e-mail address returned from PO_VENDOR_SITES_ALL for that record.

Navigate back to the Non-Catalog Request page. You need to create a field on this page that maps to Attribute15 of the view object on that region. You also need to figure the location within the hierarchy of the pages where this new item will be created. You can click About this page to discover the VO name and the nested region within which the new item will be created. In the About this page screen, click Expand All within the Page Definition and search for the existing field SupplierName as shown in Figure 9-19. You know that the new item must be created in the proximity of the SupplierName, therefore you search for the Supplier Name field in the page hierarchy.

Armed with these details, navigate back to the Non-Catalog Request page by clicking the Return to Page: Non-Catalog Request link at the bottom-left corner of the About this page screen. Now, click the Personalize Page link, and in the Style field, select Labeled Field Layout from the drop-down list and click Go. You will now be able to see the region SupplierInfoLabelRN. Click the Create Item link next to that region and enter the following details:

Field	Value	Comments
Level	Site	
ID	xxVendorSiteEmail MainField	A unique name for field created via personalization
Item Style	Message Styled Text	So that item style is display only
Prompt	Vendor Site Email	
View Attribute	Attribute15	The value returned from LOV will be stored in Attribute15 of the requisition line
View Instance	NonCatalogRequestVO	Name of the view object

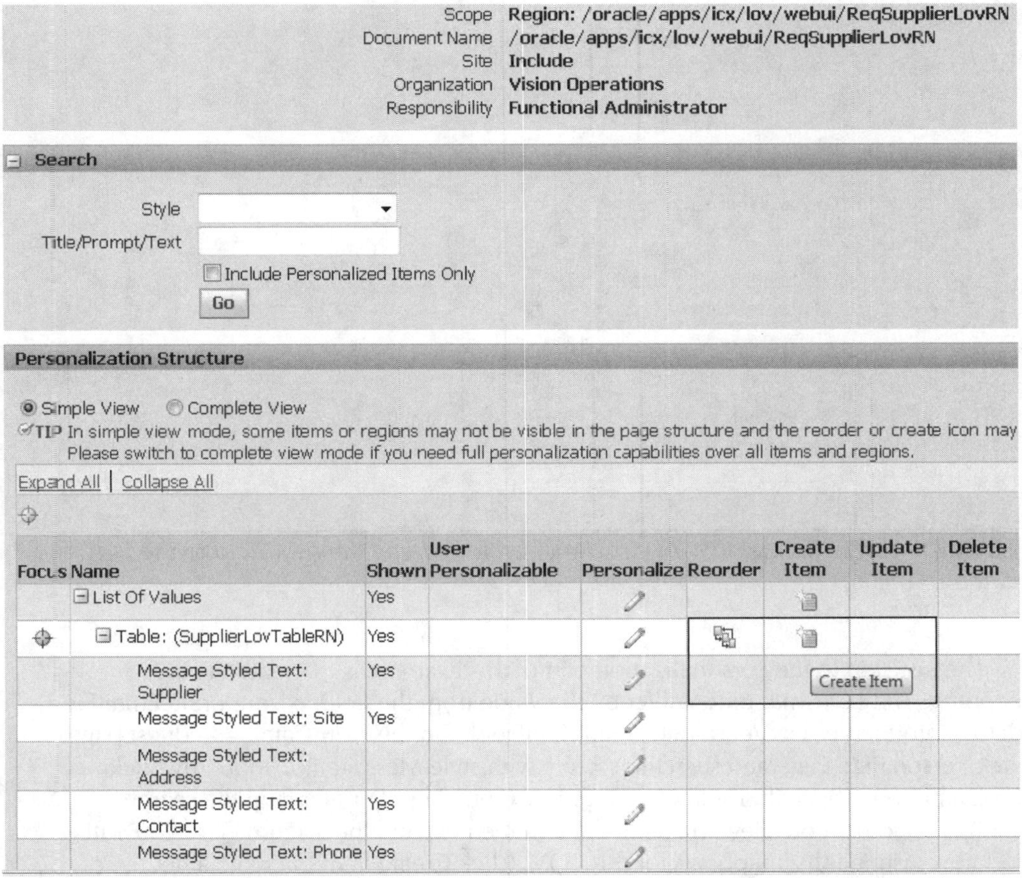

FIGURE 9-17. *Create a new item that will display the Vendor Site Email at runtime.*

ORACLE Applications Administration

Security | Core Services | Personalization | File Manager

Application Catalog | Import/Export

Create Item

* Indicates required field

Level: Site

Item Style: Message Styled Text

Property	Value
* ID	xxVendorSiteEmailFieldLOV
Access Key	
Rendered	true
Required	no
Scope	.
Search Allowed	false
Selective Search Criteria	false
Sort Allowed	no
Sort By View Attribute	
Tip Message Name	
Tip Type	none
Total Value	false
User Personalization	false
Vertical Aligment	middle
View Attribute	xxVenSiteEmail
View Instance	ReqSupplierVO
Warn About Changes	true
Width	

FIGURE 9-18. *Minimal information required for adding the new field to the LOV search results*

The last step in the personalization part of this example is to create the LOV mapping. The LOV mapping will copy the value from the field xxVendorSiteEmailFieldLOV into the field xxVendorSiteEmailMainField. On the Non-Catalog Request page, click Personalize Page and search for items with style Message Lov Input, by clicking the Go button. This will display Message Lov Input: Supplier Name in the search results. Click the icon View In Hierarchy and then expand the + icon. Here you will find the existing LOV mappings for this LOV. Click Create Item to create a new mapping as shown in the following table:

Field	Value	Comments
Level	Site	
ID	xxVenSiteEmailLOVMap	Any unique name within the page for a field created via personalization
Item Style	Lov Map	
*LOV Region Item	xxVendorSiteEmailFieldLOV	Name of the item in the LOV region that displays supplier site e-mail
Return Item	xxVendorSiteEmailMainField	Name of the item in the main noncatalog request page that displays the value returned by LOV

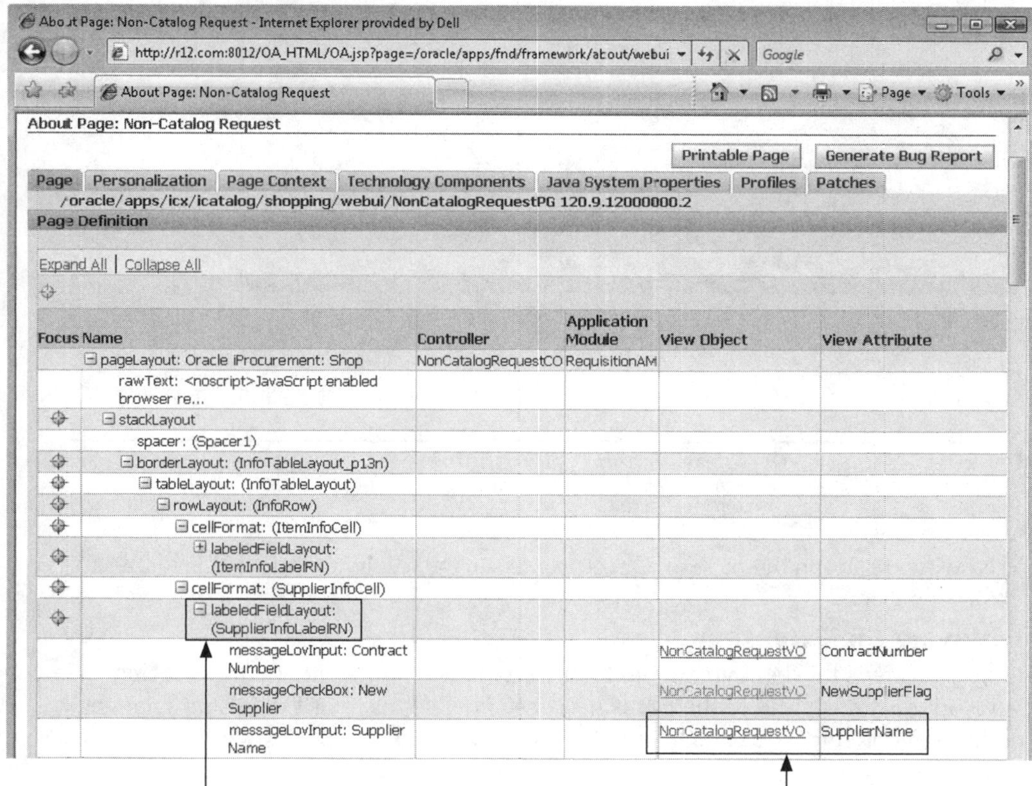

FIGURE 9-19. *How to find out the region within which the new item must be created*

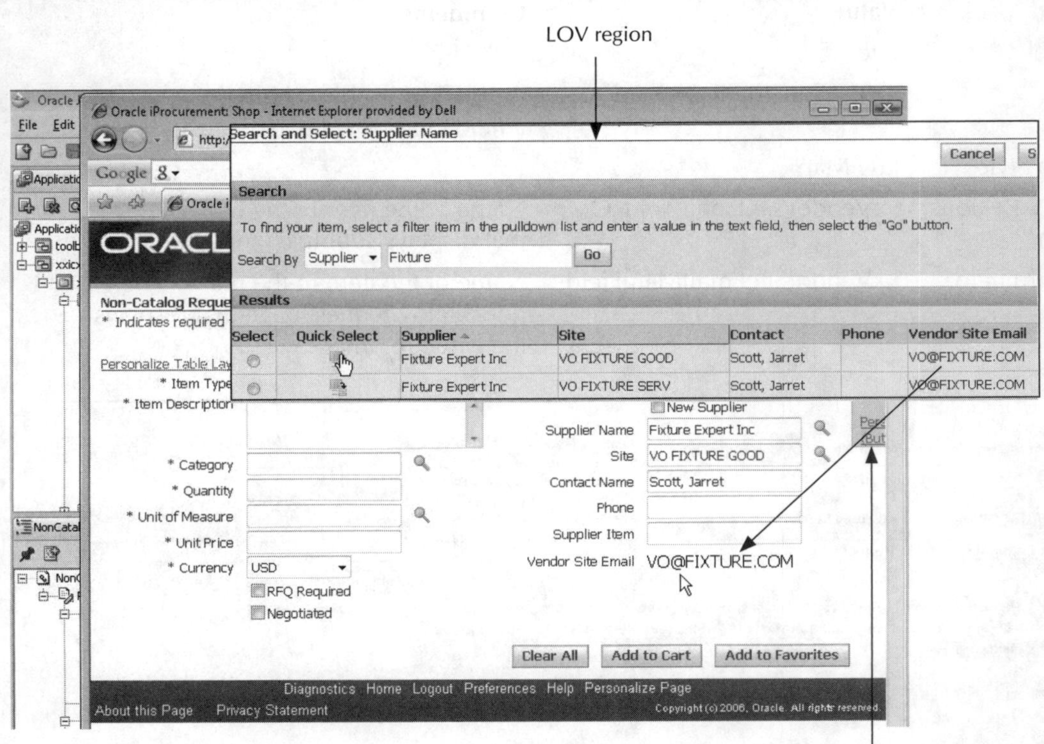

FIGURE 9-20. *Result of VO extension and LOV mapping*

Now, you can run the page in JDeveloper to see the results as shown in Figure 9-20.

Deploying the Extension

The logical steps for deployment are to ensure that each change you made using JDeveloper is transferred to the E-Business instance. Let us revisit the list of changes you implemented for the extension in the example:

Change via JDeveloper	Comments	Deployment Step
Creation of a new view object	Runtime files are in myclasses/xxcust.	Copy the entire xxcust to $JAVA_TOP so that you get $JAVA_TOP/xxcust on the server. This needs to be done on each midtier unless the code directories are shared across the midtiers.
Personalizations to create items and LOV mapping	Even though pages are run from JDeveloper, when personalizations are done they get directly stored into the database.	They are already in the database instance against which pages were personalized when run from JDeveloper. Use the Functional Administrator responsibility to extract and to apply these personalizations on another EBS instance.
Substitution of a view object	Run jpximport to load the substitution into the database.	Substitution details are stored in the same layer as personalizations. Use the Functional Administrator responsibility to extract and to apply these personalizations on another EBS instance.

To summarize, the deployment will involve following steps:

1. Load substitution information into the Oracle Apps database using jpximport.
2. Transfer the entire myclasses/xxcust from the JDeveloper installation to the $JAVA_TOP/xxcust directory on all of the midtier target boxes.

You will notice that all the changes made to implement this extension are either stored in the personalization layer (not the core MDS layer) or in a file system location beginning with xx%. Oracle never delivers any object names beginning with XX in E-Business Suite.

Once the deployment is completed, you should bounce the midtier (not just the Apache) for our view object substitution to take effect. This can be done by the following command on an R12 instance. You must have an Apps schema password to run these commands:

```
$INST_TOP/admin/scripts/adstpall.sh
```

The command adstpall.sh will stop the midtier and its services. To start the midtier services, run command adstrtal.sh:

```
$INST_TOP/admin/scripts/adstrtal.sh
```

OA Framework Extensions Tips

In this section, we will discuss miscellaneous items that could be useful while working on OA Framework extensions. The majority of the suggestions and recommendations are products of practical experience from field work and working with numerous clients.

Personalizations with SPEL and Other Options

Some of the common personalizations performed by E-Business Suite implementation teams are to hide or show items or regions on a page, make items read only, and make fields mandatory or nonmandatory. Typically, these properties can be assigned the following values: TRUE, FALSE, or SPEL. SPEL (Simplest Possible Expression Language) is an expression that returns a Boolean value, either TRUE or FALSE.

We made up a scenario to help you understand how SPEL works. Let us assume that in one of the pages, a person's details are displayed along with salary information. In addition to that, assume that the business requirement is to display the salary of that person only if the currently logged-in person is a supervisor of the person record being displayed. Obviously, it will not be possible to hard code either TRUE or FALSE against the property Rendered for the Salary field through the personalization as there is a condition attached to it. To overcome this problem, you can use the SPEL expression that can be applied to the property Rendered for the Salary field. The SPEL expression will equate to TRUE if the currently logged-in person is the manager of the person record being displayed. Assuming that the underlying view object's name is personDetailsVO and it has a Boolean attribute called isCurrentUserSupervisorOfPerson, we can build a SPEL expression that reads: ${oa.personDetailsVO.isCurrentUserSupervisorOfPerson}. This SPEL expression can then be attached to the property Rendered of the Salary field using personalization. Whenever the person's manager logs in to see the record, he or she will be able to see the Salary field, as this expression will return TRUE. For all other users, the salary information will be hidden, thanks to the personalization framework, as this expression will return FALSE.

One of the biggest assumptions made in this example is that Oracle will have already delivered a Boolean view object attribute that will meet the need of your SPEL syntax. Of course, that may not always be true. In such cases, you can either extend that view object to create the new view object attribute or you may decide to extend the controller. In the extended controller, you would first call super().processRequest(), and then execute your custom code. The following snippet shows what the controller code may look like:

```
OAMessageStyledTextBean personSalary = (personSalary)oawebbean
.findChildRecursive("SalaryFieldName");
if (/*expression-current person is supervisor of person record being
displayed*/)
{ personSalary.setRendered(true); }
else
{ personSalary.setRendered(false); }
```

Embedding Custom Region into Standard Pages

This is one of the most popular extensions techniques for embedding extra functionality into the standard OA Framework pages. With this technique, you can build any custom XML region that has its own custom Application Module (AM) and a number of custom view objects (VOs). Of course, this custom region can leverage standard AM and VO as well if applicable. One thing to keep in mind is that the custom region must be a StackLayout type of region. The controller attached to this region will be passed the pageContext object of the top-level region of the page into which it gets embedded. The custom region can therefore get a handle to the parameters being passed to the main page itself. In addition to that, you can also use a pageContext object to get a handle to the top-level Application Module for that transaction by invoking the getRootApplicationModule() method.

Here is the list of the steps that you need to perform in order to embed a custom region:

1. Create a stackLayout region in JDeveloper and attach Application Module and nested regions as per your business requirements.

2. Load the custom region into the MDS repository using the XML Importer utility. Transfer the objects from the myclasses JDeveloper directory to $JAVA_TOP/xxcust on the midtier box. Note down the full path of the custom region that has been loaded into database. The full path will be similar to /xxcust/oracle/apps/fnd/framework/toolbox/tutorial/OrderDetailsRN.

3. Personalize the page into which the custom stackLayout region will be embedded. Create a new Flexible Layout item using personalization and give it a unique name/ID.

4. While in the personalization hierarchy page, locate the Flexible Layout that you have created in the previous step and create a new Flexible Content item within it. Give this item a unique name and ID and in the Extends field enter the full path of the custom region you wish to embed.

By following these steps, you will be able to embed a custom region into the standard page. The custom region may not necessarily have to be a read-only region. By using this approach, you can link an independently developed region into the standard page. To the end user, the custom region will appear as a normal region and will be consistent with the overall look and feel of the standard page.

Working with Nested Application Modules

Let us assume that a single transaction involves three pages: Page1, Page2, and Page3. In this example, we'll also assume that Page1 AM is AM1; Page2 AM is AM1, with its nested shared region using AM2; and Page3 AM is AM1 with a shared nested region based on AM3. When a user navigates from Page1 to Page2 to Page3 while retaining the AM, then on Page2, AM1 will remain the root AM, whereas AM2 will become a nested AM. Similarly, on Page3, AM1 will remain the root AM, whereas AM2 and AM3 will become nested AMs. This is known as implicit nesting because nowhere at the time of defining Application Modules did we create a relationship between the three Application Modules.

Explicit nesting is different, whereby you navigate to the Application Module property in JDeveloper and attach further Application Modules for reference.

In case of implicit nesting, if you need to get a handle to the nested AM, you cannot simply do pageContext.getRootApplicationModule().findApplicationModule ("AM2"). This is because the OA Framework dynamically nests AM2 and AM3 at runtime, and in the process of doing so these nested AMs get their names on the fly.

For example, if you wish to get a handle to nested AM in the controller code written at the top level, use the following code snippet:

```
String amName = "";
String nestedAMArray[] = pageContext.getRootApplicationModule()
.getApplicationModuleNames();
System.out.println("Root AM=>"+pageContext.getRootApplicationModule()
.getName() + " Child AMs=>"+ nestedAMArray.length);
for(int i = 0; i < nestedAMArray.length; i++)
{
amName = nestedAMArray[i];
System.out.println("Nested AM Name=>"+amName);
ApplicationModule  am =pageContext.getRootApplicationModule()
.findApplicationModule(amName);
if ( am != null )
  System.out.println("Found Handle to Nested AM " + amName );
}
```

This code will produce the following results:

```
Root AM=>AM1 Child AMs=>2

Nested AM Name=>region10_region1_oracle_apps_fnd_framework_toolbox_
    tutorial_server_AM2

Found Handle to Nested AM region10_region1_oracle_apps_fnd_framework_
    toolbox_tutorial_server_AM2

Nested AM Name=>region11_region1_oracle_apps_fnd_framework_toolbox_
    tutorial_server_AM3

Found Handle to Nested AM region11_region1_oracle_apps_fnd_framework_
    toolbox_tutorial_server_AM3
```

When writing code to get a handle to nested AMs, you will have to be aware that nested AMs cannot always be located by their original names.

Listing the Page Parameters

When working in an extended controller, or when developing a controller for the stackLayout region that will be embedded, it is important to know the list of all the parameters that are available to the page; as mentioned previously, this can be achieved with the pageContext object. With the simple code snippet shown next, you will be able to display all the parameters that are available to the controller.

First, add the import statement:

```
import java.util.Enumeration ;
String xxParamName;
for(
Enumeration enumeration = pageContext.getParameterNames();
enumeration.hasMoreElements();
System.out.println ("Parameter Name=>" + xxParamName + " Parameter
Value=> " + pageContext.getParameter(xxParamName))
)
{xxParamName = (String)enumeration.nextElement();}
```

Using Profile Options to Achieve Server-Level Personalization

In Oracle E-Business Suite, there is a Preferences function that can be made available to all the users. Let us assume that you have embedded a custom stackLayout region xxPrefstackLayoutRN to this page. This region also dynamically displays messages and instructions (text) to the end user.

Your business requirement is that when the Preferences page is accessed by an internal user (such as staff), the page should display the embedded region so that your internal staff can read the desired message and instructions. However, as per your business requirements, the same preference page must not show the custom embedded region when the Preferences page is accessed externally from the Internet (hosted by externally facing midtier). The limitation of the personalization framework is that you cannot define personalization at the server level. However, we do know that a profile option called Node Trust Level is set to a value of External (internal value 3) for External midtiers.

In this case, you can add the following code to the controller:

```
OAStackLayoutBean oastacklayoutbean = (OAStackLayoutBean)webBean
   .findChildRecursive("xxPrefstackLayoutRN");
if ((oastacklayoutbean != null) &&pageContext.getProfile("NODE_TRUST_
LEVEL").equals("3"))
     oastacklayoutbean.setRendered(false);
```

The extended controller must then be attached to the standard page via personalization. After the extension is complete, the users accessing the Preferences page from the external middle tiers will not be able to see the embedded custom region.

View Object Extension/Substitution but Not at Site Level

You have seen that extended view objects substitute the standard view objects at the site level. Effectively this means that all users across all the responsibilities will see the effect of the view object extension. How do you deal with this if your business requirement dictates that a view object extension must be applicable for only a certain set of responsibilities? In that case, the approach listed next can be implemented, assuming the name of the VO being extended is SequencePickListVO:

1. Create a profile option XX Switch VO SequencePickListVO.
2. Set this profile to No at the site level but to Yes at the required responsibility level.
3. Now create an extended VO in which the UNION ALL operator can be used in the SQL Statement. The first part of UNION ALL will return records as per custom conditions when the profile option is set to Yes. This part of the SQL Statement will have in its WHERE clause a fnd_profile.value(XX_SWITCH_VO_SPLV)='Y' condition.
4. The second part of the UNION ALL operator can have a WHERE clause with the fnd_profile.value(XX_SWITCH_VO_SPLV)='N' condition appended to it. The other WHERE clause conditions will remain the same as in the standard view object's SQL Statement.

Passing Parameters Between Pages

There are various ways of passing parameters from one page to another. The most common practice is to use a HashMap object. However, if you are building a custom application that has transactions spanning multiple pages, HashMap has to be built each time with the desired parameters and values. Some developers use an alternative such as creating session variables by invoking pageContext .putSessionValue (nameOfSessionVariable,valueOfSessionVariable). To retrieve the value method, pageContext.getSessionValue(nameOfSessionVariable) can be used. The problem with session variables is that their values are retained even after the transaction has been completed: effectively, as long as the user session remains active, the session variable values are retained.

In such cases, another option can be considered. Let us assume that you wish to retain the value of all the parameters so long as the transaction remains active, that is, as long as the RootAM is not released. In this case, you can create a custom view object with transient attributes. You can create one transient attribute for each parameter and such a view object will have only one record. To set the parameter values, you can invoke the set<Attribute> method to set view object attribute values. This view object can thereafter be attached to the root Application Module. In this case, so long as the AM is retained from one page to another, this view object will remain available and therefore parameter values can be accessed from any of the pages that belong to this transaction.

Clearing the MDS Cache

OA Framework caches flexfield, value set definitions and other AOL objects to improve performance. Therefore, you must clear the MDS cache if you make changes to any of these objects. The MDS cache can be cleared from the Functional Administrator responsibility by following this navigation path:

(N)Functional Administrator>(Tab)Core Services>(SubTab)Caching Framework (SideNav)>Global Configuration(B)Clear All Cache

This step is also useful when you create new items or LOV mappings using personalizations; note that sometimes the global cache must be cleared for certain kinds of personalization changes to take effect.

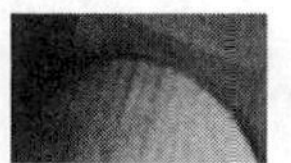

TIP

Changes made to XML and Java class files within $JAVA_TOP or to any files within CLASSPATH do not become effective by clearing the global cache. For changes made to files within CLASSPATH, you should bounce the Apache in E-Business Suite version 11i. For version R12, instead of bouncing the Apache, you should bounce the oacore ocj4 using the script $INST_TOP/admin/scripts/adoacorectl.sh.

Personalizations When Running Pages from JDeveloper

It is possible to perform a personalization when running the pages from JDeveloper. JDeveloper runs the OA Framework pages within embedded OC4J (Oracle Components For Java). However, even if pages are run from JDeveloper, the personalizations are still stored in the database MDS repository.

For example, the OA Framework extension example in this chapter adds an item xxVendorSiteEmailFieldLOV to the LOV region. Even if you were to perform this personalization while running that page from JDeveloper, the definition of this new item would still get registered with the MDS repository. This new item references a view object attribute xxVenSiteEmail in the view object ReqSupplierVO. During development, the extended xxReqSupplierVO existed in the JDeveloper myclasses directory, and hence a reference to xxVenSiteEmail was found when running the page from JDeveloper. However, if the same LOV page were run from the application by logging into the iProcurement responsibility, then the user would get an error. This is because even though personalizations get directly stored in database, the extended view objects must still be copied across to the midtier. To resolve this issue, the deployment steps must be completed immediately after testing the changes from JDeveloper.

Missing server.xml in Release 11i

In some rare cases, you will notice that server.xml might be missing from one of the packages in $JAVA_TOP. If you are intending to extend a view object, then it must first be opened in JDeveloper. If you find that its package does not have server.xml, then you can manually create server.xml using a text editing tool such as Notepad.

Also if you wish to open just one single view object in JDeveloper, then you may opt to create just one entry in server.xml on your desktop. You do not need to deploy the edited server.xml back to the middle tier. A sample server.xml is shown next:

```
<?xml version="1.0" encoding='windows-1252'?>
<!DOCTYPE JboPackage SYSTEM "jbo_03_01.dtd">
<!-- $Header: server.xml 120.5 2005/08/04 02:19 sosingha noship $ -->
<JboPackage
 Name="server"
 SeparateXMLFiles="true"
 PackageName="oracle.apps.icx.poplist.server" >
<DesignTime>
  <Attr Name="_version" Value="9.0.3.13.56" />
  <Attr Name="_ejbPackage" Value="false" />
</DesignTime>
<Containee
  Name="CategoryTypeVO"
  FullName="oracle.apps.icx.poplist.server.CategoryTypeVO"
  ObjectType="ViewObject" >
</Containee>
</JboPackage>
```

Of course, when building your own server.xml, you will use the relevant package name, Containee Name, Fullname, and ObjectType. Permissible object types in server.xml are the different types of BC4J objects, that is, Entity, AppModule, ViewObject, ViewLink, and Association.

Filtering the Contents in JDeveloper 10g for R12

The Application Sources node in JDeveloper displays all the OA Framework pages, BC4J objects, and other objects that are present in the myprojects folder of JDeveloper. However, you may wish to restrict the list of components displayed for each project. For example, you may wish to restrict contents displayed in Application Sources to icx and xxcust objects. To achieve that, you can click Project Properties in JDeveloper and select the Project Content node on the left-hand pane. Within the Project Content under the Include/Exclude tab, you can add the list of objects that you wish to display in the Application Sources node.

Debugging Techniques in OA Framework

The most common debugging requirement is to be able to see the SQL Statements that are being executed from OA Framework pages. For this, SQL Trace can be initiated from the Diagnostics link when running the page. Of course, the FND: Diagnostics profile option must be set. When you click the Diagnostics link, you will be presented with a drop-down list labeled Diagnostics. To run SQL Trace of OAF Session, select the Set Trace Level option. In order to see the bind variable values, select the Trace with the binds and waits option.

Another way of seeing all the SQL Statements is by enabling BC4J trace in JDeveloper. However, to do so you will have to run the page from JDeveloper itself. Prior to running that page, append -Djbo.debugoutput=console to the Runner property for the project in JDeveloper. After setting this property, you will be able to see all the SQL Statements in the JDeveloper console while running the page.

Sometimes at runtime you get an error message with the complete Java error stack. In such cases, look out for the text containing "## Detail," which usually pinpoints the source of the error. This error stack message also lists the line number from which the error was thrown. If the error originates from a Java class for which you do not have access to source code, then, subject to your country's regulations for using Java decompilers such as JAD, you can run jad -lnc abc.class, where abc is the name of the class. The -lnc option will produce a decompiled text file containing the line numbers from original Java source code. This allows easy debugging for the root cause of the error.

JDeveloper has a very powerful built-in debugger that can be used to set breakpoints to debug the pages when run from JDeveloper.

Lastly, in rare cases you will receive the error message, "You have encountered an unexpected error. Please contact the System Administrator for assistance."

In such cases, you can enable the profile options FND: Debug Log Level to Statement, FND: Debug Log Enabled to Yes for your username, and FND: Debug Log Module to %. Once you set these profile options using the Functional Administrator responsibility, log out and log back in to reproduce the error. After reproducing the error, query on table FND_LOG_MESSAGES for your FND user_id. After completing your debugging, reset these profile options if you wish to disable FND logging.

Summary

You learned the basic fundamentals of OA Framework technology. You saw how JDeveloper can be set up to perform development and extensions in OA Framework. To keep the custom code safe from upgrades and patches, it must be ensured that all custom code resides in a custom package. The name of the custom package and objects must begin with xx<cust>, where cust is the short name of the company. Good naming conventions also facilitate quick recognition of the custom code. It is important to develop and unit test all the extensions via JDeveloper itself before deploying all the extensions to the server. The login context of Oracle E-Business Suite is simulated in JDeveloper by specifying the FND User and responsibility details in the project properties.

The example undertaken in the extensions exercise also covered personalizations. Extensions almost always involve some level of admin-level personalizations. We also saw that OA Framework also allows for end users to perform user-level personalizations. User-level personalizations can be done by the end users themselves to create personalized views of the queried data.

Lastly, you saw the steps involved in deploying OA Framework extensions to E-Business Suite. Given the CLASSPATH feature of Java, it is possible to create the xxcust package in a custom directory location, instead of customizations being stored underneath $JAVA_TOP. In such cases, a new environment variable named XXCUST_JAVA_TOP can be created by the DBAs. By making the XXCUST_JAVA_TOP directory available within CLASSPATH, you can avoid the need to modify any of the contents within $JAVA_TOP.

CHAPTER 10

Custom Look and Feel

An ability to completely customize the appearance of the HTML-based user interface is probably one of the most underutilized features in E-Business Suite. This feature is referred to as Customizing Look and Feel, or CLAF for short, and is available as of the 11.5.10 (Cumulative Update 2) release of Oracle Applications. A typical scenario where you can use CLAF is in externally facing E-Business Suite applications such as iRecruitment, iSupplier, and other modules that are Internet facing. It is reasonable to expect that the appearance of the Internet facing HTML-based application conforms to the corporate UI standards and looks similar to the rest of the corporate website. To give you an even better idea, consider the Internet facing pages of the iRecruitment module; it is not uncommon that iRecruitment is successfully implemented in an organization, but its appearance is completely different from the rest of the corporate website. This is quite usual because the default look and feel that is shipped with Oracle Applications is normally very different from the external appearance and branding standards for a corporate website.

In this chapter, we'll outline the process of creating a completely new GUI theme for HTML-based applications in Oracle Applications. Throughout this chapter, we'll refer to this process as CLAF (Custom Look and Feel). You may also hear some people refer to this process of application branding as *skinning* (creating custom skins), and in the context of this book they mean the same thing.

In the following sections, we'll give a high-level overview of UIX (User Interface XML) technology, which is the underlying technology that makes it possible to create custom skins in Oracle Applications; we'll also provide a practical guide with example templates and the best practices on how to create a custom skin in both R11i and R12.

UIX: CLAF Enabling Technology

In OA Framework, the presentation layer in R11i and R12 is built on Oracle's UIX (User Interface XML) technology. Prior to the broad adoption of ADF (Application Development Framework) Faces in Oracle's current products, UIX was Oracle's main framework for building web applications, and is still used in E-Business Suite R11i and R12. Using a framework such as UIX enables developers to design their applications with a consistent look and feel, which is one of the main reasons for its broad acceptance across many of Oracle's web-based products.

With UIX, you can create web pages where you specify page layout, data sources, and user interface events. In E-Business Suite, OA Framework takes care of data binding and events, making the process of web page design much easier; without OA Framework, this needs to be done by an application developer.

A UIX page can be conceptualized as a hierarchical tree of user interface nodes. User interface nodes can be familiar web components such as headers, tables, tabs, input text boxes, and others. They can also be UIX-specific components such as pageLayout, stackLayout, and corporateBranding. User interface nodes can also have one or more child nodes that can be both visible and invisible on the web page. Visible components are web widgets that you see on web pages such as submit buttons, text boxes, radio buttons, and others. Invisible components usually serve as containers for other components such as the pageLayout UIX component. You use uiXML code structures to create UIX pages. Figure 10-1 shows a UIX page code structure and rendered page layout. From the example, you can see that the pageLayout component serves as a container for other components and also organizes the content within the UIX page. A typical page layout is divided into several main areas:

- Branding
- Navigation
- Global
- Buttons
- Page content
- Footer

Coding of UIX pages can be a fairly complex affair and, as we mentioned earlier, it is obsolete and replaced by newer ADF technologies in the latest versions of JDeveloper 11g. The good news is that you only need to be aware of some aspects of UIX technology to be able to successfully create a custom look and feel in Oracle Applications. It is beyond the scope of this book to discuss the features and coding techniques used to create UIX applications. UIX is documented in the older versions of JDeveloper 9i; we suggest taking a look at tutorials that are bundled with JDeveloper 9i for more details on UIX.

UIX technology enables the customization of the appearance of OA Framework pages by allowing you to specify your own definitions of custom styles, custom icons, or custom renderers for UIX components. There are two look and feels (LAFs) that UIX provides out of the box: Base LAF and Simple LAF. These are parent LAFs that can be extended to create a custom LAF in applications that rely on UIX at the page rendering and presentation layers. A custom LAF inherits the style definitions from the parent LAF, and properties that define a custom LAF are kept in a look and feel configuration file.

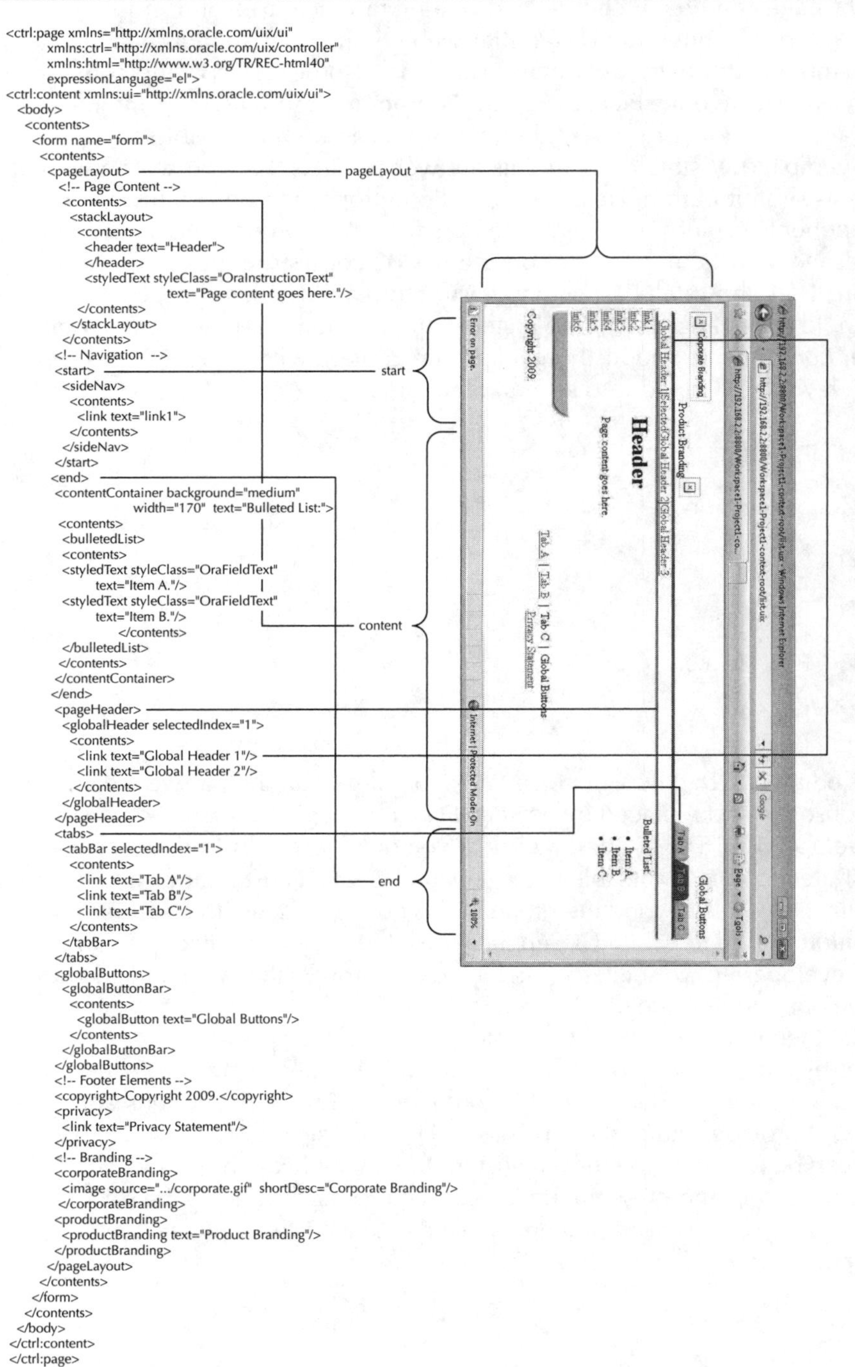

```
<ctrl:page xmlns="http://xmlns.oracle.com/uix/ui"
        xmlns:ctrl="http://xmlns.oracle.com/uix/controller"
        xmlns:html="http://www.w3.org/TR/REC-html40"
        expressionLanguage="el">
<ctrl:content xmlns:ui="http://xmlns.oracle.com/uix/ui">
  <body>
   <contents>
    <form name="form">
     <contents>
      <pageLayout>
        <!-- Page Content -->
        <contents>
          <stackLayout>
            <contents>
              <header text="Header">
              </header>
              <styledText styleClass="OraInstructionText"
                          text="Page content goes here."/>
            </contents>
          </stackLayout>
        </contents>
       <!-- Navigation -->
       <start>
         <sideNav>
           <contents>
             <link text="link1">
           </contents>
         </sideNav>
       </start>
      <end>
       <contentContainer background="medium"
                   width="170" text="Bulleted List:">
        <contents>
        <bulletedList>
        <contents>
        <styledText styleClass="OraFieldText"
              text="Item A."/>
        <styledText styleClass="OraFieldText"
              text="Item B."/>
                   </contents>
        </bulletedList>
        </contents>
       </contentContainer>
      </end>
       <pageHeader>
         <globalHeader selectedIndex="1">
           <contents>
             <link text="Global Header 1"/>
             <link text="Global Header 2"/>
           </contents>
         </globalHeader>
       </pageHeader>
       <tabs>
         <tabBar selectedIndex="1">
           <contents>
             <link text="Tab A"/>
             <link text="Tab B"/>
             <link text="Tab C"/>
           </contents>
         </tabBar>
       </tabs>
       <globalButtons>
         <globalButtonBar>
           <contents>
             <globalButton text="Global Buttons"/>
           </contents>
         </globalButtonBar>
       </globalButtons>
       <!-- Footer Elements -->
       <copyright>Copyright 2009.</copyright>
       <privacy>
         <link text="Privacy Statement"/>
       </privacy>
       <!-- Branding -->
       <corporateBranding>
         <image source=".../corporate.gif" shortDesc="Corporate Branding"/>
        </corporateBranding>
       <productBranding>
         <productBranding text="Product Branding"/>
       </productBranding>
      </pageLayout>
     </contents>
    </form>
   </contents>
  </body>
</ctrl:content>
</ctrl:page>
```


FIGURE 10-1. *Anatomy of a UIX page*

UIX Custom Style Sheets

The style sheet definitions in UIX are conceptually similar to CSS (Cascading Style Sheets) and are a standard way of defining the appearance of HTML-based pages such as fonts, colors, and other attributes. However, UIX style sheets are defined in XML style sheet language (XSS) document with an .xss extension. The styles from the parent LAFs are automatically inherited into a custom LAF. Here is an example:

```
<styleSheetDocument xmlns="http://xmlns.oracle.com/uix/style"
  version="2.0" documentVersion="1.0">
 <styleSheet>
  <style selector=".OraInstructionText">
   <property name="color">black</property>
   <property name="font-family">Arial,Verdana,sans-serif</property>
   ...
   ...
  </style>
<style name="HeaderText">
   <property name="color">#660099</property>
   <property name="border-width">1px</property>
   <property name="border-color">#660099</property>
 </styleSheet>
</styleSheetDocument>
```

The example shows that styles are either selector (.OraInstructionText) or name based (HeaderText). During runtime, UIX reads the XSS style sheet file and converts it into a CSS style sheet; selector-based style definitions appear in the generated CSS with the same name, while name-based styles are not included in the generated CSS. Named-based styles are actually a collection of shared properties between multiple selectors. In the example, we define OraInstructionText style to change the text color and the font family. Property names and values are the same as defined in a CSS specification; therefore, familiarity with CSS style sheets is a prerequisite to creating custom styles in UIX and Oracle Applications.

UIX Custom Icons

With UIX, you can include your own icons within the definition of your custom look and feel. However, there is a caveat to this: there is a limited number of customizable icons. In Oracle Applications, you can easily access the list of customizable icons through the Customizing Look and Feel responsibility. We'll take a look at this in the sections that follow.

The definitions of custom icons are added to the CLAF configuration file and enclosed within an <icons> tag:

```
<icons>
<icon name="tabBarEnabledStart">
<context-image width="8" height="20"
```

```
uri="cabo/images/xxcust_claf/tbes.gif">
</context-image>
</icon>
...
</icons>
```

The capability to specify your own custom icons makes it really easy to design your own buttons, tabs, and other customizable components that are created with images (icons).

UIX Custom Renderers

For complete control over the look and feel of applications based on UIX, you can consider using custom UIX renderers. A renderer is a Java object such as the renderer for the UIX table component; it is responsible for creating the output, usually HTML markup, from UIX components. The renderers come in two flavors: Java renderers and UIX XML template (UIT) renderers.

Java Renderers

Every component renderer in UIX implements the Renderer.java interface:

```
public interface Renderer
{
  //Render a UINode in a RenderingContext.
  public void render(
    RenderingContext context,
    UINode           node) throws IOException;
}
```

Components within a UIX page are conceptualized as UINodes. Java renderers get attributes from UINode; if needed, the renderer can call OutputMethod from the RenderingContext object to write some output content such as HTML markup. Here is an example of a custom Java renderer that extends the renderer for the standard separator UIX component:

```
import java.io.IOException;
import oracle.cabo.ui.RenderingContext;
import oracle.cabo.ui.UINode;
import oracle.cabo.ui.io.OutputMethod;

public class XxCustSeparatorRenderer extends SeparatorRenderer
{
  protected void renderContent(
    RenderingContext context,
    UINode           node
    ) throws IOException
```

```
  {
    OutputMethod out = context.getOutputMethod();
    out.writeRawText("< Raw HTML markup goes here >");
  }
}
```

In the example, we override the renderContent method from the original SeparatorRenderer class and call the writeRawText method in the OutputMethod object to return our custom HTML code for the separator UIX component. The separator component normally renders the <HR> HTML tag, but you can utilize Java inheritance to override that behavior. If the code is successfully compiled and placed on the target environment, you need to create a new entry in the LAF configuration file which points to your custom renderer:

```
<renderers>
<renderer name="separator">
<class name="xxcust.ui.laf.desktop.XxCustSeparatorRenderer"/>
</renderer>
</renderers>
```

It is strongly advised not to use custom Java renderers; the code in Java renderers can be very complex, and the internals of the rendering mechanism are scarcely documented. In addition to this, UIX is obsolete in Oracle's technology stack, so the costs of coding and maintaining of custom Java renderers are normally difficult to justify. On that note, we'll swiftly move on to template-based renderers, which offer a similar type of flexibility without having to write a single line of code.

Template Renderers

The template renderers use UIX XML constructs to declaratively create a layout template for the UIX components. When implementing template renderers in Oracle Applications, you are most likely to modify the pageLayout component. Here is an example of the pageLayout template-based renderer that strips out all of the pageLayout components aside from the page header and main contents:

```
<?xml version="1.0" encoding="UTF-8"?>
<templateDefinition xmlns="http://xmlns.oracle.com/uix/ui"
                    xmlns:data="http://xmlns.oracle.com/uix/ui"
                    xmlns:ui="http://xmlns.oracle.com/uix/ui"
                    xmlns:html="http://www.w3.org/TR/REC-html40"
                    xmlns:demo="http://www.example.org/demo/templates"
                    localName="pageLayout">
  <content>
    <!-- The contents of pageLayout is placed in HTML table -->
    <tableLayout>
      <contents>
        <!-- Render the pageHeader named child -->
```

```
          <rowLayout hAlign="center" width="100%">
                <contents>
                  <cellFormat hAlign="center">
                    <contents>
                      <ui:rootChild name="pageHeader"/>
                    </contents>
                  </cellFormat>
                </contents>
              </rowLayout>
          </contents>
         <!-- Render page contents-->
          <rowLayout>
            <contents>
              <cellFormat>
                <contents>
                  <rootChild name="contents"/>
                </contents>
              </cellFormat>
            </contents>
          </rowLayout>
        </contents>
      </tableLayout>
</content>
</templateDefinition>
```

The template renderer for pageLayout in the example creates tableLayout and places pageHeader and contents named UIX components into it. The named components are included within the <rootChild> tag.

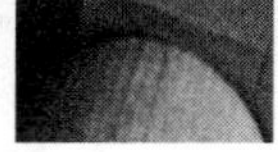

NOTE
A template with only contents and pageHeader components wouldn't be of much use in Oracle Applications; we'll shortly provide the full example of a pageLayout template renderer that could be used in most implementations of CLAF in Oracle Applications.

It is possible to include standard HTML code within UIX templates; most people are probably more familiar with the standard HTML rather than constructs allowed in UIX pages and templates. The previous example is easier to read if you use the standard HTML within the UIX content tag in the template-based renderers:

```
<?xml version="1.0" encoding="UTF-8"?>
<templateDefinition xmlns="http://xmlns.oracle.com/uix/ui"
                    xmlns:data="http://xmlns.oracle.com/uix/ui"
                    xmlns:ui="http://xmlns.oracle.com/uix/ui"
```

```
                    xmlns:html="http://www.w3.org/TR/REC-html40"
                    xmlns:demo="http://www.example.org/demo/templates"
                    localName="pageLayout">
  <content>
    <!-- pageLayout is placed in standard HTML table element -->
    <table xmlns="http://www.w3.org/TR/REC-html40"
           cellpadding="0" cellspacing='0" border="0">
      <!-- Render pageHeader -->
      <tr><td><ui:rootChild name="pageHeader"/></td></tr>
      <!-- Render the pageLayout contents -->
      <tr><td><ui:rootChild name="contents"/></td></tr>
    </table>
  </content>
</templateDefinition>
```

The definition of template-based renderers needs to be registered in the LAF configuration file and enclosed within the <renderers> tag:

```
<renderers>
  <renderer name="pageLayout">
   <template name="pageLayout.uit"></template>
  </renderer>
 </renderers>
```

How to Create CLAF in Oracle Applications

In this section, we'll outline the practical steps that you need to perform in order to create a CLAF in Oracle Applications. We'll also provide a full version of the pageLayout template renderer that could be used in most implementations; obviously, you can modify it to meet your requirements, and we'll discuss how this could be achieved.

Before we start going through the practical steps, it is worth mentioning that the technique we are about to discuss here is applicable to both releases of Oracle Apps R11i (11.5.10 CU2+) and R12. The CLAF files in both releases are placed under the $OA_HTML/cabo directory.

Oracle Applications 11i are delivered with Oracle's corporate Browser Look and Feel, also known as BLAF. As of R12, Oracle Applications are shipped with a look and feel called SWAN. In our demonstration, we are going to use R12; however, the same techniques can be applied to R11i. Technically, the SWAN look and feel is an extended version of BLAF from R11i; for the purposes of this book, we are going to refer to the default Oracle Applications look and feel as BLAF.

Before you start creating a CLAF, you need to assign a Customizing Look and Feel Administrator responsibility to a user who will be performing the customization. Figure 10-2 shows the initial Look and Feel Configuration screen.

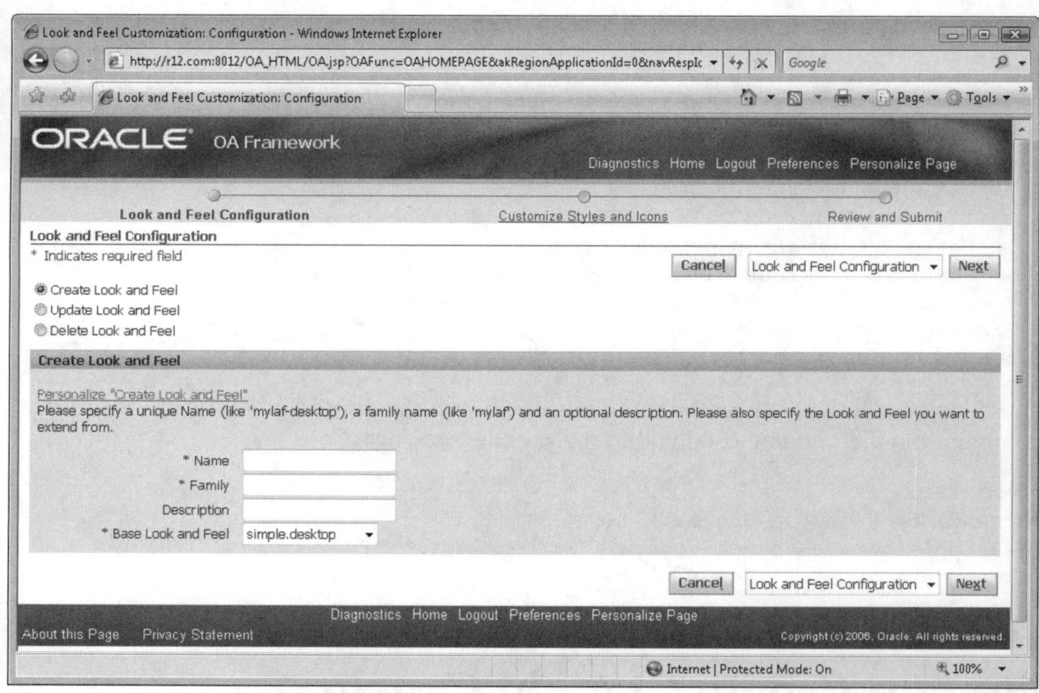

FIGURE 10-2. *Look and Feel Configuration screen*

Creating Custom Styles and Icons

The first step is to specify the name and family of your CLAF in the Look and Feel Configuration screen. We provided the values xxcust-laf-desktop for the Name field and xxcust for the Family field. When you are creating a CLAF for the first time, you extend Simple LAF (simple.desktop); if you have other LAFs defined, you can choose them as your parent LAF. In our example, we extend simple.desktop. It has a somewhat minimalistic appearance, but we can extend it to include our own styles.

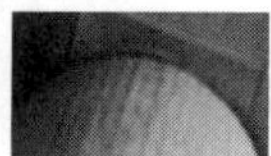

NOTE
Although many people would like to extend BLAF or SWAN directly, this is not possible in Oracle Applications. At the moment, you can only extend Base LAF, Simple LAF (simple.desktop), or a previously defined custom LAF.

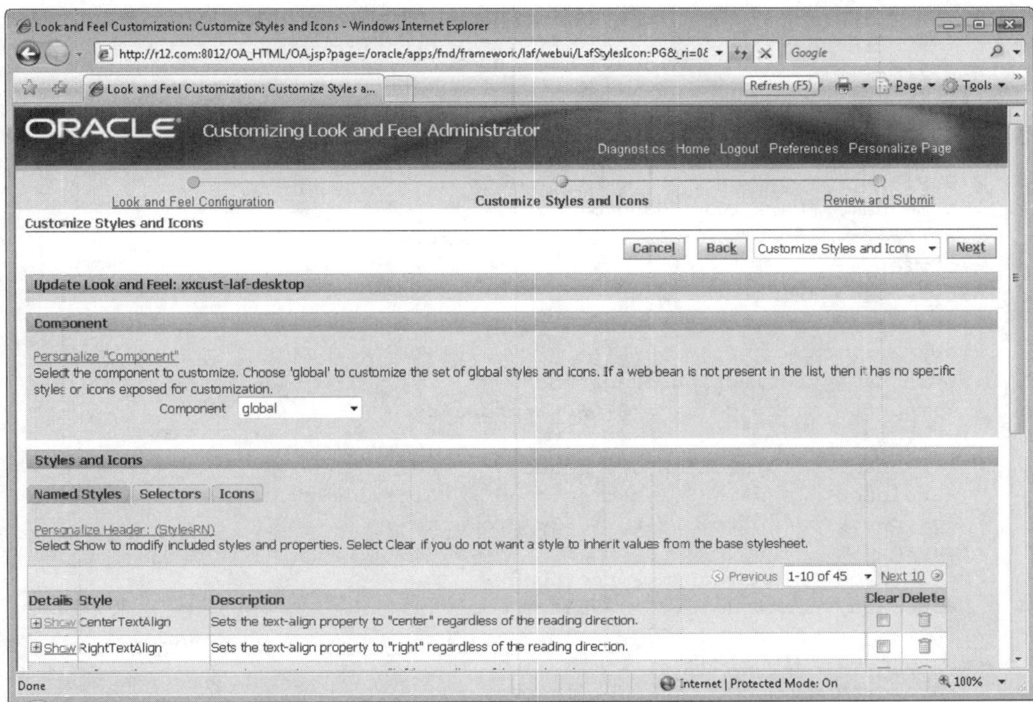

FIGURE 10-3. *Customize Styles and Icons screen*

When you click the Next button, you navigate to the Customize Styles and Icons screen (Figure 10-3), where you can specify the majority of our styles and customizable icons.

We suggest that you specify as many styles and icons as possible through the Customize Styles and Icons screen rather than manually updating the resulting XSS file. When you click the Next button again, you are presented with the opportunity to preview your style changes in the Review and Submit screen. If you are happy with your custom styles, you can click the Finish button and create your CLAF.

The definitions that we used are generated in an XSS style sheet file xxcust-laf-desktop.xss:

```
<styleSheetDocument xmlns="http://xmlns.oracle.com/uix/style"
version="2.0" documentVersion="_125">
  <styleSheet>
    <style name="DarkBackground">
      <property name="color">#FFFFFF
      </property>
      <property name="background-color">BLACK
      </property>
    </style>
```

```
<style name="DarkAccentBackground">
  <property name="color">#ffffff </property>
  <property name="background-color">#DDDDDD</property>
</style>
<style name="LightAccentBackground">
  <property name="color">BLACK</property>
  <property name="background-color">#F6F6F6</property>
</style>
<style name="DarkForeground">
  <property name="color">#000000</property>
</style>
<style name="LinkForeground">
  <property name="color">BLACK</property>
</style>
<style name="ActiveLinkForeground">
  <property name="color">#FF6600</property>
</style>
<style name="VisitedLinkForeground">
  <includeStyle name="LinkForeground"> </includeStyle>
  <property name="color">#333333</property>
</style>
<style name="DisabledLinkForeground">
  <property name="color">#999900</property>
</style>
<style name="GlobalHeaderItem">
  <property name="color">RED</property>
  <property name="text-decoration">none</property>
</style>
<style name="GlobalHeaderLink">
  <property name="color">RED</property>
  <property name="text-decoration">none</property>
</style>
<style selector=".OraGlobalHeaderBody">
  <property name="padding">6px</property>
</style>
<style selector=".OraTabBarEnabled A">
  <property name="padding">5px</property>
</style>
<style selector=".OraTabBarSelected A">
  <property name="padding">5px</property>
</style>
<style selector=".OraTabBarEnabled">
  <property name="padding">5px</property>
</style>
<style selector=".OraTabBarSelected">
  <property name="padding">5px</property>
</style>
<style name="GlobalHeaderItem">
```

```
      <property name="color">RED</property>
      <property name="text-decoration">none</property>
    </style>
    <style name="GlobalHeaderLink">
      <property name="color">RED</property>
      <property name="text-decoration">none</property>
    </style>
    <style selector=".OraGlobalHeaderBody">
      <property name="padding">6px</property>
    </style>
    <style selector=".OraTabBarEnabled A">
      <property name="padding">5px</property>
    </style>
    <style selector=".OraTabBarSelected A">
      <property name="padding">5px</property>
    </style>
    <style selector=".OraTabBarEnabled">
      <property name="padding">5px</property>
    </style>
    <style selector=".OraTabBarSelected'>
      <property name="padding">5px</property>
    </style>
  </styleSheet>
</styleSheetDocument>
```

Our CLAF (xxcust-laf-desktop) can now be applied at the site, responsibility, application, organization, or user level by setting the profile option Oracle Applications Look and Feel (APPS_LOOK_AND_FEEL). The result is shown in Figure 10-4.

CLAF Files and Directory Structure

The CLAF definitions are stored on the file system on the middle tier. Here is a summary of the files that get created:

- $OA_HTML/cabo/lafs/xxcust-laf-desktop.xss

  This is CLAF main configuration file. Because we haven't defined any template renderers or custom icons at the moment, it contains only a look and feel style sheet declaration:

  ```
  <?xml version='1.0' encoding='ISO-8859-1'?>
  <look-and-feel style-sheet-name="xxcust-laf-desktop.xss"
  xmlns:xxcust-laf-desktop="http://xmlns.example.org/laf/xxcust"
  xmlns="http://xmlns.oracle.com/uix/ui/laf" family="xxcust"
  extends="simple.desktop" id="xxcust-laf-desktop">
  </look-and-feel>
  ```

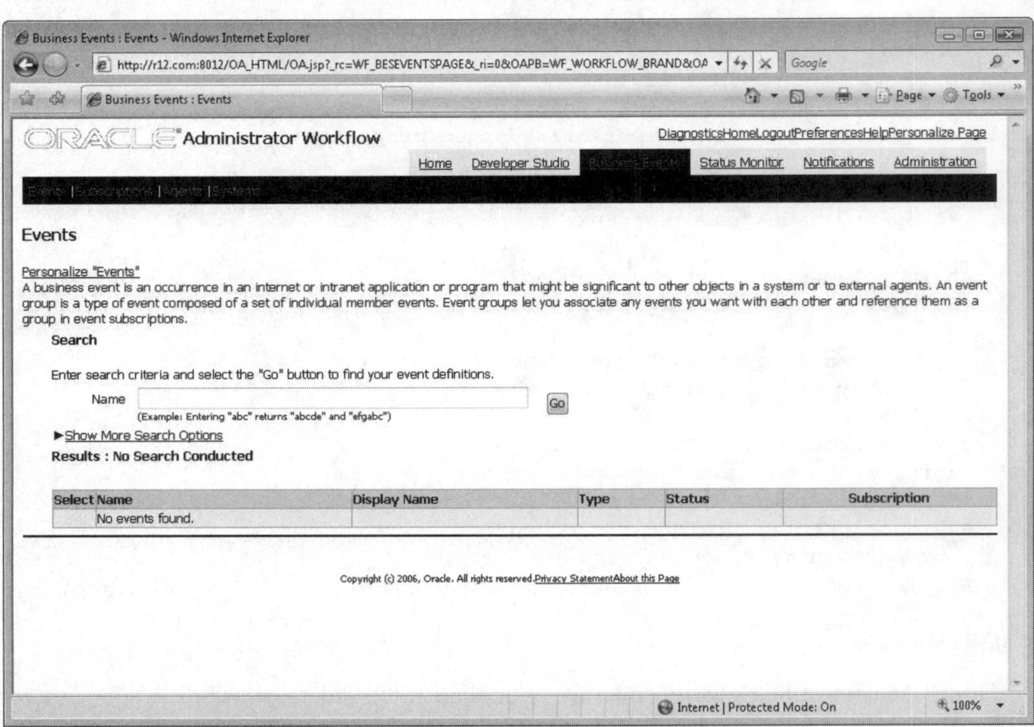

FIGURE 10-4. *New look and feel after applying the styles*

- $OA_HTML/cabo/styles/xxcust-laf-desktop.xss

  This is the XSS style sheet definition (as just listed).

- $OA_HTML/cabo/images/<LookandFeelId>/, where <LookandFeelId> is a CLAF name.

  We didn't have any images in our example CLAF; if you need to include them, you would save them in the $OA_HTML/cabo/images/xxcust-laf-desktop directory.

- $OA_HTML/cabo/templates/<LookandFeelId>/, where <LookandFeelId> is a CLAF name.

  We are going to create a pageLayout template in the next section, and the directory for our example where custom templates are saved is $OA_HTML/cabo/templates/xxcust-laf-desktop.

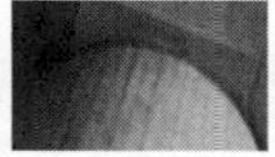

TIP

If you are struggling to figure out what styles need to be customized, we suggest you use a Firefox add-on such as Firebug, which allows you to inspect any element on the web page. Then you can go to the $OA_HTML/cabo/styles/cache directory and pick the names of dynamically generated CSS style selectors. UIX dynamically generates CSS style sheets in the cache directory and this is a good place to start investigating if there any problems with your styles.

Adding a Custom Template Renderer

It is great to be able to change properties such as colors and fonts and even introduce custom icons, but that still doesn't allow you to completely control the layout of the page components such as global buttons, tabs, corporate branding, and others. In addition to that, because of your requirements to meet the corporate standards in terms of appearance, you will likely need to include some kind of page header such as a corporate web page header that includes a logo or links to other parts of the website. This problem can be solved by introducing a custom template renderer; in most cases, it is sufficient to create a pageLayout template renderer that allows you complete control over what and where components get displayed on the page affected by your CLAF. The most common case is to include a custom piece of HTML code to include, for example, a custom page header on the top of the standard Oracle Applications content.

As mentioned earlier, the definitions of the custom template renderers for our example are stored in the $OA_HTML/cabo/templates/xxcust-laf-desktop directory. Because you are customizing the pageLayout template renderer, save it as pageLayout.uit in the $OA_HTML/cabo/templates/xxcust-laf-desktop directory. Here is the definition of our pageLayout.uit:

```
<?xml version="1.0" encoding="windows-1252"?>
<!-- Template definition file.  -->
<templateDefinition xmlns="http://xmlns.oracle.com/uix/ui"
                    xmlns:data="http://xmlns.oracle.com/uix/ui"
                    xmlns:ui="http://xmlns.oracle.com/uix/ui"
                    xmlns:html="http://www.w3.org/TR/REC-html40"
                    xmlns:demo="http://www.example.org/demo/templates"
                    targetNamespace="http://www.example.org/demo/
                        templates"
                    localName="pageLayout">
  <!-- Define a pageLayout as base attribute -->
  <type base="ui:pageLayout">
    <!-- Important: Adding title attribute -->
    <attribute name="title" javaType="string"/>
```

```
</type>
<!-- Content section definition-->
<content>
  <stackLayout>
    <contents>
    <!-- Adding our custom Header via urlInclude -->
    <urlInclude source="/OA_HTML/xxcust_header.html"></urlInclude>
      <tableLayout cellPadding="0" cellSpacing="0" width="100%">
        <contents>
          <rowLayout>
            <contents>
              <cellFormat hAlign="start">
                <contents>
                  <!-- image source="/OA_MEDIA/FNDSSCORP.gif"/ -->
                </contents>
              </cellFormat>
              <cellFormat hAlign="start" wrappingDisabled="true">
                <contents>
                  <!-- rootChild name="productBranding"/ -->
                </contents>
              </cellFormat>
              <cellFormat hAlign="end" vAlign="top" width="100%">
                <contents>
                  <rootChild name="globalButtons"/>
                </contents>
              </cellFormat>
            </contents>
          </rowLayout>
        </contents>
      </tableLayout>
      <spacer height="10"/>
      <tableLayout width="100%">
        <contents>
          <rowLayout styleClass="OraTableBorder0001">
            <contents>
              <cellFormat hAlign="end">
                <contents>
                  <rootChild name="tabs"/>
                </contents>
              </cellFormat>
            </contents>
          </rowLayout>
          <rowLayout hAlign="center" width="100%">
            <contents>
              <cellFormat hAlign="center">
                <contents>
                  <ui:rootChild name="pageHeader"/>
                </contents>
```

```
          </cellFormat>
        </contents>
      </rowLayout>
      <rowLayout hAlign="center" width="100%">
        <contents>
          <cellFormat>
            <contents>
            </contents>
          </cellFormat>
        </contents>
      </rowLayout>
    </contents>
  </tableLayout>
  <tableLayout width="100%">
   <contents>
    <rowLayout>
      <contents>
        <cellFormat hAlign="end">
          <contents>
            <ui:rootChild name="messages"/>
          </contents>
         </cellFormat>
       </contents>
     </rowLayout>
   </contents>
</tableLayout>
  <spacer height="10"/>
  <tableLayout width="100%">
   <contents>
    <rowLayout>
     <contents>
      <cellFormat hAlign="end">
       <contents>
         <ui:rootChild name="pageButtons"/>
       </contents>
      </cellFormat>
     </contents>
    </rowLayout>
   </contents>
  </tableLayout>
  <tableLayout width="100%">
   <contents>
    <rowLayout>
     <contents>
      <cellFormat hAlign="start">
       <contents>
         <header size="0" data:text="title@ui:rootAttr" />
       </contents>
```

```
    </cellFormat>
   </contents>
  </rowLayout>
 </contents>
</tableLayout>
<tableLayout width="100%">
  <contents>
    <rowLayout>
      <contents>
        <cellFormat vAlign="top">
          <contents>
            <ui:rootChild name="start"/>
          </contents>
        </cellFormat>
        <cellFormat width="100%" vAlign="top">
          <contents>
            <rootChild name="contents"/>
          </contents>
        </cellFormat>
        <cellFormat vAlign="top">
          <contents>
            <ui:rootChild name="end"/>
          </contents>
        </cellFormat>
      </contents>
    </rowLayout>
  </contents>
</tableLayout>
<tableLayout width="100%">
 <contents>
  <rowLayout>
   <contents>
    <cellFormat hAlign="end">
     <contents>
       <ui:rootChild name="returnNavigation"/>
     </contents>
    </cellFormat>
   </contents>
  </rowLayout>
 </contents>
</tableLayout>
<spacer height="10"/>
<tableLayout width="100%">
 <contents>
  <rowLayout>
   <contents>
    <cellFormat hAlign="end">
     <contents>
```

```
                <ui:rootChild name="pageButtons"/>
              </contents>
            </cellFormat>
          </contents>
        </rowLayout>
      </contents>
    </tableLayout>
   </contents>
  </stackLayout>
 </content>
</templateDefinition>
```

Generally, in the page layout template, you place your components within the tableLayout component (this is an HTML table without borders) using a <rootChild> tag. In our pageLayout.uit, we have deliberately decided to omit some components that normally render in the standard Oracle Applications such as corporate branding, a privacy statement, and a footer, as well as the product branding. More importantly, we have used the urlInclude component to include our custom HTML code on the top of the page:

```
<urlInclude source="/OA_HTML/xxcust_header.html"></urlInclude>
```

The code listing for xxcust_header.html is as follows:

```
<!-- Custom Header START -->
<style type="text/css" media="screen">@import url(xxcust_menu.css);
</style>
<div id="nav-menu">
<ul>
<li><a href="#">BBC</a></li>
<li><a href="#">Reuters</a></li>
<li><a href="#">CNN</a></li>
</ul>
</div>
<!-- Custom Header END -->
```

We also demonstrate that you can even import CSS definitions as you would in the standard HTML code. The xxcust_menu.css is defined as follows:

```
#nav-menu ul
{
list-style: none;
padding: 0;
margin: 0;
background-color: grey;
}
#nav-menu li
{
```

```
float: left;
margin: 0.5em 0.5em;
}
#nav-menu li a
{
float: left;
background-color: red;
height: 3em;
line-height: 3em;
width: 12em;
border: 0.2em solid black;
display: block;
color: black;
text-decoration: none;
text-align: center;
}
#nav-menu
{
width:100%;
}
```

Both xxcust_header.html and xxcust_menu.css need to be placed in the $OA_HTML directory. The last step is to add the renderer definition into the CLAF configuration file. This is done by adding the renderers section. Our $OA_HTML/lafs/xxcust-laf-desktop.xml now looks like the following:

```
<?xml version='1.0' encoding='ISO-8859-1'?>
<look-and-feel style-sheet-name="xxcust-laf-desktop.xss"
xmlns:xxcust-laf-desktop="http://xmlns.example.org/laf/xxcust"
xmlns="http://xmlns.oracle.com/uix/ui/laf" family="xxcust"
extends="simple.desktop" id="xxcust-laf-desktop">
  <renderers>
    <renderer name="pageLayout">
      <template name="pageLayout.uit">
      </template>
    </renderer>
  </renderers>
</look-and-feel>
```

After adding the definition of your custom page layout template renderer into the configuration file, you need to restart the middle-tier services for the changes to take effect. The final result is shown in Figure 10-5. Every page that is affected by the CLAF has a custom header added via the urlInclude UIX component. It is also possible to add arbitrary HTML tags such as <div> where necessary.

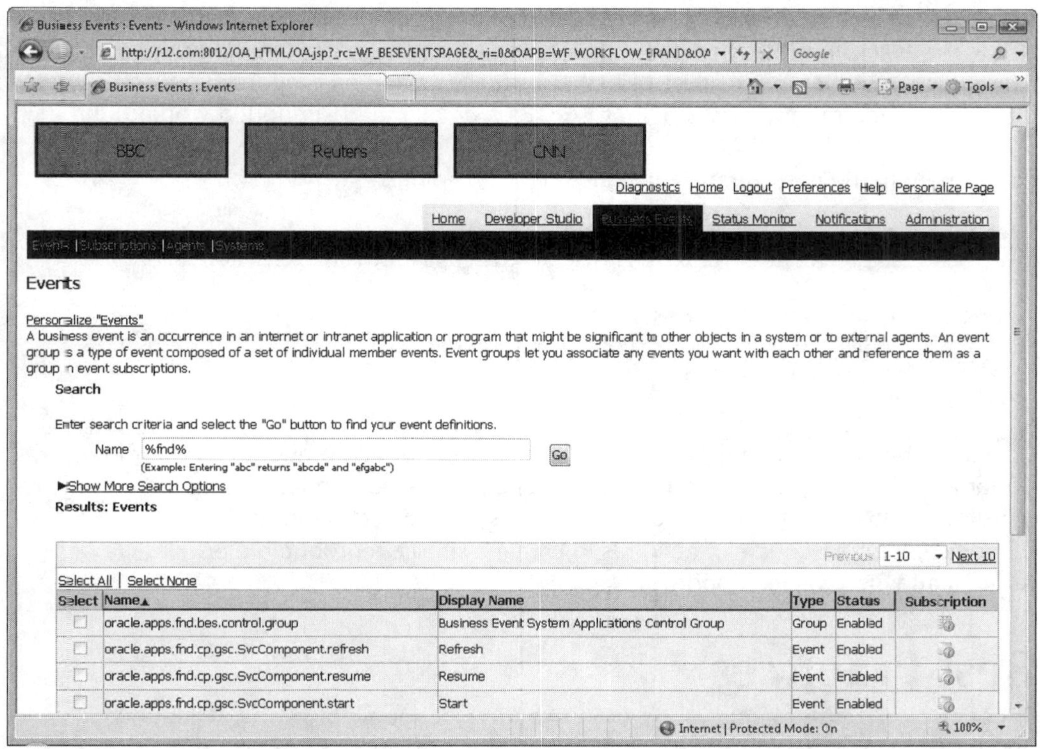

FIGURE 10-5. *A page in Oracle Applications after applying CLAF*

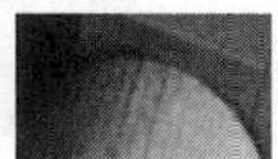

TIP

If you are deploying a CLAF on a middle-tier server that is externally Internet facing, the chances are that your Apache is configured to use SSL (HTTPS). We have discovered that urlInclude doesn't work very well over HTTPS—that is, more often than not, the HTML code that urlInclude points to does not render properly due to security exceptions. Use a rawText component in pageLayout template to work around this issue; simply put raw HTML code inside the rawText component, and that should fix the issue on middle tiers with SSL enabled.

When working with CLAF, we have discovered that sometimes the Simple LAF that we must extend does not have a corresponding web component that exists in BLAF. An example is the Rich Text Editor component that is used in iRecruitment, Contracts, and other applications. In other instances, certain components, such as check box, didn't render properly in CLAF. As a quick but unsupported workaround, you can try to include BLAF components in your CLAF by pointing to the BLAF Java component in the configuration file. Here is an example:

```
<renderer name="checkBox">
   <class name="oracle.cabo.ui.laf.oracle.desktop.CheckBoxRenderer"/>
  </renderer>
  <renderer name="richTextEditor">
   <class name="oracle.cabo.ui.laf.oracle.desktop
.RichTextEditorRenderer"/>
</renderer>
```

Please be aware that this technique doesn't work for all components, and more importantly, it is not supported by Oracle Support. The bottom line is that if there is a problem with any of the components in terms of incorrect rendering and otherwise, the best course of action is to create a simple reproducible test case and raise a call with Oracle Support.

Best Practices

In conclusion to this chapter, we would like to say a couple of words of caution about dealing with CLAF. We suggest that you initially apply CLAF to a limited number of responsibilities and that you perform careful testing of functionality. Remember that CLAF extends Simple LAF, which doesn't have the same features as BLAF (CLAF cannot extend and inherit BLAF). This implies that there is a potential loss of functionality; an example is the UIX trains component, which in CLAF doesn't have associated icons but instead renders trains as ordinary HTML links. This is because the train component in Simple LAF is implemented without icons and therefore inherits that behavior in CLAF. However, it is possible to use XSS style sheet definitions to remedy this issue to a certain extent, but please keep in mind that components in Simple LAF render differently from BLAF components in Oracle Applications' default look and feel.

If you experience an issue with your CLAF that results in web pages having a really strange and unexpected look and feel, it is most likely that either the configuration file or the XSS style sheet file is not a well-formed XML file. Load the file into an XML editor (for example, JDeveloper) and make sure that it is a well-formed XML document without any exceptions. In addition to that, it is a good idea, after changing the style, to purge the CSS cache in the $OA_HTML/cabo/styles/cache directory and retest the change by clicking Ctrl+F5 in Firefox or Internet Explorer.

This action will force the browser to use new CSS definitions rather than cached ones. When you perform changes in the CLAF configuration file such as adding a renderer, you must bounce the middle-tier application server; in R11i, that is Apache and JServ; in R12, it is Apache as well as oacore OC4J.

In the multitier installation of E-Business Suite, each middle tier should typically have CLAF-related files deployed. However, in some cases, such as external iRecruitment pages, CLAF files may be deployed only to the middle tiers that serve the target group of users such as external iRecruitment applicants in the example. We suggest deploying CLAF across all midtier machines to avoid confusion.

Summary

CLAF is one of the little publicized features of E-Business Suite that deserves greater prominence among the user community. The most common scenario is to use CLAF in externally facing OA Framework–based applications such as iSupplier and iRecruitment. In fact, any application based on OA Framework can take advantage of CLAF to customize its appearance to meet corporate requirements.

The three major UI elements that can be customized by CLAF are styles, icons, and template renderers. The combination of these three elements should allow you to customize almost any aspect of UI appearance in OA Framework–based applications.

Lastly, we point out that because any CLAF that we build is based on Simple LAF rather than the standard out-of-the-box BLAF, you need to exercise caution when applying CLAF to an application, and extensive testing is required to make sure that no functionality is lost due to the change of look and feel.

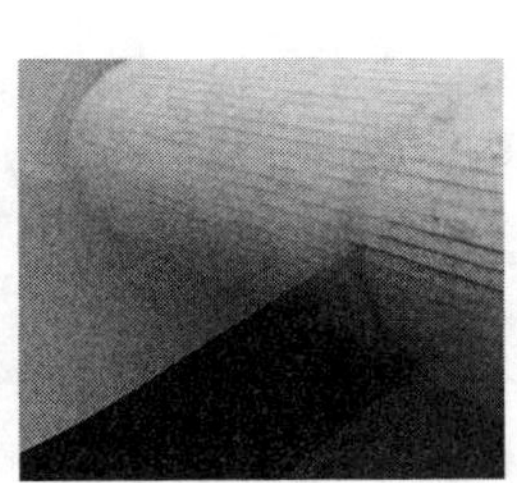

CHAPTER 11

Oracle Workflow

racle Workflow (OWF) technology is one of the key integration enablers between the applications within E-Business Suite and systems that interact with it from outside. It is often used by Oracle Applications product teams to deliver streamlined business processes that incorporate human tasks through various types of notifications and messaging such as approval e-mails and automated activities such as retrieving approval limits from the Oracle Applications database. Oracle Workflow allows you to visually capture business processes that are mapped to various functions within E-Business Suite; these standard processes that are delivered out of the box can be modified by customers to cater for specific needs and business requirements at different client sites.

In this chapter, we'll take a look at the architecture and main components, and explore how to create new and modify existing Workflow processes. We'll also provide a list of best practices to have in mind when dealing with OWF from the developer's point of view.

The sections that follow in this chapter are largely applicable to both R11i and R12 of Oracle Applications. The enhancements of the Oracle Workflow product in E-Business Suite have slowed somewhat as of release 11.5.10; nevertheless, it is important to stress that in the current releases of Oracle Applications and in the years to come, Oracle Workflow will remain one of the key tools in the developer's arsenal.

Architecture Overview and Key Components

There are two flavors of the Workflow product offering from Oracle: the standalone version and the one embedded in E-Business Suite. We'll concentrate on the latter, although from the functional and architectural point of view, they are almost the same.

Similar to other Oracle tools, Workflow consists of both development and runtime components. The main development tool is Workflow Builder, which only runs on a PC desktop as a Windows application; you can say that all the other components are Workflow server components because they are running either inside an Oracle database or application servers as illustrated in Figure 11-1.

End users interact with Oracle Workflow through either their web browser or an e-mail client. A typical task performed by end users is reviewing and replying to Workflow notifications, which can be accessed through the Advanced Worklist page in Oracle Applications; alternatively, notifications can also be delivered to users' e-mail inboxes.

Worklist is developed as an OA Framework page. E-Business Suite installation uses OAS10g (Apache + OC4J) to render an OA Framework page in Release 12. To deliver e-mails to users' e-mail clients, Oracle Workflow uses the Java Mailer component based entirely on the Java Mail API (javax.mail package), which runs as a service component in the application (middle) tier. There are also other service components, such as agent listeners that run on the middle tier.

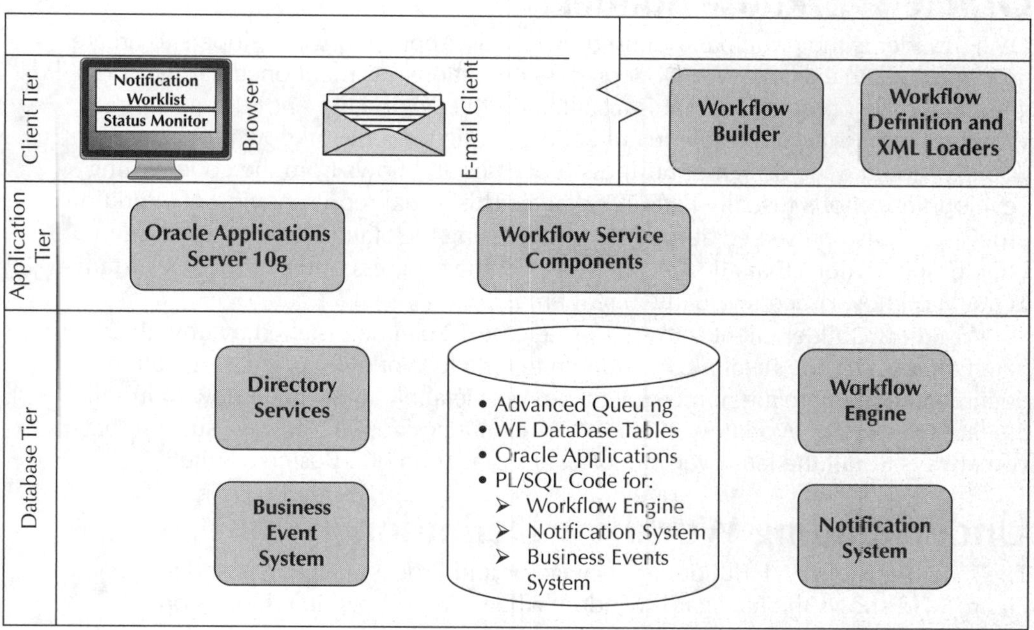

FIGURE 11-1. *Oracle Workflow components*

Workflow Engine is the key component of Oracle Workflow, and it is written in PL/SQL along with the Business Events system, the Notification system, and Directory Services. All of these major components expose public PL/SQL APIs that can be accessed from the APPS schema in the Oracle Applications database. The Business Events system and other parts of the OWF infrastructure extensively use the Advance Queuing (AQ) feature of Oracle Database for a variety of tasks such as deferring execution of Workflow activities and delivering and receiving messages to and from other applications and systems.

The WF% database tables that store the Workflow definitions and transactional data are kept in the APPLSYS schema, and you can divide them into two major types:

- **Workflow definition tables** Store the definitions of Item Types (Workflow processes).
- **Workflow transactional tables** Store transactional information used by Workflow Engine to execute the Workflow process definition as designed by developers.

Oracle Workflow Builder

OWF Builder is the principal tool used by Oracle Applications developers to create new and update existing Workflow process definitions. As mentioned earlier, it is a graphical development tool that is installed on the PC desktop and runs as a Windows application. Its main feature allows designers of Workflow processes to visually separate the design of business processes and flows from the code writing development efforts (usually PL/SQL or Java). This visual representation of Workflow processes is also preserved at runtime by accessing the Status Monitor function in Oracle Applications that allows you to inspect the progress of the particular instance of the Workflow process visually in real time.

Workflow Builder client software for Release 12 can be installed by downloading patch 4096620 from Metalink. In addition to Oracle Workflow Client Installation documentation, there are numerous articles on Metalink that explain how to install the latest version of Workflow client software on a desktop PC, and we suggest that you always install the latest version for your installation of E-Business Suite.

Understanding Workflow Definition

The main parts of OWF Builder are Navigator and Process Diagram windows. Figure 11-2 shows the Navigator window when a Workflow definition is open in Workflow Builder.

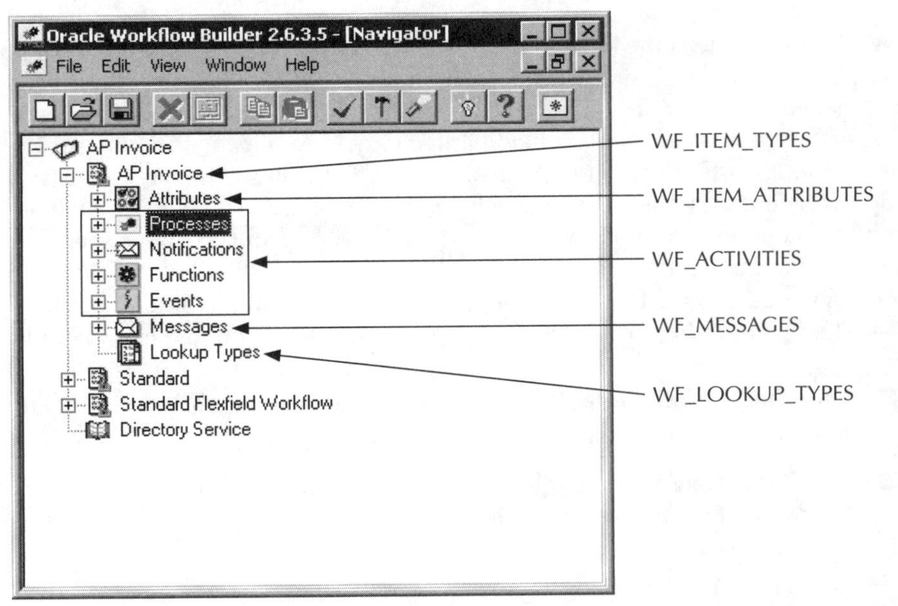

FIGURE 11-2. *Workflow definition and corresponding database tables*

In Oracle Workflow, the container that holds the definitions of processes is called item type, and it is the top level in the definition hierarchy. In other words, item type is the Workflow definition of an overall Workflow process, bearing in mind that the overall Workflow process can consist of multiple processes and subprocesses but it is usually one main process that kicks the whole process off.

Workflow Key Elements

As illustrated in Figure 11-2, the Workflow Builder Navigator window displays the elements of the Workflow structure tree. In this case, the item type that we have open in Workflow Builder is the AP Invoice Workflow process, which is available in the VISION installation.

The item type definition structure can be divided into Activity and Supporting Element groups:

- Activity Elements:
  - Processes
  - Functions
  - Events
  - Notifications
- Supporting Elements:
  - Attributes
  - Messages
  - Lookup Types

To explain the difference between item type (Workflow) activities and supporting elements used by activities, let's examine the AP Invoice item type a little more closely by connecting Workflow Builder to a VISION database and opening both the Navigator and Process Diagram windows, as shown in Figure 11-3.

In the Navigator window (left-hand side), you can see that the AP Invoice item type consists of a number of attributes (Supplier, Approver Comments, Invoice_id, and so on), two processes (Invoice Approval, Send Notifications), four functions (Check If Matched to PO, Escalate Approval, Identify Approver, Update Approval History), a Receive Event Start activity, and several Standard End activities. There are some other elements of this process such as notifications and messages that are not shown in Figure 11-3 because they are part of the Send Notifications process, which is just another process within the main process. On the right-hand side is the Process Diagram window, which displays the components of the Invoice Approval—Main process.

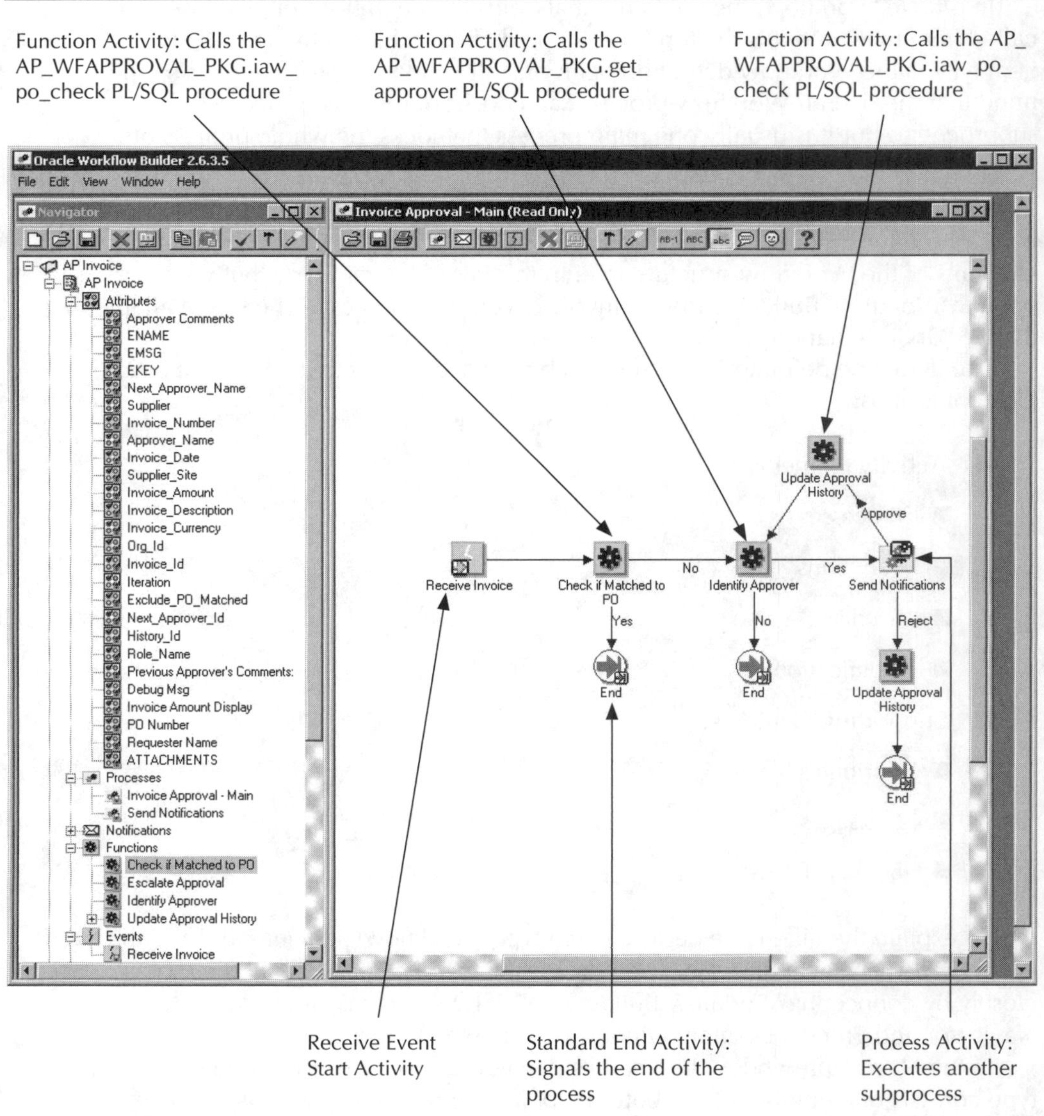

FIGURE 11-3. *AP invoice approval process*

We've chosen to examine the standard AP Invoice Workflow item type because it is representative of a typical approval Workflow process in Oracle Applications. It first checks if an invoice is matched to a purchase order (PO), in which case the process is ended. If not, it proceeds to the next activity, Identity Approver, which finds an approver for the invoice. It then proceeds to the Send Notifications process activity, which is responsible for sending the approval and other notifications to users (approvers and requestors) who interact with the system.

When designing Workflow processes (item types), you have to create at least one main process to serve as the container for other Workflow activities; in the case of the AP Invoice item type, the main process is Invoice Approval—Main. Every process consists of at least one Start and one End activity (node). The Start node marks the point where the process starts, and the End node marks where the process finishes. In the Invoice Approval—Main process, the Receive Invoice is marked as the start activity and serves as an entry point to the process; if you double-click it in the Workflow Builder and go to the Node tab, you can see that it is marked as the Start node (see Figure 11-4).

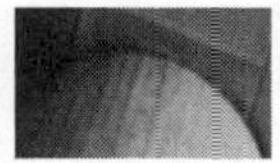

NOTE
Activities can be a Start, Normal, or End type of node.

After the Receive Invoice start activity, we have Check if Matched to PO function activity (refer back to Figure 11-3). You can think of a function activity as an automated task that performs some function within the process flow and potentially returns a result such as APPROVER_FOUND or APPROVER_NOT_FOUND. In programming terms, the function activity is a point during the process execution where

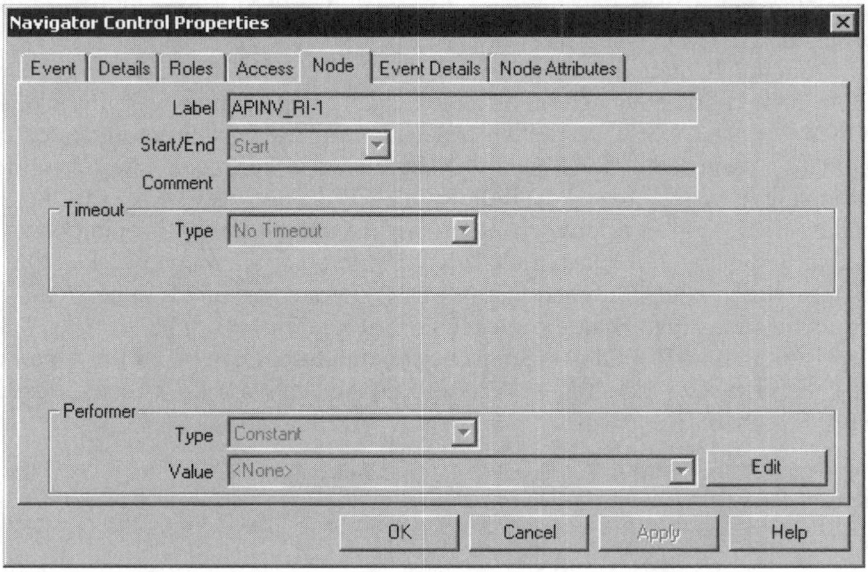

FIGURE 11-4. *The Start node is marked Start in the Start/End field.*

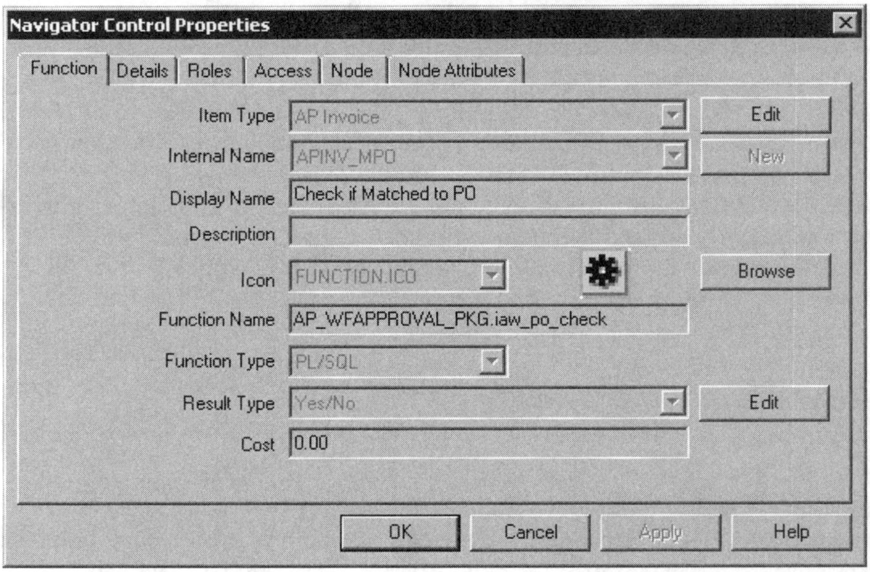

FIGURE 11-5. *The function activity calls a PL/SQL procedure.*

the Workflow Engine that executes the process calls the PL/SQL procedure specified by the function definition, as shown in Figure 11-5.

The function activity doesn't necessarily have to execute a PL/SQL procedure; for example, a function activity could be an external Java class; however, this is rarely used in practice as PL/SQL fits quite nicely with Oracle Workflow product design.

Don't get confused by the Function Name field for the Check if Matched to PO function activity, where the AP_WFAPPROVAL_PKG.iaw_po_check PL/SQL procedure name is in <*package_name.procedure_name*> format. It is important to stress that in the Function Name field, you have to enter the name of a PL/SQL procedure, not the PL/SQL function; this PL/SQL procedure needs to be coded in a specific way so that WF Engine can execute it at runtime.

To illustrate how PL/SQL code must be structured so it can be part of a Workflow process, let's have a look at the AP_WFAPPROVAL_PKG.iaw_po_check procedure in the APPS schema:

```
PROCEDURE iaw_po_check(itemtype IN VARCHAR2,
 itemkey IN VARCHAR2,
 actid   IN NUMBER,
 funcmode IN VARCHAR2,
 resultout  OUT NOCOPY VARCHAR2 ) IS
```

```
 l_po_count      NUMBER;
 l_check_PO_match VARCHAR2(3);
 l_org_id        NUMBER;
 l_debug       VARCHAR2(240);
BEGIN
--check 'Approve PO Matched' flag here
 l_check_PO_match := WF_ENGINE.GetItemAttrText(itemtype,
                                  itemkey,
                                  'APINV_AAPO');
-- we need to get the org_id until I can change
-- the raise event in the invoice workbench
 SELECT org_id INTO l_org_id
 FROM ap_invoices_all
 WHERE invoice_id = substr(itemkey, 1, instr(itemkey,'_')-1);
        -- lets go ahead and set the wf attribute
 WF_ENGINE.SETITEMATTRNumber(itemtype,
 itemkey,
 'APINV_AOI',
 l_org_id);
 --Now set the environment
 fnd_client_info.set_org_context(l_org_id);

 IF l_check_PO_match = 'Y' THEN
 SELECT count(invoice_distribution_id)
 INTO l_po_count
 FROM ap_invoice_distributions
 WHERE po_distribution_id is null
 AND invoice_id = substr(itemkey, 1, instr(itemkey,'_')-1);

 IF nvl(l_po_count,0) = 0 THEN
 resultout := wf_engine.eng_completed||':'||'Y';
                        --update invoice status
                        UPDATE AP_INVOICES
                        SET wfapproval_status = 'NOT REQUIRED'
                   WHERE invoice_id = substr(itemkey, 1,
instr(itemkey,'_')-1)
 AND wfapproval_status <> 'MANUALLY APPROVED';
 ELSE
 resultout := wf_engine.eng_completed||':'||'N';
 END IF;
 ELSE
 resultout := wf_engine.eng_completed||':'||'N';
 END IF;

 WF_ENGINE.SETITEMATTRText(itemtype,itemkey,'APINV_ADB',l_debug);
EXCEPTION

WHEN FND_API.G_EXC_ERROR
```

```
        THEN
        WF_CORE.CONTEXT('APINV','SELECT_APPROVER',
                        itemtype, itemkey,to_char(actid), funcmode);
       RAISE;
WHEN FND_API.G_EXC_UNEXPECTED_ERROR
   THEN
        WF_CORE.CONTEXT('APINV','SELECT_APPROVER',
                        itemtype, itemkey, to_char(actid), funcmode);
       RAISE;
WHEN OTHERS
   THEN
        WF_CORE.CONTEXT('APINV','SELECT_APPROVER',
                         itemtype, itemkey, to_char(actid), funcmode);
       RAISE;
END;
```

All the PL/SQL procedures that are used as function activities in Oracle Workflow must have the following signature:

```
PROCEDURE some_wf_procedure(itemtype IN VARCHAR2,
                            itemkey IN VARCHAR2,
                            actid   IN NUMBER,
                            funcmode IN VARCHAR2,
                            resultout OUT NOCOPY VARCHAR2);
```

This is because, at runtime, WF Engine (also written in PL/SQL and discussed in the next section in more detail) is designed to call the function activity Workflow PL/SQL procedures with the predefined number and type of parameters; for every AP Invoice runtime instance of the Workflow item type, the WF Engine passes to it the internal name of the item type (APINV), item key (invoice number), activity ID, function execution mode, and the result from the function activity PL/SQL code (for example, Y for Yes or N for No).

All the parameters passed by the WF Engine, apart from the function activity execution mode (funcmode), are fairly self-explanatory. The execution mode of the function activity could either be RUN, CANCEL, SKIP, or RETRY. The WF Engine tries to execute all activities in RUN mode initially. If an activity is re-executed because it is in the loop and the On Revisit flag is set to Reset, the WF Engine will execute it in CANCEL mode. An activity that is skipped or retried by the Workflow Administrator from the Status Monitor is executed in the corresponding SKIP and RETRY modes. There are a number of other scenarios that can cause WF Engine to execute an activity in either of those modes, but for now, let's focus on the fact that initially WF Engine executes all the activities in the RUN mode.

Going back to our original question about the difference between attributes and activities, you can say that attributes are used, referenced, and even modified by activities at runtime—usually by PL/SQL code, but they can also be referenced in

Notification messages and other activities. For example, in the AP Invoice item type there is an attribute called Exclude_PO_Matched, and if you double-click it in the Workflow Builder you can see that it is defined with the following properties:

Item Type	**AP Invoice**
Internal Name	APINV_AAPO
Display Name	Exclude_PO_Matched
Type	Lookup
Lookup Type	Yes/No
Default Type	Constant
Default Value	No

Within the AP_WFAPPROVAL_PKG.iaw_po_check procedure, call a Workflow API to access the value of the Exclude_PO_Matched attribute at runtime and assign it to a local PL/SQL variable:

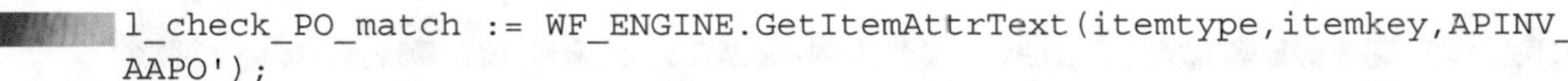

```
l_check_PO_match := WF_ENGINE.GetItemAttrText(itemtype,itemkey,APINV_
AAPO');
```

Similarly, you can use another WF Engine API to update the value of the same attribute if you are required to do so in your code.

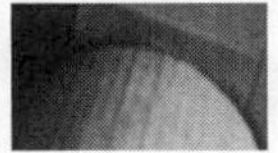

NOTE
More information about WF Engine and available APIs is in the next section.

Types of Workflow Attributes There are three types of attributes in Oracle Workflow: Item, Activity, and Message. Let's take a look at item and activity attributes; we'll come back to the message attributes later in this section.

Item attributes are defined in WF Builder by right-clicking an item type name and selecting New I Attribute. Activity attributes are created by pointing at a Function or Raise Event activity in the WF Builder Navigator screen and selecting New Attribute.

If you think of Workflow attributes as variables similar to other programming languages, then you can say that an Item attribute acts as a global variable within the runtime instance of an item type, and an Activity attribute is more akin to the concept of local variables because it is relevant only to the current activity. Item attributes can be accessed and updated by any activity within the active Workflow process. They can store various types of information, and there are several types of item attributes that can be created through WF Builder: Text, Number, Date, Lookup, Role, Attribute, URL, Form, Document, and Event type.

Workflow Function Activities Let's go back to the Check If Matched to PO activity (Figure 11-5) and its associated PL/SQL code (AP_WFAPPROVAL_PKG.iaw_po_check procedure). Activities usually return some kind of result, and in this case the Result Type is Yes/No lookup code from the Standard item type that gets shipped with Oracle Workflow. What this means is that in PL/SQL code you need to set the RESULTOUT parameter to either the COMPLETE: N or COMPLETE: Y value as this will tell WF Engine the outcome of the activity so it knows where to further branch the process. For example, in PL/SQL for the Check if Matched to PO activity, we have:

```
resultout := wf_engine.eng_completed||':'||'N';
```

As shown in Figure 11-6, the Invoice Approval item type has a couple of other types of activities: Send Notification Process activity, and within it, a few Notification activities (Approval Request, Approval Reminder, and Escalated Approval Request).

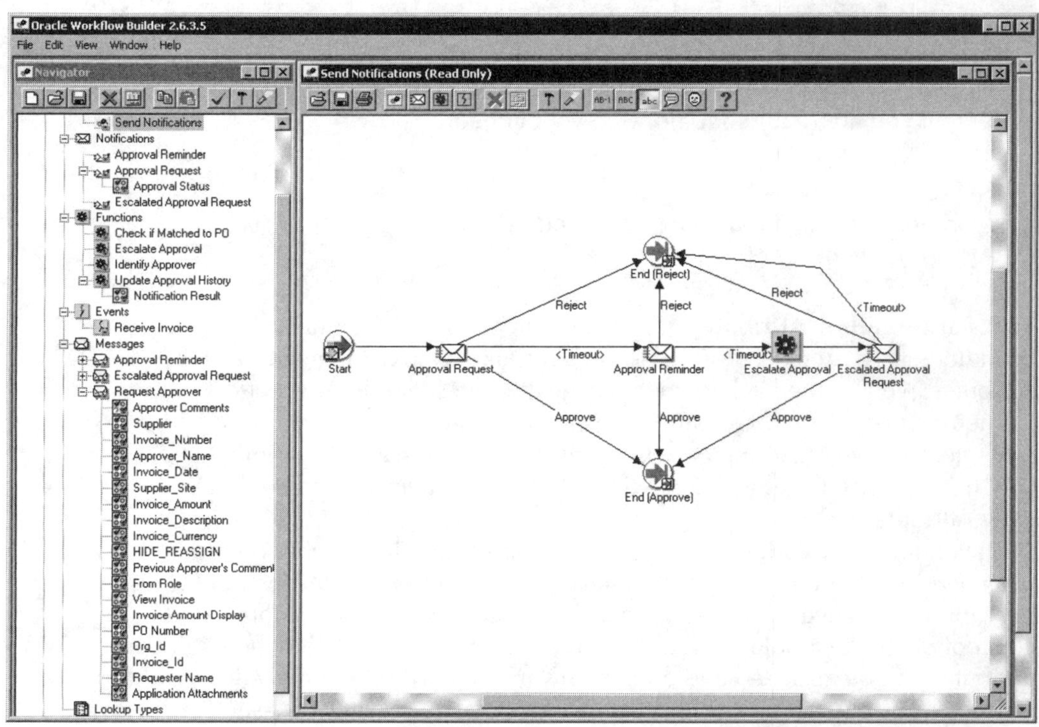

FIGURE 11-6. *Workflow notifications*

Workflow Notifications Let's take a closer look at Notifications in Oracle Workflow and how they get created in Workflow Builder by examining the Send Notification process shown in Figure 11-6.

Notifications are just another type of Workflow activity, and as with other activities, Workflow notifications can have an outcome; for example, an approval notification sent to an approver can typically result in either an APPROVED or REJECTED response.

Think of a notification as a human task within a Workflow process that needs to be completed by a person. Notifications deliver messages to Workflow roles (users). The recipients of the messages are referred to as *performers* at design time in Workflow Builder.

The messages may or may not prompt for a response; for example, a message that informs you that your holiday approval request has been approved clearly doesn't require any response, as its purpose is to provide information about the outcome. However, an approver who needs to decide whether or not to approve a holiday request usually receives a notification that requires some kind of response from the approver such as Approve or Reject.

Figure 11-6 shows the Send Notifications process and the elements that compose this process. Like any other process, it consists of at least one Start and End activity, three notifications, and one function activity. We'll now examine the Approval Request notification activity in more detail so you can understand how to create a notification activity.

Before a notification activity is created in Workflow Builder, first consider creating a message in the Navigator screen that the notification activity will send to a user. This message is then attached to the notification that you can also create in WF Builder's Navigator screen. From Figure 11-6, you can see that the Request Approver message references a number of message attributes such as Approver Comments, Supplier, Invoice_Number, and others. Message attributes are used within the message body for so-called token substitution at runtime by appending an internal attribute name to the ampersand (&) symbol as illustrated in Figure 11-7.

When the notification is sent, message attribute tokens such as &APINV_AIN, &APINV_AS, &APINV_ASSI, &APINV_AID, and others are substituted at runtime with the attribute values, that is, invoice number (APINV_AIN), supplier name (APINV_AS), supplier site (APINV_ASSI), invoice date, (APINV_AID), and other attributes.

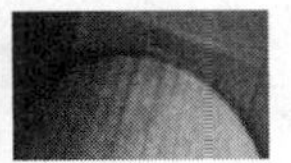

NOTE

You have to use internal attribute names (for example, &APINV_AIN) for token substitution in the message body definition.

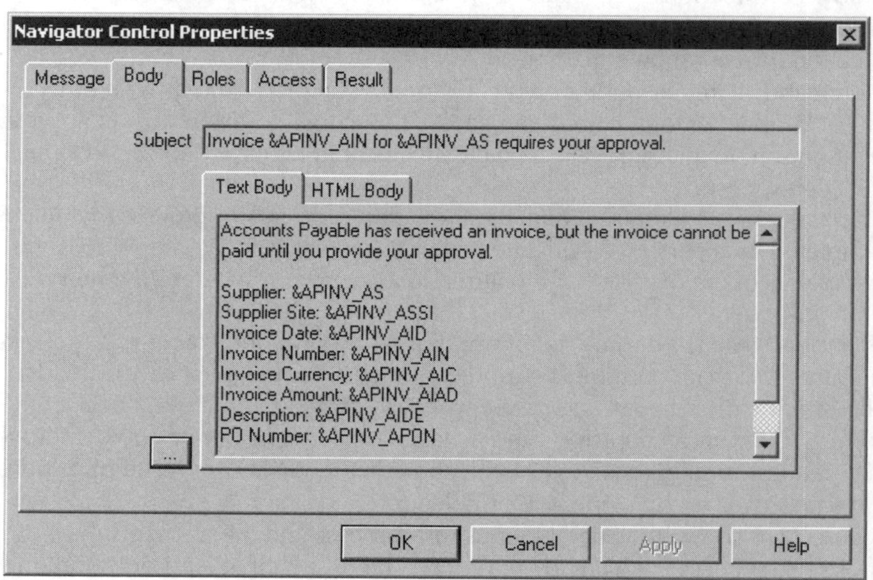

FIGURE 11-7. *Token substitution of message attributes in a Request Approver message*

Similar to item attributes, message attributes act as variables for messages. In Workflow Builder, they are defined by right-clicking a message in the Navigator screen and selecting New Attribute. You can make a reference to the existing item attribute such as the Supplier item attribute by dragging and dropping it onto the Request Approver message.

Message attributes have a Source property that determines the usage of an attribute. For example, if the Source property is set to Send, then this message attribute can be used in the subject and body of a message for token substitution. Figure 11-8 shows how this property is set for the Supplier message attribute (Request Approver message).

Alternatively, if the Source property is set to a Respond value, as is the case with the Approver Comments message attribute, the message attribute is used as a variable that stores the response from users. The presence of a Respond message attribute will create a response section within the message that is sent to the users; for example, if you want to collect the approver's comments, you store the comments in the Approver Comments message response attribute (variable). Think of the Send attributes as information that is sent to users for displaying purposes within the message (Supplier Name, Invoice Number, and so on); you can also think of the respond message attribute as a variable that collects some extra information from users such as collecting their comments and such.

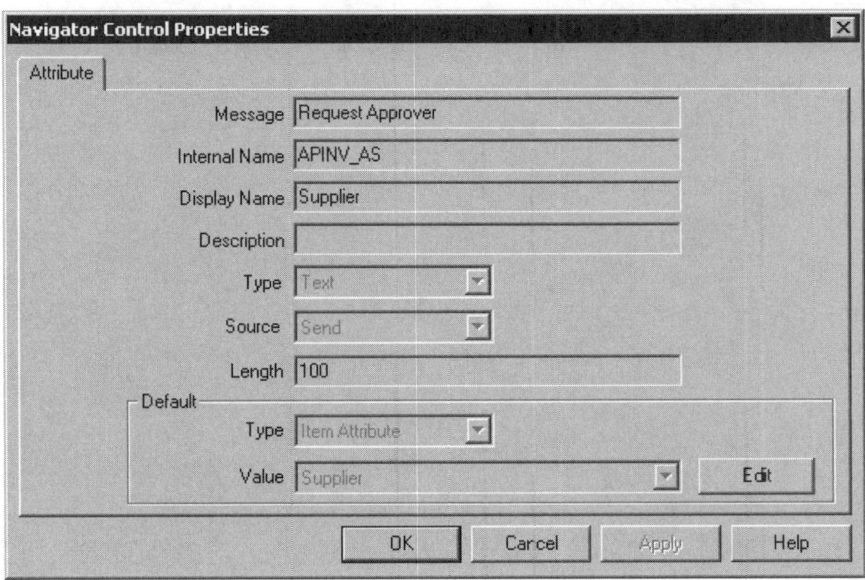

FIGURE 11-8. *Message attribute properties*

Lastly, notification messages have the Result Lookup Type property associated with messages. A Result Lookup Type prompts a user who received the notification message for a response; for example, we normally use the Approval Lookup Type (from the Standard item type), which will prompt the receiver of the notification to respond with either Approve or Reject. Figure 11-9 shows how the result type message property is set for the Request Approver notification message.

The response is then used to branch to the next activity depending on the outcome; in this case, if an approver rejects the approval of an invoice, you branch to the End activity that returns the Reject result because this End node's result property is set to Reject. This is a signal to WF Engine that the Send Notifications process is complete, with a result that equals to the REJECTED value. This result can then be used in the parent process to further route the Workflow process execution until you finally reach the end of the process.

The Request Approver message is then assigned to the Approval Request notification activity, as shown in Figure 11-10.

Lookup Types It's worth stressing that the Workflow process design quite often involves Lookup Type elements that in turn consist of Lookup Codes. You can think of a lookup type as a list or table of values; for example, the standard Approval

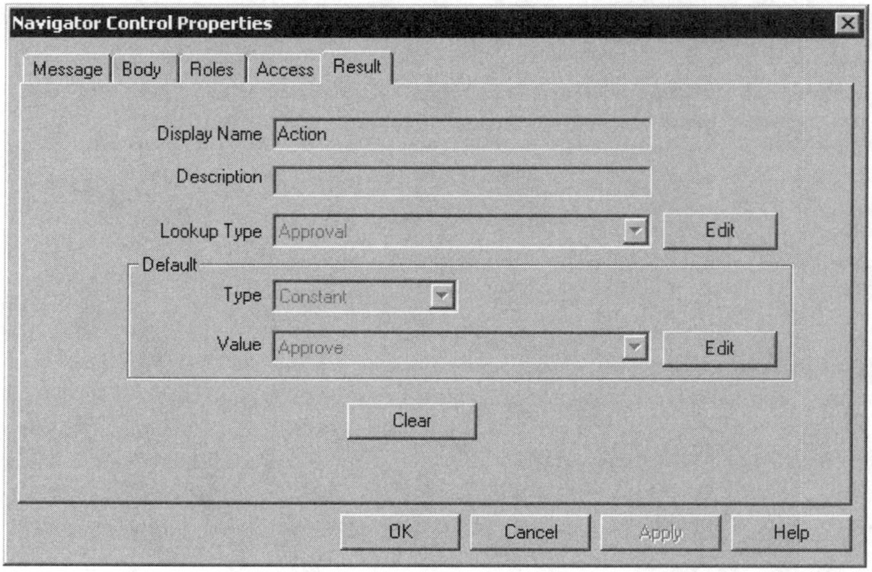

FIGURE 11-9. *Result type message property*

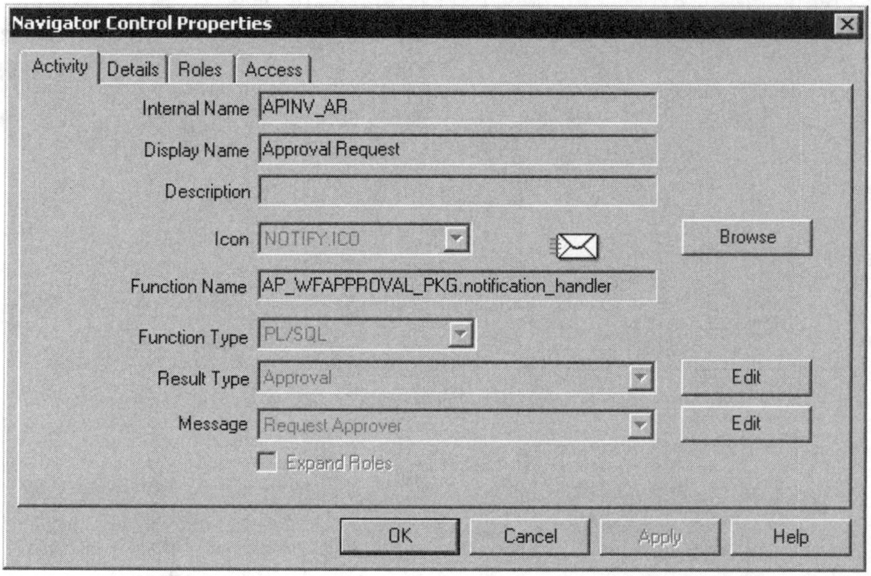

FIGURE 11-10. *Approval Request notification activity with the Request Approver message attached to it.*

lookup type in the Standard item type consists of two lookup codes: Approve and Reject (internal names are APPROVED and REJECTED).

When used by activities, lookup types provide a possible list of values as the outcome of an activity. In the example, Check if Matched to PO activity references a Yes/No lookup type in the Result Type field (see Figure 11-5); therefore, the outcome of this activity is expected to be either Yes or No in Boolean lookup code. Lookup types are also often used when defining messages, as illustrated in Figure 11-9, to prompt the responder of a notification with a list of possible responses (for example, Approve or Reject buttons).

In summary of this section about the Workflow Builder tool, you use the Navigator screen to create and display a tree-like structure of Workflow elements such as processes, functions, notifications, attributes, messages, lookup types, and events; you then drag and drop activities onto the Process Diagram window to create the process along with the transitions between the activities. Most of the time, you'll adopt the top-down approach to Workflow process design by creating a high-level graphical design of activities in the Process Diagram window and then writing PL/SQL code associated with activity functions, as well as adding other elements of your process as necessary.

In the next section, we are going to walk through a detailed example of how to create a Workflow process in E-Business Suite.

An Example: Creating a Workflow Process

We'll now take a look at how to create a simple Workflow process in a little bit more detail. As always in this book, we assume that the reader has access to a VISION installation of E-Business Suite.

First of all, let's define the requirements for our simple Workflow process. From the business perspective, our Workflow process is an approval process that accepts the details about a purchase order (PO) to be approved, and the requestor details as input parameters.

The process then executes an automated activity to find an appropriate approver (supervisor) based on the requestor's data passed to the Workflow process by the calling application that could be Form-based or OA Framework–based, or just about any other Oracle or non-Oracle application. If the approver is found, you send a message with the PO and requestor's details to the approver with an option either to approve or reject the purchase order. If the approver is not found, you simply end the process.

Next, if the approver approves the PO, you proceed to send a For Your Information (FYI) type of notification to the requestors to inform them that the PO has been approved by their supervisor; if the PO is rejected, you again end the process. Last, if the PO is approved, you update a PO Approval History table to record who has requested and approved the purchase order.

The first thing you need to do after reviewing the requirements is to establish what Workflow activities are required by the process. This could be achieved in many ways, but most people prefer to draw a diagram of the process on a piece of paper to help identify the functions, notifications, and flows.

In this example, you need the following activities:

- **Two notifications** One approval notification with the PO and requestor's details sent to the approver and one FYI notification sent to the requestor to inform him or her about the request outcome.
- **Two activities** One function activity that will execute a PL/SQL procedure to find the requestor's supervisor (approver) and one function activity that will update the custom table XX_POAPPRV_HIST to record the PO approval history.
- **Standard Start and End activities** Every process needs at least one Start and End activity from the Standard item type that comes with Workflow Builder. You'll use one Start and three End activities to mark three points where the process may complete at runtime.

Creating an XX Custom Approval Example Item Type and Supporting Database Objects

Everyone has his or her own preferences with regard to Workflow design approach; in the example, you'll create the item type, main process, item attributes, messages, notifications, and function activities, in that order. Once you have all the Workflow elements, you'll use the Process Diagram screen to draw the diagram of our process.

The following list outlines all the steps to create the example PO approval process:

1. Create the XX Custom Approval Example item type. Launch Workflow Builder from the Start menu on your desktop PC.
2. To create the item type and your main process, go to File | Quick Start Wizard and enter the following properties in Workflow Quick Start Wizard window:
   - In the New Item Type section:
Internal Name: XX_APPRV
Display Name: XX Custom Approval Example
Persistence Type: Temporary
Number of Days: 0
   - In the New Process section:
Internal Name: PO_APPR_MAIN
Display Name: PO Approval Main

   Leave the remaining default values as they are.

3. To create item attributes, in the Navigator window right-click the XX Custom Approval Example item type and select New | Attribute. You'll need to create five item attributes with the following properties:

Item Type	Internal Name	Display Name	Description	Type
XX Custom Approval Example	REQ_PERSON_ID	Requestor Person Id	Requestor Person ID	Text
XX Custom Approval Example	PO_NUM	PO Number	PO Number to be approved	Text
XX Custom Approval Example	REQUESTOR_ NAME	Requestor's Name	Requestor's Name	Text
XX Custom Approval Example	REQ_USER_ NAME	Requestor's FND User Name	Requestor's FND User Name	Text
XX Custom Approval Example	APPR_USER_ NAME	Approver's FND User Name	Approver's FND User Name	Text

4. Create notification messages that will be attached to the notifications. To create new messages in the Navigator window, right-click the XX Custom Approval Example item type and select New | Message. We'll need to create two messages:

   - PO Approval message with the following properties defined in tabs:

     Message Tab
     Internal Name: APPROVE_PO
     Display Name: PO Approval
     Description: PO Approval
     Priority: Normal
     Body Tab
     Subject: PO &PO_NUM needs your approval
     Text Body: &REQUESTOR_NAME has requested from you to approve
     Purchase Order Number: &PO_NUM
     Result Tab
     Display Name: Approve
     Description: Approve or Reject PO
     Lookup Type: Approval

From the Navigator window, select the earlier created PO Number item attribute from Attributes and drag it onto the PO Approval message. Do the same with requestor's Name attribute.

- PO Approved message with the following properties defined in tabs:

  Message Tab
  Internal Name: PO_APPROVED
  Display Name: PO Approved
  Description: PO Approved
  Priority: Normal
  Body Tab
  Subject: PO &PO_NUM Approved
  Text Body: This is FYI notification to inform you that PO: &PO_NUM has been approved by your supervisor.
  Result Tab (leave empty as it is)

From the Navigator window, select the earlier created PO Number item attribute from Attributes and drag it onto the PO Approval message.

5. Once you have messages, you can proceed and create notification activities. To create new notifications, in the Navigator window, right-click the XX Custom Approval Example item type and select New | Notification. You'll create two notifications and attach the messages that you created in the previous step:

   - To create PO Approval Notification, enter the following properties in the Activity tab:

     Internal Name: PO_APPR_NTF
     Display Name: PO Approval Notification
     Description: PO Approval Notification
     Result Type: Approval
     Message: PO Approval

   - To create PO Approved FYI Notification, enter the following properties in the Activity tab:

     Internal Name: PO_FYI_NTF
     Display Name: PO Approved FYI
     Description: PO Approved FYI
     Result Type: None
     Message: PO Approved

6. At last, you get to create two function activities: Find Approver for PO and Update PO History Table. To create new function activities, in the Navigator window, right-click the XX Custom Approval Example item type and select New | Function. You'll create two functions and attach the PL/SQL

procedures that will be created in the Oracle Applications database in one of the following steps:

- To create the Find Approver for PO function activity, enter the following properties in the Activity tab:

  Internal Name: FIND_APPROVER
  Display Name: Find Approver for PO
  Description: Find Approver for PO
  Function Name: XX_WF_EXAMPLE.FindApprover
  Function Type: PL/SQL
  Result Type: Boolean
  Cost: 0.00

- To create the Update PO History Table function activity, enter the following properties in the Activity tab:

  Internal Name: UPDATE_HIST
  Display Name: Update PO History Table
  Description: Update PO History Table
  Function Name: XX_WF_EXAMPLE.UpdateHistory
  Function Type: PL/SQL
  Result Type: None
  Cost: 0.00

7. Double-click the PO Approval Main in the Navigator window to open the Process Diagram window and create the diagram of your process. Activities can simply be dragged and dropped onto the Process window, and transitions are created by right-clicking one activity and dropping it onto the target activity. The process should look similar to the one illustrated in Figure 11-11. Do not worry if the activity icons look different—that doesn't have any functional bearing to the process execution.

8. To verify your item type definition from Workflow Builder and save it to the Oracle Applications database, go to File | Verify, and if the message "Successfully validated design" appears on the screen, you can deploy the item type definition to the database by going to File | Save As (click the Database radio button). Then you enter **APPS** in the User name field, along with the corresponding APPS schema password and the connect string to the Oracle Applications target database.

Before you can run your process and try it out, you need to create the supporting objects in the database. For demonstration purposes, we'll create both the database table and PL/SQL package in the APPS schema.

NOTE
You should not create custom tables in the APPS schema in the production environment. Custom tables are normally created in the custom schema.

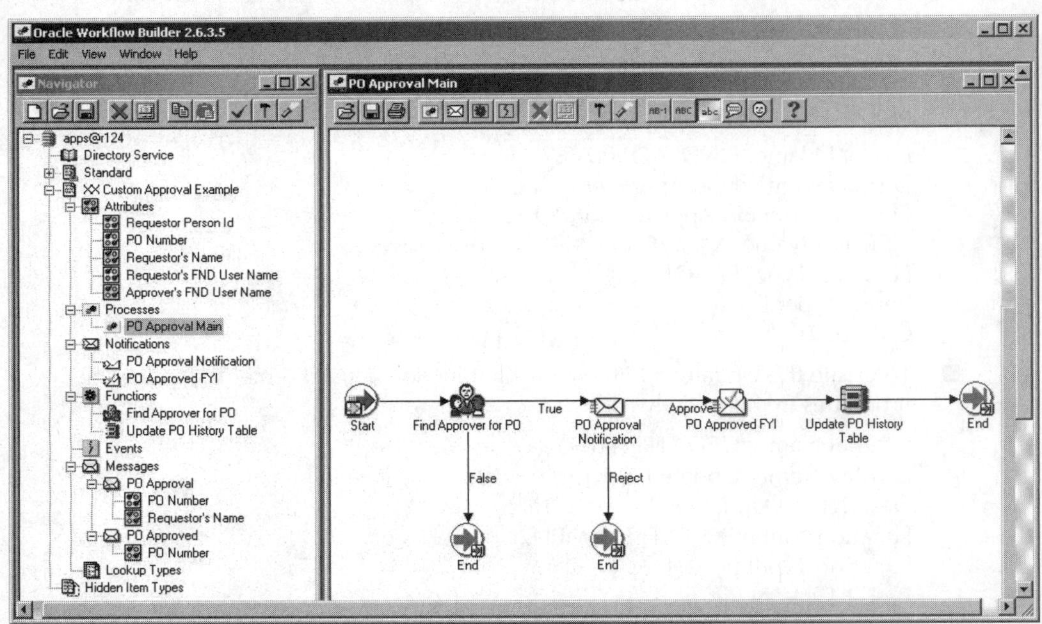

FIGURE 11-11. *Process Diagram and Navigator windows item type definition*

Log in to the APPS schema through SQL*Plus or another favorite client tool and run the following three scripts to create the XX_POAPPRV_HIST table, the XX_WF_EXAMPLE package specification, and the XX_WF_EXAMPLE package body:

```
create table XX_POAPPRV_HIST
( REQUESTOR_USERID varchar2(50)  NOT NULL
,  APPROVER_USERID varchar2(50)  NOT NULL
,  PO_NUMBER       varchar2(50)  NOT NULL);
CREATE OR REPLACE PACKAGE XX_WF_EXAMPLE
AS
PROCEDURE FindApprover
(    itemtype   IN VARCHAR2,
     itemkey    IN VARCHAR2,
     actid      IN NUMBER,
     funcmode   IN VARCHAR2,
     resultout  IN OUT VARCHAR2);
PROCEDURE UpdateHistory
 (   itemtype   IN VARCHAR2,
     itemkey    IN VARCHAR2,
     actid      IN NUMBER,
```

```
    funcmode  IN VARCHAR2,
    resultout IN OUT VARCHAR2);
END XX_WF_EXAMPLE;
/
show errors package XX_WF_EXAMPLE

create or replace package body XX_WF_EXAMPLE as
-- PROCEDURE FindApprover
-- Finds approver given the requestor's person id
-- that is passed through item attribute REQ_PERSON_ID
.PROCEDURE FindApprover
  ( itemtype  IN VARCHAR2,
    itemkey   IN VARCHAR2,
    actid     IN NUMBER,
    funcmode  IN VARCHAR2,
    resultout IN OUT VARCHAR2)
              IS
  l_requestor_person_id  VARCHAR2(50);
  op_requestor_user_name  VARCHAR2(50);
  op_requestor_display_name  VARCHAR2(50);
  op_supervisor_user_name VARCHAR2(50);
  op_supervisor_display_name VARCHAR2(50);
  l_supervisor_id number(10);
BEGIN
  -- RUN mode - normal process execution
  IF (funcmode = 'RUN') THEN
    -- get requestor person id item type attribute
    l_requestor_person_id := wf_engine.GetItemAttrText
             (itemtype => itemtype ,
              itemkey => itemkey   ,
              aname => 'REQ_PERSON_ID');
     -- find requestor's supervisor (approver) id
     SELECT ppf.person_id
      INTO l_supervisor_id
      FROM per_all_assignments_f paf ,
            per_all_people_f ppf
      WHERE paf.person_id = l_requestor_person_id
    AND paf.primary_flag  = 'Y'
    AND TRUNC(sysdate)
    BETWEEN paf.effective_start_date AND paf.effective_end_date
    AND ppf.person_id              = paf.supervisor_id
    AND TRUNC(sysdate)
    BETWEEN ppf.effective_start_date AND ppf.effective_end_date;
    -- Call WF Directory Service to get the role name for supervisor
    wf_directory.GetRoleName ( 'PER'
                              ,l_supervisor_id
                              ,op_supervisor_user_name
                              , op_supervisor_display_name);
```

```
    -- Call WF Directory Service to get the role name for requestor
    wf_directory.GetRoleName ( 'PER'
                             ,l_requestor_person_id
                             ,op_requestor_user_name
                             , op_requestor_display_name);
    -- set Approver's FND User Name attribute
    wf_engine.SetItemAttrText
           ( itemtype => itemtype,
             itemkey => itemkey, aname => 'APPR_USER_NAME',
             avalue => op_supervisor_user_name);
    -- set requestor's FND User Name attribute
    wf_engine.SetItemAttrText
           ( itemtype => itemtype,
             itemkey => itemkey,
             aname => 'REQ_USER_NAME',
             avalue => op_requestor_user_name);
    -- set resultout to TRUE (T)
    resultout  := wf_engine.eng_completed||':'|| 'T';
    RETURN;
  END IF;

IF (funcmode = 'CANCEL') THEN
  -- no result needed
  resultout := wf_engine.eng_completed||':'||wf_engine.eng_null;
  RETURN;
END IF;
EXCEPTION
WHEN OTHERS THEN
  wf_core.context('XX_APPRV'      ,
                 'FindApprover' ,
                  itemtype      ,
                  itemkey       ,
                  TO_CHAR(actid),
                  funcmode);
  raise;
END FindApprover;
-- PROCEDURE UpdateHistory
-- Updates XX_POAPPRV_HIST history table to record
-- who requested and eventually approved Purchase Orders.
PROCEDURE UpdateHistory
  (
    itemtype  IN VARCHAR2,
    itemkey   IN VARCHAR2,
    actid     IN NUMBER,
    funcmode  IN VARCHAR2,
    resultout IN OUT VARCHAR2)
              IS
  l_requestor_user_name  VARCHAR2(50);
```

```
  l_supervisor_user_name VARCHAR2(50);
  l_po_number            VARCHAR2(50);
BEGIN
  -- RUN mode - normal process execution
  IF (funcmode = 'RUN') THEN
    -- get Requestor, Approver and PO Number
    -- from attributes
    l_requestor_user_name  := wf_engine.GetItemAttrText
                                           (itemtype => itemtype
                                           ,itemkey => itemkey ,
                                           aname => 'REQ_USER_NAME');
    l_supervisor_user_name := wf_engine.GetItemAttrText
                                           (itemtype => itemtype
                                           ,itemkey => itemkey
                                           ,aname => 'APPR_USER_NAME');
    l_po_number            := wf_engine.GetItemAttrText
                                          (itemtype => itemtype
                                          ,itemkey => itemkey
                                          ,aname => 'PO_NUM');
    -- insert into PO History table
     INSERT
       INTO XX_POAPPRV_HIST
      (
        REQUESTOR_USERID ,
        APPROVER_USERID  ,
        PO_NUMBER
      )
      VALUES
      (
        l_requestor_user_name  ,
        l_supervisor_user_name ,
        l_po_number
      );
    -- no result, we return 'COMPLETE: ' string
    resultout := wf_engine.eng_completed||':'||wf_engine.eng_null;
    RETURN;
  END IF;
  -- CANCEL mode is run in the event that the activity must be undone,
  -- for example when a process is reset to an earlier point
 IF (funcmode = 'CANCEL') THEN
  -- no result needed
  resultout := wf_engine.eng_completed||':'||wf_engine.eng_null;
  RETURN;
 END IF;
  resultout := wf_engine.eng_null;
  RETURN;
EXCEPTION
WHEN OTHERS THEN
```

```
  wf_core.context('XX_APPRV', 'UpdateHistory',
                  itemtype, itemkey, TO_CHAR(actid), funcmode);
  raise;
END UpdateHistory;
end XX_WF_EXAMPLE;
/
show errors package body XX_WF_EXAMPLE
```

If the table and the PL/SQL package are created without errors, you are ready to run your Workflow process for the first time.

Running the Example Workflow Item Type

The testing of newly developed Workflow item types can be performed in two ways: you can use either the Developer Studio screen in E-Business Suite or Workflow Engine APIs to invoke the process from Oracle database client tools such as SQL*Plus. In this section, we'll demonstrate how to use the Developer Studio screen.

NOTE
In the next section, we discuss the role of Workflow Engine in more detail, along with the APIs that can be used to invoke the process from clients.

You need to log in to Oracle Applications as the user who has Workflow Administrator responsibility assigned. The user also has to be Workflow System Administrator, which you can set in the VISION environment by going to the Workflow Administrator | Administration screen and setting the Workflow System Administrator field to the required username.

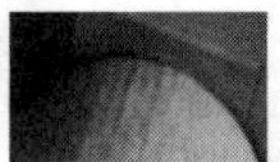

NOTE
*You can set Workflow System Administrator to *, which will allow every user to be Workflow System Administrator. Use this option only in demo environments.*

We set Workflow System Administrator to * to make things easier in our demonstration environment, and the OPERATIONS user has been assigned Workflow Administrator responsibility. Now navigate to Workflow Administrator | Developer Studio and search for your XX Custom Approval Example item type. The Developer Studio screen will find the definition of your XX Custom Approval Example item type in the database and offer an option (the Run icon) to run it from the Run Workflow screen, as illustrated in Figure 11-12.

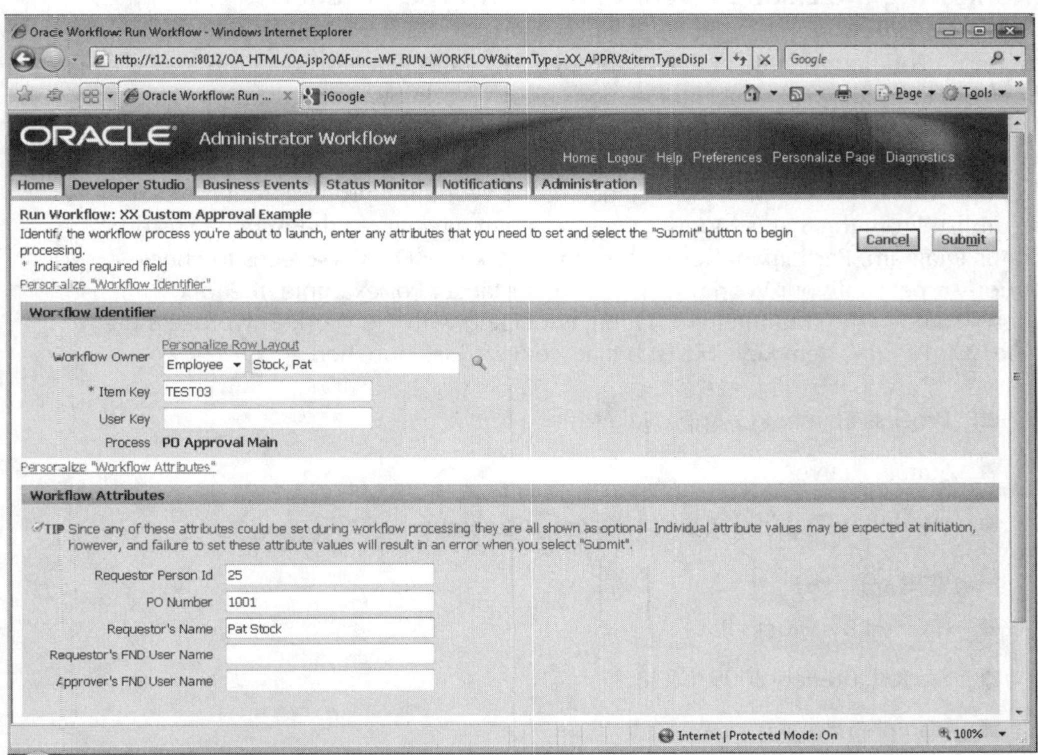

FIGURE 11-12. *Developer Studio's Run Workflow screen*

You can enter arbitrary values for Item Key, Requestor Person Id, Requestor's Name, and PO Number item type attributes that you have defined for your item type; click the Submit button to launch the process with item type attributes set to the values as entered by you.

The Run Workflow screen cannot be used to launch Workflow processes if the Start node is the Receive Event type of activity. We'll talk about Business Events a little bit later in this chapter and draw some parallels between the traditional Workflows like this example and Workflows based on Business Events.

Once the Workflow process is successfully launched through the Run Workflow screen, an instance of the Workflow item type gets created by Workflow Engine, and you can use the Status Monitor functionality to monitor the progress of the process execution.

Monitoring the Example Workflow Item Type Instance

Oracle Workflow embedded in E-Business Suite provides the functionality to monitor Workflow-related activities through the Status Monitor, which is available from the Workflow Administrator responsibility (Workflow Administrator | Status Monitor). Assuming that you are still logged in as an OPERATIONS user who has Workflow Administrator Privileges, you can query your XX Custom Approval Example item type and pick the instance of the Workflow process from the search result list. From the Status Monitor page, you can navigate to the Activity History, Status Diagram, Participant Responses, and Workflow Details screens to check various aspects of your Workflow item type instance. For example, the following list shows some of the runtime information associated with the Workflow process (item type: XX_APPRV, item key: TEST03) that we have just launched:

- Process Name: PO Approval Main
- Status: Active
- Workflow Type: XX Custom Approval Example
- Item Key: TEST03
- Owned By: Stock, Pat
- Started: 06-Feb-2009 12:28:27
- Completed:
- Status: Active
- Workflow Attributes:
    - Requestor Person Id: 25
    - PO Number: 1001
    - Requestor's Name: Pat Stock
    - Requestor's FND User Name: OPERATIONS
    - Approver's FND User Name: CBROWN

You can see that the item attributes you passed to the Workflow process are appearing as runtime values now. In addition to that, Requestor's FND User Name and Approver's FND User Name attributes are also populated; this is because the PO Approval Notification activity has executed the PL/SQL FindApprover procedure and attribute values are populated at runtime by the code.

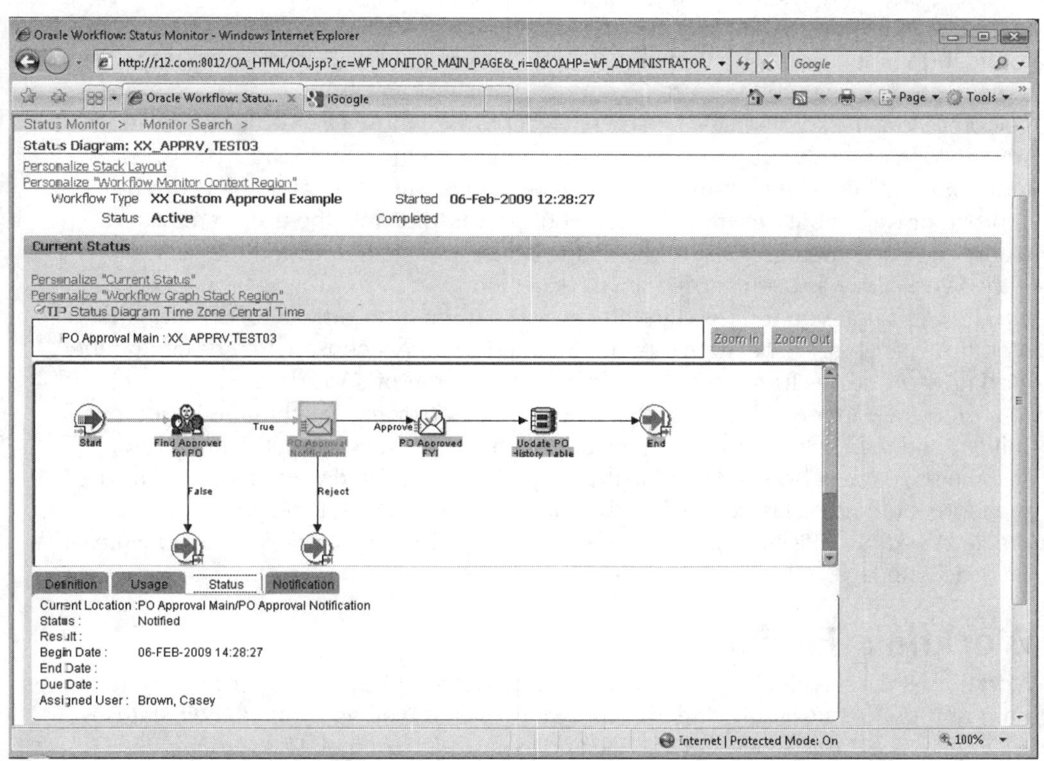

FIGURE 11-13. *Workflow Status Monitor showing the current progress*

If you click the View Diagram button from the Monitor Workflow Details screen, you can inspect the execution status of our process in the Status Diagram screen, as shown in Figure 11-13.

The Status Diagram page is the first port of call if the results of Workflow testing are not what you expect. If an activity errors out, it'll be highlighted with a red box, and the Status tab will show an error message associated with the failure.

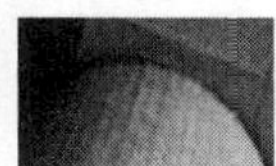

NOTE
In Oracle Workflow, exceptions that occur in the PL/SQL code that is attached to the function activities are not propagated to the client code that initiated the Workflow process.

The green color indicates successful execution. As shown in Figure 11-13, WF Engine has transitioned the process up to the PO Approval Notification activity. The notification is sent to Casey Brown (CBROWN), and until the response from the user is received, nothing will happen. If you log in as CBROWN (the default password is welcome) to the VISION instance and navigate to Workflow User Web Applications | Advanced Worklist, you should see a notification with the subject "PO 1001 needs your approval" listed within the worklist. If you open this notification, you can use Approve or Reject buttons from the page button bar to enable the user to react to it accordingly and then go back to the Status Diagram page to check if the execution of the Workflow has been carried out as expected.

The steps that you followed in this section outline just one way of creating the Workflow processes. The approach that many developers chose when designing the Workflow processes from scratch is first to draw a draft of a Workflow process either on a piece of paper or directly in the Process Diagram screen within the Workflow Builder, and then start adding basic building elements such as attributes and messages. At some stage, you also need to write the code that is associated with function activities to perform automated tasks. The code is usually written in PL/SQL; however, most of the Oracle Workflow APIs have Java wrappers which, if necessary, make it easier to write the code with Java.

Workflow Engine

Workflow Engine (WF Engine) is the central part of the Oracle Workflow module. Its main purpose is to execute and transition activities as well as manage their statuses. WF Engine is entirely written in PL/SQL and exposes its external APIs through PL/SQL, although most of the PL/SQL APIs also have corresponding Java wrappers. As with any other PL/SQL server side code in Oracle Applications, it resides in the APPS schema (the WF_ENGINE package).

We'll now take a look at how WF Engine is invoked by the client code that is issuing one of its APIs to launch an instance of the item type you built in the previous section. From SQL*Plus or another client tool, issue the following PL/SQL:

```
BEGIN
  WF_ENGINE.CREATEPROCESS( ITEMTYPE => 'XX_APPRV',
                           ITEMKEY => 'TEST04',
                           PROCESS => 'PO_APPR_MAIN');

  WF_ENGINE.SETITEMATTRTEXT ( ITEMTYPE => 'XX_APPRV',
                              ITEMKEY => 'TEST04',
                              ANAME => 'REQ_PERSON_ID',
                              AVALUE => '25');
```

```
  WF_ENGINE.SETITEMATTRTEXT (ITEMTYPE => 'XX_APPRV',
                             ITEMKEY => 'TEST04',
                             ANAME => 'PO_NUM',
                             AVALUE => '1002');

  WF_ENGINE.SETITEMATTRTEXT (ITEMTYPE => 'XX_APPRV',
                              ITEMKEY => 'TEST04',
                              ANAME => 'REQUESTOR_NAME',
                              AVALUE => 'Pat Stock');

  WF_ENGINE.STARTPROCESS(ITEMTYPE => 'XX_APPRV',
                          ITEMKEY => 'TEST04');
  COMMIT;
END;
/
```

When WF_ENGINE.CREATEPROCESS is called, an instance of a Workflow process is created, but in Oracle Workflow, we refer to it as a Workflow item. The information about a particular Workflow item is recorded in the WF_ITEMS table. The combination of ITEM_TYPE and ITEM_KEY must be unique, and the process (in the example, PO_APPR_MAIN) must be marked as runnable.

It is quite usual that in between creating and starting the process you need to initialize item type attributes with some values by calling appropriate APIs such as WF_ENGINE.SETITEMATTRTEXT, which sets the value of text item attributes, as you did in the example. The information about item attributes is stored in the WF_ITEM_ATTRIBUTE_VALUES table.

Finally, from your client code, issue a call to the WF_ENGINE.STARTPROCESS API that actually starts running the process until the first so-called blocking activity is encountered. The examples of such blocking activities are deferred and notification activities that require a response. Back in Figure 11-13, PO Approval Notification is a blocking activity because this notification requires a response (although FYI notifications are not blocking); however, WF Engine doesn't know when that will happen, as the person who is assigned this notification may act on the notification whenever he or she pleases. When WF Engine encounters such blocking activity, it marks it with an appropriate status and returns the control to the client code (the calling application usually commits at this time but doesn't have to). At runtime, WF Engine records this information in the WF_ITEM_ACTIVITY_STATUSES table.

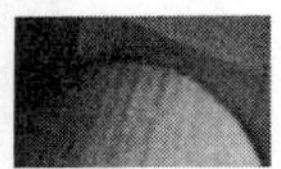

CAUTION
It is the responsibility of the client code to issue a database COMMIT. Conceptually, WF Engine internally does not commit but instead sets savepoints before every function activity that is about to execute and marks it ACTIVE before it progresses. Thus, in the case of an error, WF Engine can roll back to the correct execution point within the process. For this reason, you must not commit from your PL/SQL code that is attached to function activities, as your PL/SQL procedure is executed in the same database session as WF Engine. That means that if you issue COMMIT within your function activity PL/SQL code, WF Engine cannot roll back to the correct point if there is an error. Also, you commit the Workflow transaction data that suddenly becomes visible to the background Workflow Engine that executes from the different database session. If you really must commit within PL/SQL code, an alternative is to use an autonomous transaction.

The concept of a blocking activity brings us to an important subject of deferred activities and background engine processing that we need to examine in more detail.

Imagine that in the XX Custom Approval Example Workflow process that you looked at earlier (Figure 11-11) the function activity Find Approver for PO had a very long running piece of SQL within PL/SQL code attached to it. That would mean the client application that created an instance of the XX Custom Approval Example item type and issued WF_ENGINE.STARTPROCESS to start it would have to wait until the PL/SQL code attached to Find Approver for PO activity and other activities finished running and were marked as completed. A scenario like this wouldn't be feasible, as client applications usually initiate Workflow processing from some kind of Forms-based application at the client tier; therefore, waiting several hours or even minutes for the operator of the client application form to regain the control is normally not an option.

To resolve this issue, Oracle Workflow introduces a concept of deferred processing. When WF Engine encounters an activity that has an associated cost property set to the value that exceeds the WF Engine threshold cost, it marks that activity as deferred and returns the control to the caller (the client application). The default threshold is set to 50 (hundredths of a second), but it can be changed at runtime by changing the value for WF_ENGINE.THRESHLOD in PL/SQL. That means that if you enter the value 1.0 for the Cost attribute in Workflow Builder at design time, WF Engine will defer the execution of your Find Approver for PO activity until you run the background process from another database session. The information about the activity cost is recorded in the WF_ACTIVITIES table.

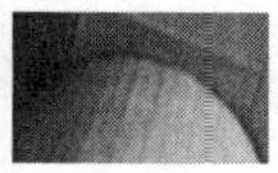

NOTE
You enter values for the Cost activity property in seconds when using Workflow Builder.

Once the activity is deferred, it is eligible to be processed by the WF Background Engine (referred to as background or deferred processing). You can think of a background engine as a specialized version of Workflow Engine that processes deferred and timed-out activities and stuck activities. The background engine can be invoked by calling the wf_engine.background() procedure, and it is important that the system administrator set up periodic running of background engine jobs as appropriate.

NOTE
The background engine issues database COMMIT every time it finishes processing a thread of execution between an eligible activity and the point where it can't proceed any further.

The timeout activity is a Workflow activity with the due date and time usually specified at design time. An item attribute of date or number type can also be used to set the activity timeout value at runtime. Oracle Applications DBAs must set up a separate background engine to process timed-out activities.

A Workflow process is in "stuck" status if its status is ACTIVE but it cannot progress any further. A typical example is if the execution thread leads to an activity within the process that is modeled not to lead to any other activity but itself is not an End activity. The background engine will mark such activity as STUCK and launch an error process. Oracle Applications DBAs must set up a separate background engine to process stuck processes.

Embedding OA Framework Regions in WF Notifications

The technique of embedding OA Framework regions in Workflow notifications has gained quite a bit of popularity when designing Workflow processes for E-Business Suite. Before this technique became available in Oracle Apps, Workflow developers used PL/SQL documents to display dynamic data within notifications. Although embedding of PL/SQL documents allows inserting of arbitrary dynamic content of almost any type, with the popularity of OA Framework–based applications, this method became increasingly obsolete. Instead, in release 11i (11.5.10, patchset OWF.G), a new feature allowing the embedding of OA Framework regions in Workflow messages became available. Obviously, knowledge of OA Framework development is a prerequisite for this technique.

The best way to learn how the embedding of OA Framework regions within Workflow notifications works is to have a look at a simple practical example. In this example, we will create a simple Workflow process that consists of only three activities: Start, Notification (with OA Framework region embedded), and End.

The notification will always be sent to the OPERATIONS user, as we will hard code the performer of this notification to the OPERATION username. Next, in the Workflow process, there is a message attribute that can be used to pass its value to the embedded OA Framework region at runtime. This will demonstrate how we can pass parameters to an OA Framework region from an instance of a Workflow process; we'll use the value of the message attribute to display it as a message within the embedded region.

First, we create a standalone OA Framework region with JDeveloper for Oracle Applications. We covered OA Framework in its own chapter in this book; here we only bring up the basic steps.

At the time of writing this book, notifications can only include stackLayout type of OA Framework regions. The region that we built in this example is a standalone stackLayout region with only one item (paramItem) included in it:

```
Begin
jdr_utils.printdocument
        ('/xxcust/oracle/apps/custom/ntf/webui/EmbedddNtfRN');
end;
/
<?xml version='1.0' encoding='UTF-8'?>
<oa:stackLayout version="10.1.3_798" xml:lang="en-US"
                xmlns:oa="http://xmlns.oracle.com/oa"
                xmlns:jrad="http://xmlns.oracle.com/jrad"
                xmlns:ui="http://xmlns.oracle.com/uix/ui"
                xmlns:user="http://xmlns.oracle.com/jrad/user"
                xmlns="http://xmlns.oracle.com/jrad"
                amDefName="oracle.apps.fnd.framework.toolbox.tutorial
                .server.HelloWorldAM"
                prompt="An Example of Embedded FWK Region"
                standalone="true"
                controllerClass="xxcust.oracle.apps.custom.ntf.webui.
                EmbeddddNtfCO">
   <ui:contents>
      <oa:messageStyledText id="paramItem"
           prompt="The value of parameter from Item Attribute:"/>
   </ui:contents>
</oa:stackLayout>
```

From the definition of the region, you can see that in our example we have "borrowed" oracle.apps.fnd.framework.toolbox.tutorial.server.HelloWorldAM from the Framework Tutorial application that comes with the VISION instance. Also, we created the EmbeddddNtfCO controller code and attached it to our stackLayout region:

```
package xxcust.oracle.apps.custom.ntf.webui;
import oracle.apps.fnd.framework.webui.OAControllerImpl;
import oracle.apps.fnd.framework.webui.OAPageContext;
import oracle.apps.fnd.framework.webui.beans.OAWebBean;
import oracle.apps.fnd.framework.webui.beans.message.
       OAMessageStyledTextBean;

public class EmbeddddNtfCO extends OAControllerImpl
{
  public void processRequest
                       (OAPageContext pageContext, OAWebBean webBean)
  {
    super.processRequest(pageContext, webBean);
    String exampleParam = pageContext.getParameter("ExampleParam");

      OAMessageStyledTextBean textBean =
        (OAMessageStyledTextBean)webBean.findIndexedChildRecursive
                                                         ("paramItem");
      if (textBean != null)
      {
        textBean.setAttributeValue(TEXT_ATTR,exampleParam);
      }
  }
}
```

The code within the processRequest method reads the ExampleParam parameter from the pageContext object and programmatically sets the text attribute of the paramItem text bean to the value from the parameter.

Now, we log in to Oracle Applications as System Administrator or Application Developer to register our region as an Oracle Applications function. We navigate to (N)System Administrator | Application | Function and create a function with the following properties:

Description tab:

- Function: XX_EMBED_NTF
- User Function Name: XX Embedded Notification Region

Properties tab:

- Type: SSWA jsp function

Web HTML tab:

- OA.jsp?page=/xxcust/oracle/apps/custom/ntf/webui/EmbedddNtfRN

Next, we open Workflow Builder and create a very simple Workflow process that consists only of a start and an end activity and one notification, as illustrated in Figure 11-14.

Now we create an item attribute with the following properties:

- Item Type: XX Embedded FWK Region
- Internal Name: EXAMPLE_FWK_RN
- Display Name: Example OA Framework Region
- Description: Example OA Framework Region

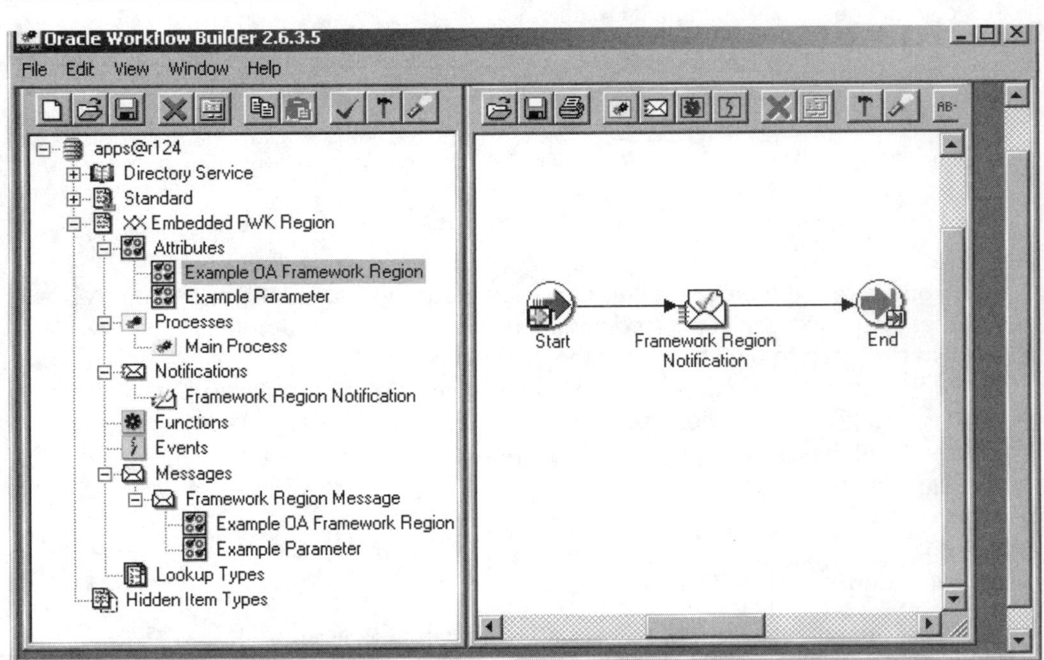

FIGURE 11-14. *Simple WF process that sends a notification with an embedded region*

- Type: Document
- Frame Target: Full Window
- Default Type: Constant
- Default Value: JSP:/OA_HTML/OA.jsp?OAFunc=XX_EMBED_NTF&ExampleParam=-&EXAMPLE_PARAM-

We also need to create another item type attribute to keep our parameter value that we set within the Workflow process or simply pass the value from the user:

- Item Type: XX Embedded FWK Region
- Internal Name: EXAMPLE_PARAM
- Display Name: Example Parameter
- Description: Example Parameter
- Type: Text

Now, we create a Framework Region Message with an internal name FWK_MSG. The HTML Body property under the Body tab should have only OA Framework region message attributes specified as tokens, as illustrated in Figure 11-15. It can also include WF_NOTIFICATION functions such as WF_NOTIFICATION (HISTORY); however, if you include any message attributes other than OA Framework region message attributes, this will result in an error message displayed on the screen.

Once the message is created, you can attach it to a notification that in our example we called Framework Region Notification.

Finally, we drag and drop Example OA Framework Region and Example Parameter item attributes onto the Framework Region Message; thus, we create two message attributes (Example OA Framework Region and Example Parameter) that reference the corresponding item attributes.

IMPORTANT
Message attributes should have the Source property set to Send.

If we now deploy both the OA Framework region and Workflow item type definition, we can test the result by logging in as a user with the Workflow Administrator responsibility and launching our Example OA Framework Region Workflow process

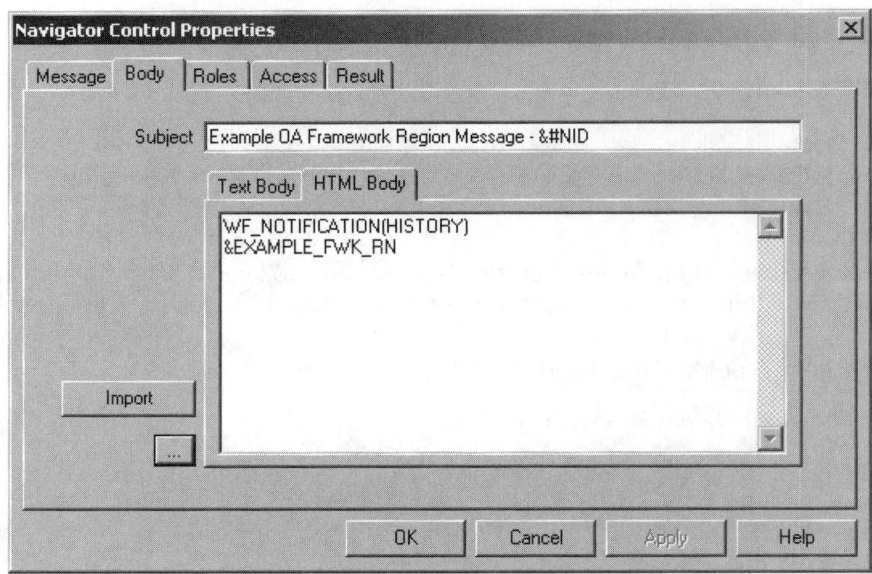

FIGURE 11-15. *OA Framework region message*

from the Developer Studio function. We pass a Hello World value for the Example Parameter item attribute before launching the process and submit. Figure 11-16 shows how the message is displayed to the OPERATIONS user when he or she accesses the Worklist.

The obvious benefit of using embedded OA Framework regions is that you can use the Personalization framework to personalize the page, in addition to receiving many other benefits of OA Framework technology, such as rendering the notifications in the standard or even custom look and feel.

Directory Service

Workflow Directory service is a type of repository that is implemented through database views in the database. The principal entities in Workflow Directory are user and role. An example of a user is the OPERATIONS user in Oracle Applications that we have referred to throughout this chapter.

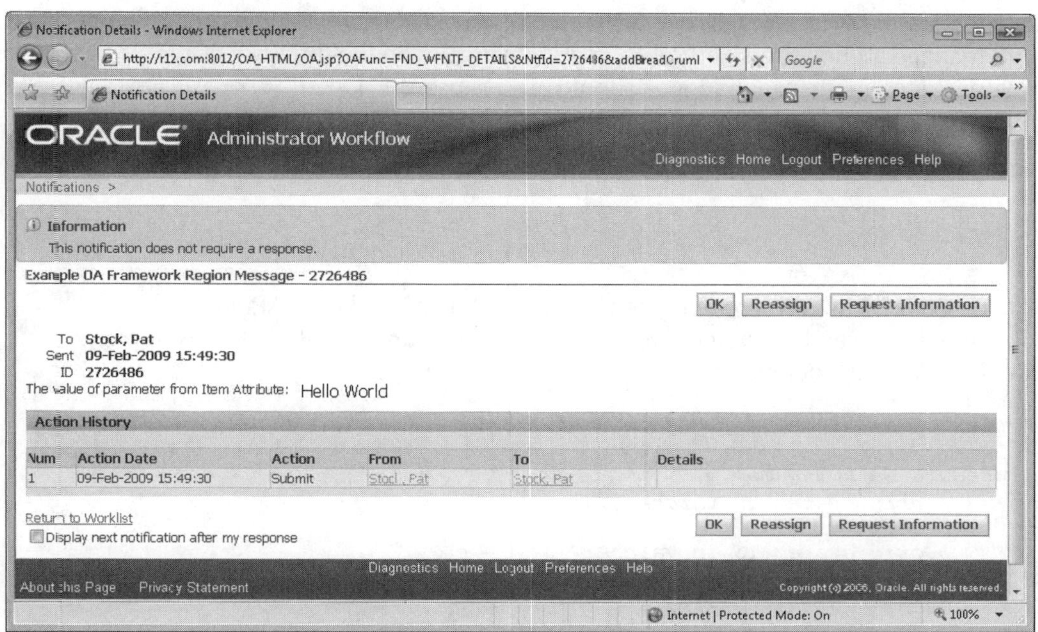

FIGURE 11-16. *Notification with an embedded OA Framework region*

The following four database views make Workflow Directory:

- **WF_USERS** Contains information about people who can receive Workflow notifications.
- **WF_ROLES** Contains information about the roles who can receive Workflow notifications.
- **WF_USER_ROLES** Contains an intersection of the users and roles from WF_USERS and WF_ROLES.
- **WF_USER_ROLE_ASSIGNMENTS_V** References assignments of users to roles.

In E-Business Suite, Oracle Workflow stores denormalized data about users and roles in local (WF_LOCAL%) tables. The data in the local tables comes from various E-Business Suite modules, and Workflow Directory views such as WF_USERS and WF_ROLES are based on the local tables.

From a development perspective, you need to be aware that Workflow Directory exposes public APIs through the WF_DIRECTORY package that allows you to create and manage ad hoc users and roles programmatically on the fly. Also, as we demonstrated in the example, you should always use WF_DIRECTORY APIs to obtain user or role information for the directory:

```
wf_directory.GetRoleName ( 'PER'
                          ,l_supervisor_id
                          ,op_supervisor_user_name
                          , op_supervisor_display_name);
```

The Workflow APIs are documented in the Oracle Workflow API Reference document that can be obtained from Oracle websites and Metalink. For example, GetRoleName is documented as:

```
Syntax

procedure GetRoleName
     (p_orig_system in varchar2,

      p_orig_system_id in varchar2,

      p_name out varchar2,

      p_display_name out varchar2);

Description
```

Returns a Workflow display name and role name for a role given the system information from the original user and roles repository.

```
Arguments (input)

p_orig_system Code that identifies the original repository table.

p_orig_system_id ID of a row in the original repository table.
```

TIP
If you need user, role, or other information in your PL/SQL code that is available through Workflow Directory, always use WF_DIRECTORY APIs rather than SQL joins to Workflow Directory views (WF_USERS and WF_ROLES). Using Workflow Directory views in SQL joins can hamper the performance.

Every notification in the Workflow item type definition must have a performer associated with it. The notification performer is simply the role (for example, an OPERATIONS user) to whom the notification is assigned or sent. Normally, we assign the performer dynamically by referring to an attribute; however, if you wanted to hard code the value for the notification performer at design time, you would need to connect to the development database through Workflow Builder and use Load Roles from Database functionality from the File menu.

Business Events in Oracle Applications

The concept of Business Events in the context of E-Business Suite plays a key role in enabling event-driven integration with other systems outside the suite (Business to Business [B2B] scenario) or even within itself (Application to Application [A2A] scenario).

In addition to that, the Business Events in E-Business Suite in particular allow for an exceptionally effective way of decoupling the standard product functionality, available out of the box, from client customizations that seek to adapt the standard product to meet customer-specific business needs. In other words, Oracle Applications developers should consider using Business Events whenever possible when configuring and customizing the standard products.

Now that we have stressed the importance of the Business Events in the life of an Oracle Applications developer, we are going to explain what they are, where and how they execute, and how to use them.

What Is a Business Event?

A Business Event is an occurrence of something important happening within an application in E-Business Suite. We usually link the Business Events with entities or objects within an application's business process flow. For example, the creation of a new employee in an HR application could be classified as a Business Event; if the occurrence of the event is somehow announced through the system, the other applications can listen or subscribe to it. Once the event happens, the subscriptions to that event specify what to do with it and how to process the information from the event; in the case of the creation of a new employee, you can decide to propagate the information about that employee to some third-party system as it happens.

From a technical point of view, the definition of Business Events is recorded in the WF_EVENTS table in the APPLSYS schema:

```
SQL> desc applsys.wf_events
 Name                                      Null?    Type
 ----------------------------------------- -------- ---------------
 GUID                                      NOT NULL RAW(16)
 NAME                                      NOT NULL VARCHAR2(240)
 TYPE                                      NOT NULL VARCHAR2(8)
 STATUS                                    NOT NULL VARCHAR2(8)
 GENERATE_FUNCTION                                  VARCHAR2(240)
```

```
OWNER_NAME                                        VARCHAR2(30)
OWNER_TAG                                         VARCHAR2(30)
SECURITY_GROUP_ID                                 VARCHAR2(32)
CUSTOMIZATION_LEVEL                      NOT NULL VARCHAR2(1)
LICENSED_FLAG                            NOT NULL VARCHAR2(1)
JAVA_GENERATE_FUNC                                VARCHAR2(240)
```

The business event definition is a record that simply declares the name of an event, usually in <company>.<family>.<product>.<component>.<object>.<event> format, status (Enabled or Disabled), the generate functions (PL/SQL or Java code that can take event key or event parameters to generate additional event data), and some other attributes.

In Oracle Applications, you can search for existing events and create new ones through the Workflow Administrator responsibility (Workflow Administrator | Business Events).

However, the events as such are not of much use on their own. You need a mechanism of listening or subscribing to them so when they happen you can do something clever with them.

The system that is at the heart of processing and managing the events in E-Business Suite is called Business Events System.

Business Events System (BES)

The Business Event System (BES) is a part of the Oracle Workflow product, but it is important to understand that BES is independent of Workflow Engine and can operate on its own.

In E-Business Suite, Oracle Applications developers use BES primarily to register potentially important events in their applications and to register subscriptions for registered events. Typically, the standard events are registered by E-Business Suite product developers and shipped to the customers, who can have their own developers create subscriptions to these events in order to achieve additional or custom functionality. Workflow Engine integrates with BES through the event activity, which is designed to handle events from BES.

Typical event processing by BES in E-Business Suite, without taking into consideration any external systems, can be summarized as follows: Oracle Applications product developers code their applications in such a way that when something important happens, such as employee creation, an event is raised. From a development point of view, raising an event is nothing more than calling either WF_EVENT.Raise() PL/SQL API or the raise() method from the BusinessEvent Java class. When the event is raised, the information that describes the event is stored in a WF_EVENT_T datatype structure in Oracle Database, provided the event is raised from PL/SQL. If the event is raised from Java code, the event information is kept in an instance of the BusinessEvent Java class. Both the WF_EVENT_T data structure and BusinessEvent object store common properties for the event such as event name, event key, correlation ID, send date, receive date, event parameter list, event payload, and some others. A separate process called Event Dispatcher, which is part of BES and implemented as server side PL/SQL, searches the WF_EVENT_SUBSCRIPTIONS table and executes any subscriptions that are defined for the event that has been raised. The process of executing a subscription can be deferred for background processing if needed.

By defining an appropriate subscription for an event, customers can execute their own code when events are raised. There are several types of actions that can be performed:

- Execute custom business logic (for example, PL/SQL code)
- Launch the Workflow item type specified in the subscription
- Receive a message from your trading partner (XML Gateway integration)
- Send a notification using standard or your own message templates
- Generate a message and send the message to your trading partner (XML Gateway integration)
- Send the event to the agent specified in the subscription (Oracle AQ integration)

An Example: Converting Existing Workflow

The easiest way to put theory into practice is to convert our existing XX Custom Approval Example item type that we created in previous sections into an item type that uses a custom event. In our existing Workflow process, we'll replace the Start node with the Receive Event start node. Once the custom event is raised, the event subscription will launch the custom Workflow process.

In order to achieve that, you need to perform the following steps:

1. Logged on as Workflow Administrator, create a custom event by navigating to Workflow Administrator | Business Events | (B)Create Event. Enter the following details:
   - Name: xxcustom.oracle.apps.po
   - Display Name: An example event
   - Description: An example event
   - Status: Enabled

2. Create a subscription for the created event: navigate to Workflow Administrator | Business Events, query xxcustom.oracle.apps.po event, and click the Subscription icon in the results region. Enter the following details in the Subscriptions page:

   - System: (enter your local system from LOV)
   - Source Type: Local
   - Event Filter: xxcustom.oracle.apps.po
   - Phase: 99
   - Status: Enabled
   - Rule Data: Key
   - Action Type: Launch Workflow
   - On Error: Stop and Rollback
   - Workflow Type: XX_APPRV
   - Workflow Process: PO_APPR_MAIN
   - Owner Name: Oracle Purchasing
   - Owner Tag: PO

   Click the Apply button to save the definition for the event subscription.

3. Now you need to modify the existing XX Custom Approval Example item type to be able to receive the custom event. Open the existing item type definition in Workflow Builder and create the following item type attributes in the Navigator screen:

Item Type	Internal Name	Display Name	Description	Type
XX Custom Approval Example	ENAME	Event Name	Event Name	Text
XX Custom Approval Example	EKEY	EKEY	Event Key	Text
XX Custom Approval Example	Event	Event	Event	Event

4. Create an Event type of activity in the Navigator screen by right-clicking XX Custom Approval Example item type, and then select New | Event. Enter the following properties:

   - Internal Name: RCV_EVENT
   - Display Name: Receive Event
   - Description: Receive event
   - Event Action: Receive

   Again, in the Navigator screen, drag and drop onto the newly created receive activity the following item type attributes: Requestor Person Id, PO Number, Requestor's Name, Event Name, Event Key, and Event. This action will create six event activity attributes.

5. Now you need to modify the workflow process to include the Receive Event activity. Open the PO Approval Main process, and in the process activity window, remove the existing Start node. From the Navigator window, drag and drop the Receive Event activity that you just created and create a transition toward the Find Approver for the PO function activity. It is important that you double-click the Receive Event in the Process Diagram window and set following properties:

   - In the Node tab, set the Start/End property to Start. This action marks your Receive Event activity as the Workflow start activity. Remember that Oracle Workflow needs at least one start and one end activity within any process.
   - In the Event Details tab, set the Event Name property to the Event Name value, Event Key to the Event key value, and Event Message property to the Event value from the drop-down list. The completed Workflow process should look like Figure 11-17.

Once you save the modified Workflow definition to the database, you can test the process by raising an event from the client:

```
DECLARE
  l_parameter_list wf_parameter_list_t;
BEGIN
  l_parameter_list := wf_parameter_list_t
                    ( wf_parameter_t ('REQ_PERSON_ID', '25')
                    , wf_parameter_t ('PO_NUM', '10100')
                    , wf_parameter_t ('REQUESTOR_NAME', 'Pat Stock') );
  wf_event.RAISE ( p_event_name => 'xxcustom.oracle.apps.po'
```

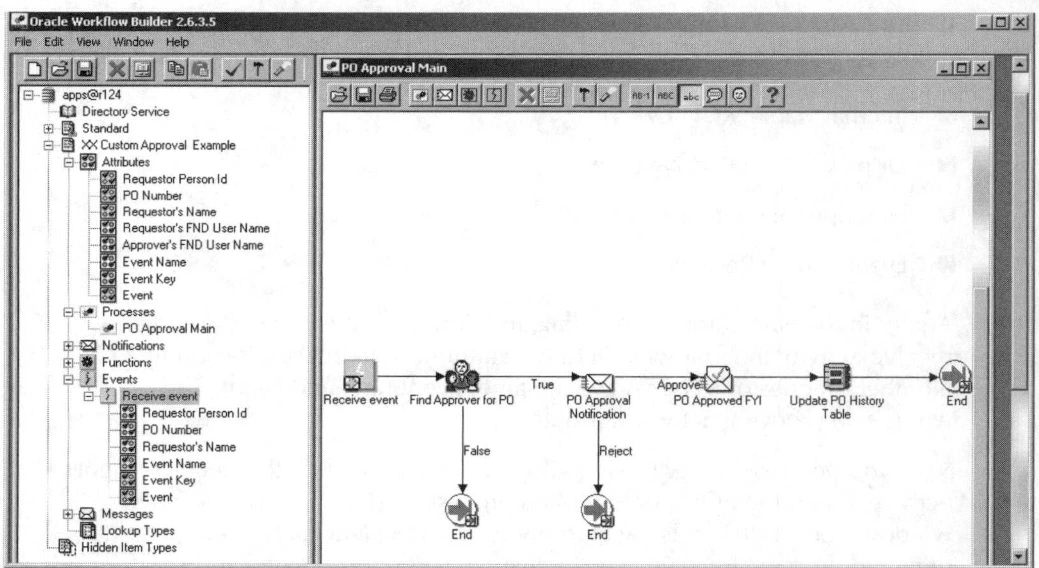

FIGURE 11-17. *Using the Receive Event to start the Workflow process*

```
                    , p_event_key => 'TEST101'
                    , p_parameters => l_parameter_list );
  COMMIT;
END;
/
```

Because you set the Phase property to 99 when you defined the subscription for xxcustom.oracle.apps.po event, the subscription will be executed immediately, and an instance of our modified Workflow process should appear in the Status Monitor screen provided that no errors occurred.

Best Practices

Summarizing the best practices for Oracle Workflow is quite a challenging task, and we'll admit that our list is limited and covers the most obvious things. Oracle Workflow product has reached a considerable level of maturity over the years; we would never pretend that the best practices list in this section covers every single aspect of the dos and don'ts of Oracle Workflow development process. The items that follow are outlined in no particular order of importance.

It is important to keep in mind that Workflow Builder can easily be used to change the existing business process to accommodate customer-specific needs; however, this powerful tool needs to be used cautiously.

Workflow Builder: Design Time

When using Workflow Builder, we advise you always to save the Workflow definitions locally (on your desktop PC) rather than opening an item type from the database and then directly saving it to a database. Not only can you inadvertently overwrite somebody else's Workflow definition when modifying the Workflow process online, but Workflow Builder can also freeze during the connection to the database. If that happens, you can lose the definition of the process that you are working on. Always work on a locally saved copy before deploying to the database.

Before doing any work on the target environment, always check that you are using the correct version of Workflow Builder.

Don't be tempted to modify the standard item type that comes with Oracle Workflow unless instructed to do so by Oracle product documentation. If you need to create a custom set of activities and Workflow objects that you often use, create a separate item type that will serve as your library item type, which you can reuse in multiple processes.

When designing the processes, be careful not to overdo the nesting of processes. A process can have any number of other processes, and excessive nesting will negatively impact the performance and render your process difficult to read and monitor.

Be mindful of how long will take to execute PL/SQL code that is attached to function activities, as this directly impacts the user experience in most cases. For example, say you are developing a purchasing approval process where the user submits a purchase order for approval from a form-based application. If this action launches your PO approval process, and within that process you have a long-running activity that executes a long-running SQL query to find an approver, the form used by the end user will appear to be hung, until the attached PL/SQL activity completes. This is easy problem to solve, as you can use the Cost property at design time to defer the problem activity to background rather than inline processing.

If your Workflow definition requires hard-coded values for the notification performers, do not type the username into the Performer field. Instead, load the roles from the database using the File | Load Roles From Database menu item, and use the loaded roles to assign the performer.

Modifications of Standards Workflow Processes

The most important rule, and we cannot stress enough how important it is, is to always read product documentation. Most of the products in E-Business Suite come with implementation guides, and there you will find what can be modified within the seeded Workflow definition. Oracle Support will not be able to help you with any customizations that are not specifically mentioned in the official documentation such as user's or implementation guides for the product in question.

Customarily, implementation consultants use one of the following methods when the seeded Workflow processes needs to be modified outside the scope recommended by the product documentation:

- Create a completely new Workflow definition and call it from the underlying application. Some E-Business Suite applications allow you to specify your own item type to be used in the business flow.
- Copy the original seeded definition and rename and modify it. The custom modified process that is renamed is then called from the underlying application. Again, to instantiate the Workflow process, consultants on site may configure the system in such a way that you can launch the modified process. Alternatively, a customization may be introduced in the underlying application to enable you to launch this custom Workflow process.
- Directly change an Oracle-delivered seeded Workflow process.

It is quite obvious that the last option is something you should definitely avoid. Unsupported modifying of seeded Workflow processes is bound to create problems in the future. Once the seeded Workflow definition is updated by an Oracle patch, the customization needs to be reapplied, and in many instances redesigned. This is something that should be avoided at all costs.

Insist on not changing the default access levels in Workflow Builder when customizing the processes. Access levels are there for a reason: to protect you from doing things that can damage the system as well as render your system unsupported by Oracle. For example, modifying a Workflow object that has a protection level less than 100 is not supported. The access level in Workflow Builder is set in the menu Help | About item. Oracle product teams protect Workflow objects because they anticipate that they may change in the future; therefore, they "lock" the definitions at design time so that customers cannot change them if they are using Workflow Builder with the correct access level value.

Remember, Oracle Applications product teams developers operate at access level 20; the customers of Oracle Applications who are using Workflow Builder to modify seeded processes should always operate at level 100 or greater. Workflow access levels are as follows:

0–9	Oracle Workflow
10–19	Oracle Application Object Library
20–99	Oracle Applications Development
100–999	Customer Organization

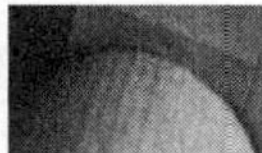

TIP

If you want to ensure that your customizations survive an upgrade of a seeded Oracle Applications Workflow process, you need to operate Workflow Builder at access level 100 or greater and ensure that both Preserve Customizations and Lock at this Access Level check boxes are checked (selected). When Oracle Applications patches are applied, they run the WFLOAD utility in Upgrade mode at an access level that is always less than 100.

Wherever possible, use Business Events to extend business processes. The Business Events allow you to decouple your customizations very elegantly from Oracle-delivered seeded code. For example, at the beginning of this chapter, we discussed the building elements of the AP Invoice item type. If you download the definition of this item type and open it with Workflow Builder, you'll notice that all activities and other Workflow objects are locked, provided you are operating the Workflow Builder at the correct access level of 100 (Help | About menu item). Now, if you need to change this process, you'll notice that the Start activity for the main process is the Receive Event activity, which indicates that this process relies on a Business Event occurrence to be launched. At this stage, you can research what Business Event will trigger the launch of the AP Invoice Approval—Main Workflow process by either checking the product documentation or querying from the Business Events screen (the Workflow Administrator responsibility). In this case, the Business Event is oracle.apps.ap.event.invoice.approval, and further analysis is probably required to figure out when this event gets fired during the business process. However, from the technical perspective, it is perfectly acceptable that customers create a subscription to this event in order to extend the standard product functionality.

Performance Considerations

From the design point of view, Oracle Applications developers need to pay special attention to the number of item type attributes used. The more item attributes are used, the poorer the performance at runtime will be, especially with regard the process startup time. Item attributes are effectively a global variable and, when the process is created, WF Engine needs to create them before the process is started.

If multiple item attributes need to be programmatically created, use the array versions of WF Engine APIs to add large numbers of item attributes programmatically. It is recommended to use the AddItemAttributeArray APIs over AddItemAttribute APIs for improved performance.

As far as message attributes are concerned, you probably guessed that it is very easy to fall into the trap of using them excessively. We recommend that you use embedded OA Framework regions where possible, as explained in the "Embedding OA Framework Regions in WF Notifications" section earlier in this chapter. For example, if you are thinking of creating a large number of message attributes in order to display an invoice data, you should consider turning this message into an OA Framework embedded region, and let OAF do the work of processing and displaying the required information.

Finally, after finishing the design of your process, discuss with your System Administrator or the DBA in charge of running the production environment how many background engines should be configured to run and at what intervals. You know the process that you designed the best; it's only fair that you brief System Administrators on how the background engines should be configured. The incorrect configuration of background processing may give an appearance of a performance issue as well as result in nonfunctioning business processes.

Deployment Considerations

As far as deployment is concerned, we advise you always to use command-line tools such as Workflow Definitions Loader and Workflow XML Loader for the promotion of Workflow and Business Event definitions between environments.

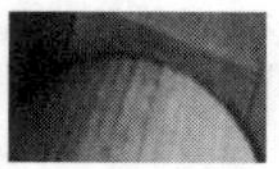

TIP
Workflow definitions can be saved as ASCII (.wft) files, which in turn can be controlled by source control.

In Oracle Applications, you should use the concurrent request type of Workflow Definitions Loader executable called WFLOAD. WFLOAD takes several parameters documented in Oracle Workflow Administrator's Guide:

- To upgrade the Workflow definition, run WFLOAD apps/pwd 0 Y UPGRADE file.wft.
  This mode upgrades to a definition specified in the input file.wft, but it preserves all customizations, taking into consideration the access level from file.wft. It is the safest mode to use.
- To upload the Workflow definition, run WFLOAD apps/pwd 0 Y UPLOAD file.wft. This mode uploads to a definition specified in the input file.wft, but it ignores all preserved customizations settings. Again, the access level from file.wft is used at runtime.

- To force the Workflow definition, run WFLOAD apps/pwd 0 Y FORCE file.wft. Do not use this option unless you know what you are doing! It forces the input file.wft to be uploaded regardless of Workflow objects protection levels. For example, Oracle Support may ask you to run WFLOAD in force mode to fix an issue caused by the patch.
- To download the Workflow definition, run WFLOAD apps/pwd 0 Y DOWNLOAD file.wft ITEMTYPE1. This mode simply downloads the definition from the database to a flat file, and it is safe to use.

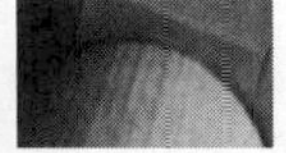

CAUTION
Be extra careful with the WFLOAD utility. Different situations call for different modes; for example, in a development environment you can run it in upload mode if you don't care about preserving of customizations. However, you wouldn't want to do that in a production environment.

Summary

Oracle Workflow is one of the key technologies in the current releases of E-Business Suite. It allows developers to design sophisticated business processes using the graphical tool Workflow Builder. At design time, Workflow developers can use many of the design constructs such as branching on a result, looping through activities, timeouts, flow branching and rendezvous, and many others to meet their requirements.

In this chapter, we discussed the main components of Oracle Workflow and Business Events System. We also provided step-by-step walkthroughs on how to build, deploy, and test a custom Workflow process from scratch; how to embed an OA Framework Region within a Workflow notification; and how to convert the existing Workflow process to use Business Event System.

Although the practical examples in this chapter will quickly get you started with Oracle Workflow in E-Business Suite, please appreciate that there is much more to Oracle Workflow that hasn't been covered in this book. For example, we haven't covered the exception handling, which is a topic that every developer needs to be familiar with. Oracle Workflow Developer's Guide, available from the E-Business Suite Online Documentation Library, provides the best reference for all of the features, including exception handling, that are not covered in this book.

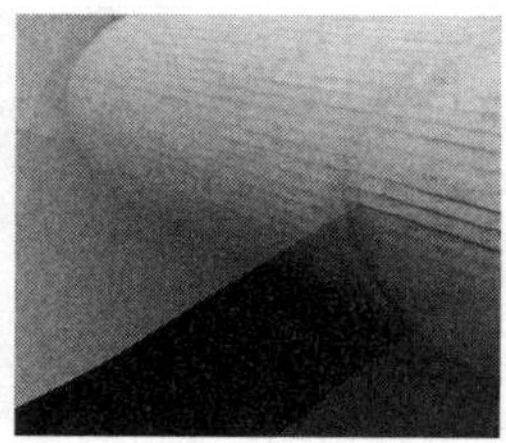

CHAPTER 12

Oracle XML Gateway

racle XML Gateway is another product that is designed to be used as both standalone and embedded within E-Business Suite product. Of course, in this book we are concentrating primarily on E-Business Suite development techniques, and therefore, in this chapter we are going to discuss how to use XML Gateway to deliver XML documents reliably to and from E-Business Suite applications.

The primary function of XML Gateway is to allow for standards-based exchanges of XML messages between E-Business Suite and other applications over the Internet or a corporate intranet. An example of one of these transactions could be a purchase order: a purchase order created by a buyer in Oracle Purchasing can easily be extracted from an E-Business Suite database and electronically sent to either a common marketplace or directly to the supplier. Likewise, sales orders from customers can be electronically delivered to E-Business Suite over the Internet through the XML Gateway module, and at the end of the order-to-cash cycle, you may also electronically deliver invoices to your customers via XML Gateway.

It is important to note that with XML Gateway any type of XML message can be exchanged between E-Business Suite and other applications and even between different applications within E-Business Suite. The messaging is not bound exclusively to exchanging business data between trading partners in a business-to-business (B2B) scenario; the content of messages can be just about anything as long as they are well-formed XML documents that comply to predefined XML Document Type Definition (DTD) for the transaction in question.

This chapter will focus on the practical aspects of building and developing from scratch both inbound and outbound transactions with XML Gateway. What we cover in this chapter is largely applicable to both releases 11i and R12, and we will highlight the important difference between the two releases when applicable.

XML Gateway Architecture Overview

The principal purpose of XML Gateway is to provide a mechanism of consuming, creating, and delivering XML messages to and from E-Business Suite. Due to the popularity and widespread use of XML-based standards, such a module allows for the standardized exchange of XML messages between diverse systems in various business-to-business (B2B) and application-to-application (A2A) scenarios.

Oracle XML Gateway is tightly integrated with Oracle Workflow and Business Events System (BES) and includes a number of other E-Business Suite and Oracle Database technology components such as Oracle Advance Queues. For instance, seeded Business Events in E-Business Suite can be used by customers to launch a workflow process that will initiate an XML Gateway outbound transaction to transmit transactional data such as purchase orders or invoices over the Internet to the trading partner.

Messaging systems such as XML Gateway essentially have to provide a reliable transport mechanism for both inbound and outbound message delivery, tools for the design of XML messages, means of generating or converting the message content at runtime, the triggering mechanisms in the applications for creating outbound messages, and a way of letting the applications involved in the inbound transaction know that the message has arrived from an outside application. Such systems also need a means of defining the application partners with whom the system exchanges messages and associating those messaging partners with a particular transaction type such as an Inbound Sales Order or Outbound Invoice.

The principal components of Oracle XML Gateway are shown in Figure 12-1 and can be classified as the following core functional components:

- Message Designer
- Transaction functional setup in E-Business Suite

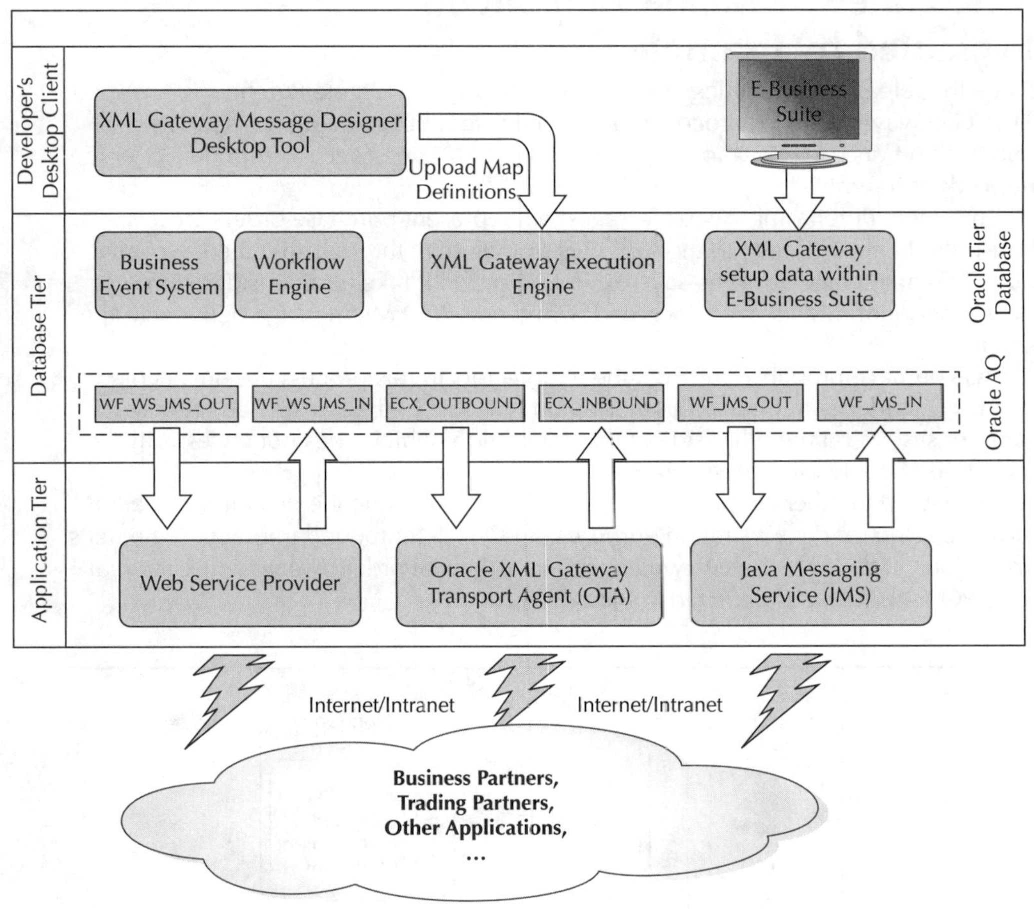

FIGURE 12-1. *Oracle XML Gateway architecture overview*

- Execution Engine Layer
- Message Transport Layer

In addition to the preceding core XML Gateway components, we already mentioned that XML Gateway is very closely integrated with both Oracle Workflow and Business Events System, and this is something we will demonstrate in our practical examples for inbound and outbound processing.

The best way to understand the role of individual components is to examine them in the context of a real and practical application. In the next section, we'll examine the seeded transaction and XML message from the Oracle Purchasing module in E-Business Suite and discuss the roles and functions of the XML Gateway components.

XML Gateway Main Components Explained by Example

Since the release of E-Business Suite 11.5.7 and higher, Oracle Purchasing has used XML Gateway in its own process models to transmit business objects such as purchase orders (POs) in a form of standardized XML messages to suppliers over the network or Internet.

In Oracle Purchasing, XML messages that represent purchase orders are transmitted either directly to the suppliers or indirectly through so-called exchange hubs or marketplaces. For the sake of simplicity, we'll take into consideration only the former option, which is concerned with direct PO XML message delivery to the supplier.

As you have probably guessed, the main actors in this process are buyers of goods and services in Oracle Purchasing on one side of the transaction and the supplier system on the other side of the transaction (which does not necessarily have to be Oracle E-Business Suite).

As we did in other chapters in this book, we will assume the default R12 VISION instance setup for demonstration purposes of PO XML outbound transaction. So, let's take a look at the XML Gateway components in logical order by examining the real XML PO transaction as depicted in Figure 12-2.

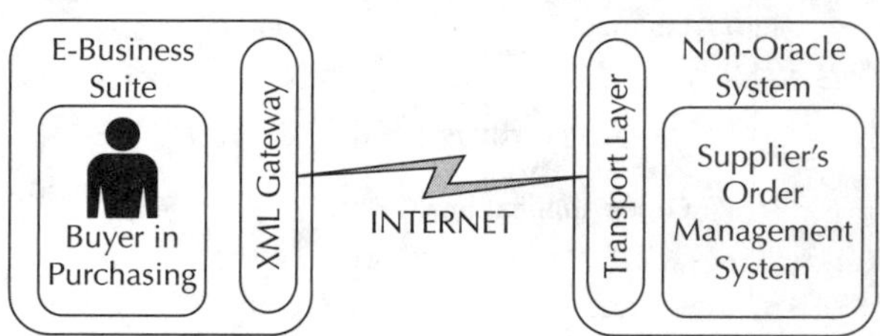

FIGURE 12-2. *Outbound XML PO transaction to a non-Oracle system*

Message Designer

Before using messages in XML Gateway, you must define your content needs by way of mapping a data source into target data format. For instance, the source of data for a message can be purchase order data in E-Business Suite database tables (PO Headers and Lines) and the target format can be an XML document that is transmitted to the supplier over the Internet. In the case of a PO outbound XML Gateway transaction, you use Message Designer to create a message map that will transform data stored in the E-Business Suite database (such as PO tables) into an XML document. With Message Designer, it is also possible to build other types of message mappings such as XML document to XML document and XML document to database types of mappings.

As illustrated in Figure 12-1, the Message Designer is a client tool installed on the developer's desktop computer. Before developers install the tool, we recommend that they check Oracle Metalink for the latest information about which version should be used for the target E-Business Suite installation in question. For example, Metalink Note 557101.1 suggests downloading client-side patch 4066964 to install XML Gateway Message Designer for R12. The installation procedure is very simple and is explained in the installation notes included in patch 4066964.

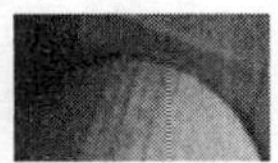

NOTE
If you are unsure what version of Message Designer should be used with your version of E-Business Suite installation, we suggest you check with Oracle Support either through Metalink portal support resources or by creating a service request with Oracle Support.

Although we are going to provide the complete step-by-step examples of creating both inbound and outbound messages from scratch in the following sections, for now we'll just briefly outline the logical order in which to approach the process of building the map using the PO XML outbound map (ITG_PROCESS_PO_007_OUT.xgm) as an example.

NOTE
The ITG_PROCESS_PO_007_OUT.xgm map definition used for a PO XML outbound transaction can be found in the $ITG_TOP/patch/115/xml/US directory in both R11i and R12. Metalink Note 412108.1 lists the changes introduced in R12. Also, for the definition of the target data, XML PO is using the 003_PROCESS_PO_007.dtd file that can be found in the $ITG_TOP/xml/oag721 directory.

Defining Data Source Map Creation or Data Definition wizards are used to create source definitions. The wizard allows you to create either a Database or XML type of the data source definition. For instance, if you select Database as the source type, the wizard will prompt you for the source database username, password, connect string, host machine, and port number. The wizard will then connect to the source database and allow you to pick database objects such as tables and views along with the desired columns that will be used in the message map. In the context of the XML PO example outbound message, the source data is an E-Business Suite database and the main parts of the message are PO Header and Lines information. For this purpose, the Oracle Purchasing product team created ITG_PO_HEADER_ARCH_V, ITG_PO_LINE_ARCH_V, ITG_PO_LINE_ARCH_V, and ITG_PO_DISTRBN_ARCH_V views in the database to extract the relevant PO header, lines, line locations, and line distributions information at runtime.

Defining Data Target Similar to defining the data source, you use the Map Creation or Data Definition wizards to create target definitions for both Database and XML types of data mapping. In the context of the XML PO example outbound message, the target data is in XML format that is validated and conforms to the standard 003_PROCESS_PO_007.dtd structure. The outline of the XML structure expressed in XML DTD terms is as follows:

```
PROCESS_PO (POORDERHDR, POORDERLIN+)
 POORDERHDR (PARTNER+, ATTCHREF*, CHARGE*, POTERM*)
 POORDERLIN (ATTCHREF*, CHARGE*, DISTRIBUTN*,
             PARTNER*, POTERM*, POBSUBLINE*, POLINESCHD*)
```

As expected, conceptually, the target data has a similar structure to the source data because for every PO header you can have multiple PO lines, distributions, and so on.

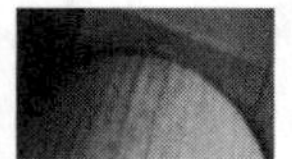

NOTE
XML Gateway uses the somewhat outdated concept of validating XML documents with DTDs instead of XML Schemas, the currently widely accepted technique of validating and defining the structure of XML documents.

Defining Source-to-Target Hierarchy (Level Mapping) In Message Designer, you can use the Level Mapping tab to relate the source and target hierarchy trees. Conceptually, both source and target parts can be either levels or elements. A level is some group of data records that is repeated within the message, such as PO Lines in the PO XML transaction; there is one PO Header in both the source and target definition, but there could be multiple PO Lines for each PO Header. The concept of levels allows the XML Gateway engine to iteratively process the data that repeats within the message. For instance, in the outbound PO XML ITG_PROCESS_PO_007_OUT.xgm map, the ITG_PO_LINE_ARCH_V level is at the source side that is mapped to the POORDERLIN target level, reflecting PO Lines in the database to PO Lines in XML level relation.

Creating Data Mappings from Source to Target Data Elements Similar to level mapping, in data mapping, the Message Designer requires that the developer map relevant individual elements such as the PO Number from source side to the target.

Defining Actions Actions in the Message Designer are activities that perform data transformation and execute different types of map execution process control. The actions can transform data at runtime by executing functions such as string and data conversion, mathematical functions, and other types of data conversion. Process control activities allow you to manipulate the map execution process. Among many process control actions, the capability of calling and executing database-specific functions such as PL/SQL functions and procedures is of particular interest. Actions in the XML Gateway can be defined for individual data elements (message elements such as PO Number), for documents (a collection of elements that form a document such as a PO), and at root level (a collection of documents). For example, on the source side, the view ITG_POHEADER_ARCH_V needs to be appended at runtime during the map execution in order to extract the PO data for an individual PO in question. This is achieved by creating an action that calls a database function to dynamically append a WHERE clause in SQL code for the view by adding an "and ITG_PO_HEADER_ARCH_V.POID = :PARAMETER4" clause on the fly.

Map and DTD Definitions Deployment Once the message map and accompanying DTD are designed, they can be deployed to the database by invoking the LoadMap and LoadDTDToClob utilities written in Java. XML Gateway also provides the utilities to delete an existing map and to load and delete DTD definitions from the database. Here are examples of how to use these utilities from the command line:

```
java oracle.apps.ecx.loader.LoadMap <DB username> <DB password>
<Hostname>:<Port>:<SID> <mymap.xgm>
```

For example:

```
java oracle.apps.ecx.loader.LoadMap apps welcome
mylinuxbox:1521:R1204 ITG_PROCESS_PO_007_OUT.xgm
```

Or:

```
java oracle.apps.ecx.loader.DeleteMap <DB username> <DB password>
<Hostname>:<Port>:<SID> <mapname>
```

For example:

```
java oracle.apps.ecx.loader.DeleteMap apps welcome
mylinuxbox:1521:R1204 ITG_PROCESS_PO_007_OUT
```

Or:

```
java oracle.apps.ecx.loader.LoadDTDToClob <DB username> <DB password>
<Hostname>:<Port>:<SID> <mydtd.dtd> <RootElementName> <Location>
```

For example

```
java oracle.apps.ecx.loader.LoadDTDToClob apps welcome
mylinuxbox:1521:R1204 003_process_po_003.dtd PROCESS_PO_003 po/xml/
oag721
```

Or:

```
java oracle.apps.ecx.loader.DeleteDTDFromClob <DB username> <DB password>
<Hostname>:<Port>:<SID> <mydtd.dtd> <RootElementName> <Location>
```

For example

```
java oracle.apps.ecx.loader.DeleteDTDFromClob apps welcome
mylinuxbox:1521:R1204 003_process_po_003.dtd PROCESS_PO_003 po/xml/
oag721
```

If you are new to the XML Gateway development process, it is quite likely that you may be confused after reading the preceding description of various parts of the Message Designer. This is because the Message Designer is a very versatile tool, and it would be impossible to describe all of its capabilities in this short overview. That said, in the sections to follow, we are going to use concrete examples to explain it step by step, so you needn't worry at this stage about the details of the message design process. Just remember that Message Designer enables you to create a message map that at runtime transforms data from the source system into the format required by the target, and that there are three type of map transformations: Database to XML, XML to Database, and XML to XML.

Transaction Functional Setup in E-Business Suite

Once you have a message map, the next step is to enable it within E-Business Suite so it can be used within a transaction. The functional setup needs to define the following:

- Message recipients for outbound and message senders for inbound transactions
- Transaction type, a corresponding message map, and message direction (inbound or outbound)
- A delivery (transport) mechanism for outbound messages such as HTTP(S), JMS, SOAP (Web Services), SMTP (e-mail), and others

In the context of the PO XML outbound transaction depicted in Figure 12-2, the buyer side of the transaction needs to set up the supplier (your trading partner) in E-Business Suite. You do this by logging in to E-Business Suite as a user with XML Gateway responsibility and navigating to the Trading Partner Setup screen: (N)XML Gateway | Define Trading Partners.

Here you can set up the trading partner details for your supplier. For this example, we chose Abbott Laboratories, Inc., on the R12 VISION instance with the values in Table 12-1.

Field in Trading Partner Setup Form	Value	Meaning
Operating Unit	Vision Operations	Our chosen operating unit. Remember that Trading Partner setup in XML Gateway is organization dependent. However, at runtime, XML Gateway is not dependent on organization setup—that is, the Trading Partners table is accessed across all operating units.
Trading Partner Type	Supplier	Our trading partner is our supplier of equipment; therefore, we select the Supplier type.
Trading Partner Name	Abbott Laboratories, Inc.	The supplier chosen by us. This is the trading partner we are sending our PO outbound message to.
Trading Partner Site	1045 Sansome St., San Francisco	The location (address) of our supplier.
Company Admin E-mail	admin@focusthread.com	Oracle Workflow will send e-mail notifications in case of errors or warnings to this e-mail address on the supplier's side.

TABLE 12-1. *Trading Partners Setup*

Field in Trading Partner Setup Form	Value	Meaning
Transaction Type	PO	In combination with the Transaction Subtype value, this is the unique short name for the New PO XML outbound transaction (PO/PRO). For PO Change, we would select a PO/POCO combination of transaction type and subtype.
Transaction Subtype	PRO	In combination with the Transaction Type value, this is the unique short name for a New PO XML outbound transaction (PO/PRO).
Standard Code	OAG	In this field, we specify the standard for XML messages. The PO XML outbound transaction is based on OAG (Open Applications Group); however, when designing your own messages, you can use other standards, including your own.
External Transaction Type	PO	In combination with the External Transaction Subtype, this is a unique transaction identifier as seen by the supplier in this case or, more generally, as seen by the receiver of the message whatever the nature of outbound message.

TABLE 12-1. *Trading Partners Setup (continued)*

Field in Trading Partner Setup Form	Value	Meaning
External Transaction Subtype	PROCESS	In combination with the External Transaction Type, this is a unique transaction identifier, as seen by the supplier, in this case, or, more generally, as seen by the receiver of the message, whatever the nature of outbound message.
Direction	OUT	For outbound transactions such as ours, the direction is OUT. For inbound transactions, the direction is IN.
Map	itg_process_po_007_out	The name of the message in the Message Repository (ECX tables in E-Business Suite) created with Message Designer as discussed in the previous section. If you needed to customize the seeded map, you would specify the name of the customized map.
Connection/Hub	DIRECT	For messages sent directly to the trading partners, you select DIRECT value.
Protocol Type	SMTP	By selecting the value for this field, you specify the transport delivery mechanism for the message transmission. It is quite useful during the development to use an SMTP value, which uses the host e-mail system to deliver the XML outbound message in the form of an e-mail.

TABLE 12-1. *Trading Partners Setup (continued)*

Field in Trading Partner Setup Form	Value	Meaning
User Name	Dummy	This field is usually used for messages that are transmitted over HTTP for server authentication purposes. If the protocol type is SMTP, we enter the value DUMMY as a workaround for an existing issue for this option.
Password	Dummy	This field is usually used for messages that are transmitted over HTTP for server authentication purposes. If the protocol type is SMTP, we enter the value DUMMY as a workaround for an existing issue for this option.
Protocol Address	vlad@focusthread.com	For SMTP, this has to be a valid e-mail address at the trading partner side (the supplier in our example). For HTTP and others, this is an end communication point at the receiving server side (for example, http://www.fochusthread.com/customServlet).
Source Trading Partner Location Code	VISION_BUYER	In our example, we use the value VISION_BUYER to identify the transmitting buyer side unique location at the receiving side. The receiver may use this information to distinguish between different senders of the same type of transaction.
Document Confirmation	0	The zero value in this field indicates that no confirmation is needed from the supplier upon message delivery.

TABLE 12-1. *Trading Partners Setup (continued)*

The data that is set up and referenced by XML Gateway is held in database tables prefixed by ECX, which is the short name for XML Gateway in E-Business Suite. The tables involved with the trading partner setup are ECX_TP_HEADERS, ECX_TP_DETAILS, ECX_HUBS, ECX_STANDARDS, ECX_EXT_PROCESSES, ECX_TRANSACTIONS, and others.

Execution Engine Layer

The Execution Engine is implemented as PL/SQL server-side code. In a nutshell, the Execution Engine applies the mapping rules and transformations from the message map that is designed with the Message Designer. It also validates the trading partner setup before executing the message map and applies code conversions if applicable.

In the PO XML outbound example, the Execution Engine will load and execute the ITG_PROCESS_PO_007_OUT map from the repository at runtime when a new PO is created and approved. The data will be extracted from Oracle Purchasing tables and transformed into XML format that complies with the 003_PROCESS_PO_007.dtd definition. After all the actions are applied, the generated message is validated with XML Parser and queued for outbound messages. Clearly, in the case of inbound messages, a message has to be queued to the inbound queue before it is processed by the Execution Engine.

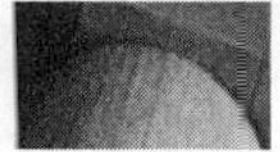

NOTE
The Execution Engine uses Oracle Workflow for error reporting and handling—keep this in mind when you're troubleshooting issues with map execution.

Message Transport Layer

As indicated in Figure 12-1, there are three principal ways of delivering messages to and from E-Business Suite via XML Gateway: Web Services, OTA (Oracle Transport Agent), and JMS (Java Messaging Services).

- **Web Services** Documents can be sent and received as document style web services. The middle-tier component on the application server contains the web service provider. The WSDL file that defines the XML Gateway web service is fixed, which in practice means that both inbound and outbound web service clients must conform to that WSDL file. In other words, your trading partner web service client code must be built based on an E-Business Suite XML Gateway WSDL file. The inbound messages are queued on the WF_WS_JMS_IN queue, while outbound messages get queued onto the WF_WS_JMS_OUT queue.

- **OTA (Oracle Transport Agent)** Implemented as a Java servlet, OTA enables a guaranteed message delivery mechanism between the two OTA servers, but it can also communicate with non-OTA servers. OTA can deliver messages over HTTP(S) with or without FND attachments. (FND attachments are a standard feature in Oracle Applications that allow additional information such as files, images, and text to be associated with E-Business Suite transactions.)
- **JMS (Java Messaging Service)** Clients that use JMS-based messaging can use JMS queues created within E-Business Suite (WF_JMS_IN and WF_JMS_OUT). Custom queues can also be created for both inbound and outbound transactions.

Practical Examples

We will now walk you through the practical examples of creating inbound and outbound transactions using XML Gateway Message Designer installed via patch 4066964 against an E-Business Suite 12.0.4 VISION instance. The steps that we'll show in detail should also work in the previous versions of Oracle Applications 11i and R12, although we have tested the examples in this chapter only against the Oracle Applications 12.0.4 VISION instance.

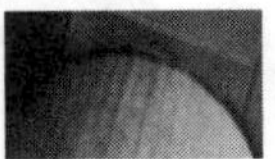

NOTE
All the database objects created in the examples are created in the APPS schema for convenience, but please remember that database objects such as tables should be created in their own custom schema rather the APPS schema. Always follow the object generation and other coding standards applicable to Oracle Applications when coding for the production environment.

Example of Creating an Inbound Message

In this example, we are going to use Trading Community Architecture (TCA) API hz_cust_account_v2pub.create_cust_account to create customer accounts in E-Business Suite for Persons (PARTY_TYPE = Person). This PL/SQL API takes the p_person_rec input parameter of the person_rec_type record type and, if the customer account creation is successful, returns a return status ("S" for Success and "E" for Error), along with other PL/SQL OUT parameters such as Account Number, Party ID, Customer Account ID, and others.

XML messages that contain new customer accounts data transmitted by a sender (our trading partner) will be received by Oracle Transport Agent (OTA) and then processed by the XML Gateway Execution Engine. During the map execution process, the Execution Engine will call our custom wrapper PL/SQL procedure, which will execute the hz_cust_account_v2pub.create_cust_account TCA API to create customer accounts. In addition to that, we'll design our inbound map in such a way that the results from a TCA API call will be recorded in a custom history table (XX_CUST_HIST) to record if the inbound transaction was successful or not. For convenience, we are going to use Abbott Laboratories, Inc., as our trading partner that will transmit XML messages to us in order to create a customer account in the VISION instance. As you probably realized, Abbott Laboratories is already set up as a supplier in the VISION database, but you could use other types of trading partners (customer, internal, or others) or even create a new one to act as your messaging peer if you wanted to.

We'll start by outlining all the steps required to create such an inbound transaction.

Step 1: Creating the Database Objects on the Target

As already mentioned, we are going to assume that the target system is a VISION instance of the E-Business Suite database. Before we can proceed with building the map for the inbound transaction, we need to create necessary supporting database objects on the target database: a custom PL/SQL package XX_XML_DEMO_INBOUND in the APPS schema that will act as a wrapper to the TCA API to create customer accounts, a custom database table XX_CUST_HIST that will keep the record of inbound transactions primarily for demonstration purposes, and a database sequence XX_CUST_HIST_ID_S that will be used by the message map to populate the primary key in our custom history table.

The following script creates the XX_XML_DEMO_INBOUND package along with its create_customer procedure that will be invoked by the inbound message map at runtime:

```
CREATE OR REPLACE
PACKAGE XX_XML_DEMO_INBOUND
IS
PROCEDURE create_customer
  (
    p_account_name   IN VARCHAR2,
    p_first_name     IN VARCHAR2,
    p_last_name      IN VARCHAR2,
    p_title          IN VARCHAR2,
    p_known_as       IN VARCHAR2,
    p_date_of_birth  IN VARCHAR2,
    p_place_of_birth IN VARCHAR2,
    p_gender         IN VARCHAR2,
    p_marital_status IN VARCHAR2,
    x_cust_account_id OUT NUMBER,
    x_account_number  OUT VARCHAR,
    x_party_id        OUT NUMBER,
    x_party_number    OUT VARCHAR2,
    x_profile_id      OUT NUMBER,
```

```
    x_return_status   OUT VARCHAR2);
END XX_XML_DEMO_INBOUND;
/

CREATE OR REPLACE
PACKAGE BODY XX_XML_DEMO_INBOUND
IS
PROCEDURE create_customer
  (
    p_account_name   IN VARCHAR2,
    p_first_name     IN VARCHAR2,
    p_last_name      IN VARCHAR2,
    p_title          IN VARCHAR2,
    p_known_as       IN VARCHAR2,
    p_date_of_birth  IN VARCHAR2,
    p_place_of_birth IN VARCHAR2,
    p_gender         IN VARCHAR2,
    p_marital_status IN VARCHAR2,
    x_cust_account_id OUT NUMBER,
    x_account_number  OUT VARCHAR,
    x_party_id        OUT NUMBER,
    x_party_number    OUT VARCHAR2,
    x_profile_id      OUT NUMBER,
    x_return_status   OUT VARCHAR2)
AS
  p_cust_account_rec HZ_CUST_ACCOUNT_V2PUB.CUST_ACCOUNT_REC_TYPE;
  p_person_rec HZ_PARTY_V2PUB.PERSON_REC_TYPE;
  p_customer_profile_rec HZ_CUSTOMER_PROFILE_V2PUB.CUSTOMER_PROFILE_
REC_TYPE;
  x_msg_count        NUMBER;
  x_msg_data         VARCHAR2(2000);
BEGIN
  p_cust_account_rec.created_by_module := 'TCA_V2_API';
  p_cust_account_rec.account_name      := p_account_name;
  p_person_rec.person_first_name       := p_first_name;
  p_person_rec.person_last_name        := p_last_name;
  p_person_rec.person_title            := p_title;
  p_person_rec.known_as                := p_known_as;
  p_person_rec.date_of_birth           := to_date(p_date_of_birth,
                                                   'DD-MON-YYYY');

  p_person_rec.place_of_birth := p_place_of_birth;
  p_person_rec.gender         := p_gender;
  p_person_rec.marital_status := p_marital_status;
  hz_cust_account_v2pub.create_cust_account( 'T',
                                           p_cust_account_rec,
                                           p_person_rec,
                                           p_customer_profile_rec,
                                           'F',
                                            x_cust_account_id,
```

```
                                                    x_account_number,
                                                    x_party_id,
                                                    x_party_number,
                                                    x_profile_id,
                                                    x_return_status,
                                                    x_msg_count,
                                                    x_msg_data);
  dbms_output.put_line(SUBSTR('x_return_status = '||x_return_status,
1,255));
  dbms_output.put_line('x_msg_count = '||TO_CHAR(x_msg_count));
  dbms_output.put_line(SUBSTR('x_msg_data = '||x_msg_data,1,255));
  IF x_msg_count > 1 THEN
    FOR I      IN 1..x_msg_count
    LOOP
      dbms_output.put_line(I||'. '||SUBSTR(FND_MSG_PUB.Get(p_encoded =>
FND_API.G_FALSE ), 1, 255));
    END LOOP;
  ELSE
    COMMIT;
  END IF;
END create_customer;
END XX_XML_DEMO_INBOUND;
/
```

We also create an XX_CUST_HIST custom table to demonstrate how to insert the data into the target database, which is often a useful technique when dealing with Open Interfaces in Oracle Applications. This table stores the history of customer accounts created through our XML Gateway inbound transactions.

```
CREATE TABLE APPS.XX_CUST_HIST
   ( ID NUMBER NOT NULL ENABLE,
 ACCOUNT_NAME VARCHAR2(2000),
 FIRST_NAME VARCHAR2(2000),
 LAST_NAME VARCHAR2(2000),
 TITLE VARCHAR2(2000),
 KNOWN_AS VARCHAR2(2000),
 DOB VARCHAR2(2000),
 PLACE_OF_BIRTH VARCHAR2(2000),
 GENDER VARCHAR2(2000),
 MARITAL_STATUS VARCHAR2(2000),
 CUST_ACCOUNT_ID NUMBER,
 CUST_ACCOUNT_NUM VARCHAR2(2000),
 CUST_PARTY_ID NUMBER,
 CUST_PARTY_NUM VARCHAR2(2000),
 CUST_PROFILE_ID NUMBER,
 API_RETURN_STATUS VARCHAR2(2000),
  CONSTRAINT "XX_CUST_HIST_PK" PRIMARY KEY (ID)
);
```

Lastly, we create a database sequence XX_CUST_HIST_ID_S that is used by the inbound transaction map to populate the primary key in the XX_CUST_HIST table:

```
CREATE SEQUENCE  APPS.XX_CUST_HIST_ID_S
MINVALUE 1 MAXVALUE 1000000 INCREMENT BY 1
START WITH 30 CACHE 20 NOORDER  NOCYCLE ;
```

Step 2: Creating an XML DTD File Used by the Inbound XML Message

Both sending and receiving systems need to agree what constitutes a valid XML message payload. The message XML payload is what is used in the Message Designer as an input from the source system. In our example, we create the newcustomer.dtd file with the following content:

```
<?xml encoding="UTF-8"?>
<!ELEMENT NEW_CUSTOMER (DATAAREA)>
<!ELEMENT DATAAREA (CUSTOMER_DATA)>
<!ELEMENT CUSTOMER_DATA (ACCNT_NAME,FIRST_NAME,LAST_NAME,TITLE,
                         KNOWN_AS,DOB,PLACE_OF_BIRTH,GENDER,
                         MARITAL_STATUS)>
<!ELEMENT ACCNT_NAME     (#PCDATA)>
<!ELEMENT FIRST_NAME     (#PCDATA)>
<!ELEMENT LAST_NAME      (#PCDATA)>
<!ELEMENT TITLE          (#PCDATA)>
<!ELEMENT KNOWN_AS       (#PCDATA)>
<!ELEMENT DOB            (#PCDATA)>
<!ELEMENT PLACE_OF_BIRTH (#PCDATA)>
<!ELEMENT GENDER         (#PCDATA)>
<!ELEMENT MARITAL_STATUS (#PCDATA)>
```

The preceding DTD file defines our inbound XML data structure that is used to create customer accounts on the target E-Business Suite system. It is used in the next step when specifying the source system data in the Message Designer.

Step 3: Creating an Inbound Map with Message Designer

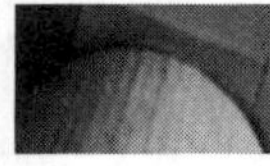

NOTE
In this section, the Message Designer Wizard window name follows the step number. Also, we provide the list of relevant fields along with the values that need to be populated in Message Designer for this example to work, although where necessary, we'll provide screen shots for added clarity.

XML Gateway Message Designer is a client-side Java application, but it looks and behaves just like any other desktop application. After opening XML Gateway Message Designer, we navigate to File | New Transaction Map in the menu to start Map Creation Wizard, which will guide us through the process of map creation. When the Message Designer Wizard Welcome window opens, we click Next to proceed to the first step:

Map Creation Wizard, Step 1: Specify a Map Name

1. Enter map name: **XX_NEW_CUSTOMER_IN**.
2. Enter map description: **New Customer Inbound Map**.
3. Click Next.

Map Creation Wizard, Step 2: Select/Create a Source Data Definition

1. Click the Create a New source data definition radio button.
2. Click Next.

Map Creation Wizard, Step 3: Specify Source Data Definition Name and Type

1. Enter the data definition name: **CUST_XML_INBOUND**.
2. Enter the data definition description: **Inbound New Customer XML Data**.
3. Select the data definition type: XML.
4. Click Next.

Map Creation Wizard, Step 4: Specify Source XML File and Root Element

1. Enter the XML Standard: **W3C**.
2. Select a DTD/XML file: newcustomer.dtd (browse for it where you saved it in an earlier step).
3. Identify the XML root element: NEW_CUSTOMER.
4. Enter the file name DTD: **newcustomer.dtd** (prepopulated).
5. Identify the runtime location of the DTD: xxcust/xml/hz.
6. Click Next.

Map Creation Wizard, Step 5: Select/Create a Target Data Definition

1. Select the Create a New Target Data Definition radio button.
2. Click Next.

Map Creation Wizard, Step 6: Specify the Target Data Definition Name and Type

1. Enter the data definition name: **CUSTOMER_DB_TARGET**.
2. Enter the data definition description: **New Customer Target Database**.
3. Select the data definition type: Database.
4. Click Next.

Map Creation Wizard, Step 7: Specify Target Database Information

1. Enter the username: **apps**.
2. Enter the password: **apps** (the appropriate value for your APPS schema).
3. Enter the connect string: **VIS** (the appropriate value for your database).
4. Enter host: **r12.com** (the appropriate value for your machine host name).
5. Enter port: **1521** (the appropriate value for your Oracle Apps database port).
6. Click Next.

Map Creation Wizard, Step 8: Select Target Tables or Views

1. Expand the APPS schema from the list of schemas to select the target XX_CUST_HIST table.
2. Shuttle XX_CUST_HIST table from Available Tables/Views list to the Selected Tables/Lists side.
3. Click Next.

Map Creation Wizard, Step 9: Select Target Columns

1. Shuttle all available columns for the XX_CUST_HIST table to the Selected Columns side.
2. Click Next.

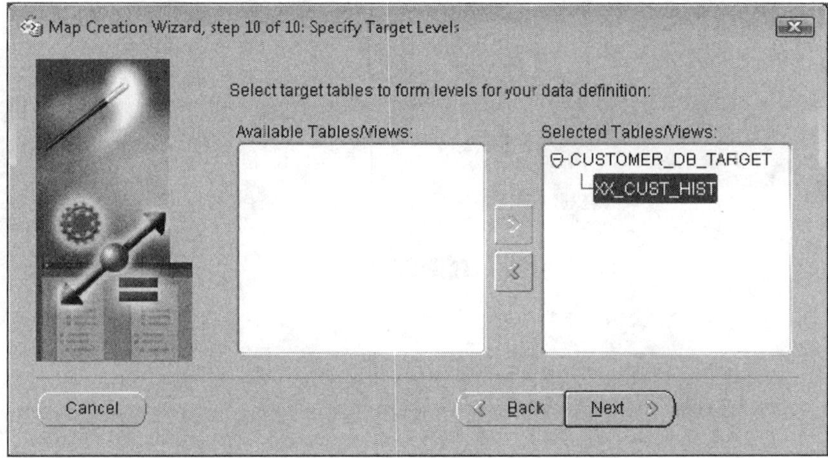

FIGURE 12-3. *Message Designer target levels reflect the target data model.*

Map Creation Wizard, Step 10: Specify Target Levels

1. Shuttle the XX_CUST_HIST table from the Available Tables/Views list to the Selected Tables/Lists side to create the CUSTOMER_DB_TARGET | XX_CUST_HIST structure as shown in Figure 12-3.
2. Click Next.

Map Creation Wizard: Summary

1. Click the Finish button to complete the wizard.

Once we exit the wizard, the initial transaction map XX_NEW_CUSTOMER_IN is created and can be saved. The first thing we need to do is to check the fields in Source and Target Definitions in our newly created transaction map by clicking the corresponding tabs in the Message Designer. Figure 12-4 illustrates what the Source Definition should look like. Here we have changed the ItemType value from Element to Level for the CUSTOMER_DATA field to reflect the fact that this item represents a level (data collection) rather than an element.

If the Target Definition is mapped correctly to the custom history XX_CUST_HIST table, we should have two fields marked with an item type of Level in the Target Definition tab: CUSTOMER_DB_TARGET and XX_CUST_HIST. The rest of the fields should be of item type Element.

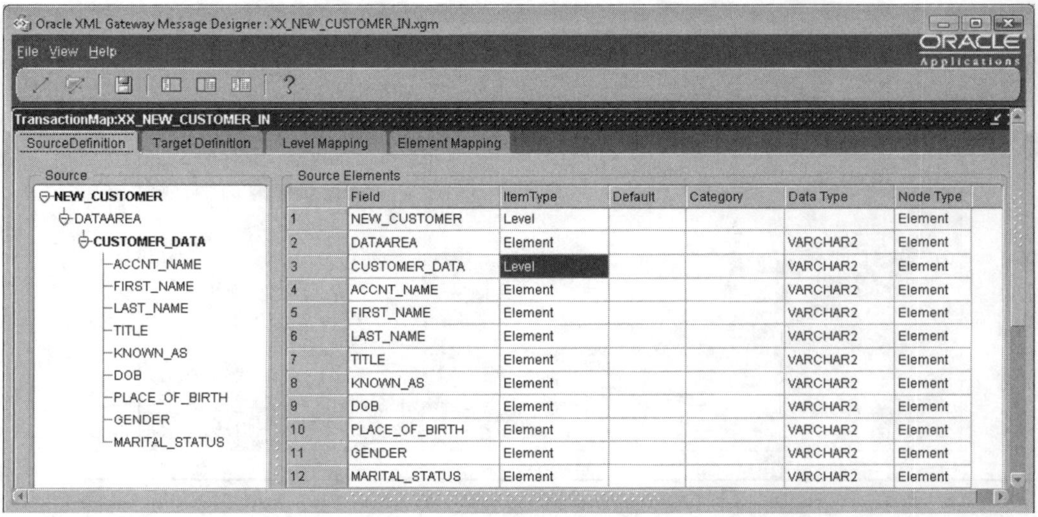

FIGURE 12-4. *Source data definition*

The next step is to perform Level and Element mappings. Level mapping in our example is a simple one and consists of associating the CUSTOMER_DATA field at the source side with XX_CUST_HIST. In the Level Mapping tab within the Message Designer, this is achieved by clicking the CUSTOMER_DATA field in the Source panel and dragging it to the XX_CUST_HIST field in the Target panel. The result is illustrated in Figure 12-5. In plain English, by doing this level mapping, we are saying that the XML data contained within the <CUSTOMER_DATA> element corresponds to the record or part of the record in the XX_CUST_HIST table.

The mapping of the individual elements is performed in the Element Mapping tab, and fields from the Source panel are mapped to their corresponding elements in the Target panel by clicking and dragging them across from Source to Target panels: ACCNT_NAME, FIRST_NAME, LAST_NAME, TITLE, KNOWN_AS, DOB, PLACE_OF_BIRTH, GENDER, and MARITAL_STATUS. By performing this action, we are mapping the individual record fields (elements) from the XML source to database columns in the XX_CUST_HIST table.

The last and probably most important step in our example is to define Map Actions. The actions within the map enable you to create variables, perform assignments, call database procedures, execute functions, concatenate strings, and perform many other similar types of actions that could be executed at runtime by Execution Engine when our map is being processed. They can be executed in Pre, In, and Post Process map execution phases. Actions are created with the Map Action Editor, which opens when you right-click an appropriate level or element in

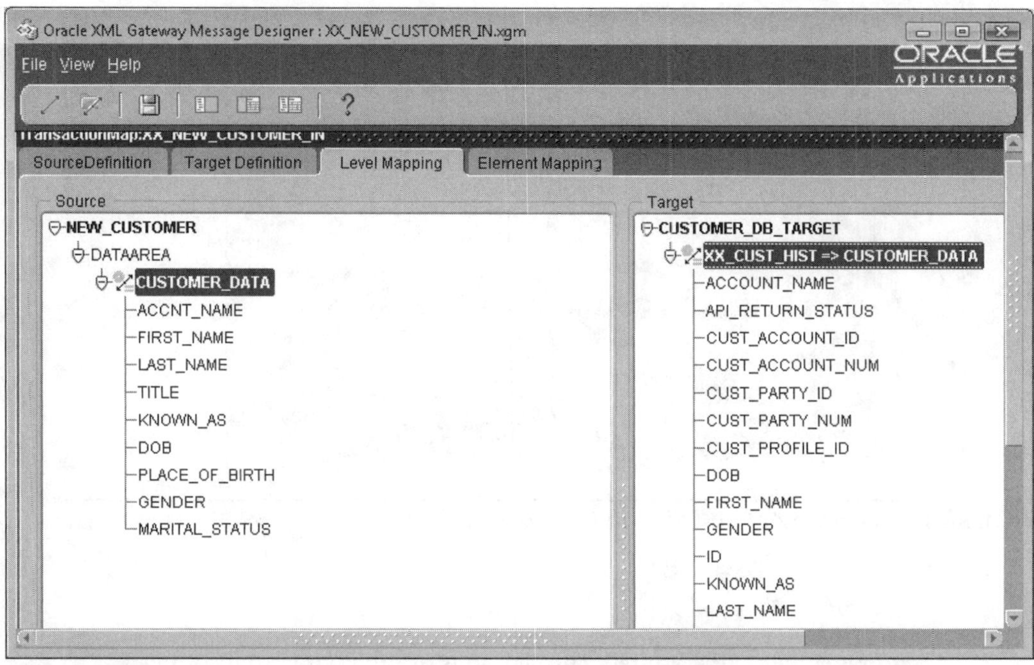

FIGURE 12-5. *Level Mapping in Message Designer*

the Target panel under the Element Mapping tab. In the example we are going to create the following actions:

1. **Create Global Variables** Our inbound map requires five global variables. To create them, right-click the CUSTOMER_DB_TARGET root element and select the Actions button to open the Map Action Editor as shown in Figure 12-6. Here you create global variables in the Pre Process phase tab by selecting Create Global Variable from Available Actions and shuttling it to Selected Actions side with the following properties:

Phase	Global Variable Name	Type	Default Value
Pre Process	GLOBAL_EVENT_PARAMETER	VARCHAR2	NULL
Pre Process	GLOBAL_HIST_ID	VARCHAR2	
Pre Process	GLOBAL_RETCODE	NUMBER	
Pre Process	GLOBAL_RETMSG	VARCHAR2	
Pre Process	GLOBAL_EVENT_KEY	VARCHAR2	DUMMY

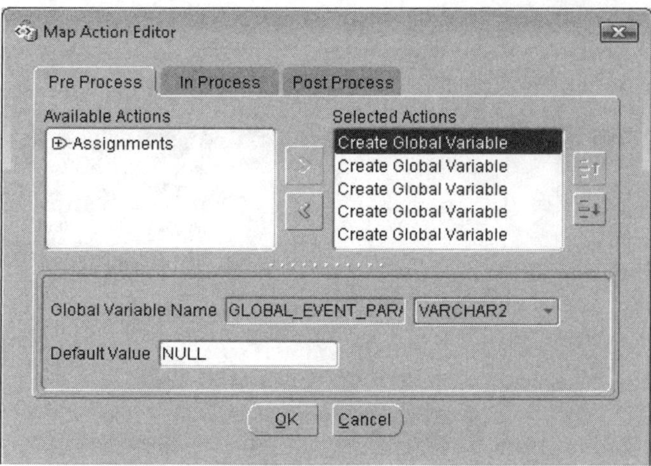

FIGURE 12-6. *Map Action Editor in Message Designer*

2. **Assign Next Sequence Value** This action is useful if you are inserting records into the target database, and in this case, it populates the primary ID key in the XX_CUST_HIST table. This time, we open Map Action Editor by right-clicking the XX_CUST_HIST element. In the Pre Process tab, we expand the Database Functions node on the Available Actions side and select and shuttle the Assign Next Sequence Value action to the right side (Selected Actions). We assign the XX_CUST_HIST_ID_S database sequence to the GLOBAL_HIST_ID variable created earlier, as shown in Figure 12-7. This action will populate GLOBAL_HIST_ID with the next sequence value at runtime.

3. **Assign Variable Value** We need to assign a unique value to the GLOBAL_EVENT_KEY variable because XML Gateway Inbound transactions require Business Events to be raised upon successful map execution. Because Business Events are raised with a unique event key, we can use the sequence number assigned to the GLOBAL_HIST_ID variable in the previous step, as illustrated in Figure 12-8. This is done in the Post Process tab, as are the rest of actions we'll create in the transaction map.

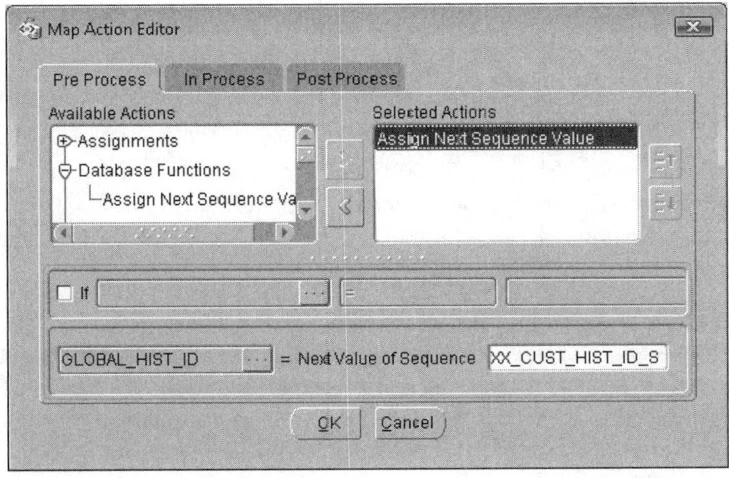

FIGURE 12-7. *Assigning the database sequence value to a variable*

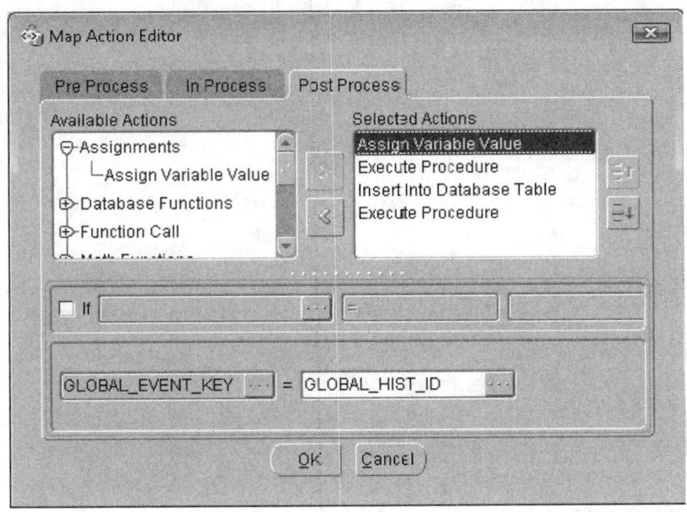

FIGURE 12-8. *Variable assignment in Map Action Editor*

4. **Execute Procedure to Create Customer Account** When Execute Procedure is selected from Procedure Call within the Available Actions list, Message Designer prompts you to log in to the target database and select a schema, PL/SQL package, and procedure name. At this stage, we call the XX_XML_DEMO_INBOUND.CREATE_CUSTOMER procedure and, in the Get Procedure Parameters window, specify IN and OUT PL/SQL parameters that are passed to and from our PL/SQL procedure, as shown in Figure 12-9. It is of great importance to map the IN and OUT parameters correctly from the Source and Target elements. Again, remember that this action is performed at the Post Process phase (XX_CUST_HIST element).

5. **Insert Into Database Table** In the Post Process tab, we select the Insert Into Database Table action from the Available Actions list and shuttle it to the Selected Actions list. This step at runtime will actually insert a customer data record into the XX_CUST_HIST table. You should make sure that this action is listed after the Execute Procedure action in the previous step.

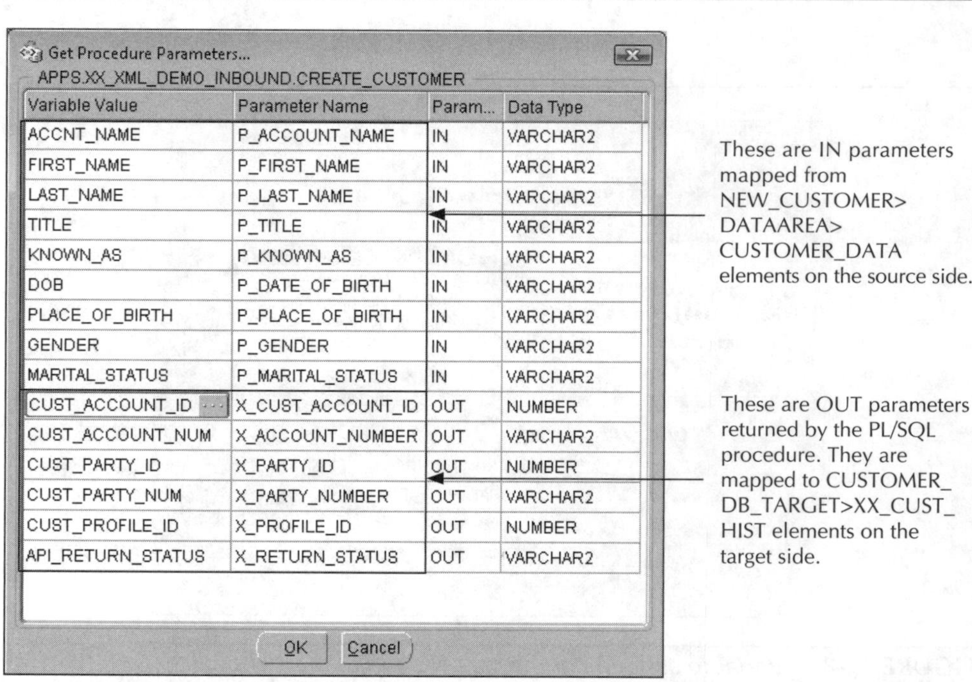

Variable Value	Parameter Name	Param...	Data Type
ACCNT_NAME	P_ACCOUNT_NAME	IN	VARCHAR2
FIRST_NAME	P_FIRST_NAME	IN	VARCHAR2
LAST_NAME	P_LAST_NAME	IN	VARCHAR2
TITLE	P_TITLE	IN	VARCHAR2
KNOWN_AS	P_KNOWN_AS	IN	VARCHAR2
DOB	P_DATE_OF_BIRTH	IN	VARCHAR2
PLACE_OF_BIRTH	P_PLACE_OF_BIRTH	IN	VARCHAR2
GENDER	P_GENDER	IN	VARCHAR2
MARITAL_STATUS	P_MARITAL_STATUS	IN	VARCHAR2
CUST_ACCOUNT_ID	X_CUST_ACCOUNT_ID	OUT	NUMBER
CUST_ACCOUNT_NUM	X_ACCOUNT_NUMBER	OUT	VARCHAR2
CUST_PARTY_ID	X_PARTY_ID	OUT	NUMBER
CUST_PARTY_NUM	X_PARTY_NUMBER	OUT	VARCHAR2
CUST_PROFILE_ID	X_PROFILE_ID	OUT	NUMBER
API_RETURN_STATUS	X_RETURN_STATUS	OUT	VARCHAR2

FIGURE 12-9. *Assigning IN and OUT parameters to a PL/SQL procedure call*

6. **Execute Procedure to Set Event Details** For inbound messages, it is mandatory to invoke the ECX_STANDARD.SETEVENTDETAILS seeded procedure that will set the details for the custom event that we are going to create in one of the next steps. We assign the following parameters in the Get Procedure Parameters window:

Variable Value	Parameter Name	Parameter Type	Data Type
xxcust.oracle.apps.hz.xml.customerInbound (Literal)	EVENTNAME	IN	VARCHAR2
GLOBAL_EVENT_KEY	EVENTKEY	IN	VARCHAR2
GLOBAL_EVENT_PARAMETER	PARAMETER1 PARAMETER2 PARAMETER3 ... PARAMETER10	IN	VARCHAR2
GLOBAL_RETCODE	RETCODE	OUT	BINARY_INTEGER
GLOBAL_RETMSG	RETMSG	OUT	VARCHAR2

Make sure that PARAMETER1 to PARAMETER10 is assigned the GLOBAL_EVENT_PARAMETER variable to avoid runtime errors.

We have now completed the design of our message map and can save it to your desktop.

Step 4: Uploading the Custom Map to the Database Repository

Before our custom map can be executed and referenced during setup, it needs to be uploaded to the database repository. To do that, log in to the middle-tier machine and access the source applications' user environment file and run the following command from the command prompt:

```
java oracle.apps.ecx.loader.LoadMap apps welcome localhost:1521:VIS
XX_NEW_CUSTOMER_IN.xgm
```

Of course, before we can run the preceding command, the XX_NEW_CUSTOMER_IN.xgm map definition needs to be transferred from the desktop to the middle-tier box. We prefer to keep custom maps and DTD files under the $XXCUST_TOP/xml directory.

Our map references the newcustomer.dtd file, which also needs to be uploaded to the database repository:

```
java oracle.apps.ecx.loader.LoadDTDToClob apps welcome
localhost:1521:VIS newcustomer.dtd NEW_CUSTOMER xxcust/xml/hz
```

If needed, the map can be removed by running the following command:

```
java oracle.apps.ecx.loader.DeleteMap apps welcome localhost:1521:VIS
XX_NEW_CUSTOMER_IN
```

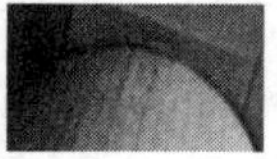

TIP
If you reload (delete and upload) a new version of the map during the development process, you have to go to Define Trading Partners (an XML Gateway responsibility) and select the map from the Map LOV (list of values) field. This is because uploaded maps get assigned a unique ID that is referenced by the trading partner setup. If you get "ORA-01403: no data found in the error stack," this is one of the first things to check, as map updates are fairly frequent during the development process.

Step 5: XML Gateway Trading Partner Setup

You perform the XML Gateway setup in E-Business Suite while logged in as a user with the XML Gateway responsibility assigned to you, and it consists of two setup steps:

1. **Define Transactions** To define our custom inbound transaction, in Oracle Applications, we navigate to the (N)XML Gateway | Define Transactions screen and enter the following details:

   - Party Type: **Supplier**
   - Transaction Type: **CUSTOM_HZ_CUST**
   - Transaction Subtype: **NEW_CUST_I**
   - Standard Code: **W3C**
   - Direction: **IN**
   - External Transaction Type: **CUSTOM_HZ_CUST**
   - External Transaction Subtype: **NEW_CUST_I**
   - Queue: **APPLSYS.ECX_IN_OAG_Q**

   Make sure that the form is submitted before proceeding.

2. **Define the Trading Partner** This step involves picking the right type of trading partner (Supplier), which is dependent on how we earlier defined our custom transaction. For this example, we pick Abbott Laboratories, Inc., as the supplier but this is a totally arbitrary choice. We navigate to the (N)XML Gateway | Define Trading Partners screen to perform the setup:

   - Operating Unit: **Vision Operations**
   - Trading Partner Type: **Supplier**
   - Trading Partner Name: **Abbott Laboratories, Inc**
   - Trading Partner Site: **1045 Sansome St San Francisco**
   - Company Admin Email: **admin@fochusthread.com**

   In the Trading Partners Details form region, we the enter following details:

   - Transaction Type: **CUSTOM_HZ_CUST**
   - Transaction Subtype: **NEW_CUST_I**
   - Standard Code: **W3C**
   - External Transaction Type: **CUSTOM_HZ_CUST**
   - External Transaction Subtype: **NEW_CUST_I**
   - Direction: **IN**
   - Map: **XX_NEW_CUSTOMER_IN**
   - Source Trading Partner Location Code: **loc123**

Step 6: Create an Event and Subscription for an Inbound Transaction

This step is mandatory. We need to create the event specified as the first parameter when we earlier defined the parameters in step 1 for the ECX_STANDARD.SETEVENTDETAILS procedure call. We log on as user with the Workflow Administrator Web Applications responsibility, navigate to the Business Events screen and click the Create button. We enter the following details:

- Name: **xxcust.oracle.apps.hz.xml.customerInbound**
- Display Name: **Custom XML New Customer Inbound**
- Description: **Custom XML New Customer Inbound**

- Status: **Enabled**
- Owner Name: **Oracle Receivables**
- Owner Tag: **AR**

We should now create a subscription to this event which can be set to be Enabled during the development phase, even if we are not going to do anything with this subscription. In other words, we create an enabled subscription with the Action Type set to Custom but the Workflow and Agent fields left blank.

Step 7: Testing the Inbound Transaction

We now finally get to test our newfound knowledge in action. The good thing about the testing of inbound messages is that XML Gateway provides a servlet that allows us to simulate an inbound transmission of XML messages from our trading partners, messaging peers, and other parties that can send messages to us.

TIP
Before testing XML Gateway transactions, we need to make sure that Workflow service components such as ECX Inbound Agent Listener, ECX Transaction Agent Listener, and others are up and running. We can check the status of Workflow services if we navigate to the responsibility Workflow Administrator Web Applications, menu path Oracle Applications Manager | Workflow Manager screen. Here, Service Components and Agent Listeners should be running.

Enter the following URL to perform manual inbound transaction testing:

```
http://<host>:<port>/webservices/ECXOTAInbound
```

This page is secured, and on the VISION instance we can log in as OPERATIONS/welcome to gain access to it. Enter the following details in this page:

- MESSAGE_ID: **204** (part of the message envelope—it has to be a unique message number).
- MESSAGE_STANDARD: **W3C** (part of the message envelope—this is the type of XML transaction we specified earlier).
- TRANSACTION_TYPE: **CUSTOM_HZ_CUST** (part of the message envelope—this is our custom transaction type).

- TRANSACTION_SUBTYPE: **NEW_CUST_I** (part of the message envelope–this is our custom transaction subtype).
- DOCUMENT_NUMBER: **204** (part of the message envelope—the document number also has to be unique).
- PARTY_ID: **601** (part of the message envelope—this is PARTY_ID for the Abbott Laboratories, Inc., trading partner who is sending us inbound messages).
- SOURCE_TP_LOCATION_CODE: **loc123** (part of the message envelope—this code has to correspond to the value we specified for Source Trading Partner Location Code in the Define Trading Partner screen earlier).
- PAYLOAD (the actual XML message that contains new customer data):

```
<?xml version="1.0"?>
<NEW_CUSTOMER>
 <DATAAREA>
  <CUSTOMER_DATA>
   <ACCNT_NAME>Joe Bloggs Holdings</ACCNT_NAME>
   <FIRST_NAME>Joe</FIRST_NAME>
   <LAST_NAME>Bloggs</LAST_NAME>
   <TITLE>Mr.</TITLE>
   <KNOWN_AS>Joey</KNOWN_AS>
   <DOB>10-NOV-1958</DOB>
   <PLACE_OF_BIRTH>Dallas</PLACE_OF_BIRTH>
   <GENDER>MALE</GENDER>
   <MARITAL_STATUS>S</MARITAL_STATUS>
  </CUSTOMER_DATA>
 </DATAAREA>
</NEW_CUSTOMER>
```

Clicking the Send button at the bottom of the screen will send the message to the OTA server on the receiving side and queue it for processing. If everything goes well, the message is processed by XML Gateway: a new record is inserted in the XX_CUST_HIST table, and a new customer account, Joe Bloggs Holdings, is created by the TCA API.

To monitor the inbound message processing progress, we can go to the Workflow Administrator Web Applications | Transaction Monitor screen and search for our message. Also, the new customer account record should be available through the Oracle Receivables | Customers screen.

Example of Creating an Outbound Message

Building outbound XML Gateway transactions is logically opposite to the way inbound transactions are created. The source of the outbound messages is usually data from E-Business Suite database tables and views converted into XML format through the Message Designer and transmitted to a trading or other partner.

In this section, we'll outline the main logical steps required to create a simple outbound transaction. The transaction will extract the data from HR_EMPLOYEES_ALL_V, which already exists in the Oracle Applications database APPS schema. In our example, we use the existing database view for convenience, but there is nothing to stop you from creating your own custom views to extract information required by your transaction. The extracted data is then mapped and converted into XML format, ready to be delivered to a trading partner, which we choose to be the existing Abbott Laboratories supplier in the Oracle Applications VISION database.

Step 1: Creating an XML DTD File Used by the Outbound XML Message

As with the inbound transaction from the previous example, both sending and receiving systems need to agree what constitutes a valid XML message payload. In this example, we are sending data about employees extracted from the source system. The format of the target XML data is defined by creating an employeedata .dtd file with the following content:

```
<?xml encoding="UTF-8"?>
<!ELEMENT EMPLOYEE (DATAAREA)>
<!ELEMENT DATAAREA (EMPLOYEE_DATA)>
<!ELEMENT EMPLOYEE_DATA (EMAIL_ADDRESS,EMPLOYEE_ID,EMPLOYEE_NUM,
                         FIRST_NAME,FULL_NAME,LAST_NAME,MIDDLE_NAME)>
<!ELEMENT EMAIL_ADDRESS   (#PCDATA)>
<!ELEMENT EMPLOYEE_ID     (#PCDATA)>
<!ELEMENT EMPLOYEE_NUM    (#PCDATA)>
<!ELEMENT FIRST_NAME      (#PCDATA)>
<!ELEMENT FULL_NAME       (#PCDATA)>
<!ELEMENT LAST_NAME       (#PCDATA)>
<!ELEMENT MIDDLE_NAME     (#PCDATA)>
```

The employeedata.dtd file will later be used in Message Designer to create the definition of the target data.

Step 2: Creating the Outbound Map with Message Designer

Similarly to what we did previously when creating the inbound message, we open XML Gateway Message Designer on our desktop, and navigate to File | New Transaction Map to start the Map Creation Wizard, which will guide us through the process of the outbound map creation. When the Message Designer Wizard Welcome window opens, we click Next to proceed to the first step.

Map Creation Wizard, Step 1: Specify a Map Name

1. Enter map name: **XX_EMPS_OUT**.
2. Enter map description: **Custom Employee Outbound XML Message**.
3. Click Next to proceed to the following step.

Map Creation Wizard, Step 2: Select/Create a Source Data Definition

1. Select the Create a new source data definition radio button.
2. Click Next to proceed to the following step.

Map Creation Wizard, Step 3: Specify the Source Data Definition Name and Type

1. Enter the data definition name: **EMP_DB_OUTBOUND**.
2. Enter the data definition description: **Outbound Employee Data from Database**.
3. Select the data definition type: Database.
4. Click Next to proceed to the following step.

Map Creation Wizard, Step 4: Specify Source Database Information

1. Enter the User Name: **apps**.
2. Enter the Password: **apps** (enter an appropriate value for your instance).
3. Enter the Connect String: **VIS** (enter an appropriate value for your instance).
4. Enter the Host: **r12.com** (enter an appropriate value for your instance).
5. Enter the Port: **1521** (enter an appropriate value for your instance).
6. Click Next to proceed to the following step.

Map Creation Wizard, Step 5: Select Source Tables or Views

1. Expand the APPS schema from the list of schemas to select the source HR_EMPLOYEES_ALL_V view.
2. Shuttle the HR_EMPLOYEES_ALL_V view from the Available Tables/Views list to the Selected Tables/Lists side.
3. Click Next to proceed to the following step.

Map Creation Wizard, Step 6: Select Source Columns

1. Shuttle all the available columns for the HR_EMPLOYEES_ALL_V view to the Selected Columns side.
2. Click Next to proceed to the following step.

Map Creation Wizard, Step 7: Specify Source Levels

1. Shuttle the HR_EMPLOYEES_ALL_V view from the Available Tables/Views list to the Selected Tables/Lists side to create the EMP_DB_OUTBOUND | HR_EMPLOYEES_ALL_V hierarchical structure.
2. Click Next to proceed to the following step.

Map Creation Wizard, Step 8: Select/Create a Target Data Definition

1. Select the Create a new target data definition radio button.
2. Click Next to proceed to the following step.

Map Creation Wizard, Step 9: Specify the Target Data Definition Name and Type

1. Enter the data definition name: **EmployeeXML**.
2. Enter the data definition description: **Employee XML Data**.
3. Select data definition type: **XML**.
4. Click Next to proceed to the following step.

Map Creation Wizard, Step 10: Specify the Target XML File and Root Element

1. Enter the XML Standard: **W3C**.
2. Select a DTD/XML file: **employeedata.dtd**.
3. Identify the XML root element: **EMPLOYEE**.
4. Enter the DTD file name: **employeedata.dtd** (prepopulated).
5. Identify the runtime location of the dtd: xxcust/xml/per.
6. Click Next to proceed to the following step.

Map Creation Wizard: Summary

1. In the Summary window, click the Finish button to complete the wizard.

The initial version of the XX_EMPS_OUT map is now completed, with HR_EMPLOYEES_ALL_V appearing in the Source Definition tab and the XML element EMPLOYEE_DATA appearing in the Target Definition tab. Before proceeding any further, we need to ensure that the EMPLOYEE_DATA field in the Target Elements region has an ItemType value set to Level (by default it is set to Element). You perform the level and element mappings much as you did with the inbound transaction map. For level mapping, click the Level Mapping tab and drag and drop the HR_EMPLOYEES_ALL_V level field from the Source panel onto the EMPLOYEE_DATA level field in the Target panel to create the HR_EMPLOYEES_ALL_V | EMPLOYEE_DATA level mapping. Similarly, for element mappings, you click the Element Mapping tab in the Message Designer and map individual elements by dragging and dropping them from the Source to Target side to form the following element mappings:

```
EMAIL_ADDRESS > EMAIL_ADDRESS

EMPLOYEE_ID > EMPLOYEE_ID

EMPLOYEE_NUM > EMPLOYEE_NUM

FIRST_NAME > FIRST_NAME

FULL_NAME > FULL_NAME

LAST_NAME > LAST_NAME

MIDDLE_NAME > MIDDLE_NAME
```

Now we are ready to create map actions. Because our requirements are very simple, we require only two map actions in the preprocess phase:

1. **Create the Global Variable** Our outbound map requires just one global variable to capture the value of the Document ID parameter passed by the calling application. This value will then be used in the WHERE clause created at runtime to select the requested record from the HR_EMPLOYEES_ALL_V view at the source side. To create a global variable, right-click the Employee root element on the target side of Element Mapping tab and select the Action button to open Map Action Editor. On the Pre Process tab, we enter the following:

Tab	Global Variable Name	Type	Default Value
Pre Process	DOCUMENT_ID	VARCHAR2	

2. **Append the WHERE Clause** This action will create the required selection criteria from the HR_EMPLOYEES_ALL_V view at the source side. At runtime, it is executed in the preprocess phase by the Execution Engine at the source transaction side. To create an Append Where Clause map action for our example, right-click the HR_EMPLOYEES_ALL_V level field

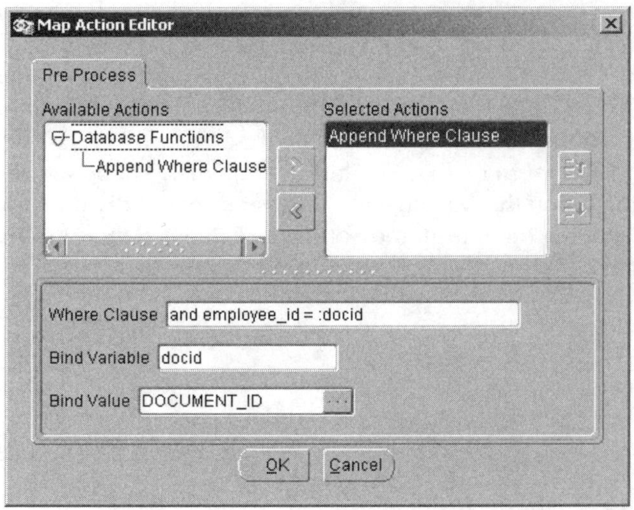

FIGURE 12-10. *Adding an Append Where Clause action to our map*

in the Source region within the Element Mapping tab, and select Actions. In the Map Action Editor, expand the Database Actions node, select Append Where Clause from Available Actions, and shuttle it to the Selected Actions side, as illustrated in Figure 12-10.

Tab	Where Clause	Bind Variable	Bind Value
Pre Process	and employee_id = :docid	docid	DOCUMENT_ID

Our map is now complete and needs to be saved locally on the desktop computer.

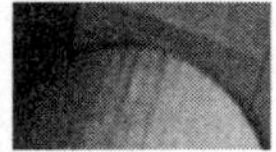

TIP
Message Designer reads MessageDesigner.properties files at startup. You can set output.dir=<your directory> to point to the directory where you want to save Message Designer–generated files (maps and data definitions).

Step 3: Uploading the Custom Outbound Map to the Database Repository

Before we can proceed to this step, we need to transfer our newly built map to an appropriate directory on the middle-tier machine. For our examples in this chapter, we choose the $XXCUST_TOP/12.0.0/xml directory, and once the transfer of the custom map and corresponding employeedata.dtd file is complete, we can execute the following commands to upload them:

```
java oracle.apps.ecx.loader.LoadMap apps welcome  \
localhost:1521:VIS XX_EMPS_OUT.xgm

java oracle.apps.ecx.loader.LoadDTDToClob apps welcome \
localhost:1521:VIS employeedata.dtd EMPLOYEE xxcust/xml/per
```

You can remove the map and its DTD file from the database repository by executing the following commands from the middle-tier machine:

```
java oracle.apps.ecx.loader.DeleteMap apps welcome \
localhost:1533:R124 XX_EMPS_OUT
java oracle.apps.ecx.loader.DeleteDTDFromClob apps welcome \
localhost:1533:R124 employeedata.dtd EMPLOYEE xxcust/xml/per
```

Step 4: XML Gateway Trading Partner Setup for Outbound Transaction

Now we need to define our custom outbound transaction as well as the trading partner. This is a required step for both inbound and outbound transactions, and the two-step process is as follows:

1. **Define the Transaction** To define our custom outbound transaction, in Oracle Applications, we navigate to the (N)XML Gateway | Define Trading Partners screen and enter the following details:

   - Party Type: **Supplier**
   - Transaction Type: **CUSTOM_PER_EMP**
   - Transaction Subtype: **EMP_OUT**
   - Standard Code: **W3C**
   - Direction: **OUT**
   - External Transaction Type: **CUSTOM_PER_EMP**
   - External Transaction Subtype: **EMP_OUT**

   Submit the form by clicking the Save button.

2. **Define the Trading Partner** We'll use the same trading partner, Abbott Laboratories, Inc., for our custom outbound transaction. In the Trading Partner Setup screen, we can set as many transactions as required for the trading partner in question. Again, we navigate to (N)XML Gateway | Define Trading Partners and select Abbott Laboratories, Inc.:

   - Operating Unit: **Vision Operations**
   - Trading Partner Type: **Supplier**
   - Trading Partner Name: **Abbott Laboratories, Inc.**
   - Trading Partner Site: **1045 Sansome St San Francisco**
   - Company Admin Email: **admin@fochusthread.com**

   In the Trading Partner Details region, enter the following details and save the record:

   - Transaction Type: **CUSTOM_PER_EMP**
   - Transaction Subtype: **EMP_OUT**
   - Standard Code: **W3C**
   - External Transaction Type: **CUSTOM_PER_EMP**
   - External Transaction Subtype: **EMP_OUT**
   - Direction: **OUT**
   - Map: **XX_EMPS_OUT**
   - Connection: **DIRECT**
   - Protocol Type: **SMTP**
   - Username: **DUMMY** (you have to enter a dummy username value for SMTP, even if it is not used)
   - Password: **DUMMY** (you have to enter a dummy user password value for SMTP, even if it is not used)
   - Protocol Address: **vlad@fochusthread.com**
   - Source Trading Partner Location Code: **FromEbiz123**

   Save the record to the database.

Step 5: Create an Event and Subscription for an Outbound Transaction

There are many ways to generate outbound transactions with XML Gateway. In this example, we use the easiest approach, which consists of creating an event and subscription that executes the ecx_rule.CreateTPMessage procedure. Later in this section, we'll suggest alternative ways of outbound message generation, along with the pros and cons of each approach.

To create the custom event, navigate to the Business Events screen and enter following details for our event:

- Name: **xxcust.oracle.apps.per.xml.employeeOutbound**
- Display Name: **Custom XML Outbound Employee Message Event**
- Description: **Custom XML Outbound Employee Message Event**
- Status: **Enabled**
- Owner Name: **Human Resources** (must be a valid application name including custom applications)
- Owner Tag: **PER** (must be a valid application short name including custom applications)

Now we create the subscription for the Custom XML Outbound Employee Message Event:

- Source: ***<your system name>***
- Source Type: **Local**
- Phase: **98** (if the phase is less than 100, then the message creation is synchronous)
- Status: **Enabled**
- Rule Data: **Key**
- Action Type: **Send Trading Partner Message**
- On Error: **Stop and Rollback**
- Priority: **Normal**
- Owner Name: **Human Resources** (must be a valid application name)
- Owner Tag: **PER** (must be a valid application short name)

Step 6: Testing the Outbound Transaction

At last, we are ready to test our outbound message creation. The message generation could be initiated by raising a Custom XML Outbound Employee Message event and passing the mandatory and optional parameters, as in the following PL/SQL block that could be executed from SQL*Plus:

```
DECLARE
  l_parameter_list wf_parameter_list_t;
BEGIN
  wf_event.AddParameterToList(p_name=>'ECX_TRANSACTION_TYPE',
                              p_value=>'CUSTOM_PER_EMP',
                              p_parameterlist=>l_parameter_list);
  wf_event.AddParameterToList(p_name=>'ECX_TRANSACTION_SUBTYPE',
                              p_value=>'EMP_OUT',
                              p_parameterlist=>l_parameter_list);
  wf_event.AddParameterToList(p_name=>'ECX_PARTY_ID',
                              p_value=>'601',
                              p_parameterlist=>l_parameter_list);
  wf_event.AddParameterToList(p_name=>'ECX_PARTY_SITE_ID',
                              p_value=>'1415',
                              p_parameterlist=>l_parameter_list);
  wf_event.AddParameterToList(p_name=>'ECX_DOCUMENT_ID',
                              p_value=>'5',
                              p_parameterlist=>l_parameter_list);
  /*
  wf_event.AddParameterToList(p_name=>'ECX_PARAMETER1',
                              p_value=>'<your parameter>',
                              p_parameterlist=>l_parameter_list);
  */
  wf_event.raise(p_event_name => 'xxcust.oracle.apps.per.xml
     .employeeOutbound',
                 p_event_key => TO_CHAR(sysdate,'YYYYMMDD HH24MISS')
                 ,p_parameters => l_parameter_list);
  l_parameter_list.DELETE;
END;
/
```

Parameters ECX_TRANSACTION_TYPE, ECX_TRANSACTION_SUBTYPE, ECX_PARTY_ID, ECX_PARTY_SITE_ID, and ECX_DOCUMENT_ID are required. By passing these parameters, we tell the XML Gateway engine what transaction needs to generate a document with a document ID that usually represents a business object such as an invoice, and who is the recipient of the message.

Executing the previously listed code should produce an outbound message that can be observed in the Transaction Monitor by searching for the most recently generated outbound transactions. The resulting XML from this example executed against the R12.0.4 VISION instance is as follows:

```
<?xml version="1.0" encoding="UTF-8" standalone='no'?>
<!DOCTYPE EMPLOYEE SYSTEM "employeedata.dtd">
<!-- Oracle eXtensible Markup Language Gateway Server  -->
<EMPLOYEE>
  <DATAAREA>
    <EMPLOYEE_DATA>
      <EMAIL_ADDRESS>kwalker@vision.com</EMAIL_ADDRESS>
      <EMPLOYEE_ID>5</EMPLOYEE_ID>
      <EMPLOYEE_NUM>4</EMPLOYEE_NUM>
      <FIRST_NAME>Kenneth</FIRST_NAME>
      <FULL_NAME>Walker, Mr. Kenneth (Ken)</FULL_NAME>
      <LAST_NAME>Walker</LAST_NAME>
      <MIDDLE_NAME/>
    </EMPLOYEE_DATA>
  </DATAAREA>
</EMPLOYEE>
```

If you configure OTA for the SMTP protocol, the specified e-mail account, vlad@fochusthread.com, should also receive an e-mail with the preceding XML content. Obviously, in real life, you are more likely to use HTTP or Web Services to deliver messages between the systems, but we find the SMTP protocol to be just fine for proof-of-concept types of projects.

Recommended Approach to Creating XML Gateway Outbound Transactions

In our example, when we created the subscription for the event that triggers our outbound transaction, we set the Action Type property to Send Trading Partner Message, which sends the message without executing a workflow process. However, in practice, you usually want to send outbound messages with a workflow audit trail. This can be achieved by using Generic Receive Event and Send Document activities from an XML Gateway Standard (ECXSTD) Workflow item type. An XML Gateway Standard item type can be obtained from a database or from the patch area on the file system at $ECX_TOP /patch/115/import/US/ecxstd.wft. Follow these steps:

1. Create a Workflow item type that consists only of the XML Gateway Standard activities Generic Receive Event | Send Document | End, where the Generic Receive Event activity is also marked as the Start node. The Send Document activity has a Send Mode node attribute that can be set to Immediate or Deferred. Set it to Immediate, as the subscription itself is deferred. If you set the Send Mode to Deferred, you'll have to wait on the Workflow Background engine to process the activity.

2. Create an event subscription with the following properties:

   - Set Phase greater than 99 (for example, 101) to defer the process of XML generation.
   - Set Action Type to Custom.
   - Set PL/SQL Rule Function to ECX_RULE.OUTBOUND_RULE.
   - Set Workflow Type and Workflow Process properties to the corresponding internal names for the item type that you created in the first step.

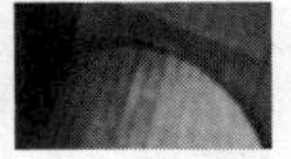

TIP
Always create a new Workflow item type to send outbound documents. This will benefit the performance of Workflow processing, as you insert only a minimal number of item attributes in the WF_ITEM_ATTRIBUTE_VALUES table if you use a simple Workflow process rather than incorporating a Send Document activity inside an existing Workflow item type, which may already contain a big number of item attributes defined for it.

Message Monitoring and Debugging

Debugging and troubleshooting XML Gateway transactions can be covered from XML Gateway transaction developer's and E-Business Suite system administrator's viewpoints. In this section, we emphasize the most important debugging techniques from the developer's perspective and provide a summary of the major debugging steps.

First, when developing both inbound and outbound messages, developers need to know how to enable logging in to XML Gateway to diagnose problems with map execution. The issues with map execution are likely to happen as you iterate through the development phase because you need to deploy the map in order to test its execution and compare the expected with the real results.

To illustrate monitoring and debugging techniques, let's assume that you have just created and deployed either an inbound or outbound message, similar to what was demonstrated in the previous section when we discussed the practical examples. In either case, after sending the initial inbound test message through the OTA servlet for the inbound transaction or by raising the event along with appropriate parameters for the outbound transaction, the first thing you need to do is to check the state of the transaction through the Transaction Monitor function available to the Workflow Administrator responsibility: (N)Workflow Administrator Web Applications | Transaction Monitor.

This screen is designed to facilitate monitoring both inbound and outbound messages by system administrators, but it can also be used by developers to check the status of transactions during the message map development process. The first thing you should look at for clues is shown next:

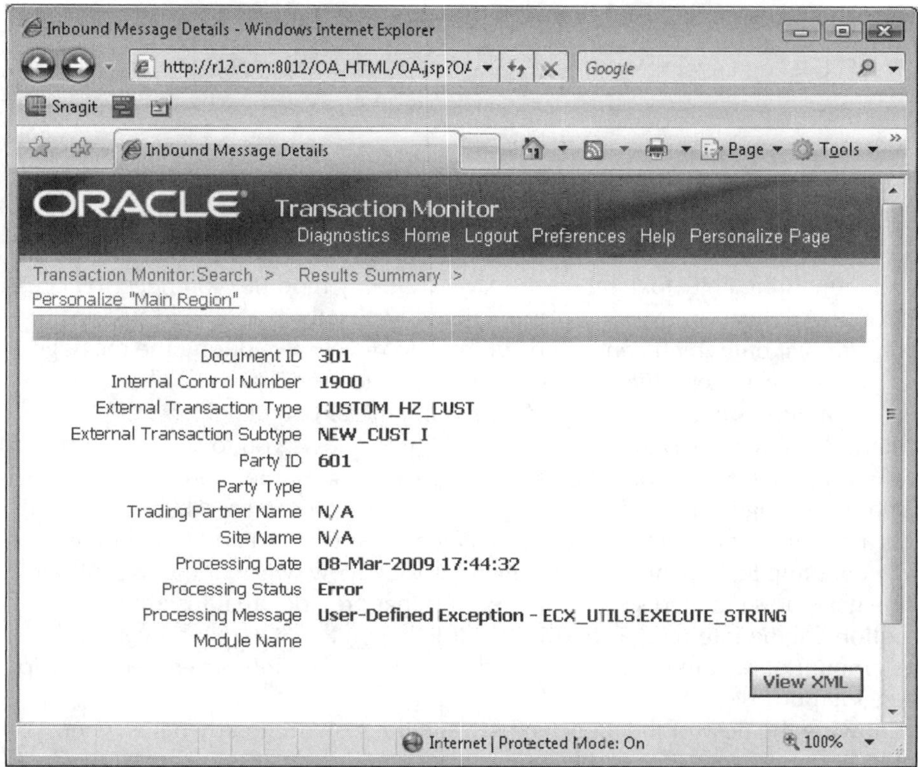

You can see that the inbound transaction CUSTOM_HZ_CUST has been processed to the point where message execution already has started, but it has failed with a user-defined exception.

This indicates that there is something wrong either with the inbound message XML data or your message map. If an error like this occurs, the next step is to take a look at the XML Gateway log files. But first, you need to enable FND logging for the XML Gateway module and reproduce the error. As of Oracle Applications 11.5.10 (patch set OWF.H) and onward, all products including XML Gateway use standard FND logging, and depending on the particular patch set level, XML Gateway logging can be enabled by setting the following profiles at the Site level as explained in Metalink Note 300298.1:

- FND: Log Module = ecx% or FND: Debug Log Module = ecx%
- FND: Log Enabled = Yes or FND: Debug Log Enabled = Yes
- FND: Log Level = Statement or FND: Debug Log Level = Statement

NOTE
You may have to bounce your R12.0.4 middle tier for changes to take effect.

After enabling FND logging for the XML Gateway module, you need to access the Oracle Applications Manager, a functionality usually available to system administrators, but which can also be granted to developers during the message build process. An alternative way of accessing Oracle Applications Manager is directly via http://<host>]:<port>/servlets/weboam/oam/oamLogin.

Here you navigate to the Logs function, which allows you to search for the XML Gateway log files by entering the value **ecx.plsql%log** for the Module search criteria. If logging is enabled at the Statement level, you can search for logs at all levels including Unexpected, Error, and Statement levels. An additional benefit of briefly enabling Statement-level logging for XML Gateway is that the Execution Engine generates detailed step-by-step entries that provide great insight into Execution Engine internals. The low level logging on the Statement level produces a huge amount of data in the database and should be used only when necessary for debugging purposes.

Knowing the flow of the message between the systems greatly helps when troubleshooting issues with XML Gateway transactions:

- Inbound messages:
  - The message was received by inbound agent ECX_INBOUND, which is a queue with an ECX_INBOUND_LISTENER_QH queue handler.
  - Agent Listener processes the message by calling WF_EVENT.LISTEN('ECX_INBOUND'), dequeues the message, and inserts the record in the ECX_DOCLOGS table.
  - Business Events System listener calls the dispatcher, which executes the ECX_RULE.INBOUND_RULE rule function, which in turn queues a message onto the ECX_TRANSACTION agent.

- Business Events System listener dequeues a message from the ECX_INBOUND agent (queue). The queue handler ECX_INBOUND_ENGINE_QH initiates the processing of the message and its payload.
- XML Gateway processes the event set in the Message Designer (ECX_STANDARD.SETEVENTDETAILS).

- Outbound messages:
  - These are usually initiated by calling the Workflow process, which in turn executes the ECX_STANDARD.SEND procedure.
  - The message is then generated by the XML Gateway and placed onto the ECX_OUTBOUND agent (queue).
  - The transport delivery mechanism, such as Oracle Transport Agent, dequeues the message from ECX_OUTBOUND and sends it to a trading partner.

Finally, we would like to highlight that there are great number of resources available on Metalink that explain how to administer and troubleshoot XML Gateway transactions. Checking Metalink regularly helps you keep up to date with both underlying technology and product changes between the releases, as this can influence the choice of message delivery and design of the message map.

Summary

XML Gateway is an E-Business Suite module that integrates both inbound and outbound XML-based messages with Oracle Applications. The product has borrowed many of its concepts from the EDI (Electronic Data Interchange) type of messaging, which has been in existence for a couple of decades to facilitate electronic exchange of the most common business documents such as sales orders, invoices, and the like. However, with the popularity of XML in today's world, EDI has almost completely been replaced by XML for exchanging of business documents over networks, including the Internet.

In this chapter, we walked through examples of creating both inbound and outbound messages. In practice, you are also likely to be asked to customize existing messages by including additional information to the custom areas of the standard messages that are shipped with Oracle Applications. As always, when customizing the standard messages, you should refer to the product user guide in the first instance to look for official recommendations.

Due to the support of Web Services as one of the transport mechanisms, XML Gateway can also be used for integration with the popular SOA (Service Oriented Architecture) platforms in various scenarios. The integration between XML Gateway and SOA platforms that provide adapters for XML Gateway is seamless; an example is Oracle E-Business Suite Adapter, which comes with the Oracle SOA Suite platform.

CHAPTER 13

Moving AOL Objects Between Instances

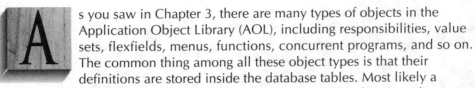

s you saw in Chapter 3, there are many types of objects in the Application Object Library (AOL), including responsibilities, value sets, flexfields, menus, functions, concurrent programs, and so on. The common thing among all these object types is that their definitions are stored inside the database tables. Most likely a developer is responsible for defining these objects; however, objects such as flexfields, lookups, and value sets can often be defined by functional staff, support staff, or administrators. These objects are first defined in the Development instance and unit tested in the same instance. Following the unit tests, these objects must get created on the UAT instance and finally are deployed on the Production instance. The challenge is how to get these changes from a development environment to production in a controlled and consistent manner.

Oracle has a utility named FNDLOAD (Generic Loader), which allows you transfer the definition of AOL objects seamlessly from one instance to another.

Brief History: Before FNDLOAD

In the initial versions of Oracle Apps, implementation teams had to either re-key the definition of AOL objects in each instance or use third-party tools to copy the definitions of these AOL objects from one instance to another. PL/SQL APIs were introduced in the later versions of E-Business Suite to transfer these objects. However, the limitation of the PL/SQL API–based approach was that the programmer had to modify or re-create the SQL scripts whenever any kind of change was made to an AOL object. Another problem with the PL/SQL API–based approach is that the developer has to write scripts or programs for each referenced or child AOL object; for example, value sets are attached to concurrent programs.

Basics of FNDLOAD

To overcome these limitations of the PL/SQL API approach, FNDLOAD (Generic Loader) was introduced by Oracle. With FNDLOAD, a developer can create AOL objects in a development instance using data entry screens. Once these objects have been unit tested for their completeness, they can be downloaded from the database into a flat file.

FNDLOAD downloads the data from the database according to the rules in a configuration (LCT) file and converts the data into a data (LDT) file. The LDT text files can thereafter be copied to UAT and the Production instance and be uploaded into the database of the destination environment. It is a good convention to create LDT file names beginning with XX to signify that it is a customization.

Generic Loader can operate in one of two modes: download or upload. In download mode, data containing the definition of an AOL object is downloaded from the database to a text file. In the upload mode, the same data is then uploaded from the text file to the database. FNDLOAD supports data structures with master-detail relationships and foreign key reference relationships. This structure is defined within the configuration file. The configuration file also contains the SQL Statements used to extract AOL definitions from the database. Additionally, PL/SQL APIs or SQL constructs are also contained within the configuration file to upload the data from the LDT file into the database.

To use FNDLOAD in the source environment, follow these steps:

1. Perform the AOL Setup in Environments using screens.
2. Run the FNDLOAD command in Download mode to download the setup. Running FNDLOAD in download mode creates a data text file (XX*.ldt).

To use FNDLOAD in the destination environment, follow these steps:

1. Run FNDLOAD in Upload mode to apply the extracted setup from LDT file.
2. Sanity test to check that the setup loaded properly.

The steps in the destination environment are repeatable across UAT, Production, or any other instance.

Advantages of FNDLOAD

FNDLOAD overcomes various challenges over manually re-keying data, as listed next:

- **Cloning development/test instances** Development instances can be cloned from a Production instance. In such cases, the AOL objects defined by the developers can be lost if their development work has not progressed to the Production instance. In this case, a developer can prepare LDT files using the FNDLOAD utility prior to the environment getting replaced from a production clone. After the cloning is complete, the AOL objects can be re-created by running the FNDLOAD scripts in UPLOAD mode.
- **Reference objects** When parent object types are downloaded using FNDLOAD, all their dependent/child objects are also downloaded into the LDT file. For example, when downloading a concurrent program or a flexfield, the value set definitions associated with the segments can be downloaded as well.
- **Auditing and testing** By using FNDLOAD, every change made to an AOL object can be audited by archiving the LDT file and the scripts into the source control system.

- **Access to UAT and production systems** Developers usually do not have access to UAT and the production environment. Therefore, FNDLOAD provides a reliable mechanism for developers to apply their AOL setup to other instances.
- **Oracle support** Oracle fully supports the usage of FNDLOAD.
- **Versioning** Given that an LDT file is a text file, it can be versioned in your source control system to track changes.
- **Cost savings** FNDLOAD helps you avoid having to buy a third-party product for moving AOL objects from one instance to another.

FNDLOAD Command

Oracle delivers various configuration (LCT) files for each AOL object. For the AOL objects, these LCT files are located in the $FND_TOP/patch/115/import directory. The syntax for running the FNDLOAD command is as follows:

```
FNDLOAD apps/appsPassword 0 Y mode lctFileName ldtFileName NameOfEntity
Parameter
```

The FNDLOAD command and its parameters are explained in Table 13-1.

Understanding the Loader Configuration (LCT) File

As is evident from Table 13-1, the key aspect of using the FNDLOAD utility correctly is the ability to analyze the configuration (LCT) file. The FNDLOAD configuration files delivered by Oracle consist broadly of three sections: Data Definitions, Download, and Upload. In the next sections, we'll look at each of these sections.

Data Definitions Section of the Configuration File

This section is for information purposes only. Here you will find the list of supported entities and their parameters, usually listed in the beginning section of the LCT file. Entities represent the object types that can be downloaded or uploaded using that LCT file. This information is useful in constructing your FNDLOAD command.

Another way to help recognize the supported entities within an LCT file is to remember that names of entities are preceded by text DEFINE. The parameters that can be passed to this entity are preceded by text KEY.

For example, affload.lct is used to download and upload flexfields. As shown from the affload.lct excerpt in Figure 13-1, the entity name for downloading a descriptive flexfield is DESC_FLEX, whereas the entity name for downloading a specific context within a descriptive flexfield is DFF_CONTEXT. Also evident is the

Parameter Name	Description
FNDLOAD	This executable is located in $FND_TOP/bin/FNDLOAD. This is the actual command for executing the utility.
apps/appsPassword	By using this credential, FNDLOAD connects to the database to Download or Upload AOL Definition. The format will be *appsusername/appspassword(@DBConnectString)*. If the connect string is left blank, FNDLOAD will connect to the database as per the value of the $TWO_TASK variable. TWO_TASK is an environment/global variable that points to the database name for that instance.
MODE	Most common values are UPLOAD or DOWNLOAD.
LCT File Name	Name of the configuration file. For example, when downloading or uploading the concurrent program, this will be $FND_TOP/patch/115/import/afcpprog.lct.
LDT File Name	Name of the loader file that is created after the extract. This file is thereafter copied to a destination instance and loaded into the target database.
Name Of Entity	The entity to upload or download. This can be left blank during upload so that everything within the LDT file is uploaded. For example, when downloading concurrent programs, the entity name is PROGRAM, and when downloading descriptive flexfields, the entity name is DESC_FLEX. Each entity has parameters that help uniquely identify the object.
Parameters	Parameters help identify the object. For example, a concurrent program can be uniquely identified by using concurrent program short name and the application to which it is registered. Parameters must always be used in combination with entity names. In order to construct the FNDLOAD for download, it is very important to analyze and understand the structure of the configuration file. A swift analysis of the configuration file will help you build your FNDLOAD command fairly quickly.

TABLE 13-1. *Construct for the FNDLOAD Command with Its Parameters*

```
# ===================================================
# Descriptive Flexfield.
# ===================================================
DEFINE DESC_FLEX
  KEY   APPLICATION_SHORT_NAME              VARCHAR2(50)
  KEY   DESCRIPTIVE_FLEXFIELD_NAME          VARCHAR2(40)
  CTX   OWNER                               VARCHAR2(4000)
  CTX   LAST_UPDATE_DATE                    VARCHAR2(50)
  BASE  TABLE_APPLICATION_SHORT_NAME        VARCHAR2(50)
  BASE  APPLICATION_TABLE_NAME              VARCHAR2(30)
  BASE  CONCATENATED_SEGS_VIEW_NAME         VARCHAR2(30)
  BASE  CONTEXT_COLUMN_NAME                 VARCHAR2(30)
  BASE  CONTEXT_REQUIRED_FLAG               VARCHAR2(1)
  BASE  CONTEXT_USER_OVERRIDE_FLAG          VARCHAR2(1)
  BASE  CONCATENATED_SEGMENT_DELIMITER      VARCHAR2(1)
  BASE  FREEZE_FLEX_DEFINITION_FLAG         VARCHAR2(1)
  BASE  PROTECTED_FLAG                      VARCHAR2(1)
  BASE  DEFAULT_CONTEXT_FIELD_NAME          VARCHAR2(200)
  BASE  DEFAULT_CONTEXT_VALUE               VARCHAR2(30)
  BASE  CONTEXT_DEFAULT_TYPE                VARCHAR2(1)
  BASE  CONTEXT_DEFAULT_VALUE               VARCHAR2(2000)
  BASE  CONTEXT_OVERRIDE_VALUE_SET_NAM REFERENCES VALUE_SET .
  BASE  CONTEXT_RUNTIME_PROPERTY_FUNCT VARCHAR2(2000)
  BASE  CONTEXT_SYNCHRONIZATION_FLAG        VARCHAR2(1)
  TRANS TITLE                               VARCHAR2(60)
  TRANS FORM_CONTEXT_PROMPT                 VARCHAR2(45)
  TRANS DESCRIPTION                         VARCHAR2(240)

  # ===================================================
  # Descriptive Flexfield Context.
  # ===================================================
  DEFINE DFF_CONTEXT
    KEY   DESCRIPTIVE_FLEX_CONTEXT_CODE   VARCHAR2(30)
    CTX   OWNER                           VARCHAR2(4000)
    CTX   LAST_UPDATE_DATE                VARCHAR2(50)
    BASE  ENABLED_FLAG                    VARCHAR2(1)
    BASE  GLOBAL_FLAG                     VARCHAR2(1)
    TRANS DESCRIPTIVE_FLEX_CONTEXT_NAME   VARCHAR2(80)
    TRANS DESCRIPTION                     VARCHAR2(240)
```

Entities in the LCT file

Parameters for the entities in the LCT file

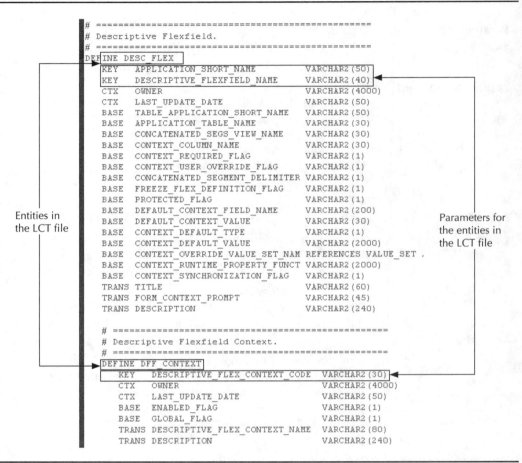

FIGURE 13-1. *Excerpt from affload.lct depicting entities and parameters*

fact that the entity DESC_FLEX can be used with the parameters APPLICATION_SHORT_NAME and DESCRIPTIVE_FLEXFIELD_NAME. Likewise, the parameter passed for entity DFF_CONTEXT is DESCRIPTIVE_FLEX_CONTEXT_CODE.

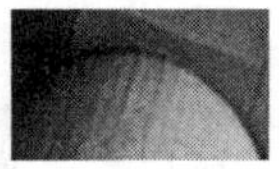

NOTE
The information in Data Definitions section must be read in conjunction with the DOWNLOAD section of LCT file, because in some cases the SQL Query that is used for downloading the object definition might depend upon other mandatory parameters that may not be documented in Data Definitions section.

As per the entities and their parameters in the configuration file for flexfields, assuming that the apps password is apps, the command to download a descriptive flexfield attached to the Lookup screen will be as shown next.

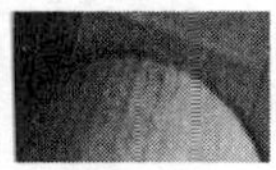

NOTE
The name of the flexfield is the Name field, not the title. This can be found in the Application Developer responsibility with the menu path /Descriptive/Register.

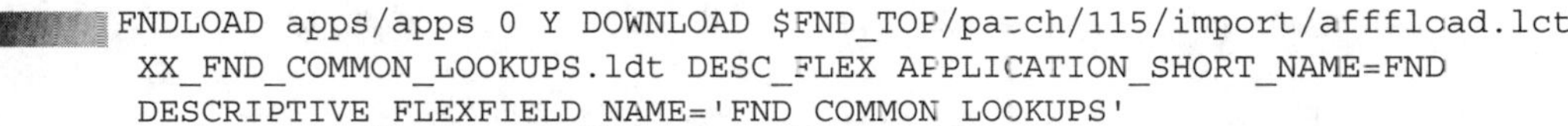

```
FNDLOAD apps/apps 0 Y DOWNLOAD $FND_TOP/patch/115/import/affload.lct
 XX_FND_COMMON_LOOKUPS.ldt DESC_FLEX APPLICATION_SHORT_NAME=FND
 DESCRIPTIVE_FLEXFIELD_NAME='FND_COMMON_LOOKUPS'
```

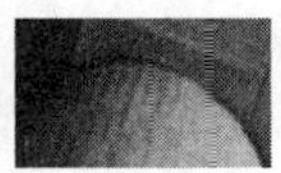

NOTE
The FNDLOAD commands in this chapter have been broken into multiple lines because of space limitations.

When using the preceding command, all the contexts against this flexfield are downloaded. This is because DFF_CONTEXT is not used in this example.

On the other hand, if you wish to download one single context of a descriptive flexfield, then the corresponding entity name (DFF_CONTEXT) and its parameter DESCRIPTIVE_FLEX_CONTEXT_CODE must also be included in the FNDLOAD command:

```
FNDLOAD apps/apps 0 Y DOWNLOAD $FND_TOP/patch/115/import/affload.lct
 XX_FND_COMMON_LOOKUPS.ldt DESC_FLEX APPLICATION_SHORT_NAME=FND
 DESCRIPTIVE_FLEXFIELD_NAME='FND_COMMON_LOOKUPS' DFF_CONTEXT
 DESCRIPTIVE_FLEX_CONTEXT_CODE='XX_OLM_USER_PERSON_TYPE'
```

In some cases, special options are available in the FNDLOAD configuration file. For example, in afsload.lct (used for menu, form, function, and so on), there are options for CUSTOM_MODE=FORCE and UPLOAD_MODE =REPLACE.

The UPLOAD_MODE option is usually used for menus. A quick examination of the afsload.lct configuration file reveals that existing menu entries will be deleted and reloaded from the LDT file when UPLOAD_MODE is REPLACE and CUSTOM_MODE is FORCE:

```
if (:UPLOAD_MODE = 'REPLACE' and :CUSTOM_MODE = 'FORCE') then
  delete from fnd_menu_entries_tl
  where menu_id = :
  (select menu_id from fnd_menus where menu_name = :MENU_NAME);
  delete from fnd_menu_entries
  where menu_id =
  (select menu_id from fnd_menus where menu_name = :MENU_NAME);
end if;
```

As a rule of thumb, FNDLOAD never performs a DELETE, with MENU being one of the rare exceptions; hence it is important to analyze the loader configuration file.

Download Section of the Configuration File

The download section of the configuration file is parsed by the FNDLOAD command for downloading the definition of the object from database. Therefore, this section consists of SQL Statements that are responsible for extracting the AOL object definitions, which are then extracted into an LDT file. The SQL Statements in this section parse the parameters passed to the FNDLOAD command. The values of these parameters are used in the WHERE clause of these SQL Statements, as shown in Figure 13-2.

As shown in Figure 13-2, if the parameter descriptive flexfield context code is not passed to FNDLOAD, then all the contexts against that flexfield will get downloaded into the LDT file because the effective WHERE clause will become as shown below:

```
WHERE a.application_short_name = :APPLICATION_SHORT_NAME
AND dfc.application_id = a.application_id
AND dfc.descriptive_flexfield_name = :DESCRIPTIVE_FLEXFIELD_NAME
AND (dfc.descriptive_flex_context_code LIKE '%' OR dfc.global_flag = 'Y' )
ORDER BY decode(dfc.global_flag, 'Y',1, 2), dfc.descriptive_flex_context_
code
```

Parameters are used in the WHERE clause of the SQL Statement

```
DOWNLOAD DFF_REF_FIELD
"SELECT /* DFF_REF_FIELD */
       dcf.default_context_field_name,
       fnd_load_util.owner_name(dcf.last_updated_by) owner,
       to_char(dcf.last_update_date,'YYYY/MM/DD HH24:MI:SS') last_update_date,
       dcf.description
  FROM fnd_default_context_fields dcf,
       fnd_application a
 WHERE a.application_short_name = :APPLICATION_SHORT_NAME
   AND dcf.application_id = a.application_id
   AND dcf.descriptive_flexfield_name = :DESCRIPTIVE_FLEXFIELD_NAME
   AND (   dfc.descriptive_flex_context_code LIKE Nvl(:DESCRIPTIVE_FLEX_CONTEXT_CODE, '%')
        OR dfc.global_flag = 'Y' )
 ORDER BY decode(dfc.global_flag, 'Y',1, 2),
          dfc.descriptive_flex_context_code "
```

FIGURE 13-2. *SQL Statements in the download section of the configuration file*

On similar lines, examination of $FND_TOP/patch/115/import/afcpprog.lct reveals that the SQL Statement used to download concurrent programs will download all the concurrent programs registered against an application if the parameter CONCURRENT_PROGRAM_NAME is not passed a value, where the parameter APPLICATION_SHORT_NAME is passed the value corresponding to the short name of an application. This usage of FNDLOAD is very useful when you wish to transfer all the custom concurrent programs registered against a custom application during implementation projects. The SQL Statement shown next is an excerpt from the download section of afcpprog.lct:

```
SELECT v.CONCURRENT_PROGRAM_NAME,.... a.APPLICATION_SHORT_NAME,
v.MULTI_ORG_CATEGORY
from fnd_concurrent_programs_vl v,

 fnd_executables me, fnd_security_groups s, fnd_application mea,
fnd_concurrent_request_class c, fnd_application ca, fnd_executables e,
fnd_application ea, fnd_application a
where ((:CONCURRENT_PROGRAM_NAME is null)
or ((:CONCURRENT_PROGRAM_NAME is not null)
and (v.CONCURRENT_PROGRAM_NAME like :CONCURRENT_PROGRAM_NAME)))
and ((:APPLICATION_SHORT_NAME is null) or ((:APPLICATION_SHORT_NAME is
not null) and (a.APPLICATION_SHORT_NAME like :APPLICATION_SHORT_NAME)))
```

Upload Section of the Configuration File

This section of the configuration file is parsed by the FNDLOAD command for uploading the definition of the object from the LDT file into the database. Therefore, this section consists of PL/SQL APIs or insert or update statements, as shown in Figure 13-3.

Some Common Examples of FNDLOAD

It will be very easy for you to write FNDLOAD commands after analyzing the configuration files, so we will cover only a few basic examples of FNDLOAD in this section. Again, we will assume that the apps password is apps in these examples.

Concurrent Programs The following command will download a concurrent program with the short name XX_GMS_ENC_FIX_CM registered against the application short name XXGMS, into a flat file named XX_GMS_ENC_FIX_CM.ldt:

```
FNDLOAD apps/apps O Y DOWNLOAD $FND_TOP/patch/115/import/afcpprog.lct
 XX_GMS_ENC_FIX_CM.ldt PROGRAM APPLICATION_SHORT_NAME="XXGMS"
 CONCURRENT_PROGRAM_NAME="XX_GMS_ENC_FIX_CM"
```

To install this concurrent program into other environments, upload this file in the destination environment using the following command:

```
FNDLOAD apps/apps O Y UPLOAD $FND_TOP/patch/115/import/afcpprog.lct
 XX_GMS_ENC_FIX_CM.ldt
```

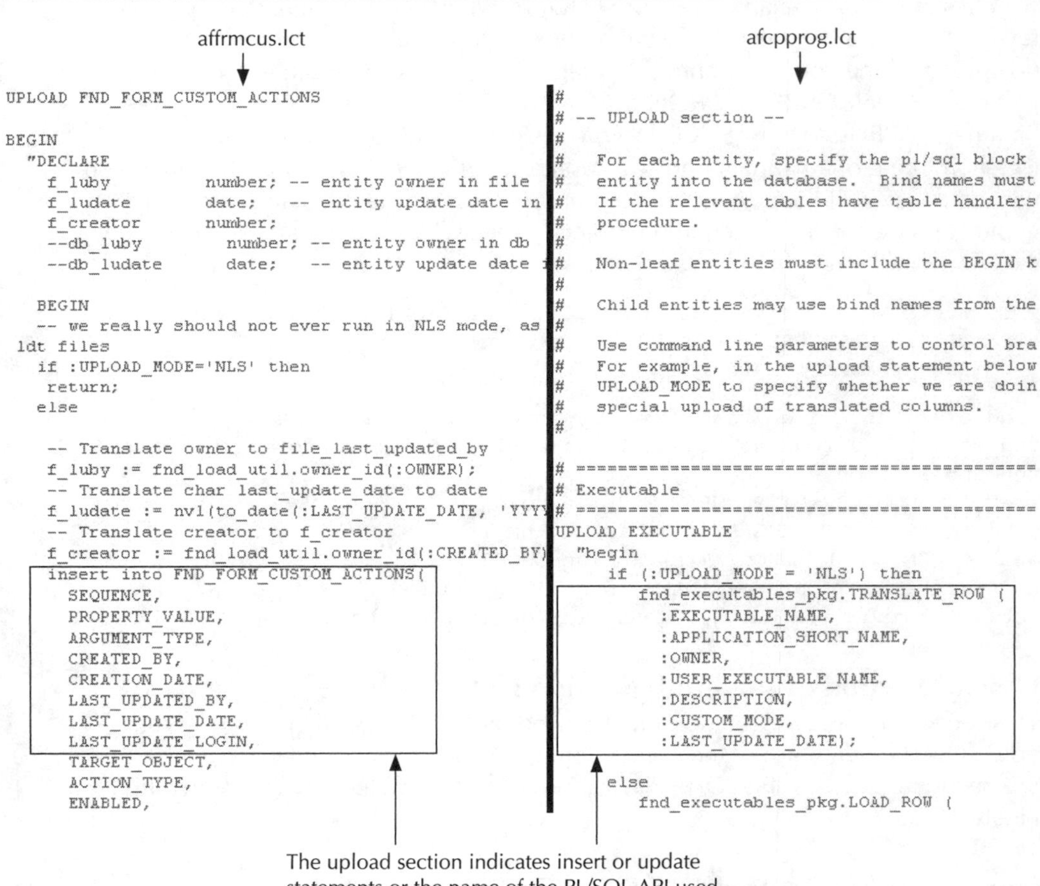

affrmcus.lct
afcpprog.lct
UPLOAD FND_FORM_CUSTOM_ACTIONS
BEGIN
"DECLARE
f_luby number; -- entity owner in file
f_ludate date; -- entity update date in
f_creator number;
--db_luby number; -- entity owner in db
--db_ludate date; -- entity update date
BEGIN
-- we really should not ever run in NLS mode, as
ldt files
if :UPLOAD_MODE='NLS' then
return;
else
-- Translate owner to file_last_updated_by
f_luby := fnd_load_util.owner_id(:OWNER);
-- Translate char last_update_date to date
f_ludate := nvl(to_date(:LAST_UPDATE_DATE, 'YYYY
-- Translate creator to f_creator
f_creator := fnd_load_util.owner_id(:CREATED_BY)
insert into FND_FORM_CUSTOM_ACTIONS(
SEQUENCE,
PROPERTY_VALUE,
ARGUMENT_TYPE,
CREATED_BY,
CREATION_DATE,
LAST_UPDATED_BY,
LAST_UPDATE_DATE,
LAST_UPDATE_LOGIN,
TARGET_OBJECT,
ACTION_TYPE,
ENABLED,
#
-- UPLOAD section --
#
For each entity, specify the pl/sql block
entity into the database. Bind names must
If the relevant tables have table handlers
procedure.
#
Non-leaf entities must include the BEGIN k
#
Child entities may use bind names from the
#
Use command line parameters to control bra
For example, in the upload statement below
UPLOAD_MODE to specify whether we are doin
special upload of translated columns.
#
==
Executable
==
UPLOAD EXECUTABLE
"begin
if (:UPLOAD_MODE = 'NLS') then
fnd_executables_pkg.TRANSLATE_ROW (
:EXECUTABLE_NAME,
:APPLICATION_SHORT_NAME,
:OWNER,
:USER_EXECUTABLE_NAME,
:DESCRIPTION,
:CUSTOM_MODE,
:LAST_UPDATE_DATE);
else
fnd_executables_pkg.LOAD_ROW (
The upload section indicates insert or update statements or the name of the PL/SQL API used.

FIGURE 13-3. *Insert statements and PL/SQL API calls in the UPLOAD section*

Lookup Definitions The following command will download a lookup type named XX_HR_EXCLUDED_PER_TYPES along with all its lookup codes:

```
FNDLOAD apps/apps 0 Y DOWNLOAD $FND_TOP/patch/115/import/aflvmlu.lct
 XX_HR_EXCLUDED_PER_TYPES.ldt FND_LOOKUP_TYPE APPLICATION_SHORT_NAME
='XXPER' LOOKUP_TYPE='XX_HR_EXCLUDED_PER_TYPES'
```

To apply this lookup in other environments, upload the file XX_HR_EXCLUDED_PER_TYPES.ldt in the destination environment using the following command:

```
FNDLOAD apps/apps 0 Y UPLOAD $FND_TOP/patch/115/import/aflvmlu.lct
XX_HR_EXCLUDED_PER_TYPES.ldt
```

Profile Option with Values The following command will download a profile option with the short name SIGNON_PASSWORD_FAILURE_LIMIT, and all its values set at each level to file XX_SIGNON_PASSWORD_FAILURE_LIMIT.ldt:

```
FNDLOAD apps/apps O Y DOWNLOAD $FND_TOP/patch/115/import/afscprof.lct
XX_SIGNON_PASSWORD_FAILURE_LIMIT.ldt PROFILE PROFILE_NAME="SIGNON_
PASSWORD_FAILURE_LIMIT" APPLICATION_SHORT_NAME="FND"
```

To apply the values of this profile option to other environments, upload file XX_SIGNON_PASSWORD_FAILURE_LIMIT.ldt in the destination environment using the following command:

```
FNDLOAD apps/apps O Y UPLOAD $FND_TOP/patch/115/import/afscprof.lct
XX_SIGNON_PASSWORD_FAILURE_LIMIT.ldt
```

Using FNDLOAD for Non-AOL Objects

FNDLOAD was initially created for moving AOL objects from one instance to another. However, given the usefulness of this utility, Oracle's various product development teams have created their own product-specific LCT files to apply some of the setups via patches. Usage of these configuration files is not documented, so the only way to use such controller files is to analyze the LCT files and download the data. These product-specific LCT files are located in $<PRODUCT>_TOP/patch/115/import. In this section, we will show sample usage of FNDLOAD in moving DQM (Data Quality Management) related setup between instances.

DQM functionality is a part of TCA (Trading Community Architecture). This functionality involves setup of various transformations rules, transformation attributes, and word replacement rules. If this setup is in progress on a development instance and being refined, then it becomes challenging to redo the entire setup assuming the development instance got cloned from production. Also, re-keying the entire setup on another instance is very time consuming and prone to error. In such cases, LCT files used by Oracle's product development team become useful.

The best way to identify such use cases is to navigate to the directory path and search for the keywords related to the functionality. If you find a set of LCT files you must test it thoroughly before using it on production. Another option is to analyze the usage of these LCT files in Oracle delivered patches.

The authors have in the past successfully used the product-specific LCT files during implementation projects for Data Quality Management, as well as for transferring Web ADI setups.

For example, the DQM LCT files are located in $AR_TOP/patch/115/import. The LDT files delivered by Oracle can be seen in the directory $AR_TOP/patch/115/import.

Use the following command to download all the transformations and custom attributes set at Party Level:

```
FNDLOAD apps/apps O Y DOWNLOAD $AR_TOP/patch/115/import/arhta.lct
XX_DQM_ATTRIBUTES.ldt HZ_TRANSFORMATION_ATTRIBUTES ENTITY_NAME="PARTY"
```

To download the DQM matching rules that contain transformation rules and scoring rules, use the following SQL. In this example, "10000" is the internal reference of the match rule defined during the implementation project. This could be a different value in your instance.

```
FNDLOAD apps/apps O Y DOWNLOAD $AR_TOP/patch/115/import/arhmr.lct
XX_DQM_MATCH_RULES.ldt HZ_MATCH_RULES MATCH_RULE_ID="10000"
```

The FNDLOAD commands to upload the transformations, match rules, and scoring rules are shown next. These commands will be run in the destination environment.

```
FNDLOAD apps/apps O Y UPLOAD $AR_TOP/patch/115/import/arhta.lct XX_DQM_
ATTRIBUTES.ldt
FNDLOAD apps/$APPS_PWD O Y UPLOAD $AR_TOP/patch/115/import/arhmr.lct
XX_DQM_MATCH_RULES.ldt
```

Using FNDLOAD: Best Practices

FNDLOAD is a very useful utility delivered by Oracle. However, in certain cases, caution must be exercised during its usage. The best practices listed below are prepared experience of authors through the practical usage of FNDLOAD over a period of many years.

1. **Menus in progress** If your team has multiple developers modifying the same menu, then untested forms and functions of other developers can accidentally be promoted to the production environment beside your own tested forms. Therefore, caution must be exercised before downloading the entire menu tree. In such cases, downloading a subset (submenu) is recommended.

2. **Independent value sets** Value sets attached to flexfields are downloaded by default when downloading the flexfields. Caution must be exercised when downloading flexfields that reference value sets with independent values for GL segment codes. It is important to avoid applying test GL codes that might not be applicable for production.

3. **Flexfields** Restrict the download and uploads to specific contexts or segments within flexfields that you are interested in. This can be achieved by applying relevant entities and parameters to the FNDLOAD command.

4. **Deletions** FNDLOAD does not support deletion, just updates and inserts. Therefore, if profile option values are being NULLIFIED, then those will not be transferred. Similarly, deleting concurrent program parameters will not be transferred either. The exception to this rule is UPLOAD_MODE=REPLACE for menus.

5. **Master environment** When using FNDLOAD, choose an environment that will be the master environment for all setups and downloads for that entity. If a functional person makes profile option changes on the test environment, then the next script released by the developer will override those changes.

6. **Avoid losing changes** Support staff may have a tendency to apply forms personalization changes directly on the test and production environments. If a developer makes further modification to forms personalizations on the development environment, then the application of those LDT files will erase the forms personalizations that were made manually for that form.

7. **Upload partial** When uploading, it is possible to partially upload specific contents within the entire LDT file. To do this, UPLOAD_PARTIAL must be used instead of UPLOAD. Some examples of UPLOAD_PARTIAL are shown next.

   To upload a single profile option from an LDT file containing all custom profile options, pass the entity name and parameters to identify the desired profile option:

   ```
   FNDLOAD apps/apps 0 Y UPLOAD_PARTIAL $FND_TOP/patch/115/import/
   afscprof.lct XX_ALL_CUST_PROFILES.ldt PROFILE PROFILE_NAME="XX_
   PURGE_DAYS_OLD_ERRORS"
   ```

   To upload just the value set definitions from the extracted concurrent program definitions LDT file, simply pass the desired entity name:

   ```
   FNDLOAD apps/apps 0 Y UPLOAD_PARTIAL $FND_TOP/patch/115/import/
   afcpprog.lct XX_GL_ENC_PROG.ldt VALUE_SET
   ```

   As shown in the preceding examples, it is mandatory to specify an entity name when using UPLOAD_PARTIAL. The FNDLOAD command signals an error when UPLOAD_PARTIAL is used without an entity name.

Summary

FNDLOAD is a very simple yet powerful utility in E-Business Suite that was developed primarily to transfer AOL objects from one instance to another. Some product development teams in Oracle E-Business Suite use this utility for transferring the definitions of non-AOL objects as well. In this chapter, you learned the inner working of the FNDLOAD utility. By understanding the underlying design of this utility, you can easily build the FNDLOAD commands for moving your custom objects across different E-Business Suite instances. As discussed in the best practices section, caution must be exercised when transferring some of the AOL objects.

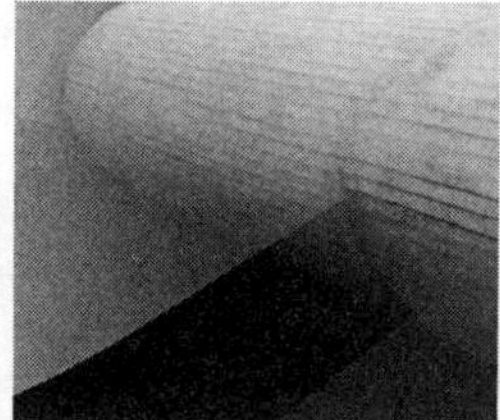

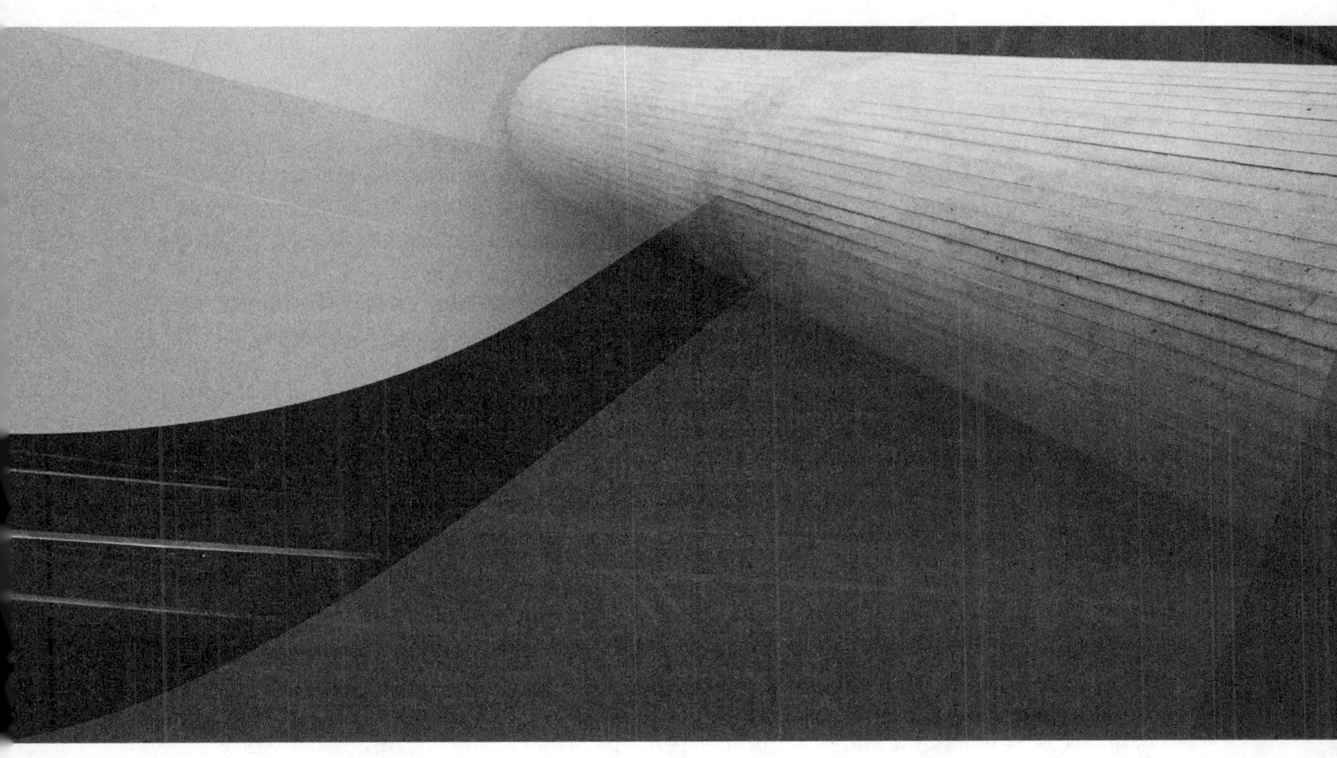

CHAPTER 14

Integration Between E-Business Suite and SOA

Service Oriented Architecture (SOA) provides an interoperability framework so that any systems, including E-Business Suite, can expose their functionality through a common interface of software services. In reality, SOA still means different things to different people at this point in time, and for that reason, we are first going to declare that, in the context of this book, by "exposing business functionality," most of the time we mean exposing E-Business Suite public APIs, open interfaces, Business Events, and XML Gateway transactions as Web Services.

We'll also touch on new developments in Release 12.1 in regard to enhanced service invocation methodology through Business Events, as well as Oracle Integration Repository enhancements. In addition, we'll walk you through a step-by-step example on how to use Oracle Applications Adapter, which is the main SOA enabler for E-Business Suite in current releases 11i and R12.

Integration Through Oracle Adapter for Oracle Applications

In the current releases 11i and R12, the easiest way of integrating E-Business Suite with SOA is through Oracle Adapter for Oracle Applications. In this book, we assume that the SOA platform is Oracle SOA Suite; however, other vendors such as IBM have their own Oracle Applications adapters with similar functionality.

Oracle Applications Adapter is an Oracle Applications Server component and can also be used with the current releases of Oracle SOA Suite 10.1.3.x out of the box. It supports the usual Web Services standards such as J2CA, XML, WSDL, WSIF, and WSIL and runs within the OC4J container.

Oracle Applications Adapter supports integration with the following functionality and services in E-Business Suite:

- Business Events
- Open interfaces
- Concurrent programs
- XML Gateway
- Public PL/SQL APIs
- EDI gateway
- Oracle Apps security

The adapter supports Integration Repository in Oracle Applications, which provides a wide-ranging list of business interfaces available in E-Business Suite.

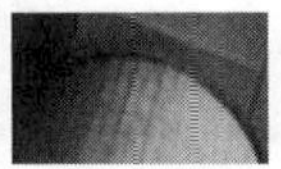

NOTE
Oracle SOA Suite comes with Database Adapter; however, when interacting with Oracle Applications, you should use Oracle Applications Adapter whenever possible.

An Example of Exposing a Business Event to SOA

In Chapter 11 about Oracle Workflow and Business Events System (BES), we highlighted some of the powerful features of BES, especially in regard to decoupling the standard product functionality from customizations. So, without further ado, let us walk you through a detailed example of exposing E-Business Suite data triggered by Business Events.

Example Process Overview and Required Software

For this example, we use the same version of JDeveloper that is currently used for OA Framework development (R12), which can be downloaded from Metalink (see Note 416708.1). Alternatively, download JDeveloper 10.1.3.3 from Oracle Technology Network (OTN). The runtime environment is SOA Suite 10.1.3.1, which we upgraded to 10.1.3.4, and the version of E-Business Suite used is R12.0.4. This example should also work with R11i.

As illustrated in Figure 14-1, raise a Business Event from E-Business Suite by calling WF_EVENT.Raise PL/SQL or an equivalent Java BES API. The event is then placed into the WF_BPEL_Q queue in the Oracle database, where it sits until it is consumed (dequeued) by Oracle Applications Adapter, which periodically polls the queue for new messages.

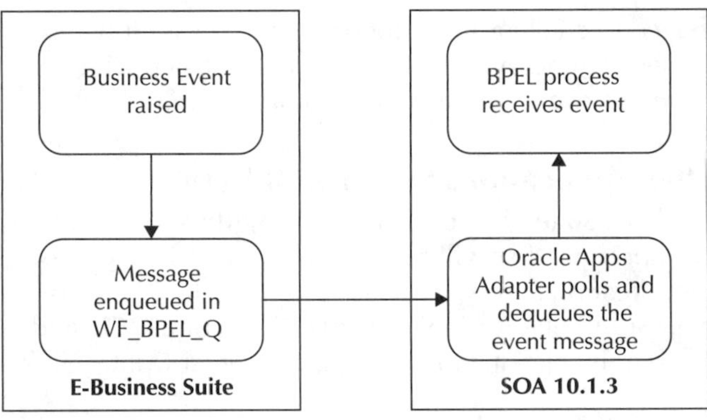

FIGURE 14-1. *Process overview*

Step-by-Step Walkthrough

In this exercise, you'll use the following components:

- **E-Business Suite** To create and raise a custom Business Event.
- **JDeveloper** Design-time tool used to create Application Server, SOA Server, and E-Business Suite database connections; configure Oracle Applications Adapter; design the BPEL process; and deploy the application to the Application Server.
- **BPEL Process Manager** To verify the successful process instantiation after raising the custom event in E-Business Suite.

Let's start with creating a custom event in E-Business Suite.

Step 1: Create a Business Event

First, log in to the E-Business Suite environment as Workflow Administrator and go to the Business Events screen: Workflow Administrator | Business Events.

Next, click the Create Event button and enter the following properties:

- Name: **xxcustom.oracle.apps.demo.integration**
- Display Name: **Custom Demo Event**
- Select status: Enabled
- Owner Name: **SYSADMIN**
- Owner Tag: **SYSADMIN**

You do not need to create a subscription for this event; it will be created automatically at design time by JDeveloper in the next step when you associate Apps Adapter with this event—no manual coding is required.

Step 2: Find the Applications Server RMI Port

When you install SOA Suite, the components of Application Server 10.1.3 are also installed. The RMI port number will be used in the next step to allow JDeveloper to connect to the Application Server.

On our server, SOA Suite is running at http://r12.com:7777, and you log in to the application server by clicking the Application Server Control link as shown in Figure 14-2.

After logging in, click the Runtime Ports link at the bottom of the page and make a note of the RMI port number, which is 12402 on the server in this example.

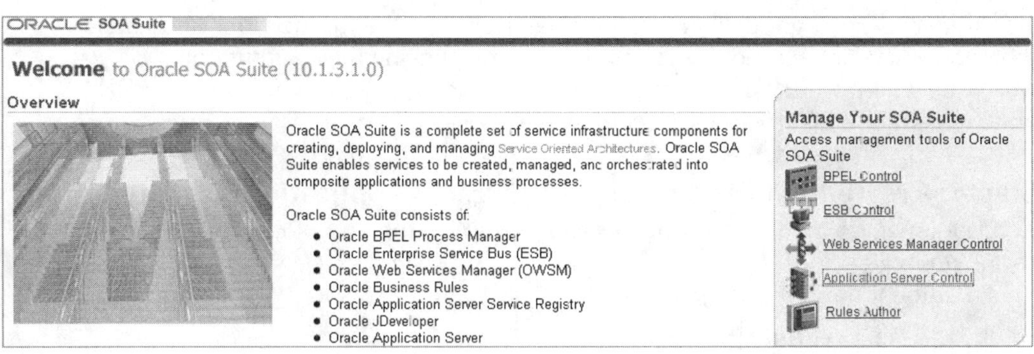

FIGURE 14-2. *Access to Application Server and BPEL Server*

Step 3: Open JDeveloper

The first thing you need to do in JDeveloper is create three connections to the Application, BPEL, and Database servers. To do that, click the Connections tab and right-click the Application Server folder as shown in Figure 14-3.

Use the RMI port for the Application Server connection (which was obtained in the previous step).

Next, create another connection to the BPEL server, but this time right-click the Integration folder and enter the connection name, host, and port number, where host is the machine name of SOA Server and port is the HTTP port of your SOA Server installation (port 7777 in the example). Make sure to click the Test Connection button to check the connection.

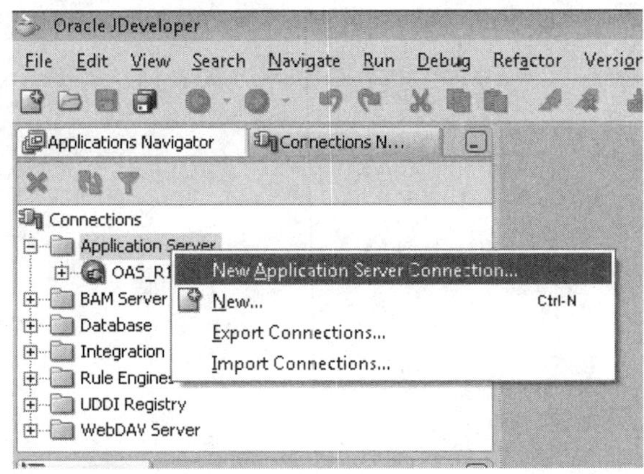

FIGURE 14-3. *Creating connections in JDeveloper*

Finally, create a database connection in JDeveloper to the E-Business Suite target database by right-clicking the Database folder in the Connections tab. Enter the connection details and test the connection by clicking the Test button.

Now, when you have successfully created the connections, you can proceed and create the BPEL Process project in JDeveloper.

Step 4: Create the BPEL Process with Oracle Applications Adapter

In JDeveloper, go to File | New and create an application and BPEL Process project as shown in Figure 14-4.

Enter the following properties for this project:

- Name: **EventIntegration**
- Namespace: **http://xmlns.oracle.com/EventIntegration**
- Select Use Default Project Settings: Checked
- Select Template: Empty BPEL Process

Click the Finish button to create an empty BPEL process.

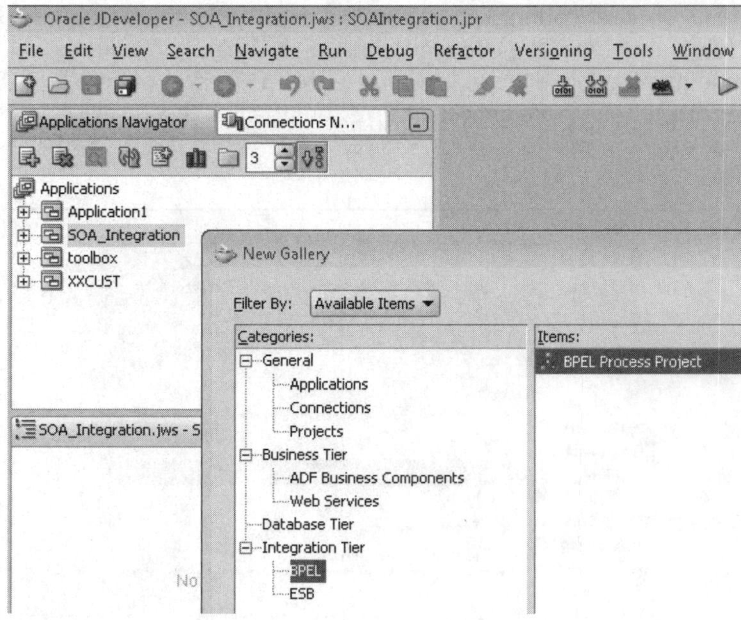

FIGURE 14-4. *Creating a BPEL Process project in JDeveloper*

Step 5: Configure Oracle Applications Adapter

Although we refer to this step as Apps Adapter configuration, it actually does not require any configuration and is a fully wizard-driven automated step. As illustrated in Figure 14-5, you simply drag and drop Oracle Applications Adapter into the Services lane for EventIntegration in the BPEL process. In Oracle BPEL, such a service is also called a partner link.

The Oracle Applications Adapter Wizard will launch automatically. Enter following details:

- Service Name: **ConsumeEvent**
- Connection: Select the database connection that you created in step 3.
- JNDI Name: **eis/Apps/R12** (It's important to make a note of the database JNDI value. It'll be used later to configure the database connection with runtime SOA Server.)

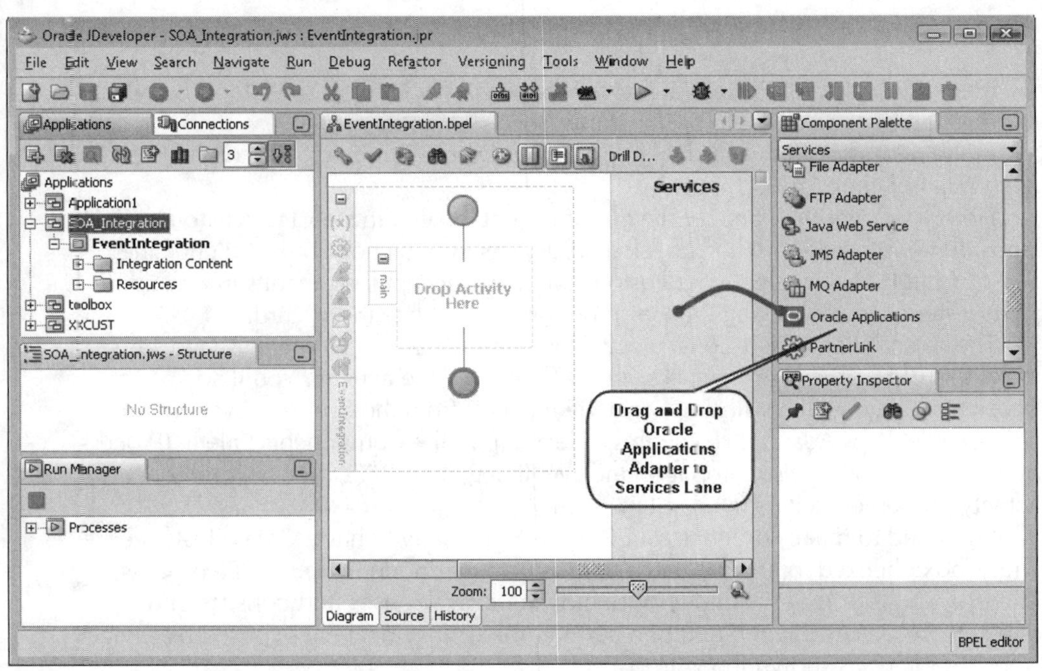

FIGURE 14-5. *Creating a BPEL partner link with Oracle Applications Adapter*

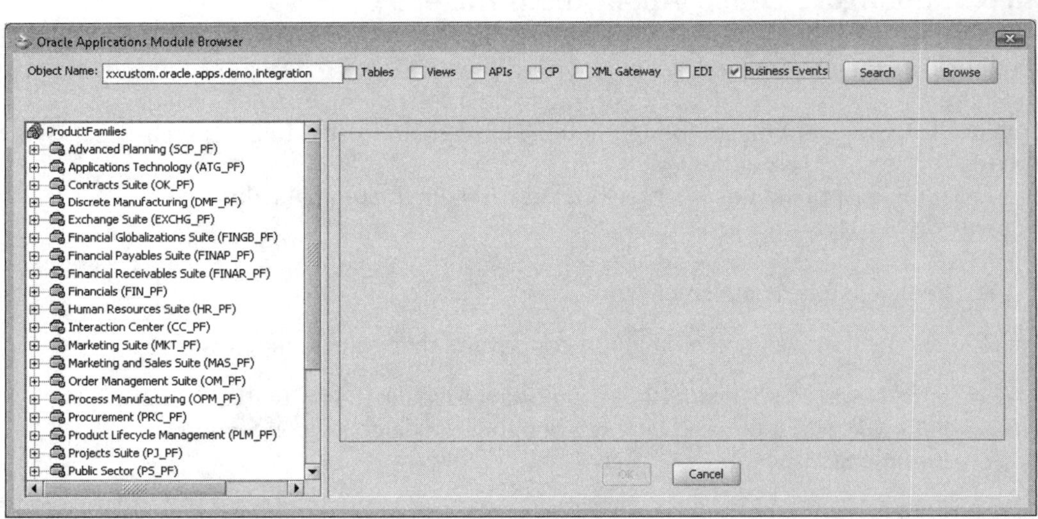

FIGURE 14-6. *Oracle Applications Adapter Module Browser*

If the IREP File Not Present dialog box pops up, click Yes and wait for the wizard to create an iRep data file. In this example, this is an optional step.

In the next step, the wizard will display the Oracle Applications Module Browser as shown in Figure 14-6.

Here you enter the name of the custom event created in step 1: **xxcustom.oracle.apps.demo.integration**. Then check the Business Events check box and click the Search button. Next, select your custom event and accept the defaults in remaining wizard steps before clicking the Finish button to complete the wizard.

The partner link called ConsumeEvent is now created in the Services lane, and to make this BPEL process executable you need at least one activity. You'll add a Receive activity, which will simply get the message from the ConsumeEvent partner link (Oracle Apps Adapter). To do this, select it from the Components Palette (Process Activities drop-down list), drop it on the EventIntegration BPEL process, and set activity properties as illustrated in Figure 14-7.

You need to make sure that your ReceiveEvent activity has a Create Instance check box checked to ensure that you have one start node in your BPEL process. The process itself is very simple for demonstration purposes and consists of only one activity (ReceiveEvent) and one partner link (ConsumeEvent exposed by Oracle Apps Adapter), as shown in Figure 14-8.

This is it, as far as JDeveloper design-time activities are concerned, and you are ready to rebuild and deploy your process by right-clicking the EventIntegration

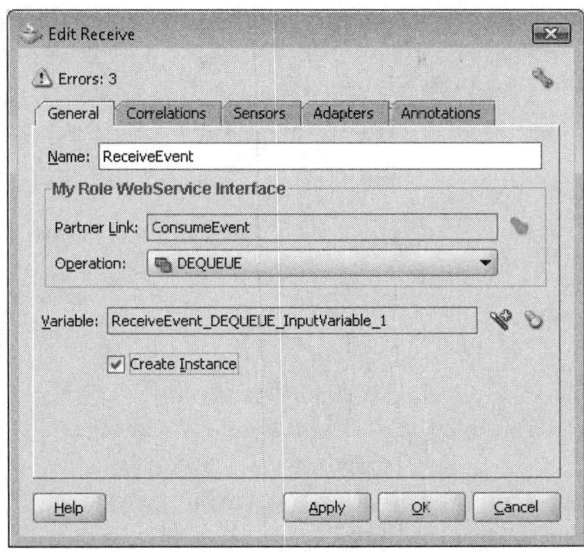

FIGURE 14-7. *Receiving BPEL process activity attributes*

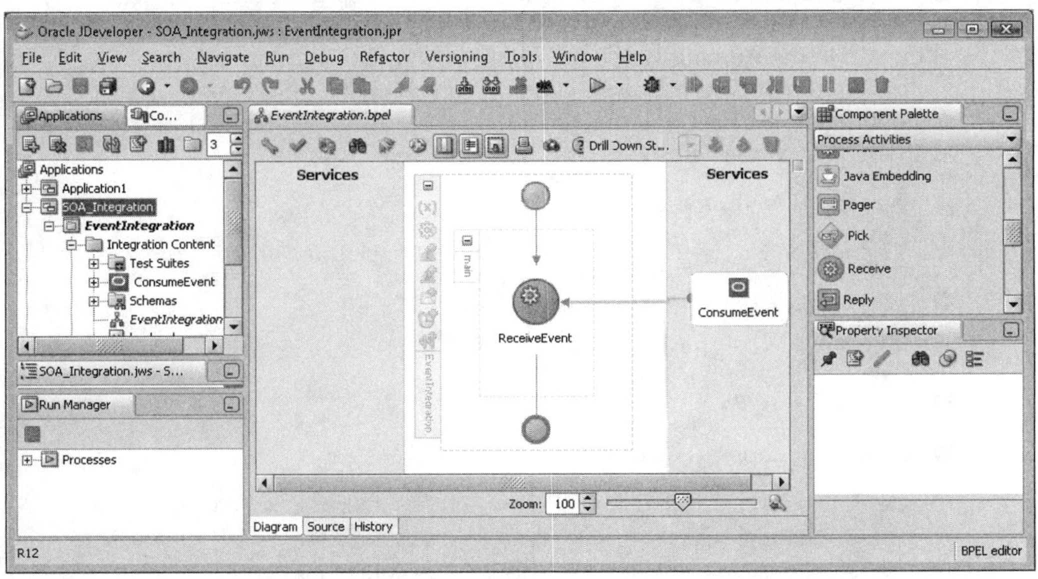

FIGURE 14-8. *BPEL Process with Oracle Applications Adapter*

project name in the Applications Navigator. If you deployed your process into the domain of your choice such as default (in our example we created domain called dhaval), upon successful deployment, you should see something similar to the following in JDeveloper's log screen:

```
[11:12:23] Successful compilation: 0 errors, 0 warnings.

Deploying to http://r12.com:7777 domain: dhaval. Please wait....

[11:12:38 AM] Please check Ant log to determine whether the project
deployed successfully.
```

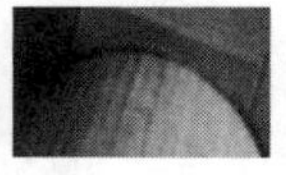

NOTE
Creating an Oracle Apps Adapter for an event partner link in a BPEL process will automatically create an appropriate event subscription at design time.

Step 6: Configure the SOA Server to Connect to the E-Business Suite Database

The SOA Server needs to be configured so that Oracle Apps Adapter can access the database at runtime. To do that, log in to the Application Server Control and perform the following actions:

1. **Create database connection pool** In the Cluster Topology screen, we drill down to the OC4J instance that hosts BPEL Server (the default name is home). In the Administration tab for that home OC4J instance, you drill down to JDBC resources, and here you can create both data sources (database connections) and connection pools. Create the connection pool with the following values:
   - Name: **r124DBConn_pool**
   - Connection Factory Class: **oracle.jdbc.pool.OracleDataSource**
   - URL: **jdbc:oracle:thin:@//r12.com:1533/R124**
   - Select the Cleartext Password radio button.
   - Username: **APPS**
   - Password: ***<apps password>***
2. **Create data source** Still in the JDBC Resources screen, click the Create button in the Data Sources region to create the database source for the E-Business Suite database and associate it with previously created connection pool:
   - Name: **r124DBDataSource**
   - Application Name: **default**

- JNDI Location: **jdbc/r124DBDataSource**
- Type: **Managed Data Source**
- Connection Pool: **r124DBConn_pool**
- Transaction Level: **Global & Local Transactions**

3. **Configure connection factory for Oracle Applications Adapter** Navigation to the connection factory for AppsAdapter is a bit tricky. The full path to it on our server, SOA.r12.com, is as follows: Cluster Topology | Application Server: SOA.r12.com | OC4J: oc4j_soa | Application: default | AppsAdapter. In the Create Connection Factory, enter the following details:

    - JNDI Name: **eis/Apps/R12** (This is the value from step 5.)
    - xADataSourceName: **jdbc/r124DBDataSource** (the data source from the previous step)

That's it, really. Now you are ready to test the functionality of Oracle Applications Adapter by either logging on to the Oracle Applications front end as Workflow Administrator and using the Test Event functionality manually or raising the event from PL/SQL or Java code. Here, we use a PL/SQL anonymous block to demonstrate how to raise our xxcustom.oracle.apps.demo.integration custom event:

```
DECLARE
  l_event_key VARCHAR2(250);
  l_event_data CLOB;
  l_event_name VARCHAR2(250);
  l_text       VARCHAR2(2000);
  l_message    VARCHAR2(10);
  l_parameter_list apps.wf_parameter_list_t;
BEGIN
  l_event_key  := TO_CHAR(sysdate,'YYYYMMDD HH24MISS');
  l_event_name := 'xxcustom.oracle.apps.demo.integration';
  l_message    := apps.wf_event.test(l_event_name);
  dbms_lob.createtemporary(l_event_data
                          ,FALSE
                          ,dbms_lob.CALL);
  l_text := '<?xml version =''1.0'' encoding =''ASCII''?>';
  dbms_lob.writeappend(l_event_data
                      ,LENGTH(l_text)
                      ,l_text);
  l_text := '<ar_customer_accounts>';
  dbms_lob.writeappend(l_event_data
                      ,LENGTH(l_text)
                      ,l_text);
```

```
  l_text := '<bank_branch_id>';
  l_text := l_text || apps.fnd_number.number_to_canonical('10001');
  l_text := l_text || '</bank_branch_id>';
  dbms_lob.writeappend(l_event_data
                       ,LENGTH(l_text)
                       ,l_text);
  l_text := '<bank_account_number>';
  l_text := l_text || 'A0001';
  l_text := l_text || '</bank_account_number>';
  dbms_lob.writeappend(l_event_data
                      ,LENGTH(l_text)
                      ,l_text);
  l_text := '<changed_by_user_id>';
  l_text := l_text || apps.fnd_number.number_to_canonical(10323);
  l_text := l_text || '</changed_by_user_id>';
  dbms_lob.writeappend(l_event_data
                       ,LENGTH(l_text)
                       ,l_text);
  l_text := '</ar_customer_accounts>';
  dbms_lob.writeappend(l_event_data
                       ,LENGTH(l_text)
                       ,l_text);
-- raise the event with the event with Bank Account Payload
  apps.wf_event.RAISE(p_event_name => l_event_name
                              ,p_event_key  => l_event_key
                              ,p_event_data => l_event_data
                              ,p_parameters => l_parameter_list);
END;
/
```

If you now log in to the Oracle BPEL Console, you should see the instances of the EventIntegration process being created every time you raise your custom event. This is shown in Figure 14-9, where three topmost processes are the result of raising our custom event three times. The XML payload is also passed to the BPEL process, which can be observed by drilling down into the individual instances of EventIntegration processes. The audit trail shows the following:

```
<process>
 <sequence>
 ReceiveEvent
 [2009/04/01 12:38:08] Received "ReceiveEvent_DEQUEUE_InputVariable_1"
 call from partner "ConsumeEvent"
 View xml document  ←------- XML Payload can be viewed here
 </sequence>
 [2009/04/01 12:38:08] BPEL process instance "70003" completed
</process>
```

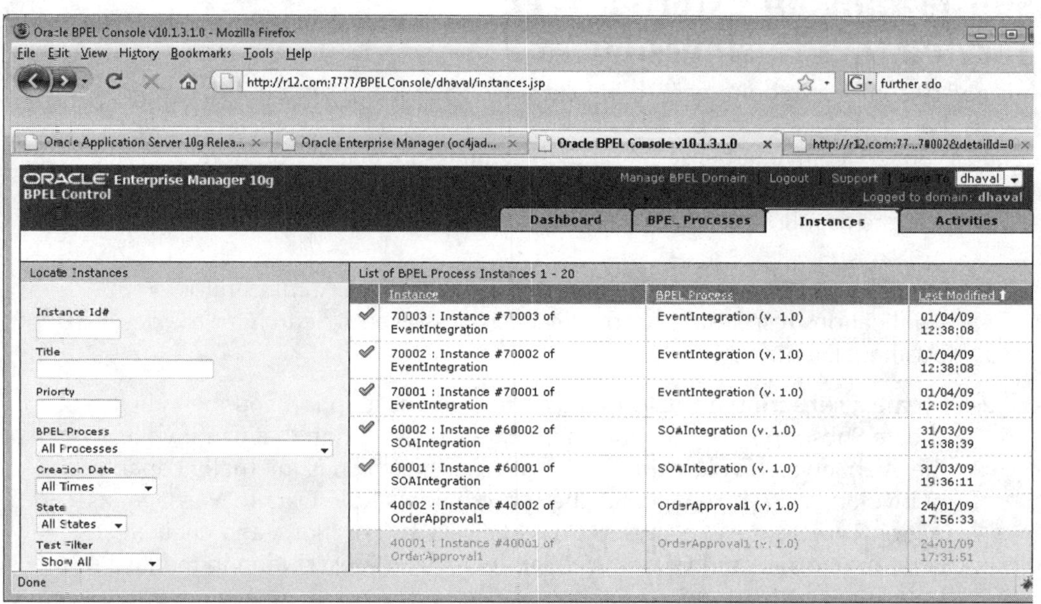

FIGURE 14-9. *BPEL console*

Once you have the XML payload from the E-Business Suite event, you can further process and transform that information using the standard and extended BPEL functionality offered by Oracle SOA Suite. Thus, data passed from E-Business Suite can easily be exposed as a Web Service and consumed by any Web Service client. JDeveloper also generates an XML schema that corresponds to the WF_EVENT_T object type.

Of course, the XML payload being passed to this event has no business context and is provided merely to demonstrate the technology in action.

New SOA Enabling Features in Release 12.1

Starting with R12, Oracle added many new features that make it very easy to integrate E-Business Suite with SOA. One of them is the SOA Invocation framework, which is a part of the Integrated SOA Gateway (ISG) in Release 12.1. This framework allows invocation of a Web Service from Oracle E-Business Suite by raising a Business Event. ISG also makes it very easy to expose PL/SQL APIs, concurrent programs, and open interface tables as Web Services. In this section of the chapter, we'll discuss the steps involved in using these features in your implementation projects.

Subscribing an External Web Service to a Business Event

It is a very common requirement to invoke a Web Service in response to certain events that take place in the business world. In R12, Oracle delivers a Java class called WebServiceInvokerSubscription that facilitates invocation of a Web Service from a Business Event subscription. The steps for invoking a Web Service using this mechanism are as follows:

1. **Identify the Business Event** Log in to the Workflow Administrator Web Applications responsibility and click Business Events. Search for the desired Business Event.

2. **Create a subscription** Click an icon named Subscription and then click Create Subscription. Here you can create a subscription that can invoke the WebServiceInvokerSubscription Java class, which is internally capable of invoking a Web Service. Set the subscription's Rule Data to Message, its Action Type to Custom, and its Phase field to 100 or more, and click Next. Enter **oracle.apps.fnd.wf.bes.WebServiceInvokerSubscription** in the Java Rule Function field.

When raising the Business Event, you must specify a number of parameters to it. These parameters with their default values can also be attached to the Business Event Subscription page.

As can be seen from Table 14-1, at the time of raising the Business Event you can specify the Web Service that you wish to invoke, along with other details.

The response from the Web Service can be placed into an inbound workflow queue that will raise another Business Event. For example, the invoking event for the Web Service can be xxcust.oracle.apps.wf.flight.reserve, whereas the response event can be xxcust.oracle.apps.wf.flight.reservationdetails.

In addition to this, you can extend WebServiceInvokerSubscription class to create your own Java class that can be used as an extended or customized subscription. Within the class that extends WebServiceInvokerSubscription, it is possible to customize the functionality by writing additional logic into the extended methods onBusinessEvent(), preInvokeService(), invokeService(), and postInvokeService(). As soon as the subscription is processed, the method onBusinessEvent() of the Subscription class is invoked. Method invokeService() uses WSIF (Web Service Invocation Framework) to invoke the Web Service dynamically, without the need of generating Java stubs.

It is also possible to invoke a BPEL or ESB process using this approach. To do so, the name of the BPEL or ESB WSDL must be prefixed with bpel:// or esb://. You will also be required to set up the profile options WF: BPEL Server and WF: ESB Server appropriately. For example, in this case you can pass a value to the parameter SERVICE_WSDL_URL as bpel://bpelServiceNameHere.wsdl or esb://esbServiceNameHere.wsdl.

Parameter Name	Description
SERVICE_WSDL_URL	WSDL of the Web Service that you wish to invoke.
SERVICE_NAME	Name of the Web Service. To identify the name of the Web Service from the WSDL, locate a text similar to <wsdl:service name="ServiceNameHere">.
SERVICE_PORTTYPE	Identifies the collection of operations that contains the method you wish to execute. This can be identified from the WSDL as <wsdl:portType name="NameOfPortType".
SERVICE_PORT	Identifies the operation that you wish to invoke in the Web Service. In the WSDL file, this can be located as <wsdl:port name="NameOfPortHere".
SERVICE_OPERATION	The method that you wish to invoke within that operation. Can be identified from the WSDL as <wsdl:operation name="NameofOperationhere".
WFBES_CALLBACK_EVENT	The Business Event that must be called to consume the response from the Web Service. The response from the Web Service will then be placed on the Workflow Queue as specified in the parameter WFBES_CALLBACK_AGENT.
WFBES_CALLBACK_AGENT	The name of the inbound queue where the response message will be placed. For example, you can pass this parameter a value of WF_WS_JMS_IN. After the Web Service invocation, the select statement select count(*) from wf_ws_jms_in will show the incremented count.

TABLE 14-1. *Parameters for Invoking Web Service via Business Events*

Developers can raise Business Events through Web Service Invocation from either PL/SQL or the Java Layer:

- **OC4J (Java layer)** Web Services can be invoked in real time from OA Framework pages using a synchronous BES subscription, provided its phase is lower than 100.
- **PL/SQL** Web Service invocations from the PL/SQL layer with both synchronous and asynchronous Business Event subscription phases will be processed in deferred mode. These subscriptions are executed by the Java Deferred Agent Listener that runs within Workflow Agent Listener Service.

The Test Business Event screen in Workflow Administrator has been enhanced in R12.1 with a new Raise in Java button to test the Business Event using the Java layer. If a Web Service is successfully invoked, this page also shows the response content from the execution of the last synchronous Java subscription in the Event Response region.

Additionally, in R12.1, the Business Event Subscription screen provides a wizard to capture the WSDL for Web Services. This user interface wizard for SOA Invocation facilitates creating a subscription with the Action Type as Invoke Web Service for an event. The wizard allows the user to enter the WSDL URL, following which services present in the WSDL file are presented for selection. Similarly, the wizard lets the user select a service port for a selected service and an operation for a selected service port, following which the user can enter a Java rule function with a specified set of parameters. The steps for using this wizard are as follows:

1. Log in to the Workflow Administrator Web Applications responsibility.
2. Select Business Events | Subscriptions for any given Business Event.
3. Provide values for System, Event Filter, and Action Type (Invoke Web Service) and click Next.
4. Parse WSDL: specify the WSDL of the Web Service and click Go, following which the wizard will parse the WSDL. After parsing it, the UI will show a region with a list of services. The user can click a radio button against a service name, following which a list of service ports will be displayed. The user can click a radio button against a service port, following which the list of operations will be shown. Finally, the user will select a Web Service operation and enter additional parameters.

Oracle Integration Repository Enhancement in R12.1

Integration Repository provides a catalog for numerous interfaces. It is a single source of truth for all interfaces that are exposed by Oracle E-Business Suite. Starting from R12.1, a responsibility called Integrated SOA Gateway can be used to access the Oracle Integration Repository. Integration Repository provides screens for developers and administrators to view, generate, and deploy a Web Service for a particular integration interface.

This responsibility allows you to service enable various components such as PL/SQL APIs, concurrent programs, XML messages, interface tables, and Business Events. For example, to expose a PL/SQL package API as a Web Service, log in to the Integrated SOA Gateway responsibility and select Integration Repository. Here you can search for a PL/SQL API and generate a WSDL for this API. Once the WSDL has been generated, it can be deployed to the application server, again by using the same user interface. By doing so, it becomes a very straightforward process to expose a PL/SQL as a Web Service.

The definition of any custom service can be downloaded into an ILDT file using the FNDLOAD command, and it can be subsequently uploaded into environments using the following command:

```
FNDLOAD apps/appspassword 0 Y UPLOAD $FND_TOP/patch/115/import/wfirep
.lct  XX_ABCD_API.ildt
```

Integration Repository also provides a mechanism to audit and monitor the incoming Web Service requests. Integration Repository administrators can find the SOA Monitor tab after logging on to the Integrated SOA Gateway responsibility. SOA Provider in E-Business Suite executes the incoming Simple Object Access Protocol (SOAP) requests for the services exposed via Integration Repository. Using SOA Monitor, it is possible to audit a Web Service's SOAP request and the corresponding SOAP response or error message. SOA Monitor can provide information about the Web Service requested, the SOAP request and response details, the status of the Web Service response, the sender's details, and so on. The administrators can periodically run a concurrent program named Purge Obsolete SOA Monitor Data to clean up the audit data. The underlying audit tables can be queried directly to monitor the Web Services requests processed by Integration Repository. These table names are FND_SOA_BODY_PIECE, FND_SOA_REQUEST, FND_SOA_RESPONSE, FND_SOA_RESPONSE_METHOD, and FND_SOA_ATTACHMENT.

Summary

In this chapter, you saw how easy it is to use Oracle Applications Adapter to expose E-Business Suite functionality to the outside world. In today's IT landscape, it is hard to avoid SOA, a type of architecture that everyone is talking about. What has been a buzz word for some time has now become a reality, and organizations are already implementing SOA on different levels of maturity.

We showed you how to use Oracle Applications Adapter with Oracle SOA Suite and glanced over the new features in R12.1. It is quite obvious that Oracle is putting a significant amount of effort to boost the capability of SOA enablement of E-Business Suite, and we are looking forward to further enhancements in the future.

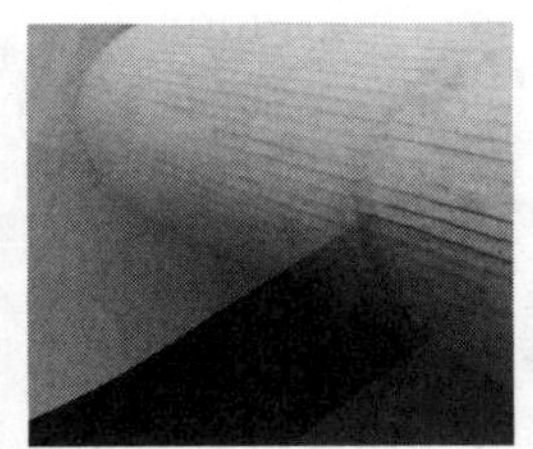

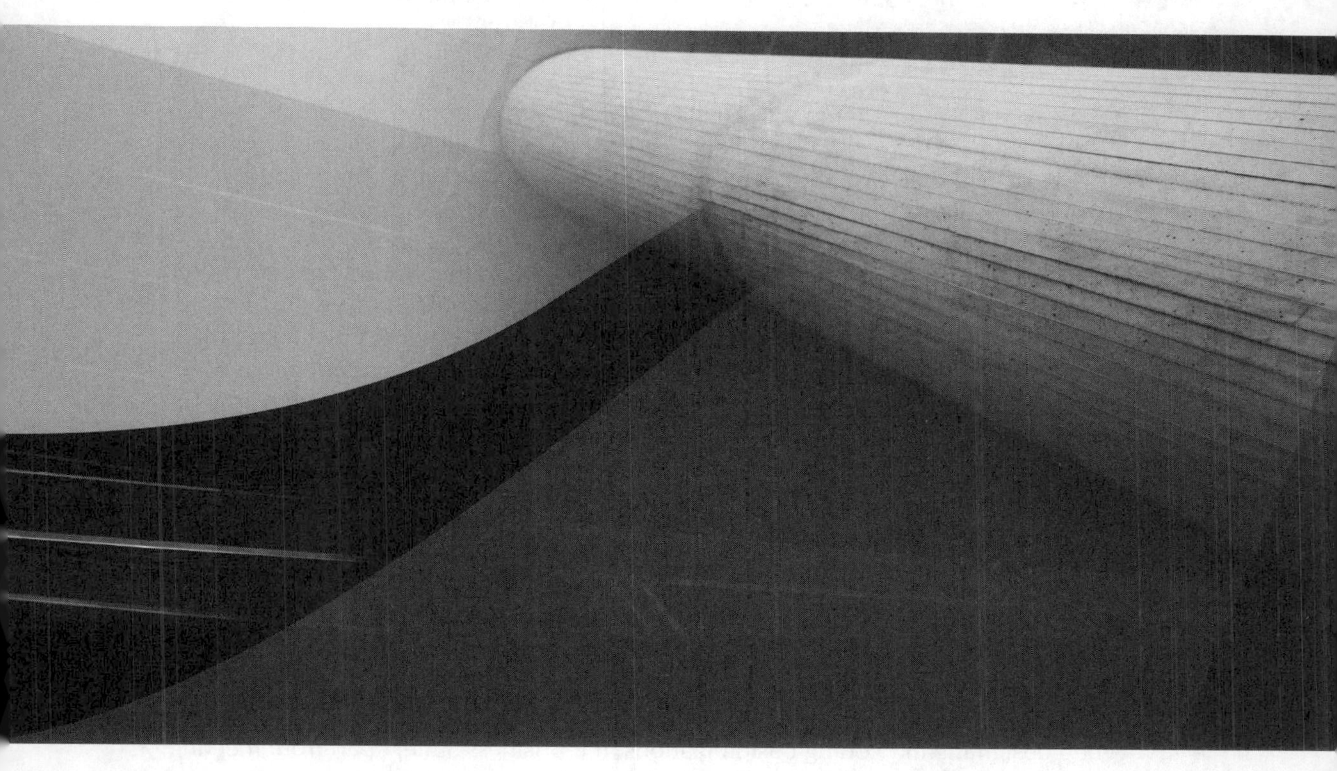

CHAPTER 15

SQL Performance Coding Guidelines

n this chapter, we provide a summary of various common practices and guidelines that help us in writing scalable SQL that performs well in our custom modules. We concentrate on SQL in particular because in the majority of cases with performance issues, poorly written SQL is the main culprit. Experienced Oracle Applications DBAs will first look for evidence of nonoptimal custom SQL code when the system exhibits performance problems, and practical advice in this chapter will help you in identifying poor SQL performance before it is deployed to a production environment. E-Business Suite modules are fairly optimized out of the box and customizations could potentially have a disrupting effect, so part of any design methodology to extend E-Business Suite must consider performance as a key requirement.

You should be aware that this chapter is not a comprehensive guide to SQL tuning in Oracle Applications but merely a quick reference to common diagnostics techniques, along with some practical guidelines.

General Considerations Before Starting Solution Design

When designing and coding customizations in E-Business Suite, apart from meeting customer requirements in terms of custom functionality, the customizations also have to satisfy the performance requirements regardless of the volume of work that needs to be performed. Typical E-Business Suite projects have various critical success criteria such as meeting tight delivery deadlines and streamlining complex business processes, but application performance can sometimes get overlooked in early stages of requirements gathering. It is therefore of vital importance to gather performance expectations before starting work on custom solution design, as this can greatly influence the amount of time and effort required to deliver the solution.

Various development techniques can be applied to different types of applications. For example, if you are creating a SQL Statement used in an online type of application (such as Forms or OA Framework UI), the priority could potentially be to bring the first set of records to the user as soon as possible. In that case, the SQL Statement should be tuned so it meets the response time expectations. On the other hand, if you are involved with building a custom concurrent program that is expected to process millions of rows of data overnight, you should tune your SQL Statements to execute in the shortest possible time so that the job finishes before online users start logging on.

Generally, when building extensions and customizations, you are either modifying the existing modules or building completely new ones. When modifying existing objects, developers need to be aware of the performance of the existing objects before modifying them further, as this could have a direct impact on performance perception of the customization. For example, if you are asked to modify a view object in a Self-Service application, you should make sure that the perception of performance for the existing object is satisfactory before extending it further. Likewise, adding more attributes to satisfy additional customized search criteria can turn a perfectly well-tuned SQL Statement into a nonperforming one.

In preparation to designing custom modules, you should gather information about at least the following items:

- **Expected response time** In broad terms, the response time is the elapsed time between an input of information into a system and initial reaction to that input. In E-Business Suite, response times are usually related to UI responsiveness of either Oracle Forms or OA Framework–based screens. For example, search screens should have mandatory and selective search criteria in order to prevent long-running queries and to show the first rows of the result set very quickly. Another example is a screen that auto queries data and renders that information when the screen is invoked; this could initially work when the number of rows in the database table is small, but as data size grows the same query may take longer and longer to execute and therefore make the screen startup very slow in the future.

  The response time expectations should also be evaluated in other than UI types of applications. Let's take an XML Gateway example: the time that elapses between the point when an inbound XML sales order message is received and when that sales order information populates Order Import interface tables could depend on many factors, including E-Business Suite configuration. If XML Gateway agent listeners that process inbound messages are configured to run once every hour, you cannot expect new inbound messages to be processed in a five-minute time frame!

- **Expected number of concurrent users** Concurrent users are all users who are accessing a custom module at the same time (concurrently). This information is important and it could affect the scalability of the custom solution and, therefore, impact the design and configuration options. The scalability of a system or module is discussed shortly in the following section.

- **Expected data volumes** The data volumes could also affect current and future application performance. In order to design the application to perform in the future as it does now, along with the current data size you need to take into consideration the growth of data in the future. In addition to that, you need to consider the distribution of data volume in time, such as establishing if the data volumes have peak times during the work hours, and, if they do, what times precisely, and similar scenarios.

Of course, these are just the starting points that need to be discussed prior to committing to an application design; the collected information will influence the technical design decisions and could have a profound impact on project delivery dates.

Scalability

In broad terms, scalable systems are those that maintain performance factors such as system responsiveness (reaction time to an input) as the load on the system increases. In the context of systems such as E-Business Suite, we usually think of scalability in respect of response times, CPU processing power, and data volumes:

- **Response time scalability** Ideally, the response time should remain constant as the number of users increases. For example, the response time of saving the same number of General Ledger Journals should remain the same as the number of concurrent users increases. In practice, all the systems and components that support them ultimately reach their scalability limit in terms of the concurrent users that they can handle. The solution is to add more resources such as Forms Servers and configuring extra OC4J instances and other resources that flatten the application response times.
- **CPU scalability** We can say that an application or system scales up if, for example, the number of transactions processed per unit of time increases linearly when you add more processors (CPUs). For instance, a custom interface that imports and processes *X* rows of data in 10 minutes with one CPU should process 4*X* rows in the same period of time (10 minutes) if you increase the number of CPUs to 4.
- **Data scalability** This refers to the processing capability of increasing volume of data in respect to time. For instance, if it takes two minutes to process *X* rows of input data by a PL/SQL block of code, it shouldn't take more than four minutes to process 2*X* rows of data.

The organization you are working for may define different types of scalability in different ways, and that is absolutely fine as long as the definitions are agreed upon and understood by all parties before solution design commences. Along with satisfying functional requirements, one of the main development goals is to write scalable applications.

SQL Coding Guidelines

SQL is used almost everywhere in E-Business Suite applications to handle and query often vast amounts of data. It is used in PL/SQL-based modules, Java-based code, Forms, Reports, BI Publisher, and just about any other tool within the suite. It is imperative that developers write efficient SQL that performs well and is scalable. In this section, we are going to outline some of the most important SQL coding guidelines specific to the E-Business Suite database. But before we do that, we'll take a brief look at how the Oracle Database server processes SQL Statements and which factors influence how it does it.

NOTE
For detailed information about Cost Based Optimizer, SQL Statement execution, and other data server concepts that affect performance and understanding of it, read Oracle Database Performance Tuning Guide and Reference *that comes with Oracle database documentation. In this book, we only provide a very brief summary for reference purposes.*

SQL Processing Overview

We start by looking at what happens when a SQL Statement is processed for the first time. Broadly speaking, SQL Statement processing consists of two steps: parsing (hard parse) and execution. Initially, an incoming SQL received by Oracle Server is checked for syntax errors, and referenced objects are checked for existence and accessibility. The output of this syntactic and semantic analysis phase is basic parse tree structure, which is passed on for further processing.

Next, the optimizer needs to decide what is the best query execution plan (route) for the statement to access the data. It initially uses methods such as view merging and SQL Statement transformation. For example, during the view merging, optimizer will try to un-nest the body of a view and merge it with the body of the parent query. This usually opens more access paths that could be considered by the optimizer to produce the best execution plan. Cost Based Optimizer, which is used in E-Business Suite, provides a means to collect statistics on objects and uses them to optimize access paths in addition to exploring different join orders and join methods.

At this point, an execution plan is generated that concludes the parse phase; the statement gets executed only during the execution phase. A handle (pointer) to the parsed SQL execution plan that can be shared and executed by multiple other sessions is called a cursor. Shared cursors use the library cache to store the SQL Statement execution plan, and the handle to this structure is derived from SQL text using a hashing algorithm. The amount of time required to parse a SQL Statement and generate the execution plan by Oracle Server is called parse time. This metric alone has profound consequences on the performance because parsing is a very expensive and CPU-intensive operation.

The process of SQL Statement parsing, compilation, and execution plan generation is called a hard parse. Oracle Server will resort to the hard parse when no cursor exists in the library cache that matches the text of the executed SQL Statement. When Oracle Server scans the library cache for a matching SQL Statement, it applies a hash algorithm to the current SQL Statement and then looks for the matching hash value in the library cache. If the match is found, the cursor is reused and a hard parse avoided, thereby massively improving the performance through reusability.

Overview of Cost Based Optimizer (CBO)

E-Business Suite uses Cost Based Optimizer (CBO), which is a component of Oracle Database server that determines the most efficient execution plan for SQL Statements. When building the execution plan, CBO uses a cost engine to assign a cost to each operation such as access methods and joins. In the sections that follow, we look at the key factors that drive CBO architecture: cost, cardinality, selectivity, access path, and join costs.

Cost

Cost is just a relative measure expressed as a number that is proportional to the amount of computing resources such as I/O, CPU, and network resources required to execute a SQL Statement. A cost is associated with access methods to each table or index that could be linked with an SQL Statement and an access path is chosen for the cheapest path. CBO optimizer then performs permutations of join orders based on all tables in the FROM clause, and again, the cost is associated with each permutation and the cheapest one is chosen. Joins are also evaluated for cost and the cheapest one wins.

The assumption is that the execution plan with the lower cost performs better than other plans that have a higher overall cost; for this reason, CBO will choose the plan with the least cost. The cost of an individual operation, is largely based on a number of I/Os needed to perform an operation, although, as of release 9i, CBO considers CPU costing as well. You can think of I/O cost as a relative cost of transferring data blocks from a disk to the main memory.

Let's take a look at how I/O influences the cost by looking at a full table scan example:

```
SQL> select value from v$parameter
where name = 'db_file_multiblock_read_count';
VALUE
--------
8
SQL> explain plan for
select po_header_id, po_line_id from po_lines_all;
Explained.
```

```
SQL> @?/rdbms/admin/utlxpls
-----------------------------------------------------------------
| Id  | Operation           | Name           | Rows  | Bytes | Cost  |
-----------------------------------------------------------------
|   0 | SELECT STATEMENT    |                | 46250 |   451K|   314 |
|   1 |  TABLE ACCESS FULL| PO_LINES_ALL | 46250 |   451K|   314 |
-----------------------------------------------------------------
SQL> alter session set db_file_multiblock_read_count = 32;
Session altered.
SQL> explain plan for
select po_header_id, po_line_id from po_lines_all;
Explained.
SQL> @?/rdbms/admin/utlxpls
-----------------------------------------------------------------
| Id  | Operation           | Name           | Rows  | Bytes | Cost  |
-----------------------------------------------------------------
|   0 | SELECT STATEMENT    |                | 46250 |   451K|   127 |
|   1 |  TABLE ACCESS FULL| PO_LINES_ALL | 46250 |   451K|   127 |
-----------------------------------------------------------------
```

The full table scan reads the whole table up to its high water mark. The high water mark is the last block in the table that had data written to it in the past. During the full table scan, multiple data blocks are read in a single I/O operation. The multiblock read is controlled by the db_file_multiblock_read_count parameter and in E-Business Suite, it is set to 8.

In the previous listing, we increased the value of db_file_multiblock_read_count from 8 to 32 for experimental purposes to show the expected reduction with regard to the cost for this operation, as fewer I/Os are needed to read the same number of blocks. In the example, the cost dropped from 314 to 127 as a result of increasing the multiblock read parameter. Please note that we used this example just to illustrate the effect of changing the db_file_multiblock_read_count parameter on the cost of one particular operation; you shouldn't change the default value of db_file_multiblock_read_count in E-Business Suite, as that would have a negative effect on performance overall.

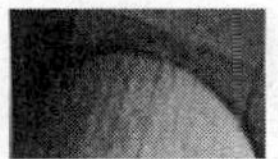

CAUTION
In E-Business Suite, the default value of the db_file_multiblock_read_count parameter is set to 8 and should not be changed unless Oracle Support instructs you to do so.

The cost is based on total and estimated cardinality; selectivity; and table, column, and index statistics. If the exact statistics are not available for the object, the optimizer uses sampled statistics or estimates. Otherwise, if no statistics are available at all, the optimizer uses hard-coded default rules.

Cardinality and Selectivity

In the context of Oracle Database Optimizer, cardinality or base cardinality is simply a number of rows in the table before applying the predicate:

```
SQL> SELECT num_rows FROM dba_tables
WHERE table_name='PO_LINES_ALL' AND owner='PO';
  NUM_ROWS
----------
     46250
```

Now, estimated or computed cardinality is slightly different in that it reflects the number of rows that CBO expects to return for a given operation. Consider following example:

```
SQL> explain plan for SELECT po_header_id, po_line_id
FROM po_lines_all WHERE po_line_id = :b1;
Explained.
SQL> @?/rdbms/admin/utlxpls
-----------------------------------------------------------------------------
| Id  | Operation                      | Name         | Rows  | Bytes | Cost|
-----------------------------------------------------------------------------
| 0 | SELECT STATEMENT                 |              |     1 |    10 |    2
|
| 1 |  TABLE ACCESS BY INDEX ROWID| PO_LINES_ALL |     1 |    10 |    2
|
|*2 |   INDEX UNIQUE SCAN          | PO_LINES_U1  |     1 |       |    1
|
-----------------------------------------------------------------------------
Predicate Information (identified by operation id):
2 - access("PO_LINE_ID"=TO_NUMBER(:B1))
```

Estimated cardinality is computed as follows:

Estimated Cardinality = Total Cardinality * Selectivity

where Selectivity is the number of rows returned by the operation divided by total number of rows in a row set. A row set can be a table, rows that passed the predicate test, the result of a join operation, and so on. For example, the selectivity of the predicate equality test PO_LINE_ID = 100 is 1/Number of Distinct Values (NDV) in column PO_LINE_ID.

In the example, we used a bind variable, and CBO used the default selectivity estimate. For equality expressions such as po_line_id = :b1, the default selectivity is 1/Number of Distinct Values (NDV), and for other types of predicates different default values are used. For the range test PO_LINE_ID > 100, the following formula is used assuming uniform distribution: 1-((high-100)/ (high-low)).

In our earlier example, the number of distinct values for po_line_id is 46250; therefore, the selectivity is 1/46250 = 2.162e-5. The estimated cardinality is then 46250*2.162e-5 = 1.

Let's look at another example containing the range expression:

```
SQL> explain plan for SELECT po_header_id, po_line_id
FROM po_lines_all WHERE po_line_id > :b1;
Explained.
SQL> @?/rdbms/admin/utlxpls
-----------------------------------------------------------------------
| Id  | Operation                  | Name          | Rows  | Bytes | Cost |
-----------------------------------------------------------------------
|   0 | SELECT STATEMENT           |               | 2313  | 23130 |  126 |
|   1 |  TABLE ACCESS BY
              INDEX ROWID           | PO_LINES_ALL  | 2313  | 23130 |  126 |
|*  2 |   INDEX RANGE SCAN         | PO_LINES_U1   |  416  |       |    2 |
-----------------------------------------------------------------------
Predicate Information (identified by operation id):
2 - access("PO_LINE_ID">TO_NUMBER(:B1))
```

When using bind variables with range predicates such as > or <, CBO uses 5 percent as the default selectivity. From the earlier expression, we have determined that the estimated cardinality in this case equals 46250 (total cardinality) multiplied by 0.05 (5 percent is the default selectivity for range predicate), which is 2312.5.

For this reason, application developers must generate an explain plan for the exact SQL that is going to be used in the real application rather than substituting bind variables with literals, as that could result in an execution plan that doesn't reflect what is going to happen at runtime.

Access Paths

Access path costs, along with costs of joins, play a major role in computing the final cost. Optimizer uses estimated cardinality based on columns selectivity for the query filter predicates, and based on that information computes the cost of table and index scans. The main access paths (in other words, the methods of data retrieval) are Full Table Scan and various types of Index Scan.

Full Table Scan In Full Table Scan, a table is scanned sequentially in multiblock mode up to the high water mark. It is usually used on very big tables but can be used on very small tables if the number of blocks is fewer than DB_FILE_MULTIBLOCK_READ_COUNT. In addition to that, it is often selected by Optimizer if there is no index on the table at all.

Index Scan Index is a sorted reference of a table's data. It stores the exact address of a table row (ROWID) along with the index key. ROWID is used to access quickly a row inside a data block. Indexes can be created on one or more table columns. Also, indexes are updated after each DML change to the underlying table, therefore affecting DML performance as the number of indexes grows.

In E-Business Suite, the most frequent type of index is a B+Tree index. The B+Tree index structure has an entry point through a root data block and can have multiple branches blocks as well as leaf blocks. When walking the index tree, branch blocks separate data ranges and locates the next branch level. The actual index data is stored in leaf blocks along with its references (ROWIDs).

There are a number of index scan types that often appear in an execution plan, but we'll list only a few:

- **Index unique scan** In the explain plan, you see the INDEX UNIQUE SCAN operation, which is used when all unique index keys appear in the equality predicates within the SQL Statement to return a single value.
- **Index range scan** This method helps with finding ranges of data usually used in conjunction with range operation such as BETWEEN, >, <, and others. The evidence of this method in the explain plan is shown by the presence of the INDEX RANGE SCAN operator.
- **Index full scan** This method is used when statistics evaluated by CBO indicate that it is more efficient than Full Table Scan if predicates do not restrict data filtering for a table.

Join Methods

Join is an operation that merges two row sources into one. When building the execution plan, the Optimizer starts off with an initial join order favoring the tables with lower estimated cardinality. It then computes the estimated cost of join operation and generates the next join permutation. This process is repeated until all permutations are completed and the join order costs evaluated. Theoretically, the Optimizer could consider n! (n factorial) join orders, where *n* is the number of tables. However, in practice, the upper number is limited to reduce the SQL Statement parsing time. The following is the list of join methods:

- **Sort merge join** Two row sources are individually sorted using the same sort key, and matching rows are merged into one. Nonmatching rows are simply discarded. Sorting could be an expensive operation, especially with a large table, which can force Optimizer to associate a high cost for this operation.
- **Hash join** With a hash join, row sources are compared and the smaller table is scanned in order to produce an in-memory hash table based on the smaller table. The hash table is then used to probe the large table for matching rows. A hash join uses a bitmap for a quick lookup. This method is particularly useful for large table joins when the estimated cardinality of one row source in the join is very big. In E-Business Suite, hash joins appear in execution plans for concurrent programs that process large amounts of data and in nonselective queries, usually from the screens that allow blind queries to be executed.

- **Nested loops join** This join method is frequently present in query execution plans. For each row in driving (outer) row source, the inner row source is probed for a match. Nested loops are efficient if the outer row source is relatively small and the filtering condition in the outer row source causes a small number of inner row source rows to be accessed. This method is optimal for selective forms or OA Framework search screen queries that return a small number of rows.
- **Merge join Cartesian** This method is used if there is an absence of joins between the row sources such as tables. CBO can select this method in some other cases—for example, when one of the row sources is very small. An example is a single row table where a Cartesian join doesn't degrade performance.

Optimizer Statistics

CBO primarily uses statistics to determine the optimal execution plan. Statistics are collected for different objects such as tables, columns, and indexes. The types of information that are collected are listed next.

Table Statistics

- Table cardinality (number of rows in a table)
- Number of disk blocks used for the table
- Calculated cost of a full table scan
- Average row length in bytes

Column Statistics

- NDV (Number of Distinct Values for a column).
- Number of NULL values in the column.
- Data distribution (histograms). CBO assumes a uniform data distribution calculated as 1/Number of Distinct Values for the column. If the column exhibits data skew, histograms are created to inform CBO about it when evaluating costs.

Index Statistics

- Number of levels in the B+Tree
- Number of leaf blocks

- Number of distinct key values
- Number of leaf blocks per key value
- Number of base table data blocks per key value

In E-Business Suite, the statistics are gathered by regularly running Gather All Column Statistics, Gather Column Statistics, Gather Schema Statistics, and Gather Table Statistics concurrent requests available to the System Administrator responsibility. The use of procedures from the FND_STATS package is mandatory in both R11i and R12 instead of the ANALYZE command or procedures from the DBMS_STATS package.

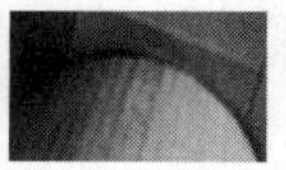

NOTE
Histograms should be created only on columns that do not have uniform data distribution and when predicates use literal rather than bind values.

SQL Tuning Tools

Our main goal is to write scalable SQL Statements that are parsed in a reasonably short time, execute efficiently time and again, do not occupy huge amount of memory, and, most importantly, are sharable. We'll discuss the guidelines that help us write efficient SQL in a short while, but before we do that, we'll remind you of the tools available at your disposal to achieve this goal.

Explain Plan

EXPLAIN PLAN is the SQL command used to obtain the execution plan for a SQL Statement. It only shows how the statement would be executed, but does not actually execute.

The output from EXPLAIN PLAN for a given SQL Statement is only relevant for the current session from which you execute the EXPLAIN PLAN command and for the database against which you execute the statement. Expect to have different results in different environments due to different database parameters, data volumes, and other factors that may affect the output from the optimizer. Before the EXPLAIN PLAN command can be run, PLAN TABLE needs to be created by executing the utlxplan.sql script from the $ORACLE_HOME/rdbms/admin directory on the database node.

Here is an example of the EXPLAIN PLAN command:

```
SQL> EXPLAIN PLAN FOR
      SELECT pha.segment1, pla.po_line_id
       FROM PO_HEADERS_ALL pha, PO_LINES_ALL pla
       WHERE pha.po_header_id = pla.po_header_id;
SQL> @?/rdbms/admin/utlxpls
```

```
-------------------------------------------------------------------------
| Id  | Operation           | Name            | Rows   | Bytes | Cost   |
-------------------------------------------------------------------------
|   0 | SELECT STATEMENT    |                 | 47195  |   921K|   459  |
|*  1 |  HASH JOIN          |                 | 47195  |   921K|   459  |
|   2 |   TABLE ACCESS FULL| PO_HEADERS_ALL  | 18878  |   184K|   137  |
|   3 |   TABLE ACCESS FULL| PO_LINES_ALL    | 46250  |   451K|   314  |
-------------------------------------------------------------------------
Predicate Information (identified by operation id):
---------------------------------------------------
1 - access("PHA"."PO_HEADER_ID"="PLA"."PO_HEADER_ID")
```

The way to read the plan is to start from the rightmost and uppermost line, which is the first operation to be executed. In the example, TABLE ACCESS FULL on PO_HEADERS_ALL is the first operation. In practice, generated plans are usually more complex, but you always start reading it from the rightmost-uppermost line and then continuing with the next level using the same rule. Consider the following example that consists of four operations: A, B, C, and D:

```
Operation A  ←------ parent operation
     Operation B  ←------ first child of A
          Operation C  ←------  child of B
     Operation D  ←------ second child of A
```

In the example, Operation C is the rightmost-uppermost one and is executed first. Next is Operation B, followed by Operation D, and finally they all feed into Operation A. The key is to remember the rightmost-uppermost rule when reading the execution plans produced by the EXPLAIN PLAN command.

An alternative way of displaying the explain plan is to use functionality from the DBMS_XPLAN package:

```
SQL> SELECT * FROM TABLE(DBMS_XPLAN.DISPLAY('PLAN_TABLE',<id>,'ALL'));
```

For example, use the syntax similar to what is shown next for displaying the explain plan

```
SQL> EXPLAIN PLAN SET STATEMENT_ID = 'apps_tune_01' FOR select
po_header_id, po_line_id from po_lines_all;
SQL> set linesize 121
SQL> SELECT * FROM TABLE(DBMS_XPLAN.DISPLAY('PLAN_TABLE',
'apps_tune_01','ALL'));
```

In Oracle Applications, you'll also find a SQL script called the afxplain.sql in FND_TOP/sql directory that is used by product teams to display the explain plan along with some other useful information.

Autotrace

Most developers prefer to use the AUTOTRACE command as a first choice tool rather than EXPLAIN PLAN. AUTOTRACE actually executes a SQL Statement and provides additional information about the execution in addition to the explain plan. Autotrace functionality is turned on and off by setting various switches of the AUTOTRACE system variable:

```
SQL> SET AUTOTRACE TRACEONLY
SQL> SELECT pha.segment1, pla.po_line_id
       FROM PO_HEADERS_ALL pha, PO_LINES_ALL pla
       WHERE pha.po_header_id = pla.po_header_id;
46247 rows selected.
Execution Plan

----------------------------------------------------------
   0      SELECT STATEMENT Optimizer=ALL_ROWS (Cost=809 Card=47195
          Bytes=943900)
   1    0   HASH JOIN (Cost=809 Card=47195 Bytes=943900)
   2    1     TABLE ACCESS (FULL) OF 'PO_HEADERS_ALL' (TABLE)(Cost=245
              Card=18878 Bytes=188780)
   3    1     TABLE ACCESS (FULL) OF 'PO_LINES_ALL' (TABLE) (Cost=562
          Card=46250 Bytes=462500)
Statistics
----------------------------------------------------------
         47  recursive calls
          0  db block gets
       6635  consistent gets
       1858  physical reads
          0  redo size
     869952  bytes sent via SQL*Net to client
      34420  bytes received via SQL*Net from client
       3085  SQL*Net roundtrips to/from client
          0  sorts (memory)
          0  sorts (disk)
      46247  rows processed
SQL> SET AUTOTRACE OFF
```

In this example, we set AUTOTRACE to TRACEONLY, which suppresses the actual output from the SQL. In comparison to the previous EXPLAIN PLAN command example, here you notice two extra columns (referred to as ID and Parent ID) that precede the operations in generated plan. They help establish the hierarchy of execution steps in the generated execution plan so that, in our generated plan, the TABLE ACCESS (FULL) OF 'PO_HEADERS_ALL' operation with ID=2 is a child of the HASH JOIN operation with ID=1, which makes it much easier to read.

SQL Trace

SQL Trace is a diagnostics tool usually used by database administrators (DBAs) for troubleshooting, tuning, and monitoring purposes. However, we recommend using it during the development and testing cycles in environments that closely reflect the production environment in terms of data volumes, concurrent users, and other factors that may affect performance.

SQL Trace generates low-level information about the number of times a SQL Statement was parsed, executed, and fetched. It also shows CPU and elapsed times, physical and logical reads, a count of rows processed, and misses on the library cache for each SQL Statement. It is the ultimate source of truth for SQL execution. Some developers also use it to reverse engineer application logic on the module they are customizing, and SQL Trace is a really fast way of figuring out how an application interacts with the database, especially if the developer hasn't got access to the source code.

SQL Trace can be enabled for a particular session (*ALTER SESSION SET SQL_TRACE = TRUE ;*), or for all sessions at the instance level (parameter SQL_TRACE = TRUE). If SQL Trace is enabled, the data server will generate trace (TRC) files and write them to the directory specified by the user_dump_dest parameter (*select value from v$parameter where name = 'user_dump_dest';*).

The generated trace files are not easy to read, so Oracle provides the TKPROF utility to format the generated raw trace files. We'll now generate a trace file for the SQL Statement from one of the previous examples and format it with the TKPROF utility:

```
SQL> alter session set timed_statistics=true;
Session altered.
SQL> alter session set sql_trace=true;
Session altered.
```

Now we run the same query for, say, three times in a row:

```
SQL> SELECT /*testA*/ pha.segment1, pla.po_line_id
     FROM PO_HEADERS_ALL pha, PO_LINES_ALL pla
     WHERE pha.po_header_id = pla.po_header_id;
SEGMENT1             PO_LINE_ID
-------------------- ----------
5366                     101918
5366                     101919
5366                     101920
<...more rows from query returned..>
SQL> /
<...all rows from the same query returned..>
SQL> /
<...all rows from the same query returned..>
```

The trace file for the current session is now produced in the directory where the user_dump_dest parameter points, and it is used as an input to the TKPROF utility in order to create formatted output:

```
[ovisr12@r12 udump]$ tkprof r124_ora_4754.trc tk4754.prf sys=no
```

The output from the previous command on the system was the tk4754.prf report file, which is what we are going to look into to analyze the statement execution from the example:

```
SELECT /*testA*/ pha.segment1, pla.po_line_id
       FROM PO_HEADERS_ALL pha, PO_LINES_ALL pla
       WHERE pha.po_header_id = pla.po_header_id

call      count      cpu    elapsed       disk      query    current      rows
-------- ------- -------- ---------- ---------- ---------- ---------- ----------
Parse         3     0.00       0.00          0        577          0         0
Execute       3     0.00       0.00          0          0          0         0
Fetch      9255     0.32       0.29          0      17024          0    138741
-------- -------  -------- ---------- ---------- ---------- ---------- ----------
total      9261     0.33       0.30          0      17601          0    138741

Misses in library cache during parse: 1
Optimizer mode: ALL_ROWS
```

We now start reading across the individual times and counts for parse, execute, and fetch phases. First, the statement was parsed three times; however, this number includes both hard and soft parses. You know that there is a huge performance penalty for hard parses, so, to differentiate between hard and soft parses, you look at the Misses in library cache during parse number, which is 1. This means that, in the example, there was one hard and two soft parses (a total of three).

The parse phase required close to zero of CPU (cpu column) and total elapsed time (elapsed column), didn't require physical disk I/Os (disk column), and used 577 logical I/Os, which are consistent read mode blocks (query column).

Next, you move onto the Execute phase, which also shows a count of three, meaning the query was executed three times. For SELECT statements, the rest of the counts are normally empty, while for an UPDATE, this is the phase where most of the work is done.

The last phase is Fetch, which does most of the work for the SELECT statement. Here you can see that the CPU and elapsed times are around 0.30 (almost identical). This indicates that this phase was mostly CPU bound. Don't get confused by the fact that the report shows CPU time being greater than the total elapsed time. This inaccuracy is due to the way the data server collects the timings for various operations, some of which execute extremely fast in big numbers. The server didn't have to bring any data from the disk (disk=0), and the query required 17024 logical I/O blocks in read consistent mode, returning the total of 138741 rows to the client.

Finally, we need to mention that Oracle provides an extended version of SQL Trace through the database event 10046:

```
alter session set events '10046 trace name context forever, level 12';
```

The traces obtained through event 10046 capture additional information about wait events, which complements the diagnostics capabilities of this very powerful and useful tool.

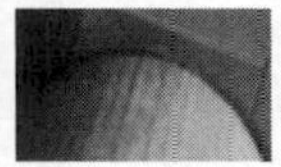

TIP
Tracing techniques specific to the E-Business Suite environment are documented extensively on Metalink. A good place to start is Metalink Note 296559.1, Common Tracing Techniques, within Oracle Applications 11i/R12.

SQL Coding Guidelines

In the following sections, we look at the most common constructs that developers need to pay attention to that could get in the way of creating effective and reusable SQL Statements.

Use of Bind Variables

To achieve cursor sharing in Oracle database, all SQL Statements must use bind variables instead of literals. The two exceptions to this rule are table columns with histograms, which we'll discuss shortly, and one-off scripts such as custom conversions that won't be used on a regular basis.

Using bind variables allows the statement to be hard parsed only once and then reused over and over again through softer types of parses. From a code writing point of view, bind variables also enable you to create SQL that is generic in nature rather than hard coded.

Earlier we stressed that hard parsing is a very expensive operation with regard to system resources and should be avoided at all costs. Here is an example that uses the po_num bind variable:

```
SELECT pha.segment1, pla.po_line_id
FROM PO_HEADERS_ALL pha, PO_LINES_ALL pla
WHERE pha.po_header_id = pla.po_header_id
and pha.segment1 = :po_num;
```

The bind variable po_num acts as a placeholder for the value that will be provided at runtime either through Oracle Forms code, Java code in the OA Framework application, or any other tool that issues SQL Statements against the Oracle database. In addition to using the bind variables, you should also ensure that the type of bind variable matches the type of database column it is bound to. In our example, SEGMENT1 column is VARCHAR2; therefore, po_num should be of the same type.

Use of Histograms

In E-Business Suite, some statements use literals in predicates such as STATUS='Approved'. Such statements with literals should be created only for columns that have data skew and no more than a few distinct values. For example, the STATUS column could have 80 percent of values with STATUS='Approved', 18 percent with STATUS='Rejected', and only 2 percent with STATUS='In Progress'. In this case, there is a clear data skew and the number of distinct values is only three, which makes this column a candidate for a histogram.

It is recommended you create a histogram for the described case because, by default, Optimizer assumes uniform data distribution, and creating a histogram will help Optimizer assign the correct selectivity for a column filter (for example, STATUS='Rejected').

IMPORTANT
Histograms should be created only when the predicate uses literal values rather than bind variables.

Use of NVL() and DECODE() Functions

NVL() and DECODE() functions should be avoided on an index column in a WHERE clause. In the following example, SEGMENT1 is an indexed column with the PO_HEADERS_U2 index:

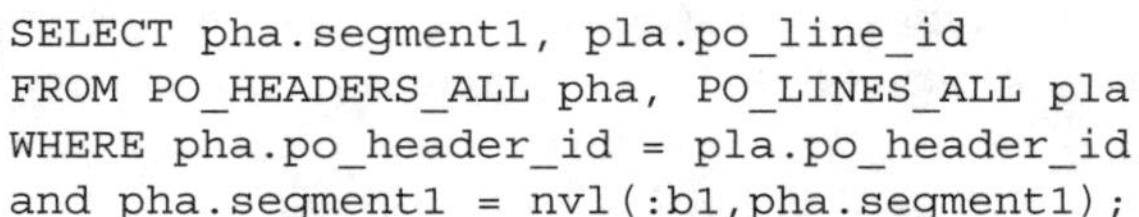

```
SELECT pha.segment1, pla.po_line_id
FROM PO_HEADERS_ALL pha, PO_LINES_ALL pla
WHERE pha.po_header_id = pla.po_header_id
and pha.segment1 = nvl(:b1,pha.segment1);
```

```
-------------------------------------------------------------------
| Id  | Operation                         | Name           | Rows  |
-------------------------------------------------------------------
|   0 | SELECT STATEMENT                  |                | 47219 |
|   1 |  CONCATENATION                    |                |       |
|*  2 |   FILTER                          |                |       |
|*  3 |    HASH JOIN                      |                | 47195 |
|*  4 |     TABLE ACCESS FULL             | PO_HEADERS_ALL | 18878 |
|   5 |     TABLE ACCESS FULL             | PO_LINES_ALL   | 46250 |
|*  6 |   FILTER                          |                |       |
|   7 |    TABLE ACCESS BY INDEX ROWID    | PO_LINES_ALL   |     7 |
|   8 |     NESTED LOOPS                  |                |    24 |
|   9 |      TABLE ACCESS BY INDEX ROWID| PO_HEADERS_ALL |     3 |
|* 10 |       INDEX RANGE SCAN            | PO_HEADERS_U2  |     3 |
|* 11 |      INDEX RANGE SCAN             | PO_LINES_U2    |     7 |
-------------------------------------------------------------------
```

It is evident from the execution plan that the use of the PO_HEADERS_U2 index is dependent on the supplied value to the :b1 bind variable at runtime. Let's now compare it with the plan where NVL() is not used:

```
SELECT pha.segment1, pla.po_line_id
FROM PO_HEADERS_ALL pha, PO_LINES_ALL pla
WHERE pha.po_header_id = pla.po_header_id
AND  (pha.segment1 = :b1 OR pha.segment1 IS NULL);
----------------------------------------------------------------
| Id  | Operation                       | Name            | Rows  |
----------------------------------------------------------------
|   0 | SELECT STATEMENT                |                 |    24 |
|   1 |  TABLE ACCESS BY INDEX ROWID    | PO_LINES_ALL    |     7 |
|   2 |   NESTED LOOPS                  |                 |    24 |
|   3 |    TABLE ACCESS BY INDEX ROWID| PO_HEADERS_ALL  |     3 |
|*  4 |     INDEX RANGE SCAN            | PO_HEADERS_U2   |     3 |
|*  5 |    INDEX RANGE SCAN             | PO_LINES_U2     |     7 |
----------------------------------------------------------------
```

Use of EXISTS and IN

EXISTS is used when the outer query uses a selective predicate and you want to do an existence check against a correlated query. If the selective predicate is in a subquery, you can use IN instead of EXISTS, and in that case, the subquery will be uncorrelated. The following query uses an EXISTS check:

```
SELECT RULE_MODE FROM PAY_LEGISLATION_RULES PLR
  WHERE LEGISLATION_CODE = :b1
AND RULE_TYPE              = 'S'
AND EXISTS
  (SELECT 1 FROM FND_SEGMENT_ATTRIBUTE_VALUES
    WHERE SEGMENT_ATTRIBUTE_TYPE = 'ORGANIZATION'
    AND TO_NUMBER (PLR.RULE_MODE ) = ID_FLEX_NUM
    AND APPLICATION_ID             = 800
    AND ATTRIBUTE_VALUE            = 'Y'
    AND ID_FLEX_CODE               = 'SCL')
-----------------------------------------------------------------------
| Id  | Operation              | Name                           | Rows    |
-----------------------------------------------------------------------
|   0 | SELECT STATEMENT       |                                |   1     |
|   1 |  NESTED LOOPS SEMI     |                                |   1     |
|   2 |   TABLE ACCESS BY
          INDEX ROWID          | PAY_LEGISLATION_RULES          |   1     |
|*  3 |    INDEX UNIQUE SCAN   | PAY_LEGISLATION_RULES_PK       |   1     |
|*  4 |   TABLE ACCESS BY
          INDEX ROWID          | FND_SEGMENT_ATTRIBUTE_VALUES   |   1     |
|*  5 |    INDEX RANGE SCAN    | FND_SEGMENT_ATTRIBUTE_VALS_U1  |   1     |
-----------------------------------------------------------------------
```

In this example, PAY_LEGISLATION_RULES is the driving outer table and is correlated with the subquery through the TO_NUMBER (PLR.RULE_MODE) = ID_FLEX_NUM condition.

You should also keep in mind that instead of NOT IN, you should always use NOT EXISTS.

Note About Outer Joins

Outer joins should be used sparingly and with great caution. When designing customizations, developers should take into consideration the use of default values in custom entities so that outer joins do not have to be issued in order to retrieve data.

When outer joins are used in queries, the tables that participate in such joins cannot be chosen by Optimizer as driving tables, which can lead to suboptimal execution plans as the choice is somewhat limited.

You should in particular avoid using outer joins with views, and especially with nonmergeable views such as those that contain more than one table (complex views), views that include a correlated subquery, and the like.

A Note About Views

Views are used in quite a few places in E-Business Suite for various purposes. They are derived from one or more base tables. When creating SQL queries in customizations, it can be very tempting to join to already existing views, but you should avoid this. SQL Statements should be created to use the base tables instead.

When creating a custom view, avoid using other views inside the custom view.

Also, calls to PL/SQL functions should be avoided if possible, as context switching between SQL and PL/SQL slows down performance. This is actually true of any SQL Statement, not just views. For example:

```
SELECT * FROM po_headers_all
WHERE org_id = fnd_profile.value('ORG_ID');
```

Calls to PL/SQL such as in our example should be avoided if possible. Instead, you should get the value of the ORG_ID profile option in the host environment and pass it on to the SQL query as a bind variable value.

SQL Tuning Tools: Common Signs of Inefficiency

Earlier in this chapter, we reminded you what tools are available that can help you build efficient and scalable SQL. Commonly, after writing an initial SQL Statement, developers use either EXPLAIN PLAN or Autotrace against a database that closely matches the production environment to examine the execution plan, although our preference is to use Autotrace rather than EXPLAIN PLAN. In addition to Autotrace, we recommend using SQL Trace and TKPROF to make sure that your SQL does not hamper performance in the overall scheme of things.

What to Look for in an Explain Plan

Let's take a look at what the most common signs of inefficiency are in SQL Statements when examining generated plans and looking for potentially problematic operations. The following table outlines the operations that need to be addressed and further analyzed if they are spotted in the explain plan.

What to look for	Why to avoid	Fix
Full Table Scan (FTS)	Not cached, which results in physical (disk) I/Os for each FTS. Even for small tables of more than 10 rows, if the statement is frequently executed by users, FTS will have a serious effect on overall performance. FTS is not scalable, as performance will degrade as the number of rows in the table grows.	If the table is to grow to more than 10 rows, change the query to use indexes, or force users to enter additional selective criteria. If less than 10 rows, FTS is usually okay.
Full Index Scan	As opposed to FTS, index blocks are cached, therefore index scans can force index blocks from other queries to be forced out from the cache. As a result, a full index scan can potentially have an even bigger negative impact on the system than FTS.	Must be avoided. Typically occurs in UI screens if the developer allows blind queries (no selective criteria) to be executed by end users. Add selective criteria to fix the issue.
Merge Join Cartesian	The most expensive operation of them all. A Cartesian join of table A with N rows with table B with M rows produces N × M rows. By definition, this is extremely bad.	Add a join condition between tables. A Cartesian join can also be the result of using NVL () and DECODE () functions in a WHERE clause. Avoid using functions such as NVL() and DECODE() in joins.
View	The word VIEW in an execution plan is evidence of a nonmergeable view. Examples of nonmergeable views are those with set operators (for example, UNION), aggregate functions (for example, SUM), and such. Nonmergeable views restrict Optimizer's options and frequently result in FTS and a nonoptimal execution plan as a consequence.	SQL Statements should avoid referencing of nonmergeable views. Also, avoid joining to views altogether—join directly to the base tables.

Row Throwaways

Row throwaways are yet more evidence of execution inefficiency. They require close inspection and SQL Statement retuning. They are the rows that have been accessed but not returned by an operation, which is illustrated next:

```
10500       TABLE ACCESS BY INDEX ROWID BIG_TABLE
10000000        INDEX RANGE SCAN
```

In this example, which we purposely made up for illustration purposes, the unselective range scan accessed 10 million rows to return just 10500 rows, which is only 0.1 percent of all accessed rows. More than 99 percent rows are discarded (thrown away); this usually happens when the most selective filters are not used first. To avoid throwaways, select the driving table with the best possible filter.

What to Look for in TKPROF

We mentioned earlier that after writing SQL, developers should monitor the behavior of SQL Statements in environments that closely match the production instance by running SQL Traces and producing TKPROF reports. TKPROF provides summaries of various counts, including logical I/Os (query + current), also known as buffer gets and physical reads (disk reads), for parse, execute, and fetch processing phases. The following table lists the most common things to look for that may signal potential problems:

What to look for	Why to avoid	Fix
A number of very similar statements that execute only once (Executions = 1)	This could be evidence of hard-coded literal values used instead of bin variables; as a result, the shared pool gets flooded with different versions. It causes latch contention and excessive memory consumption.	SQL needs to be rewritten to use bind variables instead of literal values.
Ratio between logical IOs and processed rows is big (greater than 1000)	Normally this is evidence of an inferior execution plan and could also indicate a big number of throwaways due to poor selectivity from the driving table. Excessive buffer gets consume lots of CPU.	SQL needs to be rewritten to tune the access path. For example, adding additional indexes may help, or changing the statement to use the existing may help in producing an optimal plan.

What to look for	Why to avoid	Fix
The number of fetch calls equals the number of processed rows	Indicates row-by-row processing, which badly affects CPU usage and increases latency through unnecessary round trips.	Use bulk fetches or bulk processing.
Ratio between logical IOs and disk reads is low (less than 2)	This is evidence of a nonoptimal access path that requires excessive disk I/Os. Frequent disk I/Os badly affect the disk I/O system and have a negative impact on the system as a whole.	SQL needs to be tuned to reduce disk I/Os by improving the access path.
High parse time (for example, more than 2 seconds)	Evidence of complex SQL results in high memory and CPU usage during the parsing. If flushed out frequently from the shared pool, SQL needs to be hard parsed time and again, which is very expensive.	Simplify complex SQL Statements by breaking them into simpler statements with the help of conditional logic (IF...THEN).

Generic Guidelines for UI Screens

The current releases of E-Business Suite R11i and R12 use screens that are created with either Forms Developer or Oracle Applications Framework (JDeveloper for Oracle Applications). In this section, we highlight some of the most common dos and don'ts that affect system performance:

- **Blind queries** These are the result of not entering search criteria and must be absolutely avoided as they impact the whole system. Search screens should force users to enter selective criteria when performing searches from UI.
- **Leading wildcard '%'** Prevent users from entering a leading '%' in search fields, as this will prevent index from being used.
- **Auto-queries in UI** Lists of values (LOVs) should not automatically execute queries when the user navigates to them. Also, try to avoid automatically displaying the transaction history when the user navigates to a page or a screen as, usually, it will not scale.

Summary

In this chapter, we briefly introduced SQL Statement execution and the CBO (Cost Based Optimizer) as a prelude to a discussion about the importance of execution plans and their interpretation when constructing SQL Statements. The cost is what drives CBO decisions; therefore, we stressed the importance of understanding the relationship between the cost, cardinality, selectivity, and table and index statistics. When tuning SQL Statements, the general goal is to reduce time and resources required, and this could be achieved by examining different counts provided by TKPROF reports.

In the section "What to Look for in an Explain Plan," we provided a list of the most frequent "offenders" that should be closely examined if they appear in the execution plan. In addition to that, in the section "What to Look for in TKPROF," we provided some guidelines that should be suitable for most E-Business Suite implementations.

Finally, remember that performance issues are more often than not caused by suboptimal code rather than other factors; therefore, after writing the code, you should run SQL Trace in an appropriate environment and double-check that your statements execute efficiently.

Index

A

B

C

D

E

G

H

I

J

K

L

M

N

O

P

Q

R

S

T

U

X

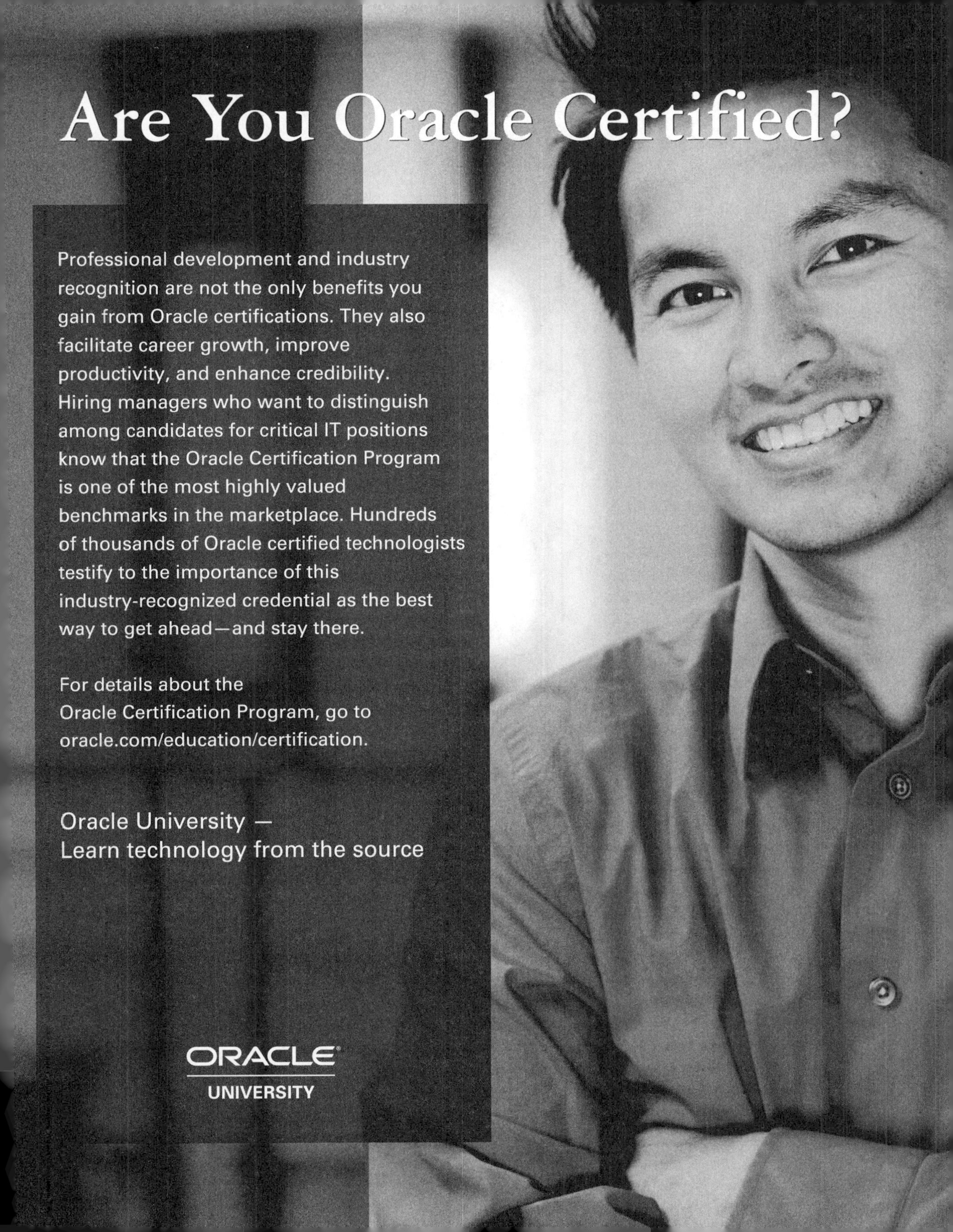
Are You Oracle Certified?
Professional development and industry recognition are not the only benefits you gain from Oracle certifications. They also facilitate career growth, improve productivity, and enhance credibility. Hiring managers who want to distinguish among candidates for critical IT positions know that the Oracle Certification Program is one of the most highly valued benchmarks in the marketplace. Hundreds of thousands of Oracle certified technologists testify to the importance of this industry-recognized credential as the best way to get ahead—and stay there.
For details about the Oracle Certification Program, go to oracle.com/education/certification.
Oracle University — Learn technology from the source
ORACLE
UNIVERSITY

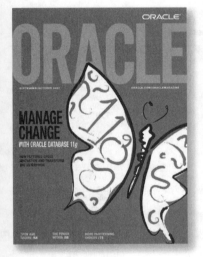